**Robert Kreider, North Newton, Kansas:**

"Harold Bender was a powerful presence in my life—intimidating and inspiring, irritating and energizing, provoking and empowering, dominating and caring. In Albert Keim's captivating study of Bender, I gained much insight into this fascinating, complex person who was one of the commanding figures among Mennonites in this century—in fact, in our entire American experience.

"This is must reading for anyone seeking to understand the Mennonite story since World War I. Here is a quality biography, rich in engaging detail, honest in providing both light and shadow. In tracing the trail of Harold Bender's focused, fast-paced, relentlessly productive life, one is left exhausted. Will anyone ever be his equal in energy, brilliance, forcefulness, and drive?

"Albert Keim presents us with a biographical case study laced with tangled issues of power and idealism, doctrine and pragmatism, freedom and obedience—all set in the context of Bender's commitment to Christ and his faith community. This is a book I could not put aside."

**Franklin H. Littell, Philadelphia:**

"Harold Bender was one of the great Christian leaders of the twentieth century of religion in America. His impact was great both in scholarship and in the life of the churches.

"He worked at a time when teachers in other denominations were moving from the uncritical and filial style to application of the scientific method in historical studies. Surmounting considerable opposition in the Mennonite fellowship, to which he remained intensely loyal throughout his life, Bender brought the critical, analytical, and comparative approach to bear upon the Anabaptist-Mennonite history and witness.

"Ever the builder as well as the intellectual, in 1926 he founded *The Mennonite Quarterly Review*—a journal still unsurpassed for both academic quality and churchly relevance. He also wrote several original contributions to Reformation studies.

"Many will remember Bender for his great service in developing Goshen College and Seminary. He also helped to strengthen or found other major agencies and institutions, all reflecting and deepening the witness and outreach of his people—in peace testimony, in missions, in social justice. He was able to listen and reach out to fellow Christians from different backgrounds, with different perspectives, without loss of charity and patience, and without compromising his own integrity and commitment.

"Bender welcomed me to Goshen and encouraged me in my Anabaptist studies, in which we shared similar convictions. For years I watched him function influentially in the American Society of Church History, where the scholars elected him president and listened to his classic statement of 'The Anabaptist Vision.'

"Brother Bender also remained unshaken in friendship when I moved into work on Christian-Jewish relations. I had become convinced that the wicked violence of Christendom was evident not only in the persecution of Christian dissenters and 'heretics' but also in the martyrdom of the Jewish people, culminating in the Holocaust.

"I am now eighty years of age, and I have known personally some of the great Christian statesmen of America and Europe. I have known no one whom I loved and admired more than Harold S. Bender—scholar, educator, statesman, and New Testament Christian. I am grateful to Al Keim for his extraordinary diligence and precise detail in presenting the life and work of this great man and Christian."

# Harold S. Bender
## 1897-1962

## Albert N. Keim

*Sponsored by*
*The Mennonite Historical Society*
*Goshen, Indiana*

Herald
Press

*Scottdale, Pennsylvania*
*Waterloo, Ontario*

Library of Congress Cataloging-in-Publication Data

Keim, Albert N.
    Harold S. Bender, 1897-1962 / Albert N. Keim.
        p.    cm.
    Includes bibliographical references and index.
    ISBN 0-8361-9084-X (alk. paper)
        1. Bender, Harold Stauffer, 1897-1962.   2. Mennonites—United
    States—Biography.    I. Title.
    BX8143.B4K45  1998
    289.7'092—dc21
    [B]                                                                                    98-11885

The paper used in this publication is recycled and meets the minimum requirements of American National Standard for Information Sciences—Permanence of Paper for Printed Library Materials, ANSI Z39.48-1984.

In using informal sources, an occasional grammatical correction or punctuation mark was added for clarity. All Bible quotations are used by permission, all rights reserved, and are from the *New Revised Standard Version Bible,* copyright 1989, by the Division of Christian Education of the National Council of the Churches of Christ in the USA; *The Holy Bible, New International Version,* copyright © 1973, 1978, 1984 International Bible Society, Zondervan Bible Publishers; or *The Holy Bible, King James Version.*

H. S. BENDER, 1897-1962
Copyright © 1998 by Herald Press, Scottdale, Pa. 15683
Published simultaneously in Canada by Herald Press,
Waterloo, Ont. N2L 6H7. All rights reserved
Library of Congress Catalog Number: 98-11885
International Standard Book Number: 0-8361-9084-X
Printed in the United States of America
Book and cover design by Gwen M. Stamm

07 06 05 04 03 02 01 00 99 98 10 9 8 7 6 5 4 3 2 1

To order or request information, please call
1-800-759-4447 (individuals); 1-800245-7894 (trade).
Website: www.mph.org

*To Leanna Yoder Keim*

# Contents

# Foreword

IN THE LIFE of the Mennonite churches and other Anabaptist-related groups in the twentieth century, few if any persons exerted influence greater than Harold S. Bender. Whether his legacy deserves applause, criticism, or some of both, it ranges deeply and broadly. Bender's influence reached into many different activities. It was wide both geographically and in the number of groups it touched, and often it set or helped to set profound new patterns. Bender's energies seemed almost boundless. Albert Keim's biography is first of all a lively story of an active person. Yet Keim also casts light on some tough questions.

By midcentury Bender was the Mennonites' dominant intellectual leader. He was both a product and a powerful agent of a renewal in Mennonite thought and faith understanding. That renewal came not only from him but also from others, who went before him, worked alongside him, or followed him, including his own students. Other scholars at times agreed or disagreed with him, but either way, he stimulated them.

Before Bender's prime years, planners of theological consultations, church-history conferences, seminars on Christian ethics, and other such events could proceed without reference to Anabaptism and its place in history. After his prime years, they could not. That change was not due entirely to Bender. Nonetheless, a symbol of the change was a decision of the American Society of Church History to honor him with its presidency for the year 1943. The duties of that office moved him to compose his most notable intellectual achievement: a presidential address entitled "The Anabaptist Vision." The address, quickly published, set forth a bold interpretation of the radical wing of the Protestant Reformation. Just as

boldly, it offered understandings of church and Christian discipleship that modern Christians might use as measures of faithfulness.

Albert Keim's engaging story tells us that Bender spent most of
his time and energy not in his study but in constant activity, as he
helped to guide the great mid-century burst of Mennonite institutions and other organized activity. At home, as a dean, Bender did
much to strengthen Goshen College in difficult times and then to
build its seminary to provide better biblical and theological education for pastors and others in his church. Meanwhile, he reached
far beyond the confines of his own Mennonite branch. As the main
builder of a Mennonite Historical Library and as leading editor of
*The Mennonite Quarterly Review* and *The Mennonite Encyclopedia*, he laid much of the groundwork for vastly increased scholarship on Anabaptists and Mennonites internationally.

In addition, his institution-building and organizational activity extended far beyond scholarship. Urged on by great forces surrounding modernization and the century's cataclysmic wars,
Bender constantly circulated in America, Europe, and sometimes
elsewhere to guide Mennonites to greater-scale and more highly
organized endeavors. Some of his efforts, as in Mennonite World
Conference, were primarily to consolidate and invigorate the family of Anabaptist-related churches. Others, such as helping to
guide the Mennonite Central Committee, reached out more broadly into worldwide service to victims of the modern world's follies.

Bender's accomplishments are large indeed; yet he was only a
man, a human, bounded by human limitations. His "Anabaptist
Vision" continues to intrigue many ordinary Mennonites, scholars, and others. One measure of its influence is that it still evokes
vigorous discussion more than fifty years after he delivered it.
However, some of the discussion is less than favorable; in general,
where Bender's ideas still stand, they stand as they have been revised. Moreover, in recent decades Mennonite church members
and their scholars have widely questioned various patterns that
now seem all too evident in Mennonite life in the vigorous, expansive mid-century decades.

Especially prominent are questions of how Mennonite leaders
in that era, Bender included, exercised authority and power. Were

those leaders' styles consistent with the pacifism and other biblical understandings of the Mennonites? Was Bender's own style consistent even with his so-called "Anabaptist Vision"? And even, despite all the language of radical faithfulness and discipleship, were Mennonites not really marching to other drums? The new institutional and intellectual achievements had deep effects. But were not the main effects less about radical discipleship than about preparing Mennonites and others of the Anabaptist family to participate more fully in modern society, become more absorbed into modern culture, and achieve greater standing in the world?

Albert Keim's book will stimulate further interpretations of Bender. One of its strong themes is how Bender related throughout life to the legacy of highly polemic debates between Fundamentalist and Modernists that pressed in on Mennonites and put their churches in great ferment during Bender's formative years. Other interpreters have emphasized how much Bender's "Anabaptist Vision" and other formulations offered an escape from the prison of those Fundamentalist-Modernist dichotomies.

Beyond those issues, the biography may foster discussions of proper styles of church leadership, the ethics of institutional accommodation, sectarianism versus interchurch cooperation, freedom versus boundaries for theological thought, and many other questions intrinsic to the concerns of Anabaptists, Mennonites, and indeed all Christians. The purpose of the biography is not to enshrine a man or to present his era as a golden age. Certainly it is not to give some final and last word. Instead, it provides data to stimulate an ongoing search for truth, and—for committed Christians who read it—an ongoing search for faithfulness.

Such is the attitude in which the Mennonite Historical Society and its Bender Project Committee offer this substantial and impressive book. We are deeply grateful to Albert Keim, to all who collaborated with him, and to those who gave financial support. Good scholarship is indeed a communal effort.

—*Walter Sawatsky*
*President, Mennonite*
*Historical Society*

—*Theron F. Schlabach*
*Chair of Bender Project*
*Committee, and Editor*

# Preface

THE SINGLE FOCUS of Harold S. Bender's life was the nurture and welfare of the Mennonite church. He was born in 1897 in Elkhart, Indiana, and as an adult he lived in the nearby town of Goshen. In the course of his life, Bender served as dean of Goshen College, dean of Goshen College Biblical Seminary, president of the Mennonite World Conference, and secretary of the Mennonite Central Committee. Those are just a few of many overlapping assignments: in 1957, at age 60, Bender carried fourteen administrative positions simultaneously, in a variety of Mennonite church organizations.

Harold Bender was also a teacher, preacher, and scholar. For thirty-eight years he taught at Goshen College or at Goshen College Biblical Seminary. After 1944, when he was ordained, he traveled tirelessly to preach in congregations, connecting with and nurturing the piety of lay Mennonites. As a scholar he gave Mennonites what he called the "Anabaptist Vision," a constructively imaged sixteenth-century lens through which Mennonites refracted their biblicist theology onto their twentieth-century experience. At mid-century, "Anabaptist Vision" became a key phrase among Mennonites and others to express a set of religious understandings and principles to guide Christian believers in the modern world.

Human life is lived as a story. Life is a series of events and experiences, refined by circumstance, ennobled by achievement and failure, and always subject to human contingency. The character and meaning of a life thus emerges as the story is told. It is possible to chronicle Harold Bender's life story on an almost daily basis for more than forty years. The biographer needed to select those events which most surely reveal the character and significance of his life as he lived it out.

This is the biography of a public man. Despite his huge written record, Harold Bender revealed almost nothing about his private life. Therefore the biography, like his life, is focused on his public persona. We see his actions and we read his ideas, but seldom are we invited to observe or share his innermost joys, hopes, and fears.

Harold Bender died in 1962. As much as anyone, Harold Bender constructed the organizations and distilled the self-understandings which have marked Mennonite life in the last half of the twentieth century. But in whichever century, Harold Bender's life becomes a guideline for testing whence Mennonites have come.

With that understanding, the Mennonite Historical Society invited the author to prepare this work. Its production has been a rich five-year journey. Harold Bender's flowing energy produced a mountain of written material. The abundant resources complicated the key responsibility of the biographer, to choose and portray prime elements of the life which explain the subject's influence.

The author is grateful to the many persons who have facilitated this project. My able research assistant Jean-Paul Benowitz worked with me for two summers, helping me comb through the massive Bender Collection at the Archives of the Mennonite Church in Goshen, Indiana. After extensive work in those archives, I owe a special debt of gratitude for the expeditious help of archivist Dennis Stoesz: he never failed to locate whatever obscure piece of information or citation I required. I am also indebted to the forty or more persons who sat with me for taped interviews and offered firsthand impressions and stories which helped me understand Harold S. Bender. The warm encouragement I received from Mary Eleanor Bender and Nancy Bender Kostick has been much appreciated.

Especially, I want to acknowledge the support and counsel of the Harold S. Bender Project Committee—Helen Alderfer, James Juhnke, Walter Sawatsky, Theron Schlabach, Mary Sprunger, and Erland Waltner. These persons supervised the project on behalf of the Mennonite Historical Society, which sponsored the undertaking and established them as the Project Committee.

Eastern Mennonite University and the Mennonite Historical

Society provided substantial financial support. The university did so extensively by funding sabbatical and research leaves for me on several occasions. The society, through its Friends of the Project Committee, ably led by chairman H. Ralph Hernley and treasurer J. Howard Kauffman, successfully raised funds to sustain the project. The project committee and I are grateful to the many friends, students, and colleagues of Harold S. Bender whose generous financial contributions made the research and the biography possible.

Finally, I want to acknowledge my particular debt to the persistent and patient work of my editor, Theron F. Schlabach. He improved the quality of the manuscript immeasurably. However, all lapses of style, fact, and interpretation are my responsibility.

—*Albert N. Keim*
   *Eastern Mennonite University*

# Time Line

1895    Elizabeth Horsch born February 7, in Elkhart, Indiana.
1897    Harold Stauffer Bender, born July 19, in Elkhart.
1907    Elizabeth baptized by immersion, Vermillion, Ohio.
1910    Harold baptized, Prairie Street Mennonite Church, Elkhart.
1913    Elizabeth graduates from Scottdale (Pennsylvania) High School, valedictorian.
1914    Harold graduates from Elkhart High School. Enters Goshen College.
1915    Elizabeth enters Hesston (Kansas) College.
1916    Harold teaches at Thorntown (Indiana) High School.
1917    Harold and Elizabeth study at Goshen College.
1918    Harold and Elizabeth graduate from Goshen College. Elizabeth begins teaching at Eastern Mennonite School in Harrisonburg, Virginia. Harold begins teaching at Hesston College.
1920    Elizabeth begins teaching at Hesston College. Harold nurses his sick father.
1921    Harold's father dies. Harold begins studies at Garrett Biblical Institute and attends Princeton Seminary. Elizabeth works as a linotypist in Pittsburgh.
1922    Elizabeth begins teaching at the Johnstown (Pennsylvania) High School.
1923    Harold graduates from Princeton. Harold and Elizabeth are married. They begin studies at Tübingen University.
1924    Harold begins teaching at Goshen College.
1927    Founds *The Mennonite Quarterly Review.* Daughter Mary Eleanor is born.

1929 Publishes *Two Centuries of American Mennonite Literature.*

1930 Does Mennonite Central Committee refugee relief work in Europe. Attends Mennonite World Conference, Danzig.

1931 Becomes assistant secretary of Mennonite Central Committee. Appointed dean of Goshen College.

1933 Daughter Nancy is born.

1935 Earns his doctor of theology degree at Heidelberg University in Germany.

1937 Writes "Peace, War, and Military Service" for the Peace Problems Committee, the statement adopted by MC Mennonite general conference.

1942 Writes *Mennonite Origins in Europe.* Becomes secretary of the MC Relief Committee, Chairman of the MCC Peace Section.

1943 Presents "Anabaptist Vision" as president of the American Society of Church History.
Elizabeth completes M.A. degree at the University of Minnesota.

1944 Harold is ordained.
Becomes dean of Goshen College Bible School.

1947 Becomes leading editor of *The Mennonite Encyclopedia* project.
The family spends a year in Europe working for MCC.

1950 Publishes *Conrad Grebel.*

1952 President of the Mennonite World Conference, meeting in Basel and Zurich.

1955 First volume of *The Mennonite Encyclopedia* is published.

1957 Festschrift in Bender's honor, *The Recovery of the Anabaptist Vision.*

1959 Publication of fourth volume of *The Mennonite Encyclopedia.*

1962 Attends Colloquy of East and West theologians at Prague.
Publishes *These Are My People.*
Harold S. Bender dies September 21.

1988 Elizabeth Horsch Bender dies March 24.

Harold S. Bender

# ❧ 1 ❧

# The Benders
# of Prairie Street

*George L. and Elsie Kolb Bender provide
the family home for Harold. George works
in Mennonite publishing and missions.*

IT WAS EARLY morning, before 5:00 a.m. on April 21, 1917.
George L. Bender was writing the weekly family letter to his son
Harold, a 19-year-old teacher at Thorntown High School in south-
central Indiana. The father reported that Aunt Cinda had returned
to Ontario, that the potatoes were all planted, and that he had
learned to drive the new Model T Ford owned by the Mennonite
Board of Missions. He ended the letter with some fatherly advice.
"Don't ever think of enlisting. You know what our doctrine is
along the war line. Be a good boy. Yours, Father."[1] Just two weeks
earlier the United States had entered World War I. The Mennonite
pacifist soul of George Bender was concerned that his idealistic
son might succumb to pressure to enlist in the war to save the
world for democracy.

In 1917 the 50-year-old George Lewis Bender was the executive officer of the Mennonite Board of Missions and Charities,
headquartered in Elkhart, Indiana. The board had missionaries in
India and was just beginning missionary work in Argentina. Bender was also the deacon of the thriving Prairie Street Mennonite
Church. George Bender was born near Grantsville, Maryland, in
1867, the son of a Mennonite immigrant father who had come to
the United States from Germany in 1852 to escape the military
draft. George was the fourth son in a family of nine children and
not robust enough to be a farmer. He had a predisposition for

housework and book learning and at eighteen became a teacher in a Maryland mountain school. In 1890 he was hired by John F. Funk, proprietor of the prosperous Mennonite Publishing Company in Elkhart, Indiana. Until his untimely death in January 1921 at age 53, Elkhart was his home.

Elkhart is located in north-central Indiana a few miles from the Michigan state line and about 120 miles east of Chicago. In the three decades after 1890, Elkhart grew from a town to a small city. By 1917 it had a population of more than twenty-five thousand people. The city was proud of its electric trolley service, paved streets, and busy railroad yards. Like many Midwestern towns of the period, Elkhart developed a consolidated public-school system during those years, with a high school and a series of elementary-grade ward schools. The children of George and Elsie Bender attended Ward 5 school near their Prairie Street home, and then Central High School.

In 1903 Andrew Carnegie gave the city a library.[2] Its twenty-five thousand books and two hundred periodicals were much used by the George Bender family, especially by son Harold. When he became a teacher at such out-of-the-way places as Thorntown, Indiana, and Hesston, Kansas, he had Elkhart library books sent to him by mail to meet his teaching needs. In 1905 Elkhart built its first large post office building. A year later George Bender became a postal clerk there, continuing until 1915, when he became a full-time employee of the Mennonite Board of Missions and Charities.

By the time young George Bender arrived in Elkhart in 1890, the city was becoming the spiritual and organizational center of the "old" (MC) Mennonite Church. In 1890 there were about twenty thousand Mennonites of Swiss and south-German origin in the United States. Some had settled in colonial Pennsylvania in the eighteenth century; more arrived in the nineteenth century. By the end of the nineteenth century, they were scattered in settlements across Pennsylvania, Ohio, Indiana, Illinois, and Iowa. Between 1870 and the First World War, this tiny pacifist sectarian church, whose history reached back to the Swiss and German Anabaptists of the sixteenth century, began a remarkable process of cultural adaptation and change. The church dropped the German language and embraced much of the spirit and style of evangelical American Protestantism. It experienced a dramatic reorientation of its life, including a surge of interest in missionary work, and the creation of a host of new organizations to manage its common life.[3]

• • •

At the center of much of the new Mennonite Church activity was John F. Funk, printer, publisher, minister, and after 1892, bishop. Born in the Franconia area of eastern Pennsylvania, Funk had lived in Chicago for ten years before relocating to Elkhart in 1867 at age 32. While in Chicago, he was converted by evangelical preaching and became an enthusiastic Sunday school worker in several city missions.

Funk's city experience was unusual for a Mennonite of the times. So was his occupation. When he moved to Elkhart, he brought a printing press with him. By the 1880s he was the unofficial publisher for the ("old") MC Mennonite Church and the Amish Mennonite church.[4] Most Mennonite books and religious materials in the United States were published by his Mennonite Publishing Company, located in a large building on the third block of north Main Street. By 1892 the company had five presses and published six periodicals with a combined circulation of thirty thousand. In the course of more than thirty years, it published 118 books, virtually all of them for the Mennonite market. By 1904 the company had eighty persons on the payroll.[5]

Funk's influence took many forms. One was the production of the *Herald of Truth* and its German-language version, *Herold der Wahrheit*. A monthly, the paper gave Funk enormous scope to promote his progressive ideas.

Funk was one of the first American Mennonite pastors of a town church. He with several others began Prairie Street Mennonite Church in 1871, and the congregation became a unique center of Mennonite progressivism. Unlike the conventional every-other-Sunday pattern of Mennonite church services, the congregation had services weekly. Sunday school was another innovation, followed soon thereafter by Sunday school teachers' meetings, to help train teachers for their roles. Children's meetings began in the 1890s. Bible readings soon became Young People's Meetings. A women's sewing circle began in 1900. By 1890 the congregation had 60 members, and at an 1892 communion service, 145 persons participated. Many were workers at the Mennonite Publishing Company.

Funk was an organizer. Among the organizations he created was the Mennonite Evangelizing Committee, which in 1892 became the Mennonite Evangelizing Board of America. In 1894 George Bender became the treasurer. The board's purpose was to collect funds to carry out general missionary work, but in the early years it served mainly as a conduit for funds to support the work of itinerant Mennonite evangelists. George Bender served as the board's unofficial executive, writing letters and directing the itineraries of numerous evangelists. In 1896 the body became the Mennonite Evangelizing and Benevolent Board, and it took on responsibility for a Mennonite mission in Chicago, which youthful Mennonites had begun three years earlier.[6]

One of Funk's most important contributions was to bring together at Elkhart a group of young men who would become important members of the next generation of Mennonite leaders. Among these was John S. Coffman, an able and eloquent evangelist from Virginia who served as associate editor of the *Herald of Truth*. By the 1890s Coffman had also become the premier Mennonite revival preacher. Another was Henry A. Mumaw, founder of the Elkhart Institute in 1894, a Mennonite academy that later became Goshen College. Others were Abram B. Kolb, Aaron C. Kolb, Dewitt Good, Benjamin Bixler, Daniel Weldy, John Horsch, and Menno S. Steiner. All of these came to Elkhart as young men invited and employed by John Funk and inclined to be active in progressive Mennonite causes. Elkhart and the Mennonite Publishing Company under John Funk became a leadership school for the MC Mennonite Church. Among those young men was George L. Bender, future father of Harold S. Bender.

•  •  •

George Bender, twenty-three years old, arrived in Elkhart in the summer of 1890.[7] There he joined another new employee at the Mennonite Publishing Company, John Horsch. Horsch was a German immigrant and son of a leading south-German Mennonite elder. Horsch and Bender became close friends. Soon after arriving in Elkhart, the two plus nearly a dozen other young men organized a boarding club. The club rented a house on Eden Street near the Prairie Street Mennonite Church, lived there, and shared expenses. They were a high-spirited group and called themselves the "dirty dozen"—after the condition of their laundry and the house in general. Their house became a center for progressive Mennonite young people in the area.[8]

The young men at the boarding club reflected a new spirit among Mennonites. While just recently off the farm, most of them had more than the usual amount of education and had imbibed, largely unself-consciously, the self-promoting, optimistic spirit of the times. George Bender caught that spirit in 1893 when he told his friend M. S. Steiner that certain eastern people thought that

**The Eden Street Boarding Club about 1892. On the porch, George Bender is the last man on the right, and John Horsch is third from the left.** Phoebe Kolb papers, AMC.

Steiner, George Bender, Bender's older brother Daniel (D. H. or Dan), and others of their set were "just the stuff."[9] These young men supported revivals, Sunday schools, prayer meetings, and mission work. Yet they also promoted a new emphasis on distinctive attire such as prayer coverings and plain dress for women and the "plain coat" for men.

George Bender's brother Dan fit the type. A successful revival preacher and promoter of progressive causes, he was also an ardent promoter of simple and plain attire. Reporting to George about one of his preaching trips in 1896, he observed that a young woman "came out" in one of the meetings, and the next evening she appeared at the meetings in a "plain dress and a prayer head covering." Several years earlier he reported satisfaction that he was getting his Somerset County, Pennsylvania, congregation "in good shape here. The sisters about all come to church with caps on." He was annoyed that several of the men continued to wear mustaches despite all of his efforts to dissuade them.[10]

The young men around Funk sometimes showed an interesting mixture of idealism and self-interest. For example, Dan Bender thought the $8.00 monthly salary his brother George received was inadequate when compared to the $20.00 to $30.00 schoolteachers received. He repeatedly urged George to leave the Mennonite Publishing Company and go where he could earn more money. Dan bragged that he himself had been offered $45.00 a month to become a school superintendent. He had turned the offer down, he explained, so that he would be free to do evangelistic work.[11]

When George Bender began work at the Mennonite Publishing Company, his first assignment was exciting: John Funk sent him to the Dakotas and the western Canadian provinces to sell magazine subscriptions to the German-speaking Russian Mennonites. George Bender spoke German, the gift of his immigrant father. The Mennonites in those areas had arrived from colonies in the Russian empire only a decade earlier. Publisher Funk hoped they would swell the subscription lists for his company's German-language papers: the *Herold der Wahrheit*, the *Mennonitische Rundschau*, and the *Christliche Jugendfreund*.[12]

• • •

On one of Bender's trips for the Mennonite Publishing Company, he met Elsie Kolb. He had become good friends with Eli S. Hallman and Menno C. Cressman, Mennonite business partners in Kitchener, Ontario, who supported progressive Mennonite concerns. On sales trips to Kitchener, Bender sometimes stayed at their homes. During a visit to the Hallmans, he first met Elsie, who occasionally worked for the family.[13]

In the summer of 1893, George joined two fellow-members of the "dirty dozen," Aaron and Abram Kolb, to ride their new bicycles from Elkhart to the Kolb brothers' home in Breslau near Kitchener. The Kolb brothers' family farm was just a quarter mile down the road from the farm of their cousin, Elsie Kolb. In the course of the visit, she and George renewed their acquaintance. Three years later they were married.[14]

The 18-year-old Elsie Kolb lived on a farm on the banks of the Grand River near Breslau, a small village three miles east of Kitchener. She was the second oldest of five children in the family of Joseph and Nancy Stauffer Kolb. The Kolb home, called Riverside Farm, would become important in the childhood experiences of George and Elsie Bender's children. When the children were young, Elsie took them to the farm for several weeks nearly every summer. The urban Bender children found the sights and sounds and smells of the farm tremendously exciting. They played with their cousins, swam in the Grand River, and learned some of the farm chores.

The children's favorite Ontario Kolb relative was Aunt Lucinda. "Cinda," or "Aunt Cinda," as the children called her, never married. A vigorous, roly-poly woman, she was a contrast to her shy and retiring older sister Elsie. Yet she and Elsie were devoted to each other, exchanging weekly letters. Cinda was a skilled seamstress and sewed many of the clothes for the Bender household.[15] After the death of George Bender in 1921, she came to stay with the Bender family each winter, to help Elsie manage the teenage boys and cope with loneliness.

The courtship of George and Elsie was mostly a long-distance affair, though George visited Ontario several times each year. They wrote letters, with George using the unromantic opening "Dear Friend" as late as four months before the wedding.[16] In February 1896 George's older brother Daniel, preaching at Breslau, reported that he "heard some fears that you might be going just a little too fast in this matter." Several months later Dan wondered how the "girl affair" was going. Dan, who loved to gossip and was aware that George and Elsie intended to marry, had apparently given away the secret; he soon wrote to ask for forgiveness. He hoped "no damage was done."[17]

The Kolbs were well pleased with Elsie's suitor. Several months after their wedding, Elsie's mother revealed that she had had a phrenologist analyze them, and the fellow had reported that they were well matched.[18] Always a frugal money manager, George assiduously saved his paychecks. When they married, they were able to move into their own house on Prairie Street.

The wedding took place in Elkhart on October 21, 1896. George had just begun teaching public school a month earlier and was unable to get away. So Elsie came to Elkhart for the wedding, accompanied by her second cousin, Titus Kolb, a former employee of the Mennonite Publishing Company and George's good friend. Due to financial problems in the Kolb family, none of Elsie's family attended the wedding.

George and Elsie were married at the Prairie Street Mennonite Church. This was an innovation since Mennonite weddings were normally held at the bride's home with only the couple's families and a few friends in attendance. In this case the entire congregation was invited and most were present. Equally innovative was a reception the couple held for their friends that evening at the home of minister John S. Lehman, one of the pastors at the Prairie Street church. George had lived with the Lehmans just prior to the marriage. The reception offered much food, including a variety of meats and fruits, and some expensive ice cream. Several years later John F. Funk, the bishop, would complain about "worldly wedding receptions," but he was present at this one.[19]

The couple settled into their home on Prairie Street. Outfitting the house cost $250.34, the biggest item being furniture. Total ex-

**Wedding picture of George and Elsie Kolb Bender, 1896, Elkhart, Indiana.**
George and Elsie Kolb Bender papers, AMC.

penses for the first year of marriage came to $906.38, including wedding costs. Also included was $4.50 to a nurse and $8.00 to Dr. Spohn for delivering a baby son, Harold Stauffer Bender, in July 1897. Later the parents spent 75 cents for baby photos and $13.20 for a baby carriage. The carriage was rather expensive in comparison to the $40 a month George earned as a teacher.[20]

• • •

George Bender began public school teaching in 1896, after working for the Mennonite Publishing Company for six years. His teacher's salary was barely adequate to support the young family. During the summer of 1900, while Elsie took Harold and a second baby, Florence, to Breslau for several months, George worked as a waiter at one of the Elkhart hotels. It was hard work, but it paid well.[21]

The turn-of-the-century years were busy ones also for George as Mennonite Evangelizing Board treasurer. From February 1896 to March 1897, he wrote 294 letters on the board's behalf, most of them responses to a variety of appeals for help. Preacher Daniel Burkhard of Ayr, Nebraska, asked for a revival preacher. Could the board help, since the congregation was too poor to cover expenses? he inquired. George made arrangements for Reuben J. Heatwole of Kansas to hold meetings there. Edward J. Berkey at the Home Mission in Chicago reported that "six came out," and that the mission needed 200 copies of J. S. Coffman's *Bible Readings* and several hundred tracts. George sent the materials.[22] After George and Elsie married, he set a rolltop desk in their bedroom and carried on his several treasurerships from there.

The family increased rapidly. Eventually there were eight children, although the youngest, George Howard, died a few days after birth. The eldest, Harold Stauffer, was born July 19, 1897. The others followed in measured succession: Florence Elizabeth on December 18, 1899; Violet Esther on November 17, 1901; Wilbur Joseph on October 15, 1903; Cecil Kolb on December 22, 1906; John Ellsworth on July 9, 1909; and Robert Leighton on March 13, 1912.

Elsie Bender apparently found birthing children fairly uneventful. The birth of Violet was the most unusual. She was born at six o'clock on a Sunday morning, headfirst in a chamber pot, to her mother's surprise.[23]

George and Elsie were devoted parents, with high ideals for their home. George, much in charge, concerned himself with all aspects of the family's life. They made a good team: Elsie, kind and gentle; George, more volatile and neurotic. He was the center around which everything revolved. He had a need to be liked and

**The George and Elsie Kolb Bender family in 1913. Harold was six-teen. From the left: Cecil, Violet, George, Harold, Robert, Florence, Elsie, John, Wilbur.** Bender Family Album.

respected, a need that affected his relationship with his children. He insisted that their behavior reflect well on his role as a father and on the family. The children sometimes resented his attitude.

The Benders were members of the new urban Mennonite middle class and took on the habits of their class. They emphasized good manners at the table and prohibited the use of slang. Doing well in school was very important, as was learning languages. In 1918 Elsie reported proudly to Harold, "Violet and Wilbur are busy; you just ought to hear them study their French." Those two were in high school. Wilbur, the second son and fourth child and a future Harvard College dean, was an amiable but uninspired student. He was "putting a little more work into his studies this year," Elsie told Harold, but he had to drop his paper route because it was too hard for them to rouse him in the morning.[24]

By 1912 there were nine mouths to feed, five of them of growing boys. The family consumed food in huge quantities. In July

1914 George spoke at a church in Middlebury, Indiana, and on Monday morning before returning to Elkhart, he bought three crates of huckleberries. Elsie canned them the next day. She canned bushels of peaches, once reporting a batch of 51 quarts in one day. In 1919 the family had two barrels of apples sent from Virginia. "We are already busy at it," she noted at another point, referring to 240 pounds of honey they had just gotten from Idaho. The twelve gallons of Smucker's apple butter from Orrville, Ohio, was not as good as homemade, Elsie observed, but "it tastes good for a change."[25]

Elsie's entire life focused fondly on her family. In 1918 the youngest son, Robert, began school, and she commented to Harold, "I miss him a lot when little errands turn up and I have to run them myself. Well, I suppose I will have to reconcile myself to seeing the children all grow up one by one. I would not have it otherwise. Well, just so they grow up to be the right kind of men and women."[26]

Elsie carried out her motherly role with wry humor. Once when Harold had bashed and lacerated his face in a rough-and-tumble basketball match at Hesston College, she told him: "I think it is up to you to look after the interests of your face more carefully when you play."[27]

After Harold left home, Elsie continued to worry about his well-being. While he was teaching at Hesston College in Kansas, she dispatched two sets of long johns to ward off the cold Kansas winter.[28] With a flu epidemic raging throughout the nation in the winter of 1918, and not getting a letter for several weeks, she feared he had been stricken. "If you do get sick," she wrote, "be sure to do as the Doctor says." During the summer she worried about Kansas tornadoes. And she missed him. "I wish you could come home for Christmas," she wrote, even though she knew he could not.[29] Elsie was a newspaper reader and often clipped editorials or news items and sent them to her son.

The Bender family grew up on Prairie Street. The house into which George and Elsie moved when married was number 1223. A few years later they bought a frame house at 1711, which was then near the edge of the city. All the children but Harold were born in that house. The Prairie Street Mennonite Church was at

1316, four blocks toward the center of town. Most of the Benders' neighbors were not Mennonites, though several Mennonite families lived on Prairie Street. The Bender children had many friends, Mennonite and non-Mennonite. They played with the non-Mennonite Dunn children just down the street, and the boys formed a neighborhood boys' club with the ominous name "Ku Klux Klan."[30] Among their best friends were the children of the John M. Brubaker family, who lived just around the corner. In 1919 the Bender family spent Christmas day at the Brubakers and ate a bountiful dinner with "the usual fixings." They were also close friends of the Joseph D. Brunks, who lived on a farm on the edge of the city.[31]

• • •

In fall 1915 the family moved into a new three-story brick house built to serve as the headquarters of the Mennonite Board of Missions and Charities at 1711 Prairie Street. The Benders' more modest house had been moved around the corner to another lot. That summer George Bender resigned from his job at the post office and became the first full-time administrator for the mission board. For George the change was dramatic. For twenty-four years he had been treasurer of the mission board in its various transmutations, but always unpaid. Now for the first time he could give the organization his full attention.[32]

The decision to hire a full-time administrator and erect the new building reflected the growth of Mennonite mission work, now in its thirty-third year. In 1915 the mission board had a dozen missionaries in India; in 1917 it would begin a mission in Argentina. It also had six home missions, several orphanages and old people's homes, and a sanitarium. Its income in 1915 was more than $150,000, and its total net holdings were above $400,000. George could no longer manage all of that business out of his roll-top desk in the bedroom, after long hours at the post office. The board needed a building with an office, space where board meetings could be held, and facilities where missionaries and board workers could stay en route to or returning from the mission field.[33]

It fell to George Bender to raise the funds for the building, and he supervised its construction. He employed his architect friend Joseph Bechtel of Germantown, Pennsylvania, to draw the plans. Joe Brunk, family friend and Prairie Street member, was the construction foreman. By fall 1915 George had raised the $12,500 needed. The building was dedicated in December, fully paid for.[34] The result was a well-planned and well-constructed building that admirably met the needs of the time.

The building of the mission board house was not without problems. To many of the board members, mostly farmer-preachers, the house seemed excessively fine. It was likely the best-designed and best-appointed house in the MC Mennonite Church at the time. Architect Bechtel had planned to paint the fine quarter-sawn oak woodwork an enamel white, a popular way to finish woodwork at the time. To placate the constituency, it received a neutral varnish. The fireplace, problematic in itself, was to be faced with marble; instead, it was finished with painted brick. The glass knobs on the doors were replaced with plain ones. The new

**The first administrative center for the Mennonite Board of Missions and Charities, and the home of the George Bender family, 1916.**
George and Elsie Kolb Bender papers, AMC.

piano in the parlor came under intense criticism, but Elsie's love of playing and her desire to teach the children the instrument prevailed over George's inclination to be all things to all people.[35]

The family income was now based on a missionary allowance, which included housing. However, the house was also the office for George and the place for meetings of the various boards connected with the mission board enterprise. It was also a major administrative center of the MC Mennonite Church. Thus Harold Bender and his siblings grew up acquainted with the Mennonite leaders of the time. They held meetings at the house on Prairie Street, frequently slept there, and always ate there when they came for board meetings. Elsie and the girls did the cooking.

The week after Christmas 1918 was typically busy. "George bro't Aaron Loucks and Sanford Yoder along home from Chicago Tuesday night, since which time preachers have been gathering in from different directions," Elsie told son Harold. "Saturday we served meals to 54. I served oyster soup to a bunch of 10 preachers Saturday evening. Papa was at the table, too, but of course he did not help to eat the oysters."[36] George did not care for oysters.

• • •

At the center of the family's life was the Prairie Street Mennonite Church. In 1916 the Sunday school class roster listed nine Benders in nine different classes. George taught Class 17 (of 22 classes), a young married and single women's group which at the time was by far the largest class. Harold, absent that year teaching at Thorntown High School, was listed on the roster of Class 18, the young men's class. George was the congregation's deacon, ordained in 1907. At various times he also served as Sunday school superintendent and for many years as church trustee. Elsie sometimes taught a class, but not in 1916.[37]

The Prairie Street congregation was one of the most progressive in the MC Mennonite Church, due largely to the young people drawn to Elkhart by the Mennonite Publishing Company and, after 1895, by the Elkhart Institute. They brought with them the vigor and creativity of youth, and a variety of customs and practices. The result was innovation but also stress and strain.

In 1913 the Prairie Street congregation had more than thirty young people but no activities specifically for youth. Pastor John (J. E.) Hartzler borrowed the college literary idea, applied it to the Prairie Street congregation, and created the Young People's Social and Literary Association. Harold Bender, at 15 years old, became its first president—his first leadership position. The YPSLA, as it was known, drew up a constitution with seven articles and fifteen bylaws, including a provision for the impeachment of any officer by a 75-percent vote of the membership, a five-cent fine for negligent members, and the summary dismissal of any member who voluntarily missed three consecutive meetings. Meetings were held monthly in the homes of parents and operated under Robert's Rules of Order.[38]

YPSLA programs included music, lectures, recitals, and social activities. An early one featured a lecture by India missionary George Lapp. The programs were surprisingly nonreligious. Roll calls were answered not by Bible verses—that began only in the 1920s—but by quotations from Longfellow or Tennyson, nursery rhymes, current events, the name of a favorite car, or some fact about Abraham Lincoln, or other such responses. Many programs featured literary, musical, and current events. In August 1915 Harold Bender, a sophomore at Goshen College that summer, came home to give an address entitled "The German Army from the German Viewpoint."[39]

In the second decade of the century, the Prairie Street congregation had not yet become conservative in attire. A photo of twenty-five young women at the 1914 YPSLA Fourth of July picnic shows not one head covering, at least seven hats, and no plain dress. A 1917 photo of the congregation's Sunshine Quartet shows two bow ties, two long ties, and Harold Bender's tie windblown over his right shoulder.[40] Yet there were efforts to promote a more conservative standard. In 1916 Bishop Jacob (J. K.) Bixler announced that six young women would be dropped from membership because they refused to conform to what Elsie Bender called "the order of the church." Elsie lamented to Harold, "It is too bad that the girls have these things to contend with. In this case the boys have less to fight against."[41]

George Bender, now the deacon, supported Bixler. He was upset when he saw one of the young women, Clara Mumaw, on the street one night. "She looked like a little girl with her skirt not so far below her knee," he told someone. Since several of the women were Goshen College students, George appealed to J. E. Hartzler, who then was the college president, to see what he could do to bring the women around. "If you can do anything with them, I for one will surely appreciate your effort," he told Hartzler. "It is the burden of my life, this little rebellion. But I do feel the church must take a stand."[42]

Elsie Bender was much more tolerant of young people's ways than her husband. "You know I don't believe in keeping young people too tightly reined in," she once told Harold, "because knowing human nature, when they get out where they are their own dictators, there is a reaction." The Bender children, especially the young women, were quite conscious of their mother's benign view about dress, but they also knew their father's practical concern that they conform to the norms of the church. When a church member complained to George that his girls went to school with two ribbons in their hair, one in each braid, the girls found comfort in their mother's sympathetic attitude. They found the requirement to wear bonnets to high school nearly unbearable, but they conformed.

Violet was especially hurt by such strictures. In 1919, as a 19-year-old, she was in charge of a program for the YPSLA. The program that evening was at the home of John B. Moyer, a conservative member of the congregation. Moyer refused to allow Violet to lead the meeting because, he said, she was not a Christian. She had not yet been baptized. Older sister Florence walked the streets with Violet for hours as Violet worked through her anger and frustration.[43]

• • •

George Bender's reputation was built on his ability to raise and manage money. Beginning in 1892 he served as treasurer of many of the new boards being created. A main function of the treasurer was to raise money, and George was good at it. It was said that he could "smell money." He was so adept that when the Mennonite Evangelizing and Benevolent Board decided to build an old people's home at Rittman, Ohio, in 1897, they took the unprecedented step of paying George to be a fundraiser. His key strategy was to solicit wealthy individuals, an approach much in vogue in the general American philanthropic community.[44]

Bender's reputation as a money manager was not built on his own accumulation of wealth; he was a man of modest means. Not trained as an accountant, he developed his own methods. What made people trust him was his strict attention to detail. On his deathbed his last words to Vernon Reiff, his successor as treasurer of the board, were characteristic of him: "I've been worrying about the annuity and endowment records. Do you have them fixed up, and are you sure you understand them?"[45]

Bender was an immensely committed and dedicated man, one of the people in every organization who make the systems work, but who do not ask questions about the fundamental bases of things. He was a progressive conservative—progressive in his support for missionary work, Sunday schools, and the organizational developments of the times in the church; but conservative in his regard for order and respect for authority. However, George was never a doctrinaire conservative: he was a pragmatic conservative who valued order, efficiency, and respectability. As a result, progressives often perceived him as one of their allies.

In early June 1916, Goshen College student Jacob (J. C.) Meyer was returning home to Smithville, Ohio. When he changed trains at Toledo, he found himself sitting next to George Bender, who was en route to an annual meeting of the Southwestern Pennsylvania Mennonite conference. The weather was terribly hot, but "with such a traveling companion, the trip did not seem long," J. C. reported. What impressed the young man were stories Bender told of his difficulties with many of the conservative members of the mission board, and of the adjustments he sometimes had to make to get things done in spite of them. Bender, Meyer decided, was a progressive.[46]

The years of George Bender's treasurership of the mission board after 1906 were rigorous. Financial strictures combined with his intense commitments exacted a price, and during the winter of 1910 he suffered a "nervous breakdown." Daughter Violet remembered him walking the floor, holding his head in his hands, and moaning, "My sins, my sins!" He did not get medical treatment, but he gradually recovered from what today would be classed as severe depression. The experience made him more rigid and religious; as a teenager Violet found herself becoming quite hostile toward him.[47]

In 1918 George Bender discovered that he had Parkinson's disease, and by 1919 he had lost the use of his right hand. He was happy to obtain the services of a secretary and a dictaphone so that he could continue his correspondence. When treatments at Johns Hopkins Hospital in Baltimore failed, he spent several months in a sanitarium at Battle Creek, Michigan. In March 1920 he suffered a nervous collapse, and on April 1 he was taken to the Norway Sanitarium in Indianapolis. His condition deteriorated swiftly. Two weeks later he was totally helpless and required constant nursing care.[48]

Writing to Harold a few weeks later, George began dramatically with "My Dearly Beloved Son," then described his mental anguish and physical pain. Referring to a recent letter from Harold, he said his heart "wept for joy when I read its beautiful sentiments. How I wish I would be in condition to further direct you." After observing, in despair, that he must now give up his position as mission board treasurer, he pronounced a benediction and passed on his fatherly mantle. "Dear Son," he wrote, "I must say I get very homesick. I have prayed daily for grace to bear my trials. My great desire would be for the Lord to take me home. You will have to take my place now and help mother raise the children."[49] For Harold, by then an ambitious young teacher at Hesston College, those words had life-changing consequences: he would not become a Mennonite Central Committee (MCC) relief worker in the Soviet Union or a missionary in Argentina. He would return home to care for his father.

Two weeks later a letter from the medical director of the sanitarium was quite discouraging. The director expected George to require continuous nursing care for the rest of his life. Moreover, George's mental instability made his care so difficult that the sanitarium frequently had to change nurses because they could not handle the stress. The future looked bleak indeed.[50]

The summer of 1920 was traumatic for Elsie Bender. George was in Indianapolis, paralyzed and suffering a nervous breakdown. Numerous church boards continued to meet at the house, and Elsie continued to provide meals and lodging. Wilbur graduated from Elkhart High School. Harold returned from Hesston College, where he had taught for two years, and soon left for a trip to visit the Kolbs in Ontario. Against the expressed wishes of her mentally distraught husband, Elsie made the arrangements and took 19-year-old Violet to Chicago's St. Luke's Hospital for an operation on her foot. In the midst of all those events, Elsie received a summons from the Elkhart chief of police: the neighbors had lodged a formal complaint, asking that the Benders be required to pen up their straying chickens.[51]

Normally a model of unflustered calm, Elsie felt herself buckling under the stress. Referring to the Bender children, she told Harold: "I feel like a driver on a high spring wagon with about 6 teams of frisky colts, trying to keep them all in check."[52] She was worried about Wilbur, just graduated from high school but too young, she felt, to take a factory job and unwilling to work on a farm. However, he could not simply hang around the house, either. The girls needed to decide whether to return to Goshen College in the fall or to hunt for teaching jobs. Returning to college would require money. George had always found a way, but he was not able to do it anymore. And there was the vexing question of what to do with her husband.

In July, Harold visited his father in Indianapolis and, in response to the sick man's importunities, brought his father back to Elkhart. There the family struggled to care for him, part of the time with the help of a trained nurse. In early January 1921, George contracted pneumonia. He died on January 17. He was 53 years old. His youngest son, Robert, was not quite 9. Harold, the oldest, was 23.

# ❧ 2 ❧

# Growing Up

*Harold grows up in Elkhart, meets Elizabeth Horsch at Goshen, graduates from Goshen College.*

HAROLD STAUFFER BENDER was born just before noon on July 19, 1897—a chubby baby who developed quickly. It took some months to find a name; George and Elsie were searching for one that could not easily become a nickname.[1] The teacher in George Bender hated slang, and nicknames were a form of slang. Harold could easily have become "Harry," but apparently he was never called by that name. At Goshen College several of his friends would call him "Hal," but the moniker did not stick.[2] Later in life, associates commonly called him "H. S.," but he always wrote his name "Harold S. Bender."

Harold Bender's life as a traveler began early. In the fall of 1897, the 22-year-old Elsie took the three-month-old baby for a visit to her parents and relatives in Ontario. It was the first of many visits Harold would make to the Kolb relatives at Riverside Farm in the ensuing years. He quickly became a favorite of Aunt Cinda. For his third birthday, she sent him a handkerchief, enjoining him to put it in his pocket and use it: "If you have no pockets in your dress, you must ask Mamma to make some." Straining to write for a three-year-old, she continued, "I wish you would come over here to spend your birthday. I know we would have lots of fun. You could help me pick currants and gooseberries, and you could watch me milking the cows and feed the calves. Don't you think that would be fine?"[3] In a letter when he was nine, she de-

**Harold S. Bender at age three, in 1900.**
George and Elsie Kolb Bender papers, AMC.

scribed in graphic detail how Uncle Irvin had killed a skunk.[4]

By the time Harold was two, he had a new sister, Florence, born in 1899; Violet was born in 1901. When Harold was five, Violet contracted polio, which left her with a crippled leg. That same year Harold began school, a few months after his fifth birthday. He graduated from high school in 1914, shortly before becoming seventeen.[5]

Harold's place in the family was always special, due partly to the gender biases of the time. Having two sisters just younger than he meant that he received more attention from his father than if there had been a close male sibling. Wilbur, six years younger, was never a rival. With the early death of the father, Harold became more like a father than a brother to Wilbur. Moreover, by the time Wilbur graduated from high school, Harold had been away from home for six years. In 1919 Harold commented to his friend Lloyd Blauch, whose brother had just died, that he had "never had a brother as a close friend, all mine being too young."[6]

To his siblings Harold became the absent older brother who sent them gifts and returned home for brief visits. Their letters to him are always warm and admiring. Florence wrote frequently, in a zesty and direct tone. In 1916 when he was teaching at Thorntown, Indiana, she advised him, "I hope you hang up your clothes every day and keep your room in order."[7] In 1918 she attended Goshen College and kept Harold posted on goings-on there. She and her roommates engaged in a series of high jinks that must have pained and amused her sober older brother.

During his elementary and high school years, Harold had a paper route, sold the *Saturday Evening Post* from door to door, mowed lawns, and for two summers during high school worked on Amish Mennonite bishop Daniel (D. D.) Miller's Cloverdale Farm southeast of nearby Middlebury. The arrangements to help on the farm were decided by George Bender and the bishop, who often cooperated on church boards. While working there, Harold learned to know one of his lifelong collaborators, Orie O. Miller. Orie was D. D.'s eldest son and managed the Miller farm during his father's frequent absences on church business. In the 1914-1915 academic year, Orie was a senior at Goshen College and Harold was a freshman.[8]

Harold attended Fifth Ward Elementary School, just a few blocks from home. He was an able student: his fifth-grade teacher claimed he was the most "brilliant" student the teacher had ever had. He was also conscientious. The story is told of a plot by his classmates to embarrass their music teacher by following all of her directions except to sing. Harold refused to go along. When the teacher brought down her baton for the opening beat, Harold burst out in a resounding solo, to the chagrin of his silent classmates. Already he possessed the conscientious persona so evident in later life.[9]

Such seriousness was evident in his first letter to the *Words of Cheer*, an MC Mennonite children's paper. Written in 1909, it was his first published writing:

Dear Readers: This is my first letter to the *Words of Cheer*. I like to read this nice little paper. I am eleven years old. I go to Sunday school every Sunday I can. I will answer some of the questions sent by the boys and girls. Jesus spoke the beatitudes. They are found in Matt. 5. Noah was 120 years building the ark. The waters prevailed 150 days on the face of the earth. The shortest chapter in the Bible is Psa. 117. The first man to get intoxicated was Noah. Abel was the first man to ascend into heaven. The longest chapter in the Bible is Gen. 32. I will close with a few questions. Who built Nineveh? How many sons did Samuel have? What were their names? How did Cain know his offering was not accepted by the Lord? How many stalls did Solomon have for his horses? How many wives did Solomon have?

Yours truly, Harold S. Bender[10]

A year later, at age 12, Harold was baptized and became a member of Prairie Street Mennonite Church. There is no record of the circumstances of his conversion. Not much given to introspection, he seems never to have made public reference to this event. But he soon became a young leader in the congregation, serving as president of a new literary society begun at Prairie Street. Harold was encouraged and mentored by J. E. Hartzler and William B. Weaver, progressive pastors at Prairie Street from 1910 to 1920. The young people perceived Weaver, who taught Bible at Goshen College during those years, as a champion of their causes.[11]

When Harold was ten, his father was ordained deacon at Prairie Street. For years George Bender had looked after the financial affairs of some of the members of the congregation, and by 1907 he had become a de facto leader of the congregation. The ordination recognized both his gifts and his role. Thus by the time Harold was ten years old, his father was a leader at both the congregational and national church levels. Church affairs permeated the life of the family.

Harold entered the new Elkhart High School in January 1911. His studies ran heavily to English and languages with seven semesters of English and Latin, and five semesters of German. He also took a lot of algebra and geometry. He sang in the school chorus and participated in a number of theater productions. His academic record was outstanding. In thirty-six courses he received only four grades lower than 90 percent.[12] He completed high school in three and a half years, graduating in June 1914, a month before his seventeenth birthday.

For the summer following his graduation, Harold went to work on the Harry Kreider farm near Sterling, Illinois. On his trip to Sterling, he traveled to Chicago in the company of the Bender family doctor, George W. Spohn. From there to Sterling he was on his own. It was his first travel adventure, and he told his parents in awed terms that Chicago must have had ten thousand streetcars and motor buses. He enjoyed watching the policemen direct traffic and was impressed by the height of the buildings. He was also quite self-conscious. "I got behind a corner to look at them [the buildings] where nobody would notice me," he told his father, "for

I did not want to act like a rube and stare at them standing still in the middle of the sidewalk."[13]

Harry and Ruth Kreider were a childless, middle-aged couple living on a 132-acre dairy farm. Harold enjoyed Ruth's cooking. "We have all the strawberries we can eat every meal almost. I have 2 big dishes full sometimes." He liked the work but was not completely at home milking cows. "He has a fine bunch of cows. I milked three (Whew!) and it wasn't so hard at that." At the end of the letter he drew a cartoon-like cow, including a switching tail, a pesky fly, and the cow saying "Moo." He wanted badly to go swimming but, he told his parents, "the only creek was so shallow that you have to lay [sic] on both sides to get wet all over and then stand on your head to get your hair wet."[14]

Each night Harold wrote letters, one of them in German to a German pen pal. When he learned that his pal had sent a card to Elkhart, he asked his mother to mail it on to him without translating it. "I can do that myself," he said. "I have become quite proficient in the German script." He missed his family, closing one of his letters with "Kiss them all for me, papa, especially mama and Robert." Robert was two years old.[15]

• • •

Harold began his studies at Goshen College in the fall of 1914. He studied there from 1914 to 1916, including two summers, and then returned to complete his degree with a major in history and social science in 1917-1918. His student days spanned the classic era of "old Goshen," the period before 1923-1924, when the college was closed and then reorganized, with a radical change in character. "Old" Goshen embraced many of the optimistic and rational conventions of American liberal arts colleges. In the 1920s Bender and his college friends of that era would speak of the "Goshen man," a reference to a style and mind-set that valued the rational and refined pursuit of knowledge.

The college promoted eloquence, and students cheered for the debate teams as if debate were a sport. There was much emphasis on classical music. The men's and women's glee clubs sang a wide range of music, from religious to whimsical and popular. The glee clubs toured among congregations, Mennonite and non-Mennonite, and were in demand for a variety of performances at secular events. Harold (and later Florence) sang in the glee clubs.[16]

The style and spirit of Goshen College when Harold Bender arrived in September of 1914 was caught by a special Goshen Choral Society dramatization of Handel's cantata "Saul." The singers, from the college and from the city of Goshen, were directed by Alvin J. Miller, who taught history at the college and was a member of the popular Rambler Quartet, a college singing group. The enactment took place on the lawn under the stars and in costume. Several soloists came from Elkhart, but most were Goshen College persons. A small orchestra and Mrs. M. C. Dow, a local pianist, accompanied the chorus. The local paper, the *Daily Democrat*, claimed it was "one of the greatest musical successes ever given in Goshen by a local organization." By popular request the performance was repeated a week later. Harold Bender missed the event; he was still milking cows in Illinois.[17]

The key figure at the college in those years was its dynamic president, John E. Hartzler. Hartzler had been pastor of Prairie Street Mennonite Church, and in 1913 he became the president of Goshen College. Until his resignation in February 1918, he set the college's tone and direction. He was nearly a generation older than Harold Bender and a genuine turn-of-the-century Mennonite progressive. Born into an Amish Mennonite family, he was reared in Missouri. Like so many of his generation, he fell under the profound influence of revivalist John S. Coffman. In 1904, at age 25, he was ordained, and he quickly became popular as an evangelist. In 1910 he graduated from Goshen College, receiving one of its first B.A. degrees. Eventually he would earn a Ph.D. at Hartford Theological Seminary.

Hartzler was an intelligent and ambitious proponent of progressive education as it was developing at the University of Chicago during his studies there. He also had a charismatic and rhetorical eloquence, developed during his work as an evangelist. But although a compelling leader, by 1918 he was too progressive for the church fathers. Moreover, his aggressive building of facilities and faculty outstripped the resources the church was willing to supply. Hence, the college's board quickly relieved him of his post. But before that happened, Harold Bender spent important and formative years of his intellectual growth and development in the shadow of J. E. Hartzler and cosmopolitan "old Goshen."

Attending Goshen College was a natural course for Harold, and with his characteristic energy, he plunged into college life. A picture in the 1915 *Maple Leaf*, the college annual produced for the first time that year, shows Harold as vice president of the freshman class, holding a pennant with his friend Orie (O. B.) Gerig, who was president. Each of the fifty-four members of the class received a descriptive caption: Harold's was "A Herald of truth, a great defender." No doubt it referred to his enthusiastic work on the freshman debate team.[18]

Harold was a member of the Oratorical Association, which managed intercollegiate debates, events generating great excitement. Usually Manchester College and Mount Morris College were the opponents, but in 1918 at the last minute, those two colleges begged wartime exigencies and reneged. Goshen's students were chagrined, and one of their debaters, Raymond Rychener, used language reminiscent of contemporary sports hype to write a droll poem for the *Maple Leaf*, accusing the colleges of dropping out because they feared Goshen's prowess.[19] Also central to much of the cultural and social activity on campus were the literary societies. The societies were organized by gender, two for men and two for women. Harold joined the Adelphians, sharing membership with such upperclassmen as Martin (M. C. or "Cliff") Lehman, Amos (A. E.) Kreider, and Samuel E. Yoder—people with whom he would work later in life. The *Maple Leaf* photo of the Adelphians includes a youthful but earnest Harold S. Bender.[20]

Bender plunged into his academic work with zest. In his English courses, he earned A's and B's. In German he earned two A's and a B under the benevolent tutelage of professor Daniel S. Gerig, a man the *Maple Leaf* characterized as "an optimist who can fully appreciate the comedy of the student's ludicrous German translation."[21] In algebra and trigonometry he earned nine credits. His professor was the austere and precise Daniel A. Lehman.

Nine hours of chemistry netted Harold three more A's under the dynamic Jonathan M. Kurtz, who attracted a large circle of students. In 1914 Kurtz organized the Chemical Society, a group open to anyone with more than nine credits of chemistry. Bender joined the Society as a sophomore and eventually earned eighteen chemistry credits, which in 1919 became a real boon as he taught the first-ever chemistry course at Hesston College. All in all, academically, Bender's first year was a resounding success. He had obtained forty-two credits of 180 needed for graduation, and earned them (in a time when B was not an easy grade) with five B's and nine A's. His academic career was off to a good start.[22]

During the summer of 1915, Harold studied full-time, earning an additional 10 credits in zoology.[23] At one point during the summer, President Hartzler brought Woodrow Wilson's Vice President Thomas R. Marshall to campus to address the college assembly. Also during the summer the city of Goshen voted on prohibition, and Goshen became a dry city.[24]

As a student Harold lived in the mission board house at 1424 South Eighth Street, just across College Avenue from the campus. The house was a residence for missionaries on furlough, and any extra rooms were rented to students. Harold usually went home to Elkhart on weekends.

• • •

In his second year, Harold came into his own on campus. The sophomore class was small; only 16 members of the original 54 freshmen returned. Sometime during the year, he began dating Gladys Weldy, an Elkhart High School senior from the Prairie Street congregation. She was a round-faced girl with widely spaced eyes, an impish expression, and a fashionable twist of hair arranged to fall over the center of her forehead. Gladys proved to be a bit worrisome to Harold's parents. "I am sure it would suit us much better if you would not have anything special to do with her," George Bender told his son.[25] Harold assured his concerned father, "We are friends just as I am with all the girls at home."[26]

The sophomore year was important for Harold's future, for

during the year he established a number of relationships important
later in his life. The "big" man on campus was J. C. Meyer. Meyer
was editor of both the college's annual, the *Maple Leaf*, and its
campus newspaper, the *Record*. He also was president of the Oratorical Association, secretary of the YMCA, vice president of the
Student Council, and member of several other organizations. He
was a bright philosophy and education major and destined to be
one of a group of pioneering young Mennonites who went to
France in 1918 for postwar reconstruction work.

Another mover and shaker was Lloyd Blauch, president of the
Student Council and a fellow history and social science major.
"Blauch" was one of Harold's roommates. Years later Harold
would close one of his letters to Blauch with "Sincerely, Your Old
Bunkie."[27] Raymond Hartzler, a classmate from Topeka and an ardent debater, was also a roommate and remained a close confidant
for many years. Jesse (J. N.) Smucker, who eventually held nearly
every student office at the college, was another bosom friend, one
of a "triangle," as Harold called his three-cornered friendship with
Smucker and Hartzler.[28] Other fellow students were important later
in Harold's life, such as Orie Miller and his younger brother
Ernest. Orie would become executive secretary of Mennonite Central
Committee, and Ernest president of Goshen College in 1940.

The academic year 1915-1916 was momentous for Goshen
College. President Hartzler pushed forward the building of a new
science hall. It was scheduled to be done in 1915, but financial
problems delayed its completion until spring 1916. The cost estimated originally at $25,000 ultimately reached $50,000. More
fateful and destructive for the long-term viability of the college was
a decision to buy and equip a farm as a laboratory for an agricultural program. Daniel Kauffman, the prominent church leader and
president of the Mennonite Board of Education, made the argument for it in his usual dogmatic fashion: "I am an ardent advocate of an agricultural annex to our schools. We want to plan for
a practical career for our young people, a career in which they will
be of practical help to the work among and for our own people
and the rural field in general. It is an absolute waste of time and
energy and a suicidal policy to fit our young people for places a

hundred miles off, where there is no opportunity to exercise their talents where they can be of practical use to the Church and the Church to them."[29]

The idea of an agriculture program appealed to church leaders. Harold Bender's own bishop, J. K. Bixler, a quite conservative churchman, wrote an article, probably at the behest of President Hartzler, for the September issue of the *Record*. In it he echoed a rural life emphasis prominent in mainline Protestant denominations at the time. Bixler believed agricultural education could become a means to rejuvenate Mennonite rural churches.[30]

From President Hartzler's point of view, agricultural education was especially attractive: at last the college was doing something that might bring rank-and-file Mennonites to support the college. So Hartzler bought an adjacent farm, erected modern buildings, equipped them with livestock and machinery, set up an agricultural curriculum, and hired faculty to operate the farm program. It was a huge investment at a time when the college was strapped for cash. And it failed. Student interest was minimal, nor did the program noticeably increase financial support.

Meanwhile, Harold Bender's second year was even more successful than his first. He studied organic chemistry, French, some history, and New Testament, and he made nearly all A's. He was elected a member of the Student Council, while his friend, L. E. Blauch, was president. Bender was also on the Students' Lecture Board, which planned an annual series of campus addresses.[31]

As a member of the Oratorical Association, Harold was involved in forensics and the annual peace contest. In the *Maple Leaf* he appeared, bow tie slightly askew, as a member of the sophomore debate team. The sophomores lost their contest to the freshmen, and Bender did not make the intercollegiate debate team. The intercollegiate team was strong in 1915-1916 and won three of its contests with Manchester and Mount Morris colleges.[32]

In his sophomore year, Bender emerged as a joiner, mover, and scholar. "With memory remarkable," the *Maple Leaf* reported, "he delves into the history of the past, devours current events, and ventures predictions for the future. What he wills he does."[33]

• • •

Harold again attended summer school in 1916. That summer his uncle Christian (C. E.) Bender, principal of the Oakland, Maryland, high school, came to Goshen to direct the summer teacher training course.[34] The program had 140 students. Harold took the course in preparation for a teaching position he had just taken at a high school in Thorntown, Indiana. Then he wrote the state normal examination required of all Indiana teachers. His principal at Thorntown would be impressed when he saw Harold's high scores in September.[35] In 1916 Harold was nineteen years old. The teaching job at Thorntown was an unwelcome detour for the ambitious young man, but his decision to take the job was prompted by his need for money to continue his education. He had borrowed as much as he could and now had to pay off some debts.[36]

However, the need to drop out of college also generated some soul-searching. Harold was searching for direction. In letters to his friend Jesse Smucker, a junior that year at Goshen, he agonized over what he called the "life-work problem." What direction should his life take? On the central point, he was clear: he was absolutely committed to Christian service. But exactly what service was not yet clear to him. Complicating everything was the "social problem," as he delicately put it, meaning young women and marriage. Should he press forward on the courtship front (apparently with a girlfriend at Thorntown) or should he put off "social" activity until he had the "life-work" business settled? Jesse, a level-headed fellow, urged his impatient friend to relax and not try to solve everything right away.[37]

At Thorntown, Bender boarded with a local family and enjoyed its good food. The cost was $5.00 per week—a bit much, he thought, since it did not include laundry. But the family had a piano that he was allowed to use. They also had a car, and on the first Sunday morning after his arrival, the family's 20-year-old daughter took him for a two-hour drive to show him the area. He admired her fast driving, but in a clear effort to allay any fears his parents might have had, he also pointed out that she would soon be leaving for college.[38]

Thorntown had a Presbyterian and a Methodist church. After visiting both, Harold selected the Methodist meetings because he liked the sermons of the tall robust pastor (also named Bender). He became active in the congregation, attending morning and evening services. On Washington's birthday, he attended a party in the church parlor sponsored by the Epworth League. He enjoyed the monthly meeting of the Brotherhood, a men's group, and he sent his father a copy of its constitution with the remark that he wished "our church might have such an organization." Communion Sunday posed a problem: should he participate? After the fact, and without revealing whether or not he had taken communion, he asked his father, "I was wondering if our church permits members to partake in such a service with other churches?"[39] In fact, his church did not.

Bender's work at school was grueling. Each forenoon he taught seven different subjects to sixth, seventh, and eighth graders. In the afternoon he had two sections of algebra, a course in German, and an American history course. In all, he taught about 140 students each day. He also coached the grade school boys' basketball team and tried to teach them volleyball. Each morning he read *Tom Sawyer* to his homeroom, except on Monday when he had a devotional based on the Psalms. There were many discipline problems. Once he rapped the knuckles of four boys who painted rings on their fingers. Harold's mother was impressed. She wished he were teaching in Elkhart so that she could visit his class and watch him teach.[40]

Harold was happy when the year at Thorntown ended and he could return to Goshen College. There was a cloud on the horizon, however. In 1917 the United States entered the World War, and Harold was an obvious candidate for the draft. He escaped with a deferment based on a promise to study theology in preparation for the ministry. The deferment actually came from George Bender's unusual ability to trade on personal relationships and his considerable charm. In this case the elder Bender happened to meet a key member of the Elkhart draft board on the Prairie Street trolley. In the course of their conversation, George expressed his concern about Harold's draft status and appealed to the draft board member for help. The encounter paid off; Harold's appeal for a draft deferment was duly expedited.[41] His way was clear to return to Goshen College.

• • •

By the summer of 1917, the financial situation of Goshen College was desperate. President Hartzler had worked strenuously to raise money, but all of his efforts fell short. In 1913 a fledgling Alumni Association had begun a ten-year drive to raise $50,000 for endowment; President Hartzler had promised to raise two dollars for each one pledged. The ultimate goal was to create a $200,000 endowment fund. After three years with little progress, Hartzler hired a professional fund-raising group, but they also failed. Eventually the college raised about $30,000, but most of that was from Hartzler's success at promoting the Musselman Fund, a memorial to a young Goshen graduate who had died just before he was to leave for a mission field. Most of that money came from the Musselman family in Pennsylvania. There was extreme shock when, despite all of the fund-raising efforts, an audit found that the college was $150,000 dollars in debt and had an ongoing operating deficit of about $4,000 per year.[42]

The financial difficulties of the college were closely linked to broader Mennonite church developments at the time. By 1915 many of the young progressives of the 1890s were the middle-aged leaders of the organizations their progressivism had created. Their challenge, as some of them saw it, was to manage the new institutions in order to control "the drift." They usually defined "the drift" in terms of theological "modernism" and worldly behavior. In 1905 the Mennonite Board of Education was created to manage Goshen and Hesston colleges on behalf of the MC Mennonite Church. By 1915 some members of the board were convinced that Goshen College was "drifting" into theological liberalism.

Efforts to stem "the drift" took a variety of forms. In 1915 the Board of Education heard a committee report on the status of the music department; the concern was about the use of musical instruments. There was concern also about the hiring of teachers who were not Mennonite. In the summer of 1917, the board's Religious Welfare Committee asked members of the faculty to write a paper stating their position on the fundamentals of the faith. And there was great concern about the use of certain textbooks.[43]

In 1917 the creation of Eastern Mennonite School (EMS) at Harrisonburg, Virginia, added another element to the mix. Conservatives now had an educational alternative. In early 1918, EMS's new president, Jacob (J. B.) Smith, wrote a vigorous letter to the MC Mennonite Church's Board of Education, challenging its members to "stand tall and stop the spread of liberalism." Among Smith's specific complaints were two articles in the Goshen College *Record*, one by President Hartzler and the other by Harold Bender's girlfriend, senior Elizabeth Horsch. Smith was a member of the Board of Education even though he presided over a rival school not under that board's jurisdiction. Despite the conflict of interest, Smith was a vociferous critic of Goshen College. His type of criticism was a major cause of the decline in the church's support for Goshen College and of Hartzler's resignation.

The premier "old Goshen" year was likely 1917-18. The *Record* and the *Maple Leaf* exhibited an exuberant spirit and style that would not soon reappear. Harold edited the *Maple Leaf*. With a long section on campus life, filled with college spoofs, humor, and literary asides, his issue lightheartedly summed up the college year. A first-year student caught the campus spirit in a piece she wrote about English professor Isaac Clayton Keller, newly arrived from Harvard and Columbia Universities:

### A Freshman Dream

I'm takin' English VI this year,
I'm just a freshman feller,
And the hardest thing I have to do
Is writin' themes for Keller.

The other night I had a date,
With my best girl—don't tell 'er,
I broke the date and stayed to home
To write a theme for Keller.

I dreamt our Sammies took Berlin,
And started hard to shell 'er,
We took old Kaiser Bill and made
Him write a theme for Keller.[44]

Harold's last year of college was clearly his best, filled with romance, a heavy academic load, and a whirlwind of activity. "Like
a mighty ocean moves this man of brains" was the way the *Maple
Leaf* described him. A quick summary of his extracurricular appointments gives some idea of his frenetic activity and a foretaste
of his future modus operandi. He was editor-in-chief of the *Maple
Leaf*, president of the
Adelphian Literary So-
ciety, vice president of
the Student Council,
secretary of the Ora-
torical Association, ad-
vertizing manager of
the Men's Glee Club,
exchange editor of the
Goshen College *Record*,
treasurer of the senior
class, assistant in chem-
istry, chairman of the
Booster Club of the
Philharmonic Chorus,
and chairman of the
Bible Study department
of the Young People's
Christian Association.
He also sang in the
Philharmonic Chorus,
the Men's Glee Club,
and the Glee Club's
quartet. Somehow he
found time to be a
member of the senior
debate team.

**Harold Bender as a student at Goshen
College in 1918.** Bender Family Album.

Academically, Bender plunged into studying the Greek language (consistent with his draft deferment), making straight A's. He did not do as well in biblical theology, where he earned B's, but he earned straight A's in economics, sociology, history, chemistry, and philosophy. By the end of the academic year, he had completed the required 180 credit hours for graduation and done so with a stellar academic record of 40 A's and 12 B's.[45]

Harold's most time-consuming activity was editing the *Maple Leaf*. He got the post even though Bernice Lehman had been the associate editor the previous year and might have expected to become editor-in-chief. With that assignment Harold's lifework as an editor began. The 1918 *Maple Leaf* was clearly better than previous ones in its design, its attractive light-green page borders, and its excellent text. It had an extended section that combined the usual college calendar with a new section on college life. The result was thirty pages of spoofs and humorous high jinks, some with a kind of joe college quality that must have brought considerable pain to college critics. One gets the impression that the midyear presidential transition from Hartzler to India missionary George Lapp may have given the students a bit freer hand than usual.

There was also romance. Harold met Elizabeth Horsch early in the fall semester. By December they were a couple, a fact highlighted by what came to be known as the "Kendallville caper." During Christmas vacation the Men's Glee Club toured Ohio. The group traveled by train, and en route to Elida, Ohio, for their first concert, they had to change trains at Kendallville, Indiana. Everyone made the change but Harold. He did arrive at Elida in time for the concert, but with Elizabeth Horsch and one of her friends in tow. His lame but much-enjoyed explanation was that he had forgotten to get off the train at Kendallville. The merriment increased when he left the Glee Club tour after only three days to visit "relatives" in Pennsylvania. He actually did visit Bender relatives in Somerset County, Pennsylvania, but everyone assumed (and his buddies insisted) that he also visited Elizabeth at her home in Scottdale. A section in the *Maple Leaf* called "Senior Tips and Quips" satirized "Harold, the leader, our editor-in-chief, while he's with his friends, train-rides are brief."[46]

**Elizabeth Horsch as a student at Goshen College in 1918.** Bender Family Album.

Elizabeth Horsch was a shy but bright and attractive member of the senior class. The *Maple Leaf* called her "dainty and brilliant."[47] In 1913 at Scottdale, Pennsylvania, she had graduated as the valedictorian of her high school class. "Our minds are given to us, but our characters we make for ourselves by slow and steady growth," she had told her classmates and their parents. It was an elegant speech—so good that the Mennonite family paper, the *Christian Monitor*, published it three months later.[48]

After two years as a Linotype operator at the Mennonite Publishing House, Elizabeth had studied for two years at Hesston College in Kansas, where she was one of seven students enrolled in the college course. In the fall of 1917 she transferred into the senior class at Goshen College. Harold later recalled that they met for the first time in Kulp Hall as she came down the steps on her way to dinner.[49] Actually, they almost certainly had met as young children in 1900, when both families lived in Elkhart: Elizabeth would have been five and Harold three. In any case, at Goshen the relationship blossomed, although it would be a slowly maturing courtship, taking five years, hindered after 1918 by distance and poverty. But for one magic year, Harold and Elizabeth were together and enjoyed each other thoroughly.

Apparently no other couple got as much good-natured joshing from their fellow students as did Harold and Elizabeth. The June-July 1918 *Record* published what the editor called a "Farce Comedy" in three acts:

> Scene—A Goshen floral shop.
> Characters—two G.C girls; one G.C. man, Mr. B. (a Senior)
> Act I—Mr. B. "Could you girls advise me as to what kind of
>     flowers to get for my mother for Easter?"
> Act II—(In pantomime) The florist gives Mr. B. a box of previously
>     ordered flowers, while the girls look on.
> Act III—(Also in pantomime) Mr. B. arrives at Kulp Hall with
>     the flowers.
> Finale—His mother lives in Elkhart,
> Therefore—[50]

No one had to guess who the characters were.

The *Maple Leaf* gleefully reported a dinner conversation between Payson Miller and Elizabeth Horsch.

> Payson—"I always feel so much at home when people call me by
>     my first name."
> Miss Horsch—(without thinking) "Yes, so do I. This afternoon
>     Mr. Bender called me by my first name, and I liked it so much."[51]

**Elizabeth by the water.** Bender Family Album.

Photos from 1917-1918 show Elizabeth arrayed in a white dress with a scarf around her neck, wearing a white-brimmed hat pulled fashionably low across her eyebrows. She and Harold were smart dressers. Harold often wore a three-piece suit, frequently with a bow tie. Many of the shots are of the couple in the woods or along the river, obviously on Sunday afternoon outings. There are many group photos, a dozen students on the banks of the river, or posing in front of one of the college buildings. In such shots Elizabeth stands out, with large, wide-

**Top: Elizabeth rowing. Bottom: Harold and Elizabeth.** Bender Family Album.

set eyes and a round face framed by soft upswept hair. At this stage of his life, Harold had a ruggedly handsome appearance, his short stature not yet accentuated by too much bulk. In one picture he holds a tennis racquet, dressed in a white suit, white shoes, and a white felt hat. Harold and Elizabeth were a handsome couple. No wonder they were the talk of the campus.

In 1917-1918 Harold was definitely the big man on campus. By contrast, Elizabeth was not a lead-

**Elizabeth Horsch.** Bender Family Album.

**Harold Bender and Elizabeth Horsch in the summer of 1918 with their friends (from the left) Mary Lantz, Jesse Smucker, and Nora Burkholder.** Bender Family Album.

er. The *Maple Leaf* characterized her as "modest, simple, and sweet."[52] Elizabeth's only office was Mission Study department chairperson for the Young Women's Christian Association, a position she held because of her interest in eventually becoming a missionary. She sang in the Women's Glee Club and in the Philharmonic Chorus. She gained a reputation for intellectual competence for an essay published in the Goshen College *Record* entitled "Ignorance vs. Error." Ideas govern the world, she argued, and are key to all progress. All ideas preexist human understanding (Plato), and humans discover ideas through impres-

**Harold Bender meditating.**
Bender Family Album.

sions (Locke). Those impressions will sometimes be in error, but error is a necessary price for knowledge.[53]

Except for a few lapses in syntactic logic, the essay was tightly argued and intellectually impressive. She had written it for a sociology course under professor Weaver, Harold's pastor at Prairie Street Mennonite Church. Weaver had the essay published in the College *Record*, a normal practice for outstanding student papers. A few weeks after the essay appeared in print, J. B. Smith of Eastern Mennonite School read it. He did not like Elizabeth's essay nor another written by President Hartzler. So Smith responded with his

The senior class at Goshen College in 1918. Front row: Ruth Yoder, Vesta Zook, Maude Byler, Harold Bender. Middle row: Elizabeth Horsch, Vinora Weaver, Bernice Lehman, Alma Warye. Back row: Robert Hartzler, Elizabeth Liechty, Payson Miller, Jesse Smucker.
Bender Family Album.

letter to the Mennonite Board of Education, six pages of impassioned prose about rampant liberalism at Goshen College.[54]

Upon learning of Smith's letter, Elizabeth's father, John Horsch, began to do damage control. Horsch was the leading MC Mennonite historian and was just establishing a reputation as a crusader against theological liberalism. In a letter to Smith, Horsch blamed Elizabeth's piece on Professor Weaver, who he said had the paper published without her consent. Furthermore, Horsch suggested, it really did not express Elizabeth's views. He claimed Elizabeth had told him that she no longer gave her own opinion in class but tried to tailor her responses to what the teacher wanted. Such temporizing, Horsch assured Smith, explained the objectionable essay. Furthermore, father Horsch argued, "the question of who has written the article is of secondary importance. The fact that it was selected by a college teacher and published in the college paper can not be explained away." Smith accepted Horsch's point: blame the liberal professor.[55]

The episode's meaning could not have been lost on Elizabeth. Neither Smith nor her father ever specified which points in the essay were so objectionable. It was simply liberal and wrong. Equally distressing must have been the realization that by blaming Professor Weaver, President Smith and father Horsch were dismissing her ideas and disparaging her integrity. For Elizabeth, this was the opening episode of a lifelong struggle to preserve her personal integrity. Her typical response became to withdraw from the fray. By contrast, Harold, usually more astute than his accusers, learned either to outmaneuver them or, more typically, to hedge his bets by accepting short-term compromise in hope of long-term gain.

At Goshen, as at most colleges, commencement was a major event. In 1918 it began on Sunday evening, June 2, with a baccalaureate sermon by the new president, George J. Lapp, and ended five days later with the conferring of degrees on Friday evening. In that year of world war, the activities took a solemn turn on Thursday evening with the reading of two letters from classmates Payson Miller and Russell Lantz, who could not be at the commencement. Both had been drafted and were struggling as conscientious objectors at the army's Camp Taylor in Kentucky. Under arrest for refusal to cooperate with the camp regimen, they had written the letters in prison tents under armed guard.[56]

• • •

With graduation behind him, Harold urgently needed to find a way to earn some quick money and pay off his considerable college debt. The war was raging, and the American economy was booming. Jobs in defense-related industries paid well. Harold learned that the Goodyear Tire Company in Akron, Ohio, paid unusually good wages, thanks to a major contract to produce rubber gas masks for the War Department.[57] So the week after graduation, he left for Akron, settled in at the YMCA hotel, and almost immediately landed a job at Goodyear, working on the gas mask assembly line. The job paid exceedingly well, with the potential (depending on how much he worked) of earning as much as $45.00 a week.

George Bender was worried, oddly, not about the compromise of nonresistance involved in war production work but instead that Harold might mishandle his money. "Remember that you have a big debt which needs to be paid, so make a special effort to do some tall financiering," he admonished. "Do not spend any more money than you must."[58]

How could Harold square working in a defense-related industry as a Mennonite? Actually, he had an answer: If drafted, he intended to take some form of noncombatant service, probably in the army medical corps. In the summer of 1918, he was not an absolute conscientious objector.[59] Four of Harold's friends from Prairie Street Mennonite Church were drafted that summer. Two entered noncombatant service and two the regular military.[60] During 1918 few if any of the young men of the Prairie Street congregation seem to have harbored strong nonresistant convictions.

Harold's friend Ernest E. Miller was much more morally torn by the issues the draft raised. He and his new bride, Ruth Blosser Miller, had been selected to go to India as missionaries, but since Ernest was of draft age, they could not legally leave the country. Miller refused a farm deferment, telling George Bender he did not want an easy way out. He had wanted to do reconstruction work in France with a Quaker unit that Mennonites were joining, but its workers had to wear a military-like uniform, and he could not do that, either. But, given all the suffering in the world, he wanted to do some sacrificial work somehow.[61] Eventually Miller went to the Near East, where he did don the uniform worn by Near East Relief workers.

Harold Bender did not take such a firm stand. His draft board left him in limbo until early September, when it summoned him for a hearing, but by then he had left for Hesston (Kansas) College. George Bender appeared before the board on Harold's behalf, "had a very nice interview," and secured another theological deferment, based on a promise that Harold would take a Bible course at Hesston as further preparation for the ministry.[62]

## ⚹ 3 ⚹

# Teaching and Courtship

*Harold teaches at Hesston, falls in love with Elizabeth, locates an intellectual middle ground.*

THE SUMMER of 1918 was busy for the Bender family. In the spring George had been hired by the MC Mennonite Board of Education to help raise money to retire the huge Goshen College debt. He was quite successful, helped by wartime prosperity and inflation. By midsummer he and several others had raised $90,000. This was not enough to meet all the needs, but enough to keep the college open and afloat.[1]

Elsie and the two little boys spent several weeks at the Kolb's Riverside Farm in Ontario. Florence began a job at the shirtwaist factory above Zeisel's store on Main Street in Elkhart. Wilbur and two friends made an overnight bicycle trip out into the country to visit some buddies. Cecil had an ulcerated tooth pulled, and Violet had an operation for an unspecified illness. Meanwhile, the mission board house was full of visitors, a George H. Rupp from Pennsylvania staying for ten days.[2]

Harold, busy at his Goodyear Rubber factory job, spent many of his summer weekends at the home of his friend Jesse Smucker, who lived near Orrville, Ohio, less than 25 miles from Akron. In July, Jesse and Harold arranged for a trip to attend a Sunday school conference at Topeka, Indiana, hosted by their former college roommate Raymond Hartzler. The trip took on special interest when the indefatigable Jesse proposed that Harold persuade Elizabeth Horsch to come to Orrville to join her friend Nora Burkholder

**Uncle Daniel Bender, President of Hesston College.** Daniel Bender papers, AMC.

(girlfriend of Raymond Hartzler), and have the foursome make the trip to Indiana in the Smucker family auto. A year later, Jesse, marooned and lonesome in a dusty village in eastern Syria as a Near East Relief worker, would remember the trip fondly.[3]

Harold's summer job in Akron was an interlude. In mid-March he had received a letter from his uncle Dan, president of Hesston College, inviting him to join the faculty there in the fall of 1918.[4] The invitation to teach at Hesston came largely because of Harold's family connections. It is doubtful that in 1918 president

Bender would have hired any other Goshen graduate. By then D. H. Bender was quite a conservative man, unhappy with Goshen College, and frankly skeptical of Harold's orthodoxy. A year and a half later, he would tell George Bender, "Harold has made some marked improvement toward conservatism, but I feel his Alma Mater still has more influence over him than we have."[5]

Harold knew he was on probation. When he filled out the Hesston faculty questionnaire, he responded to the section on his faith and doctrinal position with the comment, "I am in harmony with the expressed views of the Mennonite Church found in the Manual of the Mennonite Board of Missions and Charities"—a masterful way to place himself under the aegis of a statement his father and Dan Bender had helped write.[6]

Meanwhile, Elizabeth had been invited to join the faculty at the new Eastern Mennonite School (EMS). In this instance it seems clear that President Smith, so critical of Goshen College, would not have hired any other Goshen graduate. Elizabeth was acceptable because she was the daughter of John Horsch. So Harold and Elizabeth found teaching jobs at the two conservative Mennonite schools, separated by a thousand miles, largely on the basis of their fathers' reputations.

Harold decided to go to Hesston mainly because he had to have a paying job. Throughout much of his life, Harold would have money problems. While never deeply in debt, he never quite managed to live within his means. In that regard, his experience during the Hesston years was typical. In the fall of 1918, he still owed $550 on his school debt. At Hesston his salary was nearly $800. His goal the first year was to pay $300 on his debt and retire the entire amount by the end of the summer of 1919. He failed to reach his goal. By spring 1920 he still owed $340 but promised his father he would send or had sent $260, which left only $80. He hoped to pay the balance by the time he returned home to Elkhart in June 1920.[7]

In September 1918, Harold Bender had a college degree and a teaching position at Hesston College in Kansas, but he did not intend to become a college teacher. His goal was to become a missionary in Argentina. It was a new field: the first MC Mennonite missionaries had begun their work in 1917. In preparation for mission work, Harold planned to study at a seminary for several years. To move the plan forward, George Bender did what he did best: he raised money to help pay for Harold's first year in seminary.[8] But first Harold had to retire his college debt. From Harold's point of view in 1918, teaching at tiny Hesston College was an undesirable but necessary detour before he could get on with his life's main agenda.

• • •

In 1918 Hesston College was on the move. Begun in 1909 as an academy and Bible school, by 1918 it had become a four-year college, changing its name to Hesston College and Bible School. The expanded program offered three curricula: a college course, a Bible course, and an academy course. In 1918 it was the largest MC Mennonite school, with 14 students in the college, 115 in the academy, and 57 in the Bible school. By comparison, enrollment at Goshen in 1918-19 was 71 in the College and 63 in the academy, while EMS, the new school in Virginia, had 38 students, all at the academy and Bible school levels.[9]

The town of Hesston was located twenty miles north of Wichita, Kansas, and some six miles west of Newton, where the GC Mennonites had a college named Bethel. Hesston, the town, took its name from A. L. Hess, who owned the Hesston State Bank and operated the grain elevator and the creamery. When Hesston Academy was begun in 1909, Hess had provided the land for the campus and had served as its primary financial angel during its early years. In 1918 the school completed its second structure, the Administration building, where Harold taught his first courses. The tiny campus had only one other building, Green Gables, where Harold lived during his first year.[10]

In 1909 Harold's uncle D. H. Bender had become the school's first principal, and in 1918 he became its first president. Bible teacher J. D. Charles was the college dean. In 1919 the new college had three B.A. graduates: Menno D. Landis, Chester K. Lehman, and Noah Oyer. Eventually Lehman became dean of EMS and Oyer dean of Goshen College; eventually Harold Bender would become Oyer's successor at Goshen. In 1919 Hesston's faculty and administrators numbered only a half dozen. Other persons on the faculty or in the student body who would be significant in Harold's future were Paul and Alta Mae Eby Erb, Edward Yoder, Christian ("Chris" or C. L.) Graber, and Edward Diener.

By 1918 Hesston College was a main center of new conservative forces in the MC Mennonite church, reflected particularly by an emphasis on regulation attire and a conservative eschatological doctrine known as premillennialism. The contrast with Goshen was striking. At Hesston in 1918, all women wore the prayer veiling and many wore cape dresses. At Goshen, not one woman student wore a prayer veiling except at worship services. Many of the Hesston men, perhaps most, wore the "plain" or "regulation" coat, without lapels. At Goshen in 1918, only Arthur Slagel, who would join the faculty at Hesston in 1919, wore the plain coat.[11]

Sometime during Harold's first months at Hesston, his father urged him to don the plain coat and offered to pay for one. George was always concerned about appearances and eager to help his firstborn shed the image of Goshen liberalism. But Harold refused the offer. He told his father that he had "absolutely no conviction on the matter." If he wore it, he said, he would do so "only in deference to the wishes of yourself and Uncle Dan." Doing so had not been a condition for his coming, and if wearing it was to be a permanent practice, he was not yet ready to comply. Wearing the coat now but discarding it the next year when he went elsewhere would almost certainly be misconstrued by the church leaders, he told his father. It would hurt his reputation. How would it be if he wore "a high-cut vest"? he wondered. In any case, he promised to talk with "Uncle Dan" about it.[12]

George did not press the point. "As to the plain coat, let it rest for the present," he told Harold. "Our offer will still be open."[13] By the spring of 1919, Harold had agreed to wear the coat the following year; that was one of the conditions for his continued employment at Hesston. His "old Goshen" friend Ray Hartzler kidded him about rumors that he was wearing "the coat." He replied, "I decided that since it is expected here both at the school and in the conference and since my future might be involved, that it would be the best policy to conform for the period of my stay out here."[14]

Harold also broached the issue of premillennialism with his father, complaining that most of the faculty were "radical premillennialists and practically unchristianize and unchurch a man if he fails to agree with their view. This is true of Erb (Paul), Oyer, Charles, etc." However, he observed that Uncle Dan was not a "pre." George assured his son that "I am neither PRE or POST [*sic*]. The church has no doctrine on this subject. So neither side can call the other unorthodox. It is not essential to Salvation no matter to which side you belong."[15]

Harold exhibited a surprising degree of anxiety as the issues swirled about him at Hesston. He was glad that he did not have to share a room with anyone, he told Raymond Hartzler, because living alone made it easier to keep his own counsel. "I rather hesitate to speak freely since their prejudice especially on theology might get me in a bad way. So I am rather by myself." In fact, he was quite surprised by how different Hesston was from Goshen. Hesston people inject religion into everything, he complained. "One can't escape from it."[16]

At first Harold rebelled and got into several arguments, but as he explained to Hartzler, he soon realized that argument was futile. But "I don't know how long I can hold in when they get to talking about the world going to the dogs and how that winning the world for Christ is all right as a slogan but can never be realized and that social reform is contrary to the Bible, etc. ad infinitum in ibido." In the fall of 1918, Bender's progressive Goshen College mind-set had not yet come to terms with Hesston's conservatism.[17]

Harold's reaction to Hesston was echoed in the observations of his Goshen College friend O. B. Gerig. While teaching at nearby Bethel College in 1920, he visited Hesston and gave Harold his impressions. "I must say that while the folks all seemed to use me civilly, yet I could not help but feel that I was being pitied for my limited vision of the truth," Gerig confessed. It was all quite "annoying," he said, "to a person schooled in freer institutions."[18] He wondered how Harold had stood it. But by then Harold had been at Hesston for two years and no longer agreed with Gerig's assessment.

• • •

Harold's teaching load was heavy: nineteen class hours each week, most of them in the academy. He taught New Testament Greek, French, two sections of algebra, and geometry. He also took a biblical introduction course for college credit in order to meet the conditions of his draft deferment. The course was taught by Noah Oyer. While Harold enjoyed it, he also got the impression that Oyer was going out of his way to try to win him over to premillennialism.[19]

But not all was work and theological argument. In October, Harold transferred his church membership to the Hesston Mennonite congregation. He played basketball (once suffering a nasty eye laceration) and helped organize tennis matches. When his uncle Fred Bender came from Pennsylvania for a visit, he and Fred went

**Harold and a friend, after a rabbit hunt near Hesston in 1919.** Bender Family Album.

on a jackrabbit hunt. Harold did not go home to Elkhart for Christmas in 1918, partly to save money and partly because he could not: a record-breaking blizzard made travel impossible. He spent part of the holiday at Uncle Dan's, taking along some Bender maple syrup which they turned into taffy. In addition, he received invitations to community homes, enjoying a "fine Sunday chicken dinner at Coopriders." Throughout the year he sang in a quartet that often accompanied Uncle Dan for programs at area churches. There was also sorrow. In late November 1918, Uncle Dan's wife Sallie Miller Bender died. Harold was disappointed that his parents did not come to the funeral.[20]

In the fall of 1918, with Chester Lehman and J. D. Charles, Harold visited Mennonite conscientious objectors at Fort Riley.[21] On a Sunday afternoon in November, Chester Lehman, Paul Bender (Harold's cousin), and Harold visited the Bethel Hospital in nearby Newton and sang for the patients.[22] In January 1919, Harold was elected secretary and Paul Erb moderator of the Kansas-Nebraska Young People's conference.[23]

In February, Harold completed an article for the *Gospel Herald* entitled "Rationalism"—his first adult effort to write for a churchwide paper. He appealed for "simple faith" as the key to Christian living. Editor Daniel Kauffman was not much impressed and returned it with the comment that while "it presents a number of things worth noticing, I suppose some will find it beyond their reach." Harold had asked that his name not be attached to the article, but Kauffman refused. He also objected to Harold's use of slang, such as "Adam spilled the beans." Rewrite the piece, and we will publish it, Kauffman promised. Harold rewrote it, but it was never published.[24]

During 1918-1919, Harold kept his campus profile rather low. He rarely appeared on programs and was seldom asked to speak, especially compared to the frequent appearances of J. D. Charles, Noah Oyer, and Paul Erb. In March he did give a chapel address entitled "Principles of Good Manners," in which he argued that unselfishness and genuine love are the basic ingredients for etiquette. He outlined some essential rules of proper behavior and concluded with a homily on the character of Jesus.[25]

By the end of March 1919, Harold had agreed to teach at Hesston for another year. A few weeks later, to his profound chagrin, he received an invitation to teach history and sociology at Goshen. It was just what he had hoped for, he told Raymond Hartzler, "but the Fates have it otherwise, so I am here."[26] Harold's disappointment was not shared by his father: George Bender did not want Harold to teach at Goshen. As a member of the Goshen College board of trustees, he was disillusioned with Goshen's administrative confusion. If you want to come east, you should teach at Elkhart High School, he told his son.[27]

On Good Friday of 1919, Harold and Uncle Dan attended a founding meeting of a new MC Mennonite congregation at Yoder, Kansas. While they were there, one of the members offered Harold $7.00 a day to work on his threshing crew. To Harold, the wages seemed princely compared to his Hesston salary. "I'm going to get rich off the wheat," he joked. But it was not just the money which drew him. "One of the main reasons for going to an out-of-the-way place like that is to help in the S. S. and church work, as they need workers badly," he explained. "I think I can do some real missionary work there." And there would be other benefits. "The hard work will be good for me, and in addition I will very likely have to speak Pennsylvania Dutch all summer as the whole settlement is as Dutch as can be."[28]

When word of Harold's summer plans reached the Bender family doctor, he immediately called George to warn that Harold was physically flabby, Kansas was dreadfully hot, and threshing was hard work. Tell Harold to take it easy until he gets toughened up or he will permanently harm his health, Dr. Spohn warned. Probably with the doctor's advice in mind, George vetoed a request from Harold that younger brother Wilbur be sent out to join the threshing crew. Instead of threshing in Kansas, Wilbur spent the summer working on a farm near Sterling, Illinois.[29]

• • •

By the spring of 1919, Harold was searching for future direction. One option was college teaching. Uncle Dan wanted him to stay at

Hesston. "He is making good," Dan told George, who by then
was a patient at the Battle Creek Sanitarium. "He is an intelligent
young man, and I would like to see him held solidly for the
church."[30] Harold wanted to teach at Goshen, but his father's opposition made that course impractical in the near future.

Another option was to become a missionary in South America. In February Harold wrote to Argentina missionaries Joseph
(J. W.) Shank and Tobias (T. K.) Hershey asking for information
about the Argentine situation. Both men counseled him to complete a well-rounded graduate and seminary education before
coming. "These one-sided educated fellows make poor sticks of
missionaries," Hershey told him.[31] In June, Harold and C. K. Lehman attended the MC church's mission board meeting near Kalona,
Iowa, traveling there by way of Cass County, Missouri, and attending the dedication of a new children's home in Kansas City. At
the mission meeting, Harold's interview for a possible appointment in Argentina went well, the understanding being that he would
teach for one more year at Hesston and then attend seminary for
two years. During the summer, George was able to find a donor
who offered $400 to help cover Harold's seminary expenses.[32]

A second real option was to become George Bender's assistant
at the mission board. By 1918 the work had become more than
George could handle, and the board authorized him to hire an assistant. Upon Harold's graduation, George had offered the position to his son, but Harold turned it down. George then found
Vernon Reiff, a Kansan, who came to Elkhart in mid-March 1919
to be his full-time assistant. In September of 1919, Harold suddenly offered to become George's assistant after school was over in
1920; George must have been nonplussed.[33]

The explanation was romance. Earlier in September, Harold
had spent a week visiting Elizabeth Horsch at Eastern Mennonite
School, their first encounter since the previous summer, when
Harold had visited her at Scottdale after working at Akron, Ohio.
The visit to Virginia apparently confirmed their affection for each
other. Future Mennonite Publishing House agent Abram (A. J.)
Metzler had just arrived at EMS as a new student and was stand-
ing in his dormitory room overlooking the driveway and veranda

**Elizabeth Horsch at Eastern Mennonite School in 1918. On the left is her colleague Marian Charlton.** Bender Family Album.

of the old school building in Park Woods. He observed a red roadster with its top down, coming up the circular driveway in front of the building. As the car came to a halt, Elizabeth Horsch skipped down the porch steps with a picnic basket in her hand. The car, Metzler knew, belonged to a young local Mennonite, but the driver was Harold Bender. Harold stepped smartly out of the car, held the door for Elizabeth, and got back in the car. Off they went, north toward the mountains and an all-day outing, with Elizabeth's head scarf whipping in the breeze.[34]

Harold had marriage on his mind, though as he ruefully told his friend Raymond Hartzler, who had just recently married, he was doing his "best" to carry out his mother's advice not to get married before age 30. In that wonderfully smart "old Goshen" language used by Harold and his friends when speaking about their romantic activities, Harold told Raymond that "I have not been forgetting to improve the time in the meanwhile," but as yet "there are no secret treaties." However, he went on, "it is necessary to keep hidden the negotiations leading up to the final league [an allusion to President Wilson, at that moment negotiating the Treaty of Paris, which included a proposal for a League of Nations], "since the premature publication of the proceedings might seriously jeopardize the final outcome."[35]

Hartzler had just settled with his bride, Nora Burkholder Hartzler, into a small farmhouse near Topeka, Indiana. He found "home-making a very interesting and enjoyable experience, one which you cannot afford to miss even at the expense of marrying earlier than your mother suggests." Harold, single, on the bleak plains of Kansas, responded that Hartzler's description of home life was "quite entrancing, almost too much so in fact. A man shouldn't be tempted like that when he has so many years of preparation yet before him as I have."[36]

If Harold had settled at Elkhart to assist his father, that would certainly have made marriage to Elizabeth a possibility. George Bender liked the idea, too, but by September 1919, Vernon Reiff had already been at work as George's assistant for six months, liked his job, and did it well. George's loyalty to his son was strong, and he tried to give Reiff some broad hints that he would not try to hold him if he could get another job. Reiff, however, failed to take the hint. George had to admit that he was "at a loss to know what would be best to do," but in any case it was too late. By the spring of 1920, George was much too ill to train Harold as an assistant. Harold's future would not be in mission board administration. And marriage would have to wait.

Harold considered one other possibility. In January 1919 the Mennonite Relief Commission for War Sufferers decided to send relief workers to the Near East, and within a few weeks a contingent of nine Mennonites were on their way. In the group were two of Harold's friends, Orie O. Miller and Chris Graber. Several months later two more Goshen friends, Jesse Smucker and Ernest Miller, joined the contingent. To Bender, Hesston must have seemed like a long way from the real action.

During the fall of 1919, American Mennonites became aware of a dreadful famine in the areas where Mennonites lived in the new Soviet Union. From his father Harold learned of plans to send a relief contingent to aid the famine-stricken Mennonites in the Soviet Ukraine. The opportunity to join the relief contingent was almost irresistible, and in January 1920 Harold wrote to his father asking for information and offering his services. Gravely ill and hospitalized at the Battle Creek Sanitarium, George Bender could not bring himself to agree to Harold's request. "Personally, we would not prefer your going," he told Harold. "I believe that if you have in mind to go to school some more, that now would be the best time to go."[37] It was inconceivable that Harold would go against his father's wishes in the matter, but in any case the issue was moot. By the time the first relief workers were selected to serve in the Ukraine, Harold had no choice: he would care for his terminally ill father.

In late July 1920, a group of Mennonite leaders met at the mission board house to hammer out the details of the organization to support the Soviet work. While Harold busied himself tending to his father in the first-floor bedroom, Aaron Loucks, Levi Mumaw, D. D. Miller, P. C. Hiebert, Maxwell Kratz, Orie Miller, his uncle Dan Bender, and five others met upstairs in the second-floor conference room. There, during an intense all-day meeting, they created a new inter-Mennonite relief organization they named the Mennonite Central Committee (MCC).

Peter (P. C.) Hiebert, a Mennonite Brethren leader from Kansas, became chairman of MCC; Levi Mumaw of the MC Mennonites became secretary-treasurer; and Maxwell Kratz, a General Conference Mennonite from Philadelphia, became the vice-chair. Orie Miller, by then a young businessman in Akron, Pennsylvania, was appointed director of the relief contingent. Chosen to accompany Orie Miller to the Ukraine were Arthur Slagel, Harold's fellow student at Goshen and fellow teacher at Hesston the past year, and Clayton Kratz, a junior at Goshen College from Perkasie, Pennsylvania.[38]

Had Harold been free, he would almost certainly have been a member of the relief contingent. Two years later, Slagel, writing in a pensive mood from Alexanderovsk, recalled how they had planned to come to the Soviet Union together and regretted that it had not worked out. Harold had no way of knowing how formative this event would be in shaping his own life and in the devel-

opment of one of the most important twentieth-century Mennonite organizations. In any case he was near, but not present, at
MCC's creation.[39]

• • •

The two years of teaching at Hesston College helped establish
Harold Bender's mind-set in ways that would persist throughout
his life. The conservative emphasis at Hesston forced him to search
for his own personal worldview. Some of his "old Goshen" friends
pressed him from the other side, critical and even disparaging of
his fidelity to the "old church."

At one point Raymond Hartzler needled him: "I note that you
are getting more the church point of view" (as over against the
view Harold had held at Goshen).[40] Harold did not enjoy the
good-natured kidding. "My first reaction to what you wrote about
Goshen, Hesston, myself, et al., was to be just a bit peeved," he
told Hartzler. "This feeling was augmented by further rumors that
I had 'flopped' and changed theological skin like a chameleon. The
stuff began to pour in from all sides till I was well-nigh sick of it."
Characteristically, he put the best face on it by observing, "In a
way it did me good because it showed me that I had succeeded in
my main policy here this year and had not committed any serious
indiscretions of speech or conduct." But he was peeved that his
friends thought he was too weak "to stand on my own feet upon
coming into a new atmosphere."[41]

Already at age twenty-two, Bender was engaged in what
would be a lifelong effort to forge his own path, searching for a
balance between liberals and conservatives. A penchant to think of
himself as a liberal who was searching for a mediating position between extremes came through clearly in 1919 as he tried to explain
himself to his friends. He was glad he had come to Hesston, he
said, because he had an opportunity to get "acquainted with the
conservative viewpoint and a few of the influential men who control affairs on that side." What he really valued about the Hesston
years, he told Raymond Hartzler, was that he had learned to curb
"any tendency I had toward undue radicalism, and it made me

more sympathetic toward present church leaders and their purposes and made me more tolerant and willing to sacrifice non-
essentials for the sake of the general welfare of all concerned."[42]

Harold had a pragmatic view of how to operate in the Mennonite milieu. As he explained to his friend Hartzler, "A man can't let
petty things stand in the way and compromise his whole future position and usefulness. New things must come in gradually, but by
evolution, not by revolution, and if a man starts out by being a
rebel in our church, he usually ends up on the dump."[43] What
made good sense to Harold must have sounded to many of his
friends like blatant opportunism.

On Harold's mind must have been the somewhat acrid correspondence he had been having with his Goshen friend J. C. Meyer,
who was in France that year with a Society of Friends reconstruction unit. To Harold, Meyer seemed like a rebel. Letters from Meyer
were often ill-tempered outbursts of frustration with the timid and
other-worldly character of Mennonite church leaders. At the June
1919 MC mission board meeting, the Mennonite Relief Commission learned that some of the Mennonite men in France had been
wearing leather leg puttees and cast-off military caps.[44] So the commission had, as Meyer put it, "legislated puttees and caps off."[45]

The commission action, so far from the scene and by persons
so ill-informed, infuriated Meyer. "If these brethren had come with
some of us and worked in the rain for these weeks every day without rainproof coats, and with but one work suit, with little or no
fire at night, in rooms without windows, and with food one would
not eat in the USA—they might have forgotten that some fellows
have a pair of leather puttees and a cap and might have been
thankful for a dry coat and shirt when morning came," he told
Harold. "You see, it gets on some fellows' nerves when you are
soaked and chilly and the guy who has all the comforts one could
wish for tries to assist you by pouring cold water on your crani-
um, or by talking to you about your socks or headgear, both of
which need a good wringing out."[46]

What had set Meyer off was Harold's plaintive argument that
the commission was made up of sincere and honest men, who
might not always understand things very well, but who deserved

"sympathetic cooperation." Meyer agreed that they were sincere. Yet, he observed, "good intentions may pave a road, but it may lead where I do not want to go." Against Harold's arguments, Meyer cited Aaron Loucks as leader of the first Mennonite relief contingent to the Middle East. Meyer and others considered Loucks simply incompetent.[47]

J. C. Meyer, drafted during the war, had spent some hard time as a conscientious objector in a military camp; he often referred to that experience to justify his positions. The implication was fairly clear, although never explicit: You, Harold, took a theological education deferment arranged by your father, and you counsel me to be patient and obedient? Clearly, Bender and Meyer had drastically different ideas of how to interact with the church fathers. Over the next several years, that fact would become ever more apparent as they tried to work together in a new Mennonite Young People's Conference.

Harold saw himself as a liberal who was trying to understand the conservatives. He agreed that some of the conservative leaders were all too biased. He would "fight these things in them, but it will not be a personal fight; it will be a friendly one—as far as they permit. Furthermore, I am compelled to admire their ability in spite of myself. And just here is where I tremble for our wing of the church and the things we stand for. Where are our men who are real leaders, who can match their opponents? *Nullus gnosit* [none know]. We've got to produce men with sufficient brain power, executive capacity, hard common sense, and leadership to meet on their own grounds."[48]

The "we" in Harold's mind were clearly the faculty, students, and alumni of "old Goshen." "We," he told Raymond Hartzler, "had a wonderful opportunity in J. E. Hartzler, but neither you nor I need explain why he failed. As I get around more, I realize what a hold he really had on the people and what a wonderful chance there lay before him." The problem with Hartzler, Harold insisted, was that "he failed in execution as well as in brain power. Where are *our* men who can take his place?" he wondered.[49]

• • •

Harold's work in the Kansas harvest fields during the summer of 1919 went well. His friend Edward Yoder reported that Harold had earned "considerable money."[50] But the summer was not all work. At the Yoder Mennonite congregation, Bender led the singing and conducted a series of Sunday evening Bible lessons. In August, at the end of the harvest, he traveled home to Elkhart and then on to Scottdale to see Elizabeth. The two proceeded to Harrisonburg, where Elizabeth began her second year of teaching at EMS and Harold attended the biennial general conference of the MC Mennonites.

From Virginia, Harold returned to Kansas, arriving by train in Newton on a Sunday evening. J. D. Charles, Hesston's dean, met him at the railway station. The Newton-Hesston area had not had rain for six weeks, and the dust billowed up in huge clouds as Harold rode to Hesston in the dean's big Maxwell touring car. Harold was about to begin his second year of teaching.[51]

An upbeat mood prevailed that fall at Hesston College. Enrollment was up, and a major morale booster was the arrival of Arthur Slagel of Flanagan, Illinois. "Art," as he was known, had just graduated from Goshen in the spring with a music degree and was the head of the new music department at Hesston. Now in the fall of 1919, Harold finally had an "old Goshen" pal at Hesston. They roomed together at the Cooprider boarding house on the edge of the Hesston campus and took their meals at the home of Joe and Lizzie Hershberger, just across the street.[52]

Slagel's music transformed the atmosphere at Hesston. He immediately organized a chorus of students and faculty and in the fall produced Gaul's *David the Shepherd Boy*. Harold sang the role of Samuel. Enormously popular, the program was given several times off campus. Later in the year, the chorus performed the *Messiah*, again to rave reviews.[53]

In 1918-1919, Hesston College had an able young faculty. The dean, J. D. Charles, was a popular teacher and speaker. Other faculty members were Noah Oyer, Paul and Alta Erb, Edward Yoder, Arthur Slagel, Mary Mensch, M. D. Landis, and Harold Bender. So much young talent brought new zest to the institution. Harold began the year by introducing the first chemistry course ever offered at Hesston. The administration provided him with a sizable budget to get the chemistry laboratory set up. The *Journal* reported that the "class finds the study quite interesting." Most of Harold's classes were in mathematics and languages.[54]

Despite heavy teaching assignments, Harold, Art Slagel, and Noah Oyer began a class in Hebrew grammar with a Professor Pearson at Friends University, traveling to Wichita every other Saturday for the class. It was a rigorous course. After completing the grammar requirements, they had to learn the first chapter of Genesis by memory, in Hebrew. Tuition cost $50.00, and George Bender was none too happy about the expenditure. Harold assured his father that he would save money in the long run, by getting a head start on language study for seminary.[55]

Harold was faculty adviser to the Philomathian debate team and sponsor for the sophomore class. At commencement time, the class, realizing he was not returning the next year, gave him a special farewell party, complete with ice cream and cake. After a farewell speech, he led the group in prayer, and everyone clasped hands and sang "Blest Be the Tie That Binds."[56] Harold was also president of the tennis club, leadership he shared with Alta Mae Erb, who was vice-president. Since the ravages of Kansas weather kept Hesston's tennis courts in constant disrepair, the tennis enthusiasts spent many hours keeping them in shape. Apparently the president of the tennis club did not escape the hard labor. A family photo shows Harold posing in front of the courts, dressed in white: shirt, tie, vest, and tennis shoes. He was holding not a tennis racquet but a spade.[57]

During his second year at Hesston, Harold was more prominent in public programs. In February, he was the chairman and moderator of the annual Kansas-Nebraska Mennonite missionary conference. During the year, Harold, Edward Yoder, Noah Oyer, and Art Slagel presented special programs on "Missions" at various churches. Bender usually spoke on "Our Suffering World and Our Responsibility."[58]

The young Hesston teachers enjoyed numerous trips to Wichita. In February, Slagel, Oyer, Erb, Yoder, and Bender attended a lecture by Sherwood Eddy on "Present World Conditions: A Challenge to America." A few weeks later, the same group went to Friends University to meet a Princeton seminary representative and talk about study at the seminary. Former Hesston student Chester K. Lehman was already at Princeton. In the fall of 1920, Noah Oyer would go there, followed in 1921 by Harold.[59]

There were personal matters to attend to. Having said yes to wearing a plain coat, Harold let his parents get him one. Because his room at Cooprider's was chilly, he had his mother send his blue-and-gold basketball sweater from Goshen College days. At Christmastime he told his mother, "I put on my heavy underwear about three weeks ago and have had them on ever since." They were the same two suits he had gotten two years before, he said, and they showed no signs of wear, except that all the button holes were worn out. "It's a job that I suppose will never get done till I get a wife to do my mending for me," he told his mother.[60]

In December he was quite homesick. "The nearer Christmas

**Harold at his desk at Hesston College in 1920. Note the picture of Elizabeth on the desk.** Bender Family Album.

comes, the more I wish I could be home again, but since it is not possible, I suppose the best way would be to not think about it. I even dreamed that I received a telegram telling me to come home for Christmas and promising money for the fare."[61] He did send each family member a gift, even though his father had told him to save his money instead. For Florence and Violet, there were silver Eversharp pencils. The boys each got a book.[62]

The big Christmas gift was a watch for Elizabeth. His parents had advised against the expenditure, but he told them later that "after looking on all sides of the question pro and con, I took it and sent it along east the other day." It had, he said, "a beautiful little silver case with bracelet and 15-jewel Swiss movement; its face dial was gold, I think, and could be covered with a dime." He had gotten it at a bargain, he assured his frugal father, because it was from the previous year's stock.[63]

"One of my Christmas boxes brought me a fine warm hand-knitted sweater," Harold told his mother. It was from Elizabeth. "It is just the thing to wear around the house, and it's pretty enough to take into the best company. It's just a slip-on without arms and a cutout neck of a rich brown color, all wool too." He clearly liked it and wore it continually. His mother, for unspecified reasons, felt he did not "look quite natural with that sweater on."[64]

By spring 1920, George Bender's deteriorating health became a concern. Harold wrote his father a reassuring letter, ending with "I remember you continually in my prayers and ask God to bless you and restore you speedily to health according to his will and promise."[65] Harold must have been unsettled by George's disturbingly rapid deterioration during the spring and his transfer to the Norway Sanitarium in Indianapolis in early April.

The 1920 Hesston commencement ceremonies ended on June 3, and the next morning Harold left the campus. He was on his way home to Elkhart. Another chapter in his life had closed.

• • •

Those two years at Hesston had complex consequences for Harold Bender's life. One of his reasons for going there had been to earn money so he could attend seminary. Though he did manage to pay his debts, he returned to Elkhart in June of 1920 with only about fifty dollars in his pocket. His goal to save money to finance his seminary education remained unrealized.

Bender had gone to Hesston initially because his father wanted him there and because Uncle Dan was president. Why he stayed for the second year is unclear, but the effect was to keep him out of reconstruction or relief work. Had he chosen such a venturesome course, his life might have taken quite a different direction. That he did not elect such a course offers a clue to the character of Harold Bender. Cautious by nature, he was an unusually dutiful son. By age twenty-three, he had also become a dutiful churchman. The two-year sojourn at Hesston, even though a kind of exile from the Goshen campus where he really wanted to be, was a reasonable service he was willing to offer.

The two years at Hesston had a major significance which his father saw with great clarity. "Harold, I am so very grateful to our dear Heavenly Father that you did not get to France," his father told him. "It looks like divine intervention. The church needs our young men, but what will they amount to after they have destroyed the church's confidence in them."[66] George was delighted that "your reputation is good. I trust you will never mar it." Harold, safe in the bastion of conservatism, stood in vivid contrast to some of the impatient young men in France and the Middle East who were giving the church fathers so much difficulty.

Being at Hesston also meant that Harold was not at Goshen College, the other center of conflict in the church, and thus, to borrow George Bender's phrase, "not tainted." There is little doubt that the invitation to come to Goshen when the college reopened in 1924 was possible only because of Harold's absence during the previous stormy years. Being at Hesston shielded him from a rocky stretch of Mennonite church turmoil.

One can only regret that Harold was not more venturesome. The experience in the rough-and-tumble world of reconstructing France or relief work in the Middle East might have been an important antidote to his lifelong penchant to operate within the safe confines of a few institutions. Eventually his life pattern was to travel incessantly, but always for limited periods of time. Like a homing pigeon, he always returned quickly to Goshen. Harold Bender led a rich and fruitful life, but it never involved a sustained, years-long alternative life experience. His life orbit encompassed the United States and Europe. He made one quick trip to the Middle East and a visit to South America; but the axis of his life stayed on or near a line stretching from Chicago to Princeton to Heidelberg. His only home was Goshen, Indiana.

## ✦ 4 ✦

# Leader of Young People

*Harold learns to know John Horsch, presides
at the Mennonite Young People's Conference,
argues with John L. Stauffer.*

HAROLD arrived home late on Friday night, June 4, 1920, after
two years at Hesston College, carrying his life possessions in a set
of suitcases. He was glad to be home, but his future was quite uncertain. His hopes of going to Princeton Seminary in the fall were
just that, hopes. Overshadowing everything was the illness of his
father and the nursing George Bender would require. By early
June, the doctor diagnosed his condition as physically helpless,
perhaps requiring round-the-clock care for many years. How to
provide that care was a matter not yet settled.

On Monday, June 7, Harold plunged into the activities at
Goshen College, which combined commencement with a twenty-
fifth anniversary celebration of the institution's founding. He attended a special conference on issues and problems in the church,
addressed by the presidents of the boards of education, missions,
and publication. Late in the afternoon, he attended a meeting of
some twenty young people; several of the young men involved in
a Young People's Conference movement reported on plans for a
convention at West Liberty, Ohio, in August. It was Harold's first
meeting with the founders of a movement he would soon be elected to lead.[1]

Harold also attended a long and interesting Goshen College
twenty-fifth anniversary program. Clearly, the program was intended to reassure alumni that the college was still alive and well.

In reality, it was a last hurrah for the "old Goshen" alumni: only three years later the college would be closed for a year, a victory for the conservatives.

In the summer of 1920, however, conditions at the college appeared to be improving. The aggressive leadership of a new president, Irvin (I. R.) Detweiler, seemed to offer some new hope. What most buoyed confidence was the February 1920 accreditation of Goshen as a standard college by the state of Indiana.[2] This meant that any with a bachelor of arts degree from Goshen could enter graduate schools in Indiana without examination, and graduates of Goshen's teacher training program were accredited to teach in Indiana's public schools. In the fall of 1920, the college enrolled the largest student body in its history. But the successes could not deflect the difficulties lurking on the horizon. By the next summer (1921), president Detweiler was in deep trouble with several members of the Board of Education; by 1922 he was forced to resign.

• • •

On June 18, Harold and his mother visited George Bender in Indianapolis. After consulting with his doctor, they decided to bring him home as soon as he was strong enough to travel. It was urgent, for the medical and nursing costs at Indianapolis were astronomical, totaling more than $110 a week. The mission board was committed to paying the bills, but even the board could not manage such expensive care for long.[3]

Since his father could not come home until he regained some strength, Harold decided to use the time to visit his Kolb relatives in Ontario. On the return trip, he planned to visit Elizabeth at Scottdale. Typically, waiting until the last minute to pack his bags before catching the train, in the rush he forgot his pajamas; so his mother sent them with Phoebe Kolb, a cousin, who was traveling to Ontario the next day. She also sent some film he had left behind.[4]

Harold had not visited his mother's family in Ontario in many years, and he enjoyed the time immensely. A picture shows him posing with a yard full of relatives. His mother, sounding envious, wrote, "I suppose you are enjoying yourself. I don't see as it could be otherwise."[5] Originally, he had intended to stay only one week so that he could be with Elizabeth at Scottdale over the Fourth-of-July holiday, but he scrapped that plan and stayed in Ontario an extra week. By doing so, he could meet and help settle the "boys," his little brothers John and Robert, whom the family sent over so that they would not be underfoot when George came home.

Harold spent nearly two weeks with Elizabeth at Scottdale. A month earlier Elizabeth had returned home from Eastern Mennonite School, and that summer she was working at the Mennonite Publishing House (MPH) as the "German" linotypist.[6] It may well have been during Harold's visit that she made the decision to take a teaching position at Hesston College for the 1920-1921 school year.[7] One can only conjecture why Elizabeth decided to teach at Hesston during a time when Harold would be living in Elkhart. If propinquity was their goal, Hesston was no help. Likely Hesston was able to offer her more varied teaching assignments than EMS. Also, it may have helped that her good friend Estie Miller had just moved from Scottdale to Hesston as the bride of Edward Yoder. In any case, she would spend the next year teaching at Hesston College.

Harold's visit was his third to the John Horsch household. Aside from the romantic link, the visit acquainted him with an interesting Mennonite family. John Horsch worked as the German-language editor for MPH. Both John and Christine Horsch were

**Elizabeth (front center) at Hesston College in 1920.** Bender Family Album.

immigrants from Germany. The scholar Ernst Correll, a family friend and German immigrant who often visited the Horsch home in Scottdale, once told Elizabeth that "there is no place in America that brings me nearer home [Germany] than the atmosphere of your parental home."[8] The Horsch family spoke German and English, but for the parents the favorite was German. Christine Horsch, Elizabeth's mother, always scolded her children in German and always prayed in German.[9] All of the children spoke German in near-native fashion; Elizabeth was especially proficient.

By 1920, Elizabeth's father, 53-year-old John Horsch, had lived in the United States for thirty-three years, having come to the United States in 1887 as a nonresistant fugitive from German military conscription.[10] He was also a fugitive from his father, Jacob Horsch, a south-German Mennonite bishop and prosperous farmer. The elder Horsch had intended his son to be a farmer, a vocation for which John was temperamentally and physically unsuited. Jacob Horsch never reconciled with his youngest son and eventually disinherited him.[11]

At twenty years old, a frail, boyish-looking John Horsch had arrived, penniless and hungry, at the doorstep of the John Funk home at 520 Jauriet Court in Elkhart, Indiana. He had no money; when he disembarked at Ellis Island, he had given all of his cash to a hapless young woman with a small child. Since he had his train ticket, he was able to get to Elkhart, but he could not buy food on the trip.[12] He went to Elkhart because in Germany he had read Funk's *Herold der Wahrheit*. The hospitable Funk gave him a warm welcome. From 1887 to 1895, Horsch worked for Funk's Mennonite Publishing Company, serving as an assistant editor of the *Herold der Wahrheit* and helping to produce Sunday school quarterlies and a German-language almanac, the *Familienkalender*.[13]

During those first years, John Horsch briefly attended three colleges, studying church history, Greek, and Hebrew. His eventual goal was to teach those languages at a college. He was a good student, making excellent grades, all the while struggling to learn English. In those years he also began assembling an Anabaptist library.[14]

Elizabeth Horsch's parents had experienced an unusual court-

**John and Christine Funck Horsch at the time of their wedding in
1893.** John Horsch papers, AMC.

ship. In 1893, John Horsch was living in Elkhart and decided to
get married. He had known Christine Funck only casually—both
their fathers were elders and pastors in south-German Mennonite
congregations. How the marriage arrangements were made is unclear. Since John's father had ostracized him, it perhaps is surprising that another elder in the tiny south-German Mennonite church

would give his daughter in marriage to John. Perhaps John's mother, who remained his advocate throughout her life, helped in the arrangements.

In any case, the 23-year-old Christine Funck came to America in 1893 with a dowry and her family's blessing. John Horsch traveled to Ellis Island to meet her and brought her to Elkhart. A delightful family story recounts that the young couple traveled by day coach to Indiana; Christine, exhausted by her long voyage in steerage aboard ship, leaned her head on John's shoulder as they rode the train out of New York. Horrified, John exclaimed, "Christine, pick your head up! We are not yet married!"[15]

They were soon married, one of the conditions for marriage being that Christine wear a Mennonite bonnet, something she did with reluctance. Christine's dowry provided funds for the couple to buy a house which then became a boarding place for Mennonite Publishing Company and Elkhart Institute employees.[16] Elizabeth was born on February 7, 1895. That same year, John Horsch left the Mennonite Publishing Company over dissatisfaction with some of John Funk's business practices. It was a courageous but imprudent move, because Horsch's prospects for making a living were not good. The result was a thirteen-year period of poverty and uncertainty for the young family.

Casting about for a livelihood, Horsch first tried his hand at producing and selling a breakfast cereal, but the venture failed. When Elizabeth was two, the family moved to Madison, Wisconsin, where her father enrolled at the University of Wisconsin. Unable to financially sustain his studies, they moved back to Elkhart, and Horsch continued publishing a German-language farm paper called *Farm und Haus*. That venture also collapsed. In 1900, John Horsch became an employee of J. A. Sprunger, a charismatic, freelancing Mennonite involved in a variety of evangelical publishing and social-service projects. The Horsch family moved first to Berne, Indiana, then to Cleveland, and finally to Vermillion, Ohio, where John Horsch helped operate an orphanage. Both father and daughter were influenced by Sprunger's preaching; in 1907, when Elizabeth was twelve, Sprunger baptized her by immersion.[17]

Elizabeth had three younger brothers. Walter was born in 1898,

Menno in 1901, and Paul in 1908. The family fortunes improved by 1908. M. S. Steiner, the president of the MC's mission board and one of Horsch's friends from Mennonite Publishing Company days at Elkhart, persuaded Aaron Loucks, publisher at the new MPH in Scottdale, Pennsylvania, to hire Horsch as editor for German-language material. John Horsch had finally found his niche. He continued that appointment until his death in October 1941.

• • •

When the Horsch family moved to Scottdale in 1908, it was a boomtown, supplying coke for the expansive iron-and-steel industry in nearby Pittsburgh. By the time Harold visited Elizabeth in 1920, some of the boomtown atmosphere was gone, but it was still a bustling small city.[18] Of the thirteen churches in Scottdale, one was Mennonite. The Mennonite community was small and compact, clustered for the most part near Walnut, Grove, and Vine streets. The MPH fronted on Walnut Street, and the church building was just around the corner, on Grove Street. Elizabeth's home was within a block of both.

Mennonites had lived in the Scottdale area for most of the nineteenth century. At one time the church had more than two hundred members, but by the early 1890s, there were only twelve. Then in 1892, a young Mennonite named Aaron Loucks was ordained to the ministry, and the renewal of the congregation began. Scottdale had been built on his great-grandfather's farm. In 1897 Loucks was ordained bishop.[19] By the time Harold Bender visited Scottdale in 1920, the congregation had eighty-nine members, most of them employees of MPH. The growth of the Mennonite church in Scottdale was tied closely to the life of MPH.

After 1900 the reputation and business prospects of John F. Funk and the Mennonite Publishing Company in Elkhart, Indiana, had begun to decline. Sentiment developed to establish a publishing house owned and operated by the MC Mennonite church. The church already had official boards to manage missions and education. Surely, some church leaders argued, such a key activity as publication should not be left to private enterprise. In the fall of

1907, the MC general conference appointed a Publication Board, and the new board immediately founded the MPH, hiring bishop Aaron Loucks as general manager of the new enterprise.

Loucks brought the new publishing program to Scottdale and also hired three men who were playing or soon would play major roles in the MC church. Ohioan Levi Mumaw became secretary-treasurer of MPH. Like Loucks, Mumaw was a self-taught manager, respected for having good business sense. The two men served on many church boards, usually in a secretary-treasurer capacity. During the 1920s, they managed the business affairs of the board of education, the board of missions, and the publication board, positions which Harold Bender's father would almost certainly have held but for his untimely death in 1921.[20]

The second major church leader brought to Scottdale was bishop Daniel Kauffman, who in 1908 became editor of the new MPH paper, the *Gospel Herald*. By 1920 Kauffman had made his editorship the most influential post in the Mennonite church. Kauffman had a remarkable ability to express a conservative lay theology, helped no doubt by a rough-edged prose style which appealed to the rural Mennonite readers of the *Gospel Herald*. Daniel Kauffman was the premier Mennonite leader by 1920.

The third significant person brought to Scottdale in 1908 was John Horsch. Unlike the other men, Horsch was not a church leader in the conventional sense: he was not ordained, nor did he serve on church boards and committees. But it would not have been lost on the observant young Harold Bender that he was visiting the community and home of the Mennonite Church's most prolific writer. By 1920 Horsch had published more than 350 articles, most of them for the *Herold der Wahrheit*, the *Herald of Truth*, and the *Gospel Herald*. He had also written and published seven books and numerous pamphlets. The earliest book, the 146-page *Kurzgefasste Geschichte der Mennoniten-Gemeinden* (Brief history of the Mennonite churches), was published in 1890, just three years after he arrived in America. Then in 1903 he published *A Short History of Christianity* (340 pages). A 324-page life of Menno Simons came out in 1916. The next year a 157-page treatise on infant baptism was followed by what would become a favorite subject during the next decade, a book entitled *The Higher Criticism and the New Theology.*[21]

In 1920, Horsch published two books. *Die biblische Lehre von der Wehrlosigkeit* (The biblical teaching on nonresistance) was written for Mennonites in his native Germany, who he believed had grievously violated the principle of nonresistance during the World War. The second one was also his most successful; *Modern Religious Liberalism: The Destructiveness and Irrationality of the New Theology* eventually went through three editions and sold more than ten thousand copies.[22] While no one could have predicted its great success in July of 1920, Bender as an aspiring young scholar must have been impressed by the work Horsch had done and was doing in history and theology.

In 1908, Horsch had begun a three-decade-long crusade against theological Modernism with an article on the subject in one of the first issues of the *Gospel Herald.*[23] In the dogmatic tone which became characteristic of his pen, he embraced the major tenets of American Protestant Fundamentalism, including the inerrancy of the Bible, the deity of Christ, substitutionary atonement, Christ's bodily resurrection, and the authenticity of miracles—doctrines he insisted were being destroyed by Modernists.

The Protestant Fundamentalism which Horsch reflected and embraced was notable not so much in its theological formulations, which were generally orthodox, as in its dogmatic and militant tone. The Fundamentalist crusade, driven by a search for certainty, demanded strict adherence to code words and certain rhetorical practices which tolerated no deviations. Modernism, with its liberal relativism, embodied everything Fundamentalists feared; so it became the great enemy. Fundamentalism took on a hard-edged rhetorical militancy which set it apart from conventional conservative Protestantism.

John Horsch exhibited such a mind-set. His *Modern Religious Liberalism* won an audience far beyond Mennonites and moved him into the center of the Fundamentalist crusade. But he was not working in a vacuum; the next year (1921) the general conference of the MC Mennonites adopted a statement on "Christian Fundamentals" which, fundamentalist-like, made its first article one of the basic Fundamentalist credos, the "plenary and verbal inspiration of the Bible as the Word of God."[24] The force of the Horsch pen worked upon a Mennonite milieu which was receptive to his message.

It would be fascinating to know what John Horsch and Harold Bender discussed during the several weeks the young man spent at the Horsch home in July 1920. At that point, Harold had little formal theological education, but as he put it later, at that time he was "somewhat under the influence of liberal thinking."[25] Given Harold's cautious character and the enigmatic quality of John Horsch's personality, they may not have engaged in much theological discussion. If there was discussion, it would almost certainly have been quite guarded, at least from Harold's side. In 1920, Harold was a cautious progressive with a conventional theological cast of mind: he would have agreed with Horsch's theological propositions. But he was not a Fundamentalist.

The harsh dogmatic tone of Horsch's arguments must have offended Harold's progressive and tolerant mind. His position would be much the same five years later: in the midst of the Mennonite Fundamentalist-Modernist battles and by then theologically trained and more conservative, he felt impelled by filial loyalty to come to Horsch's defense. Thereafter, Harold made a careful distinction between his support for Horsch's theological positions and his rejection of Horsch's harsh polemics.

Harold must have been impressed by the historical library Horsch had collected. In 1920, it was almost certainly the best personal collection of Mennonitica in North America, its only rival being the library of the aging John F. Funk at Elkhart. Harold must have spent considerable time getting acquainted with it during his visit. A year later as he searched for a seminar topic in Mennonite history, he spoke knowledgeably about its holdings.[26] But it may well be that Horsch and Bender did not spend much time discussing Mennonite or Anabaptist history, for it was in 1920 that he completed the writing of his *Modern Religious Liberalism*. For thirty years Horsch had been writing about Mennonite history, in many books and short articles, but in 1920 he published not a single article on history, almost certainly because he was busy with his book on Modernism.

Throughout Bender's life, John Horsch had a profound influence on his development as a historian. In 1922-1923, Horsch spent a year in Europe, visiting his relatives in Germany and doing Anabaptist and Mennonite historical research. His months-long visit with the Dutch Mennonites convinced him that they were completely under the spell of Modernism; so it provided the impulse for one of his most polemical books, *The Mennonite Church and Modernism*, written upon his return from Europe in 1923. Prior to 1921, John Horsch had written ten articles on Menno Simons and the Dutch Anabaptists for every article he wrote about the Swiss Anabaptists. An important consequence of the Horsch trip to Europe was a shift in the focus of his historical writing from the Dutch to the Swiss and south-German Anabaptists, a focus Harold Bender would later expand in his own life and writings.

•  •  •

The home in which Elizabeth Horsch grew up was most idiosyncratic. Her parents were a study in contrasts. Her mother was tall, her father short. Her mother was outgoing and hospitable, while her father was reticent and painfully shy—a condition Elizabeth inherited and which, as she put it later, "has clung to me ever since."[27] Her mother had many friends; her father had almost none. John Horsch was an ascetic, with few social skills. A loner, he enjoyed daily solitary walks in the woods behind the Horsch home. During the summer, he sometimes stretched a tarp across some bushes in the woods, moved a desk and chair underneath, and did his writing there. A habit which frequently embarrassed the family was his insistence on going to bed at seven o'clock in the evening, even if there were visitors.[28]

Christine Horsch was the center of the family and set its lifestyle. She insisted on having an organ, and she often played German chorales early on Sunday mornings. The children later believed this was in compensation for having to sing English-language gospel songs at church. She acceded only reluctantly to the strict dress regulations being imposed at Scottdale, and sometimes she resisted. When the family moved into their new house in 1909, she put lace curtains on the windows. Neighbor Daniel Kauffman, who walked past the Horsch house each day on his way to his editorial work at MPH, objected to the curtains, insisting that they violated Mennonite standards. Christine was not awed by the powerful bishop. "When you walk to work, Daniel, look the other way, and you won't be offended by my curtains," she told him.[29]

John Horsch took little notice of such things. He wore the plain coat, sometimes with a bow tie underneath. He hoped son Paul would seek employment at MPH, and counseled him to wear the collarless coat to improve his chances. But mostly he ignored such matters, focusing on his historical and editorial work, and playing a minimal role in the family's life.[30] During much of their time at Scottdale, Christine Horsch served MPH as an unpaid proofreader for German materials. In return, Horsch was granted free time to do his voluminous writing. Thus Christine Horsch was a model for her daughter Elizabeth, who would serve as Harold's unofficial and unpaid assistant editor during much of their married life.

For a variety of reasons, none of Elizabeth's brothers became Mennonite. Surely one reason was the absence of a strong father figure in the family. Moreover, the Scottdale church was essentially a company congregation; nearly all of its members were employees of MPH. So the pressure to conform to the emerging regulations regarding plain dress was driven by the institutional needs of MPH. Since the congregation was small, its communal constraints were especially intense for teenagers. The Horsch youngsters simply could not handle the pressure. Elizabeth was fortunate: she escaped by attending Hesston College from 1915 to 1917.[31]

Unlikely as it might seem, going to tiny Hesston College in a small village in Kansas opened new vistas for Elizabeth. There she encountered the eloquent and persuasive J. D. Charles, who taught her Latin, Greek, English, and botany. Another bright leader, Alta Eby (later Erb), taught her math. Despite Hesston's strongly conservative emphasis, she found the setting religiously more free and open than Scottdale. Above all, she began to make friends and discovered the joys of social life. Since Hesston at that time offered only two years of college courses, she transferred to Goshen College in 1917. There she found a much freer intellectual and social environment and also met Harold Bender. For the shy, retiring Elizabeth, the energetic Harold brought a completely new quality to her life. After an exciting, whirlwind courtship during that senior year at Goshen, the subsequent two years of separation, with Harold teaching at Hesston and she at Eastern Mennonite School, must have seemed desolate indeed.

Now in July 1920, Harold and Elizabeth were together for a few weeks, deeply in love

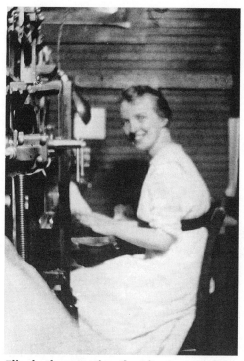

**Elizabeth operating the Linotype at the Mennonite Publishing House in 1921.** Bender Family Album.

and ready for marriage, but it could not be. Despite their joy at being together again, the brief interlude must have been somewhat sad. Harold was penniless, with much expensive schooling ahead. Even more discouraging must have been the uncertainty about his future in relation to his father's health. Until that question was settled, Harold was simply not in a position to offer her anything.

On Saturday, July 24, Harold left Scottdale by train for Indianapolis, to visit his father. On Monday he brought his father, helpless in a wheelchair, by train to Elkhart. Harold and his mother installed George in the downstairs parental bedroom and began round-the-clock care. Harold became the primary caregiver, helped occasionally by a nurse paid by the mission board.

● ● ●

On August 28-30, Saturday evening through Monday evening, Harold attended the Mennonite Young People's Conference (YPC) held at South Union Mennonite church near West Liberty, Ohio. The meetings were in a large tent on the church grounds. Several hundred young people from many Mennonite communities attended. Their theme was "Our Young People for Christ and the Church." Speakers addressed topics such as "The Present Challenge to Young People," "The Place and Aim of a Young People's Conference," "Life-Work," "Christ in Everyday Life," and "The Message of the Mennonite Church." At a lengthy business meeting, the conferees decided to hold another conference a year hence, and an executive committee and a program committee were formed. Harold was elected chairman of the new executive committee.[32]

The conference generated a lot of support among Mennonite young people and signaled the emergence of a cadre of young leaders with ideas and ambitions developed during the World War and postwar relief activities. The conflicts and tensions generated by the YPC movement eventually served as the leading edge of an emerging progressive-conservative struggle. That conflict lasted for at least a generation and resulted in some progressive Mennonites leaving the MC Mennonite orbit.

The YPC movement was begun by a group of Mennonite young men who were drafted during the war, spent time in army camps as conscientious objectors (COs), and in late 1918 volunteered to serve with Friends reconstruction units in France.[33] Within two months of the declaration of war by the United States, the Friends created the American Friends Service Committee (AFSC), and during the summer of 1917 established a relief workers' training program at Haverford College. By September, more than one hundred persons had completed an intensive six weeks of training and were ready to go abroad. Because of War Department delays, not many of the drafted men were able to leave before the armistice a year later in November 1918. But by that time, nine Mennonites had gone to France under the AFSC, and numerous others were training. Harold's good friend O. B. Gerig left in December of 1918. A month later J. C. Meyer also went to France; he had just been discharged after being interned as a CO in South Carolina military camps for six months. Soon Payson Miller, Russell Lantz, Jesse Smucker, and a dozen other Goshen graduates were in France and the Near East. By spring 1919, there were more than forty young Mennonites in France, and about twenty in the Near East.[34]

Most of the Mennonite COs furloughed to work in the reconstruction and relief projects shared a common sense of having been more or less abandoned by church leaders during their time in military camps. As they trained at Haverford College for the next phase of their wartime saga, they felt that the church still was not taking responsibility for their welfare. When they sailed, no Mennonite leader showed up to give them a send-off, and no one was designated to lead the group. So the relief workers took matters into their own hands and organized themselves.[35]

In France, the Mennonites worked in widely scattered projects. Eager to compare notes and keep in touch, eighteen of them met on March 30, 1919, at Neuvilly, where four of them were working. In the course of their meeting, they wrote an open letter to the MC Mennonite church, which Daniel Kauffman printed in the May 8 *Gospel Herald*. The message conveyed a sense of isolation from the church and frustration with the church's failure to give leadership or send representatives to visit them, even though the AFSC had offered to pay for such a visitor's travel.[36]

With the encouragement of the AFSC, the workers in France organized a conference for June 1919 that brought nearly all of them together for the first time. Eventually known as "the Clermont conference," the meeting was held on June 20-22 in a tent on a hill overlooking the Argonne forest. Thirty-eight of the forty Mennonites working for the AFSC in France attended. Also present were two Mennonite church representatives: Vernon Smucker, editor of the *Christian Monitor*, a Mennonite family paper published at Scottdale; and bishop Samuel (S. E.) Allgyer of Ohio, who represented the newly formed Mennonite Relief Commission. Also attending were Bishop Pierre Sommer of the French Mennonite church; T. Edmund Harvey, head of the AFSC in France; and Noah E. Byers, dean of Bluffton College.[37]

With a combination of inspirational and educational sessions, the meeting marked the birth of the Young People's Conference movement. What caught the attention of Mennonite church leaders were the sweeping purposes which the gathering espoused and reported:

1. To deepen the spiritual life of the Mennonite church.
2. To study our responsibilities that grow out of our attitude toward war.
3. To study the problems of the Mennonite church as regards:
   a. Church organization and administration
   b. Its relation to the social order
   c. Its relation to the state
   d. Its obligation to missionary endeavor
   e. Christian education
   f. Relief and reconstruction among stricken peoples.
4. To inspire young men and women of the Mennonite church to consecrate their lives to the conservation and extension of the principles of Jesus Christ.
5. To encourage the study of the historical development of the Mennonite church, with special emphasis on the life and writings of Menno Simons.
6. To establish a basis for closer cooperation between young people and those of maturer judgment.
7. To foster an appreciation and better understanding between Mennonites of America and Mennonites of foreign countries such as Russia, Switzerland, Germany, France, India, Holland, South America, etc.
8. To provide for the discussions of life-work problems where interviews with men of experience and training in various vocations may be had.[38]

Further, the conference elected Payson Miller, Vernon Smucker, O. B. Gerig, and J. C. Meyer to plan a Young People's Conference to be held in the United States in 1920.

The report of the conference was a bombshell waiting to explode; yet both the *Gospel Herald* and the *Christian Monitor* studiously ignored it. Neither paper ever mentioned the conference. With some difficulty, conference secretary O. B. Gerig was able to get a condensed report into the *Gospel Herald* in the guise of an announcement of the 1920 meeting. That meeting was to occur at West Liberty, Ohio, nearly a year after the Clermont conference had ended.[39]

• • •

Two young men not in France were intensely interested in the Clermont Conference report: Harold Bender and John (J. L.) Stauffer. Both attended the general conference of the MC Mennonites in 1919, where they heard the report of two of the commissioners, editor Smucker and bishop Allgyer. Harold Bender was fresh from the wheat harvest in Kansas. He had accompanied Elizabeth to EMS from Scottdale; after the conference, he had returned to Kansas for his second year of teaching at Hesston College.

That September, Stauffer began his third year of teaching Bible at EMS. Now thirty-one years old, Stauffer had served as minister at the Altoona mission beginning in 1910 and had come to teach at EMS in 1917. In an article in the *Gospel Herald* early in 1920, he expressed shock at the liberal character of the Clermont conference report. It had, as he put it, too much emphasis on "being active" and not enough on "being saved."[40] It was a scathing indictment of the men and the movement—so scathing that editor Daniel Kauffman twice returned the article to Stauffer, enjoining him to tone it down. Wisely, the YPC leaders decided not to respond to the Stauffer broadside.[41]

Harold Bender was less judicious. In a letter to Stauffer, he defended the young men and their goals. The letter was clear, strong, long, and a bit condescending. Harold clearly did not have much regard for Stauffer's ability as a theologian. Stauffer responded immediately, and a series of blistering letter exchanges followed throughout the spring of 1920. While focused on the Clermont conference statement and the men who wrote it, the argument ranged more widely, eventually involving Goshen-EMS-Hesston rivalries, regulation attire, church governance (is the church a democracy?), and specific challenges to each other to lay out their theological premises.[42]

The last letter of the exchange was waiting for Harold at Elkhart when he arrived home from Hesston on June 4, 1920. In a surprisingly conciliatory tone, Stauffer had responded to ten direct questions Harold had demanded that he answer, including one about a notorious "monkey story" which claimed that the "old Goshen" Glee Club had taken a monkey on its tours as part of its repertoire. Stauffer said he had gotten the story from evangelist Clayton F. Derstine, but conceded that since Harold was a member of the Glee Club, he would accept Harold's denial. Stauffer promised to write to Derstine and tell him to quit using the story.[43]

More substantively, the months-long confrontation must have seemed worthwhile to Harold when he read Stauffer's first paragraph: "Your confession of faith read with interest, and I am in full harmony and sympathy with this doctrinal statement. It is the clearest statement and expression of belief I have ever seen from any graduate of our oldest institution. Being given voluntarily, I think likewise it is to your credit and will so apply it."[44]

Stauffer was being a bit disingenuous, for it must have been clear to Harold that unless he made an orthodox statement, he would have a hard time shaking the "taint" he had acquired in the interchange. It was remarkable that he was able to make a doctrinal statement which was at once honest, complex, and convincing. Harold was only twenty-three years old and had studied little formal theology. Yet few Mennonites in that era could have put it better:

> I am entirely in sympathy with the doctrinal position of our church and believe it to be established on the solid rock of Gospel truth. If I did not, I could not conscientiously work with her. I love the church and the principles for which she has stood and now stands, and my life is dedicated to the service of my Master in whatever way She [sic] sees fit to use me.
>
> The historic principles of the faith, the trinity of the Godhead, divinity and humanity of Christ, His substitutionary atonement and bodily resurrection, the supernatural divine and plenary inspiration of the Holy Scriptures with their supreme authority, the authenticity and reality of the supernatural and miraculous, the new birth, justification by faith, guidance of the Holy Spirit, and the imminent bodily return of the Lord—all these have been and are and I hope will always be an integral part of my faith.
>
> By what does Christ say and does the Holy Spirit thru John say will we be judged by in the last great day—not by what we have believed—not once is it so prophesied, but by our works. As you say, "Christ and doctrine cannot be separated either by the heterodox or the orthodox theologian." I fear that a school which teaches only doctrine and no service, no loving sacrificial service, has started to separate Christ and doctrine—has lost a part of Christ.

The letter was nine pages long. It remarkably captured Harold's lifelong commitment to bringing theology and practice together.[45] A quarter century later, he would call that combination *discipleship*. Stauffer was impressed.

Harold's relief at having reached some accommodation with Stauffer suffered a severe shock a few weeks later when he arrived at Scottdale for his visit with Elizabeth. He discovered a seventeen-page handwritten letter awaiting him from George R. Brunk Sr., of Denbigh, Virginia. Brunk was an outspoken bishop of fundamentalistic bent and one of the authors of the 1921 MC Mennonite general conference report on "Christian Fundamentals." "While I am not acquainted with you, I have long known and loved your father," wrote the bishop. "I was glad to read the letters that passed between yourself and J. L. S."[46] To his dismay, Harold realized Stauffer had copied Harold's letters and sent them to bishop Brunk. What Harold had worked so hard to avoid at Hesston—putting his future at risk by taking strong public theological positions—had come to pass. One of the most powerful conservative Mennonite bishops in America had been privy to his correspondence with Stauffer!

Harold had learned a lesson; he did not reply to bishop Brunk's letter. The bishop was disappointed. In a cryptic note at the foot of his copy of the letter to Harold, he observed, "Harold promised an answer but made none."[47]

Why Harold chose to challenge Stauffer, when those most injured by Stauffer—the YPC leaders—did not, is a mystery. Given his cautious strategy at Hesston, the exchange was out of character. However, in the weeks before Stauffer's article appeared in the *Gospel Herald*, Harold had written several letters which evinced a strong interest in the Clermont conference; he seemed frustrated to be on the sidelines. So many at the front edge of the new developments were his friends. Actually, Harold was trying to be even-handed about the YPC.

In an acerbic letter to his Goshen pal O. B. Gerig, secretary of the YPC, Harold criticized the YPC leaders severely. Gerig, who had returned from France the previous September and was studying history at Harvard, thought that Harold's "invective" about the YPC movement was too strong. "I was glad for the point-blank criticisms in your letter," he wrote. "You certainly made me feel like a German pfennig several times by telling me what blatant boneheads I, with others, pulled due to my lack of balanced judgment." But he appealed to Harold to try to see some of their actions from their point of view. If you and I, who are good friends, can't treat each other with respect, how can we ever expect to make progress with those who oppose us? he asked.[48]

Harold had been especially critical of what he considered the YPC's cavalier attitude toward church authorities. Gerig, like many of his friends, found Harold's defense of church leaders frustrating in light of his experience in military camp. "MEN CANNOT BE CONSCIENTIOUS OBJECTORS AND AS INDIVIDUALS DEFEND THEIR POSITION BEFORE MILITARY AUTHORITIES UNLESS THEY HAVE BEEN IN THE HABIT OF MAKING IMPORTANT DECISIONS IN LESS MOMENTOUS TIMES," he wrote, using upper case for emphasis. "AN AUTOCRATIC LEADERSHIP THAT DISCOURAGES EDUCATION AND INDEPENDENT THINKING CANNOT DEVELOP A C.O."[49]

You would be appalled by how ignorant Mennonite young men really are, Gerig told Bender. "I heard their testimony in camp. It was pathetic."[50] The well-educated Gerig was being rather unfair, for many of the "ignorant" had been as steadfast in their CO convictions as the more articulate college men.

In any case, Gerig was relentless in his criticism of MC leaders. "The very position of pacifists renders democracy indispensable, tho' J. L. S. says democracy is not Scriptural," he told Harold. "Our church has recently become centralized. It was not originally so. Therefore, it is not unorthodox to oppose a high degree of centralization tho' it may be opprobrious to do so."[51]

Gerig had succinctly captured a key point in the conflict between the YPC movement and the church leadership. The issue of democratic church governance grew out of the experience of the young men in the World War and relief work abroad. However, its salience lay in a generational conflict between a traditional called-out leadership, based on the lot and ordination, and younger persons formed in a newer, progressive America. The latter wanted to base leadership on competence and efficiency. As Gerig stated the issue to Bender, the YPC critique of Aaron Loucks as a Mennonite leader was that YPC persons "had no confidence in their [Mennonite leaders'] ability to administer large problems."[52]

The attitude of the church leaders was nicely capsulated by Daniel Kauffman. In April 1920, Gerig persuaded *Gospel Herald* editor Kauffman to print a one-page announcement about the forthcoming Young People's Conference at West Liberty, Ohio.[53] Kauffman, uneasy about Gerig's piece, wrote an editorial in the same issue about the "Young Men's" conference. Trying hard to be noncommittal, he insisted he was neither for the conference nor against it. The only issue was the attitude of the young men toward the "standards and ideals of the church." With some justification, Kauffman was worried about their commitment to those "standards and ideals."[54]

However, the conflict was not only between two generations, an older one protecting the status quo and a younger one nibbling away at their authority. In 1920, there was also an intra-generational split. After all, John L. Stauffer, O. B. Gerig, and Harold Bender were of the same generation. In the conservative camp were J. L. Stauffer and C. K. Lehman at EMS. At Hesston were Paul Erb, J. D. Charles, Edward Yoder, and Noah Oyer, among others. They were not educated at Goshen, nor had they been drafted or in relief work, and they did not support the YPC movement.

The other group, the YPC movement supporters, were nearly all Goshen College graduates, nearly all had been drafted, and nearly all had been in relief work. The anomalies were Harold Bender, Art Slagel, and Vernon Smucker—Goshen graduates, but not drafted and not in relief work. Bender, Smucker, and Slagel became supporters of the YPC, but from their own experiential bases. Harold Bender, the dutiful son of a strong churchman-father, always found the YPC challenge to churchly authority distasteful, but he believed in its program for spiritual renewal. In 1920, Bender was a quite conservative progressive.

Yet he was a progressive. To John L. Stauffer, he wrote: "As to method, I am a progressive. To my mind, the sole test of an institution, a discipline, or a method of work, if it is Biblical, is whether it accomplishes its purpose in the most efficient way. Mere traditions and personal prejudices must yield." From that progressive stance, he lectured the more conservative Virginian: "It seems to me, Brother Stauffer, that one of the greatest hindrances from a closed system of thinking such as you and your associates hold is that it prevents the possibility of progress and acquiring new truth."[55]

Bender told Stauffer that he supported the YPC on the basis of his "progressive" platform. He also believed in the good faith of the young men in the movement: "On the whole they are true to the Bible, the Church, and her teaching. I am good friends with all of them, but I see no need as you indicate of giving up either my conservative faith or my friendship and relations with them."[56]

The Bender-Stauffer interchange was the most sustained dialogue about the YPC movement and its implications in the whole of the movement's history. By the end of the exchange, Bender was a member of the movement. It was no accident that during the August 1920 West Liberty conference, he emerged as the person to whom the YPC turned for leadership. Bender was elected chair of the executive committee. He soon perceived his main task to be allaying the suspicions of the church leaders and gaining some legitimacy for the YPC. It would prove a daunting task. The church leadership resisted his overtures, and it is remarkable that Bender sustained his commitment to the church. Some of his closest associates did not.

## ⋄⁵ ⁵ ⁵⋄

# At Garrett and Princeton

*Harold's father dies. Harold attends Garrett Biblical
Institute and Princeton Theological Seminary.*

IN THE FALL of 1920, Harold cared for his father and as a sideline
taught two courses in Greek language at Goshen College, com-
muting to Goshen several days a week on the trolley. His friend
Jesse Smucker apparently picked up some scuttlebutt that students
found Harold's courses pretty heavy. "Do not push the class too
hard; remember that few people get Greek as easily as you do,"
Jesse advised Harold. "I simply make this statement in the interest
of humanity."[1] Harold was teaching in the religion department as
a colleague of his former pastor William Weaver, who had just resigned that role at the Prairie Street congregation. The next year
Weaver would lose his job at Goshen. Critics had charged that he
was too "liberal."

Harold's sister Violet was a sophomore at Goshen in 1920. So
able was she that the *Maple Leaf* described her as a "human encyclopedia."[2] She was the news editor for the Goshen College
*Record* and an advocate of women's suffrage.

This was a good year to be at Goshen College. Enrollment in
1920-21 was high, with 234 students. The student body was unusually mature, with nearly a dozen men on campus who had been
abroad in relief and reconstruction work. Four of the men taught
on the faculty. J. C. Meyer was teaching history and social science;
in the fall he organized an overseas relief workers' organization on
campus to promote peace and relief work.[3]

Along with teaching and caring for his father, Harold practiced his lifelong hobby, fishing. On October 9 he and a friend, J. Boyd Cressman, tried their luck at a lake in southern Michigan; but as sister Violet gleefully reported, all they caught were "three magnificent minnows!"[4] Harold returned from the trip to find his good friend Jesse Smucker at Goshen. Smucker had just returned from his relief assignment in the Near East. On his trip home, he had taken a long route via India and Hong Kong. In a college chapel service, he described his experiences to the student body.[5]

For Harold, such activities must have been a welcome respite from the often-difficult task of nursing his father. George's condition vacillated. Part of the time he was reasonably easy to care for, but during particularly trying times, the family had to get the assistance of a male nurse. Harold's friends encouraged him. Paul Erb wrote from Hesston, "Your father is fortunate to have you at home to care for him." And he added, "I envy the opportunity you will probably have for much reading."[6] In addition to teaching Greek and nursing his father, Harold was also busy with YPC matters. As chair of the executive committee, he handled YPC-church relations. At the suggestion of Ernest Miller, he invited participants to comment on their experience at the West Liberty YPC conference. A ten-page paper of paragraph-long testimonials entitled "Echoes from the Young Peoples Conference" was compiled and distributed to church leaders and young people.[7]

Oscar Burkholder, pastor of Cressman Mennonite church in Breslau, Ontario, Elsie Bender's home church, responded to the "Echoes" paper. Burkholder, an emerging leader among MC Mennonites in Ontario, was critical of the conference. Bender responded to Burkholder with what friend Jesse Smucker called an unnecessarily defensive attitude.[8] Smucker was right. Yet the letter offers a window into Harold Bender's mind in the fall of 1920, just a few months before he began three and a half years of intensive seminary work.

To Burkholder's query as to why the YPC organization could not just fit into existing church organizations, Harold argued that the YPC's mission was to "give special time and thought to the young people with their problems, their difficulties, their weaknesses. No one is doing that," he pointed out, "not even the schools, because very few Mennonite young people attend the schools."[9]

The situation among young people is "serious," he told Burkholder. "Most of the younger generation are only half-hearted or wholly dubious in their church loyalty, lack spiritual power, and do not consider either their own lives seriously or the call of Christ and the church to service, or if they do consider seriously, they get so little sympathetic understanding help for their problems that they give up."[10]

At the MC's general conference in 1919, Harold had heard Daniel Kauffman offer the disturbing information that only 40 percent of Mennonite young people were staying in the church.[11] Kauffman had used the data in a call for more discipline and greater stress on standards. Harold was using the information quite skillfully to justify the YPC program.

Harold responded most defensively to Burkholder's concerns about relations between YPC leaders and church leader. All new movements are subject to suspicion in the beginning, he observed, pointing out that none of the major church boards had begun as an official agency but had become such only with time. Should not the church fathers who had led those movements give the younger generation the same opportunity? he asked. He concluded the letter with "Your Brother in the Service," and under his name offered the YPC slogan, "OUR YOUNG PEOPLE FOR CHRIST AND THE CHURCH."[12]

The letter expressed Harold's frustration with the status quo in the Mennonite church in 1920. During the next two years, his leadership of the YPC movement exhibited a persistent search for ways and means to communicate his concerns to church leaders, an effort which failed and splintered the YPC movement itself.

• • •

George Bender died on January 17, 1921. In early December, Harold had observed a turn for the worse. To his uncle Dan Bender, he remarked that George was running a constant fever, although the sick man's physical discomfort seemed to have lessened somewhat. Until George died, the need for constant care continued.[13]

Despite their difficulties, the 1920 Christmas holiday was a fairly happy time for the Bender family. It was the first time in three years that Harold was at home for Christmas. The Bender cousins from Pennsylvania all stayed at 1711 Prairie Street during the college break, as did several Ontario cousins and friends on the Kolb side; the big house was filled with young people. The day before Christmas, O. B. Gerig stopped at Elkhart for an afternoon visit. He was on his way home to Orrville, Ohio, from his teaching job at Bethel College in Kansas.[14]

By the time the holiday festivities were over, George had contracted a chronic pneumonia and was in serious condition. The last three days of his life were a nightmare: his temperature reached an extreme, 107 degrees. Years later, Violet wrote about the experience: "We were all thankful when death released him."[15]

People gathered for the funeral from far and wide. Goshen College canceled classes so teachers and students could attend.[16] Messages came from distant friends. Harold's good friend Jesse Smucker, holding revival meetings at Canton, Ohio, sent a letter: "I have just learned of the death of your father. Words are almost meaningless at such times, and I do not know what to write. But I just wanted you to somehow feel that I sympathize with you sincerely in this your great loss. Harold, I would grasp your hand and weep with you."[17]

Harold also received a letter from Aaron Loucks, written the day before George died. Loucks had heard that the end was near and composed a warm letter, commenting on his love and regard for George and expressing his admiration for Harold's devotion to his parents in their time of need.[18]

A tantalizing question for which there is no answer is whether Elizabeth accompanied Uncle Dan on his trip from Hesston to the funeral. There is no record of Harold's own reaction to his father's death. Until just a few months before George died, the common assumption was that he would live to be an old man, thus requiring many years of continual care. More than any of his siblings, Harold had been hostage to that fact. Suddenly, he was free.

Since he had a close relationship with his father, he must have pondered the ironic meaning of his father's death for his own life. Yet Harold did not leave an account of his thoughts. His only written reference to his father's death is typically oblique, dropped into a letter to the YPC executive committee two weeks after the funeral. He began, "I am sorry that due to circumstances of the last few weeks, I have been unable to attend to matters as closely as I wanted to, and some of the work has been delayed. However, I am free now and will push ahead more rapidly."[19]

• • •

The death of George Bender also changed his wife's life. George's managerial control of the family had always left Elsie under his shadow. Violet, a perceptive analyst of human nature, now saw her mother blossom as her own person. For the first time, Elsie began to express personal opinions about matters of interest to her. She became, Violet said, "fun to be with and to talk to."[20]

The quiet, imperturbable Elsie faced some serious problems. One was the status of her home. She lived in a house that belonged to the mission board. As long as George lived, it was also the home

**The Bender children in 1921 soon after the death of George Bender. From the left: Violet, Harold, Robert, Wilbur, John, Cecil, Florence.** Bender Family Album.

of her family. With George's death, his assistant became the new treasurer; hence, Vernon Reiff's family should now move into the house at 1711. The mission board was kind and allowed Elsie to continue as a housekeeper and hostess for its activities, so she lived in the house for two more years. By 1923, with only Cecil, John, and Robert still at home, she moved to a smaller house on nearby Cleveland Street.[21]

A second problem was how to earn a living. The family was not destitute, for George was not just a good fundraiser; he was also an astute money manager. Despite his meager earnings, by 1917 he had saved enough money to build a house. He and the boys (other than Harold) did a lot of the construction. His plan was to build the house and rent it until he was no longer mission board treasurer, whereupon it would become the family home. But even before the house was completed, his plan went awry when he was offered twice as much as the house had cost. He sold it and invested the money in several Elkhart banks. Thus when he died, Elsie had bank bonds in excess of $5,000, or the equivalent of more than three years of George's mission board allowance. She carefully husbanded the money, often allowing the children to borrow from the banks with the bonds as security. It was a cushion which she was able to stretch out over nearly the rest of her life.[22]

For two years Elsie continued to receive the missionary stipend George had received when he was alive. But almost immediately the family began a procedure which continued until youngest son, Robert, completed his second year in college: some of the siblings worked and supported others who went to school. Harold became the family treasurer, keeping elaborate records of who borrowed and who paid into the family fund.

The 1921-22 academic year was the most challenging financially. That year Harold was at Princeton, and Florence and Wilbur were students at Goshen College. Violet, who a year earlier had been a sophomore at Goshen, now dropped out of college and taught high school in nearby Millersburg, Indiana. Her earnings supplemented the mission board stipend her mother received. During 1922-23 both Violet and Florence worked, and their earnings went into the common treasury. So for two years, Harold and

Wilbur were in school, and Violet and Florence worked for their support.[23]

When Goshen closed in 1923-24, Wilbur got a job teaching. He and Florence supported the family, while Violet, unable to return to Goshen, completed her degree at Oberlin College. Harold and Elizabeth, now married, spent the 1923-24 year at Tübingen University in Germany, for which Harold had a scholarship from Princeton. Upon their return to Goshen in September 1924, they rented a house on Eighth Street, and Elsie, Cecil, John, and Robert moved from Elkhart to share the home with them, an arrangement which in Elsie's case would continue until her death in 1948. For some years the three boys also continued to share the house as they attended and eventually graduated from Goshen College.[24]

• • •

In early March 1921, Harold began studies at Garrett Biblical Institute in Evanston, Illinois, just north of Chicago. His goal was a bachelor of divinity degree. He chose Garrett because it had the quarter system, which allowed him to begin his work in March. Garrett was also attractive because it charged only a small entry fee and no tuition. He would have preferred to go directly to Princeton, but Princeton's semester system would have meant waiting until September. Garrett was a Methodist seminary. In 1921 it was the second-largest seminary in the country, with over four hundred students;[25] but it was not widely known in Mennonite circles.

Harold made the decision to attend Garrett before going on to Princeton for prosaic reasons, but the intellectual benefits of the experience were important for his theological development. It was his first sojourn in a non-Mennonite, urban environment. After six years at Goshen and Hesston, the difference could not have been more remarkable. He needed the change. It was immensely valuable that his first graduate-study experience should take place at one of the most dynamic liberal social-gospel seminaries in America. Bender needed exposure to alternative points of view, presented by dynamic intellects. In 1921, Garrett had a strong fifteen-member faculty, a new curriculum, and an aggressive sense of purpose under the leadership of president Charles Stuart.[26]

Harold had been at Garrett only a few weeks when he received a letter from Daniel Kauffman, inquiring about the orthodoxy of one of the professors, Harris Franklin Rall. Rall had a systematic-theology degree from the University of Berlin and was a prominent advocate of the social gospel. In 1920, Rall published *Modern Premillennialism and the Christian Hope*. Kauffman, no premillennialist himself, had read a hostile review of Rall's book. What was the standing of this professor at the school, and was Garrett a liberal school? Kauffman wanted to know.[27]

Harold responded immediately. He told Kauffman that he had Professor Rall for a class in systematic theology, but since there were more than fifty students in the class, he had not learned to know him. As for the seminary, he would place Garrett on a theological line about halfway between the liberal University of Chicago divinity school and the conservative Princeton Seminary. For example, he told Kauffman, Garrett did not hold to the orthodox theory of inspiration; it embraced the theory of evolution, and Garrett professors placed the Old Testament books rather late in history. But the professors were quite orthodox in their views of grace and Christology. Clearly trying to assuage Kauffman's suspicions, Harold assured the church leader that all the courses he was taking dealt with "fact rather than interpretation." And, he added, "I would not want to take a full course here."[28]

Harold lived in dormitory D at the institute and worked part-time as a waiter in the dining hall. In June, J. Boyd Cressman, one of Harold's old college chums and a veteran of reconstruction work in France, graduated from Goshen and almost immediately joined Harold at Garrett. They roomed together during the summer. In a letter to Orie O. Miller, who had just returned from relief work in the new Soviet Union, Bender described the summer at Garrett on the shore of Lake Michigan as "pleasant." On the Fourth of July, he and Cressman and some other Mennonites in the city had a picnic, which everyone enjoyed. Among those present was the first Dutch Mennonite whom Harold had ever met, a young seminarian named J. M. Leendertz.[29]

Harold was delighted finally to be in school. He threw himself into the work with gusto, carrying four heavy courses: two in New Testament theology, a course in biblical Aramaic, and the one in systematic theology under Professor Rall. During the summer he piled on even more work, taking five courses: two in Old Testament, one in New Testament, and two in historical theology. He made straight A's.[30]

Harold was methodical. The New Testament course was a study in "Canon and Text," and he wrote a carefully typed 34-page synopsis of the course. Today it would be called a portfolio. Requirements included reading the textbooks, doing 1,200 pages of collateral reading, writing a 4,000-word review of a major work in the field, and cataloging a set of manuscripts and facsimiles in the Garrett library with a general description of each. The point of the course was to give the student both the practice and the principles of textual criticism. Bender wrote a paper—he called it "a review with criticism"—of Casper R. Gregory's *The Canon and Text of the New Testament*. He produced a masterful critique, written with sharp precision.[31]

By May, Harold was searching for a thesis topic for a summer course in historical theology. For advice he wrote to historian C. Henry Smith at Bluffton College and to John Horsch. What could he do in seventeenth-century Mennonite history? he inquired. Horsch dismissed Harold's queries about the Amish schism or the Dordrecht Confession of Faith or a Hutterite topic as "hardly of considerable general importance." When Harold expressed interest in a topic on the social and economic conditions of Mennonites in the sixteenth or seventeenth century, Horsch insisted that Anabaptism was a religious movement and ought to be studied as such. But he was fulsome in his readiness to loan Harold any needed books. At the same time, he was clearly worried about Harold's studies at Garrett. "Glad to see that you are awake to the dangers threatening the Christian church from liberalistic theology," he wrote. "I am sure you will find lots of it in Garrett Institute. There are not many seminaries that are sound on the fundamentals."[32]

The response of the erudite C. Henry Smith, who had written the two most scholarly Mennonite histories by an American Mennonite up to that time, was more helpful. He suggested four topics which needed research, adding a reminder that all four topics required fluency in German and Dutch.[33]

At Easter, Harold visited Elkhart and ran an errand for his friend Jesse Smucker. Smucker's long-running romance with Mary Lantz, who lived near Topeka, had picked up in earnest when he returned from his relief stint in the Near East. His finances had not picked up, however: he was a young minister and struggling farmer without much cash in hand. So, unable to afford a trip to Indiana to see Mary, he arranged for Harold to deliver a bouquet of flowers to her home on Easter morning. The romantic gesture, Smucker said as he thanked Harold, had been "well worthwhile." Since Smucker was going to be in Scottdale in June, he offered to do something similar for Harold.[34]

Smucker, who would certainly have known, expected Harold and Elizabeth to get married that summer. "After that greatest of days is over and you two, now ONE [sic], are on your way, returning to your home, why be sure to stop over at Orrville and pay me a visit," he told Harold.[35] But there was no wedding that summer.

One might have expected marriage to have been Harold and Elizabeth's first priority once the uncertainty attached to caring for his father was removed as an obstacle. It is a tribute to their hard-headed pragmatism that they recognized the financial hurdles they faced, given Harold's goal to complete his graduate work in one hard push. The critical factor in the decision not to get married apparently came from Princeton: Harold learned that married men did not get scholarship aid. That policy was based on the assumption that if seminarians had enough money to get married, they had enough to pay for their education. Harold, penniless, needed the aid. So he and Elizabeth planned for a wedding a year later, in September of 1922.[36]

• • •

The YPC continued to take a great deal of Harold's time during the spring and summer of 1921. In May, several of the YPC executive committee met at Eureka, Illinois, for a day of consultation and planning. By early spring 1921, it had become clear that no conference could be held that year. The Eureka meeting confirmed the decision. The reason was clear: the opposition of church leaders was unrelenting, and there were rifts in the YPC leadership circle about how to cope with the situation. Harold characteristically argued for going slow and trying to bring the church fathers along. It was a strategy men such as J. C. Meyer, O. B. Gerig, and Paul Whitmer found too temporizing.[37]

During the summer the executive committee met in Chicago and hammered out a strategy which essentially confirmed Harold's position. A conference would be planned for June 1922 in Illinois. Jesse Smucker, who shared Harold's basic position and was highly regarded as a rising young minister in the Ohio conference, was selected as moderator of the conference and chair of the program committee. Smucker was deemed more acceptable to church leaders because he was not one of the "France men," as the Clermont conference men were called.

The Chicago meeting also laid out in general lines the conference themes. By planning a purely inspirational program, the executive committee hoped to send a reassuring message to the MC general conference, which would meet a few weeks later at Garden City, Missouri. The YPC executive committee decided not to ask for official recognition, however, since they did not believe that would be possible. As chair of the executive committee, Harold requested permission to write an informal letter to bishop Sanford C. Yoder, moderator of the MC general conference and chair of its committee on arrangements. He would inform Yoder of the YPC plans and reiterate the organization's general purposes. Yoder was perceived to be sympathetic, and the YPC leaders hoped that he would use the information to help counter criticism.[38]

Harold's letter to Yoder was an open and honest appeal to the church official to help interpret the YPC movement to his fellow church leaders. Sadly, rather than treating the letter as an informal note from Harold to a trusted church leader, Yoder read the letter to the committee on arrangements. The committee immediately made a public response, precisely what the YPC committee had hoped to avoid. The response pulled no punches. "Since the origin and present status of the Young People's General Conference are not in accord with the aforesaid standard," the committee said, "we are unable to approve of the movement."[39] Harold's critics on the YPC committees had been correct: the church leaders would not deal charitably with the YPC.

Harold chose to put the best face on it. "While the last paragraph is not just what we should like to see, yet I take it as rather a challenge than anything else. There have been some misunderstandings and misgivings about this movement on the part of some, and that feeling is reflected in the letter." Showing a great deal more magnanimity than the situation deserved, he observed, "We can well appreciate the consideration shown in their reply." He urged his committee members to remain true to the goals and aims of the movement. He, at least, was convinced that ultimately the church would accept the movement.[40]

Harold's hope in the face of such a rebuff, while inexplicable to many of his contemporaries, offers an important clue to his lifelong modus operandi. While often impatient with short-term and immediate tasks, he had an enormous ability to persist over the long haul. Throughout his life he continually outlasted his detractors. Moreover, his persistence gave continuity to his major lifelong endeavors. This character trait, shared to some degree with his parents, was a rare gift and one that was necessary for the challenging leadership roles he would assume during his life.

By 1921 the major lineaments of Harold's character were becoming clear. His regard for decorum and authority, his instinctive search for a middle ground, his aversion to risk-taking, his ability to think independently, his near-total trust in his good intentions, his comfort with conventional orthodoxy, his persistence, and his intellectual prowess—these together constituted a personality and character remarkably attuned to the needs of his particular milieu.

• • •

The summer quarter at Garrett ended in late August. Harold had to be at Princeton on September 28. He spent two weeks at home in Elkhart, and then left for the "East" via Bluffton, where he visited Paul Whitmer, J. E. Hartzler, and C. Henry Smith. It was his first visit to Bluffton and Witmarsum Seminary. From there he went to Scottdale to see Elizabeth, who had returned from Hesston in June. With the help of her brothers Walter and Menno, who were linotype repairmen, Elizabeth had found employment as a linotype operator at a company in Pittsburgh.[41]

At midnight on September 27, Harold caught a train out of Scottdale, and the next morning he met his former Hesston colleague Noah Oyer at the Lancaster, Pennsylvania, railroad station. The two traveled together to Princeton Seminary, arriving just in time to register and participate in the drawing for rooms in the dormitory. Harold drew a room in Brown Hall.[42]

To enroll at Princeton, Harold needed only his Goshen College diploma, a letter from his pastor confirming that he was in "good and regular standing" as a member, a letter from Garrett Institute listing his courses, and evidence that he had a command of the original languages of the Bible. Because of his work at Garrett the previous six months, he was able to begin his work at Princeton as a "middler."

Harold was finally where he had hoped to be ever since a cold February day in 1919 when he, Art Slagel, Paul Erb, Noah Oyer, and Edward Yoder drove from Hesston to Friends University in Wichita to talk with a Princeton representative. Chester (C. K.) Lehman, a Hesston graduate and good friend of Harold, had attended Princeton from 1919 to 1921. Now in the fall of 1921, with a Princeton Th.B., Lehman was at EMS, beginning a lifelong tenure there teaching theology. In 1923 he became dean of the college, a position he held until 1956.[43]

In 1920 Noah Oyer had begun his studies at Princeton; he completed the Th.B. in 1922. In 1924 he became dean at Goshen College. He died in 1931, and Harold succeeded him. Thus three men who would serve as Mennonite deans from the 1920s into the 1950s studied at Princeton at about the same time. Bender and Lehman would also become the founders of the two MC Mennonite seminaries.

Noah Oyer, like C. K. Lehman, arrived at Princeton with a Hesston A.B., thus needing the Th.B. degree. By contrast, Harold used his Garrett studies to move directly into the regular master's degree program. In turn, he used his Princeton studies to complete his Garrett B.D. He then took enough courses at the university (tuition was free to seminary students) to earn an M.A. Since the particular courses he took at the university also fulfilled requirements for the Th.M. at the seminary, he was able to acquire three degrees in two and a half years, including two summers. Thus by the summer of 1923, he had a B.D. degree from Garrett Institute, a Th.M. from Princeton Seminary, and an M.A. from Princeton University. He was also able to use a thesis from one of his courses as the exhibit in his application for a fellowship which supported him during his work at Tübingen University during the 1923-24 academic year. The Tübingen studies became the first installment of his work toward the doctorate at Heidelberg University ten years later. He would receive the doctorate in 1935.

The Princeton Seminary which Harold joined in September 1921 had one of the most beautiful campuses in the country. It was quite a contrast to the bleak, austere, and tiny campus of Hesston College, where he had spent the previous two years. Like Garrett, Princeton costs were modest. Everyone except married men got some financial assistance. Harold worried that he might not get the help he needed, but Noah Oyer assured him that there would be no problem. Costs per student were about $200 to $250 per year, and nearly all of Harold's fees were covered by his financial assistance. He paid no tuition. A luxury Harold enjoyed for the first time was a hot shower, available on each dormitory floor. By 1921 a renovated gymnasium offered a basketball court and boxing and wrestling facilities.[44]

The seminary students attended university athletic events. Harold reported in November 1922 that the Princeton football team had beaten Yale 3-0 and that Princeton was champion of the big three. He attended the resulting celebration, commenting on the "parade, bonfire, and all. Some sight!"[45]

The seminary normally enrolled about 200 students. Bender's graduating class in 1923 had some 50. Most were sons of farmers, merchants, and ministers. About 60 percent were Presbyterian. While the main purpose was to train ministers for Presbyterian pulpits, quite a few initially became missionaries. In Harold's graduating class, more than 20 of the 50 graduating men planned to go abroad in such service. A steady stream of "famous" missionaries (Harold's letters nearly always designated them as "famous") came to the campus and spoke to the student body, sometimes holding weeklong meetings.

Noah Oyer found the student body "congenial," but he wished for "a deeper spiritual life" among its members. Oyer was surprised by what he called their "decidedly democratic spirit." In the spring of 1921, Sherwood Eddy, Harry Emerson Fosdick, and Robert Speer were on campus to hold meetings. Oyer hoped they would have some good effect on the students' religious life.[46] In the spring of 1922, Harold attended a lecture by William Jennings Bryan on "Evolution and Revelation."

Harold was especially impressed by Robert Speer. In the fall of 1922, Speer spoke to Bender's regular Tuesday evening Bible study group about his recent trip to Asia and the Near East. He gave a "ringing message," Harold reported. "It was my first chance to hear him, and I appreciated it very much. He told us that there is the same old need for the same old transforming power of Christ in the hearts of men everywhere. He contraried recent statements by Sherwood Eddy and other leaders to the effect that the old Gospel and the old method etc. is no longer adequate. Speer certainly is endowed with power if any man is among the religious leaders of today."[47] Speer was the secretary of the Presbyterian Board of Foreign Missions and on the seminary's governing board.

Harold's years at Princeton coincided with the early skirmishes which led finally in 1929 to a rift between the conservatives and the moderates on the faculty. In 1929, the forceful spokesman for the conservatives, professor J. Gresham Machen, with three of his colleagues—Oswald Allis, Cornelius Van Til, and Robert Dick Wilson—founded Westminster Theological Seminary. Machen had earned his B.D. at Princeton in 1905, spent a year at Marburg, and returned to the faculty at Princeton in 1906 to teach New Testament. By 1921, when Harold arrived, Machen had become a leading voice in the Fundamentalist-Modernist debate. The professor was sure Modernists could not be Christian, because they denied that salvation was dependent on the historical fact that Christ had died to atone for human sin. He wrote *Christianity and Liberalism*, a book soon widely read, while Harold was taking his courses at Princeton. But Harold did not actually read the book until a year later, in January of 1924 at Tübingen.

Machen, a stimulating teacher and popular with students, was becoming a guardian of what was known as the "Princeton Theology." At its center was an insistence that God's verbal and plenary inspiration had produced an inerrant original biblical text. The Bible was a supernatural document unlike any other. While Machen was critical of the emotional excesses of revivalism, he agreed that regeneration and conversion were necessary for genuine piety. But he also believed that genuine piety was dependent on a commitment to fundamental biblical doctrine.[48]

Historian George Marsden has argued convincingly that the centerpiece of Machen's conflict with liberalism was his insistence that historical events can be known and understood with something close to their original quality. Machen was quite skeptical of liberals, who were prone to emphasize how time and memory change events from the past. For Machen, historical facts "stay put. If a thing really happened, the passage of years can never possibly make it into a thing that did not happen."[49] Furthermore, Machen believed events have a fixed significance, the significance they held in the eyes of God. In the case of the Bible, the significance of the events is revealed by God himself. Practically, this meant that the first task of the historian is to find the facts and their true significance. Humans do not create meaning, they find it. This profound difference in the understanding of historical hermeneutics, Marsden has argued, was at the heart of Machen's conflict with modernism.[50]

In his second year, Harold took Machen's "Romans Exegesis" course. Just the year before, Machen had published *The Origin of Paul's Religion*, which argued for a close continuity of thought between Jesus and Paul. As one of the course projects, Harold wrote a complicated exegesis paper on Romans 1:1-7. Machen returned the paper with the observation that "there are two classes of persons in America—(1) those who write 'thought,' 'though,' and 'through,' and those (2) who write 'thot,' 'tho,' and 'thru.' Your intellectual attainments clearly justify you in assuming to be en-rolled in the former class." Harold had routinely used "thot," "tho," and "thru," and Machen was not amused. He nevertheless gave Harold a "satisfactory"; the alternative was "unsatisfactory." In 1922 Princeton did not yet use letter grades.[51]

Harold considered Machen his most formative instructor. "I owe to him as much as to anyone a great clearing in my thinking along theological lines, as well as the clear grasp of the differences between the liberal and conservative point of view in theology," he once told John Horsch.[52] A decade later, upon learning of Machen's death, Harold told John C. Wenger, "We got to know each other intimately, and I owe my decisive theological development to him. I was somewhat under the influence of liberal thinking, and would never have been delivered from it, at least as it seems to me now, if I had not met the powerful and thoroughly Christian mind of Dr. Machen. He was the best teacher I ever had."[53]

Half of Harold's courses at Princeton were in the area of bib-lical studies, evenly divided between the Old and the New Testa-ments. In Old Testament, most of his courses were taught by Geer-hardus Vos, who had a Ph.D. in Arabic from the University of Strasbourg. Vos offered his students an attractive view of Old Tes-tament history, arguing that it is focused on God's redemptive acts and that redemptive history reaches its consummation in Christ. That view of Old Testament history eventually became a common understanding; but for Harold, this was almost certainly his first encounter with it.[54]

Old Testament professor John Davis was Harold's primary ad-viser, and Davis was the one who recommended Harold for the Green Fellowship which made study at Tübingen possible in 1923-24. In Hebrew, Harold had Robert Dick Wilson, a close collabo-rator with Machen and a die-hard conservative. One of his most interesting teachers was Charles R. Erdman, who held the chair of practical theology at Princeton. Erdman was a moderate Funda-mentalist, and during the 1920s he was Machen's chief opponent in the faculty feud. In 1925, Erdman was elected moderator of the General Assembly of the Presbyterian Church and was a propo-nent of inclusivism: he felt that holding the various groups togeth-

**The Princeton Seminary class of 1922. Harold is third from the left in the top row. Noah Oyer is on the left in the second row.** Harold S. Bender papers, AMC.

er was a greater value than an absolute insistence on classical orthodoxy. Harold never mentioned Erdman specifically, but Erdman's position in Presbyterianism was identical to the position for which Harold was striving just then for Mennonite polity.[55]

As always, Harold was a diligent student, but Princeton stretched him, especially the second year. When Elsie warned him about working too hard, he told her, "You needn't worry about me working too hard for I'm not there yet. I seldom get in more than 10 hours of study a day. It just shows how much I was loafing before." He always got to bed by midnight, he assured his mother.[56]

At the end of the first semester, Harold declared his satisfaction with the work at Princeton. He told Orie Miller, "I must say that I am enjoying the work here at the Seminary very much. There is a high standard of scholarship which combined with sound teaching and loyalty to the Bible makes this an almost ideal place to study. The only trouble comes from the fact that the place is almost too Presbyterian for a good Mennonite."[57]

• • •

In 1921, the Princeton Christmas vacation began on December 21. Harold spent the holiday at Scottdale with Elizabeth, after traveling via Baltimore and Washington, D.C. It was his first visit to Washington, and he was there to see his college friend L. E. Blauch, who had a job as a social researcher for an education organization. On January 2 several of the YPC executive committee gathered at Scottdale to begin plans for a YPC meeting in 1922. Orie Miller, Jesse Smucker, and Harold were present.[58]

The executive committee members engaged in an intense discussion about where to go with the movement. Despite two years of work, there was still no YPC constitution, due to lack of agreement among the leaders of the YPC. Harold tried to diagnose the problem for Orie Miller. Some people, like Paul Erb, for example, were loath to join the movement until it got official endorsement from the general conference, he told Miller. Until persons like them felt free to join, the movement would have an uphill road. Harold outlined four possible courses of action. One was to set up a self-perpetuating organization, and hold an annual conference on an ongoing basis. A second was to hold a 1922 conference and make one of its purposes the preparation of a petition to general conference for official endorsement. If that failed, they would fold their tents and go home.[59]

A third idea was not to hold a conference and instead wait for the MC Mennonite general conference to act. A fourth was to give up the idea of a general YPC and work with district conference youth meetings. Harold had worked with youth meetings in Kansas-Nebraska and in Indiana-Michigan conferences, and there was a lively Ohio conference movement. From those bases a churchwide conference might evolve.[60]

Harold favored holding a conference in 1922 and letting the general conference decide the future. Apparently he carried the day at the January meeting in Scottdale. The three leaders agreed that he should inform the general conference moderator, Sanford C. Yoder, of their plans, which Harold did. Yoder was blunt in his reply, the gist of which was that the leaders of general conference could not accept most of the members of the committee of the YPC as legitimate leaders. The only way the YPC could become legitimate, Yoder suggested, would be for the current leadership to resign and let the general conference appoint a new committee. In reply Harold patiently explained that a compromise could be worked out, but that to surrender completely was not possible. To surrender would mean a repudiation of principles the YPC committee believed to be important to the youth of the church.[61]

The YPC committee forged ahead. By April they had an invitation to meet at the Science Ridge church near Sterling, Illinois. The date was set for June 15-18. During April and early May, as Harold struggled to complete his course work at Princeton, he carried on a continuous correspondence to arrange the conference program. He met a lot of disappointments. Typical was the enigmatic reply from his uncle Dan. Invited to speak, D. H. Bender replied, "I will not say that I will not attend. I want to do God's will and the very best for the cause. I can make no promise now, and you had better not count on me, but I am open to conviction." It was hard to plan for a conference with that kind of nonanswer.[62]

By mid-May Harold was at home in Elkhart, after a few days' stay with Elizabeth at Scottdale en route from Princeton. The Elkhart visit offered an opportunity for a family reunion of sorts. Wilbur was just finishing his first year at Goshen. Violet was completing her first year of teaching at nearby Millersburg High School. The big event was Florence's graduation from Goshen College.

By June 10 Harold was back at Garrett Institute to complete work for his B.D. On that day the Mennonite Board of Education took the fateful step of appointing *Gospel Herald* editor Daniel Kauffman to be president of Goshen College.

As usual, Harold piled on a heavy course load at Garrett. He gave his paper for his course in intertestamental Judaism the title, "Research in the Apocrypha and Pseudepigrapha with a View to Throwing Light on the Literary History of the Psalter, Including a Catalog and Brief Study of Sundry Prayers, Poems, and Hymns Found Therein." That mind-numbing label was a long one for a paper of only seven pages, but professor Fuller liked the paper. He commented that "the results may appear meager, but the author stayed in the original sources, no secondary sources being used. This naturally meant threshing a great deal of straw to find a few grains of wheat."[63]

Harold had scarcely begun his work at Garrett before he had to leave for the YPC meeting at Sterling, Illinois. The three-day conference was a major event, with some fifty speakers and several quartets. The style of the conference showed the influence of interdenominational Bible and missionary conferences which some of the YPC leaders had attended earlier. Every participant received a "morning watch" booklet. Each morning watch included a theme such as "Loving the Lord," a Bible text, a meditation from Jowett, "My Daily Meditation for the Circling Year," a set of questions for personal examination, and a prayer.[64]

Each evening, right after supper and before the evening service, there was a "Sunset" service in the church cemetery. At least once each day, missionary Florence Cooprider led the congregation in a recitation of a motto in Hindi sent to the conference by some "India boys" from one of the Mennonite missionary schools in India. The motto was mounted on the wall of the church. Vernon Smucker led the conference in a memorial service for Mennonites who had died in missionary and relief service.[65]

There was ample music, and the sessions were long. The Saturday morning one was typical. It began with three songs, a devotional, "Still, Still with Thee" by the Conrad Sisters quartet, an address on "Personal Evangelism" by J. W. Hess, another song, and another by J. C. Meyer on "Contemporary Mennonitism." Then the Conrad Sisters sang "He Is So Near to Me," and S. F. Coffman spoke on the "Christian Faith." After three hours, the meeting finally ended—with another song, announcements, the doxology, and a closing prayer.

On Saturday afternoon the conference held a business session and passed three resolutions: affirming the need for an inspirational and educational conference, urging an effort to get general conference endorsement, and authorizing the newly elected executive committee to plan for another conference. Raymond Hartzler and Harold were nominated as candidates for chair of the executive committee. Harold was elected. His fellow committee members were John Yoder, Walter Yoder, Vernon Smucker, and Payson Miller.[66]

The Sterling conference was the last hurrah for the French relief and service men in the YPC movement. It was also the last time many of the "old Goshen" people were on the program—persons like J. C. Meyer, Lester Hostetler, A. E. Kreider, N. E. Byers, I. W. Detweiler, Jesse Smucker, Raymond Hartzler, and C. Henry Smith. New persons on the program for the first time were Oscar Burkholder, S. F. Coffman, and C. F. Derstine from Ontario. Harold was delighted that Noah Oyer had agreed to attend. Oyer spoke twice. Orie Miller gave an address on the "Mission of the Mennonite Church."

Conspicuous by their absence were major leaders such as Aaron Loucks, Daniel Kauffman, Daniel Bender, Sanford C. Yoder, or any Virginia or Pennsylvania leaders. Harold and the YPC committee had failed to bring in MC general conference leaders. Just a few weeks before the conference, Daniel Kauffman had written a rather long editorial about the upcoming conference. His main point: "Our observation has been that separate movements of *special classes* [emphasis added] within the same church are invariably divisive."[67]

The *Gospel Herald* did not comment on the meeting. For the *Christian Monitor*, Vernon Smucker wrote an editorial endorsing the YPC and describing the conference in quite positive terms. He expressed regret that the church's leaders had chosen to stay away; the YPC had offered a great opportunity for them to get acquainted with the youth of the church. In September, editor Smucker published the entire text of the conference, including synopses of the various addresses.[68]

## ✃ 6 ✄

# Princeton, Marriage, Europe

*Harold wins the Green Fellowship for study in Europe
and graduates from Princeton Seminary.
Harold and Elizabeth get married.*

FROM THE YPC sessions of June 1922, Harold returned to Garrett
Biblical Institute and plunged into his studies. Among his diversions was attendance at the Krimmer Mennonite mission in Chicago, where in July he heard a sermon by a German Mennonite minister named Michael Horsch. Horsch spoke about the work of the
German Mennonite relief organization Christenpflicht (Christian
duty), of which he was chair. He had come to the United States to
seek help from Americans for the dire needs of Germans who were
victims of the postwar collapse of their nation's economy. Michael
Horsch was Elizabeth's uncle, a brother of John Horsch.[1]

Harold found Uncle Michael quite interesting and escorted
him to the railroad station, where they talked until Horsch left for
Newton, Kansas, for more meetings. Horsch promised to visit
Bender at Garrett when he returned to Chicago in mid-August.
The encounter at the Krimmer mission became the beginning of a
long and fruitful association. It also made more tangible an idea
Harold had been pondering for some time. He decided to explore
the possibility of study in a German university for a year after
graduation from Princeton.[2]

Harold graduated with his B.D. degree on August 30 and returned to Elkhart. He had three weeks before classes began at
Princeton. Apparently sometime during the summer, Elizabeth
found a job teaching at the Johnstown, Pennsylvania, high school.

She and Harold had planned to marry during the summer of 1922, before Harold went back to Princeton. Again, the reasons for the delay are not clear. Housing for married students at Princeton was expensive and scarce, and they were not able to get financial assistance. Almost certainly, financial problems delayed the marriage for another year. And when Elizabeth got the job in Johnstown, they could not really afford to marry, especially if they wanted to go to Europe together the following year.

In far-off Soviet Union, friend Arthur Slagel read the marriage announcements in the *Gospel Herald*. He noticed that John Fisher and Alma Wayre had married, and so had Jesse Smucker and Mary Lantz. Why not Harold and Elizabeth? The letter with Harold's answer has been lost, but in October Slagel wrote, "Accept my condolement [sic] for the change in your plans. I know just a little bit how you feel about it. But I need a wife worse than you do, really."[3]

In any case, by September 26 Harold was back at Princeton, ensconced this time in Alexander Hall. Its rooms were reserved for seniors. He had one of the prized ground-floor rooms, just down the hall from the quarters of professor J. Gresham Machen, a bachelor. The rooms in Alexander were quite commodious, each with an adjoining bedroom. Maids came in daily to make the beds. Each room had a bed, pillows and sheets, a bureau, a washstand, several chairs, a table, a "looking glass," a bookcase, a floor rug, and a "clothes press."[4]

The opening seminary exercises began at 11:00 a.m. on September 27 in Miller chapel. Bender was the only Mennonite among the 215 students. That spring the *Princeton Seminary Bulletin* proudly called Princeton Seminary the "Oxford of America." Princeton meant to prepare "men" for the "work of the Master. Princeton recognizes the need for ministers who are true men." Harold Bender found the "Oxford of America" much to his liking.[5]

Princeton emphasized the spiritual and devotional life. Each day "little groups of men meet together to keep tryst with the Heavenly Father," explained a student. On Wednesdays each class met for a half hour in the morning for worship and "intercession." In the mornings, faculty members led twenty-minute chapels. On

Tuesday evening of each week, the YMCA held a meeting for special speakers who might be on campus. In the fall of 1922, Harold heard an address by missionary Charles Abel on "Work Among the Cannibals." Abel had served in New Guinea. Professor Spaeth of the university faculty spoke on "The Value of Shakespeare to the Minister."[6] Once a month there was a social evening in the Alexander Hall parlor for faculty and students.

Harold entered into campus life with vigor. During both years he sang bass in the seminary chorus. In 1922-23 he also sang in a sixteen-member glee club which, as he put it, sang "high-class sacred music." The club performed in New York and in New Jersey churches on weekends, and at many seminary events. His course work consisted mostly of electives and theses. The big project of the year was writing a thesis to support his application for the George S. Green Fellowship, with which he hoped to fund his study in Germany the following year. The Green Fellowship promoted advanced study in Old Testament literature, and in 1923-24 it was worth $900. If Harold could win the prize, it would represent more annual earnings than he had ever received in his life. To his delight he learned that he was the only applicant. For 1922-23 the topic of the paper was "The Literary History of the Hymnary Known as David," a study of the Psalms. Harold plunged in, working with professor Jack Davis, his adviser.[7]

In mid-November Harold was dismayed to discover that one of his classmates had also decided to enter the competition. He had been "double-crossed," he told Noah Oyer at Hesston. It was a mean trick. "My only chance now," he wrote, "is that [he] gives it up or that he fails to write a satisfactory paper for Davis. Secretly, I think the latter is quite possible unless his wife does it for him. She seems to have egged him on thus far."[8]

Harold's frustration was rooted both in his desire to study in Germany and the absence of a clear idea about alternatives. Teaching at Goshen the next year was almost certainly no option, in light of the college's many problems. He had thought about studying at Hartford Seminary if he could obtain a fellowship. "Perhaps I'll find a rich uncle who wants to subsidize me for a year abroad," he told Noah Oyer ruefully. "But I guess there ain't no such animal among us."[9]

The thesis had to be submitted by April 1. Harold worked feverishly, spending as much as eight hours a day on the paper during February and March. The weather, down to ten degrees almost every day, helped by keeping him indoors. As a result the paper became, as he told his mother, "a small book," 159 pages long. It was his first sustained piece of research and writing. He handed it in on March 19, well before the deadline,[10] but the presence of a rival paper added a dramatic touch to the final outcome.

The Christmas break began on Wednesday, December 19, and Harold headed like a shot for Johnstown. Before they left for Scottdale on Friday evening, he shaved off a two-month growth he had cultivated on his upper lip—a "very cute little mustache," he assured his mother, as he promised to send her a picture. "It makes me look quite distinguished."[11]

Harold and Elizabeth had a busy time at Scottdale, spending one evening with C. F. and Martha Eby Yake and another with Vernon and Mary Hostetler Smucker. Harold was so busy he found no time to go to Somerset County to visit his Bender uncles and arrange for the annual shipment of maple syrup to Elkhart. Elsie still kept George's retail maple syrup business going, though at a reduced level. Most of the syrup came from Bender relatives in Somerset County. Harold received a pongee shirt from Elizabeth. The fine silk fabric pleased him, and he told his mother, "I have been wearing it practically all week." But the collar was too big; so he sent it to Elkhart for "shrinking." Harold got Elizabeth a Princeton pillow. It was not much of a gift he admitted, but about all he could afford after paying $30 for his train fare to Scottdale and back. In addition to small Christmas gifts, Harold and Elizabeth also got their first wedding gift, a hand-worked tablecloth and six napkins from Aunt Jessie, a great aunt on the Otto side of the family. She had made the set for the wedding in the fall, and when Harold and Elizabeth called off the event, she kept it and sent it for Christmas.[12]

Harold apologized to his mother for not coming home for Christmas. Instead, he sent a five-pound box of candy plus some stamps for the boys. Aunt Cinda was with Elsie for the winter, and over Christmas the women did extensive sewing. They made Harold two pairs of pajamas as a Christmas gift. Throughout Harold's time at Princeton, he used a leather laundry bag to mail his clothes home to Elsie for washing. The twice-a-month trips were rapidly wearing out the bag, and at Christmastime Harold worried that it might not last out the last four months of travel. Since he was so strapped for cash, he decided to send the bag of laundry only once a month.[13]

• • •

On New Year's Day, Harold traveled back to Princeton. Classes began the next morning. The spring semester was relatively easy, aside from the tension of waiting for word on the Green Fellowship. In March he made a trip to Elkhart on YPC business. The YPC organizers were planning a conference for June 1923, and Harold's purpose was to meet with the Indiana-Michigan conference executive committee to get permission to hold the event at one of the northern Indiana congregations. He succeeded, wangling an invitation from bishop D. D. Miller to meet at Miller's Forks congregation in LaGrange County. The price of the invitation was that the Indiana-Michigan conference executive committee would have the right to veto suggestions for conference speakers.[14]

On April 6 professor Jack Davis announced the Green award in Old Testament had been won by Harold. A Church of the Brethren friend, Maynard Cassady, won the church history fellowship. Cassady, a graduate of Juniata College, would spend the year at Tübingen with Harold and Elizabeth. Another friend, Edward Roberts, won the apologetics award and would study at the University of Berlin in 1923-24. Years later Roberts became the dean of Princeton Seminary. Harold's final exams began on April 14 and continued for nearly two weeks, the last one on April 24.[15]

In the midst of his exams, Harold wrote a benedictory letter to Noah Oyer at Hesston. "This has certainly been a rich year for me," he told his friend, "tho I feel a need for a great deal more than I now have. How little we ever get to master compared with what we ought to have!" Harold urged Oyer to read Swete's *Holy*

*Spirit in the New Testament.* "I started out to read it as required reading but finished it as a devotional book."[16] In early May he reported his grades to Oyer, saying he was gratified with the "clean record" he had achieved, but also expressing some "doubt" about "the thoroness of the grading."[17]

The effect of the Princeton years on Harold Bender's life and thought were profound. By his second year at Princeton, Harold's sense of calling had shifted decisively toward church leadership education. Princeton, with its focus on ministerial preparation, offered Harold a working model of something he came to believe Mennonites needed. As he worked at perceiving his future calling, his current experiences were fundamental: Harold was taking seminary training while trying to lead the YPC movement to legitimacy against the opposition of inadequately educated Mennonite leaders.

Writing to Noah Oyer in the fall of 1922, Harold said he was more intensely interested in the future of the Mennonite educational program than ever before. "It seems to me to hold out the brightest hope for the future, i.e., for building the church of the next generation into the power for the Kingdom of God. None of us are interested in conserving Mennonitism for Mennonites, but I am sincerely afraid that is what may be done unless powerful forces are brought to play thru the training of the coming generation of workers and leaders."[18]

Harold responded to Oyer's query about what Bender considered the urgent needs of the hour for Mennonites; he listed "a sense of mission, a genuine vital and normal religious experience, a sense of stewardship of life and talents, and a deeper sense of the simple NT gospel, a simple piety, the doctrine of love in all affairs of men and nations, and an absolute loyalty to all the teachings of Christ." To accomplish all of that, the church needed "first and most seriously a trained leadership and a trained ministry."[19] He joked that probably Oyer would find most of "this" old or heretical, but it was where he found himself at that point. The 26-year-old Bender had found his life calling. He would devote the next forty years to carrying out the basic program he described to Noah Oyer in November 1922.[20]

Commencement at Princeton was a three-day affair, but the main event was on Tuesday morning, May 8, when the degrees were conferred at 10:30 in the large First Presbyterian church on the edge of the university campus. The faculty and graduates filed out of the May sunshine into the sanctuary to the rich sounds of Bach's "Veni Creator Spiritus." The program was filled with prayers, Scripture readings, and music. Harold's chorus sang Mozart's "Gloria in Excelsis" and the class hymn, "Lift Up Your Heads, Ye Gates of Brass." The commencement address, by James G. K. McClure, president of McCormick Theological Seminary, was entitled "The Place and Power of Christian Personality in the Ministry." The president's reception in the afternoon included the announcement of the six annual fellowship awards, one going to Harold S. Bender.[21]

The next morning, bags packed, Harold left Princeton for Scottdale. He was in a hurry: that evening he would marry Elizabeth Horsch.

• • •

Harold and Elizabeth were married at 9:00 on Wednesday evening, May 9, at the Horsch home on Walnut Avenue. Had the neighbors been watching the house, they would have noticed little to suggest the auspicious event taking place within. Yet the arrival of officiating bishop Aaron Loucks at such a late hour might have raised an eyebrow or two. There were no guests, and Elizabeth's father was absent, traveling in Europe. It was a private wedding. There had been no public announcement of the nuptials.[22]

Originally, Harold and Elizabeth had planned to marry during the second week of June, after Elizabeth's school ended at Johnstown.[23] But then they had discovered that they would not be able to get a passport in the two weeks remaining till their departure for Germany on June 19. A proper passport would need her married name. So they decided to have the wedding right after Harold's graduation. But that plan also created a problem: in 1923 the Johnstown school district did not permit its women teachers to be married, and so Elizabeth could not legally marry until the end

**Harold and Elizabeth on their wedding day, May 9, 1923.**
Bender Family Album.

of her contract year in June. As the baffled couple shared their dilemma with Elizabeth's principal, he reluctantly agreed to their marriage if they kept it a secret from his school board. Hence the unannounced wedding.[24]

For the ceremony Harold wore a new navy blue suit, bought for $20 earlier in the year, which he claimed fit him to a *T*. Elizabeth's garb seems lost to the record, except that at the last minute she had to use a safety pin to raise the neckline of her dress a bit. Somehow Elizabeth was able to get off from teaching for a few days, but she returned to her classroom on the following Monday, and Harold went home to Elkhart.[25]

Harold's mother was not happy with the turn of events. She regretted that none of the Benders could attend the wedding, and she was especially upset that after only four days of marriage, the couple would separate for nearly a month. Harold tried to mollify her. "I know it isn't the customary thing to do—leave a bride for a month," he admitted. But he had learned at Christmastime that Vernon and Mary Hostetler Smucker had been married three months before they lived together. "So," he told Elsie, "I guess we can make it for a month."[26]

Harold arrived in Elkhart on the evening of May 14. During the next month, the eager young churchman attended the annual mission board meeting at Kokomo, Indiana; the Indiana-Michigan annual conference; the Goshen College commencement; and the YPC conference. In the course of all those meetings and conferences, Harold met nearly every Mennonite church leader. The only meeting he missed was a Board of Education event which confirmed the one-year closing of Goshen College for reorganization. He missed that meeting because early on that Monday morning, he and Elizabeth left for New York en route to Germany.[27]

In addition to attending meetings and completing preparations for the June 14-17 YPC meeting, Harold helped his family move out of the mission board house at 1711 Prairie Street. During the spring of 1923, Harold and his mother had discussed their alternatives. One was to build a house, but the problem was where to build. Harold proposed building on a lot on Cleveland Avenue west of Goshen. Already they were talking about the advantages of Harold and Elizabeth living with Elsie and the boys if Harold came to Goshen College to teach, something he devoutly hoped to do. But by spring 1923, the decision to close Goshen College made the idea of Harold and Elizabeth's employment there moot. And since Harold had won the Green Fellowship, they would be in Europe for a year. Elsie decided to rent a house the mission board owned just around the corner from 1711, a small house where the Reiffs had lived.[28] The Bender family moved there in early June.

• • •

During those weeks Harold was preoccupied with the impending closure of Goshen College. He considered the Board of Education's decision regarding Goshen College to be a near catastrophe. "No one but a friend of Goshen can realize to the full the effect that the closing is having among a great part of the younger element in the middle west," he told Noah Oyer. The decision was also a crushing blow to Harold personally. By 1923 he had decided Goshen was where he would like to begin his academic career. Now that prospect was in serious jeopardy.[29]

Even more serious was the shock the closing gave Harold's sense of loyalty to the church. He poured out his frustration to Oyer. "It seems to me utter folly and criminal to once more wreck the future of the church on utterly inconsequential matters compared to the great vital truths of the gospel and the needs of the world today," he lamented. What most frustrated him was that the Goshen closing showed every sign of becoming just another Mennonite schism, based, as he put it, on "personalities and petty prejudices and on nonessential points."[30]

Harold was especially upset by one of Daniel Kauffman's *Gospel Herald* editorials. "It sounds as tho in his mind there will not be an inch of yielding to the other side. His suggested solutions are not solutions at all, but mere pious platitudes. When matters of discipline such as dress and life insurance become 'fundamental differences in doctrine and life,' how sadly have our Mennonite standards of value become perverted," he told Noah Oyer. "Pray tell me," he demanded, "is it possible in this modern day to repeat the same old mistakes and divide the Church of Christ for fundamentally the same reason that Jacob Ammann did back in Switzerland two centuries ago, on matters of pure externality!"[31]

The closing of Goshen College profoundly affected the Bender family. Not only might Harold lose a teaching career at Goshen, but Violet and Wilbur chose to find other colleges. In June 1923 Wilbur had just completed his sophomore year at Goshen. When the college failed to reopen in the fall of 1923, Wilbur got a job teaching in a Goshen city school, and in 1925-27 completed his B.A. work at Harvard College. Violet completed her work at Oberlin College. Wilbur and Violet were casualties of the Goshen closing. They would never return to the Mennonite church.

The closing of Goshen College was a prominent event in the MC Mennonite church in the 1920s. It demonstrated both a contest between generations and an argument about appropriate Mennonite cultural and social adaptations with American society.

It was only peripherally a theological debate.

The generational struggle worked itself out in two ways. By the 1920s, those who had founded the major MC Mennonite organizations had established a near monopoly of leadership positions in them: the MC general conference, formed in 1898; Goshen College, in 1903; Mennonite Board of Education, in 1905; the Mennonite Board of Missions and Charities, in 1906; the Mennonite Publishing House, in 1908; Hesston College, in 1909; and Eastern Mennonite School, in 1917.

The church institutions functioned through an interlocking system of oversight committees whose members appeared again and again in a variety of permutations. For example, in 1923 Daniel Kauffman was president of Goshen College and editor of the *Gospel Herald*, but also a member of the executive committee of the mission board and of several key committees of the general conference. Sanford C. Yoder was president both of the mission board and of the Board of Education plus being a member of the Publication Board and many other committees. Dan H. Bender was president of Hesston College and a member of the mission board, the Board of Education, and the Publication Board.

That old-boy network now found itself increasingly challenged by a group of younger men, most of them in their twenties, who had grown up under the aegis of the new organizations. Many had been formed by a Goshen College education or/and by wartime CO experience and postwar relief work abroad. For the younger generation, these experiences of Goshen education, conscientious objection, and relief work gave them a much broader view of the world. Often it also made them quite critical of the sometimes fumbling leadership provided by the older generation. Young potential leaders were eager to bring their new skills and viewpoints to bear on church institutions and life. The middle-aged leaders were uneasy about sharing their roles.

American societal forces unleashed by the World War and its aftermath accentuated the generational divide. More than at any earlier time in their 200-year odyssey in America, Mennonites in the 1920s felt exposed and threatened by the surrounding North American culture. Forces which seemed especially threatening were the newly consolidated public schools, radios, the personal mobility offered by automobiles, the availability of affordable store-bought clothing, movies, attractive insurance plans, and relative prosperity, especially for farmers. Quite frequently the lightning rod for Mennonites' unease about these cultural forces was higher education.

With the Goshen College financial debacle of 1918, the Board of Education was forced to become more responsible for the operation of the college. Increasingly, the board injected itself into the operation of the college by censoring books, requiring faith commitments of faculty members, and monitoring campus social life. Regrettably, they took a relatively inactive role in fundraising and financial support. This board activity often reflected adversely on the college, depreciating the institution's credibility in the eyes of the church. That situation in turn made the college's fundraising efforts rather difficult. It was no accident that the college had four presidents in five years.

In 1922 the board persuaded Daniel Kauffman, editor of the *Gospel Herald*, to assume the college presidency. Board members hoped his prestige would rally the church behind the college. He failed, largely because the young people perceived him as inadequate for the task and stayed away from the college in droves. Enrollment fell from a high of 204 in 1921-22 to 116 students in 1922-23.[32] Kauffman was also unsuccessful as a fundraiser. When it became clear that he could not meet the financial standards required to keep Indiana state accreditation, the jig was up.

While the Board of Education must take the primary responsibility for the outcome, some of the blame must go also to the college's faculty and staff. They were simply not able to adjust to the tightening organizational system and its control of the church by the 1920s. "Old Goshen" could be liberal and relatively free of churchly control in its first twenty-five years because the churchly oversight of Mennonite institutions was still evolving. By the 1920s the MC Mennonite general conference, through its general board committees, was exercising much more authority over the church's institutions. In a *Gospel Herald* editorial in April 1923, Daniel Kauffman asked a rhetorical question: "Shall the Church take charge of her own enterprises?" He answered his question with a resounding declaration: "Yes; let the Church assume full control of all her enterprises." It was, he argued, the "way of real progress."[33] The Board of Education's much more aggressive control of the colleges signaled a coming-of-age of the new organizational system of the MC Mennonite church.

Theological and ideological factors also played roles in these developments. In the 1920s the differences between conservatives and progressives were often played out in the church's institutions, partly because the two MC Mennonite papers, the *Gospel Herald* and the *Christian Monitor*, were controlled by the old-boy leadership and allowed little difference of opinion. Through membership on church boards, conservatives such as J. B. Smith and bishop George R. Brunk Sr. of Virginia found ideal forums for bringing their agendas to bear on the church. They were almost always able to shift matters in a conservative direction because moderate leaders were more concerned about practical organizational matters than about theology. Among those inclined to be a bit more moderate were such as Daniel Kauffman, Daniel Bender, Aaron Loucks, Sanford C. Yoder, and D. D. Miller.

All of that generation's leaders, conservative or moderate, were poorly educated, with only modest theological training, and their predispositions were fundamentally cautious. The result was that in any argument between conservatives and progressives, the church leaders almost instinctively sided with the conservatives.

By the early 1920s, the few MC Mennonite progressive leaders were either in exile at Bluffton or under siege at Goshen. The lone progressive at the publishing house, *Christian Monitor* editor Vernon Smucker, was hardly able to push a progressive agenda. In 1923 he resigned in protest when the Board of Education closed Goshen College. The absence of alternative churchly forums for debate between conservatives and progressives led to heightened conflict within the institutions over the issues. The closing of Goshen College is the outstanding example of that effect.

The reservations about Goshen and outright opposition to it were rooted also in some local Indiana-Michigan church discipline struggles, mirrored in similar skirmishes across the whole church.

**Harold and Elizabeth with his mother, Elsie Kolb Bender, in June 1923.** George and Elsie Kolb Bender papers, AMC.

Some of the issues surfaced at the 1923 sessions of the Indiana-Michigan conference. Harold Bender, busy helping his mother move out of the mission board house, took a few days off to attend the conference. What he observed there made him quite unhappy.[34]

Between 1916 and 1923, the Indiana-Michigan conference had come under the leadership of bishop Jacob (J. K.) Bixler. He was the conference moderator for four years, and a conservative organization-centralizer who led forces promoting the authority of the executive committee of the Indiana-Michigan conference at the expense of congregational autonomy. A contest between progressive and conservative parties in the conference came to a head in 1923 at those annual sessions in June. The conference appointed a special committee to enforce conference rules on dress and life insurance. Within a few weeks, six ministers were identified as recalcitrant on those issues. Among them were a former president of Goshen College, I. R. Detweiler, and two of Harold's erstwhile college friends, Raymond Hartzler and Menno D. Lantz. By the end of the summer, all three had their ordinations revoked.[35]

• • •

Harold's most pressing task in late May 1923 was to complete preparations for the upcoming YPC meeting. Since he had persuaded the Indiana-Michigan conference leaders to permit the meeting at the Forks church, he now had to make good on his promise to meet those leaders' expectations about the speakers. Of the three YPCs held in those years, this one was the most completely planned and managed by Harold. Payson Miller and Vernon Smucker were the only remaining executive committee members who had been at the original conference in France. Bender set out to demonstrate to the MC Mennonite leaders that the YPC executive committee intended to meet their fundamental concerns. But he faced an uphill struggle.

What may have been decisive in the outcome was Harold's success in persuading dean J. D. Charles of Hesston College to be the keynote speaker at the conference. Each morning Charles spoke on "Christian Verities."[36] He was a dynamic young conservative, much in demand as a speaker, and clearly a rising star in Mennonite leadership circles. His untimely death several months after the YPC conference cut short a promising career. Getting Charles on the program made it much easier to get other conservative speakers to attend the conference.

The YPC sessions were in a large tent in the yard next to the church, with the tent full to overflowing, especially on Saturday and Sunday. Even Daniel Kauffman, eager to return to Scottdale after an unhappy year at Goshen College, delayed his departure so he could attend. Harold had a lot riding on the conference. In a "Call for the Young People's Conference," a three-column announcement printed in the *Gospel Herald* just before the event, he waxed eloquent about the urgent need for the meeting. "Many of us need to get back to bed-rock experience with a firmer grip on the great spiritual realities," he declared. "Thus in a time when things are being shaken may the things that shall stand be discovered."[37] He was delighted when Daniel Kauffman proclaimed the program "well arranged" and the talks "inspiring." But Kauffman could not bring himself directly to endorse the YPC.[38]

Despite lukewarm responses from people like Daniel Kauffman, Harold's persistence had paid off. The *Gospel Herald* announced the meeting and even commented favorably on it, which it had not done for previous YPC conferences. Harold had brought some of the young conservatives like J. D. Charles and Noah Oyer onto the program, together with such notable progressives as Lester Hostetler, Raymond Hartzler, and Jesse Smucker. Yet it was one of the last times such a mixture could be achieved.

Ironically, the end of the conference on Sunday evening was also the end of the YPC movement. True, in August the MC Mennonite general conference would endorse a plan for the Young People's Conference to work with the MC's Young People's Program Committee, which had been moribund for some time. But not much would come from the conference's endorsement. The young progressives had already turned to a new forum, a journal called the *Christian Exponent.* Its first issue appeared just a half year after the last YPC conference, on January 4, 1924. During four years it was a voice for Mennonite progressives. Yet Harold did not join its effort. By the time he returned from abroad in September 1924, his superiors at Goshen College forbade him from writing for the *Exponent*; to preserve the job they proffered, he acquiesced. Eventually Harold's answer to the *Christian Exponent* was yet another journal, *The Mennonite Quarterly Review.*

But at nine o'clock on June 17, 1923, those developments were still in the future. As the last strains of "O Jesus, I Have Promised" faded and the fervent benediction of bishop Albert (A. J.) Steiner reached to the darkness at the edge of the tent, Harold must have had a deep sense of accomplishment. Four years of arduous work had brought a struggling Mennonite YPC to life. Three years of intense theological study had brought him a B.D. and two master's degrees. And now, after five years of painful separation and waiting, he and Elizabeth were married. It was only a matter of hours before they would begin the greatest adventure of their young lives. He and Elizabeth would depart early the next morning for New York and a year of study in Europe.

• • •

The ocean liner *S. S. Mauretania* sailed out past the Statue of Liberty and headed east across the Atlantic. The voyage lasted ten days. For Harold and Elizabeth, it was an idyllic and belated honeymoon. Harold had his camera, and there are shots of Elizabeth in a deck chair, reading; of Harold posing on the ladder going up to the top deck; and of the couple posing in front of a lifeboat. It was June, but the weather was cool. Both wore winter overcoats: Elizabeth's was of checked design, with large pockets and the hemline at a fashionable midcalf length; Harold's was a belted khaki coat, which made him look like a sophisticated foreign journalist. Elizabeth wore a brimmed hat. They gave the appearance of a well-bred middle-class American couple on a honeymoon.[39]

The ship docked at Rotterdam on June 28, and they went directly to Lunteren, Holland, near Utrecht, to attend the annual conference of a new Mennonite Gemeentedag-Bewegung (a church-renewal movement). The conference buildings were modest but set in a cozy pine forest, and Harold and Elizabeth were charmed by

**Harold and Elizabeth aboard ship en route to Europe in June 1923.**
Bender Family Album.

the peaceful ambience. Waiting to welcome them was Elizabeth's father, John Horsch, who had been doing historical research during a sojourn of several months in the Netherlands.[40]

Harold and Elizabeth were having their first encounter with Dutch Mennonites, and they were pleasantly surprised. The friendship was warm, and they found the spirituality deep. They were especially impressed by T. O. Hylkema, a pietistically orthodox pastor in the Giethoorn Mennonite church. More than with any other of the Dutch Mennonites, they found in Hylkema a kindred spirit. Hylkema had established the Vereeniging voor Gemeemtedagen in 1917, a renewal movement to spiritually invigorate the Dutch Mennonites. Its purpose was not theological but rather more practically to inspire lay persons to serve Christ in the world. The group sponsored an annual conference. Attending the gathering was a great opportunity for Harold and Elizabeth. "We learned to know intimately the leaders of the New Movement, Gemeentedag-Bewegung," Harold told Noah Oyer.[41]

For three weeks, Harold, Elizabeth, and father Horsch traveled in the Netherlands. Harold was surprised by the large number of Mennonites in the Netherlands (38,000 members, compared to 87,000 in the United States), their well-organized congregations, and their theological sophistication. The trio visited some of the major Mennonite centers such as Amsterdam and Haarlem. Then they went north to old Holland and across to Friesland to the "real Menno Simons country," as Harold put it. The young couple loved the quaint character of this pretourist Netherlands.[42]

Elizabeth and Harold were particularly delighted to spend several days with the T. O. Hylkemas in the village of Giethoorn in northern Holland. Giethoorn was honeycombed with canals, and Harold and Elizabeth spent several languid afternoons floating on

**Harold with T. O. Hylkema at the Gemeentedag Bewegung Conference at Lunteren, Holland, in June 1923.**
Nelson E. Kauffman papers, AMC.

**Harold and Elizabeth on T. O. Hylkema's boat near Giethoorn, Holland, in 1923.** Nelson E. Kauffman papers, AMC.

them in Hylkema's boat. One photo caught them sitting in the bow, Harold's arm protectively around Elizabeth's shoulder as she nodded off, lulled by the rocking boat. The trip through Holland was a "treat we shall never forget," Harold told Noah Oyer.[43]

From the Netherlands they traveled by train south along the east side of the Rhine River.[44] Had they known where to look, they could have spotted French gun emplacements overlooking the waterway. A few months earlier the French had occupied the Rhineland to enforce some reparations agreements they believed the Germans had violated—agreements that were part of the peace treaties following World War I. The French occupation created a major international crisis. It inflamed German patriotism, and it gave the Germans new reasons for feeling victimized by the Allies.

John Horsch, visiting his brother Michael at Hellmannsberg, Bavaria, at the time of the invasion, was powerfully moved by the event. Ten years later when Adolf Hitler reoccupied the Rhineland, Hitler would become an instant hero to John Horsch.[45]

By November the German outcry against France would also make its mark on Harold. Writing to Noah Oyer, he remarked with some heat, "It is quite evident that France is seeking the utter ruin of Germany, and it is quite evident that she will eventually accomplish it." And, he added presciently, "The devil is having his day over here just now."[46]

For John Horsch, it was a happy experience to introduce his daughter and new son-in-law to the Horsch and Funck relatives, and to show Elizabeth and Harold the haunts of his youth. They first visited Elizabeth's kinfolks in the Heilbronn area, with much conversation and eating as they got acquainted for the first time with Elizabeth's uncles, aunts, and cousins. A week later they traveled on to Hellmannsberg near Ingolstadt in northern Bavaria, where Elizabeth's uncle Michael Horsch and his family owned and operated a large farm. The visiting and eating began all over again. Through the year, the relationships with relatives developed further in many weekend and holiday visits.

In 1921 Michael Horsch had founded the Mennonite relief agency Christenpflicht, for which he had been raising money in Chicago. Its purpose was to deal with the dire needs of millions of Germans who were poverty stricken by the terrible economic conditions in their country following the war. In the summer of 1923, Christenpflicht was feeding thousands of children in cities like Nuremberg, Munich, Stuttgart, and Ulm. Much of the money for the various feeding projects came from America, through the MC's Mennonite Relief Committee (MRC).

One of Harold's assignments was to spend several weeks visiting the Christenpflicht's projects and to report to the MRC about his findings. He did so during August, then published a version of his report in the *Gospel Herald*. His commentary on the situation in Germany was rather astute. Farmers and people with jobs were doing quite well, he reported. In fact, farmers were prospering as never before, for produce prices were high. The people suffering hardship were the jobless, the middle class whose savings were wiped out by the horrendous inflation of the postwar years, and the elderly living on fixed incomes. He pleaded for more contributions.[47]

• • •

When Harold embarked for Europe, he had not yet selected a university. Earlier he had told John Horsch, "I want to avoid the big centers [universities] and keep to the central and South German group if possible."[48] That meant Jena, Göttingen, Marburg, and Tübingen. Apparently by the time they arrived at Hellmannsberg about August 1, they had decided on Tübingen University, likely influenced by size and location. The deciding factors remain obscure. Tübingen did put them close to the Horsch and Funck relatives at Heilbronn and Hellmannsberg. In late August, Harold, Elizabeth, and father Horsch visited Tübingen. There they arranged to rent a small apartment and confirmed Harold's matriculation as a student. Horsch then left for America; he had been in Europe for nearly a year. Since classes did not begin until October,

**Harold and Elizabeth visiting Horsch relatives near Heilbronn, Germany, in 1923. Notice Harold's mustache.** Bender Family Album.

Harold and Elizabeth left almost immediately for a month-long visit to the Alsace, Switzerland, and Italy.[49]

Even as novice travelers, Elizabeth and Harold were not merely tourists. Their first stop on this trip was to attend an Alsatian Mennonite Jahresfest (annual festival) at the Mennonite church at Colmar, south of Strasbourg. The Colmar church was a young congregation, only two years old. It was also progressive, with a weekly prayer meeting held in members' homes. At the Jahresfest, Harold met nearly all of the leading Mennonite ministers and elders in Alsace, Baden, and Basel; they had gathered to ordain two young men to the ministry. One was Hans Nussbaumer.[50] By the end of World War II, Nussbaumer would be the senior elder among the Alsatian Mennonites and an eager collaborator in many of Harold's postwar projects such as the Mennonite World Conference and the European Mennonite Bible School.

The couple spent several days in Strasbourg before moving on to Switzerland. There they claimed to visit "all the Mennonite centers," but they also enjoyed the Alpine beauty. Two trips they would never forget, Harold reported, were "a boat ride on Lake Luzern, and a trip from Interlaken to the Jungfrau, where we stayed overnight." But he sadly commented, "Our resources of time and money were all too limited for this wondrous beauty spot." At Zurich, Bern, Basel, and Geneva, Harold began his first limited exposure to Anabaptist sites and historical archives. Then it was on to Italy. In a week they visited Milan, Pisa, Florence, Rome, and Naples. They were delighted with Rome, especially the classical ruins and St. Peter's cathedral. They also took a tour of the catacombs. Traveling north, they visited the Italian lake country. Then they returned to Tübingen.[51]

By then it was October, and classes would soon begin. The couple had been traveling nonstop for nearly four months. Harold, his first stint of real travel completed, thought the time had been "far too short for all we wanted to do." But they were happy to settle into their "cozy little two-room flat" near the university. By having their own stove and doing their own cooking, they were able to "live somewhat cheaply," even though the price of food was going up steeply in the fall of 1923.[52]

## ⊷ 7 ⊷

# From Tübingen to Goshen

*Harold studies Old Testament theology at Tübingen*
*University and prepares to teach at Goshen College.*
*Elizabeth is pregnant.*

THE Tübingen of 1923 was beautiful. Harold's Princeton friend
Maynard Cassady, who was also there in 1923, described it as
"one of Germany's purest and finest expressions of her true cultural atmosphere." Its university was founded in the late fifteenth
century, and the town had a population of about 20,000. With its
quaint *Fachwerk* (timbered) houses built in the old three-story
style and its narrow streets, it was quite medieval.[1]

The university itself formed a special section of the city. In
1923 it had more than twenty major institutes, many devoted to
science and medicine. A new library, only ten years old, had over
a half million volumes. In the fall of 1923, the university had
around 2,500 students, about a fourth of them in theology. The
large number of theology students testified to the premier position
Tübingen held in theological studies in Germany. The town of
Tübingen was largely Lutheran, but the university had both
Lutheran and Catholic faculties. The Lutheran faculty was strong
in New Testament studies and in dogmatics; the Catholic faculty
was more focused on church history and patristics.[2]

Harold registered for twenty hours of lectures. The fall semester went from the middle of October to the end of February.
Among his fellow theological students was a 17-year-old named
Dietrich Bonhoeffer. Another fellow student was Ethelbert Stauffer, of Mennonite parentage, who in 1933 would publish the in-

**Tübingen, Germany.**
Bender Family Album.

fluential article "Täufertum und Märtyrertheologie" (Anabaptism and theology of martyrdom). Harold attended lectures on Monday, Tuesday, Wednesday, and Friday forenoons. During the fall semester, he had three lectures in each of those forenoons, the first beginning at 9:00 and the last ending at 12:00.³

While Harold had reasonable command of German, he must have struggled to comprehend the complicated syntax of erudite, scholarly lectures. During the fall he wrote most of his lecture notes in English, interspersed with German phrases; but by spring his notes were almost entirely in German. In accord with the conditions of his fellowship, his fall semester courses were primarily in Old Testament and Semitics. He took two language courses, one in Arabic and the other in Syriac. The Arabic course used the Koran as a text. He had three courses in Old Testament: one in Isaiah, a seminar in prophecy, and a course which investigated the religions of Babylonia and Assyria. Two of the Old Testament courses were taught by professor Paul Volz.[4]

Harold had mixed feelings about Professor Volz. He called him a "positive" theologian, by which he meant objective and scientific, but he found Volz "not altogether satisfying." His chief reservation was Volz's espousal of the Wellhausen theory of Old Testament history. Julius Wellhausen, who had taught most of his life at Göttingen University and died in 1918, had developed the "documentary hypothesis." That theory asserted that the books of the Pentateuch were a combination of four documents which had evolved over time and reflected the evolutionary development of the faith and culture of Israel. He postulated that the last document emerged from the postexilic period of Israel's history.

Like most conservative scholars, Harold found that nontranscendent, historically conditioned documentary hypothesis to be unacceptable. Yet he admitted that on both sides of the Atlantic, it was the prevailing way of explaining Old Testament history. In the long run, he told John Horsch, "I hope to do my part to knocking the theory out in the course of time." In January 1924, Harold saw his future as an Old Testament scholar who would earn his spurs as a critic of the Wellhausen theory.[5]

Bender's favorite course was dogmatics, taught by professor Karl Heim. Dietrich Bonhoeffer was also in the class, but at that point he was not yet famous. It is unlikely that Harold noticed or met the young man: they were only two of nearly six hundred students in the popular course. Heim's lectures surveyed the theology of Schleiermacher and Ritschl. Heim was forty-nine years old, but in 1923 he had been teaching for only three years. Earlier he had been secretary of the German Christian Student Union, a section of the World Student Christian Federation created by John R. Mott to bring Christian students together for purposes of evangelization and missions. In 1923 he had just returned from an around-the-world trip for the World Student Christian Federation. He had visited India, China, Japan, and the United States. Also in

1923 Heim had published one of his major works, *Glaubensgewissheit* (The certainty of faith).[6] Heim was at the height of his career during Harold's study with him. More than any other teacher at Tübingen, he affected Harold's theological frame of reference.

In his year at Tübingen, Harold took three courses under Heim. In addition to dogmatics, he also had a course in ethics and during the summer a course entitled "Das Wesen des evangelischen Christentums" (The nature of evangelical Christianity). Heim's theological and spiritual home was in what Ingemar Holmstrand has called "Württemberg Pietism."[7] Such Pietism was grounded in the presumption that the Bible is the basis for faith and the task of theology is to interpret the Bible. Heim saw his own task to be the development of philosophical concepts which would fit the New Testament meaning of Christ. That meaning could be found, Heim taught, in a transcendent and personal God who could be embraced by an encounter with the person of Jesus. Heim's *Heilsgeschichte* (salvation history) insisted that Jesus stands at the center of universal and human history and illuminates all human reality and experience.[8]

Heim also sought to discover points of connection between theology and contemporary thought. He tried to construct a view of reality which was rationally defensible but which did not violate the traditional content of Christian theology and belief. That viewpoint was attractive to Harold. Harold also was convinced by Heim's lectures on the work of Christ. Heim, he told Horsch, believed in the "substitutionary idea" of atonement and indeed insisted that substitutionary atonement was the *Kern* (kernel) of the Christian faith. Redemption is completed outside of any human strivings and efforts, he heard Heim arguing. Heim believed the work of Christ to be "completely objective," Harold reported to Horsch. "Christ has done it all for us as a completed work in the past." Harold was aware that he was hearing a Lutheran interpretation, for he called Heim a "thorogoing Lutheran."[9] But he clearly agreed with Heim. Thus Harold embraced a theological orthodoxy which would stand him in good stead in the theological skirmishes in his near future.

Heim had just published a small booklet whose title translates as "Peace with God." Harold sent it to Horsch, with the suggestion that it be translated and made available to the youth in the American Mennonite church. He thought it was about the best thing he had ever read on the subject. He found Heim "refreshing and spiritually upbuilding."[10]

In the midst of the Heim lectures, Harold first read *Christianity and Liberalism*, written by his antimodernist former professor at Princeton, J. Gresham Machen. John Horsch had sent him the book, apparently at Harold's request. Reading the book was like "feeling a breath of fresh air," Harold told Horsch.[11] The book was Machen's effort to lay out the lines of demarcation in the great battle for the soul of Christendom as he saw it unfolding in the twentieth century. The book was enormously successful, going through numerous printings. But by January 1924, Harold was under the influence of Karl Heim, who he believed to be a much keener and richer thinker and even, he told Horsch, more spiritually sensitive than Machen. Harold called Heim more "mystical."[12] Reading Machen in Tübingen helped Harold put the book in a perspective he would not have had if he had read it prior to going to Germany.

By January 1924 Harold was complaining that the year was going fast. But he also enjoyed the work and found it quite "profitable." However, he was so busy he had not had a chance to begin work on his doctorate. To do that, he told Horsch, would require another semester or two, and he and Elizabeth were seriously considering that possibility.[13] If Harold had been able to continue, he would almost certainly have taken a degree in Old Testament or Semitics. His interest in doing a critique of Wellhausen might have served as a dissertation topic.

• • •

By February, Harold was also communicating some interest in Anabaptist history. He had just read the newest book on Luther, Karl Holl's *Gesammelte Aufsätze* (Collected works), and he noted that Holl had "made some interesting comments on the Anabaptists." For Heim's course he had also read Albrecht Ritschl's *History of Pietism.* Ritschl, critical of Pietism, thought he saw links between the Franciscans and the Anabaptists: he believed they shared a common class origin and religious orientation. Harold was intrigued with Ritschl's thesis but dubious about it. He had also just seen a new book by Klemens Löffler, *Die Wiedertäufer zu Münster, 1534-35* (The Anabaptists of Münster), published in 1923, which he thought should be in the library at Scottdale.[14]

An important factor in Harold's new interest in Anabaptist history was his friendship with a 29-year-old Bavarian named Ernst Correll. In 1924 Correll was just completing a dissertation at the University of München (Munich), on the topic of Swiss Mennonite economic activity in the eighteenth century. Correll was the son of a Mennonite woman but was not himself a Mennonite. During the World War he had served in the German army. After the war, though penniless, he had somehow managed to begin his university studies under the renowned sociologist Max Weber. When Weber died, he continued his studies under another highly notable scholar, Ernst Troeltsch. In 1920 Correll learned to know the Mennonite Hege family who farmed a large *Hof* (farm, estate) just north of Munich near Markt. The Heges opened their home to the indigent student. "He is always hungry when he comes," Mrs. Hege told John Horsch, "and it takes a few days to fill him up."[15]

While visiting the Heges in the fall of 1922, John Horsch had met Correll. It was a case of immediate mutual friendship, built on sharing a consuming interest in Anabaptist history. John Horsch was impressed by Correll and told Harold, then studying at Princeton: "I must say that I have taken a liking to him. His knowledge of Mennonite history is remarkable; there are not many that surpass him on this point; none of his age."[16] Horsch tried to raise money to mitigate Correll's financial distress and appealed to Harold for help. Harold was himself a poor student, having just borrowed more money to complete his year at Princeton. But he did try to solicit some money for Correll from Goshen students. Whether he succeeded is not known.

In any case, soon after arriving in Germany, Harold and Elizabeth met Correll, and Correll's broad knowledge of Anabaptist scholarship put Harold on a fast track to becoming an Anabaptist scholar. During the spring of 1924, Harold's correspondence began to include frequent references to Anabaptist subjects. Early in 1924 he wrote a series of articles for the *Christian Monitor* entitled "Journeys in the Land of the Mennonite Fathers."[17] The articles described the Anabaptist movement in Zurich, Bern, Basel, Strasbourg, Augsburg, and Nuremburg. The writing was based primarily on materials from a German Mennonite encyclopedia, the *Mennonitisches Lexikon*, a work edited by two remarkable German Mennonite historians, Christian Hege and Christian Neff.

Harold learned to know Neff and Hege, further fostering his interest in Anabaptist studies. The lifework of the two men, of Harold's father's generation, closely foreshadowed that of Harold himself. Christian Hege had been born into a Mennonite family and as a young man had studied at the University of München. In 1893 he became the financial-page editor of a Frankfurt newspaper, the *Frankfurter Nachrichten*, a position he then held for forty years.[18] But his real interest was Mennonite history. He wrote constantly on historical topics for Mennonite papers. His greatest work was as coeditor of the *Mennonitisches Lexikon*, begun in 1913. In 1924 Hege and Neff were in the midst of that great project.

By 1924 Christian Neff was the leader of German and European Mennonites. He had an impressive theological education, having studied at Erlangen, Berlin, and Tübingen. Neff was both pastor of the Weierhof Mennonite church in the eastern Palatinate and the outstanding Mennonite historian in Europe. From 1891 on, he had been almost continuously either editor or associate editor of the two German Mennonite papers, the *Christlicher Gemeinde-kalender* and the *Mennonitische Blätter*. As coeditor of the *Mennonitisches Lexikon*, he was its guiding light for more than thirty years.[19] The *Lexikon* was an ambitious effort to compile systematically all known information about Mennonites, arranged alphabetically in three volumes.

In 1924, Christian Neff was busy organizing and making plans for the first Mennonite World Conference (MWC), to be held at Basel in 1925 in celebration of the four-hundredth anniversary of the Anabaptist movement. In June of 1924, Neff issued a call for a world conference. Harold translated it into English and sent a copy to John Horsch with the request that it be published in the *Gospel Herald.*

He reported to Horsch that he had tried to apprise Neff tactfully of the fact that the American "old Mennonites" could not participate unless they could do so without "tacitly recognizing the *ungläubige* [unbelieving] Mennonites as full brethren." At that time, most American MC Mennonites would have considered European Mennonites to fit the *ungläubige* category. American Mennonites might be observers but could not fully participate, Harold had told Neff, because doing so would compromise their "full gospel position." However, Harold betrayed uncertainty on the matter; he plaintively asked Horsch, "That is the case, is it not?"[20] Already his limited foray into Anabaptist history was pushing him into a nascent embrace of Mennonite ecumenicity.

Despite his heavy academic load, Harold found time to pursue some relief work with his uncle Michael's Christenpflicht. He and Elizabeth spent the first week of February at Hellmannsberg, helping to sort a large shipment of clothing from the American church-

**Elizabeth and her mother visiting Michael and Marta Horsch at Hellmansberg, Germany, in the summer of 1924.** Bender Family Album.

es. He was annoyed that another shipment was still at Scottdale. "It is quite out of place to leave it in Scottdale when thousands here would be glad for it," he told John Horsch. He reported forwarding a $395 check from the American Mennonites to Christenpflicht. To his surprise, a month earlier he had received another check for $1,000 dollars for German relief from "a brother" in Goshen. He had held back $60 to be used to feed hungry youngsters in Tübingen.[21]

Harold and Elizabeth had planned to visit Vienna during the Christmas holiday, but an enormous snowfall made even train travel impossible. As soon as the snow melted in early January, Harold and his Princeton friend Maynard Cassady accompanied Harold's uncle Michael to the Erzgebirge area of Saxony to explore possibilities for Christenpflicht relief work. Harold was horrified by the abject poverty they observed there.[22]

• • •

In the fall of 1923, when Harold and Elizabeth returned from their long trip to Switzerland, Italy, and Alsace, they found a letter from Sanford C. Yoder.[23] Yoder announced that he had been elected president of Goshen College. The 45-year-old Yoder was a bishop in Iowa and secretary of the Mennonite Board of Missions and Charities. He had chaired the general conference committee which refused to give its blessing to the Young People's Conference movement. Yoder was less doctrinaire than D. H. Bender or Daniel Kauffman, yet his election as president of Goshen College suggested that he was at least minimally acceptable to arch conservatives. Thus he received an invitation to be Eastern Mennonite School's commencement speaker in 1924. He was only meagerly educated, not earning even his B.A. degree until later, in 1927 (at Iowa State University). But he possessed great personal integrity and a homely dignity which appealed to educated and uneducated Mennonites alike. He also had a keen sense of what was possible within the narrow range tolerated by MC Mennonites in the 1920s.

Yoder's assignment was to prepare for the reopening of Goshen College in the fall of 1924, and his first order of business was to assemble a faculty. Would Harold want a position? Yoder enclosed a questionnaire which was being circulated to all prospective faculty. Such an offer was just what Harold and Elizabeth had been hoping for, and they responded immediately. "Mrs. Bender and I have considered earnestly, carefully, and with much prayer the matter of accepting [such] a call," Harold told Yoder. "Our hearts and hopes have always been in Goshen as a place to serve the church. We want to serve there if we can be used."[24]

However, Harold entered a caveat: he could not serve on the faculty if the "Board and the management" insisted that he be "an active promoter of uniform dress." He also added two financial qualifications: he needed assurance of adequate budget to buy library books for the religion department, and he wanted a reasonable salary. Somewhat cavalierly, he told Yoder: It is up to you. You decide if I am the person you want.[25]

In his reply, president Yoder challenged Harold's "take us as we are if you want us" approach. He hoped Harold would "see his way clear to make the adjustments necessary to accept the place that is open to you." Yoder refused to promise the money for books, nor would the college be able to pay people on the basis of degrees and rank. In fact, Yoder admitted that he had not even begun to talk about salaries; but he thought $1,500 a year might be about right.[26]

On the "regulation dress" question, Yoder told Harold he was going to follow the example of president D. H. Bender at Hesston. D. H. accepted the practice of the faculty member's home conference. Since at that very moment, Harold's Indiana-Michigan conference was breaking apart on such issues, Yoder's remark did not give Harold much help. Sensing Harold's frustration, Yoder went on to challenge him at his weakest point. You ought to wear the coat because "it will add to your prestige and also to the prestige of the institution," he wrote. And then he used an argument Harold found impossible to dispute. "I think, Harold, that you owe it to yourself and to your father to do all you can to use your powers to serve the church of your faith."[27] Whether that meant actually wearing the plain coat was not clear, but Yoder certainly had implied that he should be willing.

On one issue Yoder was adamant: Elizabeth would have to wear the specified kind of bonnet. "Your wife always wore a consistent bonnet when she wore it," he observed. "I can assure you that if she would come back here and work among us dressed the way she used to [be] that there would be little difficulty as far as she is concerned." He went on to say that he did not have strong convictions on the bonnet or the plain coat; while it was true that the plain coat was a new innovation, the bonnet was an old "established custom of the church." Yoder admitted that he had little patience with people who had "forced the hat question into the fore."[28]

Elizabeth and Harold were quite worried that the dress issue would make them unacceptable at Goshen. To her parents, Elizabeth expressed regret that wearing a hat while teaching at Johnstown and now in Europe was putting their future at Goshen in jeopardy. John Horsch responded with remarkable solicitude: "I notice what you say, dear Elizabeth, regarding feeling guilty for wearing a hat." But he assured her it would be much worse if she had insisted on wearing it after the church had asked her not to. Besides, he said, the church did not insist that "sisters in relief work in Constantinople wear bonnets."[29] He was referring to Elizabeth's friends Vinora Weaver and Vesta Zook, who had ceremoniously pitched their bonnets into the Atlantic Ocean on their way to Constantinople.[30] Surprisingly, Horsch's message seemed to be not to worry about wearing a hat in Europe. But he also was telling Elizabeth to wear the bonnet when she got back to the United States.

Harold's friend Vernon Smucker, the erstwhile editor of the *Christian Monitor* who had resigned over the closing of Goshen College, was not so gentle. Learning that Harold had decided to teach at Goshen, Smucker warned him that the intolerance level in the church was at an all-time high, and that Harold's effort to placate the conservatives in order to get to Goshen was sure to go wrong. Do not think, he warned Harold, that the conservatives are going to forget Elizabeth's hat-wearing and your mustache. In Europe, Harold was sporting a spiffy "Charlie Chaplin" mustache.[31]

A more intellectually and morally challenging issue emerged out of Harold's involvement with the new unofficial Mennonite journal the *Christian Exponent*. This was the periodical that some "old" Goshen alumni in the summer of 1923 decided to produce. They were disillusioned especially by the closing of Goshen College and frustrated by their inability to give voice to their concerns through official church publications. Most of the founders were originally part of the YPC movement. The venture was funded substantially by C. H. Musselman, a progressive Mennonite apple grower and apple butter maker at Biglerville, Pennsylvania. Vernon Smucker, the erstwhile editor of *Christian Monitor* who had been Harold's good friend and colleague during the YPC era, now became editor of the *Exponent*. Around him an editorial group constituted a who's who of Mennonite progressives: Lester Hostetler, N. E. Byers, J. E. Hartzler, Crissie Shank, I. R. Detweiler, Paul Whitmer, and others.[32]

Whether Harold was ever invited to join the editorial board is not known, but he apparently promised to write some articles. President Yoder realized that Harold's writing in the *Exponent* would make him an easy target for conservatives. So in the early spring of 1924, he gave Harold a gruff warning that if he was going to write for the *Exponent*, he could not be considered for the Goshen assignment.[33] It was a measure of Yoder's concern that on the same day he wrote to Harold, he also sent a letter to John Horsch, urging him to impress on Harold how dangerous any connections with the *Exponent* would be.[34] Apparently Vernon Smucker got wind of the pressure being put on Harold. "I do not want to discourage your going back to Goshen," he told Harold, "but to be frank with you, I do not see how you can be yourself and be any more acceptable there than most of the other men who have given a good part of their lives to the work there and now are turned down."[35] Apparently in 1924, Smucker still considered Harold to be thoroughly progressive.

For Harold, it was a moment of truth, and the decision was not easy. He argued to John Horsch that writing for the *Exponent* did not mean that he agreed with its theology. It was important, he told Horsch, for someone with a moderate position to counter their liberal ideas.[36] Somewhat naively, Harold assumed that the conflict about the *Exponent* was primarily a matter of theological argument—when in fact the church leaders saw the *Exponent* as a challenge to their authority as well as a forum for unorthodox viewpoints. They did not share the hopeful, liberal notion that both the *Exponent* group and Harold shared, that truth could be found in free-flowing argument. The church leaders assumed an orthodoxy which was not subject to dispute or argument: hence, their way to deal with the *Exponent* was to boycott it. And they pressured Harold to join the boycott.

For most of Harold's young adult life (twenty-seven years by 1924) he had been able to have it both ways in these ongoing liberal-conservative arguments. He had thought of himself as a progressive, with tolerance for opposing viewpoints and a large measure of optimism about human rationality. For that reason, he had almost instinctively tried to keep his relationships open to both conservatives and liberals, as the decent and sensible thing to do. It was also a somewhat tenable strategy as long as he was a student. But now the situation had changed.

The lines between his liberal and conservative friends were becoming sharper and thus more difficult to negotiate. Also, the prospect of a job at Goshen was forcing him to make a choice, not just to straddle the fence. He needed the job; he wanted the job. But to take the job would mean giving up some cherished relationships and committing heavily to the conservative agenda. The choice was not easy, particularly because if he went to Goshen, he would immediately, to some degree, find himself hostage to the conservatives. In that situation, it made little difference what one's mental reservations might be. The practical effect was that one had to pursue a quite conservative agenda.

Easing Harold's difficulties was the fact that he was predisposed to be cautious: he received no satisfaction from rocking the boat. He was in fact theologically orthodox and conservative. His forays through theological fields for nearly four years had produced remarkably little change in basic theological orientation. He was much better informed theologically than when he began, but his theological formation had always kept a conservative shape. That meant that he found himself quite comfortable with the prevailing Mennonite theological consensus. In March 1924, he said as much to Daniel Kauffman, and Kauffman was delighted. "Glad for your statement about doing your part in maintaining the old orthodox faith," Kauffman told him. "Some of our well-meaning young people are ignorantly cuckooing the ranker stuff handed out by avowed liberalists of the Kent-Fosdick-Matthews type. If they had their way, we Mennonites in North America would soon be just like the Mennonites in Holland."[37]

By April, Harold had agreed to go to Goshen on the terms set by Yoder. He told John Horsch he hoped the assignment would be permanent, but of course, he said, it all depends on whether a "moderate" policy is possible and whether the conservatives will support the school financially. He wrote to Horsch, "So far, I am told, most of them stand about with two hands in their pockets waiting to see what happens."[38]

Then came a big shock. In a *Gospel Herald* notice about the new Goshen faculty, Harold and Elizabeth learned to their amazement that Harold would be teaching history, not Bible and theology. Somehow president Yoder had failed to communicate that relevant piece of information. How could such a thing have happened? And why not Bible and theology? When Harold protested the assignment, Yoder replied, "By another year, I hope, Harold, that you will have won the confidence of the people of Northern Indiana so well and established yourself so thoroughly with the church, that we can use you in the Bible department." Then Yoder added what must have felt to Harold and Elizabeth like an ominous warning: "But I want to tell you that there is some opposition to that [Bible department assignment] just yet, and we are earnestly praying that all such opposition may be removed during the year by your attitude. I am not saying this for your discouragement but for your encouragement, as I believe you want to stand by the church, and I know it will not mean much hardship on your part to remove everything out of the way."[39]

Yoder was clear about what the period required: "This is a time when we all must come down off our high horses—I am sure I have had to—and humiliate ourselves before the Lord as brethren should if we are going to get along together." What was Yoder's humiliation? In return for allowing the college to reopen, the very conservative Indiana-Michigan conference executive committee insisted on interviewing all prospective faculty for theological orthodoxy. Already they had rejected several candidates.[40]

Yoder had to be very careful. He clearly did not think Harold could pass muster if he had to face the committee as a theologian. Bender was quite disappointed. After four years of struggle and effort, he had as much if not more theological education than any other MC Mennonite. It must have been almost more than he could bear, to be denied the opportunity to teach in his field because president Yoder feared an Indiana-Michigan conference committee.

Yet Harold accepted the situation and replied to president Yoder's strictures with remarkable magnanimity: "I appreciate your words concerning the church and school situation, and the need for caution. It is my sincere desire and purpose to adapt myself to the situation as best possible, retaining always freedom of conscience. I shall of course exercise every caution."[41]

Bender's willingness to bend to the need of the moment was not just giving in. In the fall of 1923, after completing the faculty questionnaire and feeling sure that his rejection of the dress regulations would jettison any chance of going to Goshen, he had sent a pessimistic letter to Noah Oyer. It seems sad, he wrote, that a "minor point of mere externalities" could keep one from serving the church one loves. The real sadness, he told Oyer, was that those who are thus rejected "will for the most part never find another real home."[42] In the spring of 1924, Harold decided to keep the peace and remain in his "real home."

• • •

At Tübingen, the fall semester ended on February 29, 1924. Harold and Elizabeth left immediately for Spain, where they soaked up the Mediterranean warmth after an unusually cold German winter. A photograph shows Elizabeth wearing a black hat and overcoat, feeding pigeons in the plaza of a Spanish city. They visited Madrid, Barcelona, and Toledo for two weeks and then turned north to tour France and spend part of a week in Paris. Leaving

Paris, they stopped at several Mennonite centers in the Palatinate, spending several days with Christian Neff at the Weierhof.[43]

The visit with Neff was important to Bender as he began learning the main lines of Anabaptist and Mennonite history scholarship. Harold was still three weeks away from learning that his teaching assignment at Goshen would be history. For the budding young theologian, the friendship of the pious and scholarly Neff must have been a special experience. He had no other older mentor who, like Neff, combined a warm piety and a sophisticated scholarship. Neff was a helpful alternative model for Harold—especially as he tried to relate to his father-in-law John Horsch, whose brittle piety and polemical scholarship were so different from the style of Christian Neff.

After the Weierhof visit, Elizabeth and Harold made a short trip across the Rhine River to Heilbronn, where they spent the Easter holiday with Elizabeth's Funck and Landes relatives. By mid-April they were back in Tübingen for the beginning of summer semester classes. In the pile of accumulated mail was a bit of unexpected news: Elizabeth's mother was coming to Europe and would return to the United States with them in the fall.[44]

Another reality also intruded: they were nearly out of money. Harold estimated that they had just enough to live on until time to leave for home. But that left them nothing with which to buy their steamship tickets for the voyage. The financial pinch felt even worse because, with the urging of his friend Maynard Cassady and Semitics professor Volz, Harold had conceived a plan to travel in the Middle East. The idea was to spend the month of August in Egypt and Palestine. Where could he find the money? Harold turned for help to John Horsch, but the Horsches needed all their extra cash to pay for mother Horsch's trip to Europe. In fact, Harold soon discovered that even the passage home was a problem, for when he turned to his mother for cash, she was unable to oblige. Embarrassed but desperate, he turned to Elizabeth's uncle Michael Horsch at Hellmannsberg. Uncle Michael agreed to advance the money for the steamship tickets with the understanding that as soon as Harold got back to Goshen, he would obtain a bank loan and repay his uncle.[45]

On May 13, Harold left on a weeklong trip to meet mother Horsch at Bremen. Elizabeth did not go with him. She was pregnant and having morning sickness. So while Harold fetched his mother-in-law from Bremen, Elizabeth went to Lautenbach to be with her mother's relatives. The trip took a week because Harold traveled by way of Halle, Leipzig, Wittenberg, Berlin, and Hamburg, visiting each place briefly. He spent two days in Berlin with his friend Frank Yeaworth, who had the Princeton New Testament fellowship at the university there. In Hamburg, he met Mennonite pastor Heinrich van der Smissen. By 1924 the 75-year-old van der Smissen had been pastor of the large Altona-Hamburg congregation for more than forty years. In Bender's view, he was a liberal, but Harold's contact showed his desire to know every strata of Mennonite life in Europe. Of the major European Mennonite communities in Europe in 1924, Bender had failed to visit only those in Prussia and in the Soviet Union.[46]

While Elizabeth and mother Horsch stayed with relatives during the summer, Harold attended lectures. He studied with his two favorite professors, Heim and Schlatter, and took a course in the Ethiopian language. He confessed to being hard pressed to keep up, partly because of diversions. One was an effort to help his new friend Ernst Correll find a job in America.[47] Harold persuaded president Yoder to hire Correll to teach German at Goshen. Yoder agreed, then reversed himself, and then changed his mind again. There were several problems. Correll was not a Mennonite, and he smoked cigarettes. Also, there were budget and course-load problems. Finally it was agreed that Correll would come to Goshen with the proviso that he be paid on the basis of the hours in his teaching load, which would be less than a full-time position. Harold and Elizabeth would return to America in August, accompanied by mother Horsch and by Ernst Correll.

The summer semester ended on August 1. The original plan was to spend several days in Belgium, visiting some Anabaptist sites. The travelers would then go to England for a week, meeting their ship, the SS *Ryndam*, at Southampton for the voyage home. But by August neither mother Horsch nor Elizabeth felt up to so much travel, and the trip to England was abandoned. Instead, Au-

**On the ship, returning to the United States in 1924. With Harold and Elizabeth are Christine Horsch and Ernst Correll.** Bender Family Album.

gust became a time for making *Abschied* (farewell) visits to relatives. On August 22, Harold and Elizabeth, with mother Horsch and Ernst Correll, bade farewell to the kinfolks at Lautenbach and boarded the train for Rotterdam.[48]

The ocean voyage was a relaxing time; Harold claimed that the party got "rested up." The Benders and mother Horsch arrived at Scottdale on Sunday, September 7. Harold and Elizabeth had hoped to leave for Goshen by the middle of the week, stopping en route to visit Harold's sister Florence, Vernon and Mary Smucker, and an uncle of Elizabeth—all in Ohio. But they stayed until Friday. Classes would begin on the following Wednesday; so they went straight to Elkhart. It was good to be home.[49]

• • •

Harold and Elizabeth moved into a rented house on Eighth Street in Goshen, less than a block from the college. They arrived with few worldly goods. Elizabeth's parents had worried that getting settled into housekeeping would be a big strain on Elizabeth, but Harold assured them that she was "looking fine" and that in fact she really did not have much to do.[50] Elizabeth was five months pregnant and living in her own home for the first time in her life. She must have found the fall of 1924 to be a special time, after so many years of living with no settled residence.

Despite Harold's reassurances to the Horsches, Elizabeth had an extremely difficult pregnancy. She was ill much of the time. The baby was due about New Year's Day, but failed to arrive on time, so the family moved Elizabeth to Elkhart to be near the Elkhart hospital. On Sunday, January 18, more than two weeks overdue, Elizabeth entered the hospital, and the doctor induced labor. The result was tragedy. Complications during the birthing caused the death of the baby, a boy, and for several days Elizabeth's own life hung in the balance. Thereafter, her recovery was agonizingly slow: she was hospitalized for nearly a month.[51] Harold and Elizabeth were heartbroken by the baby's death. A cherished dream, having a large family, would have to wait.[52]

Elizabeth's convalescence took many months, and her mother came from Scottdale to help care for her. By the time she fully recovered, the family had decided that Harold's mother, Elsie, and his brothers Cecil, John, and Robert would move into the house on Eighth Street with Elizabeth and Harold. Cecil and John were students at Goshen College. Elizabeth's youngest brother, Paul, a freshman at the college that fall, also joined the household. Thereafter, for much of their married life, Harold and Elizabeth had extended-family members living with them. During the first two decades, mother Elsie served as housekeeper, cook, and nanny.[53]

The arrangement offered mutual advantages. It allowed Elsie and the boys an affordable situation for living, and it freed Elizabeth to teach at the college. But it also made Harold, at twenty-eight years of age, the de facto head of a household with three teenage brothers, a 52-year-old mother, a 31-year-old wife, and an 18-year-old brother-in-law. The arrangement must have been a daunting challenge for the young man. Nor could it have been easy for the shy and retiring Elizabeth to be thrust into such a boisterous domestic establishment. Until Robert graduated from college in 1933, Harold also managed the family money. The finances were intricate, as the younger members borrowed from the older ones and from their mother to put themselves through school. Harold kept the financial records.[54]

**Harold holding daughter Mary Eleanor on the lawn of the Benders' new house in Goshen, Indiana.** Bender Family Album.

In 1926, Elsie provided the funds to build a new house on South Main Street. Harold and Elsie designed the house as a home for the extended Bender family. Initially, Harold and Elizabeth lived in a small apartment on the first floor, but in 1927, with the birth of daughter Mary Eleanor, that arrangement became impractical. So they and Elsie exchanged quarters. It proved practical to share meals, since there was only one kitchen. Elsie did most of the cooking.[55]

The house was of a Cape Cod design, with white wooden siding, two floors, a large attic, and a basement. It stood on what was at that time the south edge of the city of Goshen. In 1924, Goshen was a prosperous town of 10,000 people. Main and a few other downtown streets had been paved with brick in the first decade of the century; but the main highway south past the Benders' new house was still gravel and mud.

The best means of transportation was the trolley. A line ran on Eighth Street from downtown to the College and connected with interurban tracks which ran south through the little hamlet of Waterford and on to Warsaw. In Goshen, one could board New York Central trains to Chicago, New York, and other points; in Warsaw, one could also board Pennsylvania Railroad trains running east and west.[56] An interurban also ran from Goshen to Elkhart, where four railroad lines connected. By the 1930s, as automobiles became more plentiful, the electric trolleys became obsolete. Bender bought his first car in 1928.

Goshen was the county seat of Elkhart County and therefore an important administrative center. But its economy was based on the fertility of the surrounding farms and a number of small industrial enterprises. In the 1920s, Goshen had eighteen industrial establishments, ranging from furniture manufacturers to rubber plants, textile firms, and tool-and-die operations. The largest employed several hundred people.[57]

The town had two theaters, the Jefferson and the Lincoln. Both offered stage performances, but increasingly, especially during the summers, they also showed movies, since talkies were becoming popular during the late 1920s. The theaters also sponsored some local-talent events. One of the most notorious was a wedding portrayed by men only, some dressed as women; it was sponsored by the First Methodist Church, and played to packed audiences for several nights running in 1926. Such leisure-time attractions gave Goshen College administrators much trouble, as did Blosser's Park, on an island just southwest of the college. The park featured a shooting gallery, a bathing beach, a baseball diamond, a skating rink often used as a dance floor, and a variety of other amusements.[58]

In 1923, the city constructed a large new high school building with seventy-five classrooms, a 1,200-seat auditorium, and a 1,000-seat gymnasium. Harold's brother John graduated from the new building in 1925. "Bobbie," the youngest of the boys, followed in 1929. In 1925, Goshen's public library, four times larger than the Goshen College library, had the largest circulation of any public library in the state of Indiana—due in part to use by Goshen College students.[59]

In 1925, Tillie Stoll, assistant editor of the *Maple Leaf*, offered an up-beat if somewhat parochial and prejudiced description of the city. She observed that "in Goshen there are no negroes, very few foreigners, and very little poverty. In Goshen there are no slums. The city is beautiful, its streets lined with attractive homes and splendid trees. Goshen is a pretty, clean, modern little city and has every prospect of a big and prosperous future."[60]

The Goshen of 1924 had a Midwestern small-town ambience with many small-city amenities. However, Harold and Elizabeth lived in Goshen not because it was a pleasant town but because after four years of preparation, their desire to teach at Goshen College had become a possibility. Harold taught his first class on September 17, 1924. With only two exceptions, for the next thirty-eight Septembers, until his death on September 21, 1962, he would be on hand to begin the academic year at Goshen College.

## ✺ 8 ✺

# Goshen College and MQR

*Bender teaches at Goshen College. He and a few*
*colleagues establish* The Mennonite Quarterly Review.
*Bender visits the Soviet Union.*

IN SEPTEMBER 1924, Goshen College was quite different from the
school Harold and Elizabeth had attended during their senior year
in 1918. Gone were the Joe-college high jinks and the Ivy League
aura. Harold's 1918 *Maple Leaf* had been awash with classical literary and philosophical aphorisms; in the 1925 *Maple Leaf*, seniors invoked biblical passages as life-guiding mottoes. Also no-
ticeable were the coverings worn by Mennonite women, though
surprisingly few of the men wore plain coats. In the fall of 1924,
only president Yoder, dean Oyer, and business manager Christian
(C. L.) Graber wore the plain coat. Harold began doing so in
1927. By then, several other faculty members also wore the plain
coat, including history professor Guy F. Hershberger.

There was a noticeably chastened quality about the campus,
due in part to the institution's extremely straitened finances. While
everyone purported to be pleased with student enrollment, the
number was clearly unsatisfactory, especially compared to the
other Mennonite schools. In the fall of 1924, Hesston had 150 students, EMS 107, Bluffton 262, and Bethel 236; Goshen had only
70.[1] Of those 70, there were only seven seniors and eight juniors.

Some of the outstanding debt had been retired during the year
the college was closed. Yet there was precious little money on hand
to begin the school year. It was a time to test the faith of even the
most hopeful. But it was also a time to build. For Harold, who had

174

so single-mindedly spent the past four years preparing to teach at Goshen, it was the fulfillment of a dream.

The dream demanded a heavy workload. In addition to a full teaching assignment, Harold was also the college librarian. Located in the basement of the Administration building, the college's library had 7,400 "carefully selected" volumes. Bender supervised all aspects of the library's operation, including the student assistants and the reading room, where students studied but not always as quietly as the rules required. Once that fall when "Professor Bender" walked into the reading room, there was "suddenly a dreadful silence," the *Maple Leaf* reported.[2]

Bender was one of seventeen faculty members. Only his friend Ernst Correll had a doctorate. After Correll, Harold probably had the most years of study, although other faculty members also had master's degrees. Several faculty were not Mennonites. In that first year, it probably was safer for President Yoder to employ persons who were not Mennonite than to use Mennonites of dubious orthodoxy.

Only four of the seventeen faculty were graduates of Goshen, and only Silas Hertzler, Daniel Lehman, and Samuel Witmer had taught at Goshen prior to 1924. One purpose for closing Goshen— to rid it of unorthodox faculty—had been largely attained. Recapturing the "old Goshen" traditions thus devolved onto the shoulders of a few returning veterans. As *Maple Leaf* adviser, Harold carried part of that role. The 1925 annual was still rather somber, but by 1928 it had again become more spirited. The faculty found it difficult to control change. As early as the fall of 1925, Harold complained that some of the "Iowa girls are quite dressy." It was a real problem to know how to discipline them, he told John Horsch, but it had to be done.[3]

The administration of the college was organized around fifteen standing committees. Bender served on seven, chairing the athletics and library committees. The athletics committee was especially challenging because athletics was highly suspect in the MC Mennonite church. Given Harold's own caution and the constituency's concerns, it is surprising how quickly athletics was allowed to blossom and change at Goshen. As early as 1927, the women's basketball teams wore uniforms with plaid skirts and sailor ties, and the men wore T-shirts under cardigan sweaters monogrammed with a large GC logo. To some critics of Goshen College, these changes were surely the first steps toward intercollegiate sports. One Goshen tradition which did return was team debate, though limited to intravarsity events. In the 1930-1931 academic year, intercollegiate debates resumed, with Goshen debating teams at Taylor University and Wheaton College. Bender coached the affirmative side; Guy F. Hershberger the negative team.[4]

That first year, Bender taught elementary and intermediate New Testament Greek, numerous history courses, a course in church history, and one in Mennonite history. He was chair of the history and social science department. When Guy F. Hershberger joined the faculty in 1925, Bender moved out of history and became chair of the economics and sociology department. By 1928 he was teaching what became his enormously popular "Family" course, one of four sociology courses. That year he was also listed on the Bible School faculty as professor of Old Testament and church history. Thus after his first year, he regularly taught sociology, church history, Old Testament courses, and sometimes Greek or Hebrew. Despite the restrictions on teaching theology, he was reasonably happy with his teaching assignments.[5]

The Goshen College of 1924-31 was a nearly perfect environment for Harold Bender. It offered scope and space for his wide-ranging, restless interests beyond his role as college teacher and librarian. One interest was college finances, driven partly by his membership on the college-alumni executive committee. Orie O. Miller was also a member, and on that committee the two men began their long collaboration in Mennonite affairs. Miller was also the financial agent for the Mennonite Board of Education, and thus ultimately responsible for the financial state of Hesston and Goshen.

By 1925, the 33-year-old Miller had established a reputation as an astute businessman. Upon graduating from Goshen College in 1915, he had married fellow-student Elta Wolf of Akron, Pennsylvania, a village in Lancaster County, and entered her family's shoe manufacturing business there. He proved to be a successful salesman for the company. Within a few years, he became the firm's secretary-treasurer and eventually a co-owner. Miller had spent the year of 1919 in Middle East relief and in 1920 became the director of the first MCC relief work in the Soviet Union. He was one of Harold Bender's generation of "relief workers" who managed to win the confidence of the church fathers in the early 1920s, helped no doubt by his reputation as a successful business-man. Miller managed to slip through and around the internecine liberal-conservative conflicts of the 1920s largely because he relat-ed to Mennonite institutions at a second remove, usually in some financial capacity. He was not a scholar but a doer (several times in the lot for minister, but never ordained). He wielded enormous influence behind the scenes.[6]

Given the financial poverty of the college, it was imperative to develop new sources of support. Bender soon became disillusioned by what he felt was a lack of a clear plan by which to generate funds. He was especially impatient with the fundraising strategy used by president Yoder, who typically went from community to community and house to house, trying to raise money for operat-ing costs and to retire the annual deficits. The money thus gath-ered was simply not adequate to operate the college.[7]

Bender had a more ambitious plan. The MC Board of Educa-tion should develop a program to raise a million dollars, he told Miller. The three MC church colleges needed $250,000 for build-ings; $700,000 for endowment (he somewhat arbitrarily allocated $500,000 for Goshen and only $100,000 each for Hesston and EMS, including EMS even though it was not a Board of Education school); and $50,000 for student scholarships. How and where would they get such huge sums? Miller inquired. Bender had a plan. The funds would be raised over ten years by selling Menno-nite Board of Education lifetime bonds bearing 3% interest. The bonds would be sold to individuals and to congregations. In addi-tion, donors should be persuaded to will farms to the Board of Ed-ucation either outright or on an annuity basis. "Bluffton College, with a much smaller constituency, is raising over $100,000 per year," he told Miller. "Why cannot we do better?"[8]

Bender was also concerned about disorganized management of

the board's finances. He proposed a radical separation of its financial management from the educational and spiritual aspects of its oversight. Get some businessmen and bankers, who know how to manage large amounts of money; put them on a finance committee, chaired by you as financial agent, he urged Miller. The people would have confidence that their money was used well and therefore would contribute more generously.[9]

Bender was quite upset by the Hesston College board of trustees, who had loaned a large amount of Hesston endowment money to a relative of a board member without security. Mennonite church leaders "are often quite dumb" about money, Bender told Miller.[10] The cautious and frugal Orie Miller responded to Bender's ideas with some bemusement. "Your suggestions are always so radical that I am not yet ready to express my own reactions or opinion in regard to some of those that you have made," he told Bender. "I shall take your letter along on this week's trip and give some of them more time to soak in."[11] Bender, sensing that he may have overstepped things a bit, tried to make some amends. "Perhaps I am expecting too much. I am very much disturbed about the situation particularly in view of the strong competition Bluffton is giving us in Ohio. We may suffer if we come along too slow. Please pardon any unseemly excess."[12]

● ● ●

It was one of the most momentous decisions in Bender's life. "I have practically decided to give up my Old Testament work and work primarily in Reformation and Mennonite history," Harold told John Horsch. "I want to make my doctorate in this field." The date was Saturday, January 8, 1927. To carry out his plan, he told his father-in-law, would require at least two years of study in Europe. His specialty would be decided by where he found financial support. If the Hutterites gave him help, he would do Hutterite history. Otherwise he would probably work in south-German or Swiss history. He intended to begin his studies during the summer or fall of 1928. He thought he and Elizabeth could carry some of the expense, but he hoped either the Hutterites or the Mennonites would come to their aid. Harold was feeling expansive on that Saturday morning in 1927: The previous afternoon the first issue of a new journal of Mennonite history and opinion had been mailed to subscribers. Its title was *The Mennonite Quarterly Review*, and Harold Bender was its founding editor.[13]

Just a few weeks earlier, Bender had written nearly identical letters to Orie Miller and John Horsch outlining an aggressive historical program for the Mennonite church. We must begin, he had argued, "an organized intelligent working of our historical problem soon. The problem is a large one and one that needs large plans and vision." The goal would be to create "a Corpus Mennoniticorum," a comprehensive compilation and critical edition of Anabaptist-Mennonite sources. It would take at least "25 years to accomplish." In 1926, Harold Bender was thinking big.[14]

In early 1926 Bender wrote an article for the *Gospel Herald*, appealing for church support for work in Mennonite history. His assessment of the existing state of such work was scathing. The number of books that Mennonites are writing on their history "is so small as to be ridiculous," he wrote. It is incredible that a "denomination of over 40,000 adult members with a glorious history of over 400 years, with an average wealth above the normal, does practically nothing to further its history, either in defense or constructive work. The church has never seriously faced the problem of properly studying and writing her history."[15]

Since the recovery of Mennonite history was such a large task, and given the "broken condition of Mennonitism," Bender argued that there should be an effort to get all Mennonites around the world involved in the task. The MC Mennonites should take the lead. And he became practical: The project could be paid for by asking each Mennonite congregation for $5 per 100 members per year.[16]

In April of 1927, Bender began a series of seven articles in the *Gospel Herald* entitled "What Can the Church Do for Her Historical Work?" Mennonites needed to write their own history, he argued. Too much of it had been done by those who were hostile. As a result, he told his readers, "for hundreds of years the whole of the civilized world with very few exceptions had thought of the

Anabaptists and Mennonites as a fanatical sect of extremists, who had at various times in the past been guilty of rebellion and uprising, and who had a wholly perverted type of Christianity, a sect which was only a burden on the face of the earth and an abomination in the sight of God and all true Christians.[17]

"Mennonites are today known chiefly by the eccentricities of some minor groups, and are thought of as people with oddities instead of principles," he continued. "The Mennonite name ought to stand the world over for certain definite ideals and principles, just as the Quaker name does." Knowing his audience, Bender sagely observed that history could also help resist modernism. Some of our own brethren have used Mennonite history to make "the church out to have been liberal in its origin, a misrepresentation which has influenced many to disloyalty to the church."[18] If there were proper histories, Mennonite history could not so easily be distorted by modernists to their purposes.

With uncharacteristic bluntness, Bender cited the many resolutions made by the MC general conference urging the Mennonite Historical Committee to promote historical work. "It is with considerable astonishment that one learns that for the most part these resolutions were not carried out," he reported. *Gospel Herald* editor Daniel Kauffman was offended by Bender's critique. He sent the articles back with instructions to tone down the criticism. Frustrated, Bender circulated the articles to several people for assessment, including John Horsch. All urged him not to change anything. Bender returned the articles to Kauffman with only minor changes, and Kauffman reluctantly printed them.[19] At a time when criticism of church leaders was seen as disloyalty, Bender had taken some risk with his directness. But clearly history was a safer subject than theology.

• • •

By January 1927, Bender had decided to be a historian. With his *Gospel Herald* articles, he had become the spokesman, with John Horsch, for MC Mennonite historical work. He had laid out a vision of what the historical task should be. At that point he had not produced any significant historical writing, but neither had he been idle as a historian. The arrival of Bender and Ernst Correll at Goshen in September of 1924 had set off an unprecedented flurry of Anabaptist and Mennonite historical activity at the college. Prior to 1924, there had been little historical writing at Goshen College. By January of 1927, when Bender announced his conversion to history, there was an aggressive new program poised to produce new historical material at a prodigious pace. What had happened?

Within six weeks after their arrival at Goshen in the fall of 1924, Bender and Correll had resurrected a moribund Goshen College Mennonite Historical Society, which had been started in 1921. Harold became president, Correll the librarian. The Historical Society, whose members were faculty and students, immediately became the largest organization on campus and the agency for a huge surge of interest and activity.[20] A wave of historical consciousness swept the college. There were monthly programs attended by nearly the entire student body. Bender, Correll, and others gave frequent "illustrated lectures" on historical topics. Mennonite history activities overshadowed literaries and literary programs. Students talked and wrote Mennonite history.

Bender and Correll were a dynamic duo. Ernst Correll, with his vigorous and humorous persona and halting English, was the campus personality. Bender was the organizer and manager. Already in Europe they had conceived the idea of writing a biography of Conrad Grebel, one of the founders of the Swiss Brethren movement. When they got to Goshen, they announced that the biography would be published in time for the 400th anniversary of Swiss Brethren beginnings in 1525.[21] Unfortunately, their public relations program was more successful than their ability to produce. After all, 1925 was only a few months away. Bender and Correll compounded their problem by expanding the project to include the translation and critical editing of the Conrad Grebel letters. Since their goal was to be exhaustive, they needed to examine all possible sources to make sure they had all the material. They carried on an extensive correspondence with scholars and archivists in Europe and America. Correll traveled to libraries and archives in the United States, and in 1926 he went to Europe to search for materials there.[22]

Bender and Correll also began book collecting, a habit Bender had already developed in Europe. Now the effort moved into high gear, and every issue of the college *Record* reported on rare treasures being located in Mennonite communities and brought to Goshen College. All of this activity was reported to the campus through the Historical Society, by way of college chapels, the college *Record*, and speeches. The emphasis on Mennonite history gave the college a new ethos which separated it from "old Goshen" but which well fit its new objectives. It gave the struggling college an aura of scholarly orthodoxy its detractors could not gainsay. For the college, it was an unplanned but real boon.[23]

The striking feature of the new history was its quality: it was based almost entirely on original research in the sources. The centerpiece and best exhibit was the Grebel material. Nosing about in every conceivable place on both sides of the Atlantic, Bender and Correll acquired, in a remarkably short time, nearly the entire corpus of Grebeliana (obviously, most of it in copy form). They even found and became the first to publish a hitherto unknown letter of Conrad Grebel, printing it in the fledgling *Mennonite Quarterly Review*.[24] This was a real coup for an enterprise less than three years old. Bender, Correll, and Elizabeth brought formidable language skills to the work. Harold mentioned their mutual effort to decipher some of the more obscure Swiss dialect passages in several of the Grebel letters. They handled German and French quite well, and Dutch to some extent, although sometimes they called on John Horsch for help with translating Dutch. Augmenting their skills in Latin was the brilliant and enigmatic Edward Yoder, who was just then completing a successful doctoral program in classical languages at the University of Pennsylvania. In the fall of 1924, Yoder began translating the Latin text of the Grebel letters.

In the fall of 1925, the Benders, Correll, and Yoder were joined by young Guy F. Hershberger, whose master's thesis had been on the origins of the Anabaptist movement. Also important as supporting players were John Umble (of the English department, but with a passion for Mennonite history), and president

Sanford C. Yoder. Although not a scholar himself, Yoder recognized, respected, and enabled the scholarship of others.

Not all of the new activities went smoothly. To celebrate the 400th anniversary of the beginnings of the Swiss Brethren in Zurich, Bender and the Historical Society planned a special all-day historical program in connection with the June 1925 college commencement. The ambitious program included addresses by the premier Mennonite historian, C. Henry Smith, a former dean of the "old Goshen" who had moved to Bluffton College, and by the less well-known D. E. Harder of Bethel College. Both were GC Mennonites. Also invited to deliver addresses were John Horsch, Daniel Bender, Ernst Correll, and A. H. Newman (a Baptist Reformation scholar of Mercer University). But John Horsch, consumed by his antimodernist crusade, curtly rejected. He explained, "I do not feel free to have a part in a meeting in which a Bluffton professor would have a part."[25]

Bender was dumbfounded. He had already invited Smith and Harder, and both had accepted. "We have been put at a loss by your preference not to serve with Smith," he told Horsch. "We are put into an embarrassing situation." Hoping against hope, Bender begged his father-in-law to reconsider, noting that Smith had been invited not as a representative of Bluffton but as a historian, and pointing out that Smith had lectured at Hesston College just the year before. But Horsch was adamant, and Harold disinvited Smith. Smith accepted with good grace. And since Smith could not be invited, Bender also had to disinvite professor Harder of Bethel.[26]

That unpleasantness behind him, Bender then discovered that Horsch did not intend to present his paper in person. Horsch's reasons were partly that he found it excruciatingly difficult to speak in public, and partly that Goshen was again coming under increasing fire from conservatives in the East; Horsch did not want to be identified with the pariah institution. Only by persistent pleading did Bender persuade him to attend.[27] But Horsch had derailed an event which might have begun to bring Mennonite historians together. The foreshortened program with Horsch and Professor Newman, neither of them good speechmakers, turned out to be somewhat lackluster.

• • •

By January of 1927, Bender was ready to launch the centerpiece of his Mennonite history program at Goshen, the publication of the first issue of *The Mennonite Quarterly Review (MQR)*. The *MQR* soon became the "jewel in the crown" of his historical efforts. Bender had first broached the idea in the winter of 1924 while a student at Tübingen. A quarterly journal, he told John Horsch, "a sort of Mennonite Review," would promote interest in Mennonite history and conservative faith. We need it, Bender said, to "keep our young people away from the influence of the Bluffton element and other liberal leaders"—especially, he added, if *The Christian Exponent* turns out to be a tool of the liberals. (He had just seen the *Exponent*'s first issue.) Horsch agreed. There was "great need" for such a journal, he replied, "if a leading feature would be bold yet Christ-like opposition to the revolutionists, and defense of the old faith."[28]

Bender had also tested the idea on Daniel Kauffman in a February 1924 letter from Tübingen. Not yet aware that his own theology was under suspicion, Bender wrote: "I believe if the *Exponent* turns out to be the organ of the liberal element, the Church will have a serious problem on her hands. We must have a journal in the Church for the more educated class, especially our college young people. I have been thinking of this for a number of years, quite apart from the *Exponent*, and wonder whether this is not an opportune time to launch such a paper."[29]

Bender described the journal as "a sort of Mennonite review (monthly or quarterly)" containing first-class articles on Mennonite history, faith, current issues, biblical studies, and such matters which were usually too heavy for the *Herald* or the *Monitor*. He assured Kauffman that it should be an advocate of conservative Mennonitism. The Mennonite Publishing House could publish it, or perhaps it could be put out by the faculty of Goshen College "as the *Princeton Review* used to be." Already in 1924, Bender was setting his idea in a larger historical framework. He urged Kauffman to give such a journal "serious consideration." He hoped it could be initiated the next year, "on the 400th anniversary of Mennonitism."[30]

Kauffman rejected the idea, suggesting instead that Bender use the *Goshen College Record*. Bender was disappointed, reasoning that to use the *Record* would be only a "temporary makeshift." Bender complained to Horsch that "DK" did not understand how seriously a historical journal was needed. But he agreed that it might be good to wait until it was clear that Goshen College would survive.[31]

Thus in 1926, Bender with Umble and Hershberger edited three special issues of the Goshen College *Record* devoted to Mennonite history, labeling extra material a *Review Supplement*. The issues with the *Review Supplement* had forty-eight pages rather than the twenty of the conventional *Record*. Their decision to publish as the *Review Supplement* was sound, for it gave the fledgling new history effort immediate access to the college's alumni, a far broader audience than an entirely new journal might have had.

The first issue, January 1926, set a strong precedent, with original articles by John Horsch and A. H. Newman, a Bender and Correll translation of Conrad Grebel's "Protest and Defense" to the Zurich city council in 1525, and a survey by Bender of new Anabaptist and Mennonite historical material published in 1925. There were two book reviews, one by Bender of Correll's new book on the Swiss Anabaptists just published at Tübingen, and the second on Virginia bishop Lewis J. Heatwole's *Mennonite Handbook of Information*. Under a section entitled "Notes," Bender described another project, a "Forthcoming Biography of Conrad Grebel," and explained that the earliest the book could go to press was the summer of 1926.

The second *Review Supplement*, for May-June 1926, was remarkable. Bender wrote a three-page editorial announcing that the *Review Supplement* would now be permanent, published three times a year, and more than just a historical journal. Its goal was to comment on and contribute to the life and faith of the Mennonite church. The contents of the May-June issue, he said, give some indication of the new publication's character. There were two historical articles, one by Horsch and another by Correll. Bender commented at length on the Horsch article, "Origin and Faith of the Mennonite Church in the Netherlands." He emphasized that it offered "clear disproof of any vital connection whatsoever between the Swiss Brethren and the first Mennonites in the north. The old bridge, Melchior Hofmann, by which Anabaptism was once thought to have traveled from Switzerland to Holland, has broken down and must be abandoned." Bender's position was that scholars simply did not know how the two movements were connected.[32] A significant redirection and definition of Mennonite history had begun.

However, the key article in the May-June issue was a reprint of the first chapter of a new book by Bender's Princeton professor J. Gresham Machen, *What Is Faith?* Why print this chapter in the *Review Supplement?* Because, Bender wrote, Machen challenged the modern emphasis on "experience" which was replacing knowledge as the true basis for understanding life and faith. Observed Bender:

> This attitude in the world of religious thought has led to a decrying of all theological thinking and doctrinal formulation and has presented us with a group of modern religious leaders who tell us that our beliefs do not need to be true or rest on truth so long as we find them useful. In substance, this is a romantic agnosticism. It is the service of Dr. Machen to tear away the halo of romanticism and lay bare the hollow agnosticism behind it.

Bender expressed himself as greatly delighted that he could print Machen in the *Review Supplement.*[33] Certainly it was no accident that one of the articles was a positive review by Noah Oyer of Machen's already-popular *Christianity and Liberalism* (1923). The effusive embrace of Machen in the *Review Supplement* was a boon to Goshen College: no one could accuse Goshen of being soft on modernism.

As if to make that fact crystal clear, Bender also wrote a nine-page review of a recent book by J. E. Hartzler, *Education Among the Mennonites of America* (1925). After leaving the presidency of Goshen College, Hartzler had by 1921 become president of Witmarsum Seminary, a GC Mennonite institution associated with Bluffton College in Ohio. John Horsch considered Hartzler as the leading Mennonite modernist. Bender used the review to cut his former pastor and president down to size and, no doubt, to polish his own image as a defender of conservative orthodoxy. It was not an equal encounter, for already Bender knew more about Mennonite history than Hartzler did. Bender drove the point home by systematically citing every historical mistake Hartzler's book had made.

By the time Bender was finished, nobody could read Hartzler without suspecting his scholarly ability. Having ruined Hartzler's research credibility, Bender then attacked the man's basic propositions about Mennonite history and faith. It was a devastating and intemperate attack on a fellow Mennonite scholar.[34] After writing it and before printing it, Bender had circulated it among his faculty colleagues, asking for criticism because, Bender observed, "A review of the wrong kind may do more harm than good." Apparently his colleagues thought his attack was all right, for none suggested any changes.[35]

By the fall of 1926, Bender and the Mennonite Historical Society realized they had far more material to publish than three forty-page *Review Supplements* could handle in a year. In November, with Umble and Hershberger, Bender made a seven-point proposal to the college administration, the key points being that the *Review Supplement* name be changed to *The Mennonite Quarterly Review*, that the journal appear four times a year, and that its size be increased to seventy-two pages.[36] The response was immediately affirmative, and the first issue came out only two months later, during the second week of January 1927.

Bender was appointed editor, with three associate editors: John Umble, Guy F. Hershberger, and Edward Yoder. Subscriptions were $1 per year. By June 1927 there were almost 200 subscribers, and the paper was paying its own way. The editors printed 600 copies of the first two issues so they could send free copies to potential subscribers. Bender sent complimentary copies to all of his professors at Garrett, Princeton, and Tübingen, as well as dozens to his European friends.[37]

*The Mennonite Quarterly Review* (*MQR*) was a key element in the historical program Bender had in mind. In the first issue, he laid out its course and purpose. On the page opposite the mast-

head and table of contents, he delivered a ringing manifesto entitled "TO THE YOUTH OF THE MENNONITE CHURCH."
Bender declared,

> THE GOLDEN AGE of the Mennonite Church is not past; it is
> just ahead. The problems of the present are many; they are difficult.
> But problems are challenges. They are opportunities for consecrated
> talent. The time never was and never will be when problems are not
> present. Let vision and faith see problems as challenges.
>
> THE PRESENT GENERATION of Mennonite youth have un-
> usual talent to consecrate to the present task. The number of young
> men and women trained and in training, whose heart is set on the
> work of the Kingdom, whose loyalty is sincere, whose faith is deep,
> has never been exceeded. The Church is ready to use this talent,
> this faith, this loyalty.
>
> THE COMING GENERATION in the Mennonite Church is
> being given a carefully built, well-knit, efficient organization of ac-
> tivities. This organization is the equal of that in any Mennonite
> group, and is quite compact, has rich resources and experience be-
> hind it. It covers the field of publication, education, missions,
> Sunday school, church music, and church history.
>
> THE HERITAGE of the coming generation in faith and practice
> is sound. The faith has been kept. The historic ideals of the
> Mennonite Church are still functioning. Whatever obscuring of
> New Testament faith and practice has been found at places can be
> remedied. The Mennonite church still wishes to be a pure New
> Testament church.
>
> YOUTH OF THE MENNONITE CHURCH, the church of to-
> morrow! The heritage is yours, the organization is yours, the talent
> is yours, the problems are yours, the future is yours. Get the vision,
> follow the gleam, bend your back to the burden, consecrate your-
> selves to the task. You are needed, you are wanted, you are able.
> May God grant the will.

Here was heady rhetoric, a call to join a movement, and an affirmation of hope for the future. If there was ever a moment which
announced the beginning of the Harold Bender era, this was it.[38]
All of Bender's dreams and yearnings during the previous six years
as he struggled not to be marginalized during the YPC and seminary years found a voice in the manifesto. Finally he was in position to pursue some of his most cherished objectives.

In a rather lengthy editorial, Bender laid out his goals for the new journal. With an obvious glance over his shoulder at the *Christian Exponent*, he declared that the *MQR* was "not a journal of propaganda nor merely a journal of opinion. It has no program or pattern over which it wishes to make or remake the Mennonite Church. Its sole program is to be a servant to the truth and to the historic ideals and faith of the Mennonite church." The *MQR* would focus on "Mennonite history, thought, doctrine, life, literature, and affairs." The material was to be scholarly and of permanent value. He assured readers that doctrinal and theological articles would be "conservative, vital, biblical, and evangelical." Trying to reassure other Mennonite periodicals, he insisted that the *MQR* would fill a niche no other was filling. He hoped the other periodicals would welcome the *MQR* not as a rival but as a "necessary complement." Finally, he expressed regret that it could not be an "all-Mennonite Review," yet urged scholars from all the Mennonite groups to participate.[39]

• • •

Meanwhile, the Grebel project was running out of steam. Realizing that they could not publish without all the known sources, Correll went to Europe during the summer of 1926 to ferret out the remaining materials. Unfortunately, he became ill, so ill that he was not able to return to the United States until January of 1927, just in time for the beginning of second-semester classes.[40] During the summer of 1926, Scribner's Publishing Company expressed interest in the project, but no manuscript was forthcoming.[41] Apparently the Bender-Correll relationship was fraying. Bender, always impatient with those around him who could not operate at his speed, complained to Horsch that Correll "could work a great deal faster than he does."[42] Actually, Bender had done virtually no work on the Grebel biography either. Only two years into his work as a historian, he was caught in a lifelong habit of promising more than he could deliver.

The Grebel project had made Bender aware of the necessity of adequate bibliographical sources for serious historical work. By 1926 he realized the need for a comprehensive American Mennonite bibliography.[43] The first issue of the *MQR* carried the first installment (for 1727-1827) of what Bender entitled a "Mennonitica Americana, 1727-1927: A Critical Bibliography." During 1927, he promised, the *MQR* would publish the complete bibliography and identify and indicate the location of everything published by Mennonites in America.

It was a rash promise, since most of the work had not yet begun. Bender was apparently unable to restrain his enthusiasm and had failed to learn from the Grebel project about rosy promises of quick action. Thus he declared that in 1928 that *MQR* would publish a similar bibliography of European Mennonite literature written by Mennonites. Finally, he announced plans for a comprehensive bibliography of all materials ever written about Mennonites. He wisely did not indicate a date for that project's completion.[44]

During the following two summers (1927 and 1928), Bender traveled extensively, investigating sources in libraries and archives and particularly visiting Mennonite communities searching for books and other materials. He explained why the search for books in Mennonite communities was so necessary: "Since most of the literature of the early days was out of print and not to be had even in the shops of antiquarians, it was necessary to make a personal search in the only places where this literature was to be found, namely, in the homes of Mennonites."[45]

Bender made his most successful foray in 1927 when, during a few weeks in Pennsylvania's Lancaster County, he acquired more than 125 books from Mennonites' attics and bookshelves. Some he bought; most were gifts. He enjoyed telling the story of one Mennonite woman who had been worried about what to do with her old German books. "She could no longer read them; to throw them away was a sin; none of her friends wanted them; to sell them would have been a sacrilege. Out of a full heart, she thanked me kindly for having been so kind as to relieve her of her books."[46]

However, the aftereffect of Bender's visit to Lancaster caught him by surprise: some Lancaster leaders resented having their old books taken to Goshen, and through Orie Miller they asked to have them returned to Lancaster County. Bender demurred. "I barely touched the surface," he told Miller. "There are lots of duplicates of everything I got still in the County. Let's wait to return the books until you discover what you need from us."[47] Harold sent Orie a list of the titles he had acquired, and in truth it included no genuinely rare books of great monetary value. What had stirred the Lancastrian reaction was apparently the sheer number of books (coupled, no doubt, with bias against Goshen).

Bender's book raid had at least one positive effect: the Lancastrians realized they needed a library and a historical society of their own. Orie, partly to help deflect criticism, asked Harold to suggest a plan by which Lancaster Conference could systematically begin a book-preservation program. Harold obliged with an elaborate congregationally based plan and an offer to help organize a library.[48]

Bender's supreme coup during these book-collecting expeditions was the discovery, at a rare-book shop in Harrisburg, Pennsylvania, of the first known edition of the *Ausbund*, the great sixteenth-century Anabaptist hymnal. It was also the only known copy in existence. In a state of near ecstasy, he purchased the book and carried it back to Indiana. An original copy of the rarest Anabaptistica was again in Mennonite hands. The find was a tribute to Bender's aggressive and attentive effort to leave no stone unturned where source materials were concerned. There was literally no one else with the drive and the knowledge to do what he was doing.

During 1927 Bender was elected to the Mennonite Historical Committee, the official church committee responsible for the historical work of the MC Mennonite church. The committee decided to produce a history of the Mennonites for use as a textbook in Mennonite schools. The idea was for Horsch and Bender to collaborate on the project.[49] Bender was delighted. The committee is "ready to spend all the money necessary to secure a good book," he reported to Horsch. But he was also worried, for they wanted the book finished by September of 1929. He did not think it could be done unless he was given full time to work on it;[50] but he agreed to the assignment. So during the summer of 1928, supported by funds from the Historical Committee, Bender made an extensive research trip to Ontario and eastern Pennsylvania. Again he collected books, but now he also gathered resource materials. It was his first extensive historical research experience, and he enjoyed it immensely.[51]

In 1929 Harold published his first book: *Two Centuries of American Mennonite Literature, 1727-1927*. It was an exhaustive bibliography of material published by American Mennonites. The impulse to prepare the bibliography was triggered by the publication in 1925 of Virginia bishop Lewis J. Heatwole's *Mennonite Handbook of Information*, a bibliography which only listed 250 American Mennonite titles. Even Bender's rudimentary knowledge of American Mennonitica told him that there were far more publications than that. What was needed, he told John Horsch, was a scholarly and exhaustive list of all books published by Mennonites in America.[52]

•  •  •

By 1928, Bender was restlessly casting about for means to earn a Ph.D. degree in history. His colleague Silas Hertzler had just completed his Ph.D. at Yale, and many of Harold's friends were busy in graduate studies. Always aware of the competition, Bender told John Horsch that "in the world at large the degree counts for something. Of course, the work done would be still more important. However, it will not pay for our branch of the church to stay behind the other Mennonite groups in advanced degrees and scholarship."[53]

Bender began his quest by writing to a number of schools about requirements, especially for residence requirements. With a wife and daughter and a teaching position to maintain, his options were limited. In 1926 he inquired of Southern Baptist Seminary in Louisville, and later he wrote to Northwestern University in Evanston, Illinois.[54] In April of 1928, he wrote to professor Hans von Schubert, professor of church history at Heidelberg University, asking whether he could do a doctorate in one year and do his thesis out of the Täuferakten series of Anabaptist source materials of which Schubert was editor.[55] Meanwhile, he began looking for ways to finance such an undertaking.

In the fall of 1928, Bender made what he told Horsch was a

"desperate effort to secure one of the [Guggenheim] fellowships." The Guggenheim Foundation in New York gave forty or fifty awards per year, with princely stipends of $2,000, for a year of study in Europe. Harold proposed to study at Heidelberg University.[56] But, realizing that his chances for the Guggenheim award were limited, he was pleased when Northwestern University promised that if he came there, he could complete the degree in one calendar year. In that case, he would begin his work in the summer of 1929 and have his degree by June 1930. He would write his dissertation in church history with a Mennonite theme. Nevertheless, he clearly hoped to do his work in Europe: the problem was how to get there.[57]

Sometime during 1928, Bender had an inspiration: he would take a group of people on a trip to Europe during the summer of 1929. The tour would pay his travel expenses, and if the Guggenheim Fellowship came through, he could begin school there in the fall. The problem was that he could scarcely bear the idea of being away from Elizabeth and Mary Eleanor for such a long time.[58] But he advertised his trip and found thirteen willing takers, among them his friend Paul Erb of Hesston College. In "The Heart of Europe Tour," he promised 53 days of travel for "less than $600."[59] It was the first Mennonite tour group conducted by an MC Mennonite whose sole purpose was travel for pleasure.

The group left New York in June 1929 aboard the *SS Leviathan*, traveling third-class tourist. After three days in England, they crossed the channel. At the Hook of Holland, they were met by a new motorcoach which Harold had chartered for travel on the continent. It was quite an innovation in 1929, when most travel was still by train, and motorcoaches and highways were still rather primitive. Bender described the bus travel as "eminently satisfactory" and told Noah Oyer, "Motor-coach is the proper way to travel comfortably."[60]

The trip was an interesting mixture of visiting Mennonites and doing more conventional sightseeing. On their first Sunday in Holland, the group attended the big Mennonite Church in Haarlem where Harold's friend J. M. Leenderts, from Garrett Seminary days, was pastor. After visiting Amsterdam and the Menno Simons country in Friesland, they followed the Rhine into Germany, visit-

**The "Heart of Europe" tour group. Harold is on the far right.**
Bender Family Album.

ing Christian Neff at Weierhof and other Mennonite communities
in the Palatinate. The second Sunday they were with the Horsch
relatives near Heilbronn, where the group worshiped with several
Mennonite congregations. Then it was on to Luther country near
Eisenach and south to Nuremburg. They spent a day at Hellmansberg, visiting Uncle Michael Horsch's estate and observing "modern Mennonite farming" methods. One Sunday they worshiped
with a Mennonite congregation just north of Munich.[61]

Then followed several days in Switzerland, including a stop at
St. Gall, where Harold and Paul Erb saw some original Grebel letters in the town archives. The trip continued to Zurich and Lucerne and included worship with the oldest continuing Mennonite
congregation in the world, at Langnau in the Emmental, a valley
near Bern. One of the tour-group members, bishop Eli Frey from
Archbold, Ohio, preached the sermon. The last Sunday was spent
with the Alsatian Mennonite congregation at Colmar. Five days
visiting France and Paris ended with embarkation at Cherbourg
for the trip home. Bender was delighted with the trip and told John
Horsch that the European Mennonites had made a splendid impression on the Americans.[62]

Bender had hoped to leave home in June with the Guggenheim

Fellowship in hand, but just a few weeks before the tour left New York, he learned he would not get it. So he decided to return in August with the tour group and attend Northwestern University for a year. There he planned to do his Ph.D. in church history and write his dissertation on the history of the Amish.[63]

On an impulse Bender decided to visit Heidelberg University while his group toured the area. He was delighted to discover that professor Walther Köhler, a Swiss Reformation scholar, had just come to Heidelberg and in the new academic year would become the dean of the university's theological faculty. Bender had visited Köhler at the University of Zurich in 1924 and had sent Köhler complimentary copies of the *MQR*, so Köhler had some knowledge of the young scholar. Köhler assured him that he would need only one semester of residence at Heidelberg if his thesis were ready and accepted. And it could be in English. Bender instantly grasped the opportunity. He would study at Heidelberg during the spring semester in 1930, write his dissertation, and get his degree in August.

Immediately Bender cabled Goshen College that he intended to return to teach during the fall semester and not begin his studies at Heidelberg until the spring semester. The news unsettled president Yoder and dean Oyer, who had made their budgets for the 1929-30 academic year assuming Bender would be absent. Bender explained that this schedule was necessary because Köhler had agreed for him to do his thesis on Conrad Grebel. Hence, he needed first to return and work through the Grebel material that he and Correll had so laboriously gathered at Goshen.[64]

Bender also informed a surprised and piqued dean Oyer that he would not be returning with the tour group. He and one of the tour members, Dr. S. T. Miller of Goshen, had succeeded, against all odds, in securing visas to visit the Soviet Union. So, he told president Yoder, "I will be back in Goshen by about September 16, unless," he joked, "the Bolsheviks get me."[65]

After seeing their fellow tour members off at Cherbourg, Miller and Bender traveled to Poland, where they attended services at the large Mennonite church in Gdansk. At 5:30 a.m. on August 19, they boarded an airplane for a fourteen-hour flight to Moscow, arriving there at six o'clock in the evening. The flight was quite an adventure, given the tiny and primitive airplane (with six seats and no instruments), the trackless country they flew over, the frequent stops for refueling, and the fact that it was Bender's first time in an airplane. He enjoyed the flight and announced himself a "flying enthusiast." The trip was one of the few times he kept a travel journal.[66] It was clearly the trip of his dreams.

The plan was to go to Moscow and then secure permission to visit the Mennonites in the Ukraine. It was a historic moment to visit the Soviet Union. During the month of August, many tens of thousands of Mennonites were congregating in Moscow in a desperate effort to emigrate to escape the draconian "kulak reforms" the Stalinist regime had begun. Bender and Miller were apparently able to travel about Moscow with relative freedom. Miller, a physician, was interested in visiting hospitals, which they did the first day. On their second day, they succeeded in visiting Mennonite leaders Cornelius Reimer, Johann Dueck, and Peter Froese. In the early 1920s, Reimer had served as the bookkeeper for the Mennonite Central Committee relief work in the Soviet Union.[67] Within a few months, all of these men would be imprisoned by the authorities as part of an effort to stem the flood of German and Mennonite refugees coming to Moscow.

After a few days in Moscow, Bender and Miller visited Leningrad and then left for Finland by train. Bender was relieved to be out of the Soviet Union, noting in his diary that "the transformation from Russia to Finland was marvelous. Beautiful grounds, buildings. Everything clean, well-dressed. Our relief was great. Slept all night."[68] They traveled back to Germany via Sweden and Denmark, whereupon Miller left for a visit to England before returning to the United States.[69] Bender spent several days with the Horsch relatives at Lautenbach, then boarded the *SS George Washington* at Cherbourg for the return trip home.

The three-month trip had a remarkable effect on Bender. As the ship plowed west across the Atlantic, he had time to take stock. "During a sea journey of some length, with no companions, one usually has plenty of time to think," he remarked, typing away on a borrowed shipboard typewriter. Bender was writing an essay entitled "What of the Morrow?" offering a somewhat roseate assessment of the MC Mennonite church's future. "A generation of progress and working together has brought the church to a greater unity than we have ever had before. Our general church work is conducted under great general boards which have almost universal support. There are no parties in the Church, no large opposing group. There is greater uniformity in church polity, teaching, doctrine, worship, and activity than ever before. In methods of church work, we are as one."[70]

In missions and giving, the work of the church is soaring, Bender claimed. "The total amount of money given to the work of the church is reaching new levels. We have more volunteers than we can use. We are on the crest of a strong wave of giving to all causes and of missionary interest and work." He was delighted that "practically all of our young people are now in the church," and they have "never before been so numerous and so active." He applauded "the ministry. In doctrine they are orthodox, evangelical, sound, plain. We cherish the peace message of salvation and preach it together with the whole teaching for holy living found in the Word. Our Bible teachers are sound, our schools are safe, our literature is pure. We are awake and diligent in defense of the faith."[71] Bender ended the four-page paean with a section headed, "What lack we yet?" There he highlighted a need for greater spirituality, worried about the coming generational leadership transition, fretted about too much emphasis on the "dress problem," and urged greater "support and training of the ministry." Observing Paul's claim "I can do all things through Him," he concluded with a question, "Why be a pessimist when God is with us?"[72]

The euphoric shipboard essay was never printed, and history quickly turned it into whimsy. Just a week before Bender wrote it, the biennial MC general conference, meeting at Goshen College, created a new five-member General Problems Committee, which for the next two decades would be a divisive new force in Mennonite church polity. Nor could Bender have known that the church's touted material prosperity would be shattered fifty-nine days later on Black Tuesday, with the collapse of the stock market and the onset of the Great Depression.

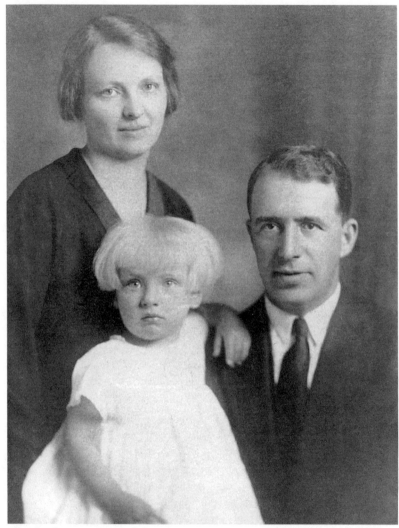

**Elizabeth, Harold, and daughter Mary Eleanor in 1929.**
Bender Family Album.

The *SS Washington* docked at Hoboken, New Jersey, on September 12, and on Saturday there was a joyous reunion with Elizabeth and Mary Eleanor at the Horsches in Scottdale. By Tuesday noon they were back in Goshen, and the next day Harold taught his first fall classes.[73]

## ৵ 9 ৵

# Defending Horsch, Helping MCC

*Bender defends Horsch but skirts Fundamentalist-Modernist controversy. He helps MCC move "Russian" refugees to South America.*

HAROLD BENDER and John Horsch had a genuine and deeply felt regard for each other, but the relationship was an interesting study in personality contrasts. Bender was vigorous, gregarious, ambitious, well educated, and in constant search of the golden mean. Horsch was shy, retiring, enigmatic, poorly educated, and preoccupied with defending absolutes. Bender had a preternatural ability to finesse problems and conflicts. Horsch blundered about, nearly oblivious to the human dimensions of the issues with which he was engaged. Both men were theologically orthodox and conservative. The contrasts had to do with style, temperament, mentality, and education.

By 1925, Bender had spent four years of study at several of the best academic and theological institutions in the world. He had acquired a high regard for careful analysis and reasoned discourse. He had learned the art of separating argument from personality. Even though he might have quibbled with the point, he really did share the liberal assumption that the search for truth was more important than its capture.

John Horsch came from quite a different milieu: he lacked the benefit of a good education. The rather brief periods he spent in American colleges had marginal intellectual consequence because he was struggling to learn English, and the colleges he attended were exceedingly weak academically. His secondary education in

Germany was vocational and narrowly focused. The result was what Bender once described to Ernst Correll as Horsch's inability to do "*systematische Gliederung*," to think systematically and analytically. And, Bender added, "I doubt whether anything can be done about the weakness."[1]

Horsch had little firsthand acquaintance with contemporary liberal ideals of dispassionate scholarly discourse. Like most of the Mennonite leaders of his generation, he was essentially self-taught.

**Harold and Elizabeth with John and Christine Horsch at the Horsch home in Scottdale, Pennsylvania, in the 1930s.** Bender Family Album.

True, he read a great deal, but narrowly. When he read a journal like *Christian Century*, which he regularly perused, he sought material to fuel his ongoing arguments with liberals. He read such literature warily, as a hazardous but necessary part of his vocation.

Horsch's inability to engage in dispassionate controversy was made worse by a chronic personal shyness. It was as though in his writing, which sheltered him from painful personal encounter, he compensated by being too resolute and forthright. Since he seldom traveled, he lacked personal acquaintance with many of his major protagonists, so personal relationships did not temper his instinct for personal attack.

Bender, on the other hand, knew, on a first-name basis virtually everyone with whom he engaged in argument. In 1926, after

Bender's scathing review of J. E. Hartzler's book in the *Review Supplement*, Lester Hostetler, the new editor of the *Christian Exponent*, accused Bender of having laid "Mennonite virtues" aside. Bender, touched to the quick, responded with an acid letter accusing Hostetler of using "somewhat cave-man tactics of the knockdown-drag-in type."[2] Shortly after the exchange, Bender visited Hostetler in Ohio. The two agreed that the matter had gotten out of hand, and they promised to forgo any future arguments in public or in writing. Bender agreed even though, as he told Horsch, he was sure Hostetler was "very sympathetic toward liberal views."[3] Horsch would not have been able to do what Bender had done.

Horsch's acid pen was also a product of deeply held convictions. He was motivated by a Christian experience which required a forceful and straightforward attack on heresy. In his first surviving letter to Bender in 1921, Horsch warned his future son-in-law against the dangers of "liberalistic theology" at Garrett and confessed, "I could not have maintained my stand for Biblical orthodoxy were it not for the continuous experience of the truth of the Christian message." At another point, when arguing with Bender about women's bonnets, he rather wistfully observed, "May the Lord lead us in the questions concerned. I am sure that I want to take the course that I am convinced He wants me to take. These are matters of grave importance, and our own likes and dislikes should not enter when it comes to a decision."[4]

In general, Horsch had an unusually pessimistic view of the interplay of good and evil, explaining to Bender at one point, "Toleration towards liberalism means the ruin of the church. Liberals can afford to have unbelievers in their church, but the reverse is not true. Evil will grow naturally while with the good it is otherwise."[5] Such a bleak view of human nature tended to reinforce Horsch's strident tendencies.

In 1929, Bender warned his friend Irvin Burkhart, who had just written a thesis on Menno Simons, that Horsch did not like what Burkhart had written. Better make sure he likes it, Bender cautioned. "You know that Horsch is rather ruthless if he believes one to be in the wrong."[6] In this case Bender interceded for Burkhart, reminding Horsch that the point of the historical study of

Menno Simons was to find out what Menno believed rather than to try to prove that Menno was always right.[7]

Horsch was a true believer. In a letter to Harold and Elizabeth in early 1924, he railed against the "liberals" in the church. "There is not a drop of martyr blood in their veins, but they tell us they are the true Mennonites and the rest of us have departed from the faith. I cannot say how despicable the position of a man is to me who does not have enough faith in his faith to confess it. In this case the Mennonites of Holland are way ahead of our liberals in America. The church must rid itself of these dangerous elements before it is too late."[8] Bender responded, as he often did, with some gentle admonition: "It is perhaps necessary to be careful in making sweeping statements about the liberals. Positive liberalism I believe is really limited to a few of the more advanced thinkers. It is possible to hurt more than help by indiscriminate condemnation."[9]

Bender was uneasy about Horsch's polemics. In the spring of 1924, the Mennonite Publishing House (MPH) printed Horsch's harshly polemical *The Mennonite Church and Modernism*.[10] Bender got the book in the midst of his heavy summer-semester work at Tübingen. He read the book in one night and the next morning wrote Horsch a six-page letter. "We [he included Elizabeth] think it is a very clear and convincing presentation of the issue, and it finds our hearty *Zustimmung* [agreement, concurrence] throughout." But, he told Horsch, "in a few places there is room for criticism."[11]

Horsch had attacked Modernists for their lack of nonresistance. Bender reminded him that "all" of the leading Fundamentalists were pro-war, and that the backbone of the peace movement was made up of Modernists. This issue he and Horsch would always argue about. What seemed a virtue to Bender (at least Modernists opposed war) simply meant for Horsch that their pacifism was suspect because they were Modernist. After a dozen pointed criticisms, Bender made the one which pained him most about Horsch's writing: You have to document your criticisms with footnotes and references. Too many of your arguments are generalizations drawn from the broader American religious culture which do not apply to Mennonites. Thus you give Mennonite Modernists an opening to defend themselves. "Only that which can be proved dare be asserted," he admonished Horsch.[12]

Bender tried hard not to be used by his father-in-law. Horsch was constantly on the lookout for anecdotes to support his war on the liberals. In 1926 he learned that Amos (A. E.) Kreider might be invited to teach at Goshen. Kreider had taught at Goshen in 1917-1918 and again in 1921-1923. He was a devout and able teacher who shunned conflict and controversy. President Yoder had hoped Kreider would return to Goshen when it reopened in 1924. By then Kreider was teaching at Witmarsum Seminary in Bluffton and chose not to return. Horsch interpreted that decision as an indication of his liberalism. In order to oppose his return in 1926, he needed evidence to prove his point, and he claimed to recall that Kreider had been one of Elizabeth's teachers and had seemed liberal to her.

Harold and Elizabeth were appalled at the prospect that Horsch would use her name, and Harold rushed a letter to his father-in-law saying that Elizabeth never had Kreider for a teacher and that the vague impression she may have had came from her roommate Mary Good, who had become a missionary in India. He assured Horsch that in fact Elizabeth and he did not consider Kreider a liberal.[13]

It is doubtful whether anything Bender might have done would have helped to tone down Horsch's crusade against Modernism, even if he had tried harder. Three things held him back. One was the son-in-law factor. Bender benefited from the relationship, which made it more difficult for Mennonite conservatives to attack him. During his 1928 book-collecting foray into Lancaster County, he visited bishop John Mosemann one evening. Mosemann and Horsch saw eye-to-eye on the Modernism threat, and Bender told Orie O. Miller he felt like he was walking into the den of a "lion." When Bender arrived at the Mosemanns, he was surprised to discover that also visiting were two other conservative "lions," bishops Noah Mack of Lancaster County and George R. Brunk (I) of Virginia. He got a "surprising reception," he told Orie Miller. They were all quite congenial and expressed their admiration for John Horsch.[14]

Bender seldom tried to defend Horsch, but there was one notable exception. In the "Open Forum" column of the *Christian Exponent*, several of the men Horsch had attacked in his *Mennonite*

*Church and Modernism* book defended themselves vigorously. Horsch then went on the offensive. He produced a pamphlet entitled *Is the Mennonite Church in America Free from Liberalism?* and sent copies to all Mennonite ministers. N. E. Byers, dean of Bluffton College and a person whom Horsch's pamphlet attacked, rejoined sharply in the *Christian Exponent*, including a disparaging reference to Horsch as a "typesetter and translator." Bender was incensed and demanded that Byers make a public apology. "Such publication would remove the growing impression that you are more interested in attacking persons than promoting facts and meeting issues," Bender told Byers. In such a case, Bender tersely pointed out, "the cleverest man will win. And every one knows that Deans of Colleges are more clever than proofreaders and translators."[15] Byers agreed that the argument had become personal and should be ended.

A second factor which made Bender sanguine about his father-in-law's polemics was their genuine, shared enthusiasm for Mennonite history. For twenty years Bender and Horsch maintained an almost weekly correspondence, with 80 percent of its content about historical matters. Bender was often critical of Horsch's lack of source citations, but he had enormous respect for the older man's knowledge of Anabaptist materials. Particularly in the 1930s, when Bender found it increasingly difficult to find the time to do serious historical work, he depended on Horsch for much of the careful research which undergirded his own writing. It was not that Horsch did specific research for Bender; instead, Horsch's prolific writing for the *MQR* provided a steady stream of new information that Bender was able to use in his own work. Thus difficulties the two men sometimes had over questions of Modernism were overshadowed by the continual mutual satisfaction they enjoyed in their shared historical work. Bender was genuinely impressed by Horsch's ability as a historian.

A third factor in Bender's sympathetic relationship to Horsch's crusade against Modernism was that for the most part he agreed with Horsch's positions. Bender's persistent trait was to be orthodox: he had genuine disdain for extreme positions on either side. The Modernism controversy was a battle over issues at the margins, and Bender instinctively reached for the middle. When he joined the fray, it was usually for reasons not intrinsic to the argument itself. He was trying to protect his own position or more usually that of Goshen College. One indication of his reluctance to get involved was that he wrote surprisingly little during the 1920s on Modernism, compared to his work in promoting history. In fact, he wrote only four articles specifically dealing with the Fundamentalism-Modernism issue, and each time he went out of his way to use his own theological definitions instead of the more conventional language of the arguments.

In a January 1926 article in the *Gospel Herald* entitled "Fundamentals Should Be Taught These Days," Bender argued that there is a "great need for definiteness and certainty. Definite certain knowledge of the few great simple teachings of Christ and the Word, the fundamentals of the faith, is sorely needed these days." There were actually, he claimed, only four fundamentals: (1) Christ as our "substitute," and complete commitment to him in "personal discipleship" and separation from the world; (2) the Bible as the God-inspired eternally true and valid Word of God, the only authority in faith and life, to be obeyed literally; (3) the Holy Spirit as a real person, not a mere symbol; and (4) the church as the body of Christ, composed of saved persons only, to be kept pure and unspotted from the world, the light of the world and the body commissioned to evangelize.[16]

In the fall of 1926, Bender wrote another article in which he categorically repudiated statements he said were made by some persons that the Mennonite church is "shot through and through with liberalism." Such statements "are absolutely unfounded and untrue. The church is sound on Modernism." Horsch was unhappy with this statement, for it called into question the basic proposition of his *Mennonite Church and Modernism*.[17]

In 1928, Bender wrote two more articles, one entitled "Biblical Tests of Orthodoxy," and the other "Detecting Modernism." The latter identified ten "elements or attitudes" which he claimed were marks of Modernism. Under his tenth point, he lumped the most common "denials" by Modernists, such as inerrant plenary inspiration of Scripture, the deity of Christ, the virgin birth, and vicarious atonement. He became somewhat demagogic in point five, arguing that one can tell the Modernists because they often "slur" church organizations and periodicals. Watch out especially for those who attack and belittle such "staunch institutions as Moody Bible Institute and Princeton Seminary, but never have anything critical to say about Chicago and Union Seminaries," he warned. Except for his fifth point, he was quite evenhanded: he argued that one should take great care when attaching the "liberal" label to fellow Christians.[18]

Some of Bender's arguments on behalf of orthodoxy were meant to ward off attack. The best example was an editorial in the 1925 *Goshen College Record* entitled "Criticism, Desired and Undesired." He made his point with pithy directness: "Not everyone has the moral right to criticize. Who has the right? Only he who is a living part of the organism which he criticizes. Only he who has and keeps his life in the Church, who suffers with her, and whose spiritual fellowship with the Church is unbroken."[19]

Lancaster bishop John Mosemann, who carefully scanned each *Record* for lapses in the faith, was impressed by Bender's point. He called it a "master stroke against the liberals who are outside the Church and fighting the Church with poisonous weapons."[20] Replying to Mosemann, a delighted president Yoder noted that Bender had "come a long way and has no other intention but to stand with the church in her struggle." Then he tossed in the clincher: that Bender was "putting on the plain coat."[21] The wily president knew that nothing Bender might have done could have been more convincing.

Most of Bender's arguments with John Horsch about modernism were not about substance but rather about tone and accuracy. Harold Bender, like all MC leaders in the 1920s, was an antimodernist. But he was not a crusading antimodernist. When he spoke on the issue, it was nearly always from necessity, and he spoke or wrote with an ear for the nuances which allowed him to operate in a middle ground, albeit tilted to the antimodernist side of the equation. Ultimately the Fundamentalist-Modernist controversy among Mennonites had less to do with theology than with church order and generational transition. In that context, Bender felt at home; he was committed to the Mennonite church and its emerging organizations.

• • •

"This was a very interesting day, I can assure you. My wobbly Deutsch was put on a severe test, as well as my manners," Harold explained to Elizabeth. "I tried to watch very closely and use the proper terms of address such as Herr Regierungsrat, Herr Legationsrat, etc., and bowed endlessly and smiled and said Guten Tag and Wiedersehen until I wasn't sure whether I was Unruh or Bender or one of the dear old chaps myself. I am going to insist on being called a "Ra-t" [sic] of some sort myself when I return."[22]

The day was Monday, February 17, 1930. The place was Berlin, Germany. The "dear old chaps" were German officials in the Foreign Ministry and the Reichskammer (administrative council), agencies which handled refugee affairs for the German government. Bender had arrived in Germany just two weeks earlier. His plan was to enroll at Heidelberg University when the spring semester began in early April. In the meantime he had two other tasks: write his dissertation on Conrad Grebel and serve as the Mennonite Central Committee (MCC) representative helping Mennonite Benjamin Unruh, himself an emigrant from the Soviet Union, move "Russian" Mennonite refugees out of Germany to Paraguay and Canada. It was Bender's first MCC assignment.

In 1928, Joseph Stalin began the collectivization of Soviet agriculture and launched an all-out attack on kulaks, prosperous farmers who resisted collectivization. Most Soviet Mennonites were of that class. By spring of 1929, a brutal campaign to eliminate the kulaks was in high gear, and a group of Mennonite families traveled to Moscow seeking permission to emigrate. Sometime in August, about the time Bender and Dr. S. T. Miller were in Moscow, some of those families got such permission. When that news reached the Mennonite colonies in the Ukraine, tens of thousands of Mennonites and other Germans began converging on Moscow to get exit visas. The event became an international incident. The German government offered the refugees temporary asylum and financial help. Tragically, only about six thousand were allowed to leave, four thousand of them Mennonites. Nearly all the refugees hoped to go to Canada, but it soon became apparent that Canada would not accept many of them. Nor could they remain in Germany.[23]

Ten years earlier, in 1920 in the aftermath of the Russian Revolution, the American Mennonites had created MCC to provide aid to the Mennonites caught in the Soviet civil war. Now in 1929, Benjamin Unruh, one of four men who had come to the West in 1920 to appeal for Western Mennonite help, again appealed to the American Mennonites for aid. Unruh had been living in Germany since 1920 and had firsthand knowledge of German officialdom and the Mennonite refugee situation. His appeal to Americans stimulated immediate response from MCC leaders.[24]

Levi Mumaw, P. C. Hiebert, Sanford C. Yoder, and Orie Miller met in Chicago in December 1929 to discuss what American Mennonites could do to help. Bender's trip to Moscow just a few months earlier was fresh on the minds of these MCC leaders. They invited Bender to join them; it was his first MCC meeting. Out of the meeting came a three-person Colonization Committee with an assignment to study the feasibility of settling the Mennonite refugees in either Paraguay or Brazil. Bender was on the committee.

On January 18, 1930, the committee, whose report Bender wrote, recommended Paraguay.[25] Bender opposed an alternative plan which would have sent the refugees to Brazil because that country offered no guarantee of freedom from compulsory military service. No doubt the decision was also based on the fact that a group of Mennonites from Canada had settled in Paraguay in 1927 under a comprehensive special agreement, a "Privilegium" which the Paraguayan government had offered. In any case, Bender lobbied hard for Paraguay and apparently convinced Miller and other MCC members. Thus MCC became the primary agent for settling refugees in Paraguay. It arranged to buy a large block of land from an American corporation, in a remote, interior area called the Chaco. It then sent Kansan G. G. Hiebert to Paraguay to prepare for the refugees' reception. Because he spoke German, MCC sent Harold Bender to Germany to help Benjamin Unruh arrange the refugees' departure.[26]

**Benjamin Unruh and Harold Bender in 1930.**
Harold S. Bender papers, AMC.

The German government paid for the transport, but it was Bender and Unruh's task to arrange it, purchase supplies and equipment, and negotiate the visas and permits necessary to move stateless persons from one continent to another. For the young academician from Goshen College, it was a daunting undertaking. For the first time, he had to organize and manage a large and complex operation involving thousands of people and many thousands of dollars. His terse telegrams reflected the urgency and the excitement: "REQUEST EIGHT THOUSAND DOLLARS IN MARKS HAMBURG BY MONDAY." "SIXTY-NINE FAMILIES THREE HUNDRED FIFTY-TWO SOULS SAILED SIXTEENTH APRIL HAPAG GENERAL BELGRANO. . . . REQUEST INCREASE THIRD AUTHORIZATION FROM SIXTY TO EIGHTY FAMILIES AS NECESSARY TO FILL TRANSPORT SAILING BREMEN."[27] The challenge stretched Bender and enhanced his already considerable self-confidence.

The most difficult task was persuading the refugees that they should go to Paraguay since they all wanted to go to Canada. They were in three camps, and Unruh and Bender went from camp to

**Harold Bender (on the left, behind the captain of the ship) and Russian refugees about to depart from Bremen, Germany, for Paraguay in 1930.** Harold S. Bender papers, AMC.

camp, making their case. Bender wrote to Elizabeth about one camp: "We held a general meeting with all the refugees [about 1,000 people]. Unruh and I made addresses. Unruh outlined the general situation, and I spoke on Paraguay. Now you can imagine the sort of speech I made, in a language I do not master on a subject on which I am ill-informed."[28] Whatever the difficulties, the refugees were well organized, and their leaders greatly impressed Bender. Refugee leaders themselves did much of the persuasion.

For three months Bender kept traveling from the camps to Hamburg to Berlin to Karlsruhe (where Benjamin Unruh lived) to Lautenbach, Willenbach, and Hellmansberg, where he stayed with the Horsch relatives. While in Hamburg, he lived in a hotel—and chafed at having to pay two dollars a day for his room and a dollar for each meal.[29] At the beginning of April, he took a few days off to enroll at Heidelberg University. But the first group of refugees did not get off for Paraguay until March 15, and the last finally sailed on July 12. So he was able to attend lectures only sporadically. He attended his first lectures on April 29 and that same afternoon moved into a room near the university. He ate his meals in the huge old university dining hall with its thick walls and arched ceiling. Bender was a big eater and loved the food. And, he told Noah Oyer, meals cost only fifteen cents.[30]

As a student Bender had four lecture courses: one under professor Jelke in ethics, another with professor Beer in Old Testament, a third with professor Martin Dibelius in New Testament, and the fourth with professor Walther Köhler in church history.

Bender learned a great deal from professor Dibelius's discussion of the idea of the kingdom of God. "I am surprised at the way he destroys the old liberal conception of the kingdom of God, as a gradual evolutionary making-over of the world," he told Horsch. "When I came to examine my own notion of the Kingdom, I found that it was still pretty much of the old-fashioned liberal notion—it is no longer so, however. I have not yet clearly worked it out, but I see more clearly than ever that the view of Christianity characteristic of most of American Christianity is untenable, and is certainly not 'New Testament.' The danger is of giving up the world as hopeless and accommodating oneself too much to it."[31]

However, the course in which Bender reveled was professor Köhler's Reformation history. He found the professor to be a genuinely fine, impartial historian. Bender's appraisal was no doubt influenced by a point Köhler made in his lectures. He insisted that the Anabaptist movement had begun in Zurich and that southern Anabaptism had a history quite separate from the north-German and Dutch movements. This was a matter of exceedingly great importance to both Horsch and Bender, eager as they were to sever all connections with the disastrous Münster episode of 1535. Bender also discovered that Köhler, as he told Horsch, "agrees with me that the *Gemeinde-Princip*" is the normative factor in the Anabaptist movement.[32] Bender first expressed this idea in a 1924 "Open Forum" article in *The Christian Exponent.* He declared that the Anabaptists were not early modern individualists, but had deliberately made commitment to the church community the central principle of their movement.

During the spring of 1930, Köhler was completing a book on Reformation-era Swiss Reformed church discipline. He had just found an interesting case of *"Bann und Meidung"* (ban and shunning) in the Reformed church in Basel which, Köhler told Bender, was as strict as the teachings of Menno Simons.[33] One night Köhler invited Bender to his house for dinner. There Bender discovered that Köhler was rather deaf and, to Bender's surprise, a Lutheran. He was amazed at how critical Köhler was of Luther's ethical theology. The professor told Bender, "*Die Kritik der Täufer war nicht überspannt*" (the criticism [of Luther] by the Anabaptists was not overdrawn).[34]

By July it was clear that Bender would not be able to get his degree at the end of the summer semester. The obvious reason was the refugee project: he had missed more than half of his lectures and simply had not had time to do his academic work. Another reason was a month-long delay in the arrival of his trunk, carrying Grebel project materials and books. Bender was nearly beside himself with anxiety, but the trunk finally arrived. Mainly, what made it so impossible to complete the degree came, Bender told Ernst Correll, from his intention to "verify everything and solve all the unsolved problems if possible." The result was that on July 31, the first draft of the dissertation on Conrad Grebel was only as far as 1522. He had not even begun writing about Grebel and the Reformation.[35] Bender would not be able to finish the work in time to get the degree that summer.

So Bender decided to return to Goshen for the fall semester. President Yoder and dean Oyer were dismayed, for they had made the year's budget on the assumption that Bender would not return until January 1931.[36] Bender had little choice, for he was out of money. He had received no salary while in Europe. Moreover, shortly after he left for Germany, Elizabeth (who was teaching courses part-time at Goshen College academy), had to have expensive surgery. She was hospitalized for several weeks in a Chicago hospital and earned little during the spring semester. The Benders had already borrowed $500 from father Horsch: they did not want to borrow any more. So there simply was no way Bender could afford to stay for study in the fall. Professor Köhler suggested that he come back for the spring semester in 1931 and finish the degree. That became the plan.[37]

In early July of 1930, Bender spent two days with his old college classmate and YPC colleague O. B. Gerig. By 1930 Gerig had completed a Ph.D. in history at Harvard and was working for the League of Nations in Geneva. Bender and Gerig arranged to meet in Munich, and then they drove to Heidelberg in Gerig's new American car. "We discussed everything under the sun," Bender told Oyer, "he usually being the liberal and I the conservative—the first real keen discussion I have had for a long time. Served to waken me a bit out of the sloth one gets into when all is on one's own side." Bender was intrigued that Gerig, so worldly-wise, was still so intensely interested in Mennonite questions. "We old Mennonites are somewhat like the Jews, it seems to me. We are almost a race, as well as a Church," Bender remarked.[38]

Apparently somewhat homesick, Bender was eager for news from home. Somewhere he had learned that bishop George R. Brunk was seriously ill. Rather irreverently, he told Oyer, "I have no unchristian feelings in this matter, but I thought perhaps the hand of Providence was intervening to overrule earthly arrangements." On another subject he urged, as adviser to the *Maple Leaf*, that the student he preferred be given consideration for editor; and he loudly protested being dropped as a member of the Lecture Committee.[39]

Bender also raised a ruckus when he noticed that Verna Graber, college business manager C. L. Graber's sister, had been hired to teach academy Latin and other language courses. Those were courses Elizabeth had been teaching and planned to teach again. Why, he demanded, should Verna Graber be hired to supplant Elizabeth? "This is a serious injustice, and we shall protest very vigorously," he warned Oyer. What is the problem? "Has the Principal in the Academy a private grudge?"[40] Bender was vehement because the family finances were parlous: it seemed absolutely essential that Elizabeth be employed. President Yoder tried to reassure Bender that Elizabeth's position was secure; but the episode heightened Bender's suspicion that Yoder was a careless administrator.[41]

At every possible opportunity, Bender traveled to investigate Grebel and Anabaptist historical sources. For that purpose he made two trips to Zurich. There, for the first time, he met professor Fritz Blanke, who had just come to the University of Zurich to take the place left vacant when professor Walther Köhler had moved to Heidelberg. In 1930, Blanke and Bender began a friendship and a collaborative relationship in Anabaptist history which lasted a lifetime.

Bender made a number of visits from Heidelberg to nearby Weierhof to visit historian Christian Neff. On one of those visits, he learned that the original Jan Luyken copperplates used to illustrate the 1685 edition of the *Martyrs Mirror* had been found. Bender visited the person in Munich who had the plates and discovered that he was asking four thousand marks for them. Bender urged that MPH buy them, and was frustrated when it did not act on his suggestion.[42]

During the summer Bender also began correspondence with an Austrian historian of Anabaptism named Robert Friedmann. Ten years later, in 1940, Friedmann would come to Goshen College and help Bender develop the ideas which soon became Bender's famous "Anabaptist Vision." Bender had learned of Friedmann in 1930 when the latter reviewed a book about Pilgram Marpeck. Their correspondence accelerated when it became apparent that Friedmann might be able to help Bender acquire some rare Anabaptist sources from the library of a famous scholar of the Austrian Reformation, Rudolf Wolkan. In 1930 Friedmann was also working on Hutterite history, a field in which he would soon become an expert and in which John Horsch was already an acknowledged authority. Bender sized up the young scholar for John Horsch. "I believe he will become a very valuable *Täufer*-Scholar, and one who will have appreciation and sympathy for the *Täufer* (Anabaptists)," he judged.[43]

• • •

It was a day in early May just after another group of refugees sailed out of Bremerhaven harbor en route for Paraguay. Bender and a director of the north German Lloyd ship line were chatting about matters relating to the next transport of refugees. The director learned that Bender was a registered travel agent for the north German Lloyd company in Chicago and that he was extremely homesick for his family. To Bender's surprise, the director offered to bring Elizabeth and Mary Eleanor to Europe and return them free of charge. He would also give them free rail transportation on the continent. All this would be in second-class rather than the third-class accommodations the Benders always selected.[44]

So on July 24, just a week before lectures ended at Heidelberg, Elizabeth and three-year-old Mary Eleanor arrived at Bremen on the *SS Columbus* for a joyful family reunion. Bender took them to one of the refugee camps on some business and then on to Heidelberg. There they took Mary Eleanor to an eye specialist. Then they went out to nearby Lautenbach, where Elizabeth's relatives entertained them warmly while Harold returned to Heidelberg for the final week of lectures. One of their fond hopes had been to attend the Passion Play at Oberammergau, but they simply could not afford the tickets. So, Bender told Ernst Correll, instead they would "start the rounds of the *Vetterstrasse* (visiting the relatives)."[45]

On August 30 the Benders boarded a train for Danzig, Poland, to attend a three-day worldwide Mennonite conference. This second Mennonite World Conference (the first had been in 1925 at Basel) focused on Mennonite relief activity, especially on the tragic plight of the Soviet Mennonites. Bender spoke twice, reporting on the work he and Benjamin Unruh had just completed with the Russian refugees. He proposed a resolution which the conference adopted: that all Mennonite churches take up a special offering on a Sunday in November 1930 to aid Mennonite refugees.[46]

The conference was an important event in Bender's life. He not only met and learned to know nearly all of the major Mennonite figures in the European world, but for the first time he also met Cornelius (C. F.) Klassen. Klassen had escaped from the Soviet Union only in 1928, and had settled in Winnipeg. Prior to 1928 he had been in Moscow and had served as a spokesman for the Soviet Union's Mennonites. During the 1930s and 1940s, he became widely known among Canadian Mennonites in his role as a collector on the debts incurred by Russian immigrants during their 1923-27 migration to Canada. Later, after World War II, C. F. Klassen, Orie Miller, and Bender would emerge as the three major leaders of MCC.[47]

The seven-month sojourn in Europe did not net Bender the

Ph.D. he had hoped for. It was a symptomatic outcome, pregnant with meaning for his future. He had let the practical work for the Mennonite peoplehood crowd out his scholarship, as would happen continually for the rest of his life. But his time in Europe and his attendance at the Danzig conference had also established him as the American Mennonite who had firsthand acquaintance with all the important Mennonite leaders in the world. No other Mennonite in America in 1930 had such an advantage. Because of those contacts, the executive committee of MCC, stirred out of their moribund state by the Soviet refugee crisis, made Bender a member of that committee with the title of assistant secretary. With his language skills and breadth of contacts, they made him responsible to carry on all foreign correspondence for MCC. Other executive committee members in 1930 were P. C. Hiebert, a Mennonite Brethren high school teacher from Kansas; M. W. Kratz, a General Conference Mennonite lawyer from Philadelphia; Henry Garber, a Lancaster County minister; Levi Mumaw, business manager at MPH in Scottdale, Pennsylvania; and Orie Miller.[48]

On September 9 the Benders boarded the *SS Europa* at Bremen, and six days later they landed in New York. After a one-day visit at Scottdale, they hurried on to Goshen. The next day Mary Eleanor broke out with measles: Bender called them "authentic German measles." She had apparently picked up the virus during their travels.[49]

• • •

Harold and Elizabeth returned to a parched and fearfully hot Indiana. The drought was a foretaste of troubles to come. In the fall and winter of 1930-31, the Great Depression was only beginning to be felt in the great American heartland. Ominously, in early February 1931, the State Bank of Goshen collapsed, and the Mennonite Historical Society lost funds deposited there. However, enrollment at the college fell only slightly in the fall of 1930; two more years would pass before the financial situation at Goshen College became critical. Now, in September of 1930, the students streamed back to campus, the women reveling in a newly refurbished Kulp

Hall dormitory. Goshen College had reached a kind of equilibrium: for several years the student body had been stable at about 300 students.[50] While the acrimonious attacks of conservatives continued, a substantial reservoir of support had been established. Financially, the college was still fragile, but as an institution, it had an increasingly solid place in Mennonite life. Winning that place had been a struggle.[51]

Perhaps no event better captured the difficulties the college had faced after its reopening than a letter to the college from the faculty of Eastern Mennonite School in early 1927.[52] The fundamental issue was rivalry over recruitment of students and funds. In reopening Goshen College in 1924, the Board of Education had determined that the MC Mennonite church could not afford more than one four-year college, that Goshen should be that college, and that Hesston and EMS should be feeder schools for Goshen. Goshen had been delighted with the plan, but the plan gave Hesston and especially EMS new leverage for their discontent with Goshen. By threatening to advise their students to attend other-than-Mennonite schools to complete their education, EMS could exert significant leverage on Goshen.

In 1927 EMS used its lever. In its faculty's letter to Goshen College, president Amos (A. D.) Wenger and dean C. K. Lehman stated that unless eight changes were made, "we are inclined to withhold our support until Goshen College demonstrates her ability to effect desired changes. As things stand," the letter declared, "we will send our students to schools which hold to 'Fundamentalism' because such a school is far less dangerous to Mennonite students than Goshen." The letter complained that athletics were given too much emphasis, there was too much intercollegiate activity (debating), the dress question was not being handled well, there was not enough Mennonite doctrinal emphasis, the alumni association was still administered by "Old" Goshen persons, the *Maple Leaf* was objectionable, and the campus brought in too many "outside" speakers.[53]

A "Dear Brethren" letter from president Yoder and dean Oyer tried to answer the charges and to convey a spirit of independence. The Goshen faculty "was very much grieved, when your letter was placed before them," dean Oyer wrote. He pointed out that if Goshen was to try to push its spirit and ideas on the "East" the way the "East" pushed their ideas on the "West," there would be big trouble. Oyer also expressed regret that the letter was circulated to a large number of ministers at the same time as it was mailed to Goshen, thus turning the episode into a power play. On the other hand, Oyer conceded, if Goshen was serious about being the Mennonite standard college, they really did need to heed the concerns of their more conservative brethren in the East.[54]

In addition to worsening the relationships between the two schools, the episode had one consequence for Harold Bender: he decided to wear the regulation coat. It was apparently in the context of some of these stresses and strains that Bender's sister Violet urged him to consider leaving Goshen for better employment elsewhere. Bender's reply reveals his state of mind and his basic commitments. "It would take much to move me," he told Violet. "I consider the privilege of teaching in a small college with a cul-

**Harold and siblings with their mother, Elsie, in the early 1930s. From the left: Cecil, Florence, Wilbur, Elsie, Robert, Violet, Harold, John.**
Bender Family Album.

ture and atmosphere of its own, based on a Christian philosophy, a privilege. The barren life of our modern educational factories does not attract me any more than the thin thinking of our modern sophisticates. I might earn a living elsewhere. But it would not be living a life."[55]

Bender sometimes lost patience with his brother Wilbur at Harvard and with Violet, with her Oberlin degree, when they cast aspersions on Goshen College or the Mennonite church. Live-in brother-in-law Paul Horsch enjoyed the fireworks at Sunday dinners when Wilbur and Harold debated the relative merits of a Harvard or Goshen College education.[56]

Harold and Wilbur also disagreed about politics. In 1928 Bender was quite disgusted with Wilbur when he learned that Wilbur had broken with a girlfriend over politics. Harold told Violet that Wilbur had the idea "she is not intellectual because she expects to vote for Hoover. Wilbur is now a Harvard sophisticate (on the surface) and plays the part by legging for [Democratic candidate Al] Smith." Bender favored Hoover.[57]

By 1928 Bender was committed to Goshen College and the Mennonite church, and he had a clear idea about his own abilities and gifts. When he applied for the Guggenheim Fellowship in order to study in Europe in late 1928, he listed his father-in-law John Horsch as a reference. Horsch had no idea how to write a reference: he had never done such a thing. So he sent the materials to Bender with a plea: Please write what is needed, and I'll sign my name to it. Bender was aghast, but he desperately needed the reference. So he wrote the recommendation, sending it to Horsch with the admonition to take out anything he could not say with a "clear conscience."[58]

The ghost-written document declared:

> I gladly comply with your request for a statement regarding the qualifications of Dr. [sic] Harold S. Bender, candidate for one of the Guggenheim Fellowships, and for an estimate of the worth of the project he proposes as his theme for research.
>
> I have known the candidate personally and intimately for the past eleven years. We traveled together in Europe in the summer of 1924; we have been closely associated in research in the field of

Reformation and Anabaptist History—the field of his proposed research project—for the past five years. We have cooperated in the collection of a library in this field, and we have collaborated and continue to collaborate in the writing and publication of material in this field. On the basis of this association, I am prepared to give the Guggenheim Foundation a thoroughgoing endorsement both of the candidate and his project. I might say that my judgment of the project is based on my own forty years of experience in research and authorship in the field.

First the candidate. In character and personal virtues, above reproach. The candidate is a thorough Christian gentleman. He was a leader in his college as a student and has since his university days become a leader in his chosen fields, college teaching, and in his religious work. A fine type of intellect, thoroughly trained, balanced, with attractive qualities of mind and heart, a sound personality. He is enthusiastic for his work, yet mature and sound. To my mind he represents the best type of scholarship, not pedantic, nor narrow, not lost in the technical detail of his specialty, broadly cultured yet equipped for painstaking and accurate research. Above all I should say that he is gifted with that imagination which alone can lift a scholar from the plain of mediocre plodding to the realms of creative interpretation and synthesis. I should certainly say that he possesses and has demonstrated unusual capacity for productive scholarship in the brief span of his career to the present.

Fitness of the candidate for research project proposed. From my own research and acquaintance with workers in the field, I am lead [sic] to the conviction that the candidate is well-qualified for his proposed project. He has had a deep and permanent enthusiasm for the field. He has made it his major interest apart from professional duties for the past five years. He is thoroughly at home in the German language in which the material for the project is to be found almost exclusively. He is qualified to use French, Dutch, and Latin in his studies. He has mastered the literature and material in the field thoroughly, having had at his disposal the best library of Anabaptistica in the country. I can confidently say that he has been recognized by his co-workers in the field and by his denomination as well as others, as one of the two or three authorities in the field of Anabaptist history. His college and his church have accorded him high recognition as an historian by his elevation to important posts and official positions. His publications within the past five years, though not extensive, are of the highest quality as pieces of historical writing, and they with his other achievements give unusual promise of further productive scholarship of a high order. His writings are written in a clear simple style, stimulating, and show evidence of careful investigation and analysis. I consider him the most capable man in the field today either in America or Europe, to whom an assignment of a project for research in this field could be made.

The project. My own life-time study in the field of Reformation and Anabaptist History convinces me that Anabaptist history is just coming into its own, and that the accumulation of material is such that the time is ripe for a new synthesis, and one that will be sincerely appreciated by historians, both in the field of social history and religious history. Very little of this work has been done since the material of the past two generations has been accumulating, and the misconceptions of the past cry for a scholarly and thorough treatment. Further, the nature of the Anabaptist [sic] is such as to be of great interest to the social historian and sociologist. In this movement lie the roots of much that is best in modern life, such as separation of church and state, emphasis on personal rather than institutional religion, religious freedom, Christian pacifism, ethical earnestness, social application of religion, reform of the economic system, etc. A comprehensive investigation and illuminating presentation of this material would be a much appreciated contribution to the cultural history of the Reformation and post-Reformation period. I can not help but think of Albert Hyma's *Christian Renaissance* as a splendid example of what might be expected as the fruit of such a project. For instance, the Dutch Anabaptist or Mennonite movement was closely connected with the development of civil freedom and progress in that land and consequently throughout Europe. The work of Grotius shows the influence of the group, and Rembrandt's genius was molded by it to some extent. If the Guggenheim Fellowships have not yet been devoted to such projects in the history of culture and religion, in social and religious history, I confidently believe that a real contribution in the way of productive scholarship would be made by the devotion of a fellowship to such a project as this.

I hope it may be possible to confer a fellowship upon Professor Bender for prosecution of research in this valuable project.

Very truly,
John Horsch[59]

This morally problematic exercise in self-description suggests the intense urgency Bender attached to his pursuit of a Ph.D.; it also offers a wonderful window into Bender's self-perception in late 1928. Both the language and the tone suggest how completely Bender could drop the self-effacing humility of his contemporary Mennonite ethos and adopt the posture of an ambitious and talented American academician intent on making his mark in the world. That Bender could live and thrive in the Mennonite ethos of the 1920s and also exhibit such an alternative style suggests something about the facile quality of his mind and a remarkable ability to assume several contradictory identities at the same time.

Bender certainly had a healthy regard for his own talents and abilities, and he was not far off the mark: but he also exaggerated at points. In 1928 he was becoming a specialist in Anabaptist history, but surely was not yet one of its "two or three authorities." His reference to his ability to do "painstaking research" was certainly vindicated by his *Two Centuries of American Mennonite Literature*, which he had just completed. Nonetheless, he had not yet demonstrated, at least not in historical writing, that he had the imagination which would "lift a scholar from the plain of mediocre plodding to the realm of creative interpretation and synthesis." His first major scholarly article would not be published until 1933.[60]

What Bender had accomplished by 1928 was much painstaking translating and editing of source materials, plus some short pieces which, although interesting, were too limited really to demonstrate ability as a writer of monographs. He was the competent editor of an obscure new historical journal whose scholarly credibility had not yet been established. In 1928 he had little substantial scholarship to show in support of his Guggenheim proposal. In any case, despite his unusual effort, his application for a Guggenheim was denied. It would be many years before he finally gained his Ph.D.

## ❧10❧
# Dean of Goshen College

*Bender becomes dean of Goshen College,*
*modernizes the curriculum, and hires new faculty.*
*The college is accredited.*

THE FUNERAL COLUMN moved in a solemn procession from the Oyer residence down Goshen's Eighth Street and across College Avenue to the college's Chapel Hall. The mourners, on foot, were led by president Yoder and College Mennonite Church pastor C. L. Graber. At the head of the procession was the casket, carried by six faculty members: Harold S. Bender, Samuel W. Witmer, John S. Umble, Silas Hertzler, Guy F. Hershberger, and Glen R. Miller.[1]

It was Saturday afternoon, February 28, 1931. The grieving college community was burying its revered dean, Noah Oyer. Oyer had succumbed after a three-month bout with typhoid fever. He had come to Goshen as dean when the college reopened in 1924 and quickly became the most respected figure on campus. He had been one of Harold Bender's best friends and one of the few persons with whom Bender was ever totally candid. Oyer's untimely death, at age 40, was a severe blow to the college community and to Bender personally.[2] "It will be impossible to replace him," Bender told his father-in-law.[3] Oyer had been exceptional as a mediator and facilitator. His kindly disposition had made him popular with students, and his relational skills had made him an irenic presence among the intimate and sometimes conflicting relationships of faculty and staff.

Since the fall of 1930, there had been mounting dissatisfaction among the faculty with the quality of governance at the college. In early January Bender vented his frustrations to Orie O. Miller, a member of the Board of Educations's executive committee and its financial agent. "I do not think the Board is aware of the amount of inefficiency here, and the amount of dissatisfaction it creates," Bender told Miller. One reason for the inefficiency is the "unwillingness of certain persons to learn to cooperate. We simply must have teamwork at a place like this."[4]

Bender did not say who those persons were, but Miller and several other members of the board met with some of the faculty and administrators to discuss the problems. Bender reported to Miller a week later that "Sanford [president Yoder] has had talks with all of us involved," and the talks had brought "a satisfactory understanding on the personal matters which stood between us." One outcome was the reorganization of the administrative committee: from now on it would include the president, the dean, the registrar, Guy F. Hershberger, and Harold Bender. The committee had been meeting only on a desultory basis, but now it met regularly and "does business," Bender informed Miller. "Our meetings have been very pleasant and profitable. Surely the Lord was in this place, and we knew it not."[5]

Just why Bender was added to the administrative committee is unclear. However, his appointment a month before Oyer's death meant that the Board of Education's executive committee recognized his abilities and perceived him as a campus leader.[6]

By 1931 Bender's career was beginning to take its mature form. His travels, his work with the Mennonite refugees, his historical-editorial work, his growing churchmanship: all pointed to an emerging career of significant proportions. He had more energy than did many of his colleagues and a more comprehensive understanding of most issues. Usually he framed those understandings in a compelling way. He was becoming a big fish in a small pool. But the qualities which impressed the board were not necessarily apparent to Bender's faculty colleagues. Many faculty did not consider him ideal for academic leadership.

Speculation about a successor to the well-regarded Oyer began almost immediately after his death. On March 13 Ernest Gehman, a teacher at Eastern Mennonite School, visited John Horsch at

Scottdale and suggested that J. L. Stauffer would like to see EMS dean Chester K. Lehman become dean of Goshen. John Horsch liked the idea. "It would go far to satisfy the conservatives," he told Bender, and urged that Bender broach the idea with his colleagues.[7]

Bender did not like the idea. It might be worth considering, but are you sure it would satisfy the "conservative critics of Goshen?" he inquired. After all, Bender argued, Lehman had "been under fire somewhat by Brunk and others at EMS." Nor did Bender favor India missionary Martin Clifford (M. C. or "Cliff") Lehman whose name had surfaced as a possible candidate. He was also opposed to another India missionary (and future Goshen president), Ernest E. Miller.[8]

In his hesitation to endorse any of the obvious candidates, Bender almost certainly saw himself as Oyer's logical successor. Later, after he was chosen, he claimed, "I did not want at all to have the work of the Dean of the college."[9] But given Harold's near-total commitment to Goshen and his impatience with what he considered lax administration on the part of president Yoder, it is hard to believe that he did not want the position.

As usual, Orie Miller played the key role. In March, Miller visited Goshen during a business trip to Chicago and talked with Bender about becoming dean. When Bender agreed, Miller passed the word to the Board of Education.[10] The Board concurred.

A surprised and dismayed faculty heard of the appointment from the board's chairman, bishop David (D. A.) Yoder. They had not been consulted. Registrar Silas Hertzler recorded in his diary that the announcement generated "extreme opposition. . . ." Several faculty members had expressed themselves to Hertzler, and "more came to Pres. Yoder and voiced their disapproval."[11] The next day Hertzler recorded that the "faculty and student body are still alive with opposition" but that Bender himself "was quite meek and submissive today."[12] The dissatisfaction clearly was strong enough to worry Yoder. Opposition was "quite general," the president advised Orie Miller. "Among some groups" it was "very intense." Yoder felt "very sorry for Bender," for "under the circumstances" he faced "a tremendous task to make things go."[13] Bender's main supporter on campus was business manager C. L.

Dean Harold S. Bender and President Sanford C. Yoder of Goshen College, 1938.
*Maple Leaf.*

Graber. But even Graber shared president Yoder's fear that faculty resistance would make Bender's task all but impossible.[14]

Bender's faculty colleagues found him pushy and impetuous. His high energy and ill-concealed impatience often irritated them. President Yoder had hoped to take a leave of absence during the 1931-32 academic year. But now Yoder changed his mind in light of, as he put it, "the faculty situation. Bender has by no means won his way yet. He tries hard to do what is best, but his judgment fails him at the time he needs it most."[15]

President Yoder had just had an illustration of Bender's "failed judgment." On the very day of his death, dean Oyer had received a letter from Lancaster bishop John Mosemann which Bender described as "shameful for self-righteousness and the evil language used."[16] Mosemann had gotten stirred up by some student behavior at a college Halloween social affair and had used the opportunity to attack the college. The letter, coming at such a traumatic time, caused quite a stir. Bender impetuously took it upon himself to answer Mosemann, and in doing so he set off a series of bitter exchanges during and following his appointment as dean. Despite Orie Miller's effort to get Bender to back down, the acrimony continued into late summer. Where the reputation of Goshen College was concerned, Bender could be tenacious, in this case unwisely.[17]

• • •

The year 1931 was not propitious for becoming dean of Goshen College. By then the Great Depression was taking its toll. On May 1, just two weeks after Bender's appointment, the college failed to meet its payroll. By the end of the summer, many of the faculty had received only half of their salaries. There was simply not enough money to meet expenses.[18] The budget for 1931-32 was equally dismal. Despite heroic efforts to slash expenses, including an effort to have every two-person department arrange for one person to be off-salary for one semester, administrators forecast a substantial deficit.[19]

On June 1, at the last faculty meeting of the 1930-31 academic year, dean Bender had more bad news: projected enrollment was drastically down. Only 13 sophomores planned to return, compared to 50 the previous year.[20] By the end of the summer, the situation was so bad that, to relieve the college of his own salary, president Yoder decided to go to Northwestern's Garrett Seminary to work on his master's degree. He did not relinquish his title, but for all practical purposes, Bender became acting president. In a further budget-balancing move, the faculty agreed to a 10 percent cut in their salaries for the year.[21]

The college crisis also created problems for the Bender family finances. By May 1932 Bender had received only about half of his salary for the year, and the family was out of money. Bender appealed to Orie Miller for a personal loan of $300, but Orie refused, citing a $1,500 note he held from the college which had not been paid. "These are surely times that try men's souls," he commented laconically. Neither his words nor attitude did much to ease the Benders' finances.[22] Miller also heard from president Yoder. On July 28 Yoder telegraphed: "We can't keep going beyond August 1; what course shall we take?"[23]

During the fall of the 1932-33 school year, none of the faculty received more than 50 percent of the scheduled monthly salary. Although there was also some drop in prices, the situation was excruciating. For the month of December, many received only $20 in pay. During the spring semester, everyone received a flat $31.50 a month. It was not enough to keep a family in food, Bender told Miller.[24]

In January 1933 the desperate financial situation came to a head. A faculty committee—Yoder, Bender, John Umble, Paul Bender, and C. P. Martin—prepared a two-page "Resolution to the Executive Committee of the Board of Education." They took it to the full faculty for endorsement before sending it on. The resolution, while almost cloyingly deferential, was actually a complaint against board inaction. The document proposed that the college make C. L. Graber its "financial executive and field representative." The faculty even offered to reduce their scheduled salaries to make Graber's employment possible. Convinced that the college could not depend on president Yoder for its financial leadership, Bender lobbied hard with Orie Miller for Graber's appointment. Miller resisted: his solution was to cut costs. Bender disagreed: his plan was to raise revenue and manage efficiently, and he believed C. L. Graber could do it. But even more than Bender, Graber was a risk-taker, and Miller rather distrusted him.[25] Nevertheless, the board accepted the faculty plan.[26]

If the appointment was a victory for Bender, it was also good for president Yoder. Some of the pressures of management now shifted to Graber, making him a focus for certain voices of the discontent. For Goshen College, it was a historic juncture. The trio of Yoder, Bender, and Graber worked together with remarkable success. Yoder's strengths were his pastoral and churchmanly qualities. Bender brought academic and intellectual abilities. Graber provided fiscal management and entrepreneurial skills. Moreover, the three got on quite well. In 1934 Graber reported to Orie Miller that there was "no civil war as yet between H. S. Bender, Sanford, and myself, altho we have some brass tacks talk once in a while, ha!"[27]

Graber was in fact Bender's personal financial adviser, a close friend, and one of his closest confidants. He was Harold's pastor, and since the Grabers' house was just across the yard from the Benders, they were next-door neighbors. Their children were playmates. Close friendship strengthened their professional relationship.

Graber shared Bender's aggressive take-charge style, so different from the diffident, humility-laden manner of president Yoder and his generation. To Orie Miller, Graber once remarked, "I have given quite a bit of thought to Goshen reorganization with Bender. Sanford is simply not in it on this stuff. He just says to Bender, 'You and Chris go ahead. I am with you.' This is a fine spirit but not very constructive."[28] Bender and Graber gave Goshen a definite advantage, and in the 1930s, it developed into a viable modern college, largely due to their leadership.

Bender's and Graber's task might have been even more difficult but for the pervasive influence of Orie Miller. As financial agent for the Board of Education, he was a constant "gray eminence" in college affairs. During the 1930s he made the college his central concern and was its largest single financial contributor; in 1933, struggling to keep the college afloat, he gave it nearly all of his rather considerable charitable contributions.[29]

Equally important was Miller's administrative role. Graber laid down a condition for his becoming the college's "financial executive." Because of his disdain for president Yoder's administrative ability, he demanded the creation of an administrative committee that Miller would chair. Graber hoped that Miller would eventually replace Yoder as president, an idea to which Miller apparently gave some thought. In a letter to Bender, Miller mused about how tempted he was to give up his business pursuits and give his life full-time to the work of the church. The prospect horrified Bender. No, he told Miller. The church needs Christian businessmen who are willing to use their resources on the church's behalf.[30]

From 1933 to 1935, Miller chaired the administrative committee; the other members were Yoder, Graber, and Bender. The

arrangement was remarkably successful. Graber and Bender operated the college, and Miller used his connections on the many
church boards to promote college interests. When he teamed his
prestige as a successful businessman with Graber's aggressive and
astute fundraising, the financial situation at Goshen began to improve. Equally important: since Miller was one step away from the
campus, he served as a voice of cautious reason for those some-
times-incautious managers Bender and Graber.

The lowest point of Goshen's finances, like that of the national economy, came in late 1932 and the spring of 1933. In 1931
Graber and his family had gone back to his native Iowa, where he
reorganized a depression-stricken bank. In the fall of 1932, they
returned to Goshen. With his arrival, and with the Roosevelt recovery taking hold, Goshen's finances began to rise slowly. Graber
and Miller laid out an aggressive fundraising plan, including a program to enroll several hundred "hundred-dollar-a-year men" who
would commit to an ongoing annual contribution to the college.[31]

Graber also began an aggressive plan to collect delinquent student accounts, and within a year he had collected nearly all of
them. He shrewdly dedicated all such monies to payment of overdue faculty salaries, a plan which helped raise faculty morale.
Graber discovered that many students would come to college if
they could get part-time work, so he began a shirt factory on campus to employ students. He also rented cows from neighboring
farmers and hired students to milk them, thus reducing costs at the
dining hall. He installed a diesel generator to reduce the college's
electric bill. And he raised student fees.[32]

By increasing revenue, containing costs, and increasing enrollment, Graber set the stage for Goshen's financial recovery. By summer 1936, Graber happily reported a $2,100 surplus for the bud-
get year. That fall Goshen enrolled 310 students, the most in its
history. Goshen College was still desperately poor, but it had
turned a financial corner.

The achievements of the Yoder-Graber-Bender team were reflected in comparative enrollments of Mennonite colleges between
1931 and 1944, the years of Bender's deanship. Table 1 offers the
data. By 1943-44, Goshen stood in first place.

Table 1. Mennonite College Enrollments[33]

| 1931-32 | | 1943-44 | |
|---|---|---|---|
| 1. Bluffton | 316 | 1. Goshen | 468 |
| 2. Bethel | 244 | 2. Bethel | 270 |
| 3. Goshen | 236 | 3. Bluffton | 141 |
| 4. Tabor | 45 | 4. Tabor | 137 |
| 5. EMS | 34 | 5. EMS | 86 |
| 6. Hesston | 20 | 6. Hesston | 45 |

• • •

Characteristically, Bender moved into his new role as dean without hesitation and wasted no time asserting leadership. In his second week, he edited the new *Goshen College Bulletin*, the annual college catalog. For the first time it listed the academic credentials of the faculty and staff. Gone was the effort at humility by a minimal display of credentials so evident in earlier editions. The editing and layout were also much sharper. The new catalog was clearly meant to impress its readers with the college's academic prowess. It looked like a typical American college catalog.

However, the *Bulletin* was also more intentionally religious. During the spring of 1931, Bender led the faculty to adopt a "Goshen College Statement of Fundamentals," a ten-point doctrinal statement which replaced a brief hundred-word affirmation of spiritual "Aims." For the first time in its history, Goshen College had a formal creed. When Daniel Kauffman in 1933 urged Bender to "make it clear that it [Goshen] is to be a Fundamentalist institution," Bender happily reminded the church leader of the new catalog statement.[34]

Bender's idea of what a college should be was heavily influenced by Princeton University. He had loved Princeton's academic, athletic, and musical traditions. But it was hardly possible to make Goshen over in the image of Princeton. So Bender took a different tack and, perhaps unconsciously, harked back to the "old" Goshen traditions. In 1933 he wrote "A Program for Goshen College," which offered some indication of his ideals for the school. In a section on "Objectives," he argued that the college should be "a liberal arts college offering a liberal cultural education," to which all professional education should be subordinated.[35]

The "Program" was partially affected by a visit Bender had made only a few weeks earlier to Calvin College, a Christian Reformed Church college in Grand Rapids, Michigan. He was impressed by how singularly Calvin College focused on service to the Reformed church, especially by preparing pastors for its congregations and teachers for its parochial schools.[36] Bender described Goshen's first task as service to the Mennonite church, conceived, as he put it, not in a "narrow and limited service," but to prepare and train workers "who can participate sympathetically and efficiently in all the activities of the church."[37]

In 1933 Bender envisaged Goshen College as a modern liberal arts college serving the Mennonite church. By 1944, when he left the college deanship, he and his colleagues had largely accomplished that goal. While many persons contributed to the outcome, Bender's leadership was key. His willingness to try new ideas, his urge to be contemporary, and his intuitive feel for the liberal arts—these all helped to move the process along.

During the 1930s Bender led Goshen in four specific areas of modernization. One area was basic curricular reform: changing the grading system, developing a general-education program, designing a divisional structure, and creating a Bible department. The second area was faculty recruitment and credentialing. The third project was the building of a new library. The fourth area was accreditation by the North Central Association of Colleges and Schools.

• • •

Bender pushed curricular change in the weekly faculty meetings. While it was normal for the president to chair the meetings, Yoder traveled continually and was seldom present. In Yoder's absence, Bender presided. He usually opened the meeting with silent prayer and closed it with an audible "petition," as faculty secretary J. C. Wenger once put it. Moreover, as dean, Bender assumed the chair of the course of study committee, which managed the curriculum and all academic matters. Already in 1926 Bender had called for honors courses to stimulate student scholarship. In the fall of 1931, he returned to the honors idea and persuaded the committee to publish a "Student Scholarship List" at the end of each semester. In the fall of 1932, the faculty adopted the proposal.[38]

Publishing such a list required a numerical system of quality points. In 1921 the college had adopted a quality-point system, but Noah Oyer had opposed the idea when he became dean in 1924, so the system never took effect. In the fall of 1934, Bender made the quality-point system operational.[39]

Actually, modernizing the curriculum had begun before Bender became dean. Beginning in 1927, each student had to declare a major and earn forty-eight upper-level hours of credit for graduation. By 1935 all B.A. and Th.B. students had to take at least four semesters of language. The next year the faculty adopted a new general-education curriculum for the freshman year.[40]

A faddish but significant recasting of the curriculum came out of a proposal Bender wrote in 1937: "The Integration of the Curriculum into Unities Higher Than Departments." He was influenced by the widely shared assumption that American colleges should teach general liberal arts rather than specialized subjects. Bender proposed a new five-division system of "Language, Literature, and Fine Arts"; "The Social Sciences"; "The Natural Sciences"; "Bible and Philosophy"; and "Teacher Education."[41] Prior to this, Goshen had always been structured as a college of liberal arts, with the second division being the Bible School. Now the Bible School became a part of the division of Bible and philosophy, with Bender as division chair.

With the new organization came a new general-education requirement in Bible. Now, to graduate, every student had to take eight hours of Bible (reduced to six in 1940). In addition, all Mennonites had to take the "Mennonite History and Principles" course. All freshmen took "Introduction to Christianity," a course Bender redesigned in 1939 with the help of J. C. Wenger and Paul Mininger.[42] For five years Bender taught the Christianity course nearly every semester. Most students also took a course in New Testament, and many elected a course in systematic theology. The expansion of the Bible curriculum began in 1931 when eleven courses were offered. By 1936 there were thirty-three Bible courses (not including other religion courses), and the number of students taking Bible courses had jumped from sixty-five in 1931 to one-hundred thirty in 1936.[43]

In 1938 all of these changes were embodied in a new, larger, and more-attractive catalog. The catalog also featured a growing and changing faculty. The big change was in academic degrees and in the new people who came to the faculty in those years. In 1931 only Silas Hertzler in education and Glen Miller in science had Ph.D. degrees. Within a year, Hesston's financial problems gave Goshen the gift of two more persons with Ph.D. degrees: Edward Yoder, a Latin classicist, and Paul Bender in Natural Science. By 1944, eleven faculty members had Ph.D. degrees, including Bender. Bender worked assiduously at what would later be called "faculty development," especially by encouraging doctorates.

•  •  •

Recruiting faculty for Goshen College had special problems in the 1930s. In 1938 Bender and president Yoder were trying to lure Samuel (S. A.) Yoder, a Mennonite and Goshen alumnus who was teaching English at Wheaton College. The problem was that S. A. Yoder insisted he would come only if he was guaranteed, as president Yoder put it, "that he would always get his salary." We really dare not promise him that, the president told Bender.[44]

Bender's approach to S. A. Yoder was to appeal to his altruism. "Goshen cannot compete with other colleges in salary and does not expect to," he told the Wheaton professor. "Those who teach at Goshen must be willing to forgo certain material advantages for the sake of the cause. You are not the first one nor will you be the last one of our number to be faced with the temptation to follow the larger financial inducement."[45]

Bender cited science professor Glen Miller as an example. Miller had been offered $3,000 a year elsewhere but had accepted Goshen's $1,500. "Goshen College would not exist without that spirit," Bender told Yoder. "If you come to Goshen College, you

The faculty of Goshen College in 1935. Harold Bender, Sanford C. Yoder, and C. L. Graber are in the center of the front row. Elizabeth Horsch Bender is the fourth person from the left in the third row.
Sanford Calvin Yoder papers, AMC.

will not be able to have financial security. You will rather find yourself in the fellowship of [those who] press on in faith and trust that God's provision through the church will be adequate." S. A. Yoder decided to come to Goshen.[46]

Sometimes Bender's recruiting failed. In 1934 he needed a theology professor to replace Gustav Enss, who had resigned. Bender was convinced that the only person with the stature and training Goshen required was dean C. K. Lehman of EMS. Lehman was the sole amillennialist at EMS and sometimes felt oppressed by the ardent premillennialism espoused at the school. When approached, Lehman expressed interest in the idea, but his colleagues at EMS urged him not to make the move. Undaunted, Bender enlisted John Horsch to woo Lehman on behalf of Goshen. Horsch, also an amillennialist, admired Lehman and was delighted to help. He reported to Bender that Lehman would consider the offer if S. C. Yoder, Bender, Daniel Kauffman, and Orie Miller went to EMS and met with president Wenger and bishops George Brunk and

Noah Mack. The purpose would be to discuss how Goshen might become more strictly conservative so that EMS students might again be able to finish their educations at Goshen.[47]

Bender saw the plan for what it was: a power play to protect Lehman's reputation as a conservative, and a way for conservatives to exert influence on Goshen College. No, Bender bluntly told Horsch. "We would not consider having anyone of our faculty dictated to by outside forces, especially of men of the type of Wenger and Brunk."[48]

So Lehman refused. Bender was quite disappointed. Nor was he amused by a jocular suggestion from C. L. Graber. "Let's ordain Bender," Graber chuckled to Orie Miller, "make someone else Dean, and appoint him [Bender] to teach Bible and theology!"[49]

Bender worked hard to find faculty with academic credentials who could pass the scrutiny of conservative critics. He once explained his method to Daniel Kauffman: "It is not possible to pick faculty like one picks pressmen or office-clerks, particularly when it comes to filling places in a Mennonite church school. We have to get men ready."[50] As dean he worked hard to "get men [and a few women] ready." Two notable cases were those of John C. Wenger and Carl Kreider.

Wenger graduated from Goshen in 1934. He had planned to study medicine, but at Bender's suggestion, he decided instead on theology. Bender hoped to prepare Wenger to return to teach Bible and philosophy. Over a four-year period, Bender mentored Wenger through his theological education, always careful to see that Wenger's credentials would be orthodox. No longer certain about the orthodoxy of Princeton Seminary, he sent Wenger to a Fundamentalist institution, Westminster Seminary in Philadelphia.

While studying at Westminster, Wenger established himself as Bender's protégé by writing a history of the Franconia Mennonite Conference. It was an exhaustive work of more than five hundred pages, a remarkable achievement for a young scholar. Bender was delighted with it. "Nothing equal has yet been done in our Mennonite historiography," he told Wenger. "You deserve a doctor's degree for it."[51]

However, Bender had more ambitious goals for young Wenger

than a degree from Westminster. In the fall of 1936, Bender suggested that the young scholar should seek a doctorate at the University of Zurich. There he could study under Bender's friend Fritz Blanke, the Reformation scholar. Blanke had been much influenced by John Horsch's book on nonresistance. As Bender told Wenger, Blanke was "spiritually very near to Mennonites."[52]

Wenger was eager to comply, but a week after he got Bender's suggestion, he found himself in the "lot" for possible ordination for the Mennonite congregation at Norristown, Pennsylvania. Furthermore, having said yes to being in the "lot," Wenger found that he could remain in the "lot" only if he stopped attending Westminster. The Franconia Conference leadership was opposed to seminary training for ministers. Wenger protested, but the bishops were adamant. "These men are made of stern stuff," Wenger told Bender. "What shall I do?"[53]

The query put Bender in a quandary. If he told Wenger to continue at the seminary, Goshen College would be attacked for meddling in local church affairs. If Wenger dropped out of seminary, he would not be able to come to Goshen later as a teacher. Bender's surprising advice was to be clever: Don't promise *never* to go to school. Agree to drop out of seminary for now. And, he told Wenger, don't ever show this letter to anyone.[54] As it turned out, the matter was moot: the lot did not "fall" on Wenger. He had been saved for Goshen College.

Bender had urged Wenger to begin his studies at Zurich in April of 1937. Then Wenger announced that he was going to be married and hoped to take his new wife, Ruth Detweiler, to Zurich with him. Bender was annoyed. But he decided to make the best of what he considered a bad situation. He urged Wenger to leave his bride behind and have her join him later in the year. Wenger was so thoroughly under Bender's spell that he agreed, despite the pain of leaving Ruth only a week after their wedding.[55] Equally stressful for the cautious and fearful Wenger was the fact that frequent letters to Blanke had never been answered.[56] Bender was sending Wenger to Zurich with absolutely no confirmation that he would be able to study there.

Nevertheless, it all worked out. Blanke became Wenger's doctoral adviser, and Ruth Wenger joined her husband later in the spring. J. C. Wenger was even able to spend the spring semester at the University of Basel, studying with the renowned theologian Karl Barth. Best of all, Blanke accepted the Franconia history as Wenger's doctoral dissertation, totally on the advice of Harold Bender. Actually, Blanke asked Bender to write a critique of Wenger's "history," which Bender did.[57] Blanke used the Bender critique to convince his faculty colleagues that Wenger's Franconia history was a worthy doctoral dissertation.[58]

John and Ruth Wenger returned from Europe in the summer of 1939, just a few months before the German invasion of Poland. In late August they arrived in Goshen to begin lifelong service on the faculty of Goshen College. Harold's four-year tutelage had paid off. He had his professor of Bible and philosophy.

Economics professor Carl Kreider joined the faculty in the fall of 1941. Kreider, from the Bethel Mennonite congregation near Wadsworth, Ohio, had graduated from Goshen in 1936. An outstanding student, he had excelled in every area of academic and college life. During the summer after his graduation, he worked as an accountant in a B. F. Goodrich office in Cleveland, Ohio. He was earning money to pay his way through his first year of graduate study at Princeton University, where he hoped to study economics.[59]

Suddenly, with no warning, the Bethel congregation elected Kreider to be their pastor. To everyone's surprise, Kreider declined. When word reached Bender at Goshen, he immediately rushed off a letter urging Kreider to reconsider. "Almost the only way for a man to come into a position of larger influence and leadership in our church is through the ministry," he told Kreider.[60] But Kreider, a decisive man, was not moved. He believed he had scholarly ability, and he wanted to teach at a Christian college. Kreider felt no call to preach.

That fall at Princeton, Kreider received another letter from Bender. E. Raymond Wilson, one of the secretaries at the American Friends Service Committee, had just told Bender that the AFSC had an annual scholarship which supported graduate study abroad. Bender believed that Kreider's record combined with his interest in the study of economics from a Christian viewpoint would make him a strong candidate for the award. Bender suggested that Kreider apply, and indicate the London School of Economics as his choice for study. Bender also wrote a letter to Clarence Pickett, executive secretary of the AFSC, urging Pickett's help. He pointed out the wonderful opportunity a scholarship for Kreider might offer for Friends-Mennonite cooperation.[61] To Kreider and Bender's immense delight, Kreider won the award. So during 1938-39, Bender had two protégés in study abroad: Carl Kreider in London, and John C. Wenger in Basel and Zurich.

Kreider's year abroad was highly successful. Upon his return it led, again with Bender's help, to a Brookings Institution fellowship. Sometime in early 1939, Bender startled Kreider by implying that he was being considered for the faculty at Goshen. In one of the many administrative glitches which frustrated Bender, president Yoder had failed to get out a letter officially inviting Kreider.[62] So he was surprised.

Kreider completed his Ph.D., and in the summer of 1941, he and his wife, Evelyn Burkholder Kreider, moved to Goshen. The courtship and recruitment of Wenger and Kreider for Goshen College was remarkable not only for the skill with which Bender arranged their progress through graduate school but also for his ability to identify talent. Others were recruited during those years: Paul Mininger, S. A. Yoder, Lois Winey, Olive Wyse, Roman Gingerich, H. Clair Amstutz, Mary Royer, Viola Good, Paul Erb, Walter E. Yoder, Levi Hartzler, Ernest Miller, Lois Gunden. They came with stories not unlike those of Wenger and Kreider.[63]

Several considerations were paramount in Bender's mind as he recruited Wenger and Kreider. He had specific ideas about what he was preparing them for, in Wenger's case to teach Bible and philosophy in the new division with that name. Bender was also concerned that the two men's education be acceptable to conservative critics. This was badly needed in Wenger's teaching area. None of the several Bible teachers of the 1930s had quite satisfied conservatives. Bender was determined that Wenger would qualify.

In Kreider's case, orthodoxy meant something a bit different. While Bender sold the overseas fellowship for Kreider to the

Quakers with an ecumenical argument, he actually feared that the ecumenism might backfire. In the letter announcing Kreider's appointment, the Friends expressed hope that the award might indeed help strengthen ties between themselves and Mennonites.[64] Bender knew that in the hands of Mennonite conservatives, such a statement could devastate Kreider's future service. So Bender tried to keep the announcement private and gently lectured Kreider against falling in with Quaker ideals. "Friends are for the most part very liberal in their theology with an excessive emphasis on the social aspect of Christianity," he observed. "I hope that nothing in your experience as a result of this opportunity" would cause any shift from Mennonitism toward the Friends' position.[65]

• • •

Harold Bender's ten-year dream had come true. Behind him rose the brick Georgian facade on the new Memorial Library. In front of him stretched a large crowd of faculty, students, and alumni. It was a warm Saturday afternoon during commencement week at Goshen College, in June of 1940. Bender had just been introduced by his friend Orie Miller, who was chairing the dedication ceremonies for the new "Memorial Library" building. The dean was making the dedicatory address. He entitled his remarks "The Use of the Small College Library."

The new library was beautiful: a visitor called it "a little jewel."[66] Surely it was a great improvement over the boxlike architecture of other campus buildings. Bender had set his sights on a new library building soon after he became dean in 1931, but not until 1936 did the college's financial situation allow him even to imagine its construction. During that year, he visited libraries and consulted with architects and librarians. By 1937 a South Bend architect had drawn up a floor plan which provided for housing 50,000 books and for seating 150 students in a large, well-appointed reading room.[67] The entire ground floor was designed to be an archives and to serve the burgeoning Mennonite history collection, "destined," as Bender immodestly put it in the fund-raising brochure, "to become the greatest library of its kind in America if not in the world."[68]

A groundbreaking ceremony on September 13, 1939, signaled that the funding goal was reached. Construction took one year. The new library building was an enormously important addition to the campus. It set the stage for Bender's greatest achievement as dean: the accreditation of Goshen College by the North Central Association of Colleges and Schools (NCA).

• • •

In early May 1934, Bender attended the NCA's annual meeting in Chicago. He was there to learn what Goshen College would need if it were to become an accredited liberal arts college. The advantages of accreditation were obvious: graduate schools and other institutions would accept the college's academic transcripts at face value, and the college itself would become a bona fide member of the higher education community.

Those same considerations led many Mennonite leaders, determined to preserve Mennonite nonconformity to the world, to be chary of accreditation. In 1938 Bender circulated a questionnaire among church leaders to assess how they felt about Goshen's performance as a church school. His purpose, he wrote, was to bring the college "more completely in line with the more conservative standards of the Church." But *Gospel Herald* editor Daniel Kauffman made the questionnaire an occasion to critique the drive for accreditation. "I have never been enthusiastic about the idea of Goshen College going into the North Central College Association," the powerful church leader wrote to Bender privately. "The hook-up between our schools and other schools—that is, the atmosphere common to all—makes the fight for separation hard enough as it is, to say nothing about membership in an association that draws us still closer and comes dangerously near being a violation of the Scriptural admonition 'Be ye not unequally yoked together with unbelievers.' "[69] But even Kauffman's opposition did not deter Bender.

The greatest barrier to accreditation of Goshen College had always been financial: Goshen simply could not meet the NCA's minimum financial-endowment standards. But the Great Depression changed all that. In the 1930s many small colleges found themselves in financial difficulty. So in 1934 the NCA announced that it was drastically lowering endowment requirements. Bender immediately saw the implications for Goshen. Suddenly what had seemed insurmountable might be possible. He rushed back to his campus, called a special faculty meeting, and—as faculty member Edward Yoder observed—"spoke enthusiastically and optimistically of the possibilities of Goshen College making successful application to the Association."[70] Even the cautious Edward Yoder thought it might be done, although he calculated it would take more than the three years Bender optimistically predicted.

Yoder was right. Not until February 1940 was Bender able to hand-carry the accreditation documents to the secretary of the NCA. Later that year, in December, the applications for membership were filed. With surprising speed, the NCA announced an inspection-team visit to the college in February 1941.

Ernest E. Miller, by then the college's president, jokingly ordered all administrators to send their suits out to the cleaners in preparation for the NCA team's visit. To students' delight, dean Bender announced he was not sending his: he was buying a new one, an "NCA suit."[71] When the team completed its inspection in February, Bender was optimistic. "The visit has been quite satisfactory," he reported to Orie Miller. A guess might be hazardous, but Bender thought that the "long road we started to travel on seven years ago" was about to have "a happy ending."[72] Bender's hunch was correct: the college was accredited. Word of the accreditation arrived, and the campus erupted with excitement. A student parade through downtown Goshen ended on campus with a huge celebratory bonfire.[73] For Bender, the celebration marked the near completion of another cycle in his life. The date was March 27, 1941.

Bender had been dean of Goshen College almost exactly ten years. In that decade, the deanship had been the consuming center of his life. Yet other matters also engaged his attention.

## ❧ 11 ☙

# Th.D. Finished; Travels

*Bender completes his Th.D. degree at Heidelberg,*
*attends Mennonite World Conference, visits*
*Mennonites in Brazil and Paraguay.*

WHEN HAROLD BENDER began his graduate education in 1921, he could not have imagined how long it would take to earn his doctoral degree. Ten years later, in 1930, after his semester at Heidelberg, he was sure he would have it completed within a year. But then he became dean of Goshen College. Under normal circumstances, he might have bargained for a leave to complete his degree before starting as dean. But the extraordinary financial problems at the college and his own straitened family finances made that impossible.[1]

With the decision in 1934 to work for NCA accreditation, the need for more faculty with doctoral degrees became acute. Certainly the dean had to have the degree if Goshen's efforts were to have any credibility. Thus Bender made plans to study at Heidelberg during the spring and summer of 1935. In characteristic overoptimism, he hoped to take courses, write his dissertation, and pass his doctoral examination in one six-month spasm of effort.

Elizabeth's cousin Christian Landes wanted to buy a new car and offered to buy a Ford if Bender brought one from the United States. With that encouragement, Bender decided to trade his four-year-old Chevrolet on a new V-8 Ford coupe. They would use the car in Europe and then sell it to cousin Christian.[2]

For Americans to live in Germany in 1935 was amazingly cheap. The Benders would be able to cover their expenses with

$1,000 Bender drew from the college as back pay. Finances would be tight but possible.[3]

On March 22, 1935, the family left Goshen. After stopping for two nights with the Horsch grandparents at Scottdale, they reached Heidelberg on April 6, a week after classes had begun at the university. Cousins Walter and Helene Landes helped them find a place five miles up the Neckar River, a house with a fine garden and lawn and a wonderful view of mountains. They even had a maid, and a washerwoman came in several times a week to do laundry and clean. Settling in, they hired young Trudy Klassen, one of the Landes cousins, as a nanny for the girls. Both Elizabeth and Harold began taking classes at the university.[4]

Elizabeth took nine hours of lectures and a special course for foreigners, all in philology and German literature. Harold overloaded himself with six courses and twenty lecture hours a week.[5] He profited little from his lecture courses: he took them merely to meet the residence requirement. At his first conference with Köhler, he learned that if he was to have any chance of taking his oral examination early enough to return home in the fall, he would have to present his dissertation entirely finished by August 1.[6] He had just fourteen weeks to write the thesis, in addition to passing the lecture courses. But there was more bad news: the Hitler regime had decreed that all dissertations written at German universities had to be done in German. Bender's ability to write in German was adequate for correspondence, but hardly for a dissertation. Undaunted, Bender launched an aggressive campaign to get the thesis done. During April, May, and June, he attended lectures sporadically—just enough to be able to pass the end-of-semester exams. Even then, by late June he realized he was not moving fast enough on the dissertation to get it finished by August 1.

So on the first of July, Harold and Elizabeth gave up the beautiful house on the Neckar River and rented two rooms near the university. To their great delight, mother Elsie Bender, urged on by son Wilbur (who paid her way), had decided to come to Germany for the summer. She arrived in early June, and she and the children moved to nearby Willenbach to be with Walter and Helene Landes. Bender stopped attending classes, and for four weeks he and

Harold and Elizabeth at the Hof Willenbach near Heidelberg, Germany, in 1935. From the left: Elizabeth with Nancy, Harold, Mary Eleanor, Trudy Klassen, Cornelius Krahn, Elsie Bender, unidentified person, Helene Landes with her son, Walter Landes, unidentified person. Bender Family Album.

Elizabeth worked feverishly on the thesis, scarcely stopping to eat and sleep. As Harold hand-wrote the original text in English, Elizabeth translated, typed, edited, and polished it into satisfactory German.[7]

Bender entitled the thesis "Conrad Grebel, der erste Führer der Schweizer Täufer" (Conrad Grebel, the first leader of the Swiss Brethren). On August 1, with some elation, he delivered the nearly five-hundred page tome to the office of the dean of the theological faculty. With it he delivered a payment of 240 marks and a promise to publish at least thirty-two pages in a scholarly journal within a year. He also had to deliver twenty copies of the work to the theological faculty.[8]

Professor Köhler was impressed. He thought the dissertation was "a splendid work, unusually well researched." In fact, he told Bender, it was so good it could be published without any changes. Bender hoped Köhler's high regard for the work would be helpful during his oral examination.[9]

There was one pressing question: Could Köhler arrange the oral examination in time for Bender to return for the fall semester at Goshen? August-September was sacred vacation time for German university professors. But to Bender's delight, professor Köhler was able to persuade the other three professors on his committee to hold the *Examen* on September 21.

With the date settled, the family and mother Bender took a three-week vacation. During a week in Switzerland, Harold and Elizabeth were able to visit rural Mennonite areas for the first time, thanks to their Ford car. They also spent a day with "old Goshen" friend Ben (O. B.) Gerig and his family at Geneva, where Gerig worked for the League of Nations. From Geneva they drove north over the high Alpine passes via Interlaken and Lucerne and through Bavaria, to visit Uncle Michael Horsch at Ingolstadt.[10]

The Benders spent the following two weeks with the Horsch and Funck relatives in Bavaria and Württemburg—including a wedding of two Landes-Funck cousins of Elizabeth. The relatives used the occasion to celebrate Bender's thirty-ninth birthday, which had come and gone practically unnoticed during that frenetic month of July when the thesis was being written. One of the relatives wrote a droll sixteen-verse poem about Bender which the whole assembly sang boisterously to the tune of "Dort unten der Mühle" (Down below the mill).[11]

Elsie Bender was warmly welcomed by the Horsch relatives and enjoyed the visit immensely. Eight-year-old Mary Eleanor began a lifelong fascination with the German language. Bender proudly reported to the Horsch grandparents that "Mary Eleanor speaks the dialect German very well." She had lots of opportunity to learn German: her playmates during much of the summer were the five Landes children, ages three to eleven. During the summer baby Nancy learned to walk, acquired twelve teeth, and began to say a few words. The relatives doted on the girls.[12]

On August 24 the family left the Landes *Hof* (farm) at Lautenbach in the Ford, accompanied by a young cousin, Elizabeth Binkele, who was going to study at Goshen College. By noon on August 26, the women and children were on board ship in Antwerp, ready for the trip home to America. Harold had to stay behind to complete his oral exam in September.[13]

Bender traveled back to Heidelberg by way of the Netherlands, where he spent several days with Dr. J. ter Meulen and T. O. Hylkema at the annual conference of the Dutch Mennonite Peace Group. Bender was much impressed by what he saw and heard. Dutch Mennonites are becoming more theologically conservative, he told John Horsch. He was especially pleased to find that his good friend Hylkema, the most conservative pastor in the Netherlands, had been appointed pastor at the Singel church, a large and historic congregation in Amsterdam.[14]

While in the Netherlands Bender also scouted for books, finding some rare Menno Simons editions—which he did not buy, however, because he lacked the money. Actually, he had quite a lot of money in his pocket, but the money was already committed to buy a car in Goshen. His cousin had decided not to buy the V-8 Ford, so he had sold it in Amsterdam. He received less for it than he had hoped, yet he later told his brother Wilbur that overall it had been a bargain, because it had given the family mobility that they could not otherwise have had.[15]

When Harold and Elizabeth first arrived in Heidelberg in the spring, they had been surprised to find that a young Russian Mennonite was also completing work in Anabaptist history under professor Köhler. His name was Cornelius Krahn, and during June he finished a thesis on Menno Simons. Köhler was bemused to find himself supervising two Mennonites writing about two leading founders of what became the Mennonite wing of Anabaptism.[16] Bender and Krahn struck up a warm friendship, and Bender immediately offered to publish Krahn's thesis as a Studies in Anabaptist and Mennonite History volume.[17] He rushed a copy to father Horsch, hoping somewhat naively that Horsch would endorse the work. Horsch would not. The work was "offensively superficial, to say the least," the older man informed Bender.[18]

Bender had set himself up for embarrassment: he could not possibly publish the book against Horsch's opposition. But he was also unprepared for Krahn's displeasure at the rejection. It was not an auspicious beginning for what would be a quarter-century of shared, albeit sometimes contentious, historical work. Fortunately, in this case Bender was able to offer Krahn an olive branch: he would publish an article out of Krahn's thesis in the 400th anniversary issue of the *MQR* commemorating Menno Simons' conversion to Anabaptism in 1536. This helped Krahn meet his need to publish something out of his thesis to complete his doctoral work at Heidelberg University.[19]

Unlike his opinion of Krahn's work on Menno Simons, Horsch was almost effusive in his praise of Bender's work on Conrad Grebel, declaring that "nothing that has appeared before can be compared with it as to thoroughness and reliability. It is very good."[20] While some of Horsch's praise can be discounted as loyalty from an admiring father-in-law, he was actually correct. Bender's dissertation was quite thorough and reliable.

It was not perfect. The dissertation lacked breadth and style. Even after more than ten years of research on Conrad Grebel, the outcome was hostage in some degree to Bender's work habits. Instead of steady careful research, his work had been spasmodic. He had done a good bit of it in 1925, some more in 1930, and then rushed to complete it in a few months in 1935. He had gone to great lengths to establish the chronology, dates, and details of Grebel's life, all necessary work which had never been done before. But he worked with a kind of tunnel vision, focusing too much on the theological track of the story, and failing to place Grebel in the larger Anabaptist-Reformation picture.[21]

Perhaps Bender's graduate education was partly at fault. In his four-and-a-half years of graduate study, he had taken only five courses in church history. At Tübingen he had taken no courses in church history because he intended to become an Old Testament scholar. He took two church history courses at Heidelberg under Köhler, but only one on the Reformation, and in that 1930 course, he lacked the time to pay more than superficial attention to the course content. His only original research was on Grebel. He had never done much serious Reformation study beyond that of the Swiss Brethren. Thus he lacked strong academic grounding in his primary scholarly field. Had he ranged more deeply and widely in Reformation history, he might have set the life and work of Conrad Grebel in a broader context.

Bender also came to his Grebel work with a particular point of view, illustrated by the effect of his careful reading of a book recommended by professor Fritz Blanke at the University of Zurich. That book, published in 1931 by Dr. Annemarie Lohmann, was *Zur geistigen Entwicklung Thomas Müntzers* (On the spiritual development of Thomas Müntzer). Lohmann argued that before late summer 1524, Thomas Müntzer was a peaceful nonrevolutionary Anabaptist.[22] As a result of reading the book and talking with Blanke, Bender decided to deal with the Grebel-Müntzer relationship in two ways: First, he would deny any personal acquaintance between Grebel and Müntzer; and second, he would show that the Müntzer whom Grebel had known through Müntzer's writings was not a revolutionary but, as he put it, "rather a fairly decent sort of Lutheran preacher." Thus Grebel, as the "best sort of Anabaptist," would not be tarnished by his connections with Müntzer. Such was Bender's strategy, as he explained it to John Horsch, a strategy the latter heartily endorsed.[23]

In May 1935 Bender had cut his classes at Heidelberg and made a hurried three-day trip to Zurich, where he had met professor Fritz Blanke for the first time. It was a fateful meeting for both men, for they instantly recognized each other as kindred spirits. Blanke had been appointed to the church history chair at Zurich when Professor Köhler had gone to Heidelberg in 1929. The 35-year-old Blanke had been a follower of the communitarian Eberhard Arnold during his early student days, but two other men had influenced him profoundly. One was Karl Holl, a Luther scholar who was his teacher at the University of Berlin, where Blanke did his doctorate. Holl had led Blanke back into Lutheranism. The other man was John Horsch. As a result of reading Horsch's 1920 book, *Die biblische Lehre der Wehrlosigkeit* (The biblical teaching on nonresistance), Blanke had become *wehrlosig* (nonresistant).[24]

Bender found Blanke to have the "genuine spiritual *Biblicismus* which the *Täufer* (Anabaptists) represent." He has an *innerlich* (inner) understanding and feeling for the Anabaptists which few people have, Bender told Horsch. "Blanke is going into *Täufer* history rather strongly, and I think he will be the coming man for us in this field in Europe."[25]

However, Bender's regard for Blanke was not just as a kindred spirit and a fellow historian. During their conversation in May 1935, Blanke offered Bender information which if true would greatly increase Grebel's stature as a Swiss Brethren leader. At that moment Blanke was writing the critical notes on one of Ulrich Zwingli's important pamphlets, the *Elenchus*, which attacked the Anabaptists. The notes were to be published in *Zwingli Werke*, a comprehensive series on all of Zwingli's works. During the days Bender was visiting him, Blanke had just come to the conclusion that the document which Zwingli quoted and refuted point-by-point, by an unnamed Anabaptist, was by none other than Conrad Grebel. Blanke's conclusion was based on internal evidence and deduction, and therefore not conclusive; but Bender wanted to be convinced, and he was. When he got back to Heidelberg, he inserted Blanke's argument into his dissertation.[26]

When Professor Köhler read Bender's dissertation, Köhler remembered that Basel Reformation leader Heinrich Bullinger had identified the author of the pamphlet cited by Zwingli in the *Elenchus* as Conrad Grebel. Bender's too-eager embrace of circumstantial evidence had been vindicated. His esteem for Blanke was complete.[27]

Walther Köhler, Bender's dissertation professor at Heidelberg University. Bender Family Album.

Bender returned from Amsterdam to Heidelberg in early September and began preparing for the oral examination, scheduled for the twenty-first of the month. While he was gone, a letter had arrived from Ernst Correll, offering some tips on what to expect. They are sure to question you on the Erasmus-Grebel connection, Correll warned. And be ready for questions about the Erasmus-Bucer relationship as it affected the English Reformation. They will also surely want to have you talk about American church history, so be sure to review American Lutheran history: your professors are all Lutheran. But do not be too concerned, Correll assured him, for you will do quite well. Bender too was sure he would pass, but he did not expect to pass with any distinction.[28]

He was wrong. Bender's oral examiners were very impressed by his knowledge of biblical theology, a product of his extensive biblical studies during his graduate work. The cable to Elizabeth on the evening after the examination announced that he was now a "Doctor theologiae Heidelbergensis, summa cum laude!" It was extraordinary, Ernst Correll told Elizabeth, for such a high honor to be conferred upon a "foreigner."[29] Father Horsch was also impressed, congratulating Bender on "making your doctor, cum magna laude."[30] From Christian Neff at Weierhof came a fatherly exclamation of satisfaction with Bender's achievement. "*Ich freue mich besonders über deine Arbeit*" (I am very pleased with your work), Neff wrote. He had just read the dissertation and found it outstanding. "There are things in it no one has ever known before," he told Bender. "You have pushed our knowledge of our history forward a huge step. *Vivant sequentes!*" (let the sequels have life).[31]

The oral examination had taken place on a Saturday morning. Right after lunch Bender caught a plane out of Mannheim for Amsterdam, to worship at Hylkema's Singel "*kerk*" the next morning. On Monday he went by train to Antwerp and boarded the SS *Ilsenstein* for home. The *Ilsenstein* was a slow boat, and due to stormy weather, the normal ten-day trip became eleven. Bender usually reveled in the Atlantic crossing, but this time he could hardly wait to get off the ship. He was homesick for Elizabeth and the girls.[32]

• • •

One of the pleasant journeys the Ford car made possible during the Benders' 1935 sojourn in Germany was a trip to Holland in May 1935. Accompanying Harold and Elizabeth were Christian and Lydia Neff. The 74-year-old Christian Neff had been the organizer of the first two Mennonite World Conferences in 1925 and 1930. Now in May 1935, he and Bender traveled to Holland to meet with several Dutch leaders. Their purpose was to begin planning a third conference, scheduled to meet in the Netherlands in 1936, in celebration of the 400th anniversary of Menno Simons' conversion to Anabaptism.[33]

Bender's involvement was purely coincidental and personal. True, by 1935 he was the best-known American Mennonite in Europe. Much more than just a visiting graduate student, he was the dean of Goshen College and assistant secretary of Mennonite Central Committee (MCC); so he was an American Mennonite leader. But he was also a member of a branch of Mennonites who vigorously opposed ecumenical connections with European Mennonites. Hence, his unofficial role may have been accidental, but in fact no MC Mennonite could have taken an official role in such an undertaking. So Bender represented no one. He just happened to be at Heidelberg, near Neff's home at Weierhof, and so Neff invited the young man to attend the meeting in Holland. Bender, in possession of an automobile, offered to take the Neffs to the meeting.

However unofficial, Bender entered into the planning with his usual gusto and quickly put his stamp on the proceedings. He was quite conscious of American MC Mennonite opposition to a Mennonite World Conference, so he pushed hard to have the gathering be neither "official" nor "representative." Thus the conference invitation would come from the Dutch Mennonites, but no Mennonite group would be invited to participate in any official capacity. In fact, the committee would assign speakers to the program on the basis of the most appropriate person for a given topic. Shunning theological traps, the conference would educate participants about each other with sessions on Mennonites in Canada, Mennonites in Germany, etc. Some sessions would be devoted to relief work, missions, and youth. And some would deal with history, especially of the Dutch Mennonites and Menno Simons.[34]

The conference-planning experience was good for Bender. It was his first involvement on an international committee and the first time he interacted with Dutch Mennonite leaders on a task. They impressed him. Thereafter he found it more difficult to blithely use the stereotypes which American Mennonites, particularly John Horsch, were so prone to make about their Dutch coreligionists. He was especially aware that precisely when German Mennonites were being drawn into the Nazi orbit and forsaking nonresistance, the Dutch were moving in the other direction. For him, it was an instructive lesson, if difficult to accept.

The planning committee made Bender responsible to invite American Mennonite speakers and attendees. He was to select two persons from each of the four largest Mennonite branches in the United States. As he did so, he learned to know other-than-MC Mennonite leaders in a way he had not known them before. Part of that learning came from the hurt feelings of leaders offended because they were not consulted in the choice of who would attend. This was especially true of some GC Mennonite leaders.[35]

Bender's entrepreneurial instincts also came into play. He decided to offer a European tour in connection with the world conference. Since he was going to have to pay his own fare—he could not ask for help from any of the organizations he served—one way to get a discount was to arrange for others to travel with him. He now formally established the "Bender Travel Service" to serve conference travelers. Unfortunately, he got few inquiries, but he did sell the steamer tickets for the seven Americans who attended the conference. They traveled together on a Hamburg-America-line ship.[36]

The sessions convened at the venerable Singel church in Amsterdam, on June 29, 1936. More than 2,000 people attended the opening session. Nearly 350 persons registered as active participants, 145 of them from Germany. The seven from the United States were Orie and Elta Miller and their daughter Lois (who had just graduated from Goshen College), Harold Bender, C. Henry Smith of Bluffton College, P. C. Hiebert of the Mennonite Brethren church, and P. R. Schroeder, president of the General Conference Mennonite church.

The conference met for two days in Amsterdam, and then the entire group boarded a ship and crossed the Ijselsee to Friesland and a Dutch Mennonite conference center at Elspeet. There the conference continued for another day. The last day of the conference was spent visiting the Menno Simons monument at Witmar-

**Harold Bender at the 1936 Mennonite World Conference in the Netherlands. Bender is the second seated person from the left. C. F. Klassen and P. C. Hiebert are fifth and sixth seated from the left.**
Mennonite Life, June 1978.

sum, with a final worship service at the Menno Simons church in that town.

After the conference a small group of Dutch Mennonite peace leaders and the Americans met to discuss mutual concerns for a worldwide peace movement. Out of the meeting came an International Mennonite Peace Committee. Bender was elected chairman. The committee's primary purpose was to assist persons who were persecuted for refusing to serve in the military. The group also endorsed a "manifesto" which the Dutch peace group had produced.[37]

Bender and Miller wrote a report of the conference which was published in the *MQR*, the *Gospel Herald*, and a number of other church papers.[38] They were enthusiastic about the symbolic benefits flowing from the conference. Indeed, the conference was an important milestone in the reconvergence of world Mennonitism, although World War II would derail the process for a dozen years.

The conference also highlighted the emerging role of Harold Bender as a Mennonite leader. There was widespread agreement that the next world conference should be held in the United States. If the Amsterdam conference had elected a leader to plan it, Bender would almost certainly have been selected. He was the only person at the conference with truly international credentials and experience. The Dutch and Germans had many able leaders, but none had experience beyond the boundaries of their own coun-tries. In the course of a decade, Bender had established personal acquaintance with virtually all Mennonite leaders in the world. As editor of the *MQR*, he presided over the only Mennonite scholar-ly journal read by Mennonites abroad. His Heidelberg dissertation on Grebel was widely known by the time of the 1936 conference. His scholarly credentials impressed the Europeans. From the Eu-ropean point of view, his role in the 1930 refugee relocation pro-gram had certified his churchly credentials.

The Mennonite World Conference illustrated Bender's ambigu-ous role in his own MC Mennonite context, as was true for Orie Miller as well. Why were they the only MC leaders at the confer-ence? One reason was a generational leadership transition taking place during the 1930s. Few were left of the original group of Men-nonite organizational pioneers, peers of Bender's father, who had emerged in the first decade of the century. Only Daniel Kauffman, editor of the *Gospel Herald*, and S. C. Yoder, president of Goshen College and secretary of the MC Mennonite church's mission board, were still in their original roles. In 1935, president A. D. Wenger of EMS and Levi Mumaw of Scottdale had died, and Aaron Loucks had relinquished his position as publishing agent. In the early 1930s, Harold's uncle Daniel Bender had resigned as presi-dent of Hesston College because of a sex-abuse scandal. Who the next generation of leaders would be was only becoming apparent in 1936. The presence of Harold Bender and Orie Miller at Amster-dam, though unofficial, signaled their emergent leadership status.

That no other MC Mennonite leaders attended highlighted the conservative, parochial sentiment among American MC Menno-nites. Fellowship with liberal European Mennonites was simply not acceptable, a sentiment given expression by Daniel Kauffman in a *Gospel Herald* editorial. Predictably, conservative Lancaster conference bishop John H. Mosemann also weighed in with a crit-ical article in the *Gospel Herald*.[39]

Perhaps most symptomatic of the MC Mennonite attitude to-ward other Mennonites was the refusal of John Horsch and Daniel Kauffman to let Bender and Orie Miller announce a possible fourth world conference to be held in North America in 1940 or

1941.[40] American MC Mennonites in the 1930s were quite ready to help Soviet Mennonite refugees, as they did in an admirable way during the 1930 crisis. But they simply were not prepared for the ecumenical fellowship of a Mennonite World Conference. It would take the tragic and dramatic events of the Second World War and the massive Mennonite relief operation in the aftermath of the war to bring MC Mennonites to embrace European Mennonites in spiritual fellowship.

• • •

Elizabeth, Nancy, and Mary Eleanor watched as the plane raced down the runway at the Indianapolis airport. It was noon on June 14, 1938, and Harold Bender was beginning the second and longest plane trip of his life.[41]

By evening, Bender was in Miami, and early the next morning he began a four-day flight on Pan American Airways, with landings in Cuba, Haiti, Puerto Rico, and Trinidad before reaching Rio de Janeiro, Brazil, on June 19. For many years he had longed to make a visit to the Mennonite colonies in Brazil and Paraguay. He had last seen those people in the spring and summer of 1930 as they boarded ships at Bremerhaven on their long journey from the Soviet Union to South America. Then he had been their expediter on behalf of European and American relief committees. Now, eight years later, he was eager to see the fruits of his labor.[42]

The trip was especially poignant for Bender because it was his first opportunity to assess the wisdom of a decision for which he had been primarily responsible. In January of 1930, he had written the report for the executive committee of MCC which designated Paraguay as the preferred destination for the refugees. The alternative had been Brazil. What had tipped the scales in favor of Paraguay had been a Paraguayan guarantee of freedom from military conscription, despite evidence that Brazil seemed more economically desirable.[43]

About a third of the 1930 refugees had opted for Brazil, nearly one-half went to Paraguay, and about a thousand were able to enter Canada. Those who went to Brazil were financially supported by the Dutch Mennonites: the Paraguayans were funded by MCC.

Throughout the 1930s there had always been an undercurrent of unease about MCC's decision in favor of Paraguay.[44] The 1938 trip was Bender's first chance to assess the situation firsthand.

Reporting to the MCC executive committee on his return, Bender found it hard not to be biased in favor of Paraguay. His abridged report published in the *MQR* and in the *Gospel Herald* was especially slanted that way.[45] Bender's finding in favor of the Paraguayans was not just the need to vindicate a decade-old decision: he had a genuine fascination with the patriarchal, communal, agrarian quality of life of the Mennonites in Paraguay.

His sharpest criticism of the Paraguayan Mennonites was aimed at those who had defied colony authorities and struck out on their own. So he wrote quite negatively of 145 families who had left the original Fernheim colony in 1937 to establish themselves in a better location—better land, better climate, better transportation—even though their undertaking had scarcely had time to get under way. By contrast, his evaluation of MCC's Fernheim settlement was glowing. "This is the best organized, the most prosperous, and spiritually the soundest Mennonite colony in Paraguay," he said, "and in my judgment, the outstanding colony in all of South America."[46]

Bender spent two weeks in Brazil, visiting many of the settlements and meeting many of the people he had learned to know briefly in Germany in 1930. His report made much of the economic hardships the settlers were experiencing. But he was especially worried by a spate of anti-German legislation Brazil had passed to close German-language schools and promote assimilation. "The Mennonites of Brazil, as everywhere else in the world, must keep themselves rather separate from the surrounding world if they expect to maintain their faith," he observed. "But in Brazil they face the further danger of assimilation in a culture and way of life which is morally, intellectually, socially, and in every other way much lower than their own." Bender shared prevailing biases about Latin culture.[47]

On July 2 Bender flew from Curitiba, Brazil, to Asunción, Paraguay. He spent the month of July in the colonies in the Chaco, that vast hot dry part of northern Paraguay where the Mennonites were slowly and laboriously hacking out a living from an inhospitable wilderness. His chief task was to exhort and encourage, and to conclude the arrangements, begun the previous year during a visit by Orie Miller, whereby MCC and the colonists regularized their financial situation. The previous year MCC had bought out the Corporación Paraguaya, which had sold the original land to the Mennonites. It thereby acquired all of the corporation's assets, including some 300,000 acres of land.[48]

The acquisition was a tremendous advantage to all concerned, reducing the price of the land for the colonists and thus their debt. However, it encumbered MCC with a large debt, to be repaid by the colonists over a long period of time. Since MCC held first mortgage rights to the land, law required it to become a limited liability organization, and so in August 1937 it became a legal corporation. Bender was one of the original eight incorporators. The new executive committee was P. C. Hiebert, president; Maxwell Kratz, vice-president; Orie Miller, secretary-treasurer; and Harold Bender, assistant secretary.[49]

The legal reorganization of MCC was fortuitous, for within a few years the Second World War would stretch the agency to the breaking point. The 1930s were a school which refined MCC's expertise and helped prepare it for the challenges ahead.

Bender returned to the United States via Peru and Colombia, arriving in Goshen on August 10.[50] The trip was his first encounter with what would come to be known as the third world, although his experience with Latin culture was marginal. The Mennonite colonies were, after all, intensive little outposts of German civilization. The trip did not seriously interrupt Bender's lifelong sojourn within the confines of Germanic culture.

The trip did leave one legacy: by the time Bender arrived in Goshen, he had a life-threatening case of typhoid fever. During late August and into September, he was extremely sick, and his temperature spiked to above 104 degrees. He was often delirious. His brother Cecil, now practicing medicine in Goshen, was his physician. The illness frightened the campus community, for everyone remembered that the last dean of the college had died of the same disease. Harold and Elizabeth were especially touched when the students packed the front lawn outside his bedroom window on Sunday evenings to sing for him.[51]

A major problem was to keep him quiet once he was feeling better. During the last week of September, he had his secretary come to the house, where he dictated a stack of letters. He also had Guy Hershberger come in and spent several hours working on *MQR* matters. As a result, he had a relapse. His friend and neighbor C. L. Graber reported to Orie Miller that the relapse discouraged Bender. "He should know better than to exert himself," Graber observed. "However, his wife permitted it, and so I keep still."[52]

In general, Bender was remarkably healthy throughout his life. His only persistent affliction had to do with what he and his mother always described as "boils," which were quite painful. In the 1930s there seemed to be no good remedy. John Horsch once told Bender that he had heard that eating lots of raisins sometimes helped.

In 1934 Bender had an especially bad case while he and Graber were on a trip to Pennsylvania. Interestingly, Bender had arranged to take Graber with him on the trip in order to get Graber out of the office: Bender was afraid Graber was working too hard and would have a "nervous collapse." He thought a road trip might be good for him.[53]

They drove Bender's car, but by the time they got to Gettysburg, Bender was so sick with boils that he had to be hospitalized. Graber, too impatient to sit at his bedside, went on to Lancaster County and spent three quite successful days raising money for Goshen College. Then he returned to Gettysburg for Bender, and they continued their trip to Philadelphia. Graber, who described himself as so nervously exhausted that he was not "worth ten cents," enjoyed his little triumph over his normally indestructible friend.[54]

• • •

If Bender had devoted himself single-mindedly to scholarship, he might have become a prolific academic scholar. By 1930 he was poised for such a career, but then he became dean of Goshen College. What might have been, simply never developed for want of time. Even with time, perhaps his restless energy and his need to be involved in practical affairs would not have allowed him to focus on scholarship. Saying yes to the deanship foreclosed many of his scholarly options, particularly when combined with his MCC and churchly involvements.

Nonetheless, by the end of the 1930s, Bender had established himself as a leading scholar of Anabaptist history. That reputation was supported by his dissertation on Conrad Grebel and his editorship of *The Mennonite Quarterly Review*.

Bender had invented the *MQR*, designed its form, determined its content, and steered its evolution. More than any other object of his creation, the *MQR* remained an expression of his beliefs and his idiosyncrasies. He managed it nearly single-handedly, with obvious consequences. In August of 1934 he was hospitalized for an appendectomy at precisely the time he had intended to edit the July issue (already two months late). As dean he had to open a new academic year, so he did not get the July issue out until late in October. When it appeared, it had only 43 pages. And the October issue appeared two months late.

Because Bender was unable and unwilling to delegate responsibilities to his associate editors, production of almost every issue of the *MQR* became a last-minute crisis. Since the text was produced at Goshen and the printing was done at Scottdale, just getting final proofs was a hurdle and made his last-minute editing even more crisis-driven. Edward Yoder, an associate editor, observed Bender's frenetic efforts with the wry comment that about all one can do is watch and give advice.[55]

What especially bothered Robert Friedmann was the absence of any method by which material was chosen for the journal.[56] Each issue was built around whatever was available at the time. Few articles were written specifically for the *Review*. Most articles emerged from conference addresses or were excerpts from book and dissertation manuscripts. There were exceptions. Bender wrote several original articles: one on Germantown; another on literature and hymnody in Lancaster County; and a historiographical survey of historical writing on Anabaptism. In 1940-41 he edited a 118-page series in five issues on the Palatine Mennonite census lists of 1664-1774. Ernst Correll also wrote a few articles specifically for the *Review*. But such cases were exceptions.

Bender actually published surprisingly little during the 1930s. His own most extensive scholarly publication was four installments of his dissertation on Conrad Grebel. Several of his conference addresses were published, and he wrote many book reviews. But even in that department, despite several announcements that the *Review* would survey all published materials on Anabaptist and Mennonite history, the journal never kept that promise. Sometimes a year or more went by without a single book review, due not to lack of suitable books but to failure in appointing reviewers.

Actually, the improvisational nature of the *MQR* gave the journal a refreshing spontaneity. There was a sense that one was getting fresh new material and that it had contemporary relevance. Compared to its stuffy younger cousin, *Church History*, the MQR was alive and vibrant. Bender wrote wonderfully pithy editorial introductions to each issue which provided perspective and context. The intermixture of original source materials (such as the Palatine lists) and more conventional monograph material offered readers a richly textured diet.

Clearly the *MQR* would have been quite a different journal but for the voluminous contributions of John Horsch. In the fifty-eight issues between 1927 and 1940, Horsch had major articles in twenty-six. In only two years did he fail to contribute: 1937 and 1938. Nearly all of his *MQR* writing would appear later in his book on the Hutterites and in his *Mennonites in Europe*. Horsch's last article was published in the October 1941 issue, a few weeks after his death on October 7. Several other major contributors, although publishing much less, were Goshen College professor John Umble on American Mennonite and Amish subjects; Guy F. Hershberger on peace topics; Edward Yoder on a variety of American Mennonite topics; Benjamin Unruh on Russian Mennonite topics; and after 1937, John C. Wenger, who introduced Pilgram Marpeck and added him to the pantheon of the *MQR*'s Anabaptist heroes. Wenger, who wrote easily and quickly, also became a prolific book reviewer.

Wenger's diligence was rewarded in 1939 by his appointment as the youngest and eighth member of the *MQR*'s board of editors—a post that put him in the company of Christian Neff of the Weierhof; Benjamin Unruh of Karlsruhe, Germany; C. Henry Smith of Bluffton College; Abram Warkentin of Bethel College; Ernst Correll of American University; and Guy F. Hershberger and Edward Yoder of Goshen College. Yoder and Hershberger had some limited influence on the *MQR* in the 1930s, especially when Bender was abroad.

The *MQR* carried almost no serious theological articles, and the few which it did print created trouble for Bender. In 1930 Irvin Burkhart published two articles on Menno Simons' view of the incarnation, based on his master's thesis for the University of Pittsburgh. John Horsch was unhappy with Burkhart's treatment of Menno's views on the sinfulness of the human body.[57] Bender thought Burkhart had it about right, but reluctantly persuaded him to write a clarification which acceded to Horsch's complaint.

More serious was the response to an article by Goshen College professor Gustav Enss in 1932. Entitled "Christianity and Religion," Enss' piece claimed that Christianity was not a religion.[58] The assertion offended "the Lion in the East," as Bender called bishop George R. Brunk Sr. Acting in character, the bishop demanded that Enss retract the article's main point. Bender had little respect for either George Brunk's theology or his good sense: "I begin to wonder whether the critic is really well-balanced mentally." He decided to challenge the bishop by submitting Enss' article to several prominent Fundamentalist theologians, asking them to authenticate its orthodoxy. The theologians obliged, much to Bender's relief.[59] Bender then allowed Enss, a tenacious advocate in his own right, to write a three-page "Note" elaborating on his use of the term "religion."[60] But he refused to print two additional articles Enss had prepared on the subject.

The *MQR* was warmly received by scholars. Roland Bainton of Yale University told John Horsch that "the journal maintains a high standard. The best work on Reformation history in this country, it seems to me, is done by the Mennonites."[61] But admiration did not translate into subscriptions. To promote subscriptions, Bender printed endorsements by distinguished scholars in a promotional brochure; yet there were only 401 subscribers in 1945. The journal required a continuous subsidy from the Mennonite Historical Society.[62]

In 1941 Bender's control of the *MQR* was challenged for the first and last time. A. J. Metzler, who became publishing agent at the Mennonite Publishing House (MPH) in 1935, was a careful manager. In 1941 he noticed that the *MQR* was getting the same special low printing rates as the in-house church papers, despite the fact that it was owned by the Mennonite Historical Society, a private organization connected to Goshen College. If MPH continues to subsidize the *MQR*, should it not come under church-wide sponsorship and evaluation, just like all other church papers? Metzler inquired.[63]

Bender was irked by the query but neatly circumvented the clear intent of Metzler by suggesting that the *MQR* be evaluated annually by the Historical Committee of the Mennonite Church, an official church committee of which Bender was secretary. He also offered to give up the Studies in Anabaptist and Mennonite History book series to the Historical Committee. In return, he suggested that Metzler and MPH give the Historical Committee more financial support. "In this way we will be moving in the direction which you have indicated," he told Metzler.[64] Bender had cleverly checkmated Metzler.

It was an interesting exchange, but for both men it was mainly a ploy. Metzler was under pressure from church conservatives to bring the *MQR* under some churchwide control, but he did not want to commit to the financial obligations Bender proposed. For his part, Bender was using the opportunity to try to get some money out of the publishing house for more historical work, while at the same time yielding nothing and preserving control of his beloved *MQR*.

The *MQR* gave Bender and Horsch the scholarly visibility that they—especially Horsch—could have gotten in no other way. But more importantly, by the end of the 1930s, Mennonites had a well-established historical scholarship with a specific explanation of the meaning and significance of their history. Bender's "Anabaptist Vision" address in 1943 would become an eloquent summation of the historical work of the previous decade, gathered up best in the pages of the *MQR*.

## ·৫·12·৯·

# Family Life; Peace Activism

*The Benders thrive in the 1930s. Bender chairs
the Peace Problems Committee.
Goshen College elects a new president.*

IN 1936 the Goshen College yearbook editors invited president
Yoder and dean Bender to select poetic epigrams to place beneath
their pictures in the *Maple Leaf*. Bender quoted Tennyson's
"Ulysses" (1842):

> I am a part of all that I have met;
> Yet all experience is an arch wherethrough
> Gleams that untraveled world, whose margin fades
> Forever and forever when I move.
> How dull it is to pause, to make an end,
> To rust unburnished, not to shine in use!

For Bender, the year 1936 seemed like a new beginning. The
long journey to the Heidelberg doctorate had begun fifteen years
earlier, shortly after the death of his father in 1920. Now the degree was in hand and its first fruit—the Grebel biography—was
being published by installments in the *MQR*. I am quite "proud"
of those issues, Bender told his brother Wilbur.[1] Of all of his
achievements, the Heidelberg doctorate and the Grebel biography
would always be his most cherished academic accomplishments.

The years from 1936 to 1940 marked a transition in Bender's
life, an interlude between his strenuous years of preparation during the 1920s and early 1930s and burdensome new responsibilities in the 1940s. In 1936 Bender could have had no premonition

of what was to come, but he certainly agreed with Tennyson: "How dull it is to pause, to make an end / To rust unburnished, not to shine in use."

In 1936 Bender was 39 years old. His hair was thinning in front, and he was putting on weight. By now he wore his plain coat continually, but often with a black tie underneath. The tie was a tiny act of defiance against a "restriction" he always found irksome. Bender found little time for recreation during the 1930s. But in 1939 he took a two-day fishing trip to Fairview, Michigan, with his brothers Cecil and Robert and chemistry professor Glen Miller. Bender caught a twelve-inch perch.[2]

A second daughter, Nancy, was born in November 1933. She was a big baby, nearly eight pounds at birth. Writing to the Horsch grandparents, Bender joked that "she looks quite plump, more like her father and mother every day."[3] Harold and Elizabeth wanted more children, but the difficult circumstances of Nancy's birth made that prospect impractical.[4]

The Benders enjoyed seeing the girls grow. In 1939 Bender wrote bemusedly to Elizabeth's uncle Michael: "*Uns geht es gut. Die Kinder werden gross, and wir werden älter*" (we are well. The children grow tall, and we grow older).[5] Daughter Mary Eleanor was twelve in 1939.

The girls experienced the normal vicissitudes of childhood. In April 1938 four-year-old Nancy broke her arm while riding a new tricycle, a gift from her Horsch grandparents.[6] In December 1936 she was very ill and had her tonsils removed.[7] Swarms of mosquitoes in northern Indiana summers made life tough for Nancy: when she was three, a

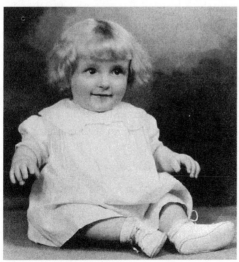

**Nancy Bender in 1935.** Bender Family Album.

sting just below the right eye produced a huge swollen bump. Mary Eleanor had frequent colds; in 1936 Elsie reported to Harold, who was attending the World Conference at Amsterdam, that Mary Eleanor was "doing a lot of coughing." More happily, the girls loved a new cocker spaniel puppy Aunt Florence gave them at Christmas in 1936. In 1937 Mary Eleanor was working hard at mastering a new violin.[8]

During the 1930s, Elizabeth was preoccupied with child-rearing, punctuated by nearly continual teaching (usually part-time), in mathematics and in languages. Bender sometimes irked his colleagues by pushing too hard for assignments for her. When Goshen's regular German teacher left in 1934, Bender insisted that Elizabeth should replace her. The faculty and S. C. Yoder opposed the idea. Yoder explained that she had been "an excellent teacher," but in the last few years her work had been less satisfactory. "I would be glad to use her if she did her work well and if it did not create a problem with the rest of the faculty," he told Orie Miller.[9]

Yoder's remarks were unfair, for he was referring to an excruciatingly difficult time when Elizabeth had been pregnant with Nancy. The following year she took three courses at Heidelberg in German language, thus sustaining Bender's claim that she was better prepared to teach German than anyone else on the faculty. In any case, after 1935 she was regularly listed in the college catalog as the instructor in German language. In 1936 she also taught algebra and trigonometry.[10]

Elizabeth shared her father's retiring nature and found it difficult to keep up with her husband's fast-paced public life. She was almost certainly conscious of the low-grade resistance of some of the faculty to her teaching. That must have been a particular burden for her.

Harold and Elizabeth were deeply involved in the Goshen College congregation. During much of the decade of the 1930s, Bender was on the church council. In 1930 he pushed hard to create a committee to plan for activities for the young people. Often he was chair of the committee. Elizabeth taught in the Sunday school, and for several years Harold was superintendent.[11]

In 1936 Harold's brother Cecil graduated from medical school and set up a practice in Goshen. That same year his youngest brother Robert was at Harvard Medical School, but spent the summer at home. He was courting Carolyn Lehman, daughter of M. C. and Lydia Lehman, former missionaries in India. M. C. was just then teaching at Goshen College. Bender's brother John was in Philadelphia, trying to get a teaching job in a city high school. Wilbur had married Louise Fay, daughter of Harvard historian Sidney B. Fay, and in 1936 he was appointed to the Harvard history faculty.[12] Harold's sister Violet, after several years of teaching in a school in Beirut, Lebanon, had returned to the United States to marry Sheldon Turner; in 1936 they were living in Frederick, Maryland. In 1936 Harold's sister Florence moved to Indianapolis, where she had just landed a job as Indiana State Director of Nursery Schools under the Works Progress Administration. She often spent weekends at the Bender house, especially after she bought a car "at a good bargain," in a deal arranged by Harold.[13]

The Bender family finances were always tight. It was hard for the household to live within the meager income the college was able to supply. On Christmas Day 1933, Bender apologized to the Horsches for sending no gifts. "Perhaps you can count your newest granddaughter as our Christmas present," he said, referring to four-week-old Nancy.[14] Between 1932 and 1937, Bender and Elizabeth together earned a total of $11,180, but by 1937 they had collected only $8,049. Of the $11,180, Elizabeth had earned $2,380. Her best earning year was 1936-37, when her salary was $1,050, compared to Bender's $1,800 that year.[15]

As college finances improved, the finances of the Benders also became a bit easier. In 1936 the house was ten years old, and they spent some money on maintenance, repainting inside and out and putting up new window shades. They also installed a new rug in the living room. In 1938 they redecorated the kitchen. The point of all the redecorating was, as Bender explained tongue-in-cheek to Florence, so "things will be in shape to receive honored guests like yourself."[16] In 1937 they bought some new furniture so they could rent several of the bedrooms to college students.[17]

Like many other Americans in the 1920s and 1930s, the Bender's began buying gadgets for their home. In 1927 they acquired a

gasoline-powered washing machine, and in the early 1930s up-
graded to an electric one from Montgomery Ward.[18] In 1937 they
bought a new electric refrigerator, a six-cubic-foot porcelain model
from Brilhart Hardware, a Mennonite-owned store in Scottdale; it
cost $180, a major expenditure, representing one-tenth of Bender's
annual salary. The first evening after its arrival, they made a frozen
dessert, which Bender pronounced "very good."[19] Bender was also
much interested in movie-film cameras; in 1936 he bought one and
took it along to the Amsterdam Mennonite World Conference.
When Elizabeth's brother Paul and his wife, Madeleine, had their
first baby, Bender offered to send them the camera so they could
take moving pictures of little Gretchen.[20]

Bender had to borrow money to buy successive cars, and during the 1930s the money usually came from father Horsch. In
1932 he bought a new Chevrolet, and he had not completed re-
payment in 1935 when he traded the Chevrolet for the new Ford
which he took to Europe. Upon his return from Europe, he bought
a Dodge, even though he still owed money on the Chevrolet. When
the Horsches needed money, Bender rushed a payment of $150 to
them with the query, "How much do I still owe?"[21]

Harold and Elizabeth's greatest lifetime expenditure came in
1938, when they bought the house from mother Bender for $5,000,
borrowing the money from the Mennonite Board of Education Endowment Fund.[22] It was a fine investment. In 1937 the city of
Goshen had resurfaced Main Street with new concrete right up
past the college campus. That raised the value of their property.

For several years after his return from Europe in 1936, Bender
gave speeches on the subject of Germany. He usually received payment for his services, normally $15 plus travel expenses. He de-
veloped a reputation as a speaker who gave "delightful lectures"
on world and German affairs. In the course of a typical year, he delivered as many as a dozen such talks to groups such as the Mother's Club of Elkhart, the Elkhart Farmer's Institute, Kiwanis Clubs
all over northern Indiana, Farm Bureau meetings, public high
school commencements, Rotary Clubs, and the Elkhart Ministerial Association.

In 1938 one of his popular lectures was entitled "How to Keep

America out of the War." Often the topic was "Hitler's Germany" or "Church and State in Hitler's Germany." Usually he tried to explain what he considered the "typical German's" view of Hitler and events in Germany. A sample of Bender's views on Hitler is carried in a report by the *Goshen News-Democrat* of an interview he gave in October 1935 after his return from Heidelberg. "I went into Germany with serious doubts as to the ability and sincerity of Hitler, but now am convinced that he is one of the great statesmen of our times in spite of the fact that I do not agree with his program," he told the reporter. "I believe he will be a determining factor in European and world history because he is the absolute master of Germany and has the vision and the constructive ability of a statesman. I do not agree with his attitude toward the church and toward the Jews."[23]

However, that assessment of Hitler was in strong contrast with Bender's reaction to the views of his father-in-law John Horsch. Horsch was all too enthused about Hitler, and Bender rebuked him sharply. In 1935 Horsch was much upset by a series of highly critical commentaries on Hitler in the "World Affairs" section of the MC Mennonite journal *The Christian Monitor*. In a letter to the Peace Problems Committee, Horsch complained of what he called "lying propaganda by Jews against Hitler."[24] He believed editor C. F. Derstine (from Canada) was a victim of such propaganda, and he asked the committee to investigate.

Bender was the committee's secretary and wisely handled Horsch's letter privately. Although hard at work on his doctoral dissertation at Heidelberg University, he took time out to defend Derstine's critique of Hitler, pointing out that both Hitler's program for the church in Germany and his treatment of Jews had to be condemned by any right-thinking Christian. He also pointed out that Horsch had to be careful when he quoted German Christians about events in Germany. With the suspension of all press freedom, the Germans knew less about German public affairs than did those on the outside. And he took Horsch to task for using statements by a notorious right-wing American preacher and publisher, Gerald Winrod of Kansas. Never, before or after, did Bender write so sharply to his father-in-law.[25]

In 1935 no one, including Bender, could have known where Hitler's program would lead. During his sojourn at Heidelberg in 1935, Bender had been impressed by what seemed like the positive effects of the Nazi economic program. "Conditions have visibly improved in Germany over five years ago," he told S. C. Yoder, a reference to Bender's sojourn in Germany in 1930 before Hitler had come to power.[26] Bender's firsthand knowledge of the dreadful conditions in Germany in the 1920s and early 1930s and his high regard for German culture made him respectful of Hitler's early accomplishments. That fact helps explain this kind of a remark: "In political and social life as well as in military and economic affairs, Hitler's movement is a democratizing movement, an Americanizing movement in a certain sense. I believe this aspect of Hitler's work is more important than some of the superficial obnoxious things such as anti-Semitism, etc."[27] Certainly such remarks sound obtuse and surreal, now that we know about the concentration camps and gas ovens. But Bender made those remarks in 1935. He did not know then what he and the world would know in 1945.

Most of Bender's speaking engagements were church-related. He frequently spoke at Sunday evening meetings in churches in northern Indiana and at special Sunday school and district church meetings of various kinds. Often he served as a speaker at the popular Young People's Institutes held throughout the church in the 1930s. In 1937 he was the main speaker at three such institutes.[28] A first in Bender's speaking career came in 1939. The pioneer Mennonite radio preacher William Detweiler invited him to preach a sermon on Detweiler's weekly *Calvary Hour* radio broadcast. Detweiler was pastor of the Oak Grove Mennonite church in Wayne County, Ohio, a congregation with strong ties to Goshen College.

• • •

Most of Bender's energies went into his job as dean and teacher. He spoke frequently in chapel, sometimes on subjects such as "Present Day Trends in Education." Although usually his chapel talks were lucid and inspirational, one in 1934 on the immortality of the soul was a real flop. His loyal but critical colleague Edward Yoder wrote a diary entry describing the talk as a series of metaphysical "somersaults and handsprings" of which none of the students could make any sense. Even worse, the speech generated a volley of queries from the college's constituency, questioning the dean's orthodoxy.[29]

In the fall of 1936, Bender was senior-class sponsor. By tradition one role of the sponsor was to facilitate the "Senior Sneak," an annual event of seniors slipping off in the dead of night for a day off-campus. The seniors reported that "with Dean Bender's aid we escaped, leaving our dignity and the juniors behind us." As commencement time approached, Bender hosted the graduating seniors at a breakfast on the Bender lawn. For many years Harold and Elizabeth were cosponsors also of the "Deutsche Verein" (German club), sometimes holding the group's monthly meetings at the Bender home.[30]

Each fall Bender gave a "Mennonite Principles and Practices" talk to the college men, in which he exhorted them to practice Christian decorum. In 1936, when he gave a similar talk to the college women, he itemized seven ideals: "a definite personal religious experience; full obedience to Christ and the Word; real, definite holiness which produces strictness with oneself on the question of sin; a real application of the Christian principles to the whole of life, business, home relations, and amusements; a true separation from the world in spirit and life; true simplicity of life; and peace and love, not only with regard to nonresistance in time of war, but in all our personal relations."[31] Interestingly, he was not explicit about attire.

Over the years Bender taught an array of courses in history, sociology, church history, and Bible. By the 1930s, with the coming of historians Willard H. Smith and Guy F. Hershberger, he no longer taught history. Beginning in 1926, he taught "The Family" course annually for several decades. In 1938 he explained the course in some detail to professor Alfred Kinsey (later famous for the Kinsey Reports), describing its practical applications to all phases of marriage and family, except for one area. "I have never gone into the purely physical aspects of the marriage relationships," he told Kinsey. "I have a definite conviction that a course such as this should keep strictly clear of 'sex' as it is frequently dragged into college courses on marriage."[32]

Bender also taught the "Christian Doctrine" course. In 1938 he used John Horsch's new edition of *Modern Religious Liberalism* as the text, a reflection of how conservative his theological impulses really were, and no doubt an act of filial respect as well.

Bender had a reputation as a no-nonsense teacher, but on April 1, 1940, he pulled a joke on his students. Walking into his "Church History" class a few minutes late, he announced without ceremony, "I think it's about time to have a little quiz." Pausing just long enough to savor the agonized silence his words had evoked, he cried, "April fool!"[33]

As dean he worked hard to recruit students and funds, traveling to various Mennonite communities. Registration was always a hectic time for Bender. Originally, dean Noah Oyer had registered all students, but when Silas Hertzler became registrar in 1928, Hertzler took over the assignment. Within a year of becoming dean, Bender took back the task, seeing it as a dean's prerogative, much to Hertzler's disgruntlement. It made sense when enrollment was small, but by the late 1930s, with enrollment in the hundreds, it became impossible. Increasingly, Bender gave registration over to the new division heads. As chair of the division of Bible and philosophy, he registered students in that division.

• • •

If the centerpiece of Harold Bender's life in the 1930s was Goshen College, a prime field around his work was the Mennonite church. The decade 1934-45 shows the many-layered quality of history. A new generation of Mennonite leaders emerged: Harold Bender, Guy F. Hershberger, and C. L. Graber at Goshen; Orie Miller at MCC; A. J. Metzler at the Publishing House; Joseph (J. D.) Graber at the Mission Board; and Paul Erb as the editor of *Gospel Herald*. Also, the forms and practices of church life and faith established by Bender's father's generation finally became the norm.

Perhaps no one summarized the posture of the MC Mennonite

church more succinctly and authoritatively than did Daniel Kauffman in a 1932 letter to Bender. The occasion was to advise Bender
about some personnel problems at the college. Given Kauffman's
magisterial position in church affairs, the letter expressed the principles which animated Mennonite church polity. "In the first place,
we must reckon the cause of Christ and the Church of greater importance than that of any institution, congregation, or individual,"
Kauffman told Bender. "With us it is God first, the Church second,
next the institutions and activities of the Church, and lastly ourselves as individuals." He called this a "vision of relative importance" in which the individual placed himself at the disposal of
"The Cause."[34]

Kauffman went on: "We hold that the standards of the Gospel
should also be the standards of the Church, wholeheartedly supported by the institutions and members. As a Mennonite Church,
we have espoused and maintained standards in faith and life that
are more or less peculiar to ourselves, that have been ignored or
opposed by most other churches, and which have come to be
known among ourselves as distinctive doctrines."[35]

Kauffman's credo stressed loyalty, nonconformity, and discipline. The Mennonite organizational and theological revolution
begun in the 1890s was nearly complete by the 1930s. The ideals
in Kauffman's letter to Bender reflected his concern that those
ideals and practices be perpetuated. Daniel Kauffman was clearly
intent on schooling the young college dean in the key rubrics of
"The Cause." Bender was quite content with "The Cause," but in
the 1930s, the effect of his roles, if not his ideas, led him toward
innovations which once in motion would unsettle the Kauffman
consensus. That was true in his historical work and also in his
MCC and Mennonite World Conference activities. It was certainly true for his modernization of Goshen College. In the 1930s, it
was true also of his peace activities.

• • •

At dusk on August 15, 1937, Harold and Elizabeth and the girls
boarded the train at Goshen for a three-day trip to Paso Robles,

California. There they visited some of Elizabeth's Horsch relatives. From California they traveled north to Oregon, where they had arranged to spend a few days with the Orie Miller family, who were also traveling on the West Coast. On August 25 both families traveled to Turner, Oregon, to attend the biennial MC Mennonite general conference.[36]

Bender and Miller were the only "lay delegates" at the conference. Normally only ordained men could be delegates, but Miller and Bender qualified by virtue of their various committee and board assignments. Miller was chair of the Young People's Problems Committee and a member of numerous other committees. Bender was chair of the Peace Problems Committee (PPC) and secretary of the Historical Committee.[37]

Because of the increasingly tense international situation, the PPC decided to put the MC Mennonite church on record regarding its position on war. As chair of the PPC, Bender wrote the original draft of a peace statement on the train en route to the West Coast. After some refinement by other PPC members, the General Conference adopted it. Entitled "Our Position on Peace, War, and Military Service," it pulled no punches. "War is sin," it declared forthrightly. "We are constrained as followers of Christ to abstain from all forms of military service and all means of support of war, and must consider all members who violate these principles as transgressors and out of fellowship with the church."[38]

The statement urged obedience to the "laws and regulations of the government in all things" and promised to "love and honor our country." Regarding how nations might avoid war, it specifically endorsed a "policy of neutrality and non-participation in disputes between other nations." That phrase drew considerable opposition from conservatives like J. L. Stauffer and George R. Brunk Sr. of Virginia, who believed the church should address government only to "explain to them our position on nonresistance" and not to give advice on how government should behave.[39]

It was the first time the MC Mennonites had adopted an official statement during peacetime specifically on war and peace. The document was symptomatic of a new effort by the Peace Problems Committee to sharpen the Mennonite peace testimony. The initiative had come from new persons on the committee. Bender had been elected to the PPC in 1933, and in 1935 the committee's long-time chair, bishop Eli L. Frey of Fulton County, Ohio, chose not to be reelected. In his place C. L. Graber was elected to be a committee member along with Orie Miller and Bender, and Bender became chair. There were also three Canadians on the committee, but the creative force was the trio of Bender, Miller, and Graber. In retrospect, the developments were fortuitous. Those three soon became the leaders of the MC Mennonites in a broader Historic Peace Church effort that developed a conscientious objector program for World War II, known as Civilian Public Service (CPS).

Bender's peace activities during the 1920s had been relatively limited. He had helped start the Goshen College Peace Society as an adjunct of the Mennonite Historical Society, though apparently the real impetus came from Guy F. Hershberger. In the spring of 1932, Bender published his first systematic comments on peace in the *Gospel Herald.* His article, two pages long, was entitled "In Time of Peace, Prepare for War." The context was the Japanese invasion of Manchuria in 1931. It was one of Bender's best early writings.[40]

Bender argued that nonresistance is more than refusal to bear arms: it must be a peacetime lifestyle which validates conscientious objection during war. "Nonresistant people should represent the highest type of citizenship to the State so that the State may feel glad and willing to make room for conscientious objection," he wrote.[41]

Bender's key point was that modern wars organize and regiment the entire nation; no one can simply refuse to serve. Nonresistant people must find an equivalent service, which he called "alternative service." He suggested it might be in the form of agricultural, forest, or reconstruction service, and he invoked a history of Mennonites' forestry service in Russia as an example. Mennonites, he insisted, must be "prepared to finance" such an endeavor. Predicting a high probability of war in the near future, he concluded: "Under such conditions, the beast of war may yet clasp the world to his breast. What then will the nonresistant Christians do if they are not prepared to live, to die, for their principles?"[42]

Bender's sense of urgency to prepare the church and its young people for what he feared would be a new war was rooted partly in his own experience during the First World War. "I was one of those who believed in noncombatant service," he told some friends in 1936, whereas "my friends became absolute conscientious objectors believing that it is impossible to go to war." He went on to say that his friends' experiences had "absolutely convinced" him in favor of nonparticipation. "The issues of noncombatant service should be cleared up," he continued. "Moral defeats come because we are not ready to make a decision before the crisis comes. We should be ready to give some concrete advice of what ought to be done."[43]

At Bender's urging, the PPC sponsored a major conference at Goshen College on war and peace, convening in February 1935. The two-day marathon provided little theological reflection: only one session dealt with peace theology. Instead, the conferees focused on peace education and other practical matters. Even John Horsch attended and read a paper. The most prescient paper was one by Guy F. Hershberger: "Is Alternative Service Possible or Desirable?" In a remarkable way, and much in the vein of Bender's 1932 article, Hershberger described a plan which practically outlined the Civilian Public Service program formed for conscientious objectors during World War II.[44]

A month after the conference, the Benders were on their way to Heidelberg. Within a month of their return, Bender attended another historic peace gathering, this time in Newton, Kansas: the first meeting of the Historic Peace Churches. Bender and Orie Miller represented the PPC. To promote further cooperative activities, the conference created a continuation committee of one representative from each of the Historic Peace Churches—Quaker, Brethren, and Mennonite. The committee was Robert Balderston of the Friends, C. Ray Keim of the Church of the Brethren, and Orie Miller of the Mennonites. It was the first time the MC Mennonites had linked up formally with the Brethren and the Friends.[45]

Bender's trip to Brazil and Paraguay in 1938 had impressed him with how poorly organized and educated Mennonites were regarding peace issues, given the parlous condition of world affairs. At his suggestion the executive committee of MCC convened a meeting of representatives from seven Mennonite groups to discuss how to address issues raised by the emerging international crisis. It was the first time in American history that representatives of nearly all American Mennonite groups got together in one room to talk about peace issues. Bender, Hershberger, Miller, Graber, and Jesse B. Martin of Ontario represented the MC Mennonites. From the Mennonite Brethren came P. C. Hiebert, C. F. Klassen, John W. Warkentin, and B. B. Janz. The General Conference Mennonites were J. Winfield Fretz, E. L. Harshbarger, D. C. Kirchhofer, Carl Landes, and David Toews. H. E. Bertsche, C. E. Rediger, D. M. Hofer, P. G. Schultz, Emanuel Troyer, and Harry Yoder represented a variety of other Mennonite groups. That such a diverse group of leaders could be convened indicates how anxious Mennonites were in 1939 about their pacifism.[46]

Representatives of the three largest groups—P. C. Hiebert, E. L. Harshbarger, and H. S. Bender—were appointed to plan another meeting in the fall of 1939. The meeting occurred on September 30, 1939 (four weeks after Germany invaded Poland), and formed a new Mennonite Central Peace Committee (MCPC). Its executive committee drew up a plan for responding to a military draft, dubbed the "Plan of Action." Bender became the MCPC's executive secretary.[47]

One person absent from the Chicago meeting of the MCPC was Harry A. Diener, moderator of the MC Mennonite general conference. He had hoped to attend, but his executive committee was so negative toward such inter-Mennonite cooperation that he stayed away. Diener's absence startled Bender, Miller, and Graber. Suddenly they realized they were running ahead of the ordained MC Mennonite church leadership. To help remedy the situation, the PPC and moderator Diener called thirty MC conference representatives to meet at Goshen in October 1939. There the MCPC "Plan of Action" was presented, discussed, and unanimously approved. Even J. L. Stauffer, the incoming moderator, approved.[48] However, he would become a vociferous critic of the CPS program when it actually took shape a few years later.

In the midst of all the peace activity of 1939, Bender made a significant trip (his first) to Winnipeg, Manitoba, where he represented the PPC at an all-Canada Mennonite peace meeting. In Winnipeg he stayed with C. F. Klassen and spoke at the peace meeting, in German. The depth of nonresistant convictions among the Mennonites and Hutterites in Canada impressed him. The meeting passed a resolution calling on all Mennonites to refuse to participate in war. The visit established lines of communication with Canadian leaders, lines that would soon be important during and after World War II.[49]

Thus in the course of a half-decade, Bender, Miller, and Graber, with help especially from Guy F. Hershberger and Edward Yoder, had moved the MC Mennonites from an implicit peace commitment to an official and explicit position. By 1940 the church had a document which formally established its position on war and peace: the 1937 Turner, Oregon, MC Mennonite general conference statement, "Our Position on Peace, War, and Military Service." It also had a blueprint for response in case of war: the 1939 MCPC "Plan of Action."

The trio had also helped create the organizational links with other Mennonite groups and with the Church of the Brethren and Friends, connections necessary to meet the challenges of World War II. They had changed the previously passive PPC into being an active agent for MC Mennonite peace work.

What the MC peace advocates had not yet created in 1939 was a well-developed theological statement of the Mennonite relation to the state and to war. But they had inaugurated a process toward that end: in 1937 they commissioned Guy F. Hershberger to produce a treatise on nonresistance. Seven years later, his effort produced the now-classic book *War, Peace, and Nonresistance.*[50]

Bender's peace activity and leadership in the 1930s was a remarkable achievement, reflecting both skill and sound leadership. Harold Bender had come a long way from his lukewarm pacifism during World War I. In the process he had helped the MC Mennonite church, and to a degree other Mennonite groups, achieve a state of readiness for the fearful challenge of World War II. The contrast with the situation of the Mennonites at the outset of World War I could hardly have been greater.

• • •

Bishop D. A. Yoder could not have been more surprised. Standing on the doorstep of his farmhouse west of Goshen were eight Goshen College students. They politely inquired whether they could talk with him. The tall gentle president of the Mennonite Board of Education invited them in. They told him they had come because they had heard rumors that S. C. Yoder was resigning from Goshen's presidency. Their preference, they said, was for Yoder to stay. One reason was that they believed Yoder was the best man for the job; but another was that they were sure that Bender wanted the job and would in all likelihood get it. The eight students said that opinion on campus ran strongly against dean Bender. One student had even declared, "If Bender becomes president, I'll pack up and leave."[51]

What students disliked about Bender was his rigid application of college rules. They also detected that the relationship between dean and president was not the best, nor were relations between the dean and some of the faculty. And they did not think Bender would be helpful in a role at which they thought president Yoder was especially adept: promoting good relations with the Mennonite church.[52]

The rumors the students had heard were true. The college board of overseers and the administrative committee had arranged for president Yoder to become the first recipient of a new sabbatical policy Bender and Graber had established in 1937. The plan was for the president to do a year of graduate study at Gordon College of Theology and Missions. Upon his return, he would teach in the Bible department.[53]

For years Bender and Graber had hoped to replace president Yoder. His old-style administrative methods seemed inadequate to the needs of the modernizing Goshen College of the 1930s. But their efforts had never succeeded because Orie Miller, the financial agent on the Board of Education and a primary financial angel of the college, had opposed such a move. Now in the spring of 1938, Miller had changed his mind and had told Bender and Graber, "Decide what kind of setup you want, and come to some agreement as to whom you would support for President."[54] Bender and Graber had immediately acted on the opening Miller offered.

Surprisingly, the plan of Bender and Graber was not to create a new streamlined hierarchy with a president at the top. Instead, they proposed an administrative committee of four, with Graber in charge of finances, Bender as dean, Ernest E. Miller as director of personnel, and Paul Mininger as president. Ernest Miller was a younger brother of Orie and a former missionary in India. Paul Mininger, son of a well-respected city missionary, had come to the faculty in 1937. He was an ordained minister, and Graber and Bender wanted him to work on college-church relations. It was assumed that either Graber or Bender would serve as chair of the administrative committee and coordinate the administration of the college. Mininger might have the title of president, but the real authority would reside with the chairman of the administrative committee.[55]

President Yoder did not like the proposal. "I am not in favor of running the college with an administrative committee as a permanent thing," he told Orie Miller. And he was certainly not in favor of appointing a new president who would merely be one member of an administrative committee. "We have two people within the school right now beside myself who about halfway feel that they are President," Yoder told Miller. "Bender and Graber like to assert authority, and with a committee they find it much

**President Ernest E. Miller of Goshen College, in 1943.**
*Maple Leaf.*

more easy to usurp what belongs to another office." Yoder warned Orie Miller that Bender may say he is willing to give over some of his responsibilities, but he had never been able to do so in the past. Yoder was pessimistic about his doing so in the future.[56]

Yoder's candidate for president was Ernest E. Miller. Miller had returned from India in 1937, where he had been in charge of a missionary school for nearly twenty years. Learning of his return, Bender had helped Miller get into a Ph.D. program at New York University during 1938-39, with the understanding that he would join the Goshen faculty in 1939. At Goshen, Miller soon established himself as a capable faculty member, popular with students and good at church relations. By the time the administrative committee had persuaded president Yoder to resign, Miller had emerged as a possible candidate.

The other candidate was Paul Mininger, but Mininger had no experience in administration. Orie Miller, the real decision-maker behind the scenes, finally agreed to Ernest Miller, despite some squeamishness about supporting his brother. In June of 1940, during commencement festivities, Ernest E. Miller was inaugurated as Goshen College president.[57]

Whether Bender wanted to be president remains obscure. He was not a supporter of Ernest Miller for president, and he soon discovered that the characteristic he had so deplored in president Yoder—slack administration—now seemed attractive. Ernest Miller was an aggressive administrator who actively managed affairs, and he soon made clear that he intended to supervise the dean. For instance, whereas president Yoder had paid no attention to Bender's travel schedule, Miller insisted that Bender clear his schedule with the president. Soon after taking office, Miller became annoyed when Bender returned from a meeting in Washington about military conscription in order to speak to the Rotary Club in Elkhart. Bender had sent Graber to Washington to finish the work Bender had begun. President Miller reminded Bender that the dean had no authority to send Graber on the trip: Bender should have canceled the Rotary speech and stayed in Washington until the work was done. Miller was especially upset when he learned that the Rotarians had paid Bender a nice stipend. But being told to clear his schedule with the president did not sit well with Bender.[58]

Bender was also annoyed by Miller's insistence that he as president receive copies of any letters about college business written by college personnel. Miller believed he needed to know what was going on; Bender saw it as interference. Moreover, with a president and a dean who were off-campus so frequently, delayed and neglected correspondence had always been a chronic problem, often causing acute embarrassment. So Miller insisted that all mail be opened by secretaries and that in the absence of college officers, urgent matters be handled by subordinates.[59] Bender had great difficulty accepting such delegation of authority.

President Miller brought important strengths to his new role. He was popular with the students and helped manage discipline problems in a better way. He was a good student recruiter, and enrollment grew in his early years as president. He also had sound administrative skills and made the college operate more efficiently. And he was a good fundraiser, helping fashion a carefully orchestrated Mennonite Board of Education fund drive to retire the long-term debt of Goshen and Hesston, a goal which succeeded remarkably well. It was a substantial achievement, preparing the college for a decline in enrollment which came with World War II. Miller was Goshen's first modern president. He brought the college administrative system up to par with the academic system Bender had already created.[60]

To a substantial degree, Bender lacked the very strengths Miller brought to the presidency. He not only lacked the necessary personal qualities of patience and forbearance, but he did not know how to be a modern manager. Bender was progressive, but he was a committee administrator, not a systems manager. He knew how to run committees, arrive at decisions, and carry them out. But he did so in a highly personal way, which is how MCC, the Peace Problems Committee, the Mennonite Relief Committee, and the *MQR* functioned. He had little skill or knowledge about bureaucratic process and was nearly incapable of delegating authority.

In college matters, the coming of Ernest Miller to the presidency changed Bender's relationship to Orie Miller. Bender had always been free to voice his frustrations to Orie, even about president Yoder, and had done so continually. But with Orie's own brother as president, Bender no longer felt free to confide in that way. The result was a significant diminution of Bender's influence and authority at the college. Now the relatively free hand he and Graber had developed to run the college in the 1930s was not only restricted by a more assertive president, but the president even had the ear of the ultimate decision-maker behind the scenes. The new milieu substantially reduced Bender's freedom of action.

# ᴓ13ᴓ

# Designing CPS, Surveying Europe

*Bender helps design Civilian Public Service, visits Europe on behalf of MCC, meets Robert Friedmann.*

IN THE EARLY 1940s, the most significant challenges for Bender came not from within the college but from the national and international scene. At daybreak on Friday, September 1, 1939, C. L. Graber was pulling weeds in the family garden before walking across the street to his office at Goshen College. Straightening up to rest his back, he was suddenly aware of Harold Bender striding across the yard from his home next door. By the look on Bender's face, something was gravely wrong. "The Germans just invaded Poland," Bender told Graber. Bender had just heard the report on the radio.[1]

For the two Mennonite Peace Problems Committee members, it was a moment of truth. Suddenly the press of work waiting for them at the college across the street seemed less urgent: preparing for the arrival of the students in a few days, arranging for a groundbreaking ceremony for the new library, and orienting Ernest Miller to be the new personnel director. Events had vindicated the work of the past several years in preparing Mennonites for the coming war. The two men had helped plan for a September 30, 1939, meeting to create a coordinating committee that would represent Mennonite peace interests; now that planning seemed prescient. For the next six years, the Mennonite response to the war and military conscription would occupy much of Bender's and Graber's energies.

In the fall of 1939, Bender was chairman of the MC Peace Problems Committee (PPC) and executive secretary of the new inter-Mennonite Central Peace Committee (MCPC). He worked with the Brethren and the Friends as a member of the Continuation Committee of Historic Peace Churches. The Mennonites had a fairly clear direction for action. Two weeks after the war began, Bender told M. R. Zigler of the Church of the Brethren that the "Mennonites are definitely planning to carry out a program of alternative service."[2]

The Brethren and Friends were less well prepared and lacked consensus on how to respond in the event of war. But now coordination between the historic peace churches became a necessity. On September 17 at Bender's invitation, a small group of Brethren, Friends, and Mennonites met at Goshen to discuss next steps. Out of the meeting came three initiatives: a Historic Peace Churches (HPC) delegation would visit President Roosevelt; the HPCs would explore doing relief work in Europe; and they would develop a common position paper on military conscription.[3]

Two weeks later the MCPC met in Chicago and wrote the basic document called a "Plan of Action." The plan urged conscientious objectors to register if a draft came, but to be sure to indicate their conscientious objection to military service. It also called for some form of alternative service under civilian control "acceptable to our Christian conscience and conformable to the principles of the Gospel."[4]

At the end of October, Bender took the plan to Rufus Bowman of the Church of the Brethren and to the venerable Friends leader Rufus Jones. Those two leaders approved. "Rufus Jones stands foursquare for the program," Bender reported. Jones was working on the arrangements for a meeting with U.S. president Franklin Roosevelt.[5]

By December the document, the Mennonite "Plan of Action," had been circulated to the HPC groups for their approval. A consensus had been reached. But then the developments hit a snag: some members of the American Friends Service Committee (AFSC) wanted to include a strong statement on behalf of conscientious objectors (COs) who chose noncooperation, who would refuse to register or have anything to do with the conscription system. Bender knew that few Mennonites would agree to such a radical refusal to cooperate with the government. But for Bender, it was more than practical church politics. He genuinely believed in registering for the draft as a signal of pacifists' "positive good will" to the government. He saw registration and cooperation as a sign that pacifists wanted to do something positive for the nation.[6]

Bender's position upset the AFSC's E. Raymond Wilson, who wondered if "to some of our young people the proposed statement will not smack very much of the historic peace churches trying to be quite sure to save their skins from the rigors of conscription without much thought of either what influence it might have on public opinion or the war itself. I suppose there is something of irony in the fact that the Mennonites who have looked askance at our emphasis on political action and political participation, now find us wondering why they are unwilling to go to a logical extreme of political noncooperation in time of war."[7] By the end of December, the AFSC was solidly opposed to the HPC statement based on the Mennonite plan, but the peace-church delegation was running out of time.[8] The meeting with President Roosevelt was scheduled for January 10, less than two weeks away.

Bender tried hard not to make any concessions on the matter, but the Friends were adamant. They also had a constituency to consider. So the peace-church representatives worked out a compromise: to present a general statement of principles, and then a confidential memorandum outlining procedures for COs with a paragraph on the absolutist position. Bender, P. C. Hiebert, and E. L. Harshbarger signed the statement for the Mennonites. Hiebert was chairman of the Mennonite Central Committee and also Mennonite Brethren; Harshbarger was a professor at Bethel College and a General Conference Mennonite.

Bender and Hiebert were the Mennonites in the delegation to see the president. It was Bender's first visit to the White House, and Roosevelt successfully swayed the delegation with his characteristic charm. They left believing they had made a great impression. Hiebert, often given to hyperbole, commented to Harshbarger, "I visualize an almost incalculable amount of suffering and heartache warded off."[9] Actually, Roosevelt did not like COs, and nearly all of his own actions were inimical to their welfare.

The effort to develop the common statement for the president impressed Bender with how difficult it would be for Mennonites to cooperate with the Friends. It made him a strong and early supporter of the idea that Mennonites must administer their own part of the soon-to-be-created Civilian Public Service (CPS) program for COs.

On the other hand, the visit to the president highlighted the importance of HPC collaboration. In early 1940 the Brethren created a Brethren Service Committee (BSC) with M. R. Zigler as the executive secretary, and the Friends established a War Problems Committee. Thus by spring 1940, each group had a working committee with a responsible executive to coordinate responses to the draft.

The sense of urgency to obtain commitments from the government about conscription was driven, especially for the Mennonites and Brethren, by memories of their inadequate preparation and performance during World War I. Both Harold Bender and M. R. Zigler had been only lukewarm pacifists in that war. But both had vivid memories of the hardships that World War I COs had experienced, partly due to inadequate church leadership. The new leaders were consciously trying not to repeat the past.

In the spring of 1940, the peace-church planners were running far ahead of the government itself. Until late June of 1940, the administration was firmly opposed to conscription. Roosevelt's hand was forced when a New York military lobbying group calling for a draft managed to get the "Burke-Wadsworth bill" introduced in Congress on June 20, the same day the Germans entered Paris. During the summer, CO initiatives regarding the proposed draft legislation were largely in the hands of the Friends' War Problems Committee. On July 9 that committee posted Quaker journalist Paul Comly French to Washington, D.C., to lead the HPC efforts against the draft. It soon became apparent that a draft bill would pass in some form, so the HPCs shifted their strategy to trying to protect the interests of COs in whatever law emerged.

• • •

In late November 1939, a few months after Germany occupied Poland, MCC sent M. C. Lehman to Germany to try to get a relief project started in Poland.[10] In March of 1940, Ernest Bennett, who had been working in Spanish relief, moved to southern France to begin work there. Just as the invasion of the Low Countries began in May, another MCC relief worker, Theodore Claassen, arrived in France. With the invasion of France, he moved to England. Thus by the summer of 1940, MCC had three workers in Europe.[11]

Sometime during the fall of 1939, Bender and Orie Miller had conceived the idea of opening a permanent MCC center in Europe, possibly in Basel, Switzerland. The plan called for Harold and Elizabeth to go to Europe during the summer or fall of 1940 to establish the center. Bender hoped to use his sabbatical for that purpose and to begin research on a history of the Amish. Orie Miller and his family then planned to do a six-month stint in 1941. The MCC center was to "serve the Mennonites of Europe in a larger way," as Bender put it.[12] However, their plans were changed by the Germans' rapid advance in the spring of 1940, their blitzkrieg.

The sudden invasion of Scandinavia, the Low Countries, and France came as a shock to Bender. The day after the Germans occupied the Netherlands, Bender told P. C. Hiebert, "I have thought much yesterday and today about our Mennonite people in Holland. They too must now suffer the horrors of war. It will be a severe test for the peace group among our Dutch Mennonites. Perhaps we shall need before long to think of helping our Dutch people both in regard to the peace testimony and in regard to relief."[13]

Hitler's invasion of the Netherlands was even more traumatic for John Horsch. Horsch was already ailing from a serious heart condition. Now, when he learned of Germany's latest action, he suffered a stroke. Since World War I, he had shared the German sense of injustice at the way Britain, France, and the United States had charged Germany with guilt for starting World War I, and he had rejoiced at Hitler's success in redressing those grievances. Yet during the interwar years, Horsch had maintained a warm personal correspondence with the queen of The Netherlands, who was quite interested in Mennonite history. Horsch had a history of heart trouble, and apparently Hitler's ruthless attack on The

Netherlands was more than he could handle. On October 7, 1941, after a lingering illness, he died.[14]

In its June 1940 meeting, the executive committee of MCC decided to send Bender to Europe to survey the situation and make decisions about what work to take up there. By the time Bender was ready to leave, the war was raging in northern France, and all steamship sailings to Europe had been canceled.[15] But Bender was undeterred. Unable to get a visa for Germany in Washington, he decided to trust his luck in getting it after he got to Europe. On July 21 he left for Washington, D.C., visiting the ailing John Horsch en route. In Washington he met Orie Miller to consult on matters of the draft. To their dismay, he and Miller learned that the Burke-Wadsworth conscription bill was going to become law, and that it contained not one improvement over the 1917 draft law. "All our endeavors so far have failed to get our new plan of action included," Bender wrote to C. L. Graber. "Orie and I consider the situation very grave and have wired Hiebert and Harshbarger to come to Lancaster by Saturday noon for a conference."[16] That Bender left the country in the midst of such a crisis is surprising.

On July 25 Bender left New York for Lisbon, Portugal, aboard the *SS Excambion*. In the summer of 1940, Lisbon was the only gateway into Europe. From Lisbon he flew to Barcelona and managed to get a visa to enter Vichy France. Once in France, he was able to visit the young Mennonite relief worker Ernest Bennett, as well as some American Friends and Brethren relief workers at Toulouse. The news was all bad: a great number of refugees and a pervasive fear and expectation that the Germans would occupy all of France, Spain, and Portugal. It was urgent that Bender get to Switzerland before all travel became impossible. To obtain a visa, he had to go to Lyons. He arrived there by train late at night, was unable to get a hotel, and slept on a barroom floor.[17]

The visa processing dragged on for nearly a week. Bender, impatient even under normal circumstances, felt trapped. Finally, on August 16 he was able to cross the border into Switzerland and arrived in Zurich after midnight. Early the next morning, he applied for a visa to Germany. Again there was interminable delay. The first day he visited rare bookstores in Zurich. The next day—Sunday—he went to the Mennonite church in Langnau and was invited to preach. The next morning he returned to Zurich and spent part of the day with his friend professor Fritz Blanke, the Anabaptist scholar. There was still no sign of a visa.[18]

So Bender caught a train to Basel, shopped for rare books, and spent the night with his friend bishop Samuel Nussbaumer. In 1924 Bender and Elizabeth had attended the ordination of Nussbaumer's son, Hans, in Alsace. Samuel Nussbaumer gave him the interesting news that two Mennonite ministers were serving as German army officers in occupied Alsace. One of them, Christian Schnebele of Karlsruhe, had preached in Hans Nussbaumer's church a few weeks earlier. The next morning Bender returned to Zurich and bought some more books. It was not until the following forenoon that the visa finally arrived. Within the hour Bender was on a train for Berlin. There he was met by M. C. Lehman and Elizabeth's uncle Michael Horsch, who was still head of the German Mennonite relief organization Christenplicht.[19]

Bender spent the next three days in Berlin, helping Lehman and Horsch plan for relief work. He also visited his friend Ernst Crous, the Mennonite pastor and historian. On Sunday morning he attended the famous Lutheran Dom church, where he heard a war sermon. One night while returning from a visit to the Crouses, he was caught in a British air raid and spent three hours in an air-raid shelter. For him, the war had become immediate and real.[20]

Much of Bender's energy while in Germany went to mediating a long-standing disagreement between uncle Michael Horsch and Benjamin Unruh. As head of Christenplicht, Horsch wanted to lead the relief efforts. Unruh, on a stipend from MCC and with the best access to officialdom in Berlin, was equally aggressive about his prerogatives. The controversy came to a head during planning for the distribution of food packages in Poland. The plan was for M. C. Lehman to buy the food and have a Mennonite firm in Berlin, A. P. Fast Company, package and deliver the food for a modest fee. Horsch wanted his congregation at Ingolstadt to do the packaging and Christenplicht to do the deliveries.

Bender favored Horsch's plan, but the problem was what to do with Unruh. Bender realized that the amount of food distribution the Germans were allowing was exceedingly limited: Lehman disbursed only about $7,000 worth of relief during his two years in Germany, with an overhead cost of more than $3,000. So Bender cast about for an alternative assignment for Unruh. He remembered his conversation with bishop Nussbaumer in Basel. Perhaps Unruh could arrange a child-feeding operation in Strasbourg. Unruh was a friend of the Nazi *Gauleiter* (provincial governor) in charge of the German occupation of Alsace, a man named Wagner, who lived in Karlsruhe. So Bender thought Unruh might be able to go into the area as an MCC relief worker. Unruh accepted the assignment.[21]

Bender also settled another matter. M. C. Lehman agreed to stay in Berlin for another year if he could return to the states to visit his family over the Christmas holidays. Bender agreed. His work finished, Bender and Uncle Michael took the train to Hellmansberg, Michael's home in Bavaria. There Bender spent the next day in meetings with Michael Horsch and Christian Hege, the German Mennonite historian. Then he went on to Zurich, where he arranged for Swiss dried milk to be sold to Lehman in Berlin and to Bennett in France as part of the relief effort.[22]

Bender caught an overnight train and visited Bennett at Perpignon, France. Then he tried to cross into Spain, only to find the border closed. The next day he succeeded. After making his way to Barcelona, he managed to get on a plane to Lisbon. There he spent several days in consultation with Ted Claassen, who had come over from England, where he was managing the MCC work. On September 4 he left by ship for home. He disembarked at New York and went immediately to the Waldorf Astoria Hotel, where he spent an hour reporting to Herbert Hoover on his findings. Hoover was head of a National Committee on Food for the Small Democracies.[23]

Waiting for Bender at the hotel was a check and a letter from Orie Miller, summoning him to Newton, Kansas, for a meeting of the executive committee of MCC the next day. The check was for the plane ticket to get him there. The executive committee wanted him to deliver his report in person. Two days later Bender and Orie Miller traveled back to Goshen together. The next morning in a

Goshen College chapel, Bender described his trip to the students. The students were impressed. "We're pretty lucky to have him home, safe, again!" the editor of the *Maple Leaf* observed.[24] Over the next five months, Bender repeated the story of his trip in thirty public speeches. Not many people made the trip to Berlin, and in the fall of 1940, Bender's journey was big news.[25]

That trip convinced Bender that, despite the dangers and difficulties, MCC relief in Europe should be stepped up and more volunteers sent out. By 1941, MCC had six American Mennonites in France, working largely in child-feeding projects. In October 1940, John Coffman, Bender's assistant in the Historical Library, left for England to join Ted Claassen. They were joined by Peter Dyck in 1941, and by Elfrieda Klassen and Edna Hunsberger in 1942.[26]

With the entry of the United States into the war in December of 1941, M. C. Lehman was interned by the Germans, then repatriated to the United States in the summer of 1942. In late 1942 the Germans occupied all of France and interned MCCers Lois Gunden and Henry and Beatrice Buller at Baden-Baden. Those MCCers were not released until February 1944.[27]

• • •

During Bender's eight-week absence in Europe, much had transpired on the draft legislation front. The Burke-Wadsworth bill finally passed in Congress on September 14, the day Bender was making his report on his trip to the MCC executive committee in Newton, Kansas. President Roosevelt signed the bill two days later. The conscientious-objector provisions were not all that the Historic Peace Churches had sought; they did not provide for absolutist COs. The pacifists also thought that the law gave far too much discretion to local draft boards in deciding who would qualify as a CO. Nonetheless, HPC people saw Burke-Wadsworth as a vast improvement over the World War I law. Specifically, Burke-Wadsworth let COs be put in "work of national importance under civilian direction," an alternative service program. That meant that COs had a choice other than noncombatancy within the military. The law based CO exemption on individual conviction rather than on membership in a recognized peace church. (However, it still recognized only conscientious objection based on "religious training and belief," thereby discriminating against some socialist and other secular pacifists.)[28]

What Burke-Wadsworth did not do was define the shape and form of the alternative service program. During September it became apparent that the government was not going to design one. So the HPCs decided to take the advice of soon-to-be Director of Selective Service, General Lewis B. Hershey: "Get your groups together, and draw up some proposals. No one in government has given much thought to the problem."[29] Hershey's advice forced three issues to the surface: What form should the program take? What body should take the lead? Who would pay for the program?

To settle such questions, the HPCs met in Chicago on October 4-5. As chair of the MC Peace Problems Committee, Bender was worried about going into an HPC meeting without some prior consultation with his fellow PPC members. The committee had not met for nearly a year. "Events are coming upon us so rapidly that we cannot do this unless we meet for personal exchange of thought and conviction," he told Orie Miller.[30] He was especially concerned to bring church leaders along with PPC thinking. He pointed out to Miller that the two persons managing the emerging CO program (Bender and Miller) were laymen, in a church whose institutional leadership was almost entirely ordained; that seemed like a strange anomaly. The point had been driven home several months earlier by the *Gospel Herald* editor: Daniel Kauffman had suggested that a bishop should be added to the Peace Problems executive committee.[31]

Kauffman's proposal had made Bender uneasy. When Orie Miller wondered if Bender was exaggerating the problem, Bender was moved to quick response. "It is altogether possible that you and I and Graber will be able to make such wise decisions that the church will accept our program without question," Bender told Miller. "However, I personally could not be satisfied to ask our leadership to act merely as rubber stamps, post facto."[32] Bender's two-decade long church experience told him that it was important to keep the church leadership abreast of events. His sense of urgency was heightened by a torrent of requests for information from pastors after the conscription bill was passed in early September 1940. There was great anxiety among Mennonites about the new draft program.

Despite Miller's foot-dragging, Bender prevailed. So a dozen Midwest church leaders met with the PPC on the forenoon of October 4, prior to the larger meeting of the Historic Peace Churches. The MC Mennonite leaders decided on several basic issues: they wanted to direct their own program, and they would pay for it.[33]

The MCs then joined sixty-five Brethren, Friends, and other Mennonites for two days of discussion. Out of the meeting came a coordinating organization called the National Service Board for Religious Objectors (NSBRO). Based in Washington, D.C., it would become the liaison body for the new alternative service program called Civilian Public Service (CPS). As it eventually evolved, CPS was directly managed by the peace churches, albeit under the general oversight of the national Selective Service System. In the course of World War II, more than twelve thousand COs worked in some 150 camps and units. Much of the work was in forestry and conservation projects in various parts of the country, but after 1943 many of the men worked as orderlies in mental hospitals. The first Mennonite camp opened at Grottoes, Virginia, in May of 1941.

• • •

As it developed, the CPS program was a unique arrangement between the American government and the HPCs. The government provided the campsites, buildings, furnishings, equipment, and technical staff. The churches paid all costs related to the care and maintenance of the men. The latter was a practical necessity since Congress almost certainly would not have appropriated money for such a purpose. Moreover, the pacifists, especially the Mennonites, wanted to show they would go the "second mile." Some Mennonites were worried about the funding commitment, but Orie Miller was sure it would be no problem. Mennonites will "gladly pay their share of the bill," he told AFSC leader Clarence Pickett. "They would do it even though every Mennonite farmer had to mortgage his farm."[34]

Bender was not nearly as sanguine as Orie Miller about Mennonite financing of the CPS program. He sensed that the number of Mennonite COs would be much higher than for the Brethren and Friends, "in proportion to membership and wealth." So he searched for some alternative. Bender wrote to Paul Comly French, now head of the NSBRO, and to Orie Miller, arguing that if the government could provide mattresses and beds for the COs, why could it not also provide "consumable food or its equivalent?" He cited the methods Goshen College had used during the New Deal period, when it employed students paid by the National Youth Administration (NYA). The remuneration could be tied to the value or amount of a standard army ration. Twelve dollars per person per month could save the peace churches a lot of money, he maintained.[35]

Paul Comly French was quick to respond. No doubt we could get the government to finance us, but do we want to? he asked. Where government money goes, so does government control. "The whole thing comes down to what our groups want and whether they wish to have a free hand in the program at some financial sacrifice to themselves," he told Bender.[36] Bender was sure French was wrong about the government's eagerness to follow its money and exercise control. It had not happened during the NYA period; why should it now? he countered.[37] But he soon realized that he was in no position to push the idea in the face of French's opposition, so he gave it up. It was an interesting example of Bender's aggressive assertiveness where government was concerned.

The new CPS program challenged the management acumen of the Mennonites. The new generation managing the church colleges, publishing houses, and mission boards had learned how to use modern administrative methods. But the superstructure of the MC Mennonite Church, the general conference organization, was still a committee system operated almost entirely by ordained men. Committee persons made decisions and carried them out personally, nearly always ad hoc.

In 1941 MCC also operated by the committee system with ad hoc administrators. Its chair was P. C. Hiebert, a teacher at Sterling College in Kansas. The vice-chair was Abraham Warkentin, dean of Bethel College. The secretary-treasurer was Orie Miller, a shoe manufacturer who kept the books and did most of the MCC administration out of his business office in Akron, Pennsylvania. Bender, dean of Goshen College, handled MCC correspondence out of his dean's office. A fifth member, Allen Yoder, was a farmer-preacher in Elkhart County, Indiana. There was no salaried staff.

Ostensibly, the conscription issues for the Mennonites were to be managed by the MCPC. It had fourteen members from various Mennonite groups. P. C. Hiebert was its chair; Bender was executive secretary, and managed MCPC affairs also out of his dean's office. As long as the work was mostly a matter of attending meetings and drawing up papers, such an informal system seemed to work—especially since Bender, as assistant secretary of MCC, executive secretary of MCPC, and chair of the PPC, functioned as a one-man coordinator. But as the CPS program emerged, the ad hoc system soon broke down.

In theory the MCPC was to serve as the coordinating body and communication conduit to the churches. Orie Miller—also as a member of MCC, MCPC, and the PPC—was to do the liaison work with the government in Washington and with the Brethren and Friends. But the volume of work soon required Miller to hire assistants. He first hired GC Mennonite pastor Henry Fast from Kansas to be his eyes and ears in Washington. Then he brought in C. K. Lehman, dean of EMS, to manage the MCC office in Akron, Pennsylvania. Meanwhile in Goshen, Bender was trying to respond to a flood of requests for information on draft and CPS matters. It was a struggle to keep the whole system together.

Henry Fast reflected the situation's troublesome tensions and anomalies. People are always writing to me about CO matters, he told Bender. "I cannot very intelligently reply at times because I do not know what the MCPC is doing. I do not want to work at cross-purposes with your committee. In any case, it appears to me that in this strategic place you have helped put me, I ought to be put on your regular mailing list."[38]

By the end of 1941, nearly all the work and activity related to CPS had shifted to the new MCC office at Akron. Bender and the MCPC were largely sidelined. So at the annual MCC meeting in

Chicago on January 2, 1942, the MCPC was dissolved and MCC took over its activities by creating a new MCC Peace Section. Bender was elected chairman. The Peace Section office was located at MCC's Akron headquarters, with a full-time secretary.[39]

All operational aspects of CPS were put under a separate CPS administrative structure. The new Peace Section became the policy committee on all peace-related issues facing Mennonites. From the point of view of Bender and Miller, the new arrangement also had an extra advantage: it put two MC Mennonites—themselves—in effective control of the wartime peace program. Since both were also on the executive committee of MCC and on the MC Peace Problems Committee, all Mennonite CPS, peace-action, and related policy had to receive their imprimatur.[40]

As the CPS program took shape in the fall of 1940, Bender's role and responsibility remained uncertain. To the dismay of Ernest Miller, by then the new president at Goshen College, Bender announced that he would have to take a lot of time off from his college responsibilities for CPS work. He envisioned his role as similar to that of Aaron Loucks during the first World War, when Loucks had functioned as a kind of freelance troubleshooter. President Miller did not like the idea at all: he needed a full-time dean.[41]

To Bender's discomfiture, president Miller gave him three alternatives: focus on being dean and do CPS work only on weekends; take a leave of absence from the college and work full-time on CPS; or have the president take over much of the dean's work. Bender, insulted and distressed by the ultimatum, appealed to Orie Miller for advice. Orie told him to stick to the dean's work; Bender grudgingly agreed. President Miller, by now aware of how difficult it was to manage or control Bender, was delighted with Orie's support, but he was also pessimistic. Bender, he told his brother, "agreed with your point of view and theory, but it will be difficult for him to work it out in practice."[42]

While Bender's role in the development of CPS was significant, it was not determinative. As chair of the new Peace Section and a member of the MCC executive committee, he wielded great influence, but only indirectly. For example, Orie Miller initially appointed Henry Fast to be director of CPS. When Fast resigned in

1943, Miller proposed to replace him with another GC Mennonite, Albert Gaeddert. Bender objected that Gaeddert was too liberal. Let Gaeddert share the post with MC Mennonite John Mosemann Jr. of Lancaster County; then you, in effect, be the actual director. Miller took his advice.[43]

Bender's rather continuous commentary on the performance and problems of various CPS camp leaders must have been trying to the camp directors. Just as Bender seemed to lack an ability to relate well to college students in disciplinary settings, he had similar problems relating to CPS men. He had little patience with human frailty, and that made it difficult for him to function helpfully in disciplinary matters.

Bender was concerned with the behavior of CPS men because by 1943 the CPS program was under tremendous pressure from MC Mennonite leaders upset by how the program was operated. Some of those leaders were unhappy to be associated with the HPC and their lobbying activities in Washington. Others were concerned about pacifist and socialist influence in the camps. They worried, for example, about speakers from the Fellowship of Reconciliation (FOR), a pacifist organization that many Mennonites considered to be too theologically liberal. Some MC leaders simply did not like the close association of MC men with other more "liberal" Mennonites in the camps. Minister Sanford G. Shetler of Johnstown, Pennsylvania, was sure that "it is becoming more and more apparent that "our mixture with the various Mennonite groups" will bring an end to "the distinctive teachings of the Mennonite church." Shetler believed that "when churches merge in movement or organization, the liberals are the gainers and the conservatives the losers."[44]

In 1941, at the insistence of conservative and outspoken leaders in the Virginia Conference, the MC general conference appointed a CPS Investigating Committee to explore what was wrong with CPS. To deal with the perceived problems, the 1943 MC general conference enlarged the PPC to twelve members. Bender continued as chair, Orie Miller as secretary, and C. L. Graber as treasurer; but the committee now included nine bishops, one of them being Bender's longtime nemesis, Virginia bishop J. L. Stauffer.[45] The conservatives in the church were not strong enough to banish the Bender-Miller-Graber trio from their PPC leadership roles, but in 1943 they surrounded them with a formidable group of advisers.

Bender disliked the new arrangement and cautiously expressed his frustration to general conference moderator Milo Kauffman. "It seems that our machinery is getting quite complicated, what with the Peace Problems Committee, General Problems Committee, CPS Advisory Committee, Relief Committee, and General Conference Executive Committee all being in some way related to and working on the CPS problem. We as a Peace Problems Committee will do our best to try to understand the new setup and fit ourselves into it, but I confess I sometimes have difficulty in keeping up with the gyrations of the machinery."[46]

Given such murky lines of responsibility, Bender felt exceedingly vulnerable as PPC chair. His anxieties help explain the extraordinary efforts he made to control deviations from nonconformity in the Mennonite CPS camps. He complained at length about education directors Atlee and Winifred Beechy at Sideling Hill CPS camp in eastern Pennsylvania, who wore wedding rings. Winifred Beechy also went without stockings and sometimes used rouge, which upset some eastern conservatives. In another case a camp requested permission to subscribe to *The Call*, a Socialist party paper. Absolutely not, Bender told them. "Organs of political propaganda are out of place" in CPS camps.[47]

Movies were often a point of concern. "The charge has been made that the films are not educational, but recreational and for amusement, even including comedy," Bender advised Ralph Hernley, the director at the Wells Tannery, Pennsylvania, CPS camp. Send me a list of all the films you have shown, he told Hernley, so I can reply accurately to the persons bringing the charges.[48] While Bender was genuinely concerned about many of these issues, he also served a useful role in absorbing and often deflecting much of the criticism.

Some of the problems intruded onto the Goshen campus. During August 1943, the managers of CPS held a Relief Training School at Goshen College. The training schools were designed to prepare CPS men and some women for relief work overseas if and when that became possible. On August 14, 1943, Bender returned to Goshen from a three-week trip to western CPS camps only to discover that Arthur Swift of the FOR had just been on campus to speak to the training school people. "Since Swift is a modernist Union Theological Seminary professor as well as chairman of the FOR, I cannot understand why he was invited," Bender complained to Orie Miller. "In my humble judgment, this is one of the worst blunders the MCC and Goshen College have made for a long time. I have struggled for 18 years to keep Goshen clear of all modernist connections, and this is the first bad break in that time."

Making matters worse, the *Goshen College Record* ran a lead article featuring Swift complete with a picture. A week later the MC biennial general conference met on the campus, and a major agenda item was the report of the CPS Investigating Committee. "To have this material around will give good fuel to the flames," Bender told Orie Miller despairingly.[49]

One proposal by MC critics was that the MCs should set up camps for MC Mennonite COs only. From the point of view of CPS administrators, it was a terrible idea, and they dragged their feet as much as possible. But at Bender's insistence, an MC Mennonite camp was established at Malcolm, Nebraska, on a farm owned by the Mennonite Publication Board.[50] The camp, which opened in October 1944, was funded through the Peace Problems Committee, and Bender became its administrator. Thirty-five MC men served at Malcolm before it closed in late 1946. By early 1945 it was apparent that the war would soon be over, so the church made no effort to establish more such camps.[51]

In October of 1941, Henry Fast and Harold Bender were appointed director and dean of the educational work in the CPS camps. Each camp employed an educational director with the task of fostering appreciation for the Mennonite heritage, enhance religious experience, and promote personal growth. All Mennonites were expected to enroll in a formal "core" course which was designed to cover the objectives. Bender became the editor of a six-booklet series on Mennonites and their heritage. He wrote the first pamphlet, *Mennonite Origins in Europe*. It was an impressive series, most of it published in 1942. More than six thousand copies of each title were printed.[52]

By 1943 it became apparent that almost half of all MC Mennonite draftees were opting for some form of military service, a discovery which Bender understandably found extremely disconcerting. What the issue highlighted was one of the anomalies of the MC Mennonite experience during the war. The church was unusually fortunate in its leaders, who designed and administered a successful pacifist response to the war. To a significant degree, the CPS program met the expectations and needs of most American Mennonites. In retrospect, it is not surprising that the convictions of many young Mennonites fell short of their leaders' expectations, though it did surprise the leaders at the time. MC Mennonite young people were not immune and could not have been immune to the powerful forces pushing them to support the war. In fact, however, compared to every other group of young people in American society (or probably to youth anywhere in the world), they were remarkably resistant to the allure of the war.

Bender wanted to be more involved in the direction of the CPS program, but for the most part he had to be content to play a policy role rather than an administrative role. That was fortunate, for in 1940 Bender's scholarly role took a new turn. That change was bound up with two historians, neither one a Mennonite.

• • •

The commuters streaming out of the evening train from New York City would not have noticed the three men as they met in the waiting room of the New Haven, Connecticut, railway station. The two men waiting were small and spare, while the one getting off the train was short, heavyset, and carrying a bulging briefcase. The three greeted each other in German. All were in their forties. For the first time, Harold Bender, with the briefcase, was meeting Roland Bainton, professor of church history at Yale University, and Robert Friedmann, an Austrian-Jewish refugee. The date was May 14, 1940. It was the beginning of an enduring friendship.

The specific place and time of meeting was a product of

Harold Bender's travel schedule. Earlier in the day he had been in New York City at a Federal Council of Churches meeting about conscientious objectors. The next morning he had an appointment in Washington, D.C. A few days before the trip, he realized he could leave New York for New Haven and Yale University in the late afternoon, spend a few hours with Bainton and Friedmann, then catch a Pullman to Washington to arrive just an hour before his appointment the next morning.[53]

So Bender had come to New Haven, with just three hours between trains, to visit Friedmann and Bainton. The three men drove to the Yale Divinity School quadrangle, where Friedmann had a room. Since the tiny room only had two chairs, professor Bainton stretched out on Friedmann's bed and caught a nap while Bender and Friedmann got acquainted.[54]

**Robert Friedmann.** Sanford Calvin Yoder papers, AMC.

Bender had come to New Haven to see Friedmann. Ten years earlier he and Friedmann had begun a correspondence while Bender was at Heidelberg and Friedmann was living in Vienna. They had learned about each other through John Horsch. Horsch's Hutterite studies had caught Friedmann's attention since the Austrian was also working on Hutterite history. During his 1930, 1935, and 1936 visits to Europe, Bender had made continual promises to visit Friedmann in Vienna, but plans never worked out. Now in the spring of 1940, through no choice of his own, Friedmann was at Yale University.[55]

Friedmann was a Jewish-Christian refugee. He was forced into exile by the Nazi regime and had to leave his wife and two sons behind. During a year in England supported by a refugee-scholar organization, he wrote an eighty-page essay entitled "Anabaptism and Pietism." Many years later he told the story: "When I was through, I put it in a nice good envelope, registered mail, and mailed it to Dean Harold S. Bender in Goshen, Indiana." In an accompanying letter, he had written, "Maybe you will be interested—I would be glad if this paper could be used in the *MQR*."[56]

A month later, in late December of 1939, Friedmann had been able to come to New York City, sponsored by the American Friends Service Committee. Learning of Friedmann's whereabouts, Roland Bainton invited him to Yale as an honorary fellow at the Divinity School. A local committee helped support him, and in late spring the committee also helped bring his wife and children to New Haven. But all the support was meager at best and temporary: there were no commitments beyond July 1940.[57]

When he left Austria, Friedmann took with him a suitcase full of Hutterite letters. His hope was to edit and publish the letters as part of his ongoing work on Hutterite history. Encouraged by Bainton, Friedmann wrote to Bender in March 1940, inquiring whether the *MQR* would be interested in publishing some of the items. But Bender had just promised to publish a set of Hutterite letters edited by Professor A. J. F. Zieglschmid, a Germanist at Northwestern University. When Bender learned of Friedmann's letters, he really preferred to publish Friedmann's work. "I am in a quandary just now as to which professor I should hitch my caboose onto," he wrote Bainton. "My heart is with Dr. Friedmann, and I want to help him all I can."[58]

Bainton offered a solution. Why not collaborate—Yale Divinity School, the American Society of Church History (Bainton was its president), and the Mennonite Historical Society? They could make an appeal to the Rockefeller Foundation for funds to support Friedmann while he produced the volume of Hutterite letters.

That is, Bainton joked, "Unless you have scruples against making friends with the mammon of unrighteousness."[59] Bender had no such scruples, particularly since Bainton's idea might solve his Ziegleschmid-Friedmann problem. He could defer publishing Zieglschmid while the appeal to Rockefeller was being made, and offer the possibility of funded collaborative work to Zieglschmid and Friedmann.

Now on this May evening in 1940, Bender was at Yale for a few hours to talk over the plans for such a venture and establish the basic lines for the appeal to the Rockefeller Foundation. However, much more important for the future of Anabaptist studies and Mennonite history was the emergence of a new relationship: Bender and Friedmann liked each other immediately. When they parted a few hours later, they were friends for a lifetime. Furthermore, Bender had decided that Friedmann should come to Goshen College. The morning after he returned from his trip, and before Bainton approached the Rockefeller Foundation, Bender told Bainton, "I believe I can get one of the Mennonite organizations to guarantee $30 per month for Friedmann beginning July 1st and continuing for a year. This could probably best be handled if he should come for the year to Goshen to live."[60]

In June, Bainton had to report that his request for funds from the Rockefeller Foundation had failed. Bender immediately began an intense fundraising campaign to bring Friedmann to Goshen. The just-inaugurated president of Goshen was his first target. "Bender is very persistent about the research scholar from Germany," Ernest Miller complained to his brother Orie. Reluctantly, the president had agreed to let the Friedmanns live in the college apartment house, but under no circumstances was he going to allow the support of the scholar to become an item in the college budget. Orie Miller found it easy to agree with president Miller since by that time he had approved Bender's suggestion that the Mennonite Relief Committee commit $30 a month to the Friedmanns. By then Bender also had a $60-a-month commitment for one year from the Goshen city ministerial association.[61] The Friedmanns would come to Goshen.

In New Haven, meanwhile, the Friedmanns were in despair.

All avenues of support and employment had failed, despite dozens of letters of endorsement from Bainton and his colleagues at Yale. Thus they were utterly surprised by a telephone call from Bainton saying, "Robert, you are a lucky fellow. I just got a telegram from Harold Bender that he wants you to be a research fellow at Goshen College at its newly opened library, and he will guarantee you a house or dwelling, and $60 a month cash for one year."[62] Overjoyed, the Friedmanns accepted immediately. Two weeks later, on July 5, they arrived in Goshen.

The Friedmanns were flabbergasted by the warm welcome. "We arrived by 10:30 at night, and there at the railroad station were Harold Bender, the minister of the Eighth Street Mennonite Church, and the pastor of the Congregational church, and many, many more people," Friedmann later recalled. "Bender brought us to North hall. There we had not only a very nice two-room apartment and kitchen, but the refrigerator was full with food. There were jams and marmalades and I don't know—butter and everything. Eggs and what have you. Cake and everything under the sun. Ice Cream. It was fantastic. We couldn't believe our eyes. So we began our sojourn in Goshen. Free apartment and $60 a month."[63]

What would be his work? He had arrived just a month after the dedication of the new Memorial Library at the college. The entire basement floor was given over to the Mennonite Historical Library. During the rush of moving the historical material out of the Administration Building in early June, the books were simply piled on the floor. By 1940 there were more than 3,000 rare books in the library, none of them cataloged. Friedmann was handed the daunting task of organizing and cataloging the historical library. He described the scene in his typically picturesque fashion. "It [the historical library] was all heaps of books. That was all I could see. Nothing else. Heaps of books. Wherever you went, there were heaps of books lying around, and you opened it, and there was something new here and something new there. It was a tremendously exciting experience."[64]

The "heaps of books" were an eloquent if mute testimony to Bender's unflagging fifteen-year effort to collect rare books for the

Mennonite Historical Library. Friedmann was awed by the accomplishment. He was even more impressed by Bender's skill at
gathering books. Shortly after he arrived in Goshen, he accompanied Bender on a visit to an Elkhart County Mennonite family re-
puted to have a very old Anabaptist book. What they found surprised them. It was a sixteenth-century *Sammelband* (collection) of
Anabaptist writings, including several by the notable Michael Satt-
ler, dating from the 1530s. Friedmann realized that the book was
priceless. How could the penurious Historical Library ever afford
it? To Friedmann's complete astonishment, Bender made no mention of money: instead, he offered a free semester of attendance at
Goshen College to one of the family's daughters. The book came
to the Mennonite Historical Library.[65]

Within a few weeks of Friedmann's arrival, Bender left on his
trip to Europe for MCC. By the time he returned to Goshen in September, the Friedmanns had moved into the parsonage of the
Eighth Street Mennonite Church. Eighth Street Church was a GC
congregation and had offered the Friedmanns the free use of the
parsonage for the academic year. The Friedmanns subsequently became members there. Early in 1941 Bender was able to get a grant
of $800 from the Carl Schurz Memorial Foundation to pay Fried-
mann to continue the cataloging of the historical library. He was
able to stitch together a number of other smaller Mennonite grants
for translating chores and some help for a new Mennonite archives.
Thus the income for Friedmann was secured for 1941-42.[66]

In early 1945 Friedmann was hired to teach at Western Michigan College in Kalamazoo, Michigan, some sixty miles from
Goshen. He held the post until he retired a quarter-century later.[67]
Friedmann's arrival had begun a new stage in Bender's evolution
as a historian and scholar.

# ৶14৸

# The Anabaptist Vision

*Friedmann influences Bender. Elizabeth works
on her master's degree. Harold presents
"The Anabaptist Vision."*

ROBERT FRIEDMANN arrived in Goshen in July 1940, just six weeks after John Horsch suffered the paralyzing stroke which abruptly halted his scholarly work. For two decades Horsch had been Harold Bender's mentor. In Robert Friedmann, Bender now found another collaborator who shared his passion for historical studies. Compared to Horsch, Friedmann was more broadly informed and educated in theology and history.

Friedmann was as single-mindedly committed to Anabaptist history as John Horsch had been, but he was much more receptive to new ideas. In fact, compared to Horsch's influence, Friedmann's effect on Bender was even more telling. Horsch had always been a conservative authority-figure in the background to whom Bender needed to show deference. Friedmann appealed to Bender's more progressive instincts.

A slow reorientation of Bender's understanding of Mennonite history had begun when Friedmann mailed his essay on "Anabaptism and Pietism" to Bender in November of 1939. In his editorial introduction to the essay, in the April 1940 issue of the *MQR*, Bender caught Friedmann's key point. "Friedmann has focused a revealing light on the central problem of Christian theology and Christian living and thus contributed effectively to a critique of modern Mennonitism," he wrote. In his essay Friedmann described how Pietism's preoccupation with soul-saving piety weakened the seamless connection between faith and practice.[1]

Friedmann helped shift Bender's attention from the fundamen-talist-modernist focus on correct belief to a new concern with how belief and life could be knit together. The Protestant temptation and habit of separating salvation and ethics now became a central concern for Bender. It was Robert Friedmann who helped Bender understand how that separation might be remedied.[2]

• • •

In January 1941 Bender began an eight-month sabbatical. He planned to write the history of the Mennonites in America, which he had been assigned to do in 1927 but which he had not yet begun fourteen years later. He believed he could also do a history of the Amish at the same time. For his Amish research, he had suc-cessfully applied for a grant from the Carl Schurz Foundation. Unfortunately, he did almost no work on any history during the sabbatical; CPS and relief activities absorbed nearly all of his time.

As part of his sabbatical, Bender attended a summer workshop at the University of Minnesota sponsored by the North Central As-sociation. Goshen College had been selected as one of twenty col-leges—among seventy who had applied—to participate in a pro-gram to upgrade liberal arts instruction. The liberal arts workshop was an unusual experience for Bender, something he had never done before.[3] He enjoyed the four-week course.[4] The family rented a house in Minneapolis so that Elizabeth and the children could be with him, and Elizabeth took courses at the university in German literature.[5]

The following summer (1942) the Benders spent two more months at the University of Minnesota, so Elizabeth could contin-ue her study. She was pursuing her master's degree in German by summer work and writing a thesis on "The Mennonites in German Literature," Bender told Friedmann.[6] Bender urged Friedmann not to "tell *anyone* [his emphasis]" about this development.[7] The rea-sons for such secrecy are obscure, but Elizabeth shunned publicity and simply may not have wanted people to know what she was doing. Moreover, it was most unusual for a married Mennonite woman of Elizabeth's generation to do graduate work. Harold and Elizabeth also were aware that many faculty at Goshen thought Bender used his position as dean to promote teaching assignments for Elizabeth. Perhaps her advanced work would be seen as just one more of Bender's schemes to secure her employment.

Bender used the time in Minneapolis toward rewriting his Grebel dissertation for publication. He had been working in history for more than a dozen years, yet had never produced a book-length monograph. He must have realized it was time to do so. During the 1930s, the *MQR* had published five chapters of the dissertation, but since his dissertation research in 1935, he had done no original research which was published. Thus in 1942 his claim as an Anabaptist historian rested on his dissertation and his editorship of the *MQR*. Getting out the Grebel biography would confirm his ability to do sustained scholarly historical work.

Bender was eager to get the Grebel biography published. In the spring of 1941, he told Edward Yoder that he was "rapidly completing" the revision and proposing to print 1,000 copies. He even sent the Historical Committee $125 to subsidize the publication.[8] However, a year later, in July 1942, he had finished only five chapters. He hoped to complete the rest "in a few days"[9]—but he did not do so. Moreover, by that time, because of war shortages, no printing paper was available, even if the manuscript had been ready. Immediately after the war, Bender found neither money nor time to complete the revision. Not until 1950 did the book finally come out.[10] The same fate befell a book which Harold and Elizabeth translated and edited during 1941 and 1942, Friedmann's *Mennonite Piety Through the Centuries*, a work on Pietism and Anabaptism. It finally appeared in 1949.[11]

Bender's two colleagues John C. Wenger and Guy F. Hershberger were more fortunate. Wenger produced a small text for use in the Mennonite history course at Goshen entitled *Glimpses of Mennonite History*,[12] published in 1940. Guy F. Hershberger had been commissioned by the Peace Problems Committee in 1937 to write a book on the biblical basis of nonresistance but had found no time to get it done. Finally in 1943, Bender secured PPC funds to buy Hershberger some time. In a leave of absence from January to September 1943, Hershberger completed the work, *War, Peace, and Nonresistance.* As chair of the PPC, Bender edited Hershberger's book during the fall and winter of 1943-44.[13]

When John Horsch had a stroke in May of 1940, he left an unfinished manuscript for a book entitled *Mennonites in Europe.* Since Bender was chair also of the MC's Historical Committee, it fell to him to see that someone completed the volume. Bender enlisted Edward Yoder, who did the bulk of the work, including the bibliography and the index. For the sensitive soul of Edward Yoder, the task was an ordeal: he had to mediate conflicting advice from Bender, John and Christina Horsch, and his publisher and boss, A. J. Metzler. But by February 1942, the book was at press, and Yoder breathed a sigh of relief that the "18 months of work and worry" were at an end.[14]

The plan had been for Bender to write a companion volume on the history of the Mennonites in America; indeed, he had actually begun work on the book as early as 1928, but had never gotten far. In 1941 Bluffton College historian C. Henry Smith had published an 800-page work, *The Story of the Mennonites*, which covered the same ground as the Horsch and Bender volumes and did so masterfully. The appearance of the Horsch and Smith volumes put pressure on Bender to complete his long-delayed book of Mennonite history. So in 1943 he appealed to A. J. Metzler for publishing house funds to support his writing during the summer of 1944.[15] But once more, other tasks got in the way, and the writing remained undone.

Bender's failure to complete his major scholarly work was partly hostage to his nearly continual production of more popular material. In 1940, as part of a centenary Sunday school celebration, he published a 60-page booklet on the history of Mennonite Sunday schools. In 1942 he wrote the first booklet in the Mennonites and Their Heritage series of small books. That series was designed for a "Core Course" in CPS camps. Also, in early 1943, Bender and Edward Yoder produced a 68-page booklet again designed for CPS men, *Must Christians Fight?*[16]

Bender also wrote articles for the *Gospel Herald.* In 1941 he did one on the importance of relief work as a mission of the church. From February to April of 1943, he wrote nine articles under the general title "In the Midst of War—Thoughts for Nonresistants." His specific topics ranged from "The Farmer and Fighting" to "Money and War," "War Hysteria," and "Mennonite Men in the Army?"[17] During the same period he also published a longer *Gospel Herald* article, "The Content of the Bible School Curriculum." That article originated as a paper he had presented to the MC Board of Education as he anticipated action the board took in January of 1943, to approve a five-year Th.B. (bachelor of theology) degree at Goshen.[18]

Throughout Bender's life, serious scholarly research was always secondary to more immediate and pressing popular writing. On one level, it reflected his commitment to the church and his willingness to subordinate his personal interests to the demands the church made on him. But it was also a fact that he could write such short pieces quickly and at odd moments without interrupting his hectic, fast-paced life—a pattern that an extensive scholarly work would not allow. Never in his entire life did Bender reserve a large block of time for research and writing as did Guy F. Hershberger in 1943, when he completed his *War, Peace, and Nonresistance*. Bender could never bring himself to withdraw from his responsibilities as dean, editor of the *MQR*, secretary of the Mennonite Relief Committee, chairman of the PPC, and secretary of the MCC executive committee. The result was almost no original research but much quick and semipopular writing.

• • •

Such was the case with Bender's most influential essay, "The Anabaptist Vision." Although it became famous as a new Mennonite manifesto, it was unresearched and hastily prepared at the last minute, to meet his obligations as president of the American Society of Church History (ASCH).

By 1940 Bender had been a member of the ASCH for fifteen years. He had joined in 1925 despite objections from John Horsch, who did not think specially trained Mennonites should be members of worldly professional organizations any more than other

Mennonites should be members of labor unions or the Farm Bureau. Horsch need not have worried, for Bender's connections with the ASCH were always tenuous at best. Yet it was one of the few non-Mennonite organizations to which Bender ever belonged.

Between 1925 and 1940, Bender attended only a few of the church-history society's annual conferences. At one in 1930, he read a paper, "Recent Progress in Research in Anabaptist History," which caught the attention of Matthew Spinka, professor of church history at Chicago Theological Seminary. Spinka had just been appointed editor of a new journal the ASCH planned to begin publishing in 1932, and he invited Bender to submit the paper for the journal's first issue. But then he was embarrassed, for his editorial committee rejected the paper. He was especially chagrined because Bender had helped him negotiate a deal in which the Mennonite Publishing House would print the new journal, *Church History*, at a reasonable rate.[19] At a session in 1936, Bender read a paper on Conrad Grebel, and that paper did appear in *Church History* in 1938.[20] It was Bender's first article published in an academic journal other than *MQR*.

In 1940 Bender took Robert Friedmann to the December ASCH conference in Philadelphia. Friedmann read a paper, "Conception of the Anabaptists," an opportunity arranged for him by Roland Bainton, who was ASCH president that year. It was Friedmann's first American conference, and he enjoyed meeting many of the leading American church historians. Bainton and Bender had agreed to use the conference to showcase Friedmann for some teaching position at an American college or university. Friedmann and Bender also attended the conference to hear Roland Bainton's presidential address, "The Struggle for Religious Liberty."[21]

While at the conference, Bender was elected to the ASCH governing council, almost certainly at the behest of Bainton. Had he not taken Friedmann to the conference and had Bainton not pushed his appointment to the council, Bender would not have later become ASCH president. And had he not become president, there would have been no "Anabaptist Vision" speech, at least not in the form we know it today. Bender was unable to attend the next two annual conferences, in 1941 and 1942. Nonetheless, in

1941 the ASCH elected him to be its vice-president; thus, late in 1942 he became the president of the ASCH.

The letter from the secretary of the ASCH, Thomas C. Pears Jr., announcing his election, got lost in Bender's office. He did not learn the news until February 1943, when he received the minutes of the meeting. "I note from the minutes that I was elected in absentia. I will await instructions from you regarding my duties," he told Pears.[22] But Pears was also new to his office and did not know what the president's duties were; so he referred Bender to the outgoing president, E. R. Hardy, who taught at the General Theological Seminary in New York City.[23]

You have two jobs, Hardy told Bender: prepare a presidential address, and tell us where the meeting will be held. Since you are in the Midwest, why not have it in Chicago?[24] Bender, preoccupied with CPS, college, and church business, did not reply to Hardy until October, only two months before the conference scheduled for December. Hardy, responsible to plan the program, must have been anxious. But when Bender finally wrote on October 9, his tone was as if nothing were amiss. "After mature consideration and counseling," he told Hardy, we have decided to hold the ASCH meeting in connection with the annual meeting of the American Historical Association. "I therefore commission you to proceed with the arrangements."[25] Hardy complied. He arranged to hold the conference at Columbia University on December 28 and 29, and selected the papers to be read.

The biggest problem was the schedule of president Bender. He had to be at an MCC meeting in Chicago at noon on December 29, on the day after his presidential address. It was wartime. Trains ran chronically late, and getting a confirmed reservation was difficult and subject to military priorities. Bender could not risk missing the MCC meeting by being tied up in New York. Almost automatically, he decided not to attend the ASCH meeting. Because of difficulties with travel arrangements, "I can not guarantee being present to preside at the Church History Society program," he told Hardy on December 16.[26] But, Bender promised, "I'll get my Presidential address to you at least by the morning of the beginning of the conference."[27]

On the day before Christmas and just four days before the conference, Bender learned that he could get a plane out of New York late in the evening of December 28, catch a train out of Cleveland, and get to Chicago by noon on the twenty-ninth. The plane ticket added $10 to the cost of the trip. Would MCC pay the difference? It would, Orie Miller assured him.[28]

The next question: could Bender get a seat on an eastbound train to New York on such short notice? A railroad strike was scheduled to begin on the evening of December 28. The impending strike, combined with the usual rush of Christmas travel, made getting a reservation almost impossible. But somehow Bender secured a seat. By late in the evening of December 27, he was on a train for New York City. The train arrived late. The conference was to begin at 3:00 p.m. By the time Bender found his way to Room 104 in Millbank Hall on the Columbia campus, it was 3:20. Thirty-one people awaited his arrival.

Bender opened the meeting with prayer. His first announcement was a sad one: ASCH secretary Pears had died two days earlier. Bender requested historian Robert Hastings Nichols to write a minute which would recognize Pears's services to the ASCH.

That afternoon the conferees heard two papers, one by David M. Cory on "The Religious History of the Mohawk and Oneida Tribes of the Iroquois Confederacy." Interspersed through Cory's presentation were songs in the Iroquois language sung by two members of the Iroquois tribe. They provided a colorful accent to the otherwise staid proceedings.

At seven o'clock the society held its annual dinner at the Columbia University Men's Faculty Club. The address by president Bender followed the dinner. Bender entitled his speech "The Anabaptist Vision." Matthew Spinka noted in the minutes of the meeting that the speech was followed by "a very lively discussion which would have undoubtedly continued much longer were it not for lack of time, for President Bender had to leave soon afterwards by plane to attend a meeting in Chicago."[29]

In his last action as president, Bender appointed Roland Bainton to preside at the ASCH sessions the next day. That done, he took a taxi to the La Guardia Airport and boarded a plane for

Cleveland. There, sometime after midnight, he caught a train to Chicago. Just after lunch at 12:30 the next day, he was at his place in one of the conference rooms at the Atlantic Hotel—ready for a day and a half of MCC meetings dealing with CPS.[30]

• • •

It remains a mystery why Bender made the effort to attend the ASCH meeting. After all, this was wartime, and he might well have begged off, given the wartime restrictions on travel. He might also have excused himself for want of time to get a speech ready. The fall of 1943 was an unusually busy time for him. President Ernest Miller was on leave to study at Princeton University, and Bender was acting president. Bender found it difficult to find time to write the speech. He carried presidential duties combined with teaching two courses and coping with the pressures on him as a leader of the emerging CPS program. As usual, Bender waited until the last minute. Two weeks before the conference, it was still not written. But when he finally got to it, the week before Christmas, he wrote it quickly. Elizabeth later remembered being "just amazed how he got that whole thing done and ready to give in no time at all: two or three days."[31]

"The Anabaptist Vision" was not a carefully researched essay: there was no time for that. But it was a carefully crafted piece. Bender knew that Reformation scholars Roland Bainton and Matthew Spinka would be there. He could also expect the two leading church historians of the time, James Hastings Nichols and Kenneth Scott Latourette, to be on hand. So the paper had to have weight.

How Bender selected his topic is not known. Clearly, given the lack of time, he had to write from what was on his mind at the time. The topic had to be Anabaptism. That was his field of expertise, and Bender's sense of a historic opportunity to promote his field made that choice nearly automatic. But he surely sensed an opportunity also to establish a new definition of Anabaptism. Several years earlier, in 1939, he had told Roland Bainton, whom he had not yet met in person: "I shall look forward to the chance to discuss Anabaptist history with you. I am still struggling with the problem of how to conceive the movement in its early period. My own feeling is that no one has yet given sufficient attention to the movement to be able to trace the connections between the various geographical and ideological subgroups. I hope some one in the not too distant future will give himself to writing a real history of the Anabaptist movement. I have threatened to do so myself if no one else undertakes it."[32]

Actually, at that very time C. Henry Smith was busy writing his massive Mennonite history, *The Story of the Mennonites*, published in 1941. Smith argued that the key element of Anabaptist belief had been the freedom of the individual. Bender vigorously contested that argument in a review of Smith's history in 1942. The Anabaptists had not stressed individualism, Bender insisted, but "group solidarity and discipline."[33] When Bender wrote his "Vision" essay in December 1943, he surely had the October 1943 *MQR* in front of him, with Smith's vigorous response to Bender's review. The Anabaptists were individualists, Smith insisted, in that they believed "faith in God" was possible only through the individual conscience. "Conscience is not a collective matter, but individual," Smith pointed out. In an aside which Bender found completely unsatisfactory, Smith claimed that the Anabaptists understood the church as "merely a fellowship of congenial and like-minded believers."[34]

The same year that Smith published his *Story of the Mennonites*, Yale historian Roland Bainton had written an essay which tried to give some shape and form to the Anabaptist movement. Entitled "The Left Wing of the Reformation," Bainton developed a taxonomy of a half-dozen characteristics shared by a broad set of sixteenth-century Protestant sectarians. Bainton sought to be as inclusive as possible, using general categories such as belief in religious freedom, and separation of church and state. As a result, he found many versions of Anabaptism in the sixteenth century.[35] Bender's approach was just the opposite of Bainton's. In his essay Bender used exclusive categories, such as a disciplined church and nonresistance. As a result, Bender found only a few authentic sixteenth-century Anabaptist groups: specifically, the Swiss Brethren, and the followers of Menno Simons in the Netherlands.

To Bainton's surprise, his phrase "Left Wing of the Reformation" had quickly become a popular label for the Anabaptists. No doubt the quick acceptance of the label was helped by the prevailing war mentality; at the end of the essay, Bainton had claimed that the "cleavage between Germany and the West" was a result of the successful eradication of the "Left Wing" in Germany, whereas in England and the United States the "Left Wing" had flourished and bequeathed the benefits of religious liberty and democracy. Suddenly Bainton had made the Anabaptists not merely legitimate but central to Anglo-American culture.[36]

In his editorials in the *MQR*, Bender had often complained about the neglect of Anabaptists by church historians. Now Bender had a new problem. Bainton had developed a powerful new image of the Anabaptists and their influence in Western history. The presidential address gave Bender an opportunity to offer an alternative to Bainton's "Left Wing" thesis.

Bender began the "Anabaptist Vision" essay by disavowing Bainton's suggestion that religious liberty was Anabaptism's essence. "But great as the Anabaptist contribution to the development of religious liberty, this concept not only does not exhaust but actually fails to define the true essence of Anabaptism," he told his audience. "It is a purely formal concept with no content or plan of action."[37] He then took direct aim at Bainton's "Left Wing" label, arguing that it was too broad to be helpful. "We know enough today to draw a clear line of demarcation between original evangelical and constructive Anabaptism on the one hand, which was born in the bosom of Zwinglianism in Zurich, Switzerland, in 1525 and established in the Low Countries in 1533, and the various mystical, spiritualistic, revolutionary, and other related groups on the other hand, which came and went like the flowers of the field in those days."[38]

The true Anabaptists were the predecessors of the half-million Mennonites in the world today, Bender told his audience. "There is no longer any excuse for permitting our understanding of the distinct character of this genuine Anabaptism to be obscured by Thomas Müntzer and the Peasants' War, the Münsterites, or any other aberration of Protestantism in the sixteenth century."[39]

After citing a series of mistaken interpretations of the Anabaptist "Vision" by various scholars, Bender described the interpretation he said "is probably destined to dominate the field." That interpretation held that "Anabaptism is the culmination of the Reformation, the fulfillment of the original vision of Luther and Zwingli." The Anabaptists, Bender claimed, "retained the original vision of Luther and Zwingli, enlarged it, gave it body and form, and set out to achieve it in actual experience."[40] In effect, the Anabaptists were the quintessential sixteenth-century Protestants.

Bender then laid out the threefold content of the "Vision." The key element was "the conception of the essence of Christianity as discipleship, a concept which meant the transformation of the entire way of life of the individual believer and of society so that it should be fashioned after the teachings and example of Christ. The focus of the Christian life was not so much the inward experience of the grace of God, as it was for Luther, but the outward application of that grace to all human conduct. The great word of the Anabaptists was not faith, as it was with the other Reformers, but following Christ (*Nachfolge Christi*)."[41]

The "Vision" also embodied a new concept of "voluntary church membership based upon true conversion." Such membership rested on a "commitment to holy living and discipleship." Indeed, that commitment "was the absolutely essential heart of the concept."[42] Bender contrasted voluntary church membership with the Protestant Reformers' acceptance of a mass church. The high standard of New Testament living embraced by the Anabaptists meant separation from the world. For that idea, Bender used the term "nonconformity" and argued that the logical outcome of nonconformity was a suffering church. Conflict with the world was inevitable, and persecution by the world was normal. The Anabaptist church, Bender explained, had practiced true brotherhood, had shared possessions, and in the case of the Hutterites, had repudiated private property.[43]

The third element of the "Vision" was the ethic of love and nonresistance, applied "to all human relationships." Calling nonresistance "Biblical pacifism," Bender observed that the Anabaptists practiced it more than a century before the Quakers. Although Bender was speaking at the height of World War II, he emphasized that nonresistance was the most radical departure of all from conventional sixteenth-century Protestantism, for the Anabaptists had repudiated any participation in warfare.

• • •

Where did Bender get his ideas? By 1943 he had been a historian for more than fifteen years. He had worked in both American and Anabaptist studies. What is surprising is how little original work he had actually done in either area. Aside from his bibliographical essay, *Two Centuries of American Mennonite Literature*, published in 1929, he had produced only two freshly researched articles on American Mennonites, both published in the *MQR* in the early 1930s.[44]

On the Anabaptists, he had done only one major original research, his Conrad Grebel dissertation in 1935. Thus the Anabaptist "Vision" was not a product of either new or continuing research. Instead, it was a product of a decade and a half of continuous immersion in and knowledge of the new material being produced in Anabaptist studies.

So where and when did the ideas in the "Anabaptist Vision" emerge in Bender's thought? One key idea was in Bender's mind as early as the spring of 1924 while he was at Tübingen University and still committed to becoming an Old Testament scholar. In a *Christian Exponent* article, Bender's "old Goshen" mentor J. E. Hartzler, then the president of Witmarsum Seminary in Bluffton, Ohio, had argued that the key ideas of the Anabaptists had been religious tolerance and the freedom of the individual conscience. Hartzler probably gleaned that idea from historian C. Henry Smith's *The Mennonites* (1920), which in the 1920s offered the most up-to-date interpretation of Mennonite history.

However, Bender had insisted that Hartzler was mistaken. "Our forefathers were not a loose society of tolerant individualists, but closed communities with strict discipline and a fixed faith and firm rules of conduct," Bender argued in a letter to the *Expo-*

*nent.* "They were scarcely modern liberals. They expressed their faith and experience in simple Biblical terms, which nevertheless contained for them strict norms of faith and conduct valid not merely for the individual but for the entire *Gemeinde* [church, congregation]."[45]

Where did Bender get such an idea? Certainly not from his schooling, for at that point he had not taken a single course in Reformation history. But by the spring of 1924, he had spent many weeks with Ernst Correll and his new father-in-law John Horsch. Correll had done his graduate work under Ernst Troeltsch, was an ardent Troeltsch disciple, and was teaching Bender to be a Troeltschian—to take seriously the sociological dimensions of the Anabaptist experience. Sensitive to social forms, Correll was much impressed by the central place the congregational community had held among the Swiss Anabaptists.[46]

Equally important in the formation of Bender's idea of the "*Gemeinde*" was the role of John Horsch, whose polemical war against liberalism was at a fever pitch precisely during the years in which Bender was courting Elizabeth. Horsch used Anabaptist history to buttress his attacks on liberalism. In 1924 Horsch knew Anabaptist history (at least Swiss Anabaptist history) better than anyone else, and he was quite sure the Swiss Brethren were not sixteenth-century versions of twentieth-century liberal individualists. Bender, with no firsthand knowledge of Anabaptist history, readily embraced Horsch's point of view.

It is quite clear that Bender wrote the letter to the *Exponent* to ingratiate himself with MC Mennonite church leaders: he was putting down a famous liberal, while defending church discipline. But it is also true that the germ of his idea about the Anabaptist idea of the church as *Gemeinde,* as a gathered and disciplined community, was clearly evident. As time passed, that concept of the church found new soil; in 1930 at Heidelberg, his first graduate-level Reformation-history course under Professor Walther Köhler reinforced it. Bender liked Köhler because, as he told father Horsch, Köhler "agrees with me that the "*Gemeinde-Princip*" is the normative factor in the Anabaptist movement."[47]

In his Heidelberg dissertation on Conrad Grebel, Bender had

begun to work out the ideas which later appeared in his 1943 essay. In chapter twelve, Bender had analyzed Grebel's theology, quoting Ulrich Zwingli to support a contention that Grebel had held to the great fundamental doctrines of the Protestant Reformers. Grebel was "thoroughly evangelical in the same sense that Luther and Zwingli were," he claimed. Where Grebel differed from the Reformers was in emphasizing the gathered nature of the church, and in insisting that the church must be separated from the world. Above all, Bender argued, Grebel had maintained a definite ethical and spiritual connection between belief and works. The outline of the "Vision" was already present in 1935. What was absent were some descriptors Bender later used in "The Anabaptist Vision" essay—terms such as nonconformity, nonresistance, and discipleship.

A comparison between Bender's original German dissertation in 1935 and the English translation which was begun in 1936 and completed in 1942 shows little change in content. In 1950, when the Grebel biography was finally published, Bender added a chapter on what he called the "significance of Conrad Grebel"; in a footnote he referred to both his own "Anabaptist Vision" and to Dietrich Bonhoeffer's *Cost of Discipleship*. "In some respects, though not all, Bonhoeffer would be a good Anabaptist," he remarked. However, there is no evidence that Bender read or knew about Bonhoeffer's *Nachfolge* (the original German version, published in 1937) before it appeared in English translation in 1948.[48]

Thus Bender possessed some basics when he sat down to write "The Anabaptist Vision." He had intimate and firsthand knowledge of the major lines of research in Anabaptist history. The decade of the 1930s had seen both a sea change in the attitudes of historians toward Anabaptist studies and a huge array of new work in Anabaptist history.

A few months after Bender's return from Heidelberg in 1930, he attended the annual meeting of the ASCH and read a paper entitled "Recent Progress in Research in Anabaptist History." "The true history of this significant group, the Anabaptist movement, has not yet been written," Bender told his audience. Nearly all that was written earlier was wrong, in his opinion, because nearly all church historians had been biased against the Anabaptists. Bender recounted that his Heidelberg professor Walther Köhler had once said that when he was in graduate school in the 1890s, the professors had mentioned the Anabaptists only to give them a "good sound kick." But Köhler's generation had begun to be more evenhanded about the Anabaptists. By 1930 Bender claimed a veritable renaissance of interest in Anabaptist history, most of it since World War I.[49]

Bender praised the work of the Verein für Reformationsgeschichte, a German Reformation history society which planned to publish fifteen volumes of Anabaptist source materials in a series, Quellen zur Geschichte der Wiedertäufer (Sources for the history of the Anabaptists), informally called Täuferakten (Anabaptist sources). The first volume, a double binding of 1,200 pages, had just come from the press in 1930. The Verein's work will provide the raw materials for a "comprehensive and authoritative history of the [Anabaptist] movement," Bender told his audience. He clearly hoped he might be the one to produce that history. He envisioned a large tome.[50]

Bender's development as an Anabaptist historian (1924-40) thus coincided with a dramatic shift among historians from ignoring or excoriating Anabaptists to taking them seriously as a subject for Reformation research. There was a flood of new monograph material. An example was Johannes Kühn's *Toleranz und Offenbarung* (1923), which eventually, through Robert Friedmann, became an important influence on Bender. The early 1930s also saw much new material on the chiliastic Thomas Müntzer and the Swiss and south-German Anabaptists. There were many Münster studies and numerous biographical works on figures such as Pilgram Marpeck, Menno Simons, Conrad Grebel, and David Joris. The Hutterites also received a great deal of attention in the 1930s.

Two studies especially influenced Bender: one by Ethelbert Stauffer, *Märtyrer-theologie und Täuferbewegung* (1933); and another by Rudolf Heyer, *Der Kirchenbegriff der Schwärmer* (1939). Then there was John Horsch's *Mennonites in Europe*, finally published in 1942, a year after his death. It was Horsch's final and best effort to establish his lifelong argument that the Swiss Brethren were the original and authentic Anabaptists, that all others were

somehow flawed, and that there was no organic connection between the Swiss and the Dutch movements.[51]

Thus Bender's "Anabaptist Vision" emerged out of an era of
rich historical study which validated Anabaptist history as a legitimate part of Reformation history. It was a process in which
Harold Bender had been both a participant and an observer. The
next great surge of interest in Anabaptist studies would come in
the 1950s, when the students of Fritz Blanke, Roland Bainton, and
Harold Bender would complete their graduate studies.

•  •  •

Robert Friedmann was almost certainly the single most formative
influence on the shape and form of Bender's "Anabaptist Vision"
address. Friedmann was the one who challenged Bender on the
question of what was central about Anabaptism or, as Bender
sometimes put it, "regulative." In the spring of 1940 while still at
New Haven, Friedmann wrote an article for the ASCH journal,
*Church History*, entitled "Conception of the Anabaptists."[52] Just
down the hall from him was Roland Bainton, writing his "Left
Wing of the Reformation" essay. Friedmann would have encouraged Bender to offer an alternative to Bainton.

In his article on "Conception of the Anabaptists," Friedmann
introduced Johannes Kühn's *Toleranz und Offenbarung* (1923).
Kühn identified five Anabaptist "types." He called his third type
*"täuferische Nachfolge."* Friedmann translated *"Nachfolge"* as
"discipleship" and defined it as "the great freedom of conducting
one's own life in the spirit of the Gospel." That spirit, Friedmann
argued, meant both the practice of love and the experience of the
cross (suffering). And it required or presumed a church that was a
close-knit community.[53]

Friedmann also developed the Nachfolge idea in two articles
entitled "Anabaptism and Pietism," published in the *MQR* during
1940. Harold and Elizabeth translated the essays, those Friedmann writings which first introduced Bender to the Kühn-Fried-
mann concept of discipleship. Bender probably saw the Kühn
book in John Horsch's library in the 1920s, but it is doubtful that

he understood Kühn's ideas until he read Friedmann in 1940. When Bender rewrote his last chapter of the Grebel biography in July of 1942, he used the term "discipleship" and cited Johannes Kühn. There is no reference to either in the original dissertation manuscript of 1935.[54]

Bender called Friedmann's "Anabaptism and Pietism" essay "one of the most significant pieces of work in Anabaptist history in recent years."[55] Friedmann was clearly marking out new ground for Bender, or perhaps more accurately, offering him new language and new theological categories. Here Bender learned that Pietism and Anabaptism were antithetical. Friedmann argued that the effect of Pietism was to blunt the prophetic voice of faith, and that the turn inward led to making peace with the world, or at least to becoming innocuous to the world.

Friedmann described the process thus:

> It [Pietism] begins with the thought of one's own depravity and the consciousness of sin in the sense that the theologians, especially Luther, have conceived it. It is followed by the struggle for repentance (*Busskampf*), an exclusively mental labor with oneself, which is quite apart from all thought of love. Then comes the process of the new birth, the consciousness of redemption and of a sure possession of salvation, and the freedom of enjoyment of this new possession. This is also a joy, . . . not the joy of the confessor and disciple of Christ, but the joy of one who has been "blessed" with the gifts of grace. This experience does not call into question the life of this world, since one has already overcome the demons individually and privately. One seeks therefore edification and uplift, but not a change of the world. The Pietist never finds himself in such severe testing as the Anabaptist, for his way is a way of much less conflict and therefore much more easy to tread.[56]

By contrast, Friedmann argued,

> the Anabaptist brethren indicate their readiness to follow the hard and difficult way of discipleship (*Nachfolge*). That is to say, they declare their readiness to follow a way which has as its final goal the kingdom of God. . . . The Anabaptist knows no compromise. He is altogether radical, since he is out to change the world. . . . Hence the new birth means for the Anabaptist a great obligation

and task—everything else but a peaceful possession. . . . "Following Christ" (*Nachfolge Christi*)—that is the central word of the Anabaptists.[57]

Perhaps the most explicit evidence of Friedmann's influence on Bender's thought is Bender's use of Pietism in the "Anabaptist Vision" essay. Near the end of the essay, he discussed several specific aspects of Anabaptism by comparing their belief to Catholicism, Lutheranism, *and Pietism*. If he had not learned about Pietism from Friedmann, he would almost certainly not have included it in that context. In the spring of 1942, Bender wrote *Mennonite Origins in Europe*, the first booklet of the six-pamphlet series for the CPS "core" course. A year and a half later when he wrote the "Anabaptist Vision" essay, he must have had that piece in front of him, for he used many of the pamphlet's phrases nearly verbatim, including the word "vision," which appears frequently. For some reason he had not used the word "discipleship" in the pamphlet. Instead, his term was "holiness of life." The "great central foundation stone" for the Anabaptists, he wrote, was "holiness of life."[58] Why did he not use "discipleship"? Perhaps Bender wanted ed a term more familiar to the CPS men. In 1942 "discipleship" was not yet a Mennonite word.

More likely Bender had not yet actually embraced "discipleship" as his word. He seems finally to have grasped the word's meaning as the central "*Kern*" (kernel) of Anabaptism while attending an August 1942 Conference on Mennonite Cultural Problems at Winona Lake, Indiana. Friedmann read a paper entitled "The Anabaptist Genius and Its Influence on Mennonites Today." The Anabaptists had been preoccupied with Jesus rather than Paul, he insisted. "They did not use the Paulinic language as the Reformers did." Their concern was with Jesus and his teachings. From Jesus, Friedmann argued, the Anabaptists had derived the central concepts of *Nachfolge* and obedience. "Without obedience simple and un-twisted," Friedmann told the conferees, "there can be no discipleship.[59]

By now Friedmann was a member of the circle of Goshen historians, and after the conference he told Bender that he was quite unimpressed by the event. "They just rambled around without any concrete knowledge. What then is all this speaking of the 'faith of our fathers' if nobody exactly knows what it really was?" In that context, Bender began to use the term *discipleship*, and by the time he wrote his "Anabaptist Vision" paper a year later, it had become his key idea.[60]

Two days before Christmas in 1943, as Bender was in the midst of writing the "Anabaptist Vision" essay, he received a note from John C. Wenger. Wenger, always attentive to the needs of his mentor, told him: "In your 'Anabaptist Vision' address, you ought to make use of Zwingli's *Elenchus*. I think you'll find that the potential *Täufer* [Anabaptist] came to Zwingli and appealed to him to issue a gospel call for those who wished *Christus nachzufolgen* [to follow after Christ] to come to his side. They spoke of choosing a new *Rat* [discipline] when the gospel course had been taken."[61]

Wenger went on to quote his Zurich University professor Fritz Blanke: "Die Täufer wollten einen *kirchlichen* Rat bilden, der die kirchlichen Sachen bestimmen wollte. Sie brachten ein ganz klares Program, zwar aus der Apostelgeschichte Urkirche als Vorbild." (The Anabaptists wanted to create a true *churchly* counsel, . . . following the original church of the Acts of the Apostles as a model [Wenger emphasized *churchly*].)[62]

Wenger's note indicates that a new concept of the church was being discussed at Goshen in 1943. At least one of Bender's colleagues at Goshen was thinking along lines similar to those Bender would incorporate in the essay. And the title of the essay had circulated enough to generate some response from the ever-helpful Wenger.

• • •

Bender wrote "The Anabaptist Vision" at a point in his evolution as a historian when the influences of persons like Bainton and Friedmann were formative. They helped him jell his ideas. But the formulation was finally his. By artfully weaving together the ideas of discipleship, fellowship of believers, and nonresistance, he created a conceptually convincing argument that the Swiss Brethren represented what he called a "consistent evangelical Protestantism."

Bender's key purpose in the "Vision" essay was to convince his academic historian colleagues to give the Anabaptists the credence and respect they deserved, and to distinguish between various Anabaptist groups. Bender sought to give the Anabaptists respectability by insisting that at least some of them—the Swiss Brethren—were simply carrying the magisterial Reformers' programs to their logical conclusion.

Bender believed the Anabaptists were a corrective for the failure of the Reformers. The "Anabaptists," he insisted, were concerned most of all about a "true Christian life, . . . a life patterned after the teaching and example of Christ." By contrast, "the Reformers did not secure among the people true repentance, regeneration, and Christian living as a result of their preaching." The Anabaptists had found the Reformation emphasis on faith to be "good" yet "inadequate." They insisted that "without newness of life, faith is hypocritical." By identifying discipleship as the central element in true Anabaptism, Bender was bolstering his argument that Anabaptism was the "culmination" of the Reformation.

In 1943 Bender had not yet grasped the theological meaning Friedmann gave to discipleship. He had a conventional Mennonite's concern for "holiness of life," but he had not moved much beyond the prevailing formulations found in Daniel Kauffman's *Bible Doctrines.* Kauffman described a sequential process that moved through "the plan of salvation," to an affirmation of a series of doctrinal formulas, and a life of "restrictions." Obedience to the restrictions was to be evidence of a life nonconformed to the world and committed to Christ. "Holiness of life" was understood as evidence of obedience to the Bible and the church. For Friedmann, discipleship was a much more complex idea than "holiness of life." It was a dialectical process of commitment, discovery, and growth—all interactive with the teachings and example of Christ.[63]

On the main points of Christian orthodoxy, Bender's essay was quite conventional. That conventional theological content accurately reflected Bender's limited theological work up to that time. Actually, in this period no Mennonites were doing much serious theological work, nor did their church encourage or desire it. Through the 1930s and 1940s, the magisterial sway of Daniel Kauffman's *Bible Doctrines* was nearly complete.

By contrast to theological work, the amount of historical work by Mennonites was considerable. History was a safe endeavor. It fitted easily into orthodox formulations. By 1943 the writings of John Horsch and Harold Bender had established the sixteenth-century Swiss Brethren as the theological baseline for Mennonite orthodoxy. The "Anabaptist Vision" was a synopsis or summing-up of that baseline. By the 1940s nearly all theological discussion by Mennonites was supported through reference to the Anabaptists. Sixteenth-century Anabaptism, specifically the Swiss Brethren, became the orthodox filter through which Mennonites received their theological orientations.

● ● ●

Bender had written the essay in a hurry, without notations. Realizing that presidential addresses were routinely published in each March issue of *Church History*, he now had to do his documentation. Sometime in January of 1944, a Goshen College student saw Harold and Elizabeth and John C. Wenger sitting at a table in the Historical Library, surrounded by great mounds of books, intently searching for references. The student remembered Wenger's gleeful chuckle as he announced, "I've found another one."[64] Elizabeth and J. C. were helping get the "Vision" essay ready for publication.

The essay appeared in the March 1944 issue of *Church History* and was then reprinted in the April 1944 *MQR*. Several thousand offprints were distributed to CPS men in the fall of 1944.[65] Eventually it would be reprinted many times in at least five languages.

It was Bender's calling to articulate a new interpretation of history which influenced how historians understood the Anabaptists. Only after the fact did he come to understand that he had also provided his fellow Mennonites with a new self-definition of who they were and whence they had come. He gave Mennonites a "usable past." Ultimately, that feature would become the most important effect of his essay.

Fundamentally, the "Anabaptist Vision" reflected Bender's

preoccupations during his emergence as a preeminent Mennonite leader. In the midst of a popular war in which Mennonites were often identified as shirkers, Bender's formulation reassured them, telling them that they were not heirs to an odd sect but instead the descendants of respectable participants in the Protestant Reformation. But there was more. In Bender's masterful "Vision," the Anabaptists, as Hans-Jürgen Goertz has put it, "became contemporaries. The chasm between the sixteenth century and the twentieth century seemed to have miraculously disappeared. The picture of the Anabaptists blurred into that of contemporary Mennonites— perhaps it was drawn, stroke by stroke, from a contemporary model."

Thus the "faith of our fathers" had taken on a familiar definition with which Mennonites could identify. It was usable history in a familiar mode. But, as Goertz observed, making the past usable nearly always does violence to that past.[66] Bender's essay both blurred the differences and foreshortened the distance between sixteenth-century Anabaptists and twentieth-century Mennonites.

Bender's definition of discipleship offered a newly emerging generation of Mennonite leaders a dynamic and theologically rich alternative to the old doctrinal and discipline-driven formulas their fathers had invented in the years after the 1890s. The fellowship-of-believers church concept provided a welcome antidote to the patriarchal authoritarianism sometimes evident in the MC Mennonite church in the first part of the twentieth century.

• • •

"The Anabaptist Vision" was only the first of three essays which Bender believed laid out the essence of the Anabaptist "great vision of truth," as he put it in 1944. He published the other two essays in the January and the July 1945 issues of the MQR. The first was by Donovan Smucker, a GC Mennonite who had been the Mid-West Fellowship of Reconciliation secretary during the late 1930s and early 1940s. Then, because of views he more and more espoused, he became one of the Goshen historians' favorite young GC Mennonites. By the mid-1940s, Bender had become the young man's mentor. Smucker had left the FOR and begun seminary studies at Princeton, with Bender's blessing.

Just six months after he read Bender's "Vision" essay in the *MQR*, Smucker wrote "The Theological Triumph of the Early Anabaptist Mennonites: The Re-Discovery of Biblical Theology in Paradox." In his *MQR* editorial comments, Bender introduced Smucker's essay effusively. "Don Smucker has systematized for the first time the whole of Anabaptist theology in a sweeping series of great basic concepts of Biblical theology in paradox," he told his readers.[67]

Smucker insisted that his essay was simply "an extended footnote" on Bender's "Vision." He added, "I consider 'The Anabaptist Vision' the most impressive and convincing survey now available."[68] He drew heavily from Bender, Horsch, Hershberger, Smith, Krahn, and Edward Yoder as sources. His foil was what he called "chastened liberalism," with its evolutionary and too-optimistic belief in human progress. Anabaptists were "pessimistic optimists," he insisted. They were pessimists because they took human fallenness seriously and thus understood the need for divine grace. They were optimists in that they believed in the possibility of a kingdom of peace and love embodied in the fellowship of Christian believers.[69]

The Anabaptists had "re-discovered the theology of the Bible!" Smucker declared. A valid theology of the Bible was "desperately difficult to maintain" because biblical truth is clothed in paradoxical form. Paradox, Smucker explained, "unites seeming contradictions in a single strand of truth." The paradoxical form occurs when God's infinite knowledge attempts to connect with the finite understanding of human reason. "Jesus," Smucker observed, "did not outrage reason: He outran it."[70]

In a footnote Smucker acknowledged that his understanding of paradox was shared by neo-orthodox theologians Niebuhr, Tillich, Kierkegaard, and Barth. He gave special credit for his insights to Ralph W. Sockman's *The Paradoxes of Jesus* (1939).[71] Sockman was a most unlikely source of inspiration for an *MQR* article. He was the popular pastor of Christ Church, a famously affluent and progressive Methodist congregation in New York City, a president of the Federal Council of Churches, and a good friend of the outspokenly liberal Harry Emerson Fosdick.

Bender's warm embrace of Smucker's essay as one of a pantheon of three which explained the "Anabaptist Vision" suggests that he was now paying less attention than previously to Mennonite conservatives. He was beginning a more progressive approach to Mennonite theology. Whether or not he was aware of doing so, Bender was exposing Mennonites to a broader theological universe.

The third essay in the "Anabaptist Vision" series was Ethelbert Stauffer's "The Anabaptist Theology of Martyrdom." Bender called it "an attempt to lay hold upon the central ideas of Anabaptism."[72] Stauffer had first published the essay in 1933.[73] Bender had almost certainly seen it when he was completing his Grebel dissertation, but he did not cite it. Nor had John Horsch ever cited it, not even in his 1938 study of Anabaptist martyrdom. It was listed in the bibliography of Horsch's *Mennonites in Europe*, but likely had been added by Edward Yoder as he completed the book in 1942.

Stauffer, son of a Palatinate Mennonite family, was professor at the University of Bonn in Germany during the 1930s. After a decade of neglect, Bender suddenly rushed to publish Stauffer's article, even though the war prevented him from getting Stauffer's permission. The war was nearly over, and so Bender might have waited a few more months and gotten that permission. But instead he went ahead, hoping, as he said in his editorial introduction to the article, that Stauffer would "indulge the editor's freedom for the sake of a Tübingen student comradeship of twenty years ago." During Bender's year at Tübingen in 1923-24, he and Stauffer had been fellow students.[74]

In 1945 Bender was self-consciously supplementing his "Vision" essay with the Smucker and Stauffer additions. The content of the Vision has been "described by Bender and Smucker," he explained editorially. Stauffer's article, he suggested, "might be thought of as giving the background of the picture of Anabaptism, or the '*Grundton*' [foundation-tone] of the music."[75] Bender liked Stauffer's essay because it offered an explanation for the heroic martyrdom so pervasive in the Anabaptist story. The Anabaptists assumed the cross of Jesus to be the central fact, the key explanation of God's purpose in history, Stauffer explained. They insisted that *Nachfolge Christi* meant that suffering and death would continue to be the lot of the faithful follower of Christ.[76] In translating the Stauffer essay, Friedmann had rendered Stauffer's term *Nachfolge* as "discipleship."

The combined Bender-Smucker-Stauffer corpus amounted to eighty pages of interpretation which laid out a new understanding of Anabaptism. Smucker offered a new theological framework which he said existed at the heart of Anabaptist theology: the paradoxical nature of Christian faith. Stauffer provided a theology of history: the cross as the ultimate exhibit of God's method and means in a sinful world. He believed the Anabaptists practiced this theology of the cross through their heroic suffering and martyrdom. Bender's descriptive Anabaptist categories provided the scaffolding for the Smucker-Stauffer theological formulations: Christian life as discipleship, the church as a fellowship of believers, the way of love and nonresistance in human relationships. By 1945 Bender had reason to be happy about the state of Anabaptist history and theology. The recovery of the "Anabaptist Vision" had begun.

# ❧ 15 ❧

# Founding the Seminary

*Bender becomes dean of the Bible school and
is ordained. The Bible school becomes
Goshen College Biblical Seminary.*

"FOR MANY YEARS and with much desire, we have labored and
prayed together for this day to come. And now it is here." The day
was October 20, 1944. Bender was delivering his inaugural address to a crowded audience of students and faculty at a special
chapel presided over by bishop David A. Yoder, president of the
Mennonite Board of Education. Bender had just become the dean
of the newly reorganized Goshen College Bible School. A few minutes earlier, professor Carl Kreider had been installed as the dean
of Goshen College.[1]

During the previous fall semester (1943), Bender had been acting president of the college while Ernest Miller was on leave to
study at Princeton Theological Seminary. In late October Miller
had summoned Bender to Princeton for a conference. He had a
proposition. He had just completed a survey of accredited colleges
which had affiliated seminaries. In order to maintain accreditation, nearly all of them had needed to separate the administration
of the college from that of the seminary. With Goshen's new Th.B.
(bachelor of theology) degree program, which included a fifth-
year, graduate-level requirement, Miller was sure the Bible school
would have to be separated from the college program.[2]

That practical consideration reinforced a larger idea president
Miller was promoting. Miller observed that the MC Mennonite
church had one publishing house, one mission board, and one

board of education. With the new five-year Th.B. program, the Goshen College Bible School had become the one post-baccalaureate Mennonite training school for church workers. To highlight its unique role, Miller told Bender, the Bible school needed a more distinct identity, one separate from the college. To create the new identity, Miller proposed to have separate deans for the college and the Bible school. Which position would you like? he asked Bender.[3]

Nonplussed, Bender asked for time to think. His reply, which incidentally came as he was beginning to write the "Anabaptist Vision" essay, was typical of Harold Bender when faced with an unattractive choice: he offered an alternative. Why not divide the work of the dean by appointing an assistant dean who would manage the lower division in the college? The dean would then handle upper-division and Bible school matters. The obvious point: Bender wanted to keep his position as dean of the whole institution.[4]

Having made his counterproposal, Bender quickly acknowledged that "the primary consideration should be what is best for the Bible school and the college," not his own personal preferences. However, he wanted reassurance on two points: that president Miller was committed to a full, graduate Th.B. program rather than merely a pumped-up undergraduate Bible major, and that Bender's salary would not be diminished by a change in roles.[5]

Writing to Goshen faculty member Olive Wyse a few months later, Bender expressed regret at leaving the college dean's office, but he felt reassured by the obvious strengths Carl Kreider would bring. Then with the unself-conscious cynicism of a seasoned dean, he remarked, "His only handicap is his youth, and other administrative officers and faculty members may take advantage of this. I shall give him every support from my angle."[6]

• • •

For Bender to relinquish the college deanship was most uncharacteristic. Seldom in his life did he give up a role or an assignment. More typically, he simply added on more responsibility, exacerbating the already harried quality of his life. Why did he accept this change? There were several considerations. Clearly he knew his relationship with president Miller was deteriorating and that Miller wanted him out of the college deanship. He also realized that Miller would not have taken such a step without the knowledge and consent of Orie Miller. A shift to the Bible school, where he would have more autonomy, would soften some of the worst aspects of their troubled relationship.

Bender also felt a genuine calling to the Bible school deanship. I believe, he told a friend, "the call has come from the Lord Himself."[7] Bender's sense of God's purpose and call to be dean was more than pious rhetoric: it was rooted in his own personal history. After all, as a student at Princeton two decades earlier, he had prepared himself for just such an assignment, as he sensed a call to train Mennonite leaders. In 1944 Bender might well have been forgiven a touch of smugness that the young seminarian, distrusted by the church fathers in 1924 as "unsafe," had just acquired the most theologically strategic position in the MC Mennonite church.

Bender was also drawn by Miller's idea of one central Mennonite Bible school with a graduate curriculum. In 1933 the Bible school had established a four-year Th.B. program, but for Bender that choice was only a stopgap. He had hoped for a fully developed seminary program. In 1937, hoping to entice J. C. Wenger to teach at Goshen, he told Wenger that he hoped "we may be able to launch our full-fledged seminary before long."[8] Half a decade later, in 1942, while still not a "full-fledged seminary," the Bible school did begin to offer a five-year program, with students taking sixty hours of liberal arts and ninety hours of Bible credits.

When in 1942 the Board of Education agreed to the five-year program with little or no hesitation, Bender must have realized that the time was ripe. Already in July of 1943, before he knew he would become its dean, he called the Bible school "our little Mennonite Seminary." Certainly the interest was there: within a year, by 1943, thirty-two students were in the five-year program.[9]

Thirty-two students was quite an advance from the fall of 1940, when the Bible school faculty spent a long meeting discussing how to generate more interest in their program and how "our ministry" could be won over to the idea of seminary training.[10] Actually, the expansion of the Bible school's enrollment and

Goshen College Bible School faculty. Bender, Sanford C. Yoder, Paul Mininger, John C. Wenger. Bender Family Album.

curriculum had come not from new efforts on the part of the Bible school faculty, but from the effects of the war. Military draft regulations offered deferments to students who were in theological studies leading to the ministry. Goshen's four-year Th.B. program did not satisfy the draft regulations. With no graduate Mennonite theological program available, many young Mennonites, to secure their deferments, would almost certainly enter seminaries of other denominations. The Mennonite Board of Education found that possibility unacceptable. So when the Goshen College Bible faculty proposed a new five-year Th.B. program, the board agreed.[11]

The new program had its critics. J. Irvin Lehman, a minister and the editor of the newly reestablished *Sword and Trumpet* magazine from the Mennonite theological right wing, called it an "adroit move toward a professional and salaried ministry."[12] Privately, Bender responded with some heat, insisting that he did not support a "hireling ministry." But, he told Lehman, "We need to encourage a better-prepared ministry, rather than to discourage it. We expect to train those whom the Lord and the church send to us. We will not in any way seek to replace the present system of calling and ordaining ministers by any 'placement' system."[13] In his address at his installation as Bible school dean in the fall of 1944, Bender emphasized the same point. We do not believe in "the concept of a professional ministry," he had told the audience, nor in "a prerequisite of schooling for ordination."[14]

EMS president J. L. Stauffer needled Bender about Bible schools which become "preacher factories."[15] So Bender wrote an article for the *Gospel Herald* entitled "Our Bible Schools: What They Are and What They Are Not." "They are not schools for the training of a professional ministry," he wrote. "They are not schools for the selection and ordination of workers. They are not schools to force their product on the church. They are not primarily schools for the training of a city ministry, but schools where the rural church should have the foremost place in emphasis."[16]

However, the messages from Bender were somewhat ambiguous. A year and a half before his appointment as Bible school dean, he told the registrar of Eastern Baptist Seminary that the Goshen College Bible School "is now the recognized training school for candidates for the ministry in the Mennonite church, even though it does not yet have the name of a Theological Seminary."[17] That assertion hardly matched either the school's statement of purpose or the current MC practice.

Bender's own situation illustrated the ambiguity which the new Bible school program created for MC members regarding ministerial calling and ordination. When Board of Education president D. A. Yoder announced the appointment of Bender as the dean of the Bible school, he also announced, with the approval of the executive committee of the MC's Indiana-Michigan conference, that Bender would be ordained to the ministry. In a letter to Bender's College Mennonite congregation announcing the ordination, Yoder explained that the purpose was to help Bender "work among the churches in general throughout the Church."[18] Typically, ministers of that era were selected by lot, from within the congregation for specific service to that congregation. The exceptions were missionaries, who might be ordained without benefit of the lot. Bender's ordination followed the missionary pattern.

Efforts to ordain Bender had begun six months before he knew he was to be dean of the Bible school. J. C. Wenger initiated the move. "For some time I have had a burden relative to the work of our Bible school here at the college," Wenger told D. A. Yoder. "This is the fact that our Dean, Brother H. S. Bender, is not ordained. He is well qualified for the work of the ministry. As you know, he is an able Bible expositor, true to the Faith and loyal to the Mennonite Church. His usefulness would be greatly increased and the prestige (in the good sense) of our Bible school enhanced if he were ordained." Wenger went on to say that all the other teachers in the Bible school were ordained, which put Bender in an anomalous situation.[19]

Wenger also informed D. A. Yoder that he had consulted Orie Miller and that Orie had encouraged him in the matter. Aware of the tensions between president Miller and Bender, Wenger ended the letter to Yoder with "for various reasons which you will understand, I have not mentioned this topic to Brother Ernest Miller, and it would seem to be well if my writing does not come to his attention."[20]

In a church where ordination was still the most important credential, Wenger was afraid president Miller might oppose Bender's ordination. No doubt from Miller's point of view, it was hard enough to manage Bender as a lay dean, and ordination, by strengthening Bender's status, might make the dean even less manageable. Likely the prospect of ordination helped Bender agree to step aside as dean of the college, and no doubt president Miller could accept Bender's ordination if it meant he would more readily relinquish the college deanship. The outcome may well have been a practical quid pro quo for the two men. In any case, Bender was ordained, and Miller got a new college dean.

The plan to ordain Bender nearly derailed. When bishop D. A. Yoder brought the proposal to the executive committee of the Indiana-Michigan conference, it almost failed. It took J. C. Wenger to rescue the situation. With the motion for ordination on the floor, no one would second it. Finally Wenger, only recently ordained himself, and feeling out of place in the situation, offered the second. The motion then passed without incident.[21]

As the Bible school flourished, the acute issues came to be the ordination and placement of graduates. As long as the lot remained in place, how could a young person with a personal call to the ministry, backed by a Bible school degree, be called by the church? In the spring of 1945, Bender had begun thinking about the placement of Wilfred Ulrich, who would soon graduate with the Th.B. Ulrich was from a congregation at Roanoke, Illinois. In school on a divinity deferment, Ulrich needed to be ordained soon after graduation or else he would almost certainly be drafted. Choosing his words carefully, Bender wrote to Ulrich's bishop, Ezra Yordy, inquiring whether Ulrich might not be ordained and installed somewhere in the Illinois conference. He offered the suggestion, he told the bishop, because "the young men are somewhat embarrassed to offer themselves, and we as a faculty have felt that it might be better if the initial contacts were made by the dean of the Bible school."[22]

Bender realized that change in this area would be glacially slow, yet he was eager for some decision. In 1945 he began cautiously to explore the possibility of licensing young men as an initial step before ordination. As he told Illinois minister J. D. Hartzler, "Many of our conferences and congregations have not yet thought along these lines and will not move very fast. Also, we do not feel as a Bible School that we should be too aggressive in this matter and get too far ahead of general church attitudes."[23] Bender favored licensing and offered his services to help the Illinois Conference determine how to move in that direction. He did not like the lot, but in 1945 he was not making public statements expressing that dislike.

• • •

The new Th.B. program caught on quickly. In 1942-43 its enrollment was twenty-seven. In 1945 there were only seventy men enrolled at Goshen College, but half of them were in the Th.B. program. Then in 1946-47, enrollment jumped to sixty-four. In the spring of 1946, fourteen graduates received the Th.B. degree—a "splendid class," Bender called them. Four were ordained during their study, and two more after graduation. Of the fourteen, four became missionaries. There was one woman graduate, Lois Johns, daughter of an influential and conservative Ohio bishop, Otis N. Johns. Upon graduation, Johns married Glen Yoder, assistant pastor of a Mennonite congregation in Protection, Kansas.[24]

Several women had graduated with the four-year Th.B. major, notably Harriet Lapp in 1938, Ruth King in 1939, and Ella Mae Weaver in 1941. In 1944 Mary Annabelle Troyer from Fisher, Illinois, applied to become a candidate for the five-year Th.B. degree. The request produced a cryptic entry in the Bible school faculty minutes: "The question of admitting women to our Th.B. curriculum was discussed briefly. Dean Bender shall investigate the subject, take counsel as he deems advisable, and bring recommendations to the group."[25]

Six months later Bender recommended that women students be admitted but be exempt from having to take the "Homiletics" and "Work of the Pastor" courses.[26] A year later, in 1945, all women candidates for the Th.B. or the B.D. degrees were "excused" from all requirements in "Practical Theology" except courses in Christian education, missions, and evangelism.[27] Since women could not be ordained, some courses were deemed superfluous. The exemptions also helped mute any criticism that the Bible school was preparing women for ministry.

One of the strange aspects for women in the program was their exclusion from meetings of the "Th.B. Fellowship." That fellowship had begun in 1942, patterned on the "Fellowship Hour" Bender had enjoyed as a student at Princeton Seminary. Bender and three students formed a committee to organize the Th.B. Fellowship's programs.[28] Meeting biweekly, the fellowship brought senior students and the faculty together for interaction and worship, usually in a faculty home. For reasons which are not clear, the inclusion of Mary Annabelle Troyer and Lois Johns in the program required some action by the faculty. A discussion by the faculty in September of 1945 failed to resolve the question, and neither Troyer or Johns ever received an invitation to the fellowship meetings.[29]

•  •  •

With the end of the war in 1945, the seminary lost the advantage of the theological-study deferments. Now most young people coming to Goshen elected to earn the four-year liberal arts degree before committing to theological study. It became clear to Bender that a more comprehensive divinity degree was needed. The Bible school needed to offer a B.D. (bachelor of divinity) program, he reasoned, or "some of our best candidates for the ministry might be lost through non-Mennonite seminaries." In September 1945, just a month after the surrender of Japan, Bender suggested that the Bible school faculty consider introducing a three-year postgraduate B.D. degree.[30] To him, introduction of the B.D. program seemed to be the logical endpoint of the movement toward a full-fledged seminary. The program, he told the faculty, would be "the final stage of development in our preparation of ministers and full-time church workers for our constituency."[31]

The timing of Bender's B.D. proposal surely was not accidental. Just a month earlier, the GC Mennonites had begun a new Mennonite Biblical Seminary (MBS) in Chicago. It would scarcely have been possible for Bender to push so quickly for a regular B.D. curriculum but for the specter that MC students might be lured to the new GC institution. The GC's new seminary offered Bender the protection he needed from conservative MC critics of seminary education, and he grasped it immediately.

Encouraged by his colleagues, Bender drew up a proposal which not only laid out a new curriculum but also proposed a name change, to "Goshen College Biblical Seminary." Bender explained that the term "Biblical Seminary" best described "the new program as an advanced program of preparation for full-time Christian service with a strong Biblical emphasis." It also seemed "best suited to the modern situation as well as [to] the traditions of the Mennonite Church."[32]

The faculty decided to keep Goshen College in the name: the GCs had already preempted "Mennonite Biblical Seminary." For MCs, the name change and the new B.D. degree were bold innovations in 1946, but Bender went out of his way to play that fact down. The Th.B. degree will continue as the main degree program, he told his colleagues, because the seminary did not want "too wide a gap between our congregations and their ministers."[33]

The B.D. degree brought an increase in student numbers and program, which in turn demanded more faculty. In 1946 John Mosemann Jr. joined the team. Mosemann and his wife, Ruth, had been among the first Mennonite missionaries in East Africa, but World War II had forced them back to the United States. During the war Mosemann had helped administer the CPS program, then in 1946 he completed a Th.M. at Princeton. Bender must have gotten keen satisfaction from recruiting the son of his old detractor, the arch-conservative bishop in Pennsylvania's Lancaster County. With Mosemann, the seminary faculty numbered five: Mosemann, S. C. Yoder, J. C. Wenger, Paul Mininger, and Bender.

Bender's proposed B.D. program followed a fairly conventional model, including a four-part division of the curriculum into Bible, church history, systematic theology, and practical theology. What was not conventional, Bender told the board of education, were a "Bible emphasis" and a "Mennonite emphasis." About two-thirds (60) of the required 90 hours were in Bible. "The Mennonite church expects its ministers to know the Bible and to use it effectively," he explained. Within the other one-third or 30 hours, the seminary would require only one course (6 hours) in systematic theology: Bender said that Mennonites did not put much emphasis on creeds and theology. Instead of systematics, Bender proposed two yearlong courses in church history (12 hours) and three courses in practical work (homiletics, evangelism and missions, and Christian education).[34]

The centerpiece of the curriculum must be Bible and the biblical languages, Bender told the board. History showed that seminaries which neglected serious Bible study in the original languages had "gone modernistic." That was a conclusion he had gleaned from a broad survey he had made of thirty-two seminary curricula as he was forming the new Th.B. program in 1941.[35]

According to Bender, "Mennonite emphasis" meant emphasis on "holiness, love, and separation, which our fathers have taught and practiced from the beginning." The truth and value of Mennonite principles, he said, had to be expressed in specific courses, but also had to permeate the entire curriculum.[36] Bender was convinced that a Mennonite seminary was crucial for the spiritual integrity of the church. "For our pastors, preachers, evangelists, and missionaries, the Mennonite Church ought not and dare not look to outside training institutions for supply of workers, except at peril to her own safety. We should insist that our prospective workers secure their training in Mennonite schools and nowhere else."[37]

The new seminary's faculty also taught the undergraduate courses in the college's Bible department, and their workload was extremely heavy. J. C. Wenger was the Bible-faculty workhorse: he often taught sixteen hours a semester, and across the whole curriculum. By contrast, the normal course-load for students was fifteen hours.[38] As for Bender, in 1945-46 he taught eleven hours each semester, in addition to being dean and all his church work. His courses that year included church history, Mennonite history, apostolic history, Romans, ethics, biblical introduction, and biblical archaeology. Given all of his other commitments, it was a heavy teaching load.

Students complained that Bender missed too many classes and that he frequently came to class unprepared.[39] Since he too often ran out of time, his classes tended to skim the surface and some-

**Goshen College Biblical Seminary faculty in 1947. From the left: Ernest E. Miller, John C. Wenger, John H. Mosemann Jr., Sanford C. Yoder, Harold S. Bender, Paul Mininger, Howard Charles.**
Bender Family Album.

times failed to help students fathom the depths of the issues they ought to have been addressing.[40] Bender's faculty colleague Olive Wyse once told him, "I have often heard students say that when you give yourself to teaching, you are one of the best teachers they have ever known."[41] Bender was not a poor teacher: what his students deplored was his failure to give them the best of which he was capable.

The problem was not unique to Bender: all of the seminary's faculty were overworked, and one consequence was some lack of intellectual rigor at the seminary. Yet even faculty overload was not the main reason for the lack of rigor. More important was the desire and need to be cautious and noncontroversial. For twenty years Bender had embraced conventional theological understandings. It would have been quite unusual had he begun a more critical approach when he became dean of the seminary. Bender had an almost compulsive need to present himself and the seminary as safe and orthodox.[42]

Bender exhibited such a mind-set in a letter in 1944. By the grapevine he had learned that the venerable and conservative General Conference Mennonite leader P. H. Richert, pastor of the Tabor Mennonite church near Goessel, Kansas, had called Guy F. Hershberger and J. C. Wenger "modernistic in their attitude toward Scripture." It is not true, Bender told Richert. "I think you must know that our church organization purged our church, particularly Goshen College, some twenty years ago of all liberalism, and would not tolerate anything like it at the present time. I can assure you that both of the men mentioned here are 100% loyal to the Scripture and thoroughly conservative from the ground up in their entire theology. I earnestly covet that the conservatives of all Mennonite branches should stand loyally together and work toward a united front against modernism."[43]

Bender was right: both Hershberger and Wenger were theologically and biblically conservative, although probably not as conservative as Richert wished. Not until the arrival of the next generation of seminary teachers in the 1950s would the seminary begin a critical approach to theological study.

Bender's new assignment as dean of the seminary placed him

at the center of momentous historic changes in the selection and training of MC Mennonite congregational leaders. The role and functions of Mennonite ministers were changing. In fact, the creation of the seminary accelerated changes which were already beginning in congregational life. But the changes were only beginning.

In a two-part editorial in the *Gospel Herald* in September 1943, Daniel Kauffman had declared, "As for training for the ministry, we get that in the school of Christ. As for needed qualifications, God sees to that." He disparaged seminary training for the ministry as being of little use.[44] With such words the aging Kauffman, in one of his last editorials, expressed the viewpoint of his generation of MC Mennonite leaders. But at the very moment of his editorial, the effects of World War II were already at work. Mennonites shared in the prosperity generated by the war. As the Mennonite community participated in the massive postwar suburbanization of the nation, the role and work of the ministry took new shapes. Congregations were becoming more receptive to trained ministers. It would require two more decades before the traditional Mennonite lay ministry was replaced by a more conventional seminary-trained and salaried pastoral model, but the change began during the war. By 1946 the new Goshen College Biblical Seminary was poised to meet the new needs.

● ● ●

The mid-1940s were a pivotal time in Harold Bender's life. The publication of "The Anabaptist Vision," his new role as dean of the Bible school, and his ordination—these established him as a central figure in Mennonite leadership circles. In 1946, during a speech at a weekend institute for voluntary service workers at MCC headquarters in Akron, Pennsylvania, Bender reflected on his hopes for and his commitment to the Mennonite church. He noted that he had attended Methodist, Presbyterian, and Lutheran seminaries and had explored their versions of the faith. Then he told the young people in his audience, "I can honestly say to you, I have not found any faith that I believe is nearer to the whole revelation of God in the Scripture and His will for the world than the faith of my fathers. I believe in it not because I do not know any-thing else, but because I am convinced of its worth, its truth, and its value."[45]

How shall that faith of the fathers be preserved and propagat-ed? Bender asked. His answer was most remarkable. Not by build-ing walls, he insisted. That had been tried and did not work. "It is an open question," he said, "whether it is possible to maintain without undue price a complex of culture that is much different from the surrounding world, which leaves us primarily education as a means."[46]

With those few words, Bender seemed to question all of the nonconformity thinking and regulations that were so central to MC life in the first half of the twentieth century. Indeed, he seemed even to question the historic two-kingdom outlook that had been a major strain of Anabaptist and Mennonite thought ever since the Schleitheim Confession of 1527. However, he made his comment more or less in passing. His main point was that Mennonites need-ed their own high schools. He went on to say that if Mennonites' ability to maintain a distinct culture without undue price was open to question, then that "leaves us primarily education as a means." Thus, he insisted, Mennonite communities needed to build Men-nonite high schools for Mennonite youth, and Mennonite young people needed to attend Mennonite colleges.[47]

Bender was not giving up on nonconformity; but he was sug-gesting a drastic change both in Mennonites' conception of it and in how they would express and achieve it. If that was his position, albeit put forward fairly quietly and in passing, it is no wonder that the 1940s were a time of stress and strain in the MC Menno-nite church.

• • •

World War II aroused enormous concern among Mennonite church leaders about the state of MC Mennonite youth. A 1944 MCC draft census confirmed something MC leaders already knew: that a great many MC young men were electing military service, despite the relatively easy option of Civilian Public Service. The census showed that among MC youths, 10 percent chose noncombatant service and 29 percent went into military service. Only 60 percent elected CPS. The study reinforced misgivings, especially among conservatives, that the assimilative forces of American culture were breaking down the boundaries of Mennonite belief and practice. The apparent weakness of Mennonite convictions for nonresistance seemed to offer confirmation that Mennonites were drifting into conformity with the national ethos. Something had to be done to stem the tide and remedy the situation.[48]

Discontent with the prevailing direction of things in the MC Mennonite church flared up in the General Problems Committee of the MC general conference in 1943. Established in 1929, the committee had become a main vehicle to shore up MC nonconformity. It had some weighty leaders, such as bishops Daniel Kauffman of Pennsylvania, Oscar Burkholder of Ontario, Harry Diener of Kansas, D. A. Yoder of Indiana, and J. L. Stauffer of Virginia.

After a dozen years of biennial exhortations to greater nonconformity, the committee came to the 1943 MC general conference, held at Goshen, with an action plan embodied in a "Resolution." Nonconformity and nonresistance should be made tests of membership. A member could violate the doctrine of nonconformity by "holding life insurance, membership in labor unions, immodest and worldly attire (including hats for sisters), the wearing of jewelry (including wedding rings), and attendance at movies and theaters." The real clincher was a plan requiring that any district conference unable or unwilling to enforce the resolution's conditions should be dropped from MC general conference membership.[49]

The MC general conference was unable to deal with the resolution in its 1943 meeting, so it called a special session for the following year. At issue was not only the question of what forms nonconformity should take, but also whether the general conference should have the authority to impose nonconformity on district conferences. A specific case in point was whether the Illinois Conference should be allowed to continue membership in the MC general conference, given relatively lax dress standards in its district.[50]

In the spring of 1944, to help put the role and authority of the

MC general conference in context, Bender was given the unenviable task of writing two articles in the *Gospel Herald* setting forth the history of MC general conference. Trying hard to be objective and quoting liberally from general conference documents, he made the case that the general conference was "purely advisory; it was not to interfere with the work of local conferences; it was not even to consider any action which would conflict with the work or regulations of any local [district] conference." Bender quoted words of the MC general conference founding father Daniel Kauffman, that the general conference was a "conference, not a lawmaking institution." The real authority, Bender argued, lay in district conferences, which derived their authority from the congregations in their districts.[51]

Bender's second article made the point that while basic authority lay with the district conferences, their autonomy was not absolute. The bylaws of general conference gave it the authority to expel a district conference by a two-thirds majority. Thus, with a two-thirds majority vote, the Illinois conference could indeed be expelled.[52] So the issue in 1944 was not whether the general conference had the right to expel a district conference: it did. The big question was whether two-thirds of the district conferences were willing to take the drastic step of expelling one of their own over the issue of nonconformity.

The effect of Bender's argument was to put him on the side of district autonomy. On the whole, he opposed the position of the General Problems Committee on nonconformity; but he also feared the effect such an extension of general conference authority might have on other agencies in the church, particularly on the church boards. Bender revealed his concern by making an unusual and doubtful argument: that the general conference had "no authority over any one of the three Church-wide boards [Education, Missions, Publishing], or any of the institutions under the jurisdiction of these Boards." To some readers, especially conservatives, his statements must have been the last straw, confirming their assessment of the hapless state of MC polity.[53]

For Bender to advance such a drastic position was most uncharacteristic. He may have felt sure that the resolution would fail, and if it did, his claim for institutional autonomy would be vindicated. On the other hand, he may have hoped to alert his institutional colleagues to the implications of the resolution: if Illinois conference could be disciplined, so could the publishing house, the colleges, and the mission board.[54]

The special MC general conference session of 1944 was a test to see if the General Problems Committee could impose churchwide standards of nonconformity. The two-day session began in blistering-hot August weather on a Tuesday evening at Goshen College, in the Administration Building's auditorium. The roll call was answered by 124 delegates, among them Harold Bender, ordained only two months earlier and thus able for the first time to be an official general conference delegate. J. C. Wenger, newly ordained, was also an official delegate for the first time. Orie O. Miller and Guy F. Hershberger were the only "lay delegates" present.

The climax was on Thursday evening, when the General Problems Committee's resolution came to the floor for discussion. The meeting quickly lapsed into incoherent wrangling as the discussion focused on point five of the resolution: "Should any conference definitely decide that they will not work in harmony with General Conference in maintaining the standards of the same, they forfeit their place in General Conference." Conservatives saw this as a way to place the burden of proof on the conferences, for enforcing nonconformity. Progressives saw the provision as preemptive and lacking in pastoral and brotherly process. Confusion overwhelmed the delegates, tension mounted, and the meeting reached an impasse.[55]

Such a moment required a special gesture, and bishop Sanford C. Yoder rose to the occasion. Forty years later Guy F. Hershberger remembered and recounted the drama. "In response to questions and statements as to the reason for the current distrust," he wrote, "Sanford quietly rose to the full length of his 6 feet 3 inches, and in his soft-spoken voice, said words to this effect: You ask the reason for our situation? I'll tell you the reason. It is because fellowship has broken down. There was a time when we experienced the finest of Christian fellowship, but for some time this has no longer been possible. Today the feeling experienced is one of ostracism. The fellowship is gone. This is the reason for distrust and tension within the church."[56]

Hershberger continued: "When the speaker sat down, there was deathly silence. Had a pin been dropped, one could have heard it—until a brother suggested a time for prayer. Then, after a long season of prayer the conference rose from its knees and discussion was resumed."[57]

The spontaneous prayer meeting had lasted an hour and a half. Bender was so moved that he took the floor to propose that the session should conclude with a communion service. Since it was already midnight, the conferees dropped his suggestion, but Guy F. Hershberger caught the evening's significance. "As the meeting drew to a close, it was announced that the Friday morning session would be receiving a report from the Resolutions Committee, followed by action on the 1943 report of the General Problems Committee. Following the benediction, a brother said to me, 'Whatever is done tomorrow will have little meaning. The purpose of the special session of General Conference was achieved this evening.' The brother was right. The dramatic evening session had given birth to a new Mennonite General Conference. The old had died. The new was born in 1944."[58]

Hershberger gave a true assessment. During the night a Resolutions Committee softened the preemptive point five, altering it to require the General Problems Committee to work with an errant conference to avoid forfeiture of membership in general conference. The change disappointed the conservatives, but they were somewhat mollified by a second resolution which reaffirmed specifically that "the Scriptures enunciate clear principles concerning simplicity, purity, self-respect, reserve, humility, and economy in attire." The resolution authorized the publication of a pamphlet carrying J. C. Wenger's conference address: "Historic and Biblical Position of the Mennonite Church on Attire."[59]

Both resolutions passed easily, but as so often in history, at the very moment of resolving old issues, new forces for change had already begun. Only J. B. Smith of the original founding generation of general conference was at the special session in 1944. Daniel Kauffman had died six months earlier. That same year, 88-year-old D. D. Miller was gravely ill, and an ailing Aaron Loucks died.

George Brunk Sr., A. D. Wenger, and John H. Mosemann Sr. had died in the 1930s. The 1944 resolution had embodied the lifework of these men, but implementation was now in the hands of Harold Bender's generation. That generation of leaders, born at the turn of the century, was now managing the church's institutions and caring for its life.

Less than two weeks after the special general conference session, Harold S. Bender at 47 became dean of the new Goshen College Biblical Seminary. Just six months earlier, 50-year-old Paul Erb had taken over the editorship of the *Gospel Herald*. His titular boss at the publishing house was 41-year-old A. J. Metzler. Two months before the special session, J. D. Graber, at 44, had replaced Sanford C. Yoder as the executive secretary of the MC's main mission board. Ernest E. Miller, president of Goshen College, was 51. His brother Orie O. Miller, executive secretary of MCC, was 52. The president of Hesston College was 46-year-old Milo Kauffman. J. L. Stauffer was the "old" man among top Mennonite institutional leaders in 1944: he was 56.

For the next two decades, these were the men who shaped the institutional life of the Mennonite church and presided over the changes set in motion by the Second World War. The new leadership generation was less preoccupied than their predecessors with boundary maintenance and more engaged in missionary outreach, expansion of relief and voluntary service, and restating Mennonite theology, ethics, and identity. Their restatements were largely within the rubric of Harold Bender's "Anabaptist Vision."

## ๑16๖

# Mennonite Community, Encyclopedia, Postwar Relief

*Bender ponders the Mennonite community movement,*
*forms group to develop* The Mennonite Encyclopedia,
*leads postwar relief work.*

S. F. COFFMAN had supper with Harold and Elizabeth Bender on a springlike Monday evening in April 1944. The devout 72-year-old bishop from Vineland, Ontario, had come to talk about some Mennonite Historical Committee matters. Coffman was chair of the committee, and Bender was secretary. But the bishop also had an idea. The Mennonites should have a good farm paper, he told Bender, not a technical paper but one to help them maintain their rural way of life. He was especially worried about the influence of such organizations as the Farm Bureau on Mennonite farmers.[1]

Earlier Coffman had tried to interest *Gospel Herald* editor Daniel Kauffman in the idea, but to no avail. Now in 1944, Coffman was trying to revive the idea because he believed the new editor of the *Gospel Herald*, Paul Erb, was interested in Mennonite rural community issues. In fact, with some prodding from Coffman, Erb would soon begin a monthly page in the *Gospel Herald* entitled "Living Our Faith," devoted to Mennonite rural community life. In any case, Bender also gave some support to Coffman's notion, and within a few days he had organized an informal meeting of a half-dozen persons to explore the idea of beginning a Mennonite farm paper.[2]

Bender's interest in the changing economic and social forms of the Mennonite community did not begin in 1944. In 1939 he learned to know a 29-year-old graduate student at the University of Chicago named J. Winfield Fretz. Fretz was a GC Mennonite born in Bucks County, Pennsylvania, and educated at Bluffton College. In 1938 Fretz had written a Chicago M.A. thesis in sociology about Mennonite mutual aid, and in 1939 Bender published two of its chapters in the *MQR.*[3]

Writing to Orie Miller in late 1939, Bender commented that the Fretz work had "stirred some deep thoughts in my mind. These thoughts run along the line of a practical application of some of the principles we have been speaking about. Why could we not study the possibility of establishing a Mennonite community somewhere, patterned according to the ideals which we have been speaking about based primarily upon the land or farming operations, but also including some small industrial enterprise, and which could be an arena for testing out the possibility of organizing a new type of Christian community with old-fashioned Mennonite principles? I am just dropping this thought into your hopper for cogitation."[4]

Actually, Bender's reference to "some of the principles we have been speaking about" was connected to extensive work by Bender's colleague Guy F. Hershberger. In the spring of 1939, Hershberger had prepared a paper for a Peace Problems Committee conference, arguing that the rural Mennonite community was being spoiled by the modern American industrial economy. Hershberger believed that Mennonites should become more deliberate in preserving what he called "our ideal Mennonite community." He had also read the paper at the 1939 MC General Conference, and soon it appeared in the *MQR.*[5]

Within a few months after Hershberger's essay, the Second World War began, and wartime issues tended to crowd others out. But the concern to preserve Mennonite communal values did not disappear. In 1942, J. Winfield Fretz, by then teaching sociology at Bethel College, began a "Mennonite Rural Life" column in the Kansas-based *Mennonite Weekly Review.*[6] That same year historian Melvin Gingerich, also on the faculty of Bethel College, read a paper at a Mennonite cultural conference and urged the creation of a "rural life publication."[7]

In the wartime years, the concern to preserve the Mennonite

rural community came to match a broader national concern which had emerged, growing since earlier in the century. The disruptive effect of World War II strengthened a growing nostalgia for rural life and rural values. With the successful invasion of Normandy in 1944, the end of the war came into view, and responsible national leaders began to worry about how to reintegrate American GIs into American life. These leaders assumed that a severe restriction of the economy would follow the end of hostilities, and that the returning servicemen would generate massive unemployment. One idea was to settle many of these young men on small plots of land and teach them subsistence farming as a way to cushion their reentry into the American economy.

In the spring of 1945, the nascent Mennonite interest in Mennonite community life matters spawned a conference at Goshen College. The driving force behind the conference was Guy F. Hershberger. In 1939, following Hershberger's ringing address, the MC general conference had created a Committee on Industrial Relations to help Mennonites working in factories deal with an MC Mennonite prohibition against labor-union membership. Hershberger became its secretary. By 1945, the committee's purview had expanded to include the growing concern for preserving the Mennonite rural community. The two-day conference at Goshen was an MC affair, and six of the papers were by Goshen-related persons.

However, the key paper was by Oliver (O. E.) Baker, a former Agriculture Department official from Washington, D.C. Entitled "The Effects of Urbanization on American Life and on the Church," the paper projected a dismal future for Mennonites unless they found a way to revive their rural communities. Baker described a visit to Goshen College several years earlier, where he had met with a group of forty college men. Thirty-eight were farm boys, but only one intended to return to the farm after college. The rest intended to become professionals. The Mennonite church could not survive such a dramatic migration from its rural roots, Baker predicted.[8]

Bender presented a paper on "The Mennonite Conception of the Church and Its Relation to Community Building." He asserted that when Mennonites use the term *community*, they really mean church. "For have we not historically, and in our highest thought, always held that the "church" is a brotherhood of love in which all the members minister to each other in all their needs both temporal and spiritual? And what more is a Christian community than a fellowship of disciples of Christ, sharing a common faith, and under a common Lord?"[9]

Mennonite Christians are, as Bender put it, "both pessimistic and optimistic about this world." Unlike Calvinists and Catholics, Mennonites did not really believe that the world could be redeemed or that it could be transformed by good intentions as the "social gospeler" thought. On the other hand, neither did they agree with "Luther and the Fundamentalists" that it is impossible to do the will of God in the present evil world. "The Mennonite believes," Bender concluded, "that the kingdom of God can be and should be set up within the fellowship of the Church here and now. The world may be full of devils, as Luther says in his great hymn, but the life within the Christian brotherhood community is satisfyingly full of victory, peace, love, and joy."[10]

The new Mennonite concern produced a new organization, the Mennonite Community Association (MCA), begun on June 3, 1946. Hershberger was the creative force in the MCA and became its secretary. The community movement enjoyed key support from *Gospel Herald* editor Paul Erb, who became MCA president. A young CPSer from Pennsylvania, Grant Stoltzfus, a son-in-law of George R. Brunk Sr., became editor of the organization's new journal, *The Mennonite Community*.[11]

The Mennonite community movement did not match the aspirations of its founders. By the end of the war, the forces changing the Mennonite community were already too pervasive to be stanched by a national Mennonite organization. Within a decade *The Mennonite Community* magazine joined the *Christian Monitor* to become a new periodical called *Christian Living*. Its focus was the Mennonite family rather than the community.[12]

Harold Bender's flirtation with the Mennonite community movement was marginal compared to the half-dozen other aspects of his life's work. It highlights his own much more broadly conceived ecumenical Mennonite world-community vision. During the last two decades of his life, he would be preoccupied about how to knit together the disparate groups of Mennonites around the world. Thus much of his energy would go to promote Mennonite relief work, the Mennonite World Conference movement, and the project to develop a Mennonite encyclopedia.

• • •

Harold Bender was in Chicago on December 29, 1944, in his role as chair of the program committee of the American Society of Church History. With him was Guy F. Hershberger. In the course of the meetings, held in connection with the annual meeting of the American Historical Association, Hershberger and Bender had lunch with Bethel College professors J. Winfield Fretz and Melvin Gingerich, and with Bluffton College's venerable Mennonite historian C. Henry Smith. By then Fretz had earned a Ph.D. in sociology at the University of Chicago in 1941. Melvin Gingerich, an MC Mennonite, held a Ph.D. in American history from the University of Iowa. The five men shared notes, and the chemistry between them must have been creative. Out of the encounter came a proposal to create a "Mennonite Scholars Guild" to promote Mennonite scholarship. The five declared themselves charter members and identified eight other potential members to be invited to a first meeting of the guild. Bender and Fretz agreed to write up a "charter."[13]

The first meeting of the "Guild" was at the Walnut Grill Room of the Pine Restaurant in Bluffton, Ohio, on August 23, 1945. From Goshen College came Harold Bender, J. C. Wenger, S. C. Yoder, Guy F. Hershberger, and John Umble. C. Henry Smith was present from Bluffton. From Bethel College came president Edmund G. Kaufman, Melvin Gingerich, dean Abraham Warkentin, historian Cornelius Krahn, and Fretz. Also present was Robert Friedmann from Western Michigan University.

Bender chaired the meeting, and he and Fretz described what the "Mennonite Scholar's Guild" might become. It would not publish papers or hold public conferences. Instead, it was to be "an intimate fellowship of Mennonite research men [sic], a fellowship of craftsmen." The larger purpose would be to "inspire and encourage men with common interests in scholarship to use it to the glory of God and the service of the Mennonite Church." Qualifications for membership would be "communicant" membership in a Mennonite congregation, "cordial loyalty" to historic Mennonitism, and research and publication at least of a master's level of work.[14] The "Guild" was renamed "The Mennonite Research Fellowship." The group elected C. Henry Smith as president, Bender as vice-president, and J. Winfield Fretz as secretary-treasurer.[15]

However, the evening's more important business was a discussion of how to help the Mennonites in Germany complete the publication of the *Mennonitisches Lexikon* (Mennonite encyclopedia). The *Lexikon*, begun in 1913, was to be a multivolume work covering all Mennonite history from 1525 onward, in standard, topical articles in alphabetical order. After the second volume (reaching the letter *N*) was published in 1942, the war interrupted the work. One of the project's aging editors, Christian Hege, had died during the war. Now in 1945, the other editor, Christian Neff, was 82 and no longer able to carry on the work. With Europe devastated by war, the project almost certainly could not move forward without help from the Americans. The new Mennonite Research Fellowship decided to help. They named a committee of Bender, Smith, Krahn, Wenger, and Friedmann, with Bender as chairman. The main idea at the time was to get out an English-language version of those first two volumes, publishing it in America and using the proceeds to help the Europeans with their final volumes.[16]

The *Lexikon* project was particularly attractive to Bender. In the summer of 1924, just before he and Elizabeth returned to the United States from their year of study at Tübingen, they had made a visit to Christian Neff at the Weierhof in the Palatinate. At that moment Neff was writing the editor's concluding remarks for the *Lexikon*'s first volume, which was published that fall. Bender had been immensely impressed by the scope of the project and its value for the historical memory of Mennonites. Now, twenty years later, he saw the completion of the *Lexikon* as an opportunity for American and European Mennonites to cooperate on a mutually beneficial undertaking.

Trading on his good relationships with publisher A. J. Metzler at the MCs' Mennonite Publishing House, Bender proposed that the presses of the various Mennonite branches cooperate in the venture. By March 1946, he and Metzler had persuaded the publishing boards of the MC Mennonites and the GC Mennonites to meet to discuss next steps. Out of those discussions came a publishing committee made up of Mennonite publishers, who then appointed an editorial committee. The Mennonite Brethren (MBs) joined the project, and the committee became Paul Erb, H. J. Andes, A. J. Metzler, J. M. Suderman, P. H. Berg, and Orlando Harms.[17]

By spring 1946, Bender had also settled on a name for the project. "It is time to agree on an English title for the new work, inasmuch as *Lexikon* is a German word," he told the publishing committee. "We should have discussed this matter at our last meeting. However, I presume there is little choice, and that Mennonite Encyclopedia is in fact the only possible choice." He invited members to suggest alternatives, but none were forthcoming. *The Mennonite Encyclopedia* it would be.[18]

The Mennonite Research Fellowship met a second time in Freeman, South Dakota, on August 26, 1946, exactly a year after the first meeting at Bluffton. Bender arrived late. He had come by plane and landed at Sioux Falls with just twelve minutes to catch a bus to Freeman, but missed it. However, his upbeat report on the progress of the *Lexikon* project compensated for his tardiness. His committee's "assignment had been accomplished," he told the gathering, and its work completed. "The entire project [has been] put on its feet."[19]

The new committee had set the goal at three 1,000-page volumes, to sell at $18 for the set. The MCs proposed to sell 3,000 sets, the GCs 1,500, and the MBs 500, to their respective constituencies. The Mennonite Publishing House at Scottdale would do the printing and financing until the sale of the books began. An editorial committee would oversee the work: Harold Bender as chairman; C. Henry Smith as vice-chairman; J. C. Wenger as secretary along with Melvin Gingerich; and Cornelius Krahn, P. C. Hiebert, C. F. Klassen, and P. E. Schellenberg as other committee members. A large editorial council representing all Mennonite groups would also be created. Elizabeth Horsch Bender was the project translator. All three volumes were to be completed in five years.[20]

Bender announced further that he would be going to Europe within a few weeks to negotiate a contract with the owners and publishers of the *Lexikon*. He completed the report with a flourish: "A significant joint project of American Mennonite scholarship is now successfully launched." He could not know that the project would consume much of his time and energy for the rest of his life.[21]

• • •

With the end of the war in 1945, the Mennonites launched an extraordinarily aggressive relief program. By early 1947 the MC Mennonites alone had 140 persons abroad in relief work and were raising hundreds of thousands of dollars per year in financial support. Such efforts were a response to the unprecedented human suffering produced by the war. Mennonites, like most Americans, had prospered greatly during the war. They could afford to be generous.[22]

The unprecedented relief effort was also a product of the zeal of Bender's generation of new Mennonite leaders who had emerged during the Second World War. Orie O. Miller, C. L. Graber, and Ernest Miller had vivid memories of the post-World War I Mennonite relief effort in which they had participated. Harold Bender, John L. Horst, J. D. Graber, Paul Erb, J. L. Stauffer, and others had been intensely interested bystanders. In 1945, the life-changing experiences and memories of a quarter century earlier became models for what needed to be done. Mennonites did not have to invent either a new rationale or new institutions for their renewed relief activity.

In the period between the world wars, Mennonites had undertaken two substantial relief projects. One was the 1930 movement of Soviet Mennonite refugees to South America, the MCC project in which Bender had gained his first direct experience in relief administration. The second was a Spanish relief program in the late 1930s under the MC Mennonite Relief Committee. The MRC, as it was called, was established in 1926 to take the place of the

World War I-era Mennonite Relief Commission for War Sufferers. It was a committee within the larger MC Mennonite mission board at Elkhart, Indiana.[23]

In August 1936, Bender had become a member of the MRC's executive board. A few months later he received a phone call from Clarence Pickett, executive secretary of the American Friends Service Committee. Pickett invited the Mennonites to cooperate with the AFSC in relief work in Spain. The Spanish Civil War was raging, and the Quakers had made arrangements to begin relief activity on the edges of the conflict. A month later Bender heard also from Michael (M. R.) Zigler, inviting the Mennonites to join the Church of the Brethren in their relief efforts in Spain.[24] Thus the MRC faced a new opportunity.

Bender was eager to get Mennonites involved, as was Orie Miller, who in 1937 was both secretary-treasurer of MCC and chairman of the MRC. S. C. Yoder, president of Goshen College in 1937, was also a member of the MRC and, even more importantly, the secretary of its parent body, the MCs' main mission board. The treasurer of that board was D. D. Miller, Orie Miller's father. S. C. Yoder and D. D. Miller were enthusiastic about getting into Spanish relief because they were just then casting about for a new mission field, and Spain seemed promising. They saw the Spanish relief effort as a precursor to possible MC mission work there.[25]

The MRC moved quickly. By December of 1937, Goshen College staff member Levi Hartzler and furloughed Argentine missionary D. Parke Lantz were at work in Spain. Eventually six American MC Mennonites served in Spain, distributing $57,000 in relief aid. In February of 1940, MRC workers Ernest Bennett and Edna Ramseyer moved into southern France and, under the aegis of MCC, began relief work among Spanish refugees there. The MRC handed administrative direction of the program over to the MCC and helped finance MCC relief efforts in France, England, Poland, and the Middle East. Bender's 1940 trip to Europe was thus as MCC assistant secretary rather than on behalf of the MRC.[26]

In 1942 Orie Miller relinquished his chairmanship of the MRC. In the reshuffling which followed, John L. Horst, editor of the *Christian Monitor* at Scottdale, became MRC chairman. Bender became secretary and de facto administrator of the committee. For the next five years, he managed the MRC projects out of his dean's office at Goshen, recruiting workers, managing budgets, and establishing policy.

When the war forced the end of MCC relief work in Europe in 1942, the MCC and the MRC began to explore China as a new area of endeavor. In 1943 Bender and the MRC, encouraged by the mission board, sent J. D. Graber, then a missionary in India and soon to be the mission board's new chief executive, to China to investigate possibilities. Graber gave a favorable report, and Bender recruited several workers to go to China: George Beare, an India missionary; J. Lawrence Burkholder, a pastor at Croghan, New York; and Clayton Beyeler, a graduate of the new five-year Th.B. program of Goshen College Bible School. Graber recommended that the trio work for and with whatever MCC program might be developed.[27]

Graber's recommendation created a storm of opposition from conservatives in Pennsylvania and Virginia.[28] By 1943 conservative opposition to MCC, exacerbated by CPS, had led conservatives to distrust any collaboration with MCC. The China program seemed like just another instance where MC Mennonite monies and workers were being used to support what they regarded as collaboration with "liberal" brethren, a reference to GC Mennonites. John R. Mumaw, EMS teacher and secretary-treasurer of Virginia Conference, complained that while "we were hoping to get further away from MCC in our organizational relationships, this appears like another tie-up that will complicate our situation even more."[29] The Virginia Conference threatened to withhold its contributions to MRC unless changes were made. In a clear slap at Bender's management of the MRC, Mumaw urged that the MRC should set up an office at Scottdale and run its own affairs in complete separation from MCC.[30]

The man caught in the middle of the conflict was the modest and gentle MRC chairman, John Horst. In near despair he told Bender, "I am deeply concerned about this turmoil that revolves around the MCC and especially the confusion that seems to be in people's minds about the relief programs of the MCC and the

MRC." Much of the problem, as Horst saw it, was that Bender and Orie Miller's domination of both organizations made many church leaders uneasy. "Did you ever think that as chairman of our Peace Problems Committee, secretary of our Relief Committee, and soon to be minister and the head of our Bible school, it might be a good thing for you to step out of active affiliation with the MCC?" Horst asked Bender plaintively. "I think I could see some very definite advantages." It was a suggestion Bender found unthinkable.[31]

Horst's observation confirmed the fact that much of the criticism leveled at MCC, MRC, and the Peace Problems Committee came from leaders who were uneasy about the unusual interlocking organizational relationships of Bender, Orie Miller, and the Graber brothers (C. L. and J. D.). In 1944 Bender was chair of the Peace Problems Committee, Miller was secretary, and C. L. Graber was treasurer. Bender was also chair of the new MCC Peace Section. As executive secretary of MCC, Miller was a member of the Peace Section, as was C. L. Graber. Bender was secretary of MRC, and Miller and J. D. Graber were members of the committee. The MCC executive committee considered itself a relief committee. Miller was its executive secretary, Bender its assistant secretary, and C. L. Graber its relief director. Small wonder that the administration of relief operations confused lay people and frustrated Pennsylvania and Virginia leaders, who were being asked to mobilize people and money even as they felt shut out by the tight hold of the Bender-Miller-Graber-Graber quartet on administrative positions.

From the standpoint of Bender, Miller, and the Grabers, the advantage was efficiency. When one of them traveled abroad, he could represent MCC and the MRC at the same time. Thus on his 1946 trip to Europe, Bender wore his MCC hat to purchase the Basel MCC house and his MRC guise to give far-ranging direction to the programs in Belgium and in Poland. Every meeting of any of the organizations became an opportunity to do business across the spectrum. But it also meant that other leaders felt excluded or remained skeptical of policies arrived at informally by the "foursome."

The result was an unrelenting barrage of criticism from "outsiders" and a nonstop effort at damage control by the "foursome." For John Horst, who had little stomach for such tensions, the situation was terrifying. For Bender, Miller, and the Grabers, it was merely business as usual. By the 1940s they had been managing damage control for two decades, and they were adept at it.

An illustration of such damage control was Bender's response to the Virginia and Pennsylvania conference leaders' insistence in 1944 that the MRC do its own relief work and not simply support MCC. Bender called a meeting of the MRC committee and invited a number of the eastern leaders to participate. Attending were bishop Amos Horst of Lancaster, and Virginians J. L. Stauffer, Jacob Shenk, and Lewis Martin. The purpose of the meeting was to identify a field of MRC relief service as soon as the war was over. Apparently the meeting produced no program plans, but Bender perceived that the Virginians were ready to support relief work in Europe. So he proposed Belgium as a promising place for relief activity (MCC planned to be elsewhere), and he suggested that the Virginians select one of their own to visit Belgium as an MRC commissioner as soon as the war ended.[32]

As a ploy Bender's proposal worked well: in contrast to the world-traveling foursome, the Virginians were much too parochial to seize such an audacious opportunity. After some hemming and hawing, they finally suggested that MRC chair John Horst go to Europe. Bender had hoped he himself would be asked to go, but he gracefully accepted Horst, realizing that Horst would have greater credibility than Harold Bender for such an assignment.[33] Thus John Horst found himself in Europe in September of 1945. He was one of the first North American Mennonite leaders to visit Europe after the war, although MCC commissioner C. F. Klassen had arrived from Canada a week earlier.[34]

Meanwhile, Bender continued to turn up the pressure on the Virginians. He asked EMS president J. L. Stauffer to let MRC borrow a faculty member to serve as director of Belgium relief, only to have Stauffer insist that "he could not spare anyone." Frustrated, Bender went directly to faculty member John R. Mumaw, who had been pushing hard for an independent MRC operation, and urged Mumaw personally to become director in Belgium. Talk to

"Stauffer about getting a leave of absence," Bender urged Mumaw.[35] But Mumaw did not respond to the overture.

During the entire Belgium project, the only Virginia Mennonite to volunteer for service was businessman Lewis Martin, and his offer came only after the roster of workers was filled. While the criticism from the Virginians and from some Pennsylvanians continued unabated, Bender was able to report to John Horst in mid-1945 that the "Virginia Mission Board has now released one thousand dollars monthly to our relief fund, five hundred dollars for Ethiopia, and five hundred dollars for China."[36] Bender and Horst had managed to keep the Virginians' cooperation despite all their objections.

In retrospect, it is clear that none of the Virginia leaders had either the experience or the inclination to act at the level required to get an overseas project going. While it was easy to deplore the centralization of authority which took place during the 1940s in the relief, peace, and missions organizations, it is also clear that the far-flung nature of postwar relief could happen only with vigorous and imaginative leadership. The Bender-Miller-Graber "foursome" met the challenge.

• • •

More than any of his other off-campus assignments, the MRC secretaryship consumed much of Bender's time during the mid-1940s. In 1944 he made a list of all the MRC activities he was trying to manage. He noted that he was opening work in China, beginning medical work in Puerto Rico, starting Mennonite Voluntary Service (VS) units for Mennonite young people in North America, managing all MC Mennonite CPS dependency disbursements, disbursing funds for Argentine famine relief, supporting MCC relief with an MRC contribution of $3,000 per month, overseeing contributions and disbursements for relief through the Elkhart mission board office, and opening a new MRC project in Ethiopia. Given such a plethora of tasks, the MRC clearly needed a full-time administrator, and the money was there to pay for it. But typically, Bender tried to do it all himself.[37]

One of Bender's major tasks was to initiate an MRC relief project in Ethiopia. In April of 1945, he attended a meeting of the new United Nations Relief and Rehabilitation Administration (UNRRA) in New York City on behalf of MCC and the MRC. In response, he proposed that the MRC should begin distributing relief in Ethiopia and follow the relief with mission work.[38] The MRC committee quickly supported that plan. Since Orie Miller was just then departing on a trip to the Middle East, East Africa, and India, the committee authorized Miller to visit Ethiopia and report back.

Bender was impatient to get the project moving. In early May, even before Miller departed and many weeks before Miller would get to Ethiopia, Bender told Horst, "We do not know for certain that we can carry through the project, but all indications are favorable." He proposed the appointment of a director so that when Miller reported back, the program could get under way quickly.[39]

Bender had a candidate for director: G. Irvin Lehman, a young Lancaster Conference Mennonite studying at Hartford Seminary. If Lehman agrees to become director, let's ordain him, Bender suggested to Horst. If the Lancaster Conference leaders objected, Bender thought Lehman could be persuaded to move his membership to the Chicago mission, to be ordained there. The MRC had used such a scheme to ordain Clayton Beyeler before sending Beyeler to China, Bender reminded Horst.[40]

It was mid-July before Miller got to Ethiopia. His cable to Bender said "Go"; by then, G. Irvin Lehman was ready as director. Bender had also arranged for Dr. Paul Conrad to go to Ethiopia to open a clinic and perhaps a hospital. Conrad was just completing his medical internship at a Chicago hospital. In subsequent months, Bender gave much time to arranging for the departure of the workers to Ethiopia. By September, the first ones arrived, and by January of 1946, about a dozen were on site, some of them nurses. By the end of 1946, the MRC had opened a 25-bed hospital in Nazareth, Ethiopia.[41]

Meanwhile, Bender was pushing hard to begin the Belgium project. By July of 1945, the Virginia brethren had decided John Horst should go to Belgium as an MRC commissioner to determine what was needed. Horst, who had never traveled before, much less to Europe, dawdled in making his arrangements. On

August 30, 1945, Bender gently urged Horst to get under way. Again Bender had not waited for the commissioner's report. He had already negotiated with Cleo Mann of Elkhart to go to Belgium as the new unit's director. He had decided, he told Horst, who was not yet in Europe, that initially there should be three men in the unit: one from Canada, one from Virginia, and Mann from Indiana.[42] By October, Cleo Mann was in Belgium. Soon other workers followed.

Two things were driving Bender's urgency about the Belgium and the Ethiopia projects: tremendous needs created by the war, and Mennonite giving for relief at an all-time high. "The upsurge of interest in all of our churches in the U.S and Canada to help in this relief program continues to grow almost beyond our capacity to handle and manage and channel things," Orie Miller told C. F. Klassen.[43]

In the summer of 1945, the MRC had $130,000 in cash waiting to be spent.[44] Orie Miller had just established a 1946 relief budget for MCC in excess of a half-million dollars. Bender realized that if Mennonite lay interest in relief was to continue, actual projects had to begin quickly. So he aggressively pushed to get the Ethiopia and Belgium projects underway.

• • •

While managing the mobilization of MRC projects took much of Bender's time during the summer of 1945, his other large responsibility was MCC executive committee work. By early 1945 it was clear that the war in Europe would soon be over. Bender noticed the "astonishing advances of the Russian army into Germany." Writing to C. F. Klassen, he observed that "the Mennonites of the region of Danzig must be going through much suffering."[45] But he had no firsthand knowledge of either the scale or the nature of the suffering.

As the Soviet armies advanced, they pushed a vast collection of people westward, refugees fleeing for their lives. The war drew to a close, literally sweeping millions of people into the maelstrom of war and famine. Among the multitudes were many thousands of Mennonites from the Ukraine, Poland, and East Prussia.

Just a few weeks after the German surrender in May, Orie Miller departed on his four-month around-the-world trip. He was to survey conditions and needs in the Middle East, East Africa, India, and Europe. With events in the world moving so rapidly, the MCC executive committee asked Kansan P. C. Hiebert, the chairman of MCC, to move temporarily to Akron and take Miller's place while he was gone. Hiebert was a genial and devout college professor, but he had scant ability as an administrator. And he was a bit of a worrier. Being at Akron made Hiebert aware for the first time of the substantial amount of independent relief work the MRC was beginning under Bender's leadership.

Hiebert became quite upset when he learned that the GC Mennonites also were thinking about launching their own independent relief work. "This matter of individualistic undertakings portends possibilities which make me apprehensive," he told Bender. "Now, my dear Bender, you again see how I am too much alarmed and concerned, but you know the motive at the bottom of it would be none other than to accomplish the greatest good to the greatest number as we unitedly contribute to the one cause of making our light shine to the world."[46]

Hiebert, a Mennonite Brethren, brought a fresh perspective to the issue. If the GC Mennonites did what the MC Mennonites were doing, the MCC relief program could be seriously handicapped. Bender, preoccupied with MC Mennonite relief politics, had not given the problem much thought. He tried to reassure Hiebert: "We shall do our best to hold our program together so that we maintain a united front in our relief work. I would also be glad to know just what the GC Board may have in mind and why. Much depends, in my mind, on the motivation for such a venture."[47] It was clear that Bender believed the MRC relief initiatives proceeded from right motives. The situation called for doing just enough independent MRC relief programming to keep MC Mennonite conservatives from jumping completely out of the MCC ship. To Bender and Miller, the MRC activities seemed eminently sensible: to P. C. Hiebert, H. A. Fast, and C. F. Klassen, the other MCC executive committee members, they must have been a bit frustrating.

Since Orie Miller was out of the country for four months, and chairman Hiebert was somewhat out of his depth, Bender as assistant secretary of MCC stepped into the breach. By 1945 the administration of the CPS program had been largely routinized and was in the capable hands of Kansan Albert Gaeddert. The routine work of the two-year-old Peace Section, which Bender chaired, was in the hands of Jesse Hoover. After 1945 the new Relief Section, managed by C. L. Graber during its first year (1943-44), was administered by J. N. Byler.

Bender found the new MCC bureaucracy a bit daunting and feared that it would reduce the ability of the executive committee members to manage affairs. For instance, as he read correspondence passing between Byler and MCC—Europe director Sam Goering, he was upset to learn that Byler had assigned relief worker Marie Ediger to Holland because that was where she wanted to work, and done so despite an earlier decision by Orie Miller that she be assigned to France. "I would suggest that you hold up this action for review," he told Hiebert. "We need to have good grass upon our whole Dutch program and not rush in too quickly or at least not have actual assignment of workers without approval by the executive committee. I am calling you today by telephone about this matter."[48] In more simple times, such micromanagement by the executive committee might have been possible. In 1945, as the flood of MCC relief workers heightened, it became practically impossible. Bender was finding it hard to change with the times.

In early June 1945, Bender received an urgent telephone call from NSBRO director Paul Comly French in Washington. Did Bender know that among the millions of refugees in Germany were many thousands of Mennonites from the Ukraine and East Prussia, and that they were in danger of being sent back to the Soviet Union? French had gotten the news from Quakers who had just returned from Europe.[49] The situation was worrisome.

At its June meeting, the executive committee of MCC decided to send C. F. Klassen to Europe to investigate and get firsthand information. But it was difficult to get North American civilians into Germany. By the time Klassen got his passport, it was August. Ominous rumors were spreading that the Soviets were going to repatriate all East European displaced persons in Western Europe.

It was urgent to get someone into Germany. To everyone's relief, European MCC director Sam Goering was able to get to Frankfurt in the last week of August and contact military authorities about the refugee situation.[50]

Finally on August 22, Klassen left for London by plane, and by the first of September had already visited Mennonite refugees in Denmark. Meanwhile, Bender and Hiebert had begun working on possible places for European Mennonite refugee resettlement. Fortunately, during July and August the other MCC executive committee member, H. A. Fast, was in Paraguay on MCC business and managed to make some preparations for a new wave of Mennonite refugees to that country's Chaco district. With the return of Orie Miller in mid-September, Bender was able to turn to other pressing matters.

• • •

One of Bender's happiest assignments was supervising the second year of a new program he had helped initiate in 1944: Mennonite Service Units. During 1945 fifteen young people worked as volunteers for two months at three locations: an old people's home at Culp, Arkansas; an orphans' home at West Liberty, Ohio; and a mission at Canton, Ohio. The first Mennonite Service Unit of four young people had worked at the Mexican Mission in Chicago in 1944.[51]

The idea had grown out of the war experience. In 1942, as civilians mobilized for the war effort, many local communities mobilized American young people into a High School Victory Corps, which put them to work during summers in a variety of local and defense-related activities. The Peace Problems Committee and the mission board decided the church should begin its own alternative to the Victory Corps. So the MRC, with Bender's enthusiastic leadership, designed what it called "Mennonite Service Units": summer work projects for Mennonite young people, developed and funded by the MRC.[52]

The program grew rapidly. By 1946 there were seven projects and thirty volunteers. The idea was popular with both young people and church leaders, and in 1946 Bender recommended that the program operate year-round. By early 1947 Laurence Horst of Hesston, Kansas, became its director. Bender and J. D. Graber were its oversight committee.[53]

The year 1945 was one of the most frenetic in Bender's life. He spent ninety days away from Goshen. One trip, visiting western CPS camps, lasted as long as two weeks, but most were hurried journeys of a day or two, with Bender traveling by train at night. More than half were speaking trips, with many Sunday morning sermons or a series of weekend addresses. The off-campus schedule played havoc with Bender's class attendance and evoked student complaints. From September to December of 1944, when he was doing much less traveling, he missed fifteen class days, or about a fourth of his classes. Adding to his busyness in 1945, his contract required him to teach two three-week classes during summer school—one in Mennonite history, the other a New Testament book study.[54]

The summer of 1946 was equally busy.[55] In Washington, Congress was working on a new peacetime draft law to replace the old 1940 one, which would end in 1947. To the consternation of the Historic Peace Church leaders, a new bill made no mention of COs. Bender attended a conference to work at inserting CO provisions. Meanwhile, he made several trips to Washington to consult about closing down the CPS program, a process the HPC leaders found frustratingly slow.[56]

During August, Bender had a bewildering string of meetings: ten all-day meetings within a span of twenty days. At home in Goshen, he was busy getting ready for a record number of students: Goshen College enrollment jumped from 448 in 1945 to 752 in the fall of 1946. In 1946-47 the new Goshen College Biblical Seminary had fifteen new B.D. students. Eldest daughter, Mary Eleanor, was a sophomore and one of the multitude of college students living in Goshen's crowded dormitories.[57] Twelve-year-old Nancy was a sixth grader at Parkside Elementary School, a half-mile north of the Bender home. Elizabeth began her last year of teaching English at Goshen High School, an assignment she had begun in 1942 when enrollment fell at the college and the departure of teachers for war service opened a high school position.

# ❧17❧

# To Postwar Europe for MCC

*Bender visits Europe, becomes coeditor of the* Mennonitisches Lexikon, *spends a year in Europe for Mennonite Central Committee.*

DURING 1946 the MRC and MCC relief programs grew rapidly. The suffering in Europe during the winter of 1945-46 was horrible, and relief aid poured in to MCC in historic amounts. Overall Mennonite contributions to MCC jumped from one and a half million dollars in 1945 to nearly four million in 1947.[1] Mennonites were making record contributions in response to postwar need. For the first time in their lives, Bender and his MCC executive committee colleagues had ample funds for their activities. Small wonder that MCC and mission board leaders rode airplanes across the Atlantic rather than slower and cheaper ships. For a few brief years, Mennonite leaders had almost more money than they could handle.

As the MCC and MRC programs expanded pell-mell during 1946, it became clear that Bender should make a trip to Europe to survey the emerging programs. Also, it was important to clarify the terms of the Mennonite encyclopedia project with the German editors of the *Mennonitisches Lexikon.*[2]

Thus on the forenoon of September 27, 1946, Bender found himself looking down at the deep-green landscape of the Netherlands and Northwest Germany from a big four-engine Constellation, making a descent to the Rhein-Main Airport outside of Frankfurt. In the distance he could make out the Rhine River, and quite soon the city of Mainz. For the first time the magnitude of

370

the destruction wreaked on German cities by the Allied bombing campaign became clear to him. The center of Mainz had been leveled.[3]

The airliner landed just before noon. Bender had made his first trans-Atlantic flight. Whatever he may have expected upon returning to the Germany he remembered was quickly altered by what he saw as the plane taxied up to the makeshift terminal. It was clear who had won the war. He was landing at an airport run by the American army. There were GIs everywhere.[4]

Waiting for Bender on the tarmac, surrounded by a solid sea of khaki, was civilian-suited Robert Kreider, ex-CPSer and MCC's man in the American zone of Germany. Kreider was MCC's representative on CRALOG (Council of Relief Agencies Licensed for Operation in Germany), the only private group authorized to do relief work in the American zone. Kreider's special permit to be in the American zone included access to American army food and housing plus the use of an army jeep and the gas to make it run. For the next week, Kreider chauffeured Bender throughout southern Germany in the army jeep. Since it was late September, and the jeep had no glass in the windows, travel could be quite chilly. Bender was glad he had brought his winter overcoat.[5]

Bender arrived at noon and immediately departed with Kreider for the Mennonite community at the Weierhof, some 100 kilometers south of Rhein-Main in the Palatinate. They crossed the Rhine river on an Army "Bailey" bridge, since all the regular bridges across the river had been bombed. They arrived at the home of Christian Neff in time for dinner. The last time Bender and Neff had met had been in 1936 at the Mennonite World Conference in Amsterdam.[6]

A slight handsome man with a carefully groomed beard and mustache, the amiable but ailing Neff was delighted to see Bender. After dinner, eyes twinkling since he knew he was putting Bender and Kreider in an awkward position, the patriarchal Neff brought out a bottle of wine to honor the occasion.[7] Later that evening many of the Mennonite neighbors gathered at the Neff home to talk with Bender.

The visit with Neff was more than a courtesy call: Bender

**Christian Neff.** Mennonite Historical Library, Goshen College.

came with a letter from A. J. Metzler, manager of the Mennonite Publishing House, authorizing him to negotiate on behalf of the Mennonite encyclopedia project, and offering American Mennonite help in completing the *Lexikon*. The key point was to get permission to translate the *Lexikon* material for inclusion in the encyclopedia. In turn, the encyclopedia committee would help Neff and his collaborators finance the *Lexikon*.[8]

Neff, overjoyed that his life's work might now be completed, readily agreed. The two men drew up a six-point memorandum of understanding which each signed, Neff in his elegant but dainty handwriting, Bender with his robust and continuous-line signature. Neff insisted that Bender become a coeditor of the *Lexikon* and enshrined that appointment in point two of the memo. Flattered, Bender accepted.[9] Reporting a few days later to Paul Erb as chair of the encyclopedia committee, Bender was exultant. "They have appointed me successor to Christian Hege as coeditor of the *Mennonitisches Lexikon* with Christian Neff."[10] Hege, the associate editor of the *Lexikon*, had died during the war.

When word of Bender's appointment reached Bethel College, historian Cornelius Krahn was nonplussed. "Do you actually think you can take the place of Christian Hege?" Krahn demanded. That, he pointed out, would be like having a German Mennonite, living in Europe, editing our Mennonite encyclopedia. They offered the editorship to you only as a "gesture of honor"; you should thank them and turn it down. Let us be honest, Krahn went on.

They have nearly a century of research experience, and we Americans are just starting; "they sowed and we reap." Krahn agreed that the Americans should give the Europeans moral and financial support and encourage them to complete the *Lexikon*; but he wanted them to have the "honor of having done it themselves." Otherwise, he told Bender, "it will appear as though we took advantage of our brethren when they were completely down and out."[11]

Krahn had a strong point. To the feeble and ailing Christian Neff, Bender appeared a godsend, come to rescue his life's work from limbo. Neff's generous invitation was natural, but Krahn was right: Bender should have turned it down. However, on that beautiful September Saturday forenoon, amid the sights and smells of Weierhof's Mennonite barnyards and the peaceful hush of Neff's study, Bender felt at home. He could not bring himself to turn down an editorship offered by one of the few men he genuinely revered. Neff died on December 30, less than three months after Bender's visit.

After a Saturday-noon lunch, Bender and Kreider crossed the Rhine River on a ferry and headed for Heidelberg. From Neff, Bender had learned that his old university professor Walther Köhler had died during the war, and Bender hoped to visit widow Köhler. The visit was a courtesy call, with just a whiff of larceny: Bender hoped to discover what Mrs. Köhler planned to do with her husband's library. Unfortunately, the Köhler home had been requisitioned by the U.S. Army, and Mrs. Köhler could not be found. So Bender and Kreider traversed the familiar road and beautiful countryside to the Mennonite hofs Lautenbach and Willenbach, and enjoyed a reunion with Elizabeth's cousins Christian and Walter Landes.[12]

From the Landes families, Bender heard a vivid account of the war and its effects on the lives of the Horsch and Funk relatives in southern Germany. Willenbach, the beautiful centuries-old hof of cousins Walter and Helene Landes, where Bender and Elizabeth had spent so many delightful weekends in the 1920s and 1930s, was nearly destroyed in a rearguard action during one of the last days of the war.[13] Walter Landes described the fearful firebombing of Heilbronn by the Americans in the spring of 1945. One of the youthful Landes cousins, Heine, had been killed during the war while serving as a soldier. Bender distributed vitamins and insulin which Elizabeth's brothers, Walter, Menno, and Paul, had sent for the relatives.[14] The next day was Sunday, and Bender and Kreider attended church with the Landes family.

From there they went on to Eichstadt for a brief visit with Adele Hege, daughter of the late Christian Hege. Bender needed her signature on the agreement he had struck with Christian Neff. He was delighted to get to see Hege's extensive library for the first time. Adele Hege, ill and in need of special medical treatment, surprised Bender by offering to sell the library to Goshen College to raise money for her treatment. She did so even though her father's will had explicitly directed that the library stay in Germany.[15]

Bender was ready to buy the library, with the idea of taking to Goshen those books which the Goshen library lacked and using the others to establish a library at the Basel MCC center.[16] But historian Ernst Crous, who would become the new coeditor of the *Lexikon* after Christian Neff died, vigorously protested. Bender quickly realized that if he wanted to do any useful work in Germany in the future, the Hege library would have to stay intact in Germany. So it was decided to move the library to Stuttgart, where it would be available to Eberhard Teufel, another of the new editors of the *Lexikon*.[17]

Aboard the jeep again, Bender and Kreider traveled east through the medieval towns of Schwäbish-Hall, Dinkelsbühl, and Nördlingen. They were on their way to Hellmansberg-Ingolstadt to visit Elizabeth's uncle Michael Horsch and to discuss how MCC could help the German Mennonite relief organization Christenpflicht. Earlier, Horsch had suggested that Christenpflicht could use "20 American Mennonite relief workers," a proposal which Bender eagerly hoped to take up.[18] Horsch's idea was attractive to Bender and Kreider because it would have allowed them to practice an emerging MCC principle: that Mennonite relief supplies should be distributed by Mennonites personally, to witness in accord with the MCC motto, "In the Name of Christ." During 1946 the largest share of material relief delivered to the American zone came from MCC, but was distributed by a German Protestant relief organization, Evangelishes Hilfswerk. Bender and the MCC executive committee disliked this arrangement because they wanted American Mennonite involvement in the distribution itself. Unfortunately, a cooperative arrangement with Christenplicht was not worked out.[19]

One afternoon Kreider and Bender visited a refugee camp in Munich where 500 Russian Mennonite refugees were interned. Later that evening they drove through dense fog on the autobahn to Stuttgart, stopping en route to eat and refuel at an army PX. The next morning they met briefly with pastor Eberhard Teufel, a leading German scholar of Anabaptism who was on the board of directors of the German Mennonite Historical Society and an active participant in the *Lexikon* project. A highlight of the visit was Teufel's account of the death of professor Walther Köhler in 1943. On his deathbed, Teufel told Bender, Köhler expressed regret that he could not die a Mennonite.[20]

From Stuttgart, Bender and Kreider drove south to visit another of the Landes cousins, Alfred, and then made a stop at Tübingen for nostalgia's sake and for a quick visit to several bookstores, where among other items Bender found many unbound copies of Ernst Correll's book on the eighteenth-century Swiss Mennonites. He bought the whole lot.[21]

By late afternoon Kreider and Bender were in Karlsruhe for a brief visit with Dr. Benjamin Unruh, with whom Bender had worked in 1930 to move the first Russian refugees to Paraguay. Delighted to see them, the loquacious Unruh talked nonstop. Finally at dusk the two Americans crossed the Rhine River again, near Strasbourg. They were headed for Muhlhouse, where they spent the night at a large hof owned by Mennonite minister Joseph Widmer. By ten o'clock the next morning, they were in Basel at the MCC house on the Birkenstrasse.[22]

For the 27-year-old Robert Kreider, it had been quite a trip. Kreider was the eldest son of Amos E. Kreider, one of Bender's professors during his senior year at Goshen College in 1918. During a four-year stint in CPS, Robert Kreider, a GC Mennonite and University of Chicago M.A. graduate, had shown promise as a churchman and administrator. In the course of the five days of travel in the jeep through southern Germany, Bender and Kreider found that despite a twenty-year difference in age, they were kindred spirits: they shared a zestful urge to propose and plan new ventures.[23]

At Basel, Bender and Kreider tried out their ideas on Howard Yoder, the director of MCC—Europe. Yoder, a successful Wayne County, Ohio, nurseryman, was the father of one of Bender's brightest students at Goshen College, John Howard Yoder. During an all-day conference, the trio of Bender, Kreider, and Yoder made three decisions. Kreider would be named MCC director in Germany. Second, he would work out of the British zone in northeast Germany but oversee MCC relief operations in all three western zones. That plan would give German MCC relief work a single administrative head.[24]

The most fateful decision was the third: to make Basel the headquarters for MCC in Europe. "Howard Yoder, Robert Kreider, and I all feel that Basel is the inevitable and strategic center for MCC relief work for the next several years, as well as the best center for our other Mennonite work which we wish to do in Europe during the next years," Bender advised Orie O. Miller.[25]

It was not a new idea. Already in 1940, Bender and Miller had hoped to establish a center at Basel, but the war had intervened. Soon after he arrived in Europe in 1945, Kreider had proposed making Basel a study center for Mennonite students. As Bender, Yoder, and Kreider envisioned it, the new center would have multiple functions. It would be the administrative center for MCC, a rest and recuperation center for MCC relief workers, a center for research and conferences, and a residence for Mennonite graduate students at the University of Basel.[26]

Bender had been thinking about the residence function the previous day, on a visit to his old friend professor Fritz Blanke at Zurich. Blanke told Bender that "Basel is the acknowledged best university in Switzerland and has no modernism in it as Zurich [University] does." While at Basel, Bender met briefly with the dean of the theological faculty and received assurance that Mennonite students would get every "advantage" if they enrolled at the university. Bender told the dean he had two or three American Mennonite students who might come to Europe to study at Basel. They would live at the MCC center and perhaps work part-time for MCC.[27]

The administrative center for MCC—Europe would require a large building, and Bender authorized Daniel Wenger, a Basel Mennonite, to find a large house which MCC might purchase. Henry Fast, a member of the MCC executive committee, opposed the Basel location, arguing with some cogency that MCC's European headquarters should be in Amsterdam, which he believed to be more central to most MCC work. Fast was convinced that Bender's pro-Swiss, pro-German, anti-Dutch bias was distorting the practical needs of MCC. But with P. C. Hiebert, Orie Miller, and Bender favoring Basel, Fast's argument for Amsterdam got no serious consideration.[28]

• • •

Bender's second assignment on the trip to Europe was as a commissioner for the MC Mennonite Relief Committee and its unit of relief workers in Belgium. By the fall of 1946, the unit had met the need for emergency relief there, and the MRC was casting about for new assignments for its workers. Bender's task was to help identify a new project.

Virginia businessman and MRC member Lewis Martin accompanied Bender during a week in Belgium. On one of their side trips, they surveyed construction needs in eastern Belgium in the area of the Battle of the Bulge. The two men could scarcely find words to describe the devastation. From there, they visited the Luxembourg Mennonites at Oesch, and on Sunday morning attended a communion service. They drove back to Brussels in the afternoon and arrived in time for an evening service at the Belgian Gospel Mission.[29]

Out of the Belgium visit came several recommendations from Bender: to end all emergency relief work in that country by December 1, 1946; to open a children's home there, with a mission program attached; and if permission could be obtained, to transfer some of the relief workers to do emergency relief in Poland. Finally, Bender proposed the creation of a builder's unit in eastern Belgium, in the area of the Battle of the Bulge.

The last recommendation set off a discussion among J. L. Stauffer, Bender, and Orie Miller about the utility of Mennonite reconstruction projects. Stauffer believed only in relief activity which would lead to mission work. "Reconstruction units may have advertising value before men, but the opportunity to provide a spiritual witness according to Acts 1:8 is very limited," he argued. "A reconstruction unit is retrogression compared to the distribution of material aid."[30] For once Bender let Orie Miller answer Stauffer. "To my viewpoint," Miller told Stauffer, "Europe is a mission field for the Mennonite church in all its branches, and is wide open and dead-ripe." He insisted that the witness value of construction units was extremely high and would provide ample opportunities for opening mission work.[31]

On Monday, October 14, MCC bookkeeper Ray Schlichting drove Bender to Walcherin, Holland, for a visit to the MRC builder's unit there. The next day they drove to Amsterdam, stopping at the Hague to visit Jacob ter Meulen. Ter Meulen was secretary of the International Mennonite Peace Committee (IMPC), and Bender was its chairman. Bender was happy to tell ter Meulen that the MCC executive committee had just decided to help the IMPC "in every way possible," including sending an American peace representative to Europe for a year in 1947. The aim was to help promote peace interests among European Mennonites. Ter Meulen in turn reported on a meeting of the Dutch peace group just a few weeks earlier.[32]

Bender interrupted his Amsterdam visit with a quick plane trip to Basel to look at a house Daniel Wenger had located for MCC's new MCC European headquarters. After a visit to the house, Bender authorized its purchase.[33] By late November, when Atlee Beechy arrived to replace Howard Yoder as director of MCC—Europe, the deal was completed. The new headquarters was a handsome three-story fourteen-room house on Arnold Böklinstrasse, just across from the famous Pauls Kirche in the heart of the city.

After returning to Amsterdam the next morning, Bender spent several days in conference with Irvin B. Horst, the new director of

MCC—Netherlands. Horst, like Robert Kreider and Atlee Beechy, had been drafted into CPS and had soon emerged as a rising young administrator. He would also become a scholar of Anabaptism. Bender and Orie Miller had quickly settled on Horst for the Netherlands assignment. "Irvin knows MCC and the total concept of MCC and all that MCC has in mind for its future Holland relationship," Orie Miller had said when he appointed Horst. "In Robert Kreider and Irvin Horst, we feel we have two brethren of outstanding ability who know fully and thoroughly all that MCC stands for and wants to stand for."[34] Bender and Miller had found loyal and able subordinates in Kreider and Horst, and as the MCC program grew in Europe, the administrative scope of the young men grew as well.

Bender and Horst were bound together by a mutual zeal for Mennonite history and rare-book collecting. To have the bookish Irvin Horst in Amsterdam was a heaven-sent opportunity for Bender and for Goshen's historical library. But on this trip, Bender had little time for book-hunting: he bought only $46 worth.[35]

His work finished, Bender left Amsterdam on a flight for New York. By late on October 22, a Tuesday, he was back in Goshen.

By then MCC had clarified the disposition of the Russian refugees in Denmark and northern Germany: many of them would be moved to Paraguay. The problem was how to finance the travel of so many thousands of persons. After the war the United Nations had created an Intergovernmental Committee for Refugees; however, that committee could not resettle Germans. Were the German-speaking Soviet refugees of German or of Dutch extraction? The answer to that question took on practical urgency when MCC chartered a Dutch ship, the *Volendam*, at a cost of $375,000 cash. If MCC could prove that the refugees were of Dutch extraction, the Intergovernmental Committee would reimburse MCC for the entire bill.[36]

Bender, Cornelius Krahn, and C. Henry Smith sprang into action. Bender wrote a brief on the matter and hand-delivered it to Assistant Secretary of State George Warren at the State Department. He also took a copy of C. Henry Smith's book, *The Coming of the Mennonites*, as an exhibit. The first paragraph in the book made the argument for the Dutch origins of the Soviet Mennonites. To everyone's surprise, the State Department accepted the historians' arguments. The Intergovernmental Committee would pay.[37]

A number of factors influenced the decision, but Bender's personal visit to George Warren seems to have helped make the difference. In addition to its effect for refugees in Denmark and northern German, the decision also helped win the release of nearly a thousand Mennonite refugees trapped in Berlin. They were freed in time to board the *SS Volendam* for the voyage to Paraguay.[38]

Bender was elated: "The Lord changed the heart of Pharaoh," he told Ernst Correll. "One of the most interesting phases of the whole operation was the historical proof which I furnished to George Warren of the State Department. This is where historical research was very practical. It is a dramatic story which I must sometime tell you in person."[39]

• • •

Christian Neff died on the night of December 30, 1946. Bender received the news three days later. He immediately sent off a cable to MCC—Europe director Atlee Beechy: "CONVEY DEEP PARTICIPATION SYMPATHY PRAYERS TO NEFF FAMILY AND GERMAN MENNONITE BROTHERHOOD IN NAME OF MCC NORTH AMERICAN CHURCHES AND MYSELF. HAROLD BENDER." The message arrived too late for the funeral, but American MCCers Walter Eicher, Delbert and Thelma Gratz, and Atlee Beechy had attended. Neff was buried in the Weierhof cemetery next to the church.[40]

Neff's death confirmed Bender's conviction that he should spend a year in Europe. Orie Miller supported the idea, and a few weeks after Neff's death, the MCC's executive committee decided to send Bender under MCC Peace Section auspices. His assignment would be to promote peace theology and spiritual renewal among the Mennonites of Europe. While wearing his Peace Section hat, he would also carry MRC, MCC, and Mennonite encyclopedia portfolios.

Bender had brought to the MCC meeting a three-page prospectus of what his assignment might be. Under the rubric of "Survey of Status of European Mennonite Churches Regarding Mennonite Heritage in General and Nonresistance in Particular," he listed some twenty activities. The list included "personal visit to all individual Mennonite ministers and congregations outside of Holland" and attendance at all official Mennonite church conferences.[41]

Bender also proposed to make a study of all literature available to European Mennonites and to arrange translations of recent American Mennonite material on peace and nonresistance. Surprisingly, Bender's list of materials to be translated did not include his own "The Anabaptist Vision." He would also do some planning for the Mennonite World Conference, arrange visits by European leaders to America, and work to create a resource center at the Basel headquarters which would be available to all European Mennonites.[42]

In 1947, Europe was Bender's "field of dreams." It carried powerful associations: that romantic and intellectually challenging year at Tübingen; the six-month stint in 1930 when he helped move Russian refugees to Paraguay; the hectic months at Heidelberg and his hard-won degree; the Horsch and Funck family associations; the Anabaptist history connections; and the presence of living, thriving Mennonite communities. All those associations, combined with the events of the World War II and its aftermath, drew him irresistibly.

To actualize the "field of dreams," Bender had in mind a kind of Mennonite "Marshall Plan" with a focused "hearts and minds" component. American Mennonites would not only give their war-ravaged fellow believers material aid but would become agents of spiritual renewal as well. For all his extensive experience and knowledge of European Mennonites, Bender was deeply imbued with the American Mennonite notion that true Anabaptist-Mennonitism had survived only in North America. Therefore, European Mennonite renewal was a North American responsibility.

Bender would go to Europe as a North American Mennonite missionary to European Mennonites. It was a calling he held deeply, and truth be told, it was a task for which he was uniquely prepared. His knowledge of European Mennonites and connections to them gave him an entrée few other North American Mennonite leaders could match. Those relationships, combined with his spiritual and theological gifts, made him the ideal American Mennonite missionary to Europe in 1947. It was as though he had spent his entire life getting ready for the assignment.

• • •

Eager to get started, Bender formed an almost comically detailed planning process which left nothing to chance. He insisted on sorting out the most mundane details with Orie Miller. Miller was struggling to direct and control the burgeoning multimillion-dollar MCC operation with its hundreds of workers scattered across the face of the globe. Yet now he found himself advising on how MCC clothing allowances were administered and commenting on the annual cost of Bender's vitamin supplements. Wisely, Bender agreed to Miller's suggestion that he accept the regular relief worker allowance of $10 per month, plus maintenance and expenses. Since Elizabeth, Mary Eleanor, and Nancy were also going to Europe, the family would receive an additional $150-per-month dependency allowance. Miller agreed that Bender might take his 1940 four-door Dodge sedan along for his travels. After some haggling, they arrived at a mileage rate for MCC to pay.[43]

Bender also managed to take along a secretary. For the first time in his life, Bender had a nearly full-time secretary who was almost able to keep up with his pace. She was Goshen College student Lois Yake, and Bender proposed that she accompany the family to Basel. Yake was eager to go, but there was a hitch: she was too young. Female MCC workers had to be twenty-four years old, and Yake was only twenty. Bender begged for an exception, promising that "my wife will assume some motherly responsibility."[44] The capable Yake hardly needed motherly oversight, but Bender's assurances carried the day, with one condition: Yake had to accept a regular two-year MCC assignment, something she was happy to do.

Meanwhile, there was a lot of last-minute activity, including the seminary commencement and the graduation of five Th.B. graduates. Paul Mininger agreed to serve as interim dean of the seminary. J. C. Wenger was put in charge of the Mennonite encyclopedia project, just then in the midst of laying out the topics and beginning to assign writers. Bender arranged to have Wenger send him the draft proposals for sign-off before the assignments became final.

There were also many last-minute family matters to organize. During May, Harold and Elizabeth arranged to have the Ford Berg family move into the Horsch home in Scottdale to look after Christina Horsch. The H. Clair Amstutz family rented part of the Bender house, and seven college men rented several upstairs rooms plus the attic. Bender's mother, Elsie, moved into an apartment. Getting things organized was expensive. "The cash demands on my funds are so heavy right now," Bender told C. L. Graber, that he had to defer payment of the balance of daughter Mary Eleanor's tuition until September 1. Graber was to send the rent money to Basel. "I would appreciate early payment, for we will be living on a close margin," Bender told his friend.[45] Bender was not sure they could live on the MCC allowances.

Finding passage across the Atlantic in the summer of 1947 was not easy. Initially, Bender had hoped to leave with the family right after commencement in early June, but despite his best efforts, they could not get tickets. Eventually it was decided that he would fly to Europe, and Elizabeth and the girls would come later in the summer.[46]

Bender left for Europe on June 13. Overwhelmed with last-minute work, he nearly missed his train. When he got to Toledo, where he was to catch a plane to Newark, he discovered he had forgotten his tickets. Equally disconcerting was a discovery that the plane actually departed from Cleveland. Undaunted, he caught a train to Cleveland, got a plane into New York about midnight, and at 11:00 the next morning caught a Pan Am flight to Brussels. Secretary Lois Yake was left to try to explain the situation to the airlines and collect refunds for the unused tickets.[47]

In Brussels, Bender consulted with Cleo Mann, director of the Belgian MRC program, before catching another plane to Amsterdam in the evening. The next day he chaired an MCC executive committee meeting of himself, C. F. Klassen, and H. A. Fast. (Orie Miller was in Cairo, Egypt, on the homeward leg of another round-the-world trip; chairman P. C. Hiebert was the lone executive committee member in the U.S.). Also attending the meeting were MCC directors Atlee Beechy, Irvin Horst, and Robert Kreider.[48] In the course of the day, the group authorized an MCC-sponsored All-Europe Mennonite Youth Conference to be held at Basel in August. They initially planned that the conference would be a modest event, but to the surprise and delight of everyone, more than 500 persons attended from all over Europe.

No doubt the most immediately significant decision was to sponsor visits to North America by three Dutch Mennonite leaders. The idea itself was part of a larger effort to bring Americans and Europeans closer together. Practically, it was a way to bring home to American Mennonites the ongoing relief needs of the European Mennonites, and it gave the Dutch a chance to thank American Mennonites for their help.[49]

Selecting the Dutch visitors was ticklish. They had to be sufficiently orthodox to avoid alienating conservative American Mennonites, but they also had to be selected with Dutch sensitivities in mind. Bender sent a letter to Willem Frederik Golterman, chairman of the main Dutch Mennonite body, the Algemeene Doopsgezinde Sociëteit (ADS, Dutch Mennonite General Conference), announcing the appointment of ministers Tjeerd Oeda Hylkema, Nanne van der Zijpp, and Herman Craandijk. When Golterman received the letter, he inquired how the selection had been made. Harold's reply was a classic display of verbal gymnastics, but apparently it satisfied Golterman. Golterman would clearly have expected to make the trip as chairman of the ADS, but because he was of a liberal bent, he was simply not acceptable to the Americans.[50] The Dutch leader accepted the decision gracefully, but the episode alerted Bender to the need to consult the Dutch before making decisions.

Bender spent a week in the Netherlands visiting key Dutch leaders. He was happy to find a "revival of biblical nonresistance" in a Dutch Mennonite peace fellowship, the Doopsgezinde Vredesgroep, which had nearly 300 members, including about 40 percent of all Dutch Mennonite pastors. The leaders of the movement hold a position "which is now almost identical with ours," Bender reported. It even had a full-time secretary and was working to arrange an alternative service program for Dutch COs similar to CPS. However, Bender was disappointed to learn that pastor van der Zijpp, whose energy and skill as a historian he admired, did not embrace pacifism. He worried about the reaction of American Mennonites if they learned about van der Zijpp's position during the pastor's travels in the U.S. At the end of the week, he and H. A. Fast attended the annual Dutch general conference program, a valuable opportunity to meet most of the Dutch leadership.[51]

The following week, Bender and several other MCCers traveled to Alsace in France, where Bender officiated at a wedding ceremony for MCCers John Fretz and Beulah Roth. He also held a communion service for MCC workers in the area. Before he left Goshen, he had been specifically commissioned by bishop Sanford Yoder to lead communion services for Mennonite workers in Europe. Holding communion services which included GC, MB, and MC Mennonite persons was a problem which Bender finessed by ignoring it; he led the services.[52]

The next morning, Bender crossed the border into Germany, where he spent an intensive four-day session with *Lexikon* coeditor Ernst

**German Mennonite leader Ernst Crous.**
Mennonite Historical Library, Goshen College.

Crous. The last time Bender had seen Crous was in 1940, when he had visited the Crouses during his epic trip to Berlin. With the death of Christian Neff, Crous was now Bender's partner as coeditor of the *Mennonitisches Lexikon*. By the end of the four days, Bender, Crous, and several assistants had planned and designed the third volume.[53]

Later in the week, Bender flew to Belgium to pick up his car, which had finally arrived after many delays. Now Bender was free to travel at will, and travel he did. He spent ten days in Germany, a few days at Basel, and the last week of July in Holland. Then he rushed back to Germany to meet Elkhart businessman Ross Martin and Goshen physician Samuel Miller at Rhein-Main airport. Miller and Martin had somehow wangled a permit to travel in Germany. Bender spent three days conducting the two Hoosiers on visits to the Horsch, Landes, and Funck hofs. The trip ended at Basel with Martin and Miller off for more trekking in Italy and Greece. A few days later, Orie Miller arrived from the Near East, and Bender took Miller and Atlee Beechy on a three-day trip to visit MCC units in Alsace, Bavaria, and Baden. On that Sunday, Bender preached at the Mennonite church at the Thomashof near Karlsruhe before they returned to Basel.[54]

By then it was August 12, and the first young people were arriving for the All-Europe Mennonite Youth Conference at Basel. The conference was held at the Holeestrasse Mennonite church, hosted by the Swiss Mennonite churches and financially supported by MCC. Its theme was "Jesus Christ Our Lord!" More than 500 people attended, ninety of them Americans, mostly MCCers. It was a landmark meeting, offering European Mennonites their first opportunity since the 1936 Mennonite World Conference to meet face-to-face and to participate in a common event.[55]

Bender declared the conference a success. "I was quite dubious in advance, but have become enthusiastic after seeing what has happened here," he told MCC relief worker Ruth Hilty.[56] He was responding to a long letter from Hilty, who was working for MCC in Amsterdam and had done some of the preliminary planning. Hilty was quite critical of the conference, which she thought was too heavily loaded with North Americans and their ideas, and too sermon-oriented, with too little time for fellowship and personal conversation. She also thought that the Swiss had not allowed their young people to attend in sufficient numbers.[57]

Hilty concluded her critique by quoting one of the Dutch pastors who was present. "We here in Europe are happy that you, our Brethren in the U.S.A. and Canada, came to bring us help. And we sense your desire to bring us spiritual aid. But we all express the same reticence to receive your spiritual aid. We are afraid, in your wanting to give us spiritual help, that you are wanting us to adopt your American methods for meeting our spiritual needs."[58]

Bender was upset by Hilty's analysis, arguing that what seemed like a too-heavy American Mennonite hand in the proceedings was accidental. He had tried to leave the leadership of the conference in the hands of the Swiss, he told Hilty, but "the management was so uncertain that I had to come to the rescue." The Swiss had no experience with handling big conferences. And, Bender thought, there were not too many North Americans at the event: the ratio of one American to five Europeans seemed to him about right. Nor did he think there were too many sermons. He believed there had been a lot of fellowship, despite any criticism voiced by the Dutch young people. The Dutch are much more used to small meetings, Bender told Hilty, because Dutch spiritual renewal is carried by "small elite movements while the mass of the membership goes untouched. Our Basel and American methods are designed to reach everyone, whether he is of the elite or not."[59]

While characteristically challenging each of Hilty's criticisms, Bender admitted that "the strategy of our inter-Mennonite co-operation has not yet been satisfactorily worked out, and certainly we Americans need to learn much along this line. With you, I feel that more than human wisdom is required."[60]

Hilty's comments no doubt accurately reflected Dutch and North German feelings about North American Mennonite beliefs and methods. In his leading style (he was always the speaker) and in his rapid circulation through the European Mennonite brotherhood during 1947 and 1948, Bender sometimes missed subtle ways his and other Americans' assumptions offended their European brothers and sisters.[61]

The Basel conference ended on Sunday. The next morning, Bender was off to Vredeshiem, Holland, for a two-day conference sponsored by the Vredesgroep. From there Bender caught a plane to Warsaw, Poland, where he spent a week reviewing its MRC project and holding a much-appreciated communion service for the American workers. He also visited devastated Mennonite churches in the Gdansk area and literally dug rare books out of the rubble of one of them.[62]

Bender called his visit to the former Mennonite communities in Poland a "depressing experience. A terrible judgment was imposed upon this community, and I do not know just how it should be interpreted," he told J. C. Wenger. "I do know there is a great and terrible task for the Mennonites of North America to help these folks and our Russian Mennonites find new homes and rebuild their shattered church life."[63]

Bender returned to Basel for one day before driving to northern Italy to attend the annual Waldensian synod, where he preached, and also to visit an MCC unit there. He returned in time to preach at the Holeestrasse church in Basel on September 7. The next morning he flew to Copenhagen, then spent four days visiting Soviet and Polish Mennonite refugees in Denmark and conferring with MCC workers there. It was his first face-to-face visit with the Mennonite refugees. He was moved by the potential he found for spiritual renewal. "These people are eager and ready for the Gospel message in the fullest form, including nonresistance," he told Orie Miller. "It is the hour for us to strike. We should put the strongest forces we have on the field. It is genuine mission work."[64]

On his way back to Basel, Bender attended a three-day German Mennonite student conference at Karlsruhe, where he gave two speeches to the nearly one hundred university students in attendance. Touched by both their sincerity and poverty, he proposed that MCC establish a special student relief program. The American Mennonite colleges would fund it and MCC administer it.[65]

Then he rushed back to Basel: he wanted to be on hand for the arrival of Elizabeth, Nancy, and Mary Eleanor.

## ❧18❧

# Traveling and Planning
# a World Conference

*In Europe, Bender travels incessantly. Nancy*
*becomes ill. Bender helps organize the fourth*
*Mennonite World Conference.*

BECAUSE of a trans-Atlantic shipping overload during the summer
of 1947, it was mid-September by the time Elizabeth, Nancy, Mary
Eleanor, and Lois Yake were able to get passage to Europe. At the
end of September, they finally arrived and settled into the MCC
Europe headquarters house on Arnold Böcklinstrasse in downtown Basel.

Harold, Elizabeth, and Nancy had two small bedrooms on the
third floor, and Mary Eleanor lived in the building's quarters for
single women. The family lived communally with the headquarters
unit of several dozen persons, among them numerous secretaries
and bookkeepers and other support staff who lived and worked at
the center. Members ate together in the common dining room and
shared in a common daily worship service. They were a small en-
clave of North American Mennonites, sharing their lives and skills
for a few years while they managed the relief and service work of
MCC in Europe.[1]

The center was a beehive of activity, with messages arriving
and leaving daily as the staff communicated with North America
and all parts of Europe. There was a constant buzz of activity as
new workers arrived and old ones departed for their various assignments. The Bender girls enjoyed the lively atmosphere, and
Mary Eleanor, who was twenty in 1947, enjoyed the companion-
ship of the staff's women. She studied French and German, earn-

**A Mennonite Central Committee administrative staff conference at Basel, Switzerland, in 1947. In the front row are four MCC executive committee members: Bender, Orie O. Miller, C. F. Klassen, Henry A. Fast.** Orie O. Miller papers, AMC.

ing credits to transfer to Goshen College when she would return in the fall of 1949.[2]

During the year in Basel, Elizabeth began the massive task of translating the first two volumes of the *Mennonitisches Lexikon*. She worked at a small desk in her third-floor bedroom. Bender had an office in the building but made little use of it since he spent less than a quarter of his time at the MCC center.[3]

After several days of settling in, the family made a weeklong visit to the Horsch and Funck relatives in Germany. Bender called it a vacation, but he worked nearly every day, conferring constantly on MCC, the *Lexikon*, and other matters.[4] During a visit with Adele Hege at Eichstatt, he persuaded her to sell fifty books from the Christian Hege library, apparently duplicates. He was delighted to get them. "Some of them are very valuable," he told J. C. Wenger.[5] He also made arrangements for Robert Kreider to purchase six yards of diaper cloth at the United States Army PX in Stuttgart for a Landes family cousin at Hof Willenbach who was expecting a baby.[6]

In October, Bender made a lengthy trip to visit Ernst Crous in Göttingen in northern Germany. He was moved by the work Ernst and his wife, Rosa, were doing. Ernst Crous was quite ill—he had collapsed on the street the week before Bender visited them. Yet he carried on a tireless pastoral ministry to about a thousand scattered Mennonites in the Göttingen area, most of them refugees from West Prussia. He and Rosa also operated a small relief program, using MCC supplies. In addition, he was the lead editor of the *Lexikon* project. It was quite a program, operated on a shoestring out of the Crous's small apartment. Bender called Crous "the most able among the German Mennonite leaders" and recommended that MCC give him more help, especially financial aid.[7]

By October, Bender had put 7,000 miles on his car and spent more than a thousand dollars on travel expenses. Reporting to Orie Miller, he noted that he had "put in many long and hard drives on the road and used up much physical and nervous energy in the course of the operations. I will be glad to do so as long as the Lord gives me strength."[8]

Bender's effort to impress Miller with his strenuous activity was triggered by complaints from someone to Orie Miller that Bender was spending too much time on book collecting and other "diversions." Bender insisted such was not the case, but he also argued that "MCC does not expect its workers to sterilize themselves in regard to their personal or institutional connections while in MCC service." With some heat, he informed Miller that he intended to use every opportunity to build up the historical library at Goshen College, "wherever I am, as I have done for years."[9]

Bender suspected the criticism was coming from Cornelius Krahn at Bethel. If so, Krahn's concern may have been triggered by Bender's efforts to purchase a library in Amsterdam. Mennonite history professor Wilhelmus Johannes Kühler had died soon after the war, and his heirs decided to sell their father's books. When Bender came to Europe, he was intending to buy them with $500 he and president Ernest Miller had raised for the purpose. After he examined them, he was dismayed to learn that the price was not the too-cheap $500 he was prepared to pay, but nearly $1,000. Despite Bender's persuasive efforts, the Kühler sons refused to lower the price.[10] Negotiations went on for many months. Not until January 1948 was Holland—MCC director Irvin Horst finally able to announce, to Bender's relief, "I have them [the books] in my possession at Koningslaan—a great treasure."[11]

In the end, Cornelius Krahn got as many books as he could afford to buy, for Bender had to sell quite a few to help cover the higher price. But Krahn again grew anxious, because he learned that Bender was gathering books in Poland. His frustration was understandable: why should Bender use his MCC- and MRC-funded time in Europe to collect books for Goshen?[12]

Bender was amazingly careless about how he used MCC facilities and people for his book collecting. After the Kühler collection was in Horst's possession at the MCC headquarters, Bender directed Horst to have the MCC secretary, Donna Yoder, type up a list of its books for his use. In March, Bender learned of a large collection of books for sale at Leiden. Buy all of them, he told Horst, "and charge them against my account." Noting that there might not be enough in his account to cover the purchase, he assured Horst he would replenish the account as soon as he could. In the meantime, MCC funds were being used to buy Goshen's historical library books.[13]

By April 1948, books were piling up at MCC headquarters in Amsterdam, some of them a result of Irvin Horst's rather than Bender's collecting. "I have recently purchased and added to your collection," Horst wrote. "The van Braght is a honey—a super, deluxe edition—the best I have ever seen. You are fortunate to have it." A week later he plaintively told Bender, "I have a number of books which I think you will be interested in, but I have the difficulty of going ahead because of lack of funds. I don't feel free to borrow sums from MCC."[14] Bender had no such inhibitions and used funds from his MCC account, not yet replenished by his personal funds, to cover the purchase.[15]

Bender deeply appreciated Horst's help. In one of the last letters he wrote before leaving Basel to return to the United States in 1948, he thanked Horst "heartily" for Horst's "willing and faithful assistance in collecting books for the Mennonite Historical Library at Goshen." Without Horst's help, he acknowledged, "very few of these valuable accessions could have been secured." And, he added tantalizingly, "I hope that some day you will be in a position in Goshen which will permit you to use these books which you yourself have helped to select."[16] Actually, by then Irvin and Ava Horst had decided to go to Goshen to complete Irvin's college degree. Horst would indeed see the Dutch books again.

By November 1947, Bender had been in Europe for six months, and he paused briefly to take stock. He had used the time, he told his MCC executive committee colleagues, to get oriented and to diagnose the situation among the Mennonites in Europe. He had made personal visits to forty leaders, attended five official church conferences, preached in seven churches, attended and spoken at a dozen conferences, visited many refugee camps, visited Poland, and conferred with all the MCC directors and administrators. He had also read all current European Mennonite publications. But he admitted, "In spite of all this orientation, I must confess that I do not have an adequate grasp of the total situation among the European Mennonites."[17]

• • •

Bender may have been tired, but there was no letup in his activity. For several months he had been negotiating to bring a prefabricated church building from Scandinavia to be erected in Heilbronn, Germany, for use by the Heilbronn Mennonite congregation and as a relief center for MCC. Now in late October, the deal was done, and Bender delightedly announced the "gift of love from the Mennonite churches of the US and Canada," to cousin Christian Landes, who in 1947 was the president of the south-German Mennonite Verband (a regional association of congregations).[18] Getting the building constructed would become one of Bender's preoccupations in the following months.

One of Bender's most important meetings took place at the Thomashof near Karlsruhe in November 1947. There he chaired a gathering of German Mennonite leaders and MCC directors to survey the spiritual needs of the Mennonite refugees in Germany. Bender used the meeting also to interpret and explain MCC's purposes in Europe and to solidify German and American Mennonite relationships. At his persuasive best, Bender described the MCC purpose in Europe as three-pronged: relief work, spiritual witness, and refugee resettlement. It was a program the south-German Mennonite leaders heartily endorsed. The south-German Mennonites had strong leaders, and by inviting those indigenous leaders for counsel and advice, MCC enhanced its participation in German-Mennonite affairs. But there was also another agenda: preparing the German leaders for what Bender had to do the next day.[19]

The MCC executive committee had handed Bender an unpleasant task: to persuade Benjamin Unruh to accept a small pension from MCC in return for a promise that he would retire from all MCC activity. Bender and Unruh had known each other for a long time. In 1920 Unruh had been one of the four men sent to apprise the North Americans of the grievous plight of the Russian Mennonites caught in the turmoil of the Civil War after the Bolshevik Revolution. Their report led to the creation of MCC in 1920. Bender had been caring for his father during the time the Russians visited Elkhart, and he would almost certainly have met them there.

Unruh had returned to Europe in 1920 but had been unable or unwilling to return to the new Soviet Union. He eventually settled near Karlsruhe, where he became a teacher in a technical school. From there he continued to play a leading role in assisting Russian Mennonites fleeing the Soviet Union during the 1920s.[20]

When the MCC sent Bender to Germany in 1930 to assist the movement of the Soviet refugees to Paraguay, he became Benjamin Unruh's assistant, helping him negotiate with German officialdom and Russian Mennonite refugee leaders. During the 1930s, Unruh had served unofficially as MCC's representative in Europe; but since MCC was largely moribund, the activity was quite limited.[21]

After the war, Unruh insisted that he be put back on MCC's payroll. Unfortunately, serious questions had surfaced about Unruh's relationship with the Nazis. With that reputation, he was a liability to MCC, and a liability in the Soviet and Prussian refugee negotiations with the English and American occupation authorities. In any case, that assignment was being handled with great skill and success by C. F. Klassen. So the MCC executive committee decided to pension Unruh into retirement. It fell to Bender to convey the bad news.[22]

"I dealt with Bro. Unruh as kindly as possible," Bender told Orie Miller. "I presented him a plan whereby the MCC might make it possible for him to spend the rest of his days in writing and scholarly work."[23] Unfortunately, Unruh objected strenuously, and several years of unpleasantness ensued.[24]

In mid-December, Bender made a weeklong trip to Poland to plan for replacements for relief workers who would soon be leaving. This time he was wearing his MRC commissioner hat. It was a strenuous trip, involving much travel and a lengthy interview with each member of the Poland unit. For his return to the West, he caught a train to Prague and a plane to Amsterdam. When he arrived in Amsterdam, he called Elizabeth and was shocked to learn that 12-year-old Nancy was gravely ill in a Basel hospital. Desperate to get back to his family, and with no planes flying over the weekend, he managed to make train connections through Paris. He arrived in Basel early on Saturday morning, December 20, and rushed straight to the hospital.[25]

On the morning after Harold had left for Poland, Nancy had suffered a ruptured appendix. The doctors had operated, but by the time Harold returned, she had developed an extremely serious ab-

**Nancy Bender in the 1940s.** Bender Family Album.

dominal infection, and her pain was nearly unbearable. By the day after Christmas, her condition had noticeably worsened, with high temperature and severe hemorrhaging. Harold and Elizabeth both gave blood for transfusions. But her condition worsened. On December 29 Bender despairingly cabled relatives and friends that Nancy's case was "hopeless."[26]

Writing to Melvin and Verna Gingerich on December 30, he spoke the only language he knew to express his anguish, the language of faith. "Humanly speaking, her chances are not better than fifty-fifty of coming through—but we know that she is in God's hands and He can give her life if He wills it," he told the Gingerichs. "As believers we have a refuge to which we can fly, a rock in which we can hide in time of storm, a God whose changeless love we can rest in." The almost ritualistic quality of his words, while deeply felt, exhibit Bender's near inability to express himself in profoundly personal terms. He could not find the words to convey his anxiety and fear. Thus he turned to conventional religious language. Bender's affirmation of faith and hope in this case was partly spoken to himself and partly to his friends Melvin and Verna Gingerich; one of the Gingerichs' young sons had been killed several months earlier in a bicycle accident.[27]

Soon after New Year's Day, Nancy began a slow improvement, to her family's great relief. For one of the few times in his life, Bender gave up his hectic schedule. During the entire month of January, he stayed close by, as Nancy struggled for life.[28] Only in February did he resume his travel schedule. By then, Nancy's convalescence was well underway.

• • •

The idea that MCC should produce a German-language paper came from Robert Kreider in the spring of 1947.[29] By early November, the Peace Section and the executive committee had agreed to the idea. They appointed Bender to be editor, with five associate editors, all MCC directors in Europe. The managing editor was to be Herman Epp, a Prussian refugee in a camp in Denmark. Epp came with a desirable credential: he may have been the only European Mennonite imprisoned in World War II as a conscientious objector. But there were also two problems: it was difficult to get clearance for him to work in Switzerland, and as Bender put it, he was "a slave to the tobacco habit."[30]

The new paper had a large editorial council of more than 25 persons from all over the world. It would have 16 pages, appear bimonthly, and have a circulation of 4,000. According to Bender's calculations, the paper would require an annual MCC subsidy of $2,000.[31]

The first issue was to have come out in January 1948, but during January Bender was too distracted by Nancy's illness to get much work done, and the visa for managing-editor Herman Epp failed to materialize. The first issue finally came out in late March, but only because Elizabeth gave up her translating work and worked on *Der Mennonit*. The first printing of 4,000 was much too limited, Bender reported to P. C. Hiebert. "We are finding ourselves swamped with subscriptions, particularly from Germany."[32]

The instant success of *Der Mennonit* demonstrated the significant need for such a paper. It was also a tribute to Harold and especially to Elizabeth's prowess as an editor, for it was a genuinely well-laid-out, well-conceived magazine, with many pictures. Each issue had news items, faith-and-life articles, devotional and uplift essays, and historical and literary pieces. It was a well-rounded paper. To the refugees, it was a ray of hope and encouragement.[33]

The first issue was typical. C. F. Klassen and P. C. Hiebert wrote short pieces of encouragement and hope. Refugee Hermann Epp reflected on the experiences of the West Prussian churches during the Hitler period. Peter Dyck described the first two voyages of the refugees to Paraguay. A "Mennonitische Weltspiegel" covered Mennonite news from around the world. Bender wrote two pieces: a helpful summary of what he called "Our World of Mennonites," with much geographic and demographic information; and a fascinating story of his travels in Poland in 1947, including pictures. For the Prussian refugees, Bender's article must have been extremely interesting. H. A. Fast described North American nonresistance. Bender appended a sidebar with a quotation from Menno Simons denouncing Christians who go to war.[34]

• • •

"I hope that it will be possible for you to come to America [at] the time of the International Mennonite Conference which is to be held at the Mennonite church at Berne, Indiana, in the summer of 1940," Bender had told his good Dutch friend Jacob ter Meulen, secretary of the International Mennonite Peace Committee.[35] Bender had written the letter in April 1939. But within a few months, World War II had begun; convening another Mennonite World Conference became impossible.

Now eight years later, Bender was writing to another Dutch leader, W. F. Golterman, chairman of the ADS (the Dutch Mennonites' General Conference), with the message that a Mennonite World Conference was planned for the summer of 1948. It would be in North America.[36] The MCC executive committee had initiated the idea and would be providing logistical and financial help.

In North America, the idea generally received support except by some MC Mennonites and other more-conservative groups. The new moderator of the MC Mennonite general conference was J. L. Stauffer, a man staunchly opposed to all ecumenical Mennonite cooperation. For supporters of the world-conference idea, his election was untimely. Under his influence, the 1947 MC general conference voted against any organized participation in the world conference movement. Nor was Stauffer persuaded by a direct appeal from Orie Miller. "Some of these Mennonites deny the deity of Christ, and consequently they cannot have God," Stauffer told Miller. Any fellowship with them would be "disloyalty to our Savior and Lord."[37] Frustrated, Miller offered a Miller-Bender kind of solution. "Since you and I are on the executive committee of MCC," he told Bender, "we'll represent the MC Mennonites."[38]

However, Miller and Bender were also realistic. To promote broad support for a world conference, the MCC executive committee appointed its chairman, P. C. Hiebert, to travel among the American churches and test sentiment. Within a few months, Hiebert visited a dozen or more Mennonite communities and found good support. He even visited Harrisonburg, Virginia. There J. L. Stauffer received him hospitably, but the world conference idea still suffered a cool rejection. Nevertheless, MCC created a new Mennonite World Conference committee, the Committee on Counsel and Guidance. When it met for the first time in January 1948, two MC delegates were present. But they came with the caveat that they could participate only if they received assurances that all North American speakers on the program would be "evangelical," and that at least one session would be devoted to nonresistance and nonconformity. Chairman P. C. Hiebert was happy to grant those conditions.[39]

"You cannot imagine how I missed you in our deliberations, especially now as the program for the World Conference shall take form," Hiebert told Bender. "But we have stumbled along as best we could."[40] Bender no doubt wanted to be closer to the actual planning process. He wrote copious letters with suggestions about time, place, and topics. But by and large, he had to be content with a more limited assignment, that of organizing the European representation at the conference.

One thing was certain: MCC would have to help many of the European delegates with expense money. How to do so equitably became a major problem. Moreover, getting visas for the Germans to travel to the United States required many months of effort.

On January 20, Bender issued a "Mennonite World Congress, 1948, News Bulletin No. 1," which went to all European leaders and pastors. The annual meeting of the MCC had just set the conference date for August 4-10. The "Congress" would convene for two days at Goshen, Indiana, and then move to Newton, Kansas, for the last four days. Bender's use of the term "Congress" is intriguing. The Europeans had spontaneously begun calling it a world "congress," and Bender discovered he liked the title. Because "conference" meant an authoritative church body to many American Mennonites, Bender hoped "congress" would lower MC Mennonite resistance. Let us use the term "Congress," Bender urged Orie Miller. But Miller disagreed; by the time the second News Bulletin came out in June, Bender's term was "World Conference."[41]

The success of the 1948 Mennonite World Conference rested heavily on Bender's ability to give the Europeans significant places on the conference program. He worked hard to make that happen.

By April he had a dozen speakers lined up. Bender agreed with Miller and Hiebert that, for the most part, the Europeans should not be assigned doctrinal topics. He was delighted when he learned that Pierre Widmer from France would be able to attend. Widmer's views were such that Bender assigned him to speak on nonconformity. It was Bender's way to tell his conservative American Mennonite brothers and sisters that European Mennonites also believed in nonconformity.[42]

Bender was unhappy with the date set for the conference—for a surprising reason: the dates overlapped with the meeting of the World Council of Churches (WCC) meeting in Amsterdam. W. F. Golterman, president of the ADS, had arranged for Bender to be an observer at the World Council gathering. Bender badly wanted to attend, especially since T. O. Hylkema hoped to submit a Mennonite peace statement to the WCC in tandem with one from the International Fellowship of Reconciliation (IFOR). Hylkema was one of the signatories of an IFOR statement, and he hoped for a Mennonite statement as well.[43]

If I could choose, Bender told Orie Miller, I would attend the WCC over the Mennonite World Conference. If the executive committee insisted that he attend the Mennonite conference, he wanted permission to make a quick round-trip flight to the WCC meeting afterward. There was a complicating factor: he had promised Elizabeth and Nancy that he would travel home with them aboard ship. What he would really like to do, he told Miller, was skip the Mennonite event entirely, attend most of the WCC, and catch a boat home in time for the opening of the seminary. "I am eagerly—almost anxiously—awaiting your decision," he told Orie Miller in February.[44] To Bender's chagrin, Miller insisted that he attend the Mennonite conference and not return for the WCC.[45]

Bender even told Goshen president Ernest Miller that he wished he could stay in Europe for another year.[46] Had he done so, he might have addressed a piece of unfinished business, a disturbing development among the Swiss Mennonites.

While confined to Basel because of Nancy's illness, Bender had taken time to read local newspapers. Skimming the January issue of the Canton Bern state-church newspaper, he was *"bestürzt* (upset)" to read an announcement that the Langnau Mennonite congregation in the Emmental had joined the Swiss Reformed state church. "I can't believe it," Bender told his friend, Swiss preacher Fritz Gerber. "It is impossible to believe such a thing could be. Can you help me understand *diese dunkle Sache* (this dark thing)? The Emmental church is the mother church of most of the Mennonite churches in Switzerland, France, South Germany, and the Mennonites in the eastern United States," he told Gerber. "This action is going to bring heavy pain to Mennonites all over the world."[47]

•  •  •

Nancy's recovery came slowly, and the doctors recommended a lengthy sojourn in the clear air and bright sunshine of the high Alps. So in late March, the family traveled to Adelboden in the Alps Mountains southwest of Bern for a stay at a mountain hotel. It was an idyllic setting, and each day brought more color back to Nancy's face. For the family, it was a precious respite from the terrible ordeal of the previous months. Elizabeth, Mary Eleanor, and Nancy stayed for three weeks. Harold, already completely behind in his work, remained for nearly a week and then rushed back to Basel.[48] He spent the last two days of March in conferences with Orie Miller, C. F. Klassen, Atlee Beechy, and others on a variety of MCC executive committee topics.

April was busy with much travel. During the last week of April, Bender visited the Torre Pellice MCC unit in northwestern Italy, where he baptized Boyd Nelson, head of the MCC unit there. Nelson had not been a Mennonite when he joined MCC, and Bender baptized him on behalf of the Goshen College Mennonite congregation.[49]

An important meeting in May was an afternoon in Amsterdam spent with Dutch Mennonite leaders Golterman, Kuiper, Dozy, van der Veen, van der Zijpp, and Meihuizen. Also present were MCCers Peter Dyck and Atlee Beechy. It was, as Beechy put it, "an informal and brotherly discussion of the nonresistant position." None of the Dutch leaders present were pacifist, and so the North Americans spent a major part of the afternoon listening to the

Dutch reasons for skepticism about North American Mennonite nonresistance, skepticism which the Dutch based particularly on their recent struggles during the Nazi occupation of their country. Bender, persistently pro-German (although anti-Nazi), was shaken by their bitter anti-Germanism. Wisely, the Americans listened more than they spoke. All ten participants agreed it was a good way to learn to understand each other.[50]

In June, Bender spent only four days at Basel. One of those days included what he later described as an *"ausnehmend und reicher Nachmittag* (an extraordinarily wonderful afternoon)."[51] He was referring to a trip by Harold, Elizabeth, Paul Peachey, and Robert Kreider to visit professor Fritz Blanke at Zurich. The Blankes hospitably entertained the four in their home, serving what Paul Peachey later described as the best strawberries he had ever eaten. Then they took the Americans on a several-hours-long walk to visit Anabaptist sites in downtown Zurich.

One reason for the trip was to allow Bender to introduce two young, promising Mennonite scholars, Peachey and Kreider, to Blanke and to get Blanke's advice about their study in Switzerland. Peachey told Blanke he would like to do something on the sociology of the Swiss Brethren, whereupon Blanke opened a drawer in his desk and pulled out a small card on which he had jotted a title for a dissertation on the subject. Peachey went on to write a dissertation under Blanke, completed five years later in 1954 with that very title.[52]

After returning to Basel, Bender left the next morning for a seven-day trip to Bullange, Brussels, Amsterdam, Hague, Leeuwarden, Groningen, Krefeld, and back to Basel. With scarcely time to change his clothes when he returned, he left for a week, in Poland, a trip movingly punctuated for Bender when he baptized the three daughters of a Cieminski family of Mennonites at Elbing. In the course of the week, he visited nearly every Mennonite church building in West Prussia. Most were being used as barns or as living quarters for families. A few had become Catholic houses of worship. The Baptists had taken over the big church house in Danzig, now Gdansk.[53]

• • •

During July the family spent ten days visiting the relatives in southern Germany. By the time they returned to Basel and made a few quick trips to Alsace and to the Swiss Emmental, it was time to leave for the United States.

Bender had arranged for MCC to buy his eight-year-old Dodge. The deal involved skirmishing about price: he wanted $1,200, but during the year he had put 30,000 miles on the car. MCC director Atlee Beechy, after consulting with several mechanics, thought $850 was about right. Reluctantly, Bender accepted the offer. The well-worn car went to MCCer Walt Eicher, but soon afterward Eicher fell asleep at the wheel, crashed, and nearly killed himself and his passenger. The old car was a total loss.[54]

On July 21 Harold, Elizabeth, and Nancy bade Mary Eleanor and the MCC staff in Basel farewell. Mary Eleanor stayed in Basel to study German for another semester. During the spring semester of 1949, she would live with a French-speaking family and attend the University of Lausanne.[55]

The Benders took a train to Paris, and on July 23 they boarded the boat at Le Havre for New York. The seas were rough, but

The Bender siblings and spouses, 1940s. From the left: Florence Bender, Mary Eleanor Bender, Louise Fay Bender and Wilbur Bender, Elsie Bender, Robert and Carolyn Lehman Bender, Harold and Elizabeth Horsch Bender, Cecil and Alice Boren Bender. Not present: John Bender, Violet Bender. Harold S. Bender papers, AMC.

none of them got seasick. From New York they caught a train to Scottdale, where Elizabeth and Nancy stayed on for a week with Christina Horsch. Bender hurried on, arriving in Goshen late on the evening of July 31. In the previous fourteen months, he had traveled more than 50,000 miles.[56]

It was good to be back in the old familiar house. Earlier in the year, the H. Clair Amstutz family, the Benders' temporary renters, had offered to buy it. Surprisingly, Elizabeth and Harold had agreed to sell and had made arrangements to rent the Paul Mininger home until they could build a new one. But at the last minute, the Amstutzes found a house they liked better, and the Benders were spared the onerous work of moving.[57]

● ● ●

The Goshen phase of the fourth Mennonite World Conference was at the Goshen High School. Its auditorium seated 1,200, with the possibility of a loudspeaker hookup for another 1,500 in other rooms. Many of the meetings used all the space since American Mennonites flocked to the meeting in large numbers. The initial plan to have only delegates and ordained persons present had been discarded. After two days in Goshen, the conference attendees spent Friday, August 6, traveling to Newton, Kansas, for four more days of meetings.[58]

The portable conference was a blockbuster, with forty-five major addresses. The blizzard of speeches gave Mennonites opportunity to take stock of who they were and what they had in common. Not all was peace and harmony. During the trip across the Atlantic on the SS *Veendam*, hostility between the Dutch and German delegates had been so sharp that they could not meet for common worship. But apparently the conference had some effect. During the Newton phase, a former West Prussian pastor, Gustav Reimer, made a heartfelt appeal to the Dutch for forgiveness and, Bender reported, the Dutch reciprocated: ADS president Wilhelm Golterman "extended the hand of fellowship and expressed a spirit of forgiveness" to the Germans before they parted.[59]

Bender chaired a session on "Nonresistance and Peace Education." The discussion had symptomatic overtones, for by 1948 American Mennonite commitment to peace had grown to an all-time high while European peace convictions had nearly disappeared. The three-hour session featured speeches by Guy F. Hershberger, Albert Gaeddert, F. van der Wissel, and Bender.

"Mennonite Peace Action Throughout the World" was Bender's address. Apparently for the first time, he mentioned the Cold War and its implications for peacemaking. What "peace action" should Mennonites undertake in the midst of such a global conflict? he asked. His answer: All Mennonites should agree on an aggressive program of service and witness for peace. But Mennonites had not yet agreed that war is an evil in which Christians cannot participate. He hoped that by the time two more Mennonite World Conferences had come and gone, all Mennonites would be able to endorse the principle of nonresistance. He called on European Mennonite young people to embrace what their fathers had rejected, and he called on Mennonites everywhere to work for alternative service programs for their young people. It was a direct but sympathetic address to those European brethren who were not yet ready for pacifism.[60]

A brief delegate session on the last day ratified a proposal written by Bender which created a continuation committee of Mennonite World Conference delegates to be convened by the MCC within one year to plan for a conference in 1952. That conference, the resolution said, was to be "an occasion for acquaintance and fellowship without in any way assuming jurisdiction over any interests."[61]

For the most part, the North American Mennonites were quite satisfied with the conference. Speaking more or less for the MCs, the *Gospel Herald* offered an enthusiastic commentary. However, the Europeans, while enjoying the fellowship, felt the program had been too one-sided—meaning too American. Wilhelm Golterman commented that the next conference should have far fewer speeches and more study-and-discussion groups. Another European delegate quite aptly called it an "American conference with foreign guests." In 1948, the inter-Mennonite dialogue had not yet progressed much beyond polite public fellowship.

Nevertheless, a giant step had been taken. For the first time, American Mennonites had participated in a conference with the Europeans. The Europeans may have felt overwhelmed by the American-managed conference, but they also had seen the surprising vitality of American Mennonite church life. The somewhat self-righteous Americans and the defensive Europeans needed each other. Coming together occasionally for good fellowship and uplifting exhortations was essential for both. In the Cold War world, Mennonite parochialism was outmoded.

When Bender wrote a proposal for another conference, he acted out of that general understanding. No one else, not even the revered C. F. Klassen or the much-traveled Orie Miller, had the broad sense of how important Mennonite cooperation was for Mennonites on both sides of the Atlantic Ocean. Harold Bender's year in Europe had given him a new inter-Mennonite vision. It was fitting that a year later he would be elected president of the Mennonite World Conference.

## *19*

# Developing the Seminary

*Bender retains the seminary deanship,*
*rejuvenates the seminary, sadly abandons*
*a GC-MC Mennonite seminary merger.*

"I CANNOT get the consent of my conscience to reduce my connection to the seminary," a troubled Harold Bender informed Orie Miller.[1] Throughout the cold Christmas holiday of 1948, Bender had been brooding over the implications of a meeting he had held on December 18 with Orie Miller, Ernest Miller, Nelson Kauffman, and A. J. Metzler. Orie had spoken for MCC, Ernest for the college and seminary, Kauffman as president of the Board of Education, and Metzler for the Mennonite Publishing House. Their message: You are far overextended and you should give up some of your responsibilities so you can meet others better.[2]

Earlier in 1948, Orie Miller had visited Bender in Basel, after an inspection trip to MCC units in Europe. He had been awed by what Bender had accomplished during his European sojourn; in fact, he was so impressed that he urged Bender to give up his seminary deanship and spend full time writing, speaking, and working for MCC.[3] Bender had responded by writing a two-page letter, basically rejecting the idea, but at the last minute he had not mailed it. He doubted that Miller was serious about his suggestion.[4]

At the spring 1948 meeting of the Mennonite Board of Education, Paul Mininger, who was acting dean of the seminary during Bender's absence in Europe, urged the board to give priority to the seminary by relieving Bender of other duties so he could give the institution his undivided attention. Orie Miller, just back from

Europe, immediately interjected the idea he had broached to Bender in Basel a few weeks earlier. We should release Bender from the seminary deanship for "more important work," Miller argued. "Mininger and Wenger can manage the seminary." Mininger established himself as a friend of Bender for all time by arguing, as he reported to Bender, that "the biggest job in the church right now is the preparation of leaders for our local churches." Bender had to remain as dean of the seminary, Mininger insisted to the board.[5]

At Newton during the Mennonite World Conference, Orie Miller had returned to the subject, and on the train returning to Goshen, A. J. Metzler had also brought up the subject and suggested that he and several others should meet with Bender. As Metzler put it, they should talk over "your many interests and responsibilities."[6]

Metzler's concern was practical: the publishing house was waiting for five books Bender had promised to write but had never delivered. Bender admitted the problem but argued that he had not been idle. He cited a long list of editing chores which he had completed.[7] Bender's elaborate explanation only served to support Metzler's argument that he was overloaded. Nor was Metzler impressed by Bender's blithe assurance that by the end of the Christmas vacation, he would be ready to begin the "American Mennonite History." He was even vexed when Bender had the audacity to ask that the publishing house buy one of the new Soundscriber dictating machines for his use in writing that book. A bit acerbically, Metzler pointed out that Bender had first promised to write that history in 1927, "twenty years ago," and that Bender had made similar promises many times since, with still nothing to show for all the promises.[8]

In October 1948, Metzler took his complaints about Bender's failure to complete his promised work to the executive committee of the Board of Education. The board directed Metzler to convene a meeting with Bender. Bender did not want the meeting, but he agreed to it a few weeks later when Goshen College president Ernest Miller pushed hard for Bender either to commit to full-time service at the seminary or to relinquish his deanship. President Miller conveyed "a feeling that I undertake too many outside activities and that there is a consequent failure to do as well as could be done in the promotion of the seminary," Bender told Paul Mininger.[9]

Bender was clearly miffed by what he saw as collusion between the Miller brothers and A. J. Metzler. He finally agreed to the meeting but with the proviso that he be allowed to bring Paul Mininger along. "I have come to lean upon Paul for counsel in matters like this and would appreciate very much having him present to hear the entire discussion," he explained to Metzler.[10] In the end, Mininger could not attend, and Bender brought J. C. Wenger.

The conferees encouraged Bender to consider one of two alternatives. Either he should relinquish the deanship and give time to peace and relief work, historical and theological writing, and some teaching; or he should continue as dean of the seminary and, as Metzler put it, "curtail other activities."[11]

Bender agreed to think it over. But there was never any real question about his choice: he would stay with the seminary deanship. His reasons were threefold. First, "to step out of the place which I now hold as dean of the seminary will mean abandonment of a firm and effective base," he told Orie Miller. To give up his "top posts" would amount to "effective withdrawal from all policy-making and leadership functions as well."[12]

The second reason was that Bender thought the seminary needed him. In making that case to Orie Miller, he noted that S. C. Yoder was retiring, young Howard Charles needed to complete his doctorate, "your John" (Orie Miller's son John W. Miller) would not be ready yet for a few years, John Mosemann was going to become half-time pastor of the College Mennonite congregation, and Ernest Miller and Carl Kreider had sabbaticals coming in 1950 and 1951. "I should not leave again for at least four years," Bender advised. "In the next four years, we should get the seminary firmly established as to faculty, policies, finances, etc." In all the flux and change, Bender wanted to be on hand to manage things.[13]

Bender's third reason was more surprising. "With Nancy growing up, we would not be able to leave America for any length of time before she is through high school—three years from now, and possibly not for a year after that."[14] Bender did not usually give family considerations much priority. Apparently Nancy's illness earlier in the year had reminded him of the importance of his family.

Typically, Bender's own proposal to solve his overcommitments was to free himself from administrative detail by the appointment of an assistant dean or secretary of the seminary. (That proposal could have worked only if he had also been willing to forgo the management of details, which was seldom the case.) "My contribution in thought [writing] requires both withdrawal and broad contacts, but is only hindered by administrative detail," he explained. What he wanted to do was continue to sit on his committees as chairman or "counselor" but not as "administrative secretary."[15]

To A. J. Metzler, Bender proposed dropping his teaching load from ten hours a semester to three hours, thus freeing him up for more writing, conditional on the publishing house's willingness to pay him for his time. He also explained that he had appointed Melvin Gingerich to be managing editor of both *The Mennonite Encyclopedia* and the *MQR*, and that Nelson Springer was managing the historical library and the archives. All of this, he told a skeptical Metzler, would make quite a reduction in his workload.[16]

Paul Mininger, studying at the University of Pennsylvania that winter, learned from A. J. Metzler and Nelson Kauffman that Orie Miller was upset by Bender's decision. It seemed that Orie Miller had expected Bender "to give up the work of the seminary leadership," Mininger told Bender, and that Orie "was somewhat disappointed that you did not."[17]

Despite twenty years of close collaboration with Bender, the astute Orie Miller had completely misread how tenacious his friend's commitment to Goshen College and its seminary actually was. Observing Bender's incredibly energetic work in Europe and hearing his frequent complaints about not having time to do his writing, Miller had expected Bender to jump at the chance to be free of the seminary deanship. Dumbfounded by his mistake, he hastened to apologize. "I hope we can continue to be friends," he told Bender, "in spite of what has happened."[18]

Just what the episode meant to Bender is difficult to say. Certainly on the surface it made no change whatsoever in his life. But it did make him think about his future. In numerous instances during those months, he used the phrase "the next twenty years." Alluding to his "God-given" talents for writing and teaching, he told Orie Miller, "The best years of my life to bring these talents to full fruitage are the coming twenty years."[19] But he did not really remedy the problem his brethren had tried to help him solve. As usual, he finessed the issues, and the problem of overload dogged him for the rest of his life.

• • •

One reason Bender gave for remaining in the deanship was that the seminary needed his attention. Since 1946, when the B.D. degree was installed and the Bible School became the seminary, it had been largely left to run itself. Bender's best energy had gone into the European MCC and MRC relief efforts. The seminary had been fortunate to catch a postwar upsurge in enrollment—in the fall of 1948 it was 49, up from 32 the previous year. By 1951 it was 66.[20]

To improve quality, Bender recruited new faculty. In 1948, the old-timers were Bender, Wenger, Mininger, Mosemann, and Yoder. A year earlier a younger man, Howard Charles, had begun what

**Harold Bender conducting a seminary class in the 1940s.**
Bender Family Album.

would become a long tenure at the seminary. Charles came with a B.D. from Union Theological Seminary in Richmond, Virginia, and a Th.M. degree in New Testament from Princeton. Later, from 1950 to 1952, he studied at the University of Edinburgh, where he completed a doctorate in New Testament.

Norman Kraus, from Denbigh, Virginia, with a B.A. from Eastern Mennonite College, completed his B.D. at Goshen and began teaching Bible and church history at Goshen College in 1951. Bender's plan for Kraus was that he should teach for a year and then go to study in Switzerland or Germany. When that plan failed to materialize, Kraus decided to go to Princeton. Bender supplied a glowing and "unqualified recommendation" of Kraus to his old classmate, Princeton seminary dean Edward Roberts. In an aside, Bender confided to Dean Roberts that "some of our friends say we are getting too much Princeton on our seminary faculty." Professors Charles, Mosemann, J. Lawrence Burkholder, and Bender had all studied there.[21]

**Goshen College Biblical Seminary faculty about 1950. Front: Ernest E. Miller, Sanford C. Yoder, Harold S. Bender. Back: John C. Wenger, C. Norman Kraus, J. Lawrence Burkholder, Paul Mininger, John H. Mosemann Jr.** AMC.

That same year, 1952, Paul M. Miller from Lancaster County, Pennsylvania, joined the seminary faculty. He had just completed the B.D. degree at Goshen. Miller was instructor in evangelism, and director of practical work. J. Lawrence Burkholder, just back from a stint of MCC work in China, had taught undergraduate Bible for two years (1949-51) before going to Princeton to work toward his doctorate.

With the retirement of S. C. Yoder in 1951, the seminary was in dire need of an Old Testament professor. Already in 1948, Bender had decided that the new teacher should be John W. Miller. In 1950 Bender persuaded Miller to apply to Princeton in Biblical studies, but to Miller's embarrassment and Bender's chagrin, he was turned down. It took a personal letter from Bender to his old friend Dean Roberts to open the door. By 1951 Miller had earned a B.D. from Princeton and an M.A. in English from New York University and was poised to pursue a doctorate in Old Testament studies.[22]

Bender's coaching of Miller's education offers a window into Bender's own theological thinking in the early 1950s. He became concerned when he learned that nearly all of Miller's reading had been in what Bender called "neoorthodox" thinking. He was quite upset when Miller testified that neoorthodoxy had helped him find "Christ in a new way" and that it had "delivered" him from bondage to the letter of Scripture and the issues of historicity, authenticity, and infallibility. When Miller also argued that Swiss neoorthodox theologian Emil Brunner represented a "biblical faith" point of view, while the orthodox Christian view was based on "Greek propositions," Bender went into action.[23]

Be sure to read B. B. Warfield, Bender urged Miller, and especially read J. Gresham Machen's *The Origin of Paul's Religion*. Warfield, a late-nineteenth-century Princeton theologian, had been critical of liberal theology. Machen's book on Paul had been popular in fundamentalist circles in the 1920s. That Bender would press such superannuated theologians on his young protégé indicates the traditional quality of Bender's theology even in 1950. He also urged Miller to read Cornelius van Til's *The New Modernism*. Van Til taught at the Fundamentalist Westminster Seminary, founded by J. Gresham Machen in 1929. All three books represented orthodox Reformed theology, and Van Til's book was a sharp attack on neoorthodoxy. Bender also gave Miller a copy of Carl F. H. Henry's *Fifty Years of Protestant Theology*. Henry was a professor at the new, evangelical Fuller Seminary in Pasadena, California, and his book was an attempt to give evangelicalism a worldview that was less separatist than that of many out-and-out Fundamentalists.[24]

Having handpicked Miller to be Goshen's first Old Testament scholar, Bender was having some second thoughts about the fitness of his protégé to teach at the seminary. Remember that the seminary is a "training school for preachers, pastors, and evangelists for the congregations of our Mennonite church," he told Miller. It is not "a school or institute for advanced theological thinking. Our church is today completely out of sympathy with the neoorthodox position on the Scriptures." We are in the early stages of our seminary work in the Mennonite church, he continued, and "we have to win and keep the full confidence of the church in our conservative Biblical and theological position. We cannot afford to run any risks."[25]

Bender decided Miller should take his doctorate at the University of Basel, which he considered much more conservative in Old Testament studies than Princeton. To make sure Miller would be accepted, Bender visited Old Testament professor Walther Eichrodt at the University of Basel during the summer of 1950. He pronounced Eichrodt "sound" and sent Miller a Basel catalog with precise instructions regarding matriculation. Miller began studies at Basel in the fall of 1951.[26]

Bender could hardly wait to get Miller into the harness. Why was it so urgent for Miller to begin at Goshen? "We have never had a professor of Old Testament," Bender remarked, remembering no doubt that he had once prepared for just that position. But there was also a practical reason: Eastern Mennonite College had just hired G. Irvin Lehman, who was probably the Mennonite best prepared to teach Old Testament. The recently organized Eastern Mennonite Seminary had just put out an attractive brochure heralding its new faculty member.[27]

The recruitment of new faculty took nearly a half decade, but by the fall of 1955, the faculty roster was basically complete. John W. Miller taught Old Testament, and Howard Charles taught New

Testament. J. C. Wenger shifted to theology, and Bender taught most of the church history. Paul Mininger continued teaching Christian education, J. D. Graber taught missions, and Paul Miller focused on pastoral theology. J. Lawrence Burkholder taught ethics in the seminary, and he and Norman Kraus taught most of the college Bible and religion courses.

As the first generation of Goshen College Biblical Seminary graduates turned to him for advice on where to do their graduate theological studies, Bender realized that he really did not know much about American seminary programs. Someone, he told Orie Miller, ought to explore which seminaries were "sound." Orie Miller encouraged him to do that and offered to help pay the travel expenses. So Bender laid out an itinerary of seminary visits to educate himself about American seminaries and their programs.[28]

Between November 19 and November 26, 1950, Bender traveled to nine seminaries. In Chicago he visited Northern Baptist and Bethany seminaries, the latter a Church of the Brethren school. He then flew to Fort Worth, Texas, where he visited Southwestern Baptist and nearby Dallas seminaries. From there he flew to Wilmington, Delaware, to visit Faith Seminary, and that same day he also stopped at Eastern Baptist in Philadelphia. The next day he took a train to Yale Divinity School and stopped on the way back at Biblical Seminary in New York City. He ended up at Princeton, where he spent parts of two days.

En route back, Bender stopped at Lancaster, Pennsylvania, to be measured for a new plain suit by his tailor. By Sunday forenoon he was back in Goshen. After spending a week and $235 on travel, he claimed to have gained a good sense of which seminaries would best serve Mennonite student needs.[29]

Bender's visit to Princeton had been disquieting. "The Old Testament department has accepted and teaches a number of points of liberal Biblical criticism, the documentary hypothesis of the Pentateuch, second Isaiah, late Daniel, etc.," he told Ernest Miller. With this went a "denial of the older teaching of the inerrancy and infallibility of the Old Testament. The doctrine of plenary verbal inspiration of the Scripture is discarded in favor of a more general concept of revelation." He believed New Testament professors

Bruce M. Metzger and Otto A. Piper were more sound, but the general theological orientation at Princeton was alarmingly neo-orthodox. "This has brought me to the place where I feel I shall have to advise against our men going to Princeton," he told president Miller, "except for those departments where we are quite certain that the men will come through satisfactorily."[30]

He was so disillusioned by Princeton, Bender told Donovan Smucker, that he was going to send his students to Southern Baptist schools. Smucker objected that "your acceptance of the Southern Baptist schools" made him "a bit restless. . . . Never forget," he reminded Bender, "that the Southern Baptists have rationalized both slavery (in the past) and racial discrimination (in the present) and nothing could be more in conflict with the brotherhood of love of the Anabaptist Vision."[31] But Bender did not share Smucker's qualms. In 1953 he decided that Goshen seminary graduate Chester Raber should not go to Princeton but instead should enter the Th.M. program at Southern Baptist Theological Seminary in Louisville.[32]

One effect of bringing new teachers to the faculty was to raise questions about the quality of teaching at the seminary.[33] Bender admitted there were problems, but he mostly blamed them on the refusal of president Miller, despite Bender's repeated requests, to reduce loads and to charge outside agencies for off-campus work by the faculty. "I have made the deliberate choice to have our seminary men continue in their work outside at the cost of reducing effectiveness inside," he told new-teacher J. Lawrence Burkholder, one of the critics. He had done it, he said, because the church needed the expert help the seminary teachers could bring and because of the war and relief emergencies. But those situations were now over, and "we must now deliberately change our policies in this regard," he promised Burkholder. "Next year teaching loads will be reduced to 12 hours and outside commitments of faculty members will be largely terminated." That promise was rooted in a significant new development: president Miller had resigned, and seminary professor Paul Mininger would become president in mid-1954.[34]

J. Lawrence Burkholder also urged more serious attention to contemporary theological problems. "My feeling is that an emphasis on graduate studies will force a departure from the legalistic

Biblicism of our heritage to a more critical approach which will take into consideration theological developments of the Christian church in general," Burkholder told Bender. "This may be a rather difficult task in terms of the constituency, but I see no alternative. We do not want to develop a reactionary and defensive spirit in our attempt to remain loyal to the values of our tradition."[35]

While appreciating Burkholder's point, Bender was not persuaded. The habits of mind finely honed during three decades of finessing problems and honoring the tradition did not easily change. Also, Bender was being realistic. The seminary does not need much "high scholarship," he argued. It is our task to "prepare effective pastors, missionaries, evangelists, and church workers. A major purpose must be to have our men [sic] master and be mastered by the message of the Bible, and to understand how best to make this message effective in the world of needy men, and to work at the cure of souls. I fear the corroding effect of too much dissective criticism even of the good kind."[36]

In a contemplative mood, the seminary dean continued: "I dream sometimes of the kind of faculty which will be as brilliant, intelligent, and effective educationally as the best there is, and still deep in the life of the church." He wanted also to see a faculty "walking humbly with the Lord, and completely loyal to the central New Testament-Anabaptist-Evangelical heritage and witness."[37]

In 1953, Bender was not yet ready to let much contemporary theological argument into the classrooms of Goshen College Biblical Seminary. His point was well taken. In 1953, the MC Mennonite church would not support a seminary which allowed a free exchange of theological ideas in the preparation of its first generation of professional pastors.

A year later, Bender must have remembered his discussion with Burkholder when he received a letter from Eastern Mennonite College president John R. Mumaw. Mumaw claimed that, as a result of studying at Princeton, J. Lawrence Burkholder was in a process of "theological defection." Specifically, Mumaw warned that Burkholder had come under the influence of neoorthodoxy. Clearly, Mumaw's insinuations worried Bender. He wrote an elaborate two-page response, defending Burkholder's orthodoxy and giving a moving, brotherly appeal to Mumaw to exercise charity toward young men still searching for their theological grounding.[38]

• • •

Change in the seminary curriculum came only slowly, retarded by the tortured relationship between Bender and president Miller. That tension made all changes affecting the seminary difficult. Nevertheless, during the 1950-51 academic year, Bender began to modify the curriculum by introducing a new seminary and senior-level college course entitled "Christian Discipleship." Bender himself taught the course, which was lodged in the department of church history. For a textbook he assigned the recent English translation of Dietrich Bonhoeffer's book *The Cost of Discipleship*. The seminar met on Tuesday evening each week in the Bender living room. "We are trying to discover what Discipleship really means for us today," he explained to former student Julia van Delden.[39] In 1953 the course was moved into the department of theology, and J. C. Wenger became its teacher.

In the spring of 1952, the seminary faculty adopted a three-page statement entitled "The Evangelism Policy of the Goshen College Biblical Seminary." In it the faculty defined evangelism as "such witness to Christ as will bring men to faith in Him as Savior and Lord with a consequent new life of discipleship in the fellowship of His church."[40] The seminary had been criticized for not being sufficiently evangelistic in its emphasis. Interestingly, one person making the point was Board of Education member Orie Miller. Always attuned to new currents, Miller was impressed by a wave of tent revivals conducted by two Brunk brothers, George Jr. and Lawrence, sons of the founder of *The Sword and Trumpet*. During the summer and fall of 1951, the Brunks had held enormously popular revival campaigns in Mennonite communities in the districts of Lancaster and Franconia in Pennsylvania; in Wayne County, Ohio; and at Sarasota, Florida.

Suddenly a new urgency about evangelism and witness was gripping the MC Mennonite church. Orie Miller insisted that the seminary should embrace the new emphasis. His brother Ernest, president of the seminary, himself skeptical of the new enthusiasm, dumbfounded Bender by suggesting that George Brunk Jr. be invited to teach at the seminary for a few years.[41]

In that somewhat feverish context, the evangelism statement emerged. The context explains why the document concluded with a confession that the evangelistic fervor of the seminary had not been adequate. The faculty promised to "make evangelism a major concern in our spirit and work."[42]

Actually, Bender was surprisingly positive about the Brunk revival campaigns. When Winnipeg pastor J. H. Enns inquired about Brunk and what Enns called *"wilde Erweckungsversammlungen* (wild revival meetings)," Bender assured him that "Brother Brunk's work is not of this sort." But he also acknowledged some reservations: "We do not think Brother Brunk's tent campaign is the only way or even the best way to do evangelistic work, but it is one good way that has helped many people."[43]

Three years earlier, in the context of developing the evangelism policy statement, Bender had arranged for Brunk, who had his own plane, to fly to Goshen to meet with the seminary faculty as they refined that statement. The meeting had not gone well. Bender had hoped that Brunk's discussion with the faculty would make him their advocate; but that hope was jettisoned when faculty members raised some critical questions about Brunk's methods and about revivalism in general. As Brunk put it, "Some were willing to give me a very light kiss as a price for the privilege of giving me a swat." Bender apologized. "I fear you got more criticisms than positive suggestions. I am not happy about our afternoon session."[44]

On the evangelism issue, Bender himself came under criticism from a Mennonite Brethren leader. H. H. Janzen complained that in his work in Europe, Bender had neglected evangelism because he was too preoccupied with teaching nonresistance. Not so, Bender insisted. He had spoken continually about a wide range of topics related to conversion, the new birth, and the Holy Spirit. And he recounted how, some months earlier, he had preached at a church in Belgium through an interpreter. "I preached an evangelistic sermon, after which the call to confess Christ was given and fourteen people came forward for prayer and confession, a number of them finding the Lord for the first time." In a jab at Janzen's reputation for child evangelism, he noted that "they were all grown people, mostly married."[45]

The fundamental change in the seminary curriculum came in the fall of 1953, when the seminary faculty scrapped the Th.B. degree and divided the courses of study into "Upper Level" and "Lower Level" degrees. Behind the changes was a new draft law which based the ministerial deferment on matriculation in a post-graduate-level course of pastor preparation. Bender was convinced that the Th.B. did not meet the criteria.[46] The "Upper Level" continued the three-year B.D. degree, and the "Lower Level" led to a bachelor in religious education (B.R.E.) degree. The B.D. became the pastoral training track, and the B.R.E. a more general program for church-worker preparation.[47]

Bender called the new plan a "far-reaching action," and he was right. It highlighted the fact that by the mid-1950s, there was no longer any question that the main task of the seminary was to train pastors. That was a dramatic change from the situation just ten years earlier, when the seminary was first begun. In June 1952 Bender reported that the seminary had graduated more than one hundred students, with one-third working for the church abroad, one-third serving as pastors, and one-third teaching. The data confirmed Bender's longtime argument that teaching in the seminary was one of the most strategically important assignments in the church.[48]

• • •

Until Paul Mininger became president in 1954, the seminary did not have its own budget. Mininger and Bender immediately established a budget and put it in effect during the 1954-55 academic year. In 1954 Bender got a boost in funding when he persuaded his friend Ross Martin, a wealthy Elkhart businessman, to pledge an annual $4,000 gift to the seminary. Martin was not a Mennonite, but he was Bender's friend from high school days. Over the years he had been a ready source of cash when Bender overspent his available resources for rare books. Martin's gift in 1954 was especially timely: it allowed Bender to build up the theological library to meet requirements for the seminary's accreditation by the Association of Theological Schools. In 1954 Bender spent the entire $4,000 on library materials.[49]

From the beginning Bender had yearned for a seminary building. In the spring of 1947, he had presented a building plan with four classrooms, a chapel, and offices.[50] But then he went to Europe for a year, and by the time he returned in 1948, the huge new college Auditorium-Gymnasium-Student Center was under construction. Soon the seven hundred persons worshiping at the College Mennonite church began using its new auditorium for Sunday services. But it was not an ideal situation, and an ambitious plan developed to build an alternative "church-chapel-seminary" complex which would give the congregation a meeting place plus serve as a college and seminary chapel and as a seminary center. Bender became one of its primary promoters, and in the fall of 1950, he brought in a Chicago architect as a consultant; but nothing came of the initiative.[51]

A year later everything changed. Orie and Elta Miller offered a major contribution to build a "functional building, adequate for a maximum of seventy-five full-time seminary students."[52] However, they wanted a separate facility, because they believed the separation of the seminary from the college was "inevitable." They gave their gift, $85,000, in honor of their parents and made it conditional: the seminary must raise an endowment of $45,000 to maintain the building. President Miller assigned Bender to raise the money. Bender agreed, on condition that the seminary dean have more freedom to manage the seminary budget.

The seminary building soon became hostage to a decision to begin a nursing program at the college, a program close to the heart of president Miller. That meant construction of a nursing building. Even more fatefully, by 1953 and during that year much of Bender's and the faculty's energies went to selecting a successor to president Miller. Until the presidency was settled, building programs had to wait. Paul Mininger became president of the college and seminary in August 1954. The planners quickly selected a plot, directly across the street from the Bender home, for the proposed seminary building. Bender then complicated the project by attempting to raise additional money to add a library wing and a seminary chapel. The cost of the building grew to nearly $125,000.[53]

That price tag made the Millers unhappy, for with so much added funding, the building was no longer really theirs. President Mininger ordered Bender to scale back the plans. Reluctantly, Bender managed to cut the cost to $97,000, with the somewhat peevish quip that now it was again "Orie Miller's building."[54] So what had begun in 1947 as a modest proposal had grown, a decade later, into a major building project. But the building would be deferred again. Profound historical forces in the Mennonite world suddenly intruded—forces set loose by a decade of inter-Mennonite cooperation in Civilian Public Service and MCC relief work.

• • •

"Don Smucker has come to the conviction that the seminary must move out of Chicago, and he would like to have it moved to Goshen, and be affiliated with our seminary, although remaining a separate institution," Bender informed Orie Miller in awed tones. He was referring to the GCs' Mennonite Biblical Seminary (MBS).[55] By now Bender had come to expect surprises from the effervescent Smucker, but this was truly a shocker. Smucker claimed to have checked with some of his GC Mennonite friends and found that they supported the idea.[56]

In Chicago, the MBS in 1952 was affiliated with the Bethany Theological Seminary, a Church of the Brethren school. Smucker was unhappy with the association and also unhappy trying to raise a young family in the city. Bender was flattered that Smucker wanted to bring MBS to Goshen. From Smucker, Bender had also learned that one of the most promising young GC leaders, Erland Waltner, was reluctant to join the MBS faculty at Bethany Seminary because he was strongly in favor of "inter-Mennonite cooperation."[57]

In 1952 Waltner was teaching in the religion department at Bethel College in Kansas. Bender had high regard for Waltner, who for two summers had traveled with him in Europe in the ongoing MCC Peace Section work with European Mennonites. He was es-

pecially impressed by Waltner's warm evangelical piety
and his embrace of Anabaptist theology.

During the summer of
1954, Waltner, by then on
the MBS seminary board, informed Bender confidential-
ly that he had again been invited to join the faculty at
MBS and in a few years to
succeed the outgoing president, Samuel F. Pannabecker. Shall I do it? he inquired.
Yes! Bender answered. "The
seminary needs a strong,
conservative, warmly spiritual, and Mennonite emphasis which I believe you are
particularly able to give."[58]

Only a few months later,

**Erland Waltner, President of the
Mennonite Biblical Seminary, 1950s.**
MHL.

a letter from Waltner, addressed to Bender, Paul Mininger, and
Orie Miller, made a surprising query. Unofficially, but with the encouragement of both president Pannabecker and the MBS board
chairman, Arthur Rosenberger, Waltner inquired whether Goshen
would be willing to discuss possible cooperation between the two
seminaries. He suggested that the two institutions might consider
setting up a new campus at some "neutral location such as
Elkhart, Indiana." Waltner proposed that he, Pannabecker, Rosenberger, and Smucker meet with Bender, Mininger, and Orie Miller
to see if the idea had merit. The first meeting was on October 9,
1954, in Chicago.[59]

Bender went into the meeting with no expectations of success.
After the meeting, he was more hopeful. He clearly wanted to pursue the idea of a cooperative venture, and he urged that the discussions be put on an official basis by placing them with the governing boards of the two seminaries. But on one point he was

adamant: "Will your side be able to accept the Goshen location? I see no other way but the Goshen location," he told Waltner.[60]

A few days later, Bender wrote to his friend J. Winfield Fretz at Bethel College, expressing surprise that "even some of our conservative men apparently would not oppose affiliation. We are right now busy exploring all the possibilities." But he also insisted that any location other than Goshen was impossible, at least "in this generation." Hoping to send a message to some of the Bethel folks who opposed a move to Goshen, he told Fretz that ten years earlier, before MBS began in Chicago, Bethel College president Edmund G. Kaufman had "told me straight out that if we would receive the GC seminary, they would come to Goshen at once." Urge your colleagues at Bethel to support the Goshen location, he told Fretz. These developments are "definitely a leading of the Lord," but if location becomes an obstacle, it will "spoil the chances [of cooperation] for a generation."[61]

A December 1954 meeting, now officially representing the two governing boards, went well; yet stubborn problems lurked just under the surface. It became apparent that of the MBS faculty, only Don Smucker favored the affiliation. More anomalous was the discovery that Erland Waltner, by now the de facto GC leader, had no real office or formal authority to carry on his leadership role in the discussions aside from his membership on the MBS governing board and a tacit assumption that he would become president of the seminary in a few years. Bender began to have doubts, suggesting at one point that perhaps a limited cooperative plan might be the best solution.[62]

To Bender's great surprise, the fall meeting of the MC Board of Education voted overwhelmingly for affiliation. Bender described the decision to Bethel president Kaufman as "a true modern miracle." But he also admitted ruefully, "We have to insist on a Goshen location, not out of stubbornness, but out of a clear sensing of what would be possible in our group at this time without tearing us apart."[63] Two weeks later the MBS Board of Directors passed a resolution favoring "cooperative effort"; but it noted that the "opposition in our constituency to the Goshen location" made a move to Goshen impossible. The resolution proposed a sincere search for a "mutually acceptable" location.[64]

Thus despite considerable interest in affiliation (or "coopera-tion," depending on who was speaking), the location question had become the major roadblock. Bender felt, in his words, "greatly disheartened." "The action of the MBS board . . . indicates a rather complete negative on the Goshen location, and a victory for the minority opposition," he told C. N. Hostetter Jr., president of Brethren in Christ Messiah College in Pennsylvania and the new chairman of MCC. "A great dream is fading."[65]

Bender seemed oblivious to the fact that a key factor in the im-passe was his own nonnegotiable stance on location. Instead, he lashed out at the GC Mennonite side.

> We now face a crisis of confidence in the GC church. It seems the decisive leadership is still in the more liberal hands—the college presidents and their allies dominate after all. Are we not forced to conclude that in effect Waltner's leadership has been repudiated? When the leadership in the Western Conference [GC] sneaks up on him, and without any brotherly consultation, blocks what he as the new leader of the seminary movement is asking for, things look pretty bad. We would not want to join you [MBS] in Chicago or anywhere under such circumstances.[66]

Why was location so important for Bender? For one thing, he feared that any move away from Goshen would alienate many conservatives in MC ranks. If Goshen went to Chicago to join MBS, the emerging new seminary at EMC would quickly draw away many students now coming to Goshen, he explained to Hess-ton faculty member Calvin Redekop. "President J. R. Mumaw is openly and completely against the seminary affiliation plan at any location. John E. Lapp [Franconia bishop] and several other strong conservative leaders take similar positions. The whole existence of our seminary is at stake."[67]

Another factor was Orie Miller. Bender was afraid that if the Goshen College Biblical Seminary (GCBS) moved to Elkhart, the seminary would lose the Millers' $85,000 seminary construction pledge. GCBS faculty member Paul Miller, a Lancastrian, opposed any affiliation with MBS because he feared eastern Mennonites would be alienated. He urged Bender to respect Orie Miller's intuition on "Mennonite ecumenics" and Orie Miller's helpful role in maintaining a "psychological link between Lancaster conference and the West."[68]

There was also another factor at work, a deep-seated personal matter. Any "real" Mennonite seminary would have to have a good historical library, Bender told Calvin Redekop. "The only good Mennonite historical libraries are at Bethel and Goshen colleges. Do you think either could be taken away from its college and taken to Chicago? Do you think I could go to Chicago without the M.H.L.?"[69]

Bender was vexed by GC complaints that if their seminary came to Goshen, it would be "dominated" by GCBS. Why did they not feel the same about Bethany, which was much larger and stronger than Goshen? he asked. At Goshen they would have "perfect equality," he told Redekop. "This is a phony argument; in our judgment, it really reflects a college jealousy and possibly a general GC inferiority feeling."[70] Thus Bender wrote vehemently to a young man at Hesston College who he knew was in close contact with many of the people whose good faith he was impugning. The letter shows his frustration at that point in 1955. He was insulted that many GC leaders did not want to come to Goshen and found it hard to accept their opposition.

In December 1955, nineteen GC and fifteen MC leaders met for two days in Chicago to discuss the "association" of the seminaries. MCC chairman Hostetter chaired the meeting; Bender served as secretary. The encounter was intense and candid. It quickly became clear that under no circumstances would the MCs consider moving to Chicago. A critical moment of truth was a direct query by A. S. Rosenberger, chairman of the MBS board: would the MCs consider an Elkhart location? Yes, replied president Mininger. He believed his board would consider an Elkhart location.[71]

By January 1956, MBS leaders had accepted the fact that GCBS would not come to Chicago, and they were ready to discuss a new associated seminary at Elkhart. The burden was now on the MCs. One point quickly became obvious: Bender was not as willing as Mininger to consider Elkhart. Or rather, he could not bear leaving Goshen. A deep-seated, almost irrational commitment to Goshen, so evident throughout his life, made him unable to consider the possibilities offered by a new cooperative seminary in Elkhart.

On January 31, 1956, Bender and Paul Mininger met with the MBS executive committee. "We presented some serious difficulties with the Elkhart location," Bender told faculty member Paul Miller.[72] Among the "difficulties" was a detailed statement by Bender regarding the financial implications for GCBS in building a new seminary campus in Elkhart. The capital-cost share for GCBS, Bender claimed, would be in the neighborhood of $200,000, with an annual added operating cost to Goshen seminary of $6,000. Since the Millers appeared to oppose the Elkhart idea, GCBS might also lose the Orie and Elta Miller gift. Moreover, Goshen had begun a process for winning accreditation from the Association of American Theological Schools, and the merger might jeopardize it. Finally, there was the pesky problem of where to locate the Mennonite Historical Library.[73]

Several of Bender's Goshen colleagues were unhappy with his opposition. I. E. Burkhart, a college fundraiser, deplored what he called "making finances a part of our answer. $200,000 spread over 20 years is not more than $10,000 a year plus interest." Making finances a key point "weakens our case," Burkhart advised president Mininger. One might have thought, he continued, that "basic doctrinal differences" might be sticking points. "Now we come to the realization that there is no issue involved, [but only] a matter of 10 miles of geography."[74]

The man caught in the middle was Erland Waltner. In April 1956 he expressed his anguish to Bender.

> To me the breakdown of these discussions without a solution would be a real tragedy. It would be more than the failure of a proposal. It would be a failure on the part of those of us who are one in Christ and who have many bonds of history and experience uniting us. This bothers me immensely, especially because to us is given in a special sense a ministry of reconciliation. Yet while I feel this deeply, I must also confess that I am quite at a loss to know what more we can do. Perhaps even this experience of "coming to the end of our resources" is of God so that He may lead us.[75]

Better than anyone else, Waltner kept the spiritual dimensions of the negotiations in focus. In April he wrote an eloquent two-hundred word "Statement of Mutuality," a term often used by both sides in the discussions. "Mutuality is the very essence of *Koinonia*," he pointed out. "It is an expression of Christian love. It is a divine gift through the Spirit. It is the atmosphere in which those who are externally 'different and unequal' actually experience their overwhelming 'oneness in Jesus Christ' and resolve their practical problems in the abiding Presence of their common Lord."[76]

Bender was touched by Waltner's eloquence. "I was much moved by your letter, which finds an almost complete echo in my own heart," he told Waltner. "I know of no way but to cast our burden upon the Lord and watch and pray. I am beginning to understand what some people mean when they speak of a heartbreak."[77] Bender may have felt heartbreak, but it did not change his mind.

In May of 1956, the executive committee of the Mennonite Board of Education offered a "revised Plan of Cooperation." It assumed two seminaries, one in Elkhart and one at Goshen, with some exchange of teachers, some shared library resources, and cross-registering of students.[78] The new venture was a minimal association: both MBS and GCBS would build new seminary buildings, one in Elkhart, the other at Goshen. The dream of two closely affiliated Mennonite seminaries was being drastically revised. Its nuanced minimalism was subtly reflected in a comment of Mennonite Board of Education president Nelson Kauffman to MBS Board president Arthur Rosenberger. "We are ready to continue in line with the most recent plans for the Associated Seminaries being located here in Elkhart," Kauffman wrote, "*with the exception of the Goshen College Biblical Seminary, which would stay on the Goshen College campus* [emphasis added]."[79] It was, Bender told a frustrated Donovan Smucker, "the maximum attainable in our generation. It is much more than nothing."[80]

In far-off Musoma, Tanganyika, Orie Miller was visiting a Lancaster Conference mission station. The mail brought a cryptic letter from Harold Bender, who at the moment of writing was in Frankfurt, Germany, waiting for a visa so he could go to the Soviet Union. "You will be interested to know that the board of the Mennonite

**The Goshen College Biblical Seminary building, completed in 1959.**
MHL.

Biblical Seminary has unanimously decided to move to Elkhart on the basis of a slightly revised plan of cooperation which was offered by our executive committee. This revised plan follows somewhat your own suggestions to the Executive Committee."[81] Bender hoped Orie Miller would continue his building gift to GCBS, for Bender had already drawn plans for a new GCBS building on the southwest corner of the Goshen campus. The new building, to be completed in 1959, would include classrooms, offices, a chapel, and a historical library and archives.[82]

The allure of a GC-MC seminary affiliation had tempted Bender's ecumenical-Mennonite soul. It finally was detoured because he could not bring himself to break apart what was always his first love and care: Goshen College and Goshen College Biblical Seminary. The detour was also necessary because Bender's sense of what was possible in the MC Mennonite church made a "united strong Seminary" impossible in the 1950s. "We must hold our [MC] church together," he told the aging J. E. Hartzler in 1955. "It has been a miracle to get our conservative Old Mennonite group to agree to this much."[83] Bender, the practical churchman, was right. In the 1950s, a united GC-MC seminary was not yet possible, but the groundwork for a future affiliation, ten years later, had been laid. The hard work and considerable pain was not in vain.

# ❧20❧
# Bender as MWC President; Encyclopedia Production

*Bender leads the 1952 World Conference. Harold, Elizabeth, and others produce* The Mennonite Encyclopedia. *GC elects a new president.*

IT WAS A sublime moment for Harold Bender. He had just completed an address entitled "Conrad Grebel and Felix Manz: Witnesses of the Faith and Disciples of Christ."[1] Nearly a thousand Mennonites and numerous dignitaries from the city of Zurich, Switzerland, filled the seats in the formal assembly room of the Zurich Congress Hall. Responding to his speech was Hans Rudolf von Grebel, pastor of the Grossmünster Cathedral, where 400 years earlier Ulrich Zwingli had been pastor. One of Zwingli's ardent disciples had been Conrad Grebel, an ancestor of the present Hans Rudolf von Grebel.[2]

The Mennonite throng had arrived in Zurich earlier that afternoon and had already held a memorial worship service at the Grossmünster. The worshipers had made the cavernous cathedral echo to the great Lutheran hymn "Grosser Gott, wir loben dich (Great God, we praise you)" and heard a finely crafted lecture by University of Zurich church history professor Fritz Blanke on the contribution of Zurich to the Anabaptist movement. Before the service some of the throng had visited the spot, only a few hundred yards from the cathedral, where Felix Manz had been martyred in the Limmat River. The crowd had then trudged to the nearby Neustadtgasse to attach a plaque to the Grebel family house where Conrad Grebel had lived. The plaque commemorated Grebel as a founder of the Anabaptist movement.[3]

The presence of a thousand Mennonites from all over the world, walking en masse through the central part of Zurich, created quite a stir. It was a Friday afternoon, August 15, 1952. They had arrived in Zurich on a special train from Basel, where for nearly a week they had been attending the fifth Mennonite World Conference. The afternoon in Zurich demonstrated, as no other event could, the connections between the revival of sixteenth-century Anabaptist scholarship and the twentieth-century world-Mennonite rapprochement embodied in the weeklong gathering of fifteen hundred Mennonites at the fifth Mennonite World Conference at Basel.[4]

The connections had been present from the first Mennonite World Conference in 1925, when historian and German Mennonite leader Christian Neff had held a conference at Basel designed to commemorate the 400th anniversary of the beginning of the Anabaptist movement and to bring twentieth-century Mennonites together. Neff had died in early 1947. By 1952 it was clear to knowledgeable observers that his successor was Harold S. Bender. In Bender, Neff's vocation as Mennonite historian and ecumenical churchman was continued. The 1952 Mennonite World Conference at Basel represented the coming of age of a movement begun

**Some of the participants at the Fifth Mennonite World Conference at Basel in 1952.** Harold S. Bender papers, AMC.

by Neff twenty-seven years earlier.

Bender was "astonished" by the large crowds. At several meetings nearly 1,500 persons were present. The facilities for the conference at the hilltop Bible Institute called St. Chrischona, a few miles north of Basel, were taxed to the utmost. The presence of more than three hundred Americans, nearly half of them MC Mennonites, was also a surprise. American Mennonites were prosperous and thus able to travel to Europe. In addition, the wartime and postwar inter-Mennonite cooperation in CPS, relief, and refugee activity had lowered the barriers between Mennonites. The 1952 Mennonite World Conference was evidence of an emergent worldwide Mennonite identity.[5]

Christian Neff had produced the first three Mennonite World Conferences, but the 1952 event was the creation of Harold Bender. The 1948 gathering at Goshen and Newton had endorsed the idea of a conference in Europe in about five years. To get the planning underway, a preparatory commission of one member from each European conference and three MCC executive committee members was formed. At the first meeting of the preparatory commission in Basel in 1949, Bender was elected president of the commission, a title he rejected in favor of "chairman." He argued that a "president" should be elected by the world conference itself. In any case, for the next two years, the Goshen seminary dean's office became the administrative center for world-conference planning.[6]

Directing the planning challenged Bender's diplomatic skills. He could not really be sure how much support to expect from his own MC people. However, by Christmas 1951 he was delighted to find that more than 200 North Americans had already signed on as delegates and visitors—more than half of them MC Mennonites.[7]

Bender's anxieties about MC Mennonite support for the conference surfaced during an exchange with seven Mennonite graduate students who were in Europe either studying or working under MCC or the MC mission board. Pointing out that the Basel conference would be "a crowning event" after many years of growing interactions between European and American Mennonites, the seven urged that the conference should "climax in a communion service." Such a service would be a true "expression of brotherhood," the young men insisted.[8]

Bender was aghast. "The official position of the church to which you and all of the other graduate students belong is closed communion," he reminded the young men. "The same is true of a half-dozen of the other Mennonite groups who will be present. . . . To ask these groups to violate their own conference discipline is quite impossible and would torpedo the conference." Furthermore, Bender pointed out, no one, in all the years he had been connected with Mennonite World Conferences, had ever suggested such an event. "The Mennonite World Conference rests on a very slender foundation," he argued. "It has only gradually been built up to the place where practically all the Mennonite groups in America accept it. This achievement could be completely destroyed by such a proposal."[9]

Bender was feeling vulnerable. On the same day he read the students' letter, he also received an ominous note from Canadian Mennonite Brethren leader B. B. Janz. Janz complained about what he called Dutch Mennonites' "liberal, social, modernistic" influences on the conference. Bender quickly assured Janz that "the program has been safeguarded on this point."[10] Clearly B. B. Janz was one who would not have tolerated a world-conference communion service. In 1952 Bender was more realistic about the state of the Mennonite polity than were his young American graduate students in Europe.[11]

Bender's greatest diplomatic challenge was to mediate the animosities between the Dutch and the German Mennonites which had been created during the Hitler era. The Dutch were especially difficult. Their delegates attended preparatory commission meetings but virtually ignored the correspondence necessary to complete the arrangements. When they did respond, it was to criticize many aspects of the emerging program, and in one case, to veto a program speaker who they believed, mistakenly, had been a Nazi. To his credit, Bender went out of his way to accommodate them while trying to be fair to the Germans.[12]

Bender got wonderful help from H. A. Fast, who in 1951-52 was Europe—MCC director. A member of the MCC executive committee, Fast used the MCC administrative machinery in Europe to

**The executive committee of the Fifth Mennonite World Conference at Basel, Switzerland. From the left: U. Hege, Harold S. Bender, H. W. Meihuizen, C. F. Klassen, H. Nussbaumer.** Mennonite World Conference brochure, AMC.

assist the preparations. Another person helping with some of the ticklish German-Dutch diplomacy was the highly regarded C. F. Klassen, MCC refugee director in Europe. Bender's trusty confidant, MCC—Netherlands director Irvin Horst, did liaison work. He was especially good at helping Bender understand the nearly paranoid fear the Dutch had of what Horst called "American dominance."[13]

As usual, Bender tried to manage everything. In his role as chair of the preparatory commission, he carried on a huge correspondence. While reading *The Sunday School Times*, he learned that an International Council of Christian Churches conference in Geneva, Switzerland, had used a new International Business Machines device which allowed individual translation in up to five languages. He immediately wrote to ICCC president Carl McIntire and was overjoyed to learn that IBM supplied the apparatus free of charge to church groups.[14] Through the IBM office in Zurich, Bender arranged for 500 headsets for the conference.

Nor could Bender resist doing some travel arrangements, much to the chagrin of the fledgling new MCC Menno Travel Service

(MTS) in Akron, Pennsylvania. Conceding that MTS should handle the Atlantic travel and even the tours in Europe, Bender drew the line on tours for the Middle East immediately following the World Conference. MTS had planned to send a staffer to the Middle East to make arrangements, but Bender much preferred to work with an old established New York firm which specialized in Middle East travel—and which would make him tour manager, pay all his expenses, and give him a commission of $1,500. The profits from the venture, he assured Orie Miller, would be used to "finance some historical publications."[15]

Miller was not convinced. So in the end, Bender and MTS made a deal: Bender would do the cross-Atlantic travel arrangements for the more-than-100 MC Mennonite travelers, and MTS would organize the Europe and Middle East tours. The advantage for Bender was that he could apply his agent's commission to paying for his and Elizabeth's fare to Europe in May and for their return in September on the fast liner *Queen Mary*. It also let him appoint Paul Erb, Cornelius Krahn, and Guy Hershberger to be tour managers on the Atlantic crossing, which brought a substantial reduction in their fares.[16]

Bender also arranged the tours for the MC Mennonites after the conference in August and early September. He divided the MC delegation into two groups, then he himself led one of the groups, first to the Middle East, then on an Anabaptist-history tour in Europe, then back to North America. Paul Mininger led the second group, who did the Anabaptist-history and the Middle East segments in reverse order, before joining Bender's group for the return voyage across the Atlantic. It was a typical Bender plan, complex and overloaded.[17]

Harold and Elizabeth left New York on May 28, right after the close of their last second-semester classes. By June 2 they were in London. From there they detoured to Edinburgh to visit Goshen professor Howard Charles, working on his Ph.D. there. Then they flew to Amsterdam (Elizabeth's first airplane ride) to begin a two-week sojourn. After a visit to Hamburg, they enjoyed several days with Ernst and Rosa Crous at Göttingen. The Crouses had just spent a year at Goshen, where they and the Benders had become close friends. Sadly, Elizabeth suffered a serious allergy attack. By the time the Benders got to the Frankfurt MCC center on July 7, she was quite ill and had to see a doctor.[18]

At Frankfurt, Bender received a disturbing telephone call from Liesel Widmer, who was serving that summer as the World Conference secretary at the Basel MCC headquarters. Widmer told Bender that professor Fritz Blanke had just called to say that the city president of Zurich had vetoed plans for a commemorative event in his city to honor the sixteenth-century Anabaptist leader Conrad Grebel and martyr Felix Manz.[19] Bender, having planned the commemoration in connection with the world conference, was dumbfounded; but he immediately realized his mistake. The Zurich ceremonies were to include the placement of plaques honoring Grebel and Manz, and in April Bender and professor Blanke had negotiated the wording of the plaques. Blanke had firmly insisted that the Manz plaque not use the term "martyr." Bender had agreed, but only now did he understand Blanke's concern: the drowning of Manz was a blot on Zurich's image and on its foremost citizen, Ulrich Zwingli. The city fathers were not about to let a reminder to be put on public display.[20]

Realizing that he had to act quickly, Bender rushed to Zurich to confer with the city president. Out of the meeting came a compromise: the city would welcome the conference and help place the plaque at the Grebel home in the Rindermarkt, but it would not allow a plaque honoring Felix Manz near the river where he was drowned. The plaque at the Grebel house would acknowledge Manz, like Grebel, as one of the Anabaptist founders. But there would be no mention of a drowning. Bender disliked the arrangement, but he had little choice.[21]

Returning to Frankfurt, Bender found that Elizabeth was feeling better. During the last week of July, the two took a weeklong train trip—a real vacation—to Vienna, stopping overnight in Innsbruck and for a few hours in Salzburg. They spent only one day in Vienna. Then they returned to Basel, where Bender plunged into intensive last-minute preparations for the conference.[22]

Unlike previous Mennonite World Conferences, this one was quite theological, built around the theme "The Church and Her

Commission." To a correspondent, Bender posed the overriding theological question: "What is God's word for the Mennonites today?" He hoped the conference would bring a "new vision and dedication to the great commission placed by our Lord upon His church."[23]

In another departure from the past, the conference was able to agree on a joint declaration. Among other points, it called on Mennonite congregations to stress the importance of the new birth as a prerequisite for baptism, urged Mennonites to reject materialism, and called for a more concerted effort to bring the gospel to the world.[24] The statement was quite remarkable: for the first time in their history, North American and European Mennonites were able to agree on some specific spiritual and theological pronouncements. Bender could not have envisioned such a development twenty-two years earlier, in 1930, when he attended his first Mennonite World Conference.

Immediately after the conference, Bender led his group on the tour to the Middle East. The trip, lasting two weeks, was his first to the "Holy Land." Elizabeth stayed behind in Basel, translating and preparing the conference proceedings for publication. She also spent a few days visiting the Horsch relatives in Bavaria.[25]

Bender returned from the Middle East on September 2. On the fourth, he and Elizabeth boarded the *Queen Mary* at Cherbourg, and six days later they were at home in Goshen. They had just missed a major event: on the previous Sunday evening a Brunk brothers tent revival near Goshen had ended, with 7,000 people crowded into the tent.[26]

When Bender got to the office the morning after his return, he was surprised: his office had been painted and the floor waxed to a high gloss. He also met his new secretary, Joan Strauss, who had begun her new job on September 1. Strauss was nervous. A seminary student had told her the day before that right away Bender would "dictate at least fifty letters." The student had expressed sympathy for Straus in her "impossible" job.[27]

Actually, Bender had no time that day for dictation; instead, he immediately began to register seminary students for the fall semester. At the end of the day, on his way home from the office, he visited president Ernest Miller. Miller was convalescing from a hospitalization following a nervous breakdown several weeks earlier.

• • •

The five-day Atlantic crossing had been just long enough for Bender to finish proofreading the 200 pages of articles under the letter A for the text of the first volume of *The Mennonite Encyclopedia*. He was pleased by his progress. In the warm afterglow of the world conference, as the Queen Mary steamed through the North Atlantic toward New York, he could scarcely have imagined that another seven years would pass before all four volumes would be completed.

During the autumn of 1952, Harold and Elizabeth worked feverishly on the encyclopedia. "Never have we been so busy as these past few months," he told Austrian historian Grete Mecenseffy. "Preparing an encyclopedia with almost one thousand pages is an especially difficult matter."[28] By mid-December they had nearly completed *B* and hoped to begin *C* before the new year. Actually, it would be another year before the text for *C* would be completed, and two years before the first volume of the encyclopedia came off the press.

In the frame of Harold Bender's life in the 1950s, the project to produce *The Mennonite Encyclopedia* became a scholarly counterpart to his Mennonite World Conference activities. The world-conference movement blossomed at Basel in 1952, bore fruit at Karlsruhe, Germany, in 1957, and reached its high point at Kitchener, Ontario, in 1962. *The Mennonite Encyclopedia* was completed within those years. As the volumes rolled out in 1955, 1956, 1957, and 1959, they heightened the sense of shared history and peoplehood reflected in the world-conference events. The two accomplishments meshed easily, and for Bender and his Mennonite people, they were synergistic. The *Encyclopedia* embodied not only the worldwide breadth but also the historical depth of Mennonitism. Because both the world conference and the *Encyclopedia* were so inclusive and extraordinary, they had a profound effect on Mennonite self-consciousness. For Bender, the two were virtually indistinguishable, the one reinforcing the other.

In 1945, when the idea of a Mennonite encyclopedia had taken form at the meeting of the Mennonite Scholar's Guild in Bluffton, Ohio, C. Henry Smith had said that the intention was to carry forward the publication of the *Mennonitisches Lexikon*. But as the Americans had examined the *Lexikon* more closely, they saw that its treatment of the American Mennonite story was all too meager and inadequate. Furthermore, the scholarship of the first two volumes, one completed in 1924 and the other in 1938, was quite out of date. Thus what C. Henry Smith had envisioned as a translation project quickly grew into a major new scholarly effort.[29]

The enthusiasm with which the small band of Mennonite scholars embraced the idea of a Mennonite encyclopedia on that humid August evening in Bluffton reflected the coming of age of a new generation of mature Mennonite scholarship. The encyclopedia was to be, the group had decided, "scholarly rather than popular." It was to give "exhaustive coverage in all fields of Anabaptist-Mennonite history, theology, ethics, and life." For Bender and his generation, it became a way to summarize what Mennonites knew about themselves.[30]

However, getting the project underway had been tedious, delayed by the many other urgent matters facing Bender and his colleagues in the aftermath of the war. It was not until early 1948, in the midst of Bender's frenetic year in Europe, that the editorial board was finally appointed. Bender and C. Henry Smith became coeditors, and historian Melvin Gingerich moved from Bethel to Goshen College to serve as managing editor on a part-time basis. Gingerich was not able to do much on the project until 1949, because he was busy completing his *Service for Peace*, a substantial history of Civilian Public Service during World War II. Beginning in January 1947, Goshen student John A. Hostetler did an elaborate analysis of the *Lexikon* and began the process of identifying topics and subjects for the new work. During Bender's year abroad in 1947-48, Hostetler elicited lists of suggested topics from an array of scholars. Robert Friedmann sent in 290 topics, C. Henry Smith even more. Smith began writing articles assigned to him.[31]

Then in October 1948, to everyone's dismay, C. Henry Smith died. Suddenly the one person other than Bender who could move the project forward was gone. Who should succeed him? Bender's response was immediate: No one, he advised Paul Erb, was "really well qualified to take the place of C. Henry Smith as coeditor." Erb, the chairman of the encyclopedia publishing committee, was dubious. The GCs will want someone of their group to help with the editing, he told Bender; how about Cornelius Krahn? "Dr. Krahn is a historian," Bender told Erb, "but I do not consider him sufficiently well-balanced and objective to take C. Henry Smith's place."[32]

The publishing committee realized that Bender's position was untenable; so Erb persuaded Bender to accept Krahn, not as co-editor but as associate editor. Bender reluctantly agreed. Krahn was not happy with the lesser title of associate editor, but accepted it as the best he could get. At the same time, the committee designated Melvin Gingerich as the managing editor. Bender, Krahn, and Gingerich became the project's executive committee.[33]

Thus began ten years of sustained collaboration among the three men, greatly shared and aided by Elizabeth Bender. Gingerich became a much-tested but honest broker between two strong-willed associates who clashed frequently. As matters turned out, Bender was completely wrong about Krahn's ability to do sustained work. For the next ten years on an almost daily basis, Krahn carried his share of the load, writing articles (686 to Bender's 958) and doing the meticulous, critical proofreading which the editorial role demanded.

Bender soon came to appreciate Krahn's contribution. In 1951 Krahn planned to go to Europe for a year, but Bender protested. "Melvin and I would set up a real howl if you should really want to take off next year," he insisted, "and we feel that we would be so badly handicapped that the encyclopedia would be much delayed." Krahn reluctantly gave up the trip.[34]

The greater difficulty was keeping Bender on task. At one point Gingerich complained to Krahn that in a three-month period when Bender was to have spent all his time on the encyclopedia, he had actually worked on it for only five days. For Gingerich, who was cajoling contributors to get their material in on time, the failure of the editor to get his work done was a terrible problem.[35]

Bender and Krahn were tough critics of each other. When Krahn read Bender's article on "Archives," he offered a series of helpful comments but was disgusted by Bender's cavalier treatment of Bethel's collection. "How you manage to take care of the General Conference efforts in one sentence is beyond my understanding," he told Bender.[36] Bender sometimes called Krahn to task. Krahn wrote about the Russian Mennonite Selbstschutz, a paramilitary self-defense force some Mennonites formed during the civil war following the Russian Revolution. But Krahn omitted any mention of an incident in which Selbstschutz officers had killed civilians. When Bender edited the piece, he added the fact. Krahn in turn insisted that since there had been only one incident, it had been an aberration and should not be mentioned. Reluctantly, Bender took it out, but he still begged Krahn to reconsider. "As an historical encyclopedia, we should not suppress known material facts," he lectured Krahn.[37]

Bender's best critic (and cheerleader) was Robert Friedmann. From his position at Western Michigan University, Friedmann served as an assistant editor and wrote nearly 200 articles. In fact, in terms of column inches, he wrote nearly half as much as Bender, which meant that he wrote a number of major articles. As an assistant editor, Friedmann was not consulted on routine matters. But he was intensely interested in the project, and a continuous stream of encyclopedia correspondence moved between Kalamazoo and Goshen.[38]

In late 1956 Friedmann received the second volume of *The Mennonite Encyclopedia* and responded characteristically: "My admiration unconditionally. This is a great work, Harold, and a monument to you and the Mennonites. Really excellent. What a distance from the earlier experiment of Neff-Hege (all honor to them, too!)" Nearly rhapsodic, he continued: "Shall I say to which article I would give the 'blue ribbon'? It is your Grebel-article. This article is a piece of writing artistry, a most enjoyable work, written with love and passion—as it should be. (Am I right?) (NB. I do not say this for reasons of flattering you, I really mean it.)"[39]

However, in the same letter Friedmann also expressed surprise because there was no article on discipleship. "Discipleship? It is your key word!" As it turned out, the editors had simply overlooked the topic during the planning phase. Bender finally added an article on the subject in the "Supplement," at the end of the final volume, along with other overlooked or late items.

Friedmann was often Bender's scholarly conscience, particularly when Bender was tempted to take shortcuts by simply translating and printing articles from the *Lexikon*. A case in point was an article on Ernst Troeltsch written by Christian Neff in the early 1930s. Friedmann insisted that a new article should be written despite an imminent printing deadline. "Won't you be embarrassed to have such out-of-date scholarship in the *ME*?" he inquired. Harold resisted. Friedmann persisted. "The *ME* is just as near to my heart as to yours. I can see that Scottdale has to produce galley proofs, but page proofs—for God's sake, hold them until later this fall!" Bender reluctantly agreed.[40]

On at least one occasion, Friedmann's writing ran afoul of Cornelius Krahn. The Kalamazoo scholar wrote the main article on Anabaptism, drawing heavily from his 1940 essay "Concept of the Anabaptists." Krahn objected that the point of the article should not be on what *Friedmann* thought the term "Anabaptist" meant, but on what the term had meant throughout history. Bender agreed, and he and Friedmann rewrote the article, Bender explaining its sixteenth-century meaning and Friedmann its more recent usages.[41]

In an argument with Friedmann about the Swiss Brethren in Moravia, Bender sarcastically inquired, "Whom am I to believe—Robert Friedmann or the *Ausbund*?"[42] Friedmann shot back: "Now Harold, a scholar as solid as you are should never have asked a question like that. You should believe neither R. F. *nor* the title page of the *Ausbund*; this is not a question of belief, but of documentation! See Wolkan, *Lieder der WT*, pp. 27-30!"[43]

Bender benefited greatly from Friedmann's critiques. When Bender finally wrote the "Discipleship" article, Friedmann called it inadequate, although he said a later draft was much better than the first. Bender—in a big hurry—had carelessly written that the Anabaptists believed Christ's life and teachings were to be "reproduced" by his disciples. No! No! Friedmann insisted. "You don't want "*Imitatio*" (*Nachmachung*). You want *Nachfolge*—following after, living as a true disciple." Bender made the change.[44]

Bender, Krahn, and Gingerich put in yeoman service on the

**Elizabeth and Harold conferring about *Mennonite Encyclopedia* matters.**
Bender Family Album.

*Encyclopedia,* but the project would not have been completed except for the herculean efforts of Elizabeth Horsch Bender. Initially her assignment was to translate the *Lexikon,* but soon she became the real mover behind the scenes. Long before the first volume appeared, she had become the main copy editor, and Harold made her responsible for style as well. In 1955 Melvin Gingerich went to Japan for two years, whereupon Elizabeth became, for all practical purposes, the managing editor. She had able help from young Liesel Widmer. Widmer, a student from Germany studying at Goshen College, gave much time to the *Encyclopedia.* In 1956 Elizabeth was belatedly named assistant editor. In 1957 she gave up her teaching at the college, although she taught several courses at the new Bethany high school. For seven years—1952-59—she spent nearly every free moment on her editing tasks on the *Encyclopedia.* Not even Harold put in as much time as Elizabeth.[45]

Bender and a Dutch scholar, Nanne van der Zijpp, wrote more than half of the articles and half of the actual words. Van der Zijpp was incredibly productive. Over an eight-year period, he produced more than 3,000 articles on Dutch topics—a tour de force that won him an honorary doctorate at the University of Amsterdam in 1961. As for Bender's writing, more than half of what he wrote had originally been assigned to others who then failed to produce. Dashing off such articles, often late at night, and depending largely on his excellent memory for the details, Bender was in his métier. He worked well under the pressure of deadlines. When he knew too little about a topic, he wrote the best he could and sent it to someone for criticism. Often the result was quite a good article, combining Bender's style and someone else's expertise.

As with most of Bender's projects, there was never enough money. In his 1947 budget projections, Bender had vastly over-stated how quickly the project would be completed and under-stated its cost. As originally envisioned, the project was to be self-sustaining, with the sale of books covering expenditures. The problem was that instead of the whole project being finished by 1951 as Bender had projected, the first volume came out only in 1955. In his initial budget, Bender had estimated costs of getting the manuscripts to the printer—the "writing costs"—at $7,000. By 1950 the project had spent $10,000, and even the first volume was nowhere near being ready.[46]

A. J. Metzler, manager of the Mennonite Publishing House, was worried. At this rate the first volume will cost $15,000, he warned. Bender brushed off the warning and promised to redou-ble his efforts. A few years later the editors worked gratis for long periods of time to relieve the financial pinch. By the end of the project in 1959, the editorial costs alone had reached $40,000.[47] Book sales barely covered the costs of printing alone.

After the first volume was published in 1955, scholars and other users eagerly anticipated the rest. George Williams, a scholar of Anabaptist history at Harvard University, could hardly wait. On several occasions he had visited Goshen for research in the histor-ical library and had observed the *Encyclopedia* work firsthand. When the last volume appeared, a delighted Williams wrote to Bender, offering his "profound admiration to you and your wife and associates in this tremendous enterprise of scholarship." Williams knew whereof he spoke: at that moment he was hard at work on a 1,000-page tome on sixteenth-century Anabaptism which he would entitle *The Radical Reformation*.[48] The book quickly became a classic in its field.

The first copy of the fourth and final volume came off the press on August 7, 1959. On August 11 the publishing committee held a celebration dinner in the Goshen College dining hall. Cor-nelius Krahn, Melvin Gingerich, and Harold and Elizabeth were present, along with members of the committee. Harold presented

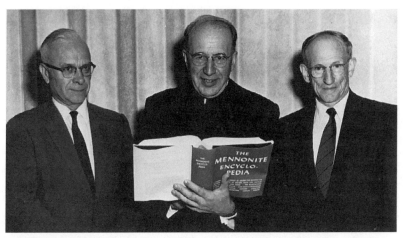

**Cornelius Krahn, Harold S. Bender, and Melvin Gingerich with the fourth volume of** *The Mennonite Encyclopedia,* **completed in 1959.**
Harold S. Bender papers, AMC.

an eight-page report on the project, including a remark that, had the committee foreseen the costs and expenses of the project, they might not have taken it on. But "mercifully," he continued, "we . . . were not given a full vision of what the demands of mind, time, energy, and money would amount to. I am sure I would personally have made different plans had I been aware in advance of what it would mean to Mrs. Bender and myself."[49]

Bender remarked to Robert Friedmann, "I have put the best part of ten years of my life and Elizabeth's into the *Encyclopedia*." And, he wrote, "we must now unload. I have other things to do yet in my life."[50]

Nevertheless, as usual, Bender could not quite end the project. He was bothered by errors and omissions. What would it cost to prepare a fifth volume of addenda, in perhaps two or three years? he inquired of A. J. Metzler. Metzler was appalled by the suggestion. "It is totally inconceivable that the publishers would be in a position to put another dollar into this project," he told Bender. "We want to turn our complete energies to the many other tasks awaiting us."[51]

*The Mennonite Encyclopedia* was Bender's magnum opus, his greatest scholarly achievement. It was a remarkable extension of the man. Universal in its scope, both historically and geographically, it summed up what Bender knew about his fellow Mennonites. Its 3,888 pages offered a sweeping explanation, rooted in history, of what Bender conceived Mennonites to be. An encyclopedia is inherently a conservative document, for it celebrates what is or was. It informs. It offers a place to stand. To an unusual degree, *The Mennonite Encyclopedia* embodied Harold Bender's relation to the Mennonite church. In the 1950s he was busy securing the heritage and mediating and moderating pressures for change. *The Mennonite Encyclopedia* was a major part of that process.

• • •

*The Mennonite Encyclopedia* was created in the midst of the hurly-burly of Bender's overcommitted life. His life was never punctuated by beginnings and endings; instead, it consisted of layered and overlapping responsibilities and activities that were ongoing. One result was that urgent, immediate items pushed long-range projects to the background. In late 1952 and during 1953, the presidential succession at Goshen College and seminary moved into the foreground.

Nelson Kauffman's January 1952 letter was as diplomatic as he knew how to make it, but president Ernest Miller was quite upset by what he called "this abrupt and surprising announcement." As president of the Board of Education, Kauffman had just informed Miller that the board would soon begin a search for a new president for Goshen College and Seminary.[52]

In 1950 the Board of Education's executive committee had proposed to replace Miller "in about three years." At that time the committee had met with Miller and advised him of their intention, but apparently Miller had not taken the news seriously. Now in 1952 he insisted he had never known of the plan. In a long letter he argued that he should stay on as president, and he accused the board of taking secret actions to which he was not privy.[53]

For years Bender had been pushing for Miller's replacement. The two men had never worked well together, a situation that vexed the Board of Education. "We deeply regret their inability to integrate their energies as well as could be reasonably expected to the common goals," a note by the board complained. The board worried that the tension might extend to college and seminary faculty and even to church leaders.[54]

I. E. Burkhart, a college and seminary fundraiser who traveled widely in the church, accused Bender of fomenting sentiment against Ernest Miller in the church.[55] Even Orie Miller was losing patience with both his brother and his longtime colleague. In a cryptic note to himself, Orie observed that "Harold isn't safe in leadership anymore—Ernest isn't able to lead further—both are ethically right and sincere but handicapped in giving their essential further contribution thru frustrations."[56]

Somehow Bender had learned of the pending Board of Education letter to president Miller. Two weeks earlier he had written a half-page, self-typed note to Orie Miller, who was a member of the board's executive committee. In what must have seemed to Orie like a rather self-serving proposition, Bender suggested that it would be necessary to find Ernest Miller "a good alternate post," for he "could hardly continue on the staff here, at least for two years after retiring." Bender suggested that the ex-president be made director of an emerging conscientious objector program now known not as CPS but as I-W service.[57]

Making the presidential change was urgent, Bender told Orie Miller. "You spoke once of signs of disintegration at Goshen. The signs are increasing. If things go too far before the change is made, it will be most difficult for any new man to swing the tiller over and recover lost ground. Somebody may get killed off in the struggle."[58] Except perhaps for their melodrama, Bender's words were not far off the mark. The somewhat fragile psyche of president Miller, struggling with the implications of the Board of Education's plan to replace him, could not handle the strain. During the August days of 1952, when most of the board's executive committee members were attending the Mennonite World Conference in Switzerland, Ernest Miller suffered a nervous breakdown and had to be hospitalized.[59]

Miller's plight forced the board to go public, and at an October 1952 meeting, the board informed the faculty of its plans. In a letter to Nelson Kauffman and Orie Miller, marked by Bender's handwritten "Not for the file," Bender reported somewhat disingenuously that the announcement provoked "practically no discussion," except "that a small group of middle-aged faculty women are highly emotionalized, to the point of bitterness, and are doing some trouble-making."[60] Actually, there was quite a lot of discussion, and by the summer of 1953, the faculty had divided into several camps: those in favor of Miller continuing, and a minority like Bender who wanted swift change.

Typically, Bender went on the offensive. In March 1953 he wrote a long unsolicited letter to the board in which he made three points. The next president of Goshen "must be a strong church man." The board should sit as a body and poll individual faculty members about whom they would like for president. And finally, Bender had heard five names mentioned "for consideration": "Paul Erb, J. D. Graber, John Mosemann, Carl Kreider, and Paul Mininger." Bender believed that "only the last three should be seriously considered."[61]

Bender's candidate was Paul Mininger. He advised college dean Carl Kreider, who was on leave to serve as dean at the International Christian University in Japan, that those members of the faculty who thought that they knew who Bender favored were "all wet."[62] But in fact, Bender's support for Mininger was such an open secret that even Mininger worried about it. "If I was president, would you also think that Dean Bender was running the school?" Mininger asked Carl Kreider. Mininger sensed that Bender's support could be a liability.[63]

In late April 1953, whether or not on Bender's advice, the board held a hearing. In two days it heard forty individual faculty members' opinions about the transition. An elaborate tally sheet revealed that more than three-fourths favored no change of president in the near future.[64] Nonetheless, a few weeks later the board approached Paul Mininger to see if he would take the job. At that, many of the faculty were upset; clearly there had been a miscommunication between the board and the faculty. The faculty assumed that if the board consulted them, their voice would determine the outcome. But the board saw the consultation primarily as a way to let faculty express their opinions. The board reserved the right to appoint whomever they desired.

Another issue was swirling about just under the surface: the board was concerned about keeping church and school connections close. Its members suspected that some new faculty whom the college was hiring were well-credentialed and professional, but might put professional values before church affinity. At least that was how J. C. Wenger understood the matter. "We are at a crucial point in the history of Mennonite higher education," Wenger told the board executive committee. "If the faculty blocks the election of the Executive Committee choice, it will not be a minor defeat of a man: it will be the defeat of church control and the perpetuation of a sound Mennonitism."[65] Wenger almost certainly reflected Bender's point of view.

In his March letter to the board, Bender had expressed what was also the board's perspective: "Is the man to be chosen as president so well informed in the problems and needs of the church, and himself spiritually so equipped, that he can effectively guide the destiny of the school spiritually and otherwise?" In Bender's opinion, the school had an able academician and administrator in dean Carl Kreider. For president, the college needed a strong churchman; and Bender was sure that Mininger fit that bill.[66]

During late summer and fall of 1953, the controversy continued to boil. With all the coolness of an undercover agent, Bender wrote two more "Not for the file" and "Discard please" notes to Orie Miller and Nelson Kauffman. "Informally, I pass on to you for information some notes about the group activity opposing the ex. com. work on change of presidency here," said one note. "This group has now shrunk considerably." The remnant group had a session "at which only six were present. This group already Tuesday had a copy of the ex. com. letter sent out from Kitchener to Board members. So they are being supplied with ex. com. communications fresh from the source."[67]

At its annual October meeting in 1953, the Board of Education elected Paul Mininger, to begin his term the next August. Bender was delighted: one of his most trusted and loyal (albeit able and independent-minded) colleagues would now be Goshen's president.

# ৵21৵

# Bender and the
# Concern Group

*Seven young Mennonites meet in Amsterdam.*
*Bender and the Concern group argue about*
*implications of the "Anabaptist Vision."*

THE DATE WAS July 19, 1957. Sitting in deck chairs aboard the *SS Saxonia*, Elizabeth and Harold Bender were enjoying a cool sea breeze. The ship was plowing through the North Atlantic one day out of Montreal, taking the couple to the sixth Mennonite World conference in Karlsruhe, Germany. It was a special day: Harold's sixtieth birthday. Elizabeth drew a brown paper-wrapped package from her handbag and handed it to him. "Harold, here is a little something for you." He assumed it was a birthday gift. It was, but the content of the package was a complete surprise. The "birthday gift" was the first copy of *The Recovery of the Anabaptist Vision*, a 360-page Festschrift, by Bender's colleagues and students in his honor. The book had been in gestation for half a decade.[1]

A Festschrift for Bender was one idea which had come out of a meeting of seven American Mennonites at Amsterdam in The Netherlands during the Easter season (April 14-25) of 1952. For two weeks the young men had worshiped and studied together, using the MCC center at Konigslaan 58 as their base. All but one had studied under Bender at some time, and all considered themselves his students. The oldest was 36. Now they were all in Europe, together for the first time. For a fortnight they reflected intensely on who they were and what they believed. Among their discoveries: that their worldview was centered squarely in Bender's Anabaptist Vision. The impulse to honor their mentor with a

Festschrift was thus a natural outcome of the meeting.[2]

Two of the men were missionaries under the MCs' board of missions: David Shank and A. Orley Swartzentruber. Shank was based in Brussels, Swartzentruber in Paris. Irvin Horst was MCC director in The Netherlands. John Howard Yoder worked for MCC in France and was a part-time student at the University of Basel. Calvin Redekop was director of MCC's new PAX program, which had American COs working at construction in Europe. John W. Miller was studying Old Testament at the University of Basel. Paul Peachey, previously MCC director in Germany, was a Ph.D. student at the University of Zurich under professor Fritz Blanke. Invited but unable to attend were Howard Charles, studying New Testament at Edinburgh; and G. Irvin Lehman, working for MCC in Greece.

During the first week, the group studied Dutch Mennonite his-

**The first meeting of the Concern group in Amsterdam in 1952. From the left: Irvin Horst, Orley Swartzentruber, John W. Miller, Paul Peachey, David Shank, John H. Yoder, Calvin W. Redekop.**
John H. Yoder papers, AMC.

tory. Each morning, after group worship, they walked from the MCC center to the Mennonite seminary, where Dutch historian N. van der Zijpp presented a series of lectures on the movement of Dutch Mennonites from radical Anabaptism to their twentieth-century Protestant orientation. Dutch Mennonite pastor Hendrik Meihuizen also lectured to the group several times. Each noon the seven returned to the MCC center for lunch. Then followed another history lecture, tea, more discussion, dinner, another lecture, tea, and bedtime. It was a strenuous regimen, which they interrupted with a weekend outing to the Menno Simons country in Friesland, staying with Dutch Mennonite families.

Back at Konigslaan for their second week, they provided their own resources for discussion and study. Paul Peachey led off with a paper on "The Decline of the West," analyzing what he saw as the collapse of "Christendom" in Europe. Other topics were communism, ecumenism, missionary strategy, and analyses of contemporary Mennonitism in Europe and America. Only one paper, John Howard Yoder's "The Anabaptist Dissent," focused specifically on Anabaptist history.[3]

The effect of the two-week seminar on the seven young men was electric. They had come together to sort out their beliefs and commitments. Being in postwar Europe made them acutely aware of how bankrupt European Christianity was. They were reassured that the Anabaptist rejection of conventional Protestantism had been correct. The problem was that working for MCC and living in Europe had also called into question the viability of the contemporary Mennonite church, on whose behalf they were serving.

By the end of the two weeks, they had come to suspect that what they called "neo-Anabaptism" (Bender's Anabaptist Vision) had become a justification for a Mennonitism which was quite deficient. It seemed irrelevant to the European situation; and it seemed to retard the necessary self-criticism the American Mennonite church needed if it was to deal with its own problems.

The seven found that they had adopted a critical posture vis-à-vis their Mennonite leaders not unlike that of the first Swiss Brethren to Zwingli. In a sense, they symbolically replicated the beginnings of the sixteenth-century Swiss Brethren, though not with rebaptisms and a communion service. They began to think of themselves as "a congregation of the Church of Christ, consciously responsible to Him."[4] Harold Bender, Orie O. Miller, and other church leaders began to seem almost Zwinglian—defenders of a religious status quo.

John Howard Yoder captured the mood of his fellows in a paper he wrote on the last day of the conference. While five of the men and their wives or girlfriends visited the Rijks Museum and Paul Peachey meditated in the Konigslaan garden, Yoder pecked away on a typewriter, summing up what he thought the group had learned. The result was "Reflections on the Irrelevance of certain Slogans to the historical Movements they represent. Or, the Cooking of the Anabaptist Goose, Or, Ye garnish the sepulchres of the righteous."[5]

In an attempt at humor, Yoder characterized the Amsterdam meeting as a "Martyrs' Synod." More tartly, he asserted that the effect of the Anabaptist Vision was not to "regain original anabaptism, but rather, with the use of anabaptism as a motto, to make possible a surprising degree of assimilation to surrounding culture."[6]

The 25-year-old's critique was relentless:

> The cultural peak of american mennonitism is represented by its colleges, where its youth is trained in art and music, literature and the good life, folk dancing and the collection of mennonitica. Its communities, instead of arising out of the city's disintegration, are consciously built in rural areas where life is simple and organization possible, not realizing that the city environment where they dare not go is the perfect picture of the moral collapse which the anabaptists took to be typical of the "world." Economically, they [the Mennonite community] are efficiently functioning units of the profit-motivated economy, with even its mission boards lending money at interest, a practice which would have sent Blaurock or Riedemann [two Anabaptist leaders] through the roof.
>
> The rapidity of this change of attitude, accomplishing in a few decades an assimilation which in Dutch mennonitism took well over a century, is thus all the more remarkable in view of the fact that it took place under the flag of the anabaptists, using the name of a people who thought themselves strangers and pilgrims, to motivate their descendants' settling down in the world for at least a long wait.[7]

The young men were convinced that Bender and his generation had created a "Corpus Mennoniticum" with little resemblance to the true Anabaptist vision. They were clearly calling much of Bender's lifework into question.

Yoder sent a copy of his report to Bender, who received it just two days before he and Elizabeth left for the 1952 Basel Mennonite World Conference. The heavily ironic tone of the paper gave Bender quite a shock. Paul Peachey reported that Bender was "perturbed" by the paper, a mood Irvin Horst observed when he met Harold and Elizabeth in London a few days after Harold had first read the paper. "He was extremely inquisitive about what we had done at Amsterdam," the irenic Horst reported to his comrades.[8]

•  •  •

The Amsterdam meeting of the seven young men ended on April 25, 1952. Six weeks later, on June 7, Harold and Elizabeth arrived in Amsterdam on their way to the world conference. The next week they attended a peace conference at Heerewegen, an MCC—Netherlands peace center. There Bender enthusiastically described an MCC plan to send one hundred young American Mennonite drafted COs to work in India under an American "Point IV" (U.S. foreign aid) program. He was surprised when there was nearly unanimous rejection of the idea by both the American MCCers and the Dutch attendees. Point IV, the critics pointed out to Bender, was a major American Cold War propaganda ploy; cooperation in it would hopelessly compromise the Mennonite peace witness and violate the Anabaptist understanding of church-state relationships. Bender had trouble appreciating their argument. The young MCCers had become more sectarian than their mentor.[9]

Even more symptomatic of the gulf between the young Americans in Europe and Bender and his generation was a meeting on August 7 in Basel. The younger group, especially the seven who had met for those two weeks at Amsterdam, eventually became known as "the Concern group," after the *Concern* series of pamphlets they began to publish, beginning in June 1954. At the 1952 Basel meeting, Calvin Redekop, John Howard Yoder, and Paul

Peachey represented the Concern group. For MCC were executive committee members Harold Bender, C. F. Klassen, H. A. Fast, Orie Miller, and C. N. Hostetter Jr., in Basel for the Mennonite World Conference the following week.

The meeting's purpose was to let the Concern men express their discontent with the way MCC administered its programs abroad. The gist of the complaints was that MCC executive committee members tried to manage everything "from the states and in quickie trips," with little chance for workers in Europe to participate in the decision-making. The Concern men thought the problem grew out of a hierarchical church structure, and that it showed how completely American Mennonite leaders had accepted a non-Anabaptist mode of organization management. The MCC executive committee had trouble understanding what the fuss was all about. So the meeting's effect was to widen the generation gap. As one Concern participant put it, "our observations were politely listened to, and politely forgotten."[10]

For the MCC executive committee, the meeting was painful. Their most talented young managers were challenging their taken-for-granted, two-decades-long way of working. Both the committee and the Concern group remembered the young men of 1919 whose challenges had run them afoul of their elders. "We have been accused of biting the hand that feeds us," John Yoder told Bender, "and [we have also been] compared to the young men who, after serving overseas under the Quakers, were no longer wanted in the (Old) Mennonite church."[11] No one, particularly Harold Bender or Orie Miller, wanted a repeat of that sad chapter in Mennonite history. Almost certainly that historical memory helped moderate the response of Bender's leadership group to the decade-long challenge which the Concern group brought to American Mennnonite church life in the 1950s.

The Concern group met two more times in Europe, once in Zurich in 1953 and again at Domburg, The Netherlands, in April 1954. Soon after the Domburg meeting, John H. Yoder tried to tell Bender how the Concern ideas had emerged. "Our reaction two years ago [at Amsterdam in 1952] was prompted by an unpleasant discovery," he explained. "We had come to believe that the Anabaptist Vision, New Testament Christianity, the Goshen enterprise, and the intentions of leaders of the "Mennonite Church" all pretty well coincided."[12] But, Yoder said, the Concern group had discovered that the four elements did not coincide:

> You have already denied having told us that the Mennonite church equals the anabaptist vision. In this form the denial is easy, but it does not change the fact that we had been led, some through CPS and some through Goshen, rather uniformly to this conclusion. Does your denial mean that in your work at Goshen for a Liberal Arts College, the Historical Library, and the *Quarterly Review*, the Bible School and Seminary, you have consciously been pursuing different aims than those of the Anabaptists or of the New Testament? We hesitate to believe this; at any rate you never told us this was the case. Be that as it may, it is in the name of the New Testament and anabaptist positions, as we understand them, that we feel obliged to express our doubts as to certain innovations in American Mennonitism.[13]

Yoder's analysis flabbergasted Bender: "John, what has happened!" he exclaimed.[14] In reply, Yoder minced no words. "What has happened to me is that in the process of growing up, I have put together an interest in anabaptism, which you gave me, an MCC experience to which you were instrumental in assigning me, and theological study to which you directed me, to come out with what is a more logical fruition of your own convictions than you yourself realize."[15] It was a biting assessment.

The tall, spare Yoder, with a mop of black hair and dark-rimmed glasses, was twenty-five years old when he attended the 1952 Amsterdam meeting. He had grown up in the Oak Grove congregation near Orrville, Ohio, in a family with many generations of Mennonite church leaders. His father, Howard Yoder, had served as MCC-Europe director right after the war. John had graduated from Goshen College in 1948 with a degree in liberal arts and immediately sought an appointment to MCC in Europe. Ever precocious, he was only twenty-one.

Orie Miller and Bender thought that John Howard Yoder was too young for a European assignment, but they were also eager to prepare the bright young man for church leadership. In August

1948, just back from Europe and in the middle of the week of busy world-conference activity at Goshen and Newton, Bender wrote Yoder a long letter. In it, Yoder's mentor urged him to consider a year of study at Goshen College Biblical Seminary before embarking for Europe. You need some "direct Bible work" and "a good basic course in Hebrew such as is required in all good seminaries such as Princeton," he told Yoder.[16] He also advised some advanced study of German and French as preparation for work in Europe.

Yoder was not eager to return to Goshen. He wanted to attend Wooster College near his home, to get some "religious philosophy with a humanist slant," he told Bender. In the spring of 1949, he hoped to attend Mennonite Biblical Seminary in Chicago for a semester. With youthful lack of guile, he told Bender that he thought he had gotten about all the Anabaptist content Goshen had to offer and that spending some time at MBS would let him hear what Donovan Smucker and Franklin Littell had to say on the subject. Plus, he said, "I'm not yet ecclesiastically inclined enough to want straight preacher-training courses like homiletics."[17]

Bender tried to dissuade Yoder. "I have high regard for Smucker and Littell. However, I am not sure that they have yet fully digested all the theology and history that they are now working on. You would profit much [more from ] . . . some contact with them a few years later than just now." What Bender really wanted was for Yoder to attend GCBS for one year to get a good grounding and then go to a European university.[18] As it turned out, Yoder spent the fall semester at Wooster and a few months at Goshen, then departed for Europe in March of 1949. Thus began a close but contentious teacher-mentor relationship. The relationship offers a window into the mind and purpose of Harold Bender during the last decade of his life.

• • •

When John Howard Yoder applied for MCC service, Bender had just returned from his year of MCC work in Europe. Bender believed there was a great opportunity for spiritual renewal among French Mennonites, especially among their young people. Yoder

**French bishop Hans Nussbaumer with Harold Bender at the Menno-nite World Conference at Karlsruhe in 1957.** Harold S. Bender papers, AMC.

became Bender's choice for such work. We are assigning you to France to do youth work and to give a peace testimony, Bender told Yoder. The idea was "a new sort of missionary work, one in which little has as yet been done, but which offers great opportunity for creative work."[19] It was a measure of the high regard Bender and Orie Miller had for Yoder that they would send such a youthful and inexperienced worker to such a difficult assignment.

In the late 1940s and the early 1950s, the French Mennonites were being split between a conservative majority and a group (primarily of young people) who sought a deeper, more expressive spiritual experience. A key part of Yoder's assignment was to help mediate the tensions between the two groups.

As Yoder soon discovered, mediation was not easy. It was complicated by the fact that the group dissatisfied with conventional French Mennonite piety was also, as Yoder told Bender, the most serious, the most ethical, the most biblical. They "want to form a pure New Testament *Gemeinde* [congregation]," Yoder reported.[20] With his characteristic logic, he posed the dilemma. "The [French] Mennonites aren't non-resistant, nor in most cases non-conformed except in the bad sense of being a closed group. . . . The dissatisfied are the ones most likely to be nonresistant, the least materialistic, the least complacent, [and] the most radical in their ethical commitment." That pattern, wrote Yoder, "puts me and MCC in an awkward position. Being Mennonite in our situation, we become somehow committed to defending Mennonitism here which isn't like ours, against an anti-Mennonitism which is in some senses more Anabaptist than the Mennonites."[21]

Yoder was especially critical of what he called "the lick-and-a-promise piety" of the leading French bishop, Hans Nussbaumer. Nussbaumer was one of Bender's best friends in Europe.[22] In 1923, while they were at Tübingen, Harold and Elizabeth had attended Nussbaumer's ordination, and Nussbaumer had become a warm supporter of the Mennonite World Conference. Now Bender found himself torn between Nussbaumer and Yoder. "I believe it is good for our own spiritual attitudes to be as gentle as possible in our witness as we try to help them," Bender admonished Yoder. "It is practically impossible in a short time to reconstruct lost group convictions."[23]

Acknowledging the problems, Bender tried to reassure his young protégé. Do not give up on the French Mennonite leaders, he told Yoder. Bender thought Yoder quite right in saying that

bishop Hans Nussbauamer was "excessively materialistic" and
that the bishop had some negative attitudes toward the new group.
Such attitudes had to change. "I will use my influence with Hans,"
Bender promised, "and insist he must integrate the group into the
life of the church and go ahead and saw wood."[24]

However, the dissatisfied members also would have to change
their attitudes, Bender insisted. They had to "love the church and
not just criticize it." To draw the two groups together, use "the
bridge of Anabaptism," Bender advised. Bring them together
around the spiritual and theological content of the original movement. Both groups need a "real anchorage in their own history."
Bender was sure the French Mennonites would find that "anchorage" only if they got help. How about a "modified form of the
'Anabaptist Vision' in translation?" he inquired.[25]

Sometime during the fall of 1950, Bender met John Yoder's father at a meeting and learned that John had begun studies at Basel
not in theology but in history and philosophy. Surprised, Bender
immediately wrote to Yoder, inquiring why he was not studying
theology. Yoder replied that actually, "apart from Jaspers on History of Christian Philosophy, I'm taking all theology." Then with
youthful nonchalance, he continued: "Being in that atmosphere
makes me feel like working on a theological *Vergegenwärtigung*
[fresh representation] of Anabaptism. . . . But it would take three
years." Yoder's view was that "from an Anabaptist point of view,
I'm not sure theology is worth that much . . . and three more years,
even though enjoyable, would hardly be justifiable if I don't plan
to be a theologian, which I don't."[26]

Now Bender was really worried. "I have often thought about
you and your further contribution to 'the Cause of Christ' and to
'Our Cause,' which I believe and hope are the same," he told
Yoder. "You may say you do not plan to be a theologian, but the
trouble is that you are one anyway. You always have been one and
you always will be. The only question is what kind of a theologian
you want to be. You do not have to be a theologian of the type of
any particular school of thought, but among the very few men
who have endowments and attitudes which enable them to be the
real theologians we need, you are one." Take the time to study,

Bender urged. Study at Zurich under Blanke, and do some work at Tübingen and Göttingen, and at Geneva—"if the Geneva faculty has some real *Christian* teachers." But get your degree from Basel, as it had the "best theological faculty in Europe." Bender mentioned a number of Basel's professors, although he failed to mention the star of the faculty, Karl Barth.[27]

Bender constantly recruited young men for the church, but he clearly sensed that Yoder had exceptional gifts and potential. "Dear John, whether you ever teach or not, or whether you ever preach or not, you can be a major servant of the cause of Christ in the Mennonite church and through the Mennonite church to the world if you are willing to be such a servant. I believe you can go through several years more of European theological study without being spoiled, and without losing your Anabaptist theology or your dedication to our cause. . . . Go right on," Bender urged Yoder. "I would be most happy to see you work on a 'theological *Vergegenwärtigung*' of Anabaptism." Bender concluded the letter with a benediction: "May you have heavenly guidance in your thinking and planning that you may find the place and the calling which has been appointed for you."[28]

Meanwhile in 1951 a budding romance developed between Yoder and a young French Mennonite, Annie Guth. Bender was overjoyed, but he wanted a direct report. "I would be happy to congratulate you," he wrote, ". . . but being a careful historian, I should have firsthand source evidence. What do you say?"[29]

Annie and John were married in 1952. In the fall they spent several months with the Yoder relatives in Wayne County, Ohio, and during the first week of November made a visit to Goshen. For Yoder the Goshen visit was a real eye-opener, after nearly four years in Europe. On a Saturday evening Bender invited some twenty-five faculty members to an informal meeting where Yoder talked about what Bender called "Mennonites and Culture." But Yoder thought most people came to get some firsthand report on the Concern meeting at Amsterdam the previous spring. Yoder refused to speak for the Concern group; but he rehearsed the sect-cycle theory, in which the sect is finally assimilated into the larger culture.[30]

"Only Sam Yoder [English professor Samuel A. Yoder] and

W. Smith [history professor Willard H. Smith] denied the sect trend," Yoder reported to David Shank in Brussels. Yoder had argued that administrative-minded leaders speed up the processes of assimilation, and spiritually minded leaders slow them down. The visit to Goshen confirmed Yoder's suspicion that Mennonite colleges speed up the assimilation process. As he told Shank, "Goshen can stimulate discipleship in individuals, just as a catholic school can, but only spontaneous revival could produce it in numbers and in intensity to enable a new sectarian beginning. We're simply afraid of a too-radical discipleship, and nothing else that organization or teaching can do will substitute for the Holy Spirit. If He comes, there'll be a brand new sect, but His coming is not likely to take place at Goshen, for there's not enough naiveté; the Brunks [tent revivalists] would come closer if their own concept of revival were more radical."[31]

Yoder met a few Goshen College students and decided "they will be much slower than the CPS generation to accept the twin (and irreconcilable) ideas of (a) discipleship as the anabaptist contribution to Christendom, and nonresistance and nonconformity as biblical; and (b) the Mennonite church as more progressive all the time, seen as a good thing."[32]

• • •

Early in 1953 John and Annie returned to Europe. By then the Amsterdam analysis which set early Anabaptism against the contemporary Mennonite church began to be tested. Part of the test was the extent to which Yoder and the others would agree to become part of the contemporary Mennonite enterprise. Bender was pressing Yoder to accept ordination so as to enhance his work among the French Mennonites. "Orie Miller and I are both convinced that you have the calling and gift for the preaching of the Gospel," Bender advised.[33] He wanted to recommend Yoder to the French Mennonite leaders. But Yoder demurred. The call would have to come from the French, he told Bender, not from MCC. And "I clearly have not for the moment a clear call to ordination," he protested. "Besides, I've been in MCC long enough, and I have my doubts about MCC ways of working."[34]

In 1952 Bender and Miller were searching for a way to bring Yoder and the Concern group into the church structures. Ordaining Yoder would be one way. Orley Swartzentruber, David Shank, and Paul Peachey were already ordained. From their side, the Concern group was not sure how to respond to the church leaders. Their hesitation came from a nagging discontent with their church, a discontent arising out of their European theological educations.

Influence from scholars like Karl Barth and Oscar Cullmann had led them to embrace a new biblical hermeneutic which took them back beyond Anabaptism to the New Testament church. The fresh understanding of the Bible provided them with a new prism through which to view both Anabaptism and contemporary Mennonitism. It also gave them powerful tools with which to critique contemporary Mennonitism. Their elders not only resisted the critique but also rejected the new theological base from which the Concern group drew their inspiration. Given their discontent with the contemporary Mennonite church, the Concern group was ambivalent about becoming part of the church's leadership cadre.

The Concern scholars generally drove their new insights in two directions. Skirting the inerrancy-infallibility issues of the fundamentalist-modernist debate, they emphasized the normative importance of the life of Jesus and the example of the New Testament church for Christian life and church practice. In 1954 John Yoder described their views to Bender. "You [Bender] see the New Testament patterns in no way normative unless there is an order given. We think the *forms* [emphasis added] of New Testament church and Christian practice are as important as the principles given in the Biblical text."[35] The effect of such an interpretive method was to emphasize the social, political, and cultural context of the New Testament narrative.[36] The second element was a new Christology emphasizing the agapeistic, or divine-love, quality of the atonement.

The emphasis on the New Testament forms and practices as normative for the contemporary church offered the Concern group a basis for criticizing current Mennonite church practice. The group emphasized a strong congregational base as a New Testament norm, compared to a more synodal model toward which they saw the Mennonite church evolving. They were especially critical of an emerging Protestant model for Mennonite pastors: one pastor for a congregation, salaried and seminary-trained. The group also had extended discussions about closed communion and the nurture of children.[37]

Actually the Concern group's concentration on the forms and practices of church polity was not unique. In the 1950s many Mennonites were preoccupied with changes underway in Mennonite church practice. In 1955 the Ministerial Committee of the MC Mennonite general conference sponsored an official study conference on "Church Organization and Administration." Three young men, Paul Peachey (teaching at Eastern Mennonite College), Howard Charles (teaching at Goshen College), and Harold Bauman (a pastor in Ohio) read prepared papers. Bishops John L. Horst, John E. Lapp, and Nelson Kauffman responded. Everyone recognized a significant increase in local congregational autonomy, and everyone expressed some discontent with the growing popularity of the salaried-pastor model of congregational leadership.[38]

In 1954 John Yoder wrote a paper in which he was critical of what he described as contemporary Mennonite congregational practice; he argued for normative New Testament congregationalism. Bender responded that Yoder was not up-to-date on what was happening in the United States and that he had misread the New Testament on church polity. There was a "strong anti-hierarchical and pro-brotherhood" movement afoot in Mennonite circles, Bender argued; a clear example was a new practice of electing lay delegates in some district conferences. He also cited what he called a "proliferation" of bishops, which had the effect of diminishing their authority. Another example was the growing popularity of church councils in Mennonite congregations, which, Bender told Yoder, were a modern counterpart of New Testament "elders." A growing practice of electing ministers rather than using the traditional lot also seemed to Bender to reflect greater lay participation. But, Bender argued, the New Testament pattern was not only congregational but also synodal and episcopal. "Who sold you on exclusive New Testament or Anabaptist congregationalism?" he demanded.[39]

Behind the argument about congregational forms was the issue of how to read the New Testament. The Concern group was trying, on the basis of new hermenuetical methods, to transcend the conventional reading of the New Testament in terms of principled (but legalistic) mandates and injunctions. How New Testament believers practiced their faith—the forms of church life—should also be binding on contemporary Christians, they insisted. Much of the argument between Bender and the Concern group on that issue had to do with how to understand the contemporary applications of New Testament practice. It was an important discussion which often left Bender defending a contemporary reality that the Concern group found unsatisfactory. Ironically, Bender felt the Concern group was frequently too legalistic in its interpretation of New Testament practice.

Bender responded more positively to the Concern group's new emphasis on Jesus as the key to understanding God's purposes in history. By April 1954 some of the original Concern seven, specifically Paul Peachey, Calvin Redekop, and John W. Miller, had returned to the United States. But a dozen American Mennonites working and studying in Europe, including John Yoder, David Shank, Orley Swarzentruber, and Irvin Horst of the original seven, met for a week in Domburg, The Netherlands, for a Concern-like seminar organized around the theme "Freedom . . . to Obey."[40]

John Yoder read a paper which served as the theological centerpiece for the seminar. Entitled "A Study in the Doctrine of the Work of Christ," the paper reflected a far-reaching new theological orientation. Yoder sought to answer a basic question: "Why did Christ have to die?" He began his answer by observing that the concept of discipleship could be as revolutionary in the twentieth century as it had been in the sixteenth. He linked discipleship with the theological work of the "neo-biblical" movement in theology, illustrated by an "Interpretation" group in the United States, and biblical scholars George Stewart and Oscar Cullmann in Europe. An exciting new perspective had developed on the meaning of the work of Christ, Yoder noted.[41]

That new theological perspective, Yoder told the group, was grounded in the Bible's insistence that humankind's fundamental condition was not depravity, but freedom. "When man [sic] faces God's command and can obey or disobey, he knows himself to be free," Yoder summarized the point. Thus God is the author of human freedom. Why did God create such radical freedom? Because, Yoder explained, God is agape, and agape respects the freedom of the beloved. The problem is that freedom also opens the door to disobedience, to sin. Sin is thus the human choice to turn away from God. So God's dilemma is how to save human beings while respecting their freedom. God, Yoder told his listeners, has chosen to be a nonresistant, noncoercive God, and his way is the way shown by Jesus, who lived in a world of sinners yet freely chose obedience to God and responded to sin without coercion. Jesus was the example of what God means human beings to become. His death on the cross revealed God's radical commitment to human freedom.[42]

Yoder explained that humans appropriate the "Work of Christ" through repentance and faith. "Repentance means ethics, not sorrow for sin: it is the turning-around of the will, which is the condition for obedience," Yoder insisted. To have faith is to identify with Christ's offering of himself in obedience to God. In other words, "faith means discipleship."[43]

However, Yoder continued, God's forgiveness does not mean annulment of our guilt, as in the ransom theory of atonement. Instead, forgiveness is the means to restore communion with God, which in turn offers the possibility of obedience to God's will. The work of Christ offers an opportunity for all humans to embrace God's purposes by restoring communion with God through obedience to his will. The cross is thus not a cure for human depravity but instead an opportunity to freely follow God's purposes. Discipleship is the mark of true repentance.[44]

In June 1954, Yoder sent a copy of the Domburg paper to John W. Miller at Goshen and urged him to circulate it for comment. By the time Bender left for Europe in July, he had read it, and sometime during the first week of August, he and Yoder discussed it at length. That encounter led Yoder to a new insight. Bender convinced me, Yoder told his Concern fellows, that a "modern (Old) Mennonite theology does not exist consciously and in a worked-out and doctrinally articulate way." The Concern group was the only group among Mennonites trying to forge a consistent and self-conscious theological blueprint, Bender told Yoder.[45] Bender's comment is interesting in light of the fact that John C. Wenger had just published a 400-page *Introduction to Theology*.[46]

In any case, Bender's affirmation greatly encouraged Yoder. We must continue to engage the Mennonite reality in dialogue, he told his Concern colleagues, but "we must adopt a teaching rather than a challenging mode."[47] Actually, the teaching mode had already begun: only a few months earlier, the first *Concern* pamphlet had been published. It featured Paul Peachey's and John Yoder's papers from the 1952 Amsterdam conference.

• • •

While recognizing the theological contributions the Concern group was making, Bender clearly remained ambivalent about it. His attitude showed in a reluctance to engage the movement in serious dialogue. In early 1955 the *Gospel Herald* published an article by John Yoder entitled "New Testament Conception of the Ministry," in which Yoder offered a critique of what he called the "salaried monarchical ministry."[48] In a letter to Yoder, Bender responded to the article with a brief defense of current Mennonite practice, arguing that the New Testament was not all that clear about the forms of ministry.[49] A few months later, Yoder and David Shank wrote a careful article entitled "Biblicism and the Church," which appeared as another *Concern* pamphlet.[50] Again Bender treated it rather lightly, jokingly calling Shank and Yoder "the Siamese twins."[51]

Yoder was insulted by what he took to be a refusal by Bender to take their work seriously, and he responded with sharp rebuke:

> What we criticize is not so much a polity as an evolution in polity; the most radical changes in present Mennonite polity are being made by present Mennonite leadership, with blithe disregard for the historical importance of the changes and often without going to the bother to advocate them strongly. It is that movement which ought to stand up and justify itself, not our advocacy of the NT pattern. When people whose only intention is to read and follow

the NT are told they are out of order, that is a pretty clear commentary on which way the Mennonite church is moving. Thirty years ago such an attempt would have been squashed by Daniel Kauffman, but he would at least have squashed it in the name of his idea of what is biblical; now we are declared out of place because the subject we are discussing is one for which the Bible doesn't matter.

It would have been helpful if you had let us know just where you think we got off the track. You have been kept fully informed on all of our thinking since the group first met, more faithfully than we have informed anyone else in the Church. Your reaction has been occasionally a caricature, occasionally a quibble about terms, but never a positive help to a better solution of the problems we have been struggling with. Since we are simply trying to be faithful to the vision of discipleship which most of us got from you, this has sometimes been disappointing, but we know that the main reason is that you are simply too busy.[52]

Stung by Yoder's criticism, Bender responded immediately with one of the longest letters he ever wrote. He admitted the truth of Yoder's observation that he had been too busy to take up the dialogue in depth, but basically denied all the other accusations. His real problem with the Concern group, he told Yoder, was that they were helping what Bender called "fringe men and movements who are beginning to open up vistas of individualistic action and constitute a disintegrating threat."[53] Just who those "men and movements" were he did not explain, nor did he identify what he meant by "disintegrating threats."

Bender criticized what he believed was a Concern-group preoccupation with church polity when the more important issues were in faith and ethics. He was also critical of what he called their "exegetical practices": their insistence that both New Testament injunctions and New Testament believers' behavior and practice be considered normative for contemporary Christians. He found their preoccupation with the "forms" of New Testament polity misplaced. Most of all, he was unhappy with their criticism of MC Mennonite church structure. He thought they made far too much of congregationalism. Do you want us to go the route of the GCs and the Old Order Amish? he demanded.[54]

Such was the discussion in mid-1955. In a 1956 *Concern* pamphlet, that issue—congregationalism—took a new turn, moving from theory to practice: C. Norman Kraus and John W. Miller developed the idea of the house church as the locus of faith and practice. Matthew 18:20 was a key text: "For where two or three come together in my name, there am I with them." They argued for a radical new understanding of the role of intimate fellowship groups in the lives of believers. Fellowship groups, Kraus and Miller proposed, would become hermeneutical communities, helping their members discern the will of God. Sometime during 1956, a few at Goshen began to meet in such a group.[55]

That development made Bender uneasy, and he eagerly sought to find out how they conducted themselves. He was nettled by their informality. They take off their shoes, they put their feet on the coffee table, and some of them sit on the floor, he complained. He found their behavior pretty undignified. And worse than being undignified, the house church began holding communion. Bender was quite upset.[56]

As for the Concern group's challenges, Bender's response remained ambivalent. He always had a high regard for new ideas—a vestige, no doubt, of his "old Goshen" liberal arts education. Moreover, in the 1950s the Concern group was a main conduit through which Bender learned about new theological currents. Located as they were at some major academic centers where new theological work was underway, Bender's unusually gifted students offered him a close-up view of contemporary theology. The new ideas were stimulating and interesting to Bender, yet worrisome from his churchmanly perspective.

The dialogue between Bender and the Concern group in fact ran two ways: the Concern group benefited greatly from the orientation Bender had given them in Anabaptist history. Anabaptism and Bender's "Anabaptist Vision" interpretation of it offered them an unusually powerful lens through which to clarify their new theological learnings. In 1957 Paul Peachey, en route to an MCC Peace Section assignment in Japan, made that very point. "We are more indebted to you than to any other man," he told Bender. "Our basic premise and point of departure was simply the Anabaptist Vision. We have never tried to revise the Vision, but have always said that if the Vision is true, then this and this must follow. The Festschrift [*The Recovery of the Anabaptist Vision*] is an expression of our esteem and appreciation," Peachey told Bender, "and a symbol of our determination to stake our existence on the Anabaptist way of life."[57] Bender could hardly have hoped for more.

Nevertheless, Bender had not only given the Concern group a historical framework: he also was a major leader in a contemporary church whose failings the Concern group was so vigorously critiquing. And therein lay much of the tension between Bender and his protégés. By the 1950s Bender had nearly perfected the art of handling criticism from conservatives who sought to preserve the status quo in the face of change. The Concern group presented a quite different challenge. Unlike the conservatives, Concern *wanted* to change the status quo, and sought to do so by combining Bender's Anabaptist Vision with contemporary hermenuetical, salvation-history, and christological theologies. The result was a critique of conventional Mennonite piety and practice from a dramatically new angle. It was a critique that Bender found it difficult to deal with.

Bender's brilliant young protégés nearly always attacked the status quo from a perfectionist, ideal-type perspective. They could do so because for the most part they were not saddled with the burdens of practical church leadership. Thus Bender found himself caught between the cogent theological and historical analyses of his students, which he found attractive, and their critique of his church, which he often found idealistic and wrongheaded. The result was an asymmetrical argument which Bender, the responsible churchman, could almost never win.

The Concern-group encounter with Bender and the Mennonite church was one of the most creative events in Mennonite history. Both Concern and Bender got it about right. The Mennonite church needed revitalization, which the Concern movement believed could come only from a new theological paradigm. They offered a paradigm grounded in a nonresistant God, whose purposes were embodied in the life and death of Jesus Christ. Bender, more clearly than the Concern group, understood the ambiguous nature of the church's struggle to embody transcendence while caught in the web of history. He also was impatient with the imperfection of the church, but he dealt with the resultant ambiguity in a manner other than theologically: he maintained a nearly complete devotion to the nurture and care of the church.

At the center of the argument between Bender and the Concern group was the issue of how completely and in what manner the church might embody the will of God. In July 1962, less than two months before his death, as Bender convalesced from cancer surgery, he received a letter from Heinz Kloppenburg, a German Lutheran churchman who had participated during the 1950s in a series of peace-theology conferences with Bender and John Yoder. Usually both Bender and Yoder had read papers at the conferences. Because of his illness, Bender had missed the most recent gathering, and Kloppenburg was reporting on it. "As usual John Yoder was brilliant," Kloppenburg observed, "but I always have the feeling that it needs at least the two of you to represent your church."[58] In the 1950s Harold Bender and John Howard Yoder embodied the dilemma, but left it unresolved. The dilemma lay in the limits of Christian perfection.

# ✧22✧

# MCC and Peace Dialogue

*Bender and his colleagues struggle to clarify MCC's role in the 1950s. Visiting the Soviet Union. Ecumenical peace dialogue.*

By 1951 C. F. Klassen had become a near-legendary figure in the Mennonite world. Among the last Mennonites to escape to Canada from the Soviet Union in 1928, he had spent many years collecting the debts the Russian Mennonite immigrants of the 1920s owed the Canadian government for moneys advanced to help them come to Canada. Despite the doleful character of his assignment, his persistence and benevolent policies had established him as a paragon of integrity. By World War II, he was the best-known Mennonite in Canada. Now, by 1951, he had spent six years directing an MCC refugee relief operation which had moved many thousands of World War II Mennonite refugees to Canada and South America. A tall, broad-shouldered man who typically wore well-tailored double-breasted suits and a fedora hat, Klassen cut an impressive figure; he also exuded boundless energy, warm piety, and good common sense.[1]

In early September 1951, Klassen had returned to the United States from Europe to attend the MCC executive committee meeting in Chicago. Afterward, on a long train ride from Chicago to his home in Abottsford, British Columbia, he had felt a new sensation. "I have never returned from an M.C.C. meeting—so downhearted is not the correct expression—dissatisfied is also not quite what I want to say—with such mixed feelings as from our last meeting," Klassen told Orie Miller. "I have observed that the unity and purpose and the joy in giving for MCC work that prevailed for so many years have gone to some extent. This worries me very much."[2]

What had gone wrong? For two decades the executive committee of Mennonite Central Committee had operated the organization with remarkable success. Orie Miller, P. C. Hiebert, H. A. Fast, and Harold Bender were joined on the committee in 1944 by C. F. Klassen. In 1948 and 1950 two newcomers were added: J. J. Thiessen of Canada (a GC Mennonite), and C. N. Hostetter Jr. (of the Brethren in Christ). Hostetter was president of Messiah College in Grantham, Pennsylvania. The expanded committee had led MCC through the breathtaking growth and global relief work of the immediate post-World War II era. But by the 1950s, MCC affairs seemed not to be going so well.

MCC was changing. The amiable P. C. Hiebert from Tabor, Kansas, with his Mennonite Brethren (MB) piety, had been chair of MCC since its beginning in 1920. In 1953 he retired and Hostetter became chair even though he was the newest member of the executive committee. His election was rather unusual. The two obvious candidates were Bender and H. A. Fast, who was vice-

The executive committee of the Mennonite Central Committee in 1951. Front row: Orie O. Miller, Peter C. Hiebert, John J. Thiessen. Back row: Henry A. Fast, Cornelius F. Klassen, Harold S. Bender, C. N. Hostetter. MCC Collection, AMC.

chair. Fast might have expected to succeed Hiebert except that both MC Mennonite and MB sentiment would have opposed him. As the next-longest-serving member after Orie Miller, Bender might have seemed the logical choice, but the members of MCC would not have agreed to have both an MC chairman and an MC executive secretary. C. F. Klassen's refugee work was too important for him to become chairman. So Hostetter became the compromise choice. Although an able administrator and a competent churchman, he lacked the weight of P. C. Hiebert.[3] Hiebert's Mennonite Brethren were the Mennonite group most lukewarm about MCC, but having him as chairman had kept the MBs connected to MCC. With his departure their support, especially in Canada, soon evaporated.

Hiebert had embodied MCC and had often been able to resolve differences simply by the warmth and generosity of his spirit. With "P. C." gone, the mix changed. H. A. Fast and Bender both had take-charge personalities and sometimes clashed. Also, by the mid-1950s, differences began creeping into the relationship between Bender and Orie Miller. Bender complained about Miller's "intuitive-snap judgments" and his habit of "throwing his weight around."[4] Hostetter confided to his diary that he was quite annoyed with the Miller-Bender "feud." "It seems," he wrote, "as tho Harold is supercritical of Orie except when someone from the G.C. attacks Orie, then Harold is there to defend him."

In one case when the two men's differences paralyzed executive committee action, Hostetter recorded, "I very frankly counseled him [Bender] about his struggle for power with Orie Miller. He received it kindly." But several weeks later, Bender had some second thoughts. "There is no feud between Orie Miller and myself, at least as far as I am concerned, and there never will be," he insisted to Hostetter. He admitted that he and Orie were not as close as they had once been, but he was sure the relationship had not deteriorated into a feud.[5]

While some of the problems were clearly personal, much of the stress and strain was due to the big ship MCC had become. In the six years since 1946, MCC had become the largest and most complex Mennonite organization in the world. In simpler times the executive committee, meeting monthly, had made virtually all administrative decisions—and Orie Miller, as executive secretary, had put the directives into effect. Now underlings were making more and more of the decisions. In effect, there was a new order, with Miller more in the role of a CEO and the executive committee increasingly advisory. Bender found it hard to adjust. He frequently indulged in Monday-morning quarterbacking, even to the point of criticizing travel itineraries of second-level managers. Such interference evoked more than a few hard feelings.

As executive secretary, an executor for a working committee rather than an actual CEO, Orie Miller often found himself in the line of criticism. In 1954, after Miller had made one of his trips, this time to visit MCC units in Europe, Bender told him that MCC workers were quite unhappy with his (Miller's) leadership. They had three main complaints, Bender told Miller: "(1) You are just too busy and the work has to suffer from [your] lack of firsthand information. (2) You have made up your mind in advance and do not really want or need their counsel. (3) They [feel that their insights are counted as] probably not too important anyway and so suppress their deeper concerns."[6]

Bender's candor, coming at almost the same time as Orie Miller's disenchantment with Bender during the Goshen College presidential election process, must have been hard for Orie Miller to take. It certainly did not help improve their relationship. Moreover, C. F. Klassen, who had always supported Miller, was also objecting that Miller dictated MCC policy. A growing testiness among executive committee members had became almost palpable.[7]

Compounding such problems in the early 1950s was a sharp decline in financial support. From a high of almost four million dollars in total contributions in 1947, the annual figure had dropped to only about one million by 1950.[8] Several factors were at work. One was a loss of confidence in MCC by Canadians. At the annual MCC meeting held in January 1951, almost no Canadian MCC members attended. Bender was alarmed that their absence came hand-in-hand with a drop in the contributions. "As you know, they did not contribute to the MCC relief program in 1950-1951," he told Orie Miller. Bender believed the Canadians had boycotted the meeting to show their discontent with the way MCC was allocating its relief budget.[9]

The Canadians wanted more money for the Mennonite refugees in Paraguay. C. F. Klassen complained to Bender that when Canadian leaders looked over the MCC budget, they saw as much being "allocated for the MCC headquarters staff in Basel as is budgeted for the Paraguayan Mennonites. . . . When they see that, they think something is radically wrong."[10] Nor were the Canadians enthused about new worldwide relief efforts in Asia and Africa which Orie Miller favored. Klassen told Miller that "understanding men" did not think MCC finances would support "spreading out too far."[11]

Canadians also expressed widespread discontent with the new Voluntary Service program MCC was developing. "And I agree with them," Klassen told Bender. "There is great danger that some of our workers stress the historical side of Mennonitism and forget the main thing, which is the emphasis on a personal commitment to Christ." Klassen's words echoed a traditional dichotomy between "evangelism" and "social gospel." Similarly, B. B. Janz, the revered Mennonite Brethren leader in Canada, opposed VS because he saw it as a humanitarian rather than a genuinely evangelical witness. Janz had helped lead the 1920s exodus from the Soviet Union and had a large following. His opinions carried weight. As for Klassen, he insisted that the only way to change the climate of opinion was for "Orie Miller to make a trip to Canada to listen to Canadian concerns and to explain MCC policy."[12]

Aggravating the decline in Canadian support was a parallel decline in U.S. giving. Bender was quite upset to learn that for 1951 the MC Mennonite church was planning to cut its previous monthly contribution of $50,000 in half. By early 1951 the cash-flow problems at Akron were chronic. At one point MCC treasurer Ura Gingerich had to stop payment on some bills because there simply was no cash. He informed Bender that on some fields, relief workers were borrowing money to keep their units going. Gingerich himself had borrowed some relief funds to keep the VS program afloat, but now in early 1951, the relief funds were depleted too.[13]

Bender reported all of this to Orie Miller as Miller traveled in

South America. He hoped his letter did "not sound too discouraging." For himself, he wrote, "I am not downcast, and will work as hard as ever to promote the good cause that MCC represents."[14] Actually, Bender was extremely worried. He published an impassioned piece in the *Gospel Herald* entitled "Our Relief Program in Danger." We are more prosperous than we have ever been, and yet our giving is lower than it has been in ten years, he told his readers alarmingly. "Brethren, this ought not so to be!"[15]

Unfortunately, the financial picture did not improve much during the next several years. In 1954 Bender wrote another *Gospel Herald* article deploring the continued decline: "Shall We Continue Our Relief Work, Voluntary Service, and I-W Service?" He argued that the service work of the church was absolutely essential to the church's evangelizing program.[16]

The Canadian and the financial problems underlined a more basic issue facing MCC in the early 1950s: how to shift from the postwar relief focus on Europe to a mixed program which deployed relief and voluntary service to many parts of the world. The shift was not easy. Bender had his own notion of how it should be done. "We must hang on to our growing fellowship with the young Mennonite church in Java, and we must continue in some form of fellowship with the Mennonites of France, Germany, Holland, and Switzerland, and we must keep a relief foothold in Europe, whatever comes, but we may have to retreat on other fronts. We must also strengthen the unity among our groups in North America. All this I believe can be done even on a reduced financial program."[17]

In 1952, brushing aside C. F. Klassen's suggestion that Orie Miller visit Canada, Bender urged Klassen to come home from Europe and spend a month visiting Canadian leaders and centers. Then Klassen might attend the March executive committee meeting to report on his findings and help the committee plan how to recover lost ground in Canada. Come home via Goshen "for a day so that we can review things completely," Bender urged.[18]

Bender wanted Klassen in North America for another reason as well. In January 1951 the Mennonite Brethren Welfare Committee had endorsed noncombatant medical corps service in the army for Mennonite Brethren conscientious objectors. "I have a first-hand report from B. B. Janz," Bender told Klassen. "Nothing has happened for a long time to give me such a heavy heart. It is of course the privilege of your conference to do this, but to do it without a thorough consultation with the rest of us disappoints me very much. No Mennonite group has ever taken this step without ultimately losing nonresistance." Bender hoped Klassen, an MB, would remonstrate with MB leaders and get the decision reversed.[19]

On the broad issue of MCC's future direction, Bender had been somewhat lukewarm about the new work MCC was opening in various parts of the world, work urged forward by Orie Miller. Miller had traveled continually across the globe since 1945, and he had a much better understanding of world needs than did Bender. Bender's focus had been almost entirely on Mennonites in Europe and America.

In any case the executive committee needed to redefine MCC's role in Europe. Paul Peachey had laid out the issues for Bender. Material aid needs in Europe had largely been met, Peachey analyzed, yet MCC continued "to work with the material aid organizational philosophy. This means a rapidly revolving staff of young volunteers without adequate long-range strategic talent at the top in Europe." What Peachey wanted was an "Erland Waltner or a J. C. Wenger" who could be in Europe for ten years and shape new programs to Europe's needs and MCC's capabilities. Such a strategic leader, Peachey argued, "would sense when an evangelist would be needed, when a teacher would be needed, [and] when the social service aspects of the program should be expanded or contracted. If we can't find such a person, our program in Europe will die a slow death." Then Peachey raised a practical issue agitating Europe-based MCC directors: whether to close the Basel headquarters and move MCC's administrative center to Frankfurt, Germany. C. F. Klassen preferred Frankfurt. Peachey and Bender favored Basel.[20]

Bender had Orie Miller's backing for the Basel center, and when H. A. Fast became MCC—Europe director in 1951, he also concurred. So Klassen, backed by the Canadians, lost the argument. For Bender and Miller, the Basel MCC center was a long-term dream they had developed in the late 1930s. Their idea had been to create a place from which American Mennonites might help their south-German and Swiss brothers and sisters recover their biblical and Anabaptist convictions. In fact, they had planned that the Orie Miller family would go to Basel in 1940 to live for a year and get the center established. The Benders would then take over during Bender's sabbatical in 1941. But the war had intervened, and not until 1946 did the dream became more real with the purchase of the Arnold Böklinstrasse house. To give up the dream in the 1950s was nearly unthinkable.

However, Bender couched his argument for Basel in Cold War terms. "It would be next to folly to move our MCC headquarters and financial resources into an occupied country [Germany] where there is a very real danger of war," he told Klassen. The executive committee had even asked Klassen and Peachey to make evacuation plans for MCC workers in Germany in case the Soviets invaded. Under the circumstances, Basel, located in neutral Switzerland, was much the better place for MCC headquarters, Bender insisted.[21]

Actually, by the late 1950s, Bender's Cold War concerns had disappeared and he had accepted an idea of Peter Dyck. As MCC's new director for Europe, Dyck proposed to combine the MCC administrative headquarters with a European Mennonite conference center—all at Frankfurt.[22] But in the early 1950s, Basel was still the center of Bender's and Miller's dream. A further reason was that Basel was the location of another of their emerging programs: a new Bible school.

The idea of a European Mennonite Bible school was born in Harold Bender's mind during his MCC term in Europe in 1947-48. The plan took root when Atlee Beechy, the MCC director at Basel in 1949, reported that three Swiss leaders had asked MCC to help them establish such a school. They and Beechy cited the fact that the Langnau Mennonite congregation in the Emmental had just established an affiliation with the Swiss state church (albeit also keeping its Mennonite ties). The Langnau action, coming from the oldest Mennonite congregation in the world, seemed to signal an urgency for more direct efforts to enhance European Mennonites' commitments to Mennonite faith and practice.[23]

**Bienenberg, the campus of the European Mennonite Bible School, near Basel, Switzerland, 1950s.** AMC.

Bender spent the summer of 1949 in Europe, including some time in Basel for a meeting of the Mennonite World Conference Preparatory Commission on August 15. He persuaded that group to spend half a day discussing the Bible school question. Significantly, Hans Rufenacht, the pastor of the problematic Langnau congregation, served as the meeting's secretary. Bender was chairman. The group agreed that a Bible school should get underway and that it should have a dual focus: to educate young people and train church workers, and to be thoroughly Mennonite. Each of five Mennonite conferences—French, Alsatian, Palatinate, Swiss, and south-German—would assign two delegates to meet in 1950 to organize a board for the school. That committee met for the first time on March 20, 1950. Bender's friend the French bishop Hans Nussbaumer was elected chairman. The board was to include representatives from the conferences and two American MCC persons, one of them C. F. Klassen.

In February, six weeks before the Bible School Committee met for the first time, Bender laid out an operating plan for 1950-51. He proposed holding short-term schools at four locations: Basel,

Belfort, Thomashof, and Hamburg. MCC would provide a teacher who would travel to all of the locations. Bender also set forth some ideas about what should be taught and how to form the organization.

Paul Peachey eloquently expressed Bender's point of view when he observed that MCC should be what Bender once called a "catalytic agent." In another metaphor, the MCC would help create an "anvil" on which to shape Mennonite beliefs. Above all else, European Mennonites needed a "faith in their own mission," Peachey told Bender. Americans could help with money and with teachers.[24] Orie Miller weighed in with assurances that the money would be forthcoming. Establish a reasonable budget, he told Guy F. Hershberger, who was spending the year at Basel as an MCC Peace Section missioner; if the budget fell short, Miller and others would cover the deficit.[25]

From November to mid-December 1950, the school met in Basel at the MCC house with twenty-eight students and five teachers (a Swiss, a German, an American, a Canadian, and a Frenchman). Peachey, who doubled as one of the teachers, declared it "highly successful." Bender's primary contribution was to recruit Cornelius Wall to become the "dean" of the school. An MB from Mountain Lake, Minnesota, Wall had gone to Europe in 1948 and worked for MCC at Gronau, West Germany. He had quickly established himself as a gifted Bible teacher with a warm evangelical pietism which had a special appeal for German-speaking Mennonites. By 1952 the Walls were back in North America, where Wall taught at the MB Bible college in Winnipeg. But Bender persuaded them to return to Europe. Perhaps more than anyone else, Wall helped move the European Bible School forward.[26]

In 1955 the Europeans installed the school in an old hotel restaurant on a hill above the town of Liestal, a few kilometers southeast of Basel. A Swiss Jura pastor, Samuel Gerber, succeeded Cornelius Wall and became the school's principal. Enrollment had climbed to seventy students per term, and the length of the school year had been greatly extended. Of all of MCC's post-World War II European undertakings, the European Mennonite Bible School was one of the most significant institutions MCC left in its wake.

From Bender's vantage point, the MCC program in the 1950s never achieved the élan of the post-World War II decade. C. F. Klassen died in 1954 after becoming director of MCC—Europe in 1953, and to Bender his death seemed an ominous portent. The main ally who shared his view of MCC's role was gone.[27]

In 1956 Orie Miller announced that by 1958 he would retire as MCC's executive secretary. His successor was Miller's understudy, William T. Snyder, a GC Mennonite. Thereupon Bender became the senior executive committee member. Though only sixty years old in 1957, he was beginning to feel the weight of age. MCC was changing rapidly, and Bender was struggling to keep up.[28]

• • •

At eight o'clock on the morning of October 27, 1956, Bender and an MB pastor, David Wiens, were enjoying a sumptuous breakfast of ham and eggs and all the trimmings. Their travel-weary bodies needed the substantial fare: they had arrived at the Hotel National in Moscow only six hours earlier, at 2:00 a.m. Now they ate hurriedly. Soon a knock on the door announced the arrival of Alexander Karev, one of the pastors of Moscow's large Baptist church. With Karev was a young woman, an Intourist guide and translator for their three-week sojourn in the Soviet Union.[29] The two North Americans were visiting the Soviet Union to make contacts with remnants of Mennonite churches scattered throughout the huge country.

In 1955, while visiting the Selly Oaks Quaker center in England, Bender had met Karev Jacob Zhidkov, executive secretary and president of the All-Union Council of Evangelical Christian Baptists. The Baptist officials had encouraged Bender to visit the Soviet Union.[30] A few weeks later, Bender learned that a delegation of British and American Baptists had actually made such a visit.

Bender immediately proposed that the Soviet Union should receive a similar visit from Mennonites, an idea which the MCC executive committee enthusiastically endorsed. Bender (MC), Wiens (MB), and Henry M. Epp (GC) were to be the delegation. Unfortunately, to get visas for the trip proved a daunting problem; eventually only Bender and Wiens could go. Bender went in his role as the ranking world Mennonite: president of Mennonite World Conference, secretary of MCC, and dean of GCBS. David Wiens, who spoke Russian, went as a representative of the Russian Mennonites in North America.[31]

Thus on a blustery Saturday morning, Bender and Wiens found themselves in Moscow, probably among the first North American Mennonites to visit the Soviet Union since Bender's visit in 1929. They had laid out an ambitious, monthlong itinerary. But despite a good-faith effort by the Canadian, German, and American embassies, they accomplished almost nothing on their itinerary. In 1955 the Soviet Union was still a very closed country, with severe restrictions on travel by foreigners. Eventually they were allowed to travel to Kiev, and to Samarkand, Tashkent, and Alma Ata in the central Asian part of the Soviet Union. By sending telegraph messages to Mennonites whose addresses they had, they were able to meet a handful of Mennonites who came to their hotels to see them. Thus they gleaned some information about the life and faith of Mennonites in that part of the Soviet Union. But Bender was deeply frustrated that a long trip to the East (eighteen hours by air, one way) netted them many long hours visiting factories and collective farms but few contacts with Mennonites.[32]

Bender's and Wien's visit no doubt sent Soviet Mennonites a signal of brotherly concern from North Americans. Unfortunately, Bender understood his role more for advocating religious freedom for Soviet Mennonites than performing spiritual ministry. Somewhat unwisely, at least in restrospect, Bender wrote a letter to the agency for religious cults, appealing for recognition of Mennonites as a religious body. That step put the safety of Soviet Mennonites at serious risk. In fact, several Mennonites who came to see Wiens and Bender were imprisoned soon after their departure.[33]

Much too optimistic, Bender tried to use the trip to open the door for more reciprocal visits. He invited the All-Union Council of Evangelical Christians to send a delegation to the next Mennonite World Conference, to be held in Karlsruhe, Germany, in 1957; and he immediately began plans for a return visit of European and North American Mennonites to the Soviet Union following the

World Conference at Karlsruhe.[34] Bender had too little understanding of the context in which Soviet Mennonites lived. In retrospect, it is clear that he badly underestimated the difficulties of
opening a channel into the Soviet Union.

• • •

Early 1950 was a time of foreboding in the Western world. Bender
expected war in Europe. "I am much concerned about the world
situation," he told Cornelius Krahn. "It seems to me likely that the
present conflict will develop into full-scale war with Russia."[35] What
made the prospect all the more frightening was the presence of atom-
ic weapons on both sides: in 1949 the Soviets had gotten the bomb.

The Cold War had begun soon after the Second World War
ended, but in early 1950 no one knew just what violence would
come of it. On June 25 such violence became all too real: a jittery
world watched as the North Korean army invaded South Korea.
Within a week American troops were in battle. President Harry
Truman signed an extension of the draft law.

In 1950 Bender was chairman of the MCC Peace Section, as
he had been since its beginning in World War II. Now, as South
Korean and American troops retreated southward in Korea, he
called on the Peace Section members "to be on a high alert." To
review the draft situation and other matters, he was calling a meeting of the main Mennonite groups. Their representatives would
gather at MCC headquarters at Akron on July 21.[36]

The Mennonites of 1950 found themselves in an unprecedented situation with regard to the draft: the law simply deferred all
conscientious objectors who based their objection on belief in a
"Supreme Being." The big question was whether public opinion
would tolerate such leniency for COs once the nation was in a
shooting war with high draft calls. On that point, Bender was pessimistic. Soon draft calls jumped from 20,000 in September 1950
to 80,000 in March 1951. By September 1951 total inductions had
reached 700,000.[37] Meanwhile, the National Council of Churches'
*News Notes* observed that criticism of conscientious objectors was
growing.[38] The Selective Service, always edgy about public sentiment, reported incidents in which patriotic citizens had painted the

barns of COs and "treated [them] shamefully in public places."[39] In January 1951 the entire draft board in Pondera County, Montana, resigned to protest the deferment of Hutterite COs.[40]

Nevertheless, when the draft law came up for renewal in early 1951, it still was not clear that the Congress and the president would end the CO deferment. Testifying before the Senate Armed Services Committee on a blustery Monday in late January, Bender urged the lawmakers simply to continue the "present provisions affecting COs." He assured Albert Gaeddert, a GC member on the Peace Section, that "the chairman, Senator Lyndon Johnson of Texas, had said that neither the Committee nor the Department of Defense was proposing any change" in the CO provisions. But Bender was uneasy. Even if CO deferment continues in this new draft law, "we should advise all our young men of draft age to volunteer," he told Gaeddert. Worried about public opinion, Bender hoped that by volunteering, the Mennonite youths could demonstrate their sincerity and loyalty.[41]

After the testimony in Washington, Bender and Harold Sherk, newly installed as executive secretary of the MCC Peace Section, caught a train to Baltimore to attend a meeting of the National Service Board for Religious Objectors. That group was working on an alternative service plan in case deferment was lost. The program, the group decided, should be civilian-administered; offer government, church, and humanitarian work opportunities; be remunerated; limit service to the same length as the military; and give complete exemption to those absolutists who would neither register nor serve.[42] The Baltimore meeting was timely: when the final bill reached the president's desk for signing, the CO deferment was gone. In its place was a provision for drafting COs to perform "civilian work contributing to the maintenance of the national health, safety and interest."[43]

A clause in the new law established a National Security Training Commission. Alarmed that standard military training had been much too slow for the Korean War emergency, the commission proposed that Congress enact a Universal Military Training (UMT) program in which all men of draft age would have to undergo six months of training. The commission assumed that more

Korea-like "police actions" would erupt throughout the world as the Cold War continued.[44]

Like many other persons, pacifist and nonpacifist, Bender feared that UMT would militarize the male population, much as had happened in Europe. At a meeting of the MC Mennonite church's general council in December 1951, he proposed that the council authorize him, as chair of the church's Peace Problems Committee, to request all MC ministers to write letters to their Congressmen, expressing opposition to the proposed law. Somewhat to his surprise, the Council agreed. Within a few days, Bender sent sample letters to each minister, listing their Congressman and Senators and urging them to write.[45]

To Bender's great relief, the UMT provision failed to pass, for whatever reason, but the new draft law did require alternative service. At issue was the form it would take. The Historic Peace Churches and Selective Service agreed on one main point: they did not want a repeat of the CPS program of World War II. When U.S. President Harry Truman finally signed Executive Order 10238 in February 1952, the new program it embodied was about what Bender had hoped for. The program was soon called I-W, the draft classification under which men in alternative service worked. Under it, COs would work in government or nonprofit organizations engaged in charitable, health, welfare, education, and scientific work. They might work as volunteers, or they could earn wages, depending on the job. If they took the initiative, they could choose their service jobs, including service abroad. The Mennonites were happy with the program.[46]

The Friends, however, decided not to cooperate with the government. Thomas Botts explained their position: "The Mennonites are willing to work with any program that will allow them to keep control of their own conscientious objectors, and they are willing to adhere to Selective Service regulations because of this. Our position is more of opposition to military purposes, and of unwillingness to be a party to the success of the conscription operation."[47] In the 1950s most MC Mennonites, especially Harold Bender, did not agree with the Friends. Bender did not believe the church should contest the right of the government to conscript its young men.

However, even among MC Mennonites, some were leaning more toward the Friends' position. In 1959 Bender and young Edgar Metzler had a remarkable exchange of opinion in the *Gospel Herald* regarding cooperation with the draft system. Metzler (son of A. J. Metzler, chief officer of the Mennonite Publishing House) had just become pastor of First Mennonite Church in Kitchener, Ontario. Before that he had served in Washington as a Mennonite staffer at the National Service Board for Religious Objectors. He was also a member of Bender's Peace Problems Committee. So he had firsthand knowledge and experience regarding the draft system. To Bender's dismay, editor Paul Erb published a front-page article by Metzler, arguing that Mennonite COs should refuse to register as the draft law required, because registering was the first act of cooperation with a militaristic system. Metzler was convinced that if Mennonites really wanted to witness against the war system, refusal to register was a place to begin.[48]

Bender quickly responded, dashing off an article entitled "When May Christians Disobey the Government?" Erb ran it, also on the *Gospel Herald*'s front page. Bender argued that Christians should refuse to cooperate with government only if the government required an act which is an evil in itself. For example, were there no alternative service, Bender would have supported COs' refusal to register. But the law's provision that the CO could opt for alternative service, he argued, made the critical difference.[49]

Bender's response expressed the MC Mennonite position quite accurately, if a bit dogmatically. Privately, Metzler chided Bender for claiming that the registration issue was a settled question. You seem "to imply that the matter has been considered. I wasn't aware this has ever been done," he told Bender.[50] As in so many of Bender's encounters with his students—students who were now becoming church leaders— he had trouble remembering that each generation has to update the legacy. For Metzler's generation, the relatively airtight compartments of church and state which had served Bender's generation were no longer obviously convincing. The universal military draft, plus the moral challenges surrounding the civil rights movement, required a more complex analysis of the Christian's relationship to government and to authority structures. It would take another ten years and the acids of the Vietnam war; only then did the MC Mennonite church officially acknowledge nonregistration as a legitimate option for Mennonite COs.

One factor fueling the debate between Metzler and Bender in 1959 was the somewhat unsatisfactory nature of the I-W program, once it began in 1952. For Mennonite young men, the program was amazingly easy to get into. One result was that the percentage of drafted young Mennonites opting for I-W service was quite high, much higher than in World War II. But a sadder result was that many Mennonite youths entered the program with only marginal convictions about nonresistance. The majority of I-W men opted for a two-year stint as orderlies in large urban hospitals. Unlike most placements under CPS, the settings left the men much on their own. By 1959 the church fathers had waged nearly a decade of effort to bring pastoral oversight and discipline to the program, but with minimal success. For young idealists like Metzler, the Mennonites' too-easy acceptance of the draft system was one of the causes for the moral and spiritual problems the I-W program exhibited. Such idealists believed a more resolute challenge to the military system would generate deeper moral conviction and a stronger peace testimony among the young draftees.[51]

• • •

Bender almost certainly saw the war-peace and church-state issues from a broader context than the argument he made in response to Edgar Metzler. During his discussion with Metzler, he was also preparing a paper for an international conference, on the "Lordship of Christ over Church and State." Bender's paper described the "peace-witness" in the United States.

The conference (Aug. 2-7, 1960) was held at Bievres, France, near Versailles, and was the third in a series known as the "Puidoux" conferences, named after the first one, at Puidoux, Switzerland, in 1955. These conferences were sponsored by the Historic Peace Churches (Brethren, Friends, and Mennonites) as a forum to discuss the theology of war and peace with representatives of the Protestant churches in Europe. An MCC Peace Section person in

Europe administered them, under the direction of a planning committee led by Heinz Kloppenburg, a leader in the German Lutheran church.[52]

Bender's really active efforts at extending the Mennonite peace witness across denominational lines had begun formally in 1950. In that year he, C. L. Graber, Amish bishop Eli Bontreger, and several other Mennonites attended a national conference on the church and war, organized by the Fellowship of Reconciliation. The moving force behind that event had been veteran peace advocate A. J. Muste. Bender read a paper which described the Mennonite position on war and peace. Out of that meeting came the creation of the Church Peace Mission (CPM), a loose organization of pacifist church groups attempting to do peace education ecumenically.[53] Bender's participation on the board of the CPM indicated that he was ready to become more broadly involved in interchurch peace concerns.

In 1948 Protestants created the World Council of Churches (WCC). Bender had wanted to attend the first meeting held at Amsterdam, but Orie Miller had said no. In its first message, the WCC urged theologians to "consider the theological issues" regarding warfare. The pacifists, unable to agree on a single statement, had responded with four statements, IFOR and the three HPCs each producing their own. Together the four became a pamphlet entitled *War Is Contrary to the Will of God*. Bender was a primary writer of the Mennonite statement, with some assistance from Dutch Mennonites. The WCC aptly inquired how the HPCs expected the WCC, with its many different religious traditions, to come to a conclusion on peace if the HPCs could not agree on one statement. Thus challenged, the HPCs brought a consensus document to the second WCC assembly, which was at Evanston, Illinois, in 1954. They entitled that statement "Peace Is the Will of God."[54]

The Puidoux conferences began in that context of ecumenical peace witness. Their general topic was "The Lordship of Christ over the Church and State."[55] Typically, the conference partners were a small group of European theologians along with representatives of the Mennonites, Brethren, and Quakers. These were the conferences at which American Mennonite theologian John Howard

Yoder developed a reputation as a seminal thinker in church-state issues. Yoder and Bender attended and read papers at each of the first three conferences. While Yoder provided the theological arguments which nearly always became the focus of the discussions, Bender's practical experience enhanced the younger man's points. The older man and the younger man complemented each other. The effect of the Puidoux conferences was to put Mennonites into serious dialogue with European churchmen and theologians—a remarkable development.

Not until the third conference in 1960 did any churchmen from behind Europe's so-called Iron Curtain attend. This introduced an East-West dimension into the conversations. Actually, in the several years before 1960, there had been a few conferences in Europe between Eastern and Western theologians, notably one in 1958 in West Germany whose participants included the archbishop of Moscow and theologians from Czechoslovakia and East Germany. Clarence Bauman, a Mennonite graduate student at the University of Bonn, had represented the MCC Peace Section at that meeting. Also in 1959 a large East-West peace conference met in Prague, Czechoslovakia.[56]

The growing traffic in East-West conferences prompted Bender, deeply interested in the dialogue with Iron Curtain theologians, to write a memo: "Guiding Principles on Participation in East-West Peace Conferences." In the poisonous atmosphere of the Cold War, he was worried that such dialogue might create some problems. He was also somewhat skeptical about the ability of the Peace Section persons in Europe to make the right moves. His memo spelled out procedures and responsibilities for MCC persons in such encounters.[57]

Bender's first actual East-West encounter came with his participation in an All-Christian Peace Assembly held at Prague in June of 1961. Bender, Peter Dyck (MCC director in Europe), and John Howard Yoder attended as Peace Section representatives. Other Mennonites present were Hendrik Bremer, a pastor from Amsterdam; Heinold Fast, pastor of a Mennonite church at Bremen, Germany; and Herbert Klassen, a Canadian student studying in London. The conference was convened by professor J. L. Hromadka, the highly regarded dean of the Comenius Theological Faculty of the Czech Brethren church. Hromadka was working to create an ecumenical peace structure that would be an alternative to the more Western-oriented World Council of Churches. The more immediate purpose was to engage in East-West dialogue and promote reconciliation. Nearly seven hundred delegates and observers attended. It was the first large ecumenical Christian gathering ever held in the Communist world. Thus it was a landmark event, as Bender pointed out in his report. In a letter to *The Christian Century*, he observed that "conversations between Eastern and Western Christians are urgently needed, and we should support them. . . . One of the great meanings of Prague" was "that there are real Christians on both sides who are not dragging their banners in the dust."[58]

Meanwhile, Bender was helping to plan an East-West theological colloquy to be held at Karlsbad in Czechoslovakia in 1962. Bender, FOR leader A. J. Muste, Church of the Brethren leader Harold Row, and Friends leader Douglas Steere—these four collaborated with dean Hromadka to set up that event. Attending from U.S. were Bender and fourteen other American churchmen—among them Eugene Carson Blake, head of the World Council of Churches; James I. McCord, president of Princeton Seminary; and John C. Bennett, dean of Union Theological Seminary. They met in January 1962 with six Europeans and twenty church leaders from behind the Iron Curtain for four days of intensive theological discussion.[59]

Douglas Steere called the experience a "fresh baptism of the common Christian life and discipleship."[60] Bender agreed, telling a friend that "I am still living under the impact of the tremendous experience at Karlsbad. I can only say Praise be to God who hath holpen us. The actuality was beyond all my expectations."[61] Aside from the spiritual benefit Bender derived from the encounter, the Karlsbad meeting signaled the emergence of Bender as a respected figure in the ranks of world Protestant leaders. In this instance it was a position he had gained largely as a result of his peace witness in ecumenical circles.

## ◦ 23 ◦

# Renaissance of Anabaptist Studies

*With Fritz Blanke, Bender leads an Anabaptist-studies renaissance. Bender writes* These Are My People. *He dies at age 65.*

ROBERT AND BETTY Friedmann had come to Goshen for the day from their home in Kalamazoo. Friedmann was delivering some overdue *Mennonite Encylopedia* articles, but his customary good cheer was visibly escalated by some news, which he relayed excitedly during lunch at the Benders. A few months earlier, in July 1955, young German Mennonite Heinold Fast and a fellow student had found an important hitherto-unknown Anabaptist document in a library in Bern, Switzerland. Entitled the "Kunstbuch,"[1] the ancient manuscript added much to the corpus of knowledge about the south-German Anabaptists and the role of Pilgram Marpeck as an Anabaptist leader.

Friedmann was impressed by Heinold Fast: Fast is "a fine young Menn. historian, the by far best and capable of all whom I know," he told Bender.[2] Bender immediately wrote to Fast, congratulating him on his "great discovery" and ordering a microfilm copy for the Goshen library.[3] Bender published a report on the "Kunstbuch" in the January 1956 *MQR*.

Fast's discovery generated a small tempest. Historian Delbert Gratz at Bluffton, who had published a history of the Bernese Anabaptists in 1953, insisted that he had discovered the "Kunstbuch" in 1950, had it microfilmed, and had brought the copy to the Bluffton College library. A bit impatiently, Bender pointed out to Gratz that what mattered was not who first found the "Kunstbuch" but who had first realized and explained its significance.[4]

The "Kunstbuch" discovery was interesting, but its real implications became apparent to Bender only the following summer. In 1956 Bender visited Europe en route to the Soviet Union, but at the last minute he was denied a visa. Since he had several weeks of free time before he could return to the United States, Fritz Blanke at Zurich invited Bender to read and evaluate a new dissertation one of his students, Jan J. Kiwiet, had just completed. Kiwiet, a Dutch Baptist pastor, was challenging Bender's understanding of Anabaptist origins. Bender was so impressed by the implications of Kiwiet's thesis that he hired a typist to reproduce the entire manuscript so he could take a copy back to Goshen.[5]

Kiwiet had made two arguments: that Hans Denck was a genuine Anabaptist, and that a substantial Anabaptist movement had developed in southern Germany independently from the Zurich Swiss Brethren. In other words, Hans Denck, whom John Horsch had always considered a renegade Anabaptist, would now have to be considered a true Anabaptist. If Kiwiet was right, then Conrad Grebel, "The Founder," as Bender had called him in his Grebel biography, would have to share that honor with Denck.[6]

Equally important was Kiwiet's argument that the south-German Anabaptist movement had begun independently from the Zurich Swiss Brethren. In this he was challenging the prevailing orthodoxy, first established by the great German historian Ernst Troeltsch in his 1912 *Die Soziallehren der christlichen Kirchen und Sekten*. Troeltsch had argued that the Anabaptists had originated in Zurich and that all subsequent groups derived from the Zurich group. He had also argued for a sharp distinction between spiritualist and Anabaptist dissenters in the Reformation era, thus pointing to the sober Swiss Brethren as the true Anabaptists. John Horsch had eagerly adopted the Troeltsch idea and made the Swiss Brethren the original Anabaptists. Harold Bender had built his entire Anabaptist understanding on that premise. Kiwiet was calling much of that into question.[7]

In the spring of 1957, Jan Kiwiet visited the United States. In a letter addressed *"To All Good Anabaptists!"* Bender announced a "one-day Anabaptist Seminar" to be held at Goshen on June 14, to take advantage of Kiwiet's presence: "Kiwiet . . . has done notable work on Pilgram Marpeck and the South German Mennonites." Signing the letter with his usual flourish, Bender added whimsically: "No Pilgramite but a Swiss Brother."[8]

The invitation went to a select group of Mennonite scholars: Robert Kreider and Delbert Gratz at Bluffton; S. F. Pannabecker, Donovan Smucker, and Cornelius J. Dyck at the Mennonite Biblical Seminary; William Klassen at Princeton; and Robert Friedmann, John Oyer, J. C. Wenger, and Guy F. Hershberger. The "Kiwiet seminar," as Bender called it, offered an opportunity to discuss firsthand what the implications of the Kiwiet thesis might be.[9]

There is no record of the conversation that day. However, Bender's jocular sign-off in the invitation and an editorial introduction he wrote for the first Kiwiet article in the October 1957 *MQR* suggest that he was not entirely convinced by Kiwiet's argument. While clearly intrigued by his thesis, Bender believed "there are still important questions and reservations" remaining. But he was also happy that Kiwiet had agreed to publish his new work in the *MQR*.[10]

Perhaps the best index to Bender's attitude was an episode at the end of the seminar. Robert Friedmann, who was much impressed by the Kiwiet thesis, remarked that "a new era" in Anabaptist research had just begun. In fact, he said, "it means the end of the Anabaptist Vision." Bender was nonplussed. "That Kiwiet has brought new light and some new points of view is true," he told Friedmann. "However, I do not see at all that this has anything to do with the *Anabaptist Vision* [Bender's emphasis] which was based on the widest possible interpretation of the central Anabaptist position, including Marpeck. Nothing that Kiwiet brought out in any way invalidates my synthesis. What do you mean?"[11]

If Friedmann offered any rejoinder, it is lost; but Bender was right. While he wrote "The Anabaptist Vision" within the Troeltsch-Horsch framework of presenting the Swiss Brethren as the original Anabaptists, his "Vision" essay did not rest on the single-origins or "monogenesis" thesis. On the other hand, it is also clear that Bender had formulated his Anabaptist Vision squarely from the Swiss Brethren nexus and that a multiple-origins or "polygenesis" model would make the somewhat narrow definitions of the Anabaptist Vision less convincing. Friedmann believed there might have been variations in the movement and that Bender's tripartite definition of the essence of Anabaptism was too narrow. There might have been additional key emphases in addition to Bender's three (discipleship, nonresistance, and a voluntary church), Friedmann seemed to imply.

• • •

During the 1950s the earth moved in Anabaptist studies. In 1958 Cornelius Krahn counted fifty-nine Ph.D. dissertations on Anabaptist and Mennonite topics either completed or in progress during that decade. About half of them were by Mennonites.[12] Bender was aware of the rush of new discoveries and interpretations. "We are truly living in a golden age of Anabaptist history," he told Fritz Blanke. "There is a tremendous amount of new material being produced about the Anabaptists."[13]

At the center of the new work was the rediscovery of two Anabaptist figures, Hans Denck and Pilgram Marpeck. Was that really one single rediscovery, or was it two? Bender was able to include brief excerpts from Kiwiet and Fast in an article on Marpeck in *The Mennonite Encyclopedia.* In 1956 and 1960, the Täuferakten-Kommission (TAK, a commission for publishing Anabaptist sources) issued the corpus of Denck material. Augmenting the Kiwiet thesis and Heinold Fast's discovery of the "Kunstbuch" was work on Marpeck done by Torsten Bergsten, a Swedish student of Fritz Blanke, and by William Klassen, a Canadian Mennonite. Both Bergsten and Klassen worked on "the Menno Simons of the South," as Bender once called Marpeck.[14]

Among the researchers at the center of much of the new work were the students of Fritz Blanke at the University of Zurich, beginning in 1953 with Paul Peachey and his dissertation. In 1955 Blanke's own little classic, *Brüder in Christo*, was published (with an English translation, *Brothers in Christ*, in 1961). Blanke's book painted a compelling picture of the first Anabaptist congregation in Zollikon, just outside of Zurich in 1525. In so doing, it also validated many of the fundamental ideas which the Concern group

had claimed as part of the Anabaptist legacy, including an emphasis on baptism as a sign of
conversion rather than as a
gateway to church membership,
and a stress on small-group fellowship as the center of Anabaptist life.[15]

In 1956 Heinold Fast com-
pleted a doctoral thesis at Heidelberg on the Swiss Protestant
reformer Heinrich Bullinger and
his relationships to the Anabaptists. Fast's adviser was Professor Heinrich Bornkamm, the
chairman of the Täuferakten-
Kommission. Bender was treasurer of TAK and in 1956 attended a TAK meeting at Bornkamm's home in Heidelberg.

**Fritz Blanke, Professor of Ana-
baptist History at the University
of Zurich.** *Zwingliana.*

Among other business at that gathering was a decision to publish
Friedmann's Hutterite epistles.[16] Friedmann himself contributed to
a surge of new Hutterite studies with his discovery of new Hutterite documents, called the Beck Collection, at Brno in Czechoslovakia.

Shortly thereafter, in 1957, John Howard Yoder, working at
the University of Basel, finished his study of Swiss Brethren dispu-
tations. In 1958 Hans Hillerbrand, a young German who had
studied at Goshen, received his degree at the University of Erlangen with a dissertation on the Anabaptists and the state. In the late
1950s, both Hillerbrand and Yoder joined the faculty at Goshen.

At the University of Amsterdam, in 1957, Irvin Horst complet-
ed a dissertation on English Anabaptism. Also during this period,
Herbert Klassen, a Bender student and Goshen College Biblical
Seminary graduate, began work on the south-German Anabaptist
Hans Hut. And in 1957 Bethel College professor William Keeney
completed a dissertation on the Dutch Anabaptist leader Dirk
Philips. Keeney's degree was from Hartford Theological Seminary.

Perhaps nothing symbolized the surge of interest in Anabaptist studies as much as did the publication of George H. Williams' *Spiritual and Anabaptist Writers* in the series Library of Christian Classics. Williams, dean of Harvard Divinity School, possessed formidable intellectual and language skills and approached Anabaptist studies from an entirely fresh perspective. In 1956 (while Harold was in Germany reading Kiwiet) he visited Goshen Historical Library and found Elizabeth in the midst of the clutter of work on *The Mennonite Encyclopedia.* She put all of the notes and files of the encyclopedia at the Harvard scholar's disposal.[17]

When Williams had decided what Anabaptists to feature in the *Writers* book, he sent the list to Bender. Bender did not like the selections and responded: Only two on your list, Conrad Grebel and Dirk Philips, are true "classic" Anabaptists. You have ignored such key people as Menno Simons, Pilgram Marpeck, and the Hutterites. "I am really disappointed in the outcome of this volume," Bender bluntly told Williams. "As your selection now stands, we could scarcely use it for our purposes, and would need to proceed with preparation of our own Anabaptist volume."[18] Bender and Friedmann had long planned to produce an Anabaptist "Reader" once *The Mennonite Encyclopedia* was completed,[19] so the threat to produce an alternative volume was real.

Knowing Bender's endorsement in the *MQR* would be critical to his book's success, Williams modified his selections to include some of Bender's suggestions. When the book came out in 1957, Bender offered some generous compliments on the volume. He also applauded Williams' new term for the Anabaptist movement: the "Radical Reformation." Bender thought that label was "by all odds the best solution of the problem of a justly descriptive term."[20]

In 1958, in two installments of *Church History*, Williams published an extensive bibliographical essay of Anabaptism. That essay prompted Bender to begin something he had long been planning to do: produce an "exhaustive Anabaptist bibliography." It will be a "bibliographically complete work, with exact titles and pages, as well as locations in libraries," he explained to Williams.[21] Bender had applied for and received a grant of $3,000 from the Foundation for Reformation Research to help the project along.

To do the actual work, Bender enlisted Hans Hillerbrand, who had just arrived to begin teaching history at Goshen College. Whatever the larger motives, Bender's plunge into the bibliography project in 1958 was a move to outflank Williams and keep the locus of Anabaptist studies at Goshen. The project, completed shortly before Bender's death in 1962, was conducted under the Institute for Mennonite Studies, a program of the Associated Mennonite Biblical Seminaries.[22]

By 1957 Bender was clearly the first among several older Anabaptist scholars, a group which included Fritz Blanke in Zurich, Roland Bainton at Yale, Robert Friedmann at Western Michigan University, Cornelius Krahn at Bethel College, and soon, George Williams at Harvard. The symbol of Bender's leadership in Anabaptist studies was that year's Festschrift in his honor, *The Recovery of the Anabaptist Vision*. Its contributors included old colleagues like Blanke and Bainton, Mennonite brothers like Krahn and Crous, and students like John Howard Yoder and J. Lawrence Burkholder. Bender was certainly pleased to have his daughter Mary Eleanor, with her new Ph.D. in hand from Indiana University, contribute an article on "The Sixteenth Century Anabaptists in Literature."[23]

Bender's preeminence in Anabaptist studies lay more in his managerial, editorial, and mentoring roles than in doing his own original research. Virtually all of his work in the 1950s was summarizing and secondary research. The titles of some of his articles suggest their derivative character: "The Anabaptist Theology of Discipleship," "The Pacifism of Sixteenth Century Anabaptists," and "The Hymnology of the Anabaptists." These were longish pieces, published in the *MQR* and designed to distill what Bender believed about the subject at hand. Almost all were spin-offs from work on *The Mennonite Encyclopedia*. His best-researched piece in the 1950s was "The Zwickau Prophets, Thomas Müntzer and the Anabaptists," first published in German in 1952 in the *Theologische Zeitschrift*, a journal produced at the University of Basel. The article was an argument against Müntzer as an Anabaptist, and for the Swiss Brethren in Zurich as the first true Anabaptists.[24]

Bender's scholarly role was thus quite different from the more

**Editor Harold Bender with the associate editors of** *The Mennonite Quarterly Review.* **From the left: Robert Friedmann, Ernest Correll, John C. Wenger, Harold S. Bender, John S. Umble, Melvin Gingerich, Cornelius Krahn, J. Winfield Fretz.** AMC.

conventional academic roles of a Fritz Blanke, a Roland Bainton, or a George Williams. They supervised graduate students who were drawn to them because of their original research. Bender's students were seminarians with pastoral goals, plus a select few whom he chose to send to graduate schools to prepare for teaching careers in Mennonite institutions. In Bender, the scholarly role was always subsumed under his role as church leader.

• • •

Despite his primary role as a churchman, Harold Bender realized that in the public mind, his image was almost completely that of an Anabaptist historian. So he had to make a disclaimer. These lectures, he told his audience, are not, as you might have expected, about the Anabaptist view of the church. "In these lectures I am working inside the framework of New Testament theology."[25]

Bender was at Eastern Mennonite College to deliver the 1960 Conrad Grebel lectures. His overall theme was "The Nature of the

Church and Its Discipleship."

When Bender had time for preparation, he enjoyed reading prepared lectures. He was a good reader, with a resonant voice which carried conviction. By 1960 he had developed a public persona—a combination of a hefty body, thinning gray hair, modest steel-rimmed glasses, and a dark plain coat with no lapels, then sometimes regarded as clerical garb. His persona lent force to his words. At Eastern Mennonite College, his reputation for scholarship inspired awe.

The high-walled chapel auditorium was well filled with attentive students and faculty. The almost worshipful attention accorded Bender was a far cry from the first visit he had made to the college forty years earlier in 1919. Then Bender had accompanied his girlfriend Elizabeth Horsch to the campus, where she was a teacher. He had felt out of place in 1919 because he considered himself much more liberal than the rigid theological conservatism which the school espoused. Now, in 1960, he was being lionized.[26]

The change was a commentary on who Bender had become, and on what Eastern Mennonite College in particular and the MC Mennonite membership in general were becoming. By 1960 Bender had become the voice of middle-ground Mennonite belief and practice. Eastern Mennonite College, long a bastion of Mennonite conservatism, was eager to join that progressive center, as was much of the MC Mennonite church. In the 1950s Bender's theological stance and that of the Mennonite church in general were nearly identical. Bender's voice was the voice of his people.

In any case, Bender found a receptive audience for his Conrad Grebel lectures, entitled *These Are My People* when published in 1962. In his presentation, Bender offered a description of the church, a masterful distillation and expansion of material from New Testament scholar Paul Minear and Old Testament scholar John Bright. One of Bright's key ideas was that in every age God calls a people into being. In the New Testament the message was that the people of God are called into being by the "gracious act of God in Christ." In the Bible, Bright insisted, when human beings respond to God's gracious act, they become members of the people of God. In New Testament terms, they become the church.[27]

While embracing Bright's idea of the people of God, Bender expanded it by insisting that the church is not just a collection of believers. What best describes the church was what Bender termed a "fellowship community, best captured by the New Testament Greek word *koinōnia.*" This insight he borrowed from Paul Minear. "Koinonia is the very essence of the church," Bender claimed. As used in the New Testament, koinonia described a people of God who engage in profound fellowship with God and with one another. In fact, Bender continued, koinonia is present only when believers come to God together with one another. And koinonia means not only shared worship, but also obedience to the will of God and care for one another. Furthermore, Bender insisted, koinonia can take different forms. One form is at the congregational level, but if the congregation is too large, it can occur in smaller fellowship groups within the congregation. Koinonia is not merely a feeling members have for each other: it requires joint action, shared experience, and serious engagement between believers.[28]

Bender claimed that the enemies of koinonia in the contemporary Mennonite church were individualism and institutionalism. Individualism undermines the relationship of the believers to one another in true fellowship. Institutionalism threatens koinonia because it puts too much authority in the hands of a few. Koinonia requires the full involvement of all in the work of the church. Bender called it "member participation."[29]

He described the church as a fellowship of believers in Jesus Christ. But the belief he had in mind was "not essentially forensic, theological, or ethical—it is personal commitment which places one in Christ, that is, in the sphere of His operation, so that one can thereby live victoriously over sin."[30] That personal commitment Bender called the essence of discipleship: the "believer follows Him in obedience, identifies himself with His cause, serves His purposes, and renounces all other loyalties."[31] While Bender cited Minear, Bright, and others, he was also invoking many of the ideas expressed during the 1950s by the Concern group. The teacher was acknowledging his debt to his students.

Bender's claim that he was doing New Testament theology was correct, but in fact his was an applied and practical form of theology without much exegetical or hermeneutical scholarship. Realistic churchman that he was, Bender knew that his "people" would not be receptive to a more scholarly approach. But neither was rigorous theological work a Bender forte. Instead, he was unusually adept at borrowing ideas and giving them new heft and context. Thus he was able to graft John Bright's "people of God" concept and Paul Minear's "koinonia" idea onto Mennonitism in a manner which offered creative new understandings that thoughtful lay people could grasp. Bender's talent was ideally suited to his roles, both as a Mennonite churchman and a Mennonite seminarian.

However, Bender was also doing something else. The koinonia concept, after all, connected with his own Anabaptist-Vision, believers-church idea and with the Concern group's idea of the hermeneutical community. Bender was giving that cluster of ideas about the church an up-to-date new term, koinonia.

• • •

By the 1950s Bender had become one of the arbiters of Mennonite faith and practice. Some other major MC Mennonite leaders who shared that role were dean C. K. Lehman and president John R. Mumaw of EMC, editor Paul Erb and publishing agent A. J. Metzler of the Mennonite Publishing House, Orie Miller of MCC, president Paul Mininger of Goshen, mission board executive J. D. Graber, and bishops Nelson Kauffman, John E. Lapp, Amos Horst, Jesse B. Martin, J. C. Wenger, C. J. Ramer, John H. Mosemann, and Allen Erb. These persons had all become adults in the early 1920s, and by the 1930s had become leaders at various levels in the church. By the 1950s they had two decades of leadership experience and were firmly in charge of Mennonite affairs. Metzler, Mumaw, Martin, Wenger, Mininger, and Allen Erb each served as moderator of the MC's general conference during the 1950s, and they served on its numerous committees. In 1954 after a redesign of the MC general conference organization, Paul Erb became its first executive secretary.

In 1949 the MC general conference created a General Council to provide continuity and coordination to its biennial general con-

FIRST MEETING OF THE GENERAL COUNCIL OF THE
MENNONITE GENERAL CONFERENCE
DECEMBER 9-10, 1949

OSCAR
CHICAGO

**The General Council of the Mennonite General Conference, 1949.
Harold Bender is on the left in the third row.** *Mennonite Historical Bulletin.*

ferences. Meeting three or four times a year, the council quickly
became the most powerful body in the general conference structure. As chairman of the Peace Problems Committee and the Historical Committee, Bender served on the council. Thus during the
1950s, he was continuously at the center of MC Mennonite general conference decision-making.

Given his high profile as president of the Mennonite World
Conference, dean of Goshen College Biblical Seminary, and popular preacher, one might have expected Bender to be elected moderator of his church; but that never happened. In the fourteen
years from 1947 to 1961, he was invited to speak at the biennial
general conference sessions only once. That was in 1959, when
J. C. Wenger was moderator and arranged for Bender's address.
During those years Bender was continuously chair of the Peace
Problems Committee and of the Historical Committee, another
anomaly since most general conference committee chairmanships
changed frequently. But he was never elected to any of the conference's other standing committees.

The failure of Bender to become moderator of the general conference lay partly in his specialized roles as theologian, historian, Mennonite ecumenist, and MCC leader. In the 1950s those roles did not readily translate into general church leadership positions. By contrast, his seminary colleagues Paul Mininger and J. C. Wenger served on a wide array of committees and both were elected moderator of general conference. But both men were also bishops and pastors. Bender was neither, and in the 1950s, those roles were still quite important for general church leadership.

Bender was also perceived as a progressive in a time when cautious conservatism was a necessary mark of Mennonite leadership. For the most part well educated, Bender's leadership generation was more progressive than their fathers' generation had been, but they were still cautious about change. That caution was tied to one of the continuities of twentieth-century MC church polity: the pressure on the MC church by three large eastern district conferences—Lancaster, Franconia, and Virginia—to maintain traditional definitions and marks of nonconformity to the world. The prominent nonconformity issue in the 1950s was clothing regulation.

Throughout his life, Bender had reluctantly complied with his church's clothing rules, but his heart was never in them. That was notably evident in the early 1950s. Addressing a nonconformity conference on the subject "Our Witness for Nonconformity in Dress in the Future," he said that where there are specific biblical injunctions, such as the prohibition against cutting women's hair or wearing jewelry, or the injunction for women to wear a prayer covering, there dare be no compromise. But, he told the conference, in the case of the regulation coat or the cape dress, the situation was different. Those were simply cultural forms with no special warrant in Scripture.[32] Although in earlier times Bender had always worn a business suit when he traveled in non-Mennonite circles, he now wore the regulation coat continuously. Nonetheless, his lukewarm embrace of the regulation coat did not commend him to eastern conservatives who often controlled nominations for general conference committees.

That conservative penchant affected much more than church polity. J. C. Wenger's 1954 *Introduction to Theology* illustrated the Mennonite leadership mind-set when applied to that important subject.[33] When Donovan Smucker reviewed Wenger's book in 1954 for the *MQR*, he tried to be kind but could not help pointing out that of 200 books cited by Wenger, two-thirds antedated 1940, and half of those were written before 1910. Of those written after 1940, half were what Smucker called "fundamentalist."[34] Wenger had managed to nearly ignore the amazing theological renaissance which had exploded among Western Christians after World War II.

Wenger was symptomatic of his generation. In 1957 the General Problems Committee of the general conference, in its biennial assessment of the state of the church, warned against "the unsound elements in much of contemporary theological writing. We do not want to accept modernism, nor do we wish the evils of Fundamentalism (rejection of Biblical nonresistance, for example). Perhaps our greatest theological hazard today is neo-orthodoxy with its low view of inspiration, relativistic ethics, and inadequate doctrine of the church."[35] Bender and Wenger agreed with such assessments.

In 1958, at the request of the MC Mennonites' Ministerial Committee, John R. Mumaw and J. C. Wenger compiled a list of "Books for the Minister's Library." Of the more than one hundred titles they selected, most were quite out-of-date, and not a single title suggested the new currents in theological and biblical studies. The list included most MC writing of Bender's generation, with three of J. C. Wenger's and two of Guy Hershberger's books. Bender did not make the list, although his Festschrift did: *The Recovery of the Anabaptist Vision*. Except for the latter, also missing from the list was any evidence of the creative new theological work of the Concern generation which had come to adulthood in the 1940s and early 1950s. Their ideas at that point had not yet affected the mind-set of most of Bender's generation of church leaders.[36]

The tight parameters of acceptable theological discourse were quite rigorously enforced by Bender at Goshen. In the summer of 1960, Paul Mininger asked J. C. Wenger to relinquish his teaching assignments in the seminary so that Wenger could assume the chairmanship of the college Bible department. Bender agreed that the change was imperative. "The Bible Department is becoming quite weak," he told Wenger. "We cannot afford to have Norman

Kraus become the chairman, and no one else is ready."[37] Bender was concerned about Kraus's theological stance.

Part of the cause for the weakness in the Bible department was the departure of J. Lawrence Burkholder, who in 1961 had taken a position at Harvard Divinity School. A few years earlier John W. Miller had not been invited to return after a leave of absence. In the late 1950s, even John Howard Yoder, the most gifted theologian of that gifted generation of Bender's protégés, was shunted to administrative assignments at MBM instead of to a teaching position at either MBS or at GCBS. The effect of all of those events was to sideline several of the most gifted new Mennonite theological voices in several generations.

Bender was more exposed to contemporary theological currents than most of his fellow leaders and therefore more conversant with what was happening theologically. But he nearly always shaped his theological understandings to the needs and possibilities of church polity, partly because he was realistic about what was possible, but also because he was serious about fidelity to the church. Bender did not embrace an individualistic church ethic. In June 1953 he read a much-discussed paper at the Ninth Conference on Mennonite Educational and Cultural Problems: "Outside Influences on Mennonite Thought."[38] He acknowledged that much of the "awakening, revitalizing, and activating" of the church during the previous several decades had come from the outside; but in a regretful note, he said that the same influences had also brought "subjectivistic, emotional, introspective, and even mystical" forms of piety into the Mennonite church, plus doctrinal importations such as "baptism by immersion, open communion, second work of grace, [and] eternal security." He also saw the realization of the church being subverted by individualism and laxity of discipline. All of this was "seriously" diluting the old Mennonite doctrines of separation, nonconformity, and simplicity.[39]

All was not gloom and doom, however. Bender assured his audience that "American Mennonitism on the whole is still sound at the core, has to a large extent recovered its sense of connection with its great past, and in general has a good balance of faith and works, inner experience, and evangelistic outreach and witnessing.

It is learning how to correct its own aberrations and accumulated deficiencies."[40] Nevertheless, there was need for vigilance. For example, Fundamentalism had to be rejected. Somewhat vaguely, Bender defined Fundamentalism as a "minority polemical and rather radical movement in American orthodox Protestantism of the past forty years." Reflexively, he hastened to assure his audience that he counted himself as "thoroughly fundamental (with a small *f*), and evangelical." He assured his listeners that he saw "no place for modernism or liberalism in any form." He believed that Mennonites had "historically been thoroughly Biblical and more completely so than Fundamentalism ever was."[41]

In Bender's view, American Mennonites faced problems of worldliness, the challenge of "full discipleship," and a need for the revival of nonresistance and nonconformity. They also needed to cure a "rampant materialism with its easy-going acceptance of modern capitalistic methods and spirit." Above all, they faced a theological challenge. "Let us take a lesson from the Church of the Brethren," who, Bender said, had lost their way theologically. He meant that the Brethren had too carelessly embraced the new postwar theologies. But despite all the challenges, he was not pessimistic about American Mennonitism. He assured his listeners, "We will find our way through to a continuing vigorous thoroughly Mennonite evangelical brotherhood, moving forward in our witness and ministry in accord with God's historic purpose for us."[42]

Like many of his generation, Bender tended to analyze the situation in terms of ideas. Had he been inclined to think more sociologically, he might have had less hope. Mennonites were being changed by powerful social and cultural forces over which they had little control. Near the center of those changes was the erosion of the Mennonite rural community following World War II. The demise of the geographically compact Mennonite community was a product of factors such as market and technological changes in agriculture. These changes required ever-greater investments of capital to achieve the economies of scale necessary to compete in the new agribusiness world. Many Mennonite farm families simply could not make the transition.[43]

Equally important were "pull" factors, which included the enticements of a burgeoning and beckoning industrial prosperity which agriculture could not match. Among Mennonite young people, this prosperity was coupled with a surge of interest in professional careers. Both factors pulled Mennonites away from their rural roots. By 1959 Goshen College professor J. Lawrence Burkholder was convinced that "the Mennonite Community is becoming a thing of the past." Concern-group member Paul Peachey insisted that "the cultural and psychic substance of Mennonite solidarity is rapidly dissolving."[44] Bender agreed with such observations, noting in 1953 that "for most of us the day of isolation is wholly past. We are increasingly in the midst of the stream of American life."[45]

In 1955 the General Problems Committee, one of the committees to which Bender was never elected, identified a long list of issues to be addressed. On it were divorce and remarriage, plus nonconformity issues such as wearing the plain coat, promoting long hair and the veil for women, and preaching against theater attendance, playing cards, dancing, tobacco, alcohol, and participation in sports. There was concern about the new I-W program for conscientious objectors, popular holiness movements, and child evangelism. The committee highlighted the need to teach stewardship to promote giving, keep church services simple, have more expository sermons, and maintain congregational kneeling for prayer. Mennonite communities were encouraged to establish and support parochial and church high schools. The General Problems Committee offered quite an agenda.[46]

One of the disappointments which World War II had bequeathed to Bender's generation was the surprisingly large number of Mennonite young men who had opted for military service during the war. Research and experience suggested that a main cause had been Mennonite attendance at public high schools. To remedy the situation, in the 1940s Mennonites established seven high schools, and in 1954 they started two more: Christopher Dock in the Franconia Conference district in Pennsylvania, and Bethany Christian High School a mile south of Goshen College. Bender led in the formation of Bethany High School, thus indicating how much he agreed with the prevailing Mennonite mood. Building high schools and parochial schools was one way to shield Mennonite young people from an encroaching world.[47]

The 1955 MC general conference, whose moderator was A. J. Metzler, also responded to a growing concern for more lay participation in church organizations and decision-making. Until the 1950s there was little lay leadership in Mennonite congregational and conference organizations. But in 1955 the general conference encouraged congregations to create lay councils to direct congregational life. It also encouraged the sending of lay delegates to the district conferences.[48]

As more congregations employed single pastors, the MC Mennonite church found that it needed to redefine ministerial titles and roles. The 1955 general conference suggested that all ordained and licensed preachers be called ministers, with the term pastor reserved for the actual spiritual leader of the congregation. The terms overseer or bishop were to apply to those who had administrative oversight over several congregations in an area. The conference also urged the use of licensing as a period of probation for young ministers before ordination, a practice Bender had been promoting for a decade.[49]

Thus the 1955 general conference illustrated how Bender's leadership generation was responding to a new era. The leaders were trying to guide the direction of change by designing pragmatic solutions to problems. But to the young men of the Concern group, that generation seemed to be temporizing rather than offering focused and forceful leadership. Bender's generation lived between their fathers' generation, which had rather arbitrarily imposed and maintained a theological and cultural orthodoxy, and the Concern generation, which was demanding a new orthodoxy. That middle generation—Bender's—was much more inclined to mediate and to direct change than to impose a new orthodoxy. It was a position neither the older generation nor the next generation found satisfactory.

Meanwhile, 1950s grassroots Mennonites were making choices that were far more powerful than any a leadership cadre could control, and those choices changed Mennonitism profoundly. While Bender's generation of leaders could not have known how deep

**Harold Bender with Nelson Springer, the curator of the Mennonite Historical Library at Goshen College.**
MHL.

and profound the changes would be, their measured and pragmatic response steadied the church during a period of great change.

Bender's own passage through the 1950s was as equivocal and complex as that of his people. Because of his responsibilities, he was at the center of several streams of influence and leadership. As editor of the *MQR* and a mentor to numerous young scholars, he shepherded an amazing explosion of new historical research in Anabaptist history. That work was challenging to the next generation, and much of it broadened the boundaries of his own original understandings of the field.

As a lecturer and writer, Bender helped shape a moderately conservative response to the acids of post-World War II theological thought. Using his masterful talent to divine what would be useful to his people, he helped to initiate the reshaping of an emerging Mennonite theological consensus, something which would come

more fully to fruition in the 1960s and 1970s. As an MC Mennonite churchman, he assisted in a measured and pragmatic response
to the powerful forces changing Mennonite life in the 1950s.

• • •

The Goshen College church bulletin carried the announcement:
"Dean and Mrs. H. S. Bender invite the congregation to attend the
marriage of their daughter, Nancy, to Eugene Hollinger Friday,
June 8, [1956,] at 7:00 P.M. in the Chapel Hall." A few days earlier a similar invitation had gone to all college and seminary faculty. Bender performed the marriage ceremony.[50] "We had a happy
wedding service," Bender informed an absent brother-in-law, Paul
Horsch. Nancy had just graduated from Goshen College a few
days earlier, after spending the fall semester of her senior year at
Eastern Mennonite College in Virginia. Within a few weeks after
her wedding, she enrolled in a master's program in music at the
University of Michigan.

Older sister Mary Eleanor had graduated from Goshen in 1950
and then entered graduate school at Indiana University, where she
studied foreign languages. By 1953 she had completed her resi-

**Harold and Elizabeth with daughters Nancy (on the left) and Mary
Eleanor.** Bender Family Album.

dency requirements and, to her parents' delight, had taken a position teaching English and languages at Hesston College. In the spring of 1955, Harold and Elizabeth made a nostalgic visit to Hesston, ostensibly to help Mary Eleanor celebrate her birthday, but also to give Elizabeth an opportunity to visit Hesston. She had last been at Hesston College thirty-four years earlier, in 1921. In 1955 Mary Eleanor moved from Hesston to Goshen for the rest of her teaching career.[51]

A major change for the Bender family had been the death of Elsie Bender in 1949. Harold's mother had lived in the Bender home since 1925. In 1954 Christine Horsch, Elizabeth's mother, moved to Goshen and joined the Bender household. On the Bender side, one of Harold's most enjoyable family events in the 1950s was a reunion in Somerset County, Pennsylvania, where his father had been born and reared.

Harold and Elizabeth hosted a continual stream of visitors, many of them internationals. Despite his busyness, Harold continued to do the family grocery shopping and often served as cook. Guests were often surprised and students amused when he greeted them at the door wearing an apron.

Especially in the 1950s, Bender developed a reputation as an erratic driver who paid scant attention to the rules of the road. The result was several accidents which dented his old Dodge car. In 1955 he had the car at the body shop to repair dents from three accidents, one of which he described to his insurance agent as "a small side-swipe."[52]

Bender continued to have his suits custom-made at Jackson's Quality Clothes Shop in Lancaster, Pennsylvania. Usually the process was as simple as a letter: "I wish herewith to give you an order for another suit made on my last measurement out of the dark oxford grey cloth which I use for my suits." The suit would arrive by mail two weeks later with a bill, in the 1950s, for $85. Bender had bought his first suit at Jackson's in 1936.[53]

In 1956 Bender finally, albeit reluctantly, closed down his Bender Travel Agency, which he had operated since 1929. Actually, he merged it with the Goshen branch office of Menno Travel Service, in return for which he was made assistant manager. The arrangement let him continue to get trans-Atlantic fare-reductions, which had always been his primary motive for operating the travel agency.[54]

During the 1950s Bender visited Europe each summer except in 1955. In 1952, 1957, and 1960 Elizabeth accompanied him, and in two of those years they were able to take genuine vacations. In 1957 they spent a rain-splattered week in a peasant home in a remote Tyrolean village, and in 1960 they spent a week at a hotel on Lake Como in southern Switzerland. But in the 1950s the never-ending work on *The Mennonite Encyclopedia* invaded even their vacations. "We took vacations as a family," Mary Eleanor remembered, "but my parents always spent most of their time reading encyclopedia proofs."[55]

During the 1950s the encyclopedia project exacerbated the mind-numbing busyness of Bender's life. In 1957 President Mininger gently suggested he should lay down some of his offices in order to reduce the pressures. Bender responded, as he had for more than twenty years, that what he really needed was a "first-class" secretary. He also assured Mininger that as soon as the encyclopedia was finished and the new seminary building in place, much of the pressure would be off.[56] At Mininger's request, he made a list of his ongoing responsibilities. The list dramatically negated his benign assumption that all he needed was better secretarial help. On his list were:

Dean, Goshen College Biblical Seminary
Secretary, MCC Executive Committee
Chairman, MCC Peace Section
Chairman, Peace Problems Committee
Chairman, Historical Committee
Member, General Council of the Mennonite General Conference
Executive Secretary, Bethany Christian High School
President, Mennonite Historical Society
Editor, *The Mennonite Quarterly Review*
Chairman, International Mennonite Peace Committee
President, Mennonite World Conference
Editor, *The Mennonite Encyclopedia*
Chairman, Division IV, Goshen College
Executive Secretary, Mennonite Research Foundation[57]

Bender's lifelong search for a "first-class" secretary was rewarded in 1958 with the employment of Ohioan Irene Hershberger, whose skills and energy were somewhat equal to Bender's demands. In 1961 Hershberger took a leave of absence to work for MCC in Frankfurt, Germany, and her replacement was an articulate and observant Ada Schrock. After her first day in the office, Schrock described herself as "bushed, pooped, exhausted, and weary to the bones!!!" Dean Bender had worked all day in one of the classrooms, largely, Schrock guessed, because there was not "even six inches of space in either office" where he might otherwise have worked. She was appalled by the "piles" which covered every level surface, including the floor. How was she ever going to locate anything in the midst of such chaos? she wondered. And how would she ever get anything done with the telephone ringing continually? "I think there should be a secretary to the secretary," she told Irene Hershberger. But she was much impressed by her new boss. "How he keeps his equilibrium and knows so much about so many things is beyond me—I'm sure the power is beyond his own too, but he does have an amazing mind."[58]

Nothing frustrated Bender and his secretaries more than the torrent of mail which engulfed his office daily, demanding response. Some of it was annoying, as when in 1953 his old adversary J. L. Stauffer, just back from a visit to Pennsylvania, reported to Bender that he had been told that Bender had called premillennialism a "damnable heresy." Is it true? Stauffer demanded to know. Bender replied that he had never in his life used the word "damnable," but he also acknowledged that he may at some point have quoted his old Princeton professor J. Gresham Machen, who had once called premillennialism a "grievous heresy."[59] After Bender returned in 1961 from the Prague Peace Conference, he gave an interview on a Goshen radio station. A listener who claimed to be a "Born Again Christian and I Know it" accused Bender of propounding a "rather Red than dead" philosophy with his peace talk.[60] Bender's reply scarcely concealed his annoyance with his detractor.

However, Bender did not merely respond. He was himself an aggressive meddler in all sorts of matters. Walking to church one Sunday morning, he noticed that students were playing tennis.

Why is that allowed? he inquired of Atlee Beechy, who by then was Goshen's dean of students.[61] He also complained about the growing tolerance for intercollegiate athletics at the college.

Sometimes his complaints had to do with turf prerogatives. In 1958 he learned that Paul Erb, the executive secretary of the MC Mennonite general conference, and Boyd Nelson, the executive secretary of the MC Relief and Service Committee (MRSC), had attended a Civil Defense meeting in Washington. Why did you do it when that sort of thing lies within the scope of my Peace Problems Committee? he inquired. Erb, unintimidated, insisted that Civil Defense had been made the responsibility of the MRSC. Besides, Erb told Bender, you are much too busy to try to deal with this new problem. You should give up some of your administrative burdens so that "you may do some of the scholarship for which you are so well prepared and which we so badly need from you."[62] It was not advice Bender was eager to hear in 1958, not even from Paul Erb.

Amid the pressures, there were many satisfactions. Harold and Elizabeth provided the prizes for the annual peace oratorical contest at Goshen College, ten dollars from Harold for the men's winner and five dollars from Elizabeth to the women's winner. Throughout the decade, Bender's students gathered their graduate degrees, to his great delight. Both Robert Kreider and Paul Peachey received their Ph.D. degrees in 1953. "May I extend to you a most cordial welcome into the corps of true Doctors in the Mennonite church," Bender told Peachey.[63] Probably nothing gave Bender greater pleasure than the Festschrift *The Recovery of the Anabaptist Vision*. Within hours of receiving it, he wrote a letter of thanks to the writers of the book. "I am completely surprised and overwhelmed by the anniversary volume," he told John C. Wenger. "It is a testimony of fellowship to the great cause we are committed to as co-laborers."[64]

• • •

It was Bender's birthday. He was sixty-four years old. As usual, he worked all day, largely to prepare his Conrad Grebel lectures for publication later that fall. He also wrote one momentous letter, which he had to type himself because Irene Hershberger had just left for a yearlong stint at the offices of MCC in Frankfurt and Ada Schrock had not yet arrived. The letter was addressed to President Mininger.[65]

Bender informed Mininger that on his next birthday, in 1962, he would be sixty-five years old. "I therefore tender to you my resignation as dean of the Goshen College Biblical Seminary, effective September 1, 1962."[66] It was a surprising, even shocking announcement from a man who had never willingly resigned from any office in his entire life. But Bender was convinced that administrators should retire at sixty-five. Only a few years earlier, he had pushed through a policy which required all MCC administrators to retire at sixty-five. Orie Miller had been the first one affected and had retired in 1958. Clearly, Bender had to follow his friend's example.

Bringing himself to resign could not have been easy. The ever-observant Ada Schrock noted that on the day of the public announcement, "the Dean" seemed pensive, preoccupied, and sad.[67] Actually, Bender had been quite tired: his ability to bounce back from the effects of long trips and many meetings had greatly diminished. After returning from a weeklong East-West Theological Colloquy in Czechoslovakia, he complained that he was feeling tired and unwell. Ada Schrock worried that he "looked pretty gray and weary, and sort of dazed part of the time." He had a severe bout with laryngitis, and Schrock suggested he stay in bed for a few days. Bender said he did not "believe in going to bed." But Schrock was worried. For the first time since she had known him, Bender seemed to suffer significant lapses of memory. "He really needs to retire," she told Irene Hershberger.[68]

However, despite Bender's diminishing physical vigor, he plunged on. One memorable day he left before sunrise for an all-day meeting in Chicago, returned late that evening, and called Schrock to come to the office to take dictation for an hour before he finally went home to bed. On that day he had forgotten to tell anyone that he would be gone. When Schrock had called to the Bender home to inquire why he had not come to the office, Elizabeth tried to reassure her with the quip "This happens to me sometimes too." Elizabeth meant, He often forgets to tell me where he's going, too.[69]

During June 1962, Bender's physical condition deteriorated, and he was persuaded to enter the Elkhart hospital for tests. He seemed to have a problem with his gall bladder, and the tests kept him in the hospital for nearly a week. It was a week he could hardly spare, since just then the last details were being worked out for the seventh Mennonite World Conference, to be held at Kitchener, Ontario, in early August. "I am carrying on from my hospital room as an office," Bender told Paul Mininger. "Ada comes over here daily." He did accede to Mininger's suggestion that John C. Wenger be appointed the acting dean of the seminary.[70]

Unfortunately, the tests confirmed not a gall-bladder problem but pancreatic cancer. Exploratory surgery at the Presbyterian-St. Luke's Hospital in Chicago revealed that the cancer was inoperable. Hoping against hope, Bender agreed to a series of cobalt radiation treatments at Memorial Hospital in South Bend. Each day during July and August, one of his faculty colleagues or a student transported him on a fifty-mile round trip for his treatment. The exertion of travel plus the radiation was extremely debilitating. By the end of July, he appeared emaciated and feeble. "He walks like an old man," Guy Hershberger told Franklin Littell.[71]

Nevertheless, Bender continued to monitor preparations for the Seventh Mennonite World Conference, an event one observer predicted would be the largest gathering of Mennonites in four hundred years. Estimates put expected attendance at more than ten thousand; when the event came, nearly fifteen thousand attended.[72] Fortunately, Bender had able assistants in C. J. Dyck, who was the conference executive committee secretary, and Erland Waltner, one of the World Conference vice presidents. The two men carried on the work Bender had to give up.

Despite a valiant effort to build up his strength so he could attend the weeklong event, Bender had reluctantly to accept the fact that at best he might be able to attend only the last weekend. It was decided that Erland Waltner would read Bender's opening keynote address entitled "Who Is the Lord?" Harold and Elizabeth were able to fly to Kitchener on the last Saturday of the conference, and on Sunday evening Bender addressed the throng gathered in the cavernous Memorial Auditorium. He titled his remarks "My Vision for the World Conference," and recounted the remarkable story of how the movement had evolved. In an unusual personal note, he observed that he was probably the only person in the hall who had been at all the world conferences since 1930.[73]

After Bender's remarks, a Brethren in Christ bishop, E. J. Schwalm, a venerable member of the MWC presidium, offered a tribute to Bender: "Your name is a household word around the world." Then he called on the audience to stand in honor of Bender's work as a churchman and a leader of world Mennonites. It was a poignant and moving moment.[74]

During the next several days, Bender was well enough to chair the MWC presidium meetings (helped by frequent rest, on a bed installed for him in the presidium office). At the last meeting of the presidium, he proposed that the presidium gather for a planning session in 1963 at the European Mennonite Bible School in Switzerland. Ever the travel agent and economizer, he urged that it be during October, to take advantage of the cheaper fares available each fall.[75]

The conference ended on Tuesday evening with an eloquent benedictory prayer by Bender, almost certainly the best-remembered Mennonite prayer ever uttered. Using King James "Thees" and "Thous" and the masculine language of the day, he addressed God on behalf of his people. "We would not finish our thanksgiving," he prayed, "without thanking Thee for all the brethren and how much they mean to us, how much they have meant to us, every one of them. Increase our love for the brethren and for the brotherhood." And in a line which brought tears to many eyes, given Bender's own precarious hold on life, he prayed: "Yes, great Jehovah, guide us, lead us, until some day we shall hear the welcome applaud: 'Come home, thou beloved of the Lord, thou servant of mine, and dwell in the house of the Lord forever.' "[76]

With Harold and Elizabeth's return to Goshen, the radiation treatments resumed, and by the end of August, Bender seemed somewhat improved. He was well enough, he thought, to attend the annual college and seminary faculty meeting at the Little Eden

Retreat Center 250 miles to the north in Michigan. At some point during the first day of the retreat, J. C. Wenger suddenly realized Bender was not with the group. Searching for him, Wenger found Bender lying on a bench in the lodge, doubled up with pain. Wenger rushed him home and helped Elizabeth put him to bed.[77]

That episode prompted Bender to cancel all of his appointments. In a letter to an Ontario pastor, he expressed regret that he would not be able to fulfill a promise to deliver his Conrad Grebel lectures in the pastor's community. Then with the dogged hope that so characterized his life, he promised to come later, after his health improved.[78]

There was, however, one obligation he could not bear to give up. He would attend the MCC executive committee meetings on September 7-8 at the Atlantic Hotel in Chicago. On the second morning of the meeting, as was their custom, Orie Miller and Harold Bender had breakfast together. For thirty-one years, with only a few exceptions, Harold and Orie had attended the four-times-a-year meetings together, Orie as executive secretary and Harold as secretary. In his role as secretary of the executive committee, Bender had developed a remarkable ability to take notes and prepare the minutes of the meeting at the same time. When a meeting ended, the minutes were ready for typing. Given the complexity and variety of the material covered in a typical meeting, it was an amazing feat.

This meeting, September 7-8, 1962, was no exception. For a day and a half, the committee dealt with a massive amount of MCC business. Present were three old-timers (C. N. Hostetter Jr., Orie Miller, and Harold Bender) and three younger men (Atlee Beechy, Robert Kreider, and William Snyder). Everyone on the committee was amazed at Bender's stamina as he filled page after page with hastily scribbled notes. However, on the second day at about 2:00 p.m., Bender suddenly suffered acute pain and realized he could not continue. He asked chairman C. N. Hostetter to appoint a secretary to take his place. Hostetter chose Robert Kreider. Ashen-faced, Bender gathered up his papers, handed them to Kreider, and without a word left the room. He had just attended his last MCC executive committee meeting.[79]

**Harold Bender at his last public meeting, September 17, 1962, in the chapel of the Goshen College Biblical Seminary. Dutch Mennonite professor J. A. Oosterbaan is addressing the seminarians. From the left: Paul Mininger, Samuel F. Pannabecker, Erland Waltner, and Harold S. Bender.** John C. Wenger papers, AMC.

Robert Krieder, reflecting later on Bender's departure that afternoon, wondered why they—Bender's colleagues—had not had the presence of mind to pause for a prayer and a benediction as their colleague and mentor departed. "We had a sense that something momentous was happening," Kreider recalled, "but somehow we let the moment pass."[80]

In subsequent weeks Bender's condition worsened, especially the pain from the malignancy. In his last public act, on Monday, September 17, he crossed the street from his house to the new chapel in the seminary building, where he introduced Dutch professor Jacob A. Oosterbaan. Oosterbaan was addressing the opening service of the fall semester at the Goshen College Biblical Seminary. Bender used the occasion to reflect briefly on the life of his Dutch friend T. O. Hylkema, who had died five days earlier.[81]

That evening Harold and Elizabeth packed his suitcase, and the next morning (Tuesday) he returned to the Presbyterian-St. Luke's hospital in Chicago. The ostensible reason was further diagnosis; but the real reason was more carefully to monitor and control his pain.

On Friday afternoon Bender's good friend, church historian Franklin Littell, visited him in the hospital and found him busy writing letters. One letter was to his longtime friend and MWC collaborator, French bishop Hans Nussbaumer. Another was to a new friend, Quaker leader Douglas Steere, whom he had learned to know during their trip together to Czechoslovakia earlier in the year. Littell found Bender lucid, thoughtful, even upbeat. But he was also realistic about his situation. "I'm ready to go home," he told Littell. "I think my work is done."[82] A few hours later, about 8:30 in the evening, he suffered a stroke. Within minutes he was dead.

After a memorial service at the College Mennonite Church, Bender was buried at the Prairie View cemetery, just over the horizon from his beloved Goshen College and Seminary.

*Great Jehovah, guide us, lead us,*
*until some day we shall hear*
*the welcome applaud:*
*"Come home, thou beloved*
*of the Lord, thou servant of mine,*
*and dwell in the house*
*of the Lord forever."*

*—Bender at the 1962 Mennonite World Conference*

# Epilogue

HAROLD S. BENDER led and nurtured his people during one of the most cataclysmic eras in human history. He and his tiny group of a half-million Mennonites, nonviolent Christians descended from Reformation-era Anabaptists, found themselves in the thick of the maelstrom. In the Soviet Union, in Nazi Germany, in occupied France and the Netherlands, in North and South America, in Africa and Asia and elsewhere—Mennonites struggled to cope with the demonic forces of twentieth-century history.

Bender became a leader of the Mennonites because the times demanded a leader and because his particular qualities of personality and character commended him to his people. His gravestone contains no epitaph. That omission is in keeping with Mennonite modesty: Harold Bender had served a people devoted to simplicity and understatement. Even to suggest that he was one of Mennonitism's most influential leaders seems somehow to violate that code of restraint. Yet therein lies Bender's most unusual accomplishment: he was able to reconcile his assertive, entrepreneurial style with the self-effacing ethos of his people.

Harold Bender had an unusual ability to speak the faith-language and practice the simple piety of ordinary Mennonites, and to do so authentically. Mennonite Central Committee administrator Peter Dyck, who traveled with Bender in relief work in post-World War II Europe, has recalled that each evening, without fail, Bender read a passage of Scripture and kneeled at his bedside for audible prayer. Perhaps no ritual among Mennonites was more pervasive than the one Peter Dyck observed. Harold Bender lived his life within the framework of conventional Mennonite tradition and piety.

However, successful leaders not only reenact the tradition: they guide the symbols and institutions which maintain it. Almost all of Harold Bender's life and energy was devoted to the care and direction of Mennonite institutions. At nearly every point in his life, colleagues urged Bender to give up his institutional leadership to practice what those advisers construed to be his true vocation, the production of ideas. He always refused. At the center of his being was a managerial urge which required many outlets. Goshen College and its Seminary, the Mennonite World Conference, and the Mennonite Central Committee became the instruments of that managerial desire. In Bender's hands those institutions became modernizing agents, helping Mennonites navigate the unsettling changes they encountered in the twentieth century.

Successful leaders must possess ideas powerful enough to shape the identity of their followers. Among the most powerful ideas are those which link a meaningful past to a purposeful future. Bender's influential 1943 essay, "The Anabaptist Vision," did just that. It forged Mennonites into a community of memory rooted in the sixteenth century, a community with strong religious impulses embodied in nonviolent service, devout discipleship, and a primary identity with the people of God, the church.

Harold Bender's life was almost entirely public. He possessed no significant personal avocations. He did enjoy travel, photography, and book-collecting, but almost always in the context of his work. He was a devoted husband, a loving father, a loyal and warmhearted friend, an engaging conversationalist. He enjoyed good food, travel, and well-fitted clothes. He was a profoundly spiritual person whose Christian faith was both experiential and rational. In short, Bender was a healthy human being. Nevertheless, some may judge that Harold Bender's life lacked proportion. He was never able to create a boundary between his personal and public life. As a result, his public life became all-consuming. It is thus no accident that a biography of Harold Bender is almost entirely the life of a public man.

Bender's oversized public persona expressed a deep-seated need to be a determining presence in the activities of the institutions he served. As a result, he continually undertook more obligations than he was able to fulfill. His time and energy never caught up with the rush of duty. Especially his time: for most of his life, what he lacked was not energy, but time. The effect was a pervasively harried style of life.

As a leader, Harold Bender acted forthrightly, but he was never a solo leader. In fact, his most normal leadership venue was a committee. Bender was a member of a generation of collective Mennonite leadership whose overlapping and interlocking relationships gave a fairly small cadre almost complete control of most major Mennonite institutions. His was a transitional generation: the fathers had invented the institutions; now, in Bender's generation, it fell to the sons (in that generation, seldom to daughters!) to refine and adapt the institutions to the vicissitudes of the middle decades of the twentieth century. For that task, Bender was almost perfectly equipped.

Bender's generation of leaders completed the organizational centralization of the Mennonite Church (MC). Those leaders' penchant to solve problems by creating central churchwide organizations may have mitigated the worst effects of powerful social forces in modern American society, for example, mass communications, consumerism, and suburbanization. Thus, as the compact rural Mennonite communities all but disappeared in the face of new social movements, central Mennonite institutions—colleges, seminaries, service agencies, retirement communities—became alternative centers of Mennonite identity. Another result of the centralization was to reduce the theological divisions within the MC. By the time of Bender's death, the East-West and conservative-progressive cleavages among MC, earlier so pervasive, had largely dissipated.

Wittingly and unwittingly, Bender and his generation forged a theological middle ground that was evangelical and somewhere between pietism and conventional Protestantism. Resting on that theological ground, the Mennonite church's network of centralized organizations and its new pattern of seminary-trained pastors admirably met the needs of a prospering, middle-class Mennonite people. Bender linked *The Mennonite Quarterly Review* and the Mennonite Historical Library to *The Mennonite Encyclopedia*, the Mennonite World Conference, and the Mennonite Central Committee. In doing so, he forged a powerful convergence of ideas, images, and institutions which gave Mennonites a surge of assertive self- confidence.

A commentator certainly might argue that a significant effect of Bender's leadership was to make the American Mennonite passage into mainstream American life somewhat less traumatic than it might otherwise have been. One consequence of his centralizing, modernizing, and historicizing work was to free Mennonites to shift from a sectarian to a denominational milieu and do so with remarkable ease and speed. He helped prepare his people for the swift, corrosive social and economic changes which engulfed them in the 1960s and 1970s.

Bender certainly did not intend to help Mennonites join mainstream America; but neither was he able wholeheartedly to embrace the system of protective nonconformity which his father's generation had fashioned. In a 1946 speech, he acknowledged as much: "It is an open question," he told his audience, "whether it is possible to maintain without undue price a complex of culture that is much different from the surrounding world, which leaves us primarily education as a means."

Bender's lifework was built on the premise that if he could change and strengthen the way Mennonites thought about their faith, they would also practice the earnest discipleship so central in his formulation of the Anabaptist Vision. To a remarkable degree, Bender succeeded in changing how Mennonites think about their faith. His most formative ideas, focused in the Anabaptist Vision, permeate contemporary Mennonite consciousness. Even Mennonites who have never heard of the Anabaptist Vision embrace its formulations. It is debatable whether that consciousness has changed Mennonite practice to the extent that Bender would have expected.

Harold Bender helped to create the institutions and the theology which carried Mennonites through perhaps their most pervasive transformation since the sixteenth century. When he died in 1962, that transformation was already underway, and during the next decade the changes continued amidst much stress and strain. The social, political, and cultural turbulence generated by the Vietnam war, the civil rights movement, and the new youth culture of the 1960s—these upheavals rippled through the Mennonite churches. In that context the dissonance among Mennonites was often generational. Youthful Mennonites were challenging older ones on a range of issues, some as mundane as counterculture dress, others as profound as resisting the draft and opposing capital punishment.

It is tempting to speculate how Bender might have responded to new changes if he had lived beyond 1962. Would he have been resilient enough to offer imaginative leadership as an elder statesman? What new institutional initiatives might he have generated? Could he have creatively adapted the Anabaptist Vision to the turbulent "baby-boomer" milieu? Perhaps nothing was more extraordinary about Bender than his amazing ability to sense the mood of his people and to respond with the care and nurture they required. The turbulent 1960s would have challenged Bender's patience; but certainly, they would not have changed his deep-seated commitments.

Robert Friedmann once called Bender "an event—a human phenomenon of unique dimension." Bender's personal endowments were certainly remarkable, and he was indeed a leader of "unique dimension." Yet his was not the leadership of a Moses leading his people out of bondage. Instead, his was the more commonplace but equally consequential opportunity to invest his people with a new self-definition. At the center of that new understanding was the refinement of an old and rather commonplace theological concept called "holiness of life." Bender offered a new term in its place—"discipleship"—and shifted the focus of Christian faith from a state of being to a quest: *"Nachfolge Christi"* (following Christ).

Bender's people, the Mennonites, found discipleship theology both liberating and convincing. By the mid-1960s the concept of discipleship had become the common property and the theological meeting place for Mennonites of virtually all theological orientations. Mennonites might disagree about the applications of nonresistance or the nature of the church. But about the centrality of discipleship in the life of the believer and of the church, there could be no dispute. As the boundaries of Mennonite communal life eroded, discipleship became the vital centerpiece around which Mennonites rallied. Bender, who had spent his entire life attempting to live and work in the middle ground of the Mennonite church, had accomplished an end fundamentally coherent with his own life. Discipleship had existed at the very heart of historic Anabaptism, and by the time of his death, it had become the central theological credo of his own people. In that development rests Harold S. Bender's greatest accomplishment.

# Abbreviations

ADS     Algemeene Doopsgezinde Sociëteit (Dutch Mennonite General
        Conference)
AFSC    American Friends Service Committee
AMC     Archives of the Mennonite Church, at 1700 S. Main St.,
        Goshen, Ind.
ASCH    American Society of Church History
Bender papers   Harold S. Bender papers, AMC
BOHC    Bender Oral History Collection, in AMC
BSC     Brethren Service Committee
CM      *Christian Monitor*
CPS     Civilian Public Service
CRALOG  Council of Relief Agencies Licensed for Operation
        in Germany
EMC     Eastern Mennonite College, Harrisonburg, Va.
EMS     Eastern Mennonite School, Harrisonburg, Va.
EMU     Eastern Mennonite University, Harrisonburg, Va.
FOR     Fellowship of Reconciliation
GC      Goshen College, Goshen, Ind.
GC Mennonite   See GCMC
GCBS    Goshen College Biblical Seminary, MC Mennonite
GCMC    General Conference Mennonite Church
GCR     *Goshen College Record*, a periodical
GCs     General Conference Mennonite people
G & EKB papers   Papers of George and Elsie Kolb Bender (parents
        of Harold S. Bender), AMC
GH      *Gospel Herald*, a periodical
Herald Press   Scottdale, Pa., and Kitchener or Waterloo, Ontario
Horsch papers   Papers of John Horsch, AMC
HPC     Historic Peace Churches
HSB     Harold S. Bender
HT      *Herald of Truth*, a periodical
IFOR    International Fellowship of Reconciliation

IMP      International Mennonite Peace Committee
*Maple Leaf*   Yearbook of Goshen College
MB **Mennonite**   Brethren (church)
MBMC   Mennonite Board of Missions and Charities, Elkhart, Ind.
         (Collection in AMC)
MBs      Mennonite Brethren people
MBS      Mennonite Biblical Seminary, GC Mennonite
MC       "Old" Mennonite Church
MCA      Mennonite Community Association
MCC      Mennonite Central Committee, Akron, Pa. (Collection in
         AMC)
MCPC     Mennonite Central Peace Committee
MCs      "Old" Mennonite Church people
ME       *The Mennonite Encyclopedia* (vols. 1-4, 1955-59; vol. 5, 1990)
MEC      *The Mennonite Encyclopedia Collection* (in AMC)
MHL      Mennonite Historical Library, Goshen College, Goshen, Ind.
ML       *Mennonite Life*, a periodical
MLA      Mennonite Library and Archives, Bethel College, North
         Newton, Kan.
MPH      Mennonite Publishing House, Scottdale, Pa.
MQR      *Mennonite Quarterly Review*
MRC      Mennonite Relief Committee
MRSC     Mennonite Relief and Service Committee
MSHLA    Menno Simons Historical Library and Archives, Eastern
         Mennonite University, Harrisonburg, Va.
MTS      Mennonite Travel Service
MWC      Mennonite World Conference (Collection in AMC)
NCA      North Central Association of Colleges and Schools
NSBRO    National Service Board for Religious Objectors
NYA      National Youth Administration
PPC      Peace Problems Committee of the MC Mennonite Church
         (Collection in AMC)
SCPC     Swarthmore College Peace Collection, Swarthmore, Pa.
SS       Steamship
TAK      Täuferakten-Kommission (a commission for publishing
         Anabaptist sources in the series Quellen zur Geschichte der
         Täufer [before 1940, Wiedertäufer]; see *ME*, 4:237-238)
UMT      Universal Military Training
UNRRA    United Nations Relief and Rehabilitation Administration
VS       Voluntary Service
WCC      World Council of Churches
YMCA     Young Men's Christian Association
YPC      Young People's Conference
YPSLA    Young People's Social and Literary Association

# Notes

## Chapter 1

1. George L. Bender to HSB, Apr. 21, 1917, f. 5, b. 1, Bender papers.

2. Abraham A. Weaver, *A Standard History of Elkhart County, Indiana* (Chicago: American Historical Society, 1916), 318-319.

3. See Theron F. Schlabach, *Gospel Versus Gospel: Mission and the Mennonite Church, 1863-1944* (Herald Press, 1980).

4. In Funk's time (and even today), Mennonites often used "old" to distinguish the largest branch of Mennonites from other groups such as the more culturally progressive General Conference Mennonites, the more traditional Old Order Mennonites, or the more revivalist Mennonite Brethren in Christ. By about the 1950s, the term "MC" (for "Mennonite Church") often replaced the nickname "old." Thus MC has become more or less the official term often used in the denomination's own documents. Old Mennonites should not be confused with Old Order Mennonites. Old Order Mennonites, like the Old Order Amish, formed around Funk's time precisely because they rejected various changes Funk was helping to bring into the "old" or MC Mennonite Church. This book uses "MC" even though the usage is partly redundant (as in MC Mennonite Church) or anachronistic. Following current usage, it will also let "MCs" identify the people of the Mennonite Church—alongside "GCs" for the people of the General Conference Mennonite Church, and "MBs" for the people of the Mennonite Brethren Church. Amish Mennonites separated from other Mennonites in 1693 in Europe. Many Amish Mennonites migrated to America in the eighteenth and early nineteenth centuries. In the latter half of the nineteenth century, some Amish Mennonites became Old Order Amish. In the course of the twentieth century, most other Amish Mennonites joined the MC Mennonite church.

5. John A. Hostetler, *God Uses Ink: The Heritage and Mission of the Mennonite Publishing House After Fifty Years* (Herald Press, 1958), 51, 57.

6. The only book-length treatment on Funk is Helen Kolb Gates, *Bless the Lord, Oh My Soul: A Biography of Bishop John Fretz Funk, 1835-1930* (Herald Press, 1964). The most accessible source of information on Funk is *ME*, 2:421.

7. John Funk to George Bender, June 28, 1890, b. 1, f. 4, G&EKB papers.

8. John Sylvanus Umble, *Mennonite Pioneers* (Mennonite Publishing House, 1940), 103. For more on George L. Bender, see the chapter on him in that book; also the record of interview with Elsie Bender, undated, f. 3, b. 15, G&EKB papers.

9. Quoted in Schlabach, *Gospel Versus Gospel* (see n. 3, above), 43.

10. Daniel Bender to George Bender: Feb. 1, 1896, f. corres. A-C, b. 1, Mennonite Evangelizing Board of America papers, AMC; and Mar. 1, 1891, b. 1, f. 5, G&EKB papers.

11. Daniel Bender to George Bender, Sept. 13, 1890, f. 4, b. 1, G&EKB papers.

12. Umble, *Mennonite Pioneers*, 104.

13. Violet B. Turner, "My Family: An Informal Narrative Written for My Children" (n.d.), b. 11, G&EKB papers.

14. Turner, 6.
15. Turner, 6.
16. George Bender to Dear Friend, June 5, 1896, f. 1, b. 14; A. C. Kolb to Elsie Kolb, summer 1895, f. 19, b. 1; G&EKB papers.
17. Daniel Bender to George Bender, Feb. 1, 1896; Daniel Bender to George Bender, May 1, 1896; f. 10, b. 1, G&EKB papers.
18. Mother to Son and Daughter, Dec. 15, 1896, f. 1, b. 14, G&EKB papers.
19. Umble, *Mennonite Pioneers* (see n. 8), 105; G. L. Bender cashbook, f. 5, b. 18, G&EKB papers.
20. G. L. Bender cashbook, f. 5, b. 18, G&EKB papers.
21. George Bender to Elsie (Kolb) Bender, Aug. 25, 1900, f. 1, b. 14, G&EKB papers.
22. Daniel Burkhard to George Bender, Jan. 27, 1896; E. J. Berkey to George Bender, Aug. 13, 1894; f. A-C, b. 1, Mennonite Evangelizing Board of America papers, AMC.
23. Turner, "My Family" (see n. 13), 6.
24. Elsie Bender to HSB, Sept. 19, 1918, f. 2, b. 2, G&EKB papers.
25. Elsie Bender to HSB: July 15, 1914; Oct. 24, 1919; Nov. 20, 1919; f. 3, b. 2, G&EKB papers.
26. Elsie Bender to HSB, Sept. 19, 1918, f. 2, b. 2, G&EKB papers.
27. Elsie Bender to HSB, Mar. 20, 1919, f. 1, b. 2, G&EKB papers.
28. Elsie Bender to HSB, Dec. 29, 1918, f. 1, b. 2, G&EKB papers.
29. Elsie Bender to HSB: Dec. 11, 1919; Mar. 20, 1919; Oct. 20, 1918; f. 1, b. 2, G&EKB papers.
30. Violet Bender to HSB, Aug., 1921, b. 11, G&EKB papers.
31. Elsie Bender to HSB, Dec. 31, 1919, f. 3, b. 2, G&EKB papers.
32. Schlabach, *Gospel Versus Gospel* (see n. 3), 92-93.
33. *ME*, 3:593.
34. Umble, *Mennonite Pioneers* (see n. 8), 110; *Goshen College Record* (Dec. 1915), 11.
35. Florence Bender, interviewed by John Bender at Elkhart, Ind., Dec. 22, 1977, tape in BOHC.
36. John Ellsworth Bender, interviewed by Albert Keim in Philadelphia, Oct. 11, 1991, tape in BOHC.
37. "Prairie Street Mennonite Sunday School" (Dec. 25, 1916), f. 10, b. 18, G&EKB papers.
38. Mary Olive Christophel, "Y. P. S. and L. A. Society," box 7, Prairie Street Mennonite Church papers, AMC.
39. Ibid.
40. J. D. Graber, *100 Years: Prairie Street Mennonite Church* (Elkhart, Ind.: The [Prairie Street Mennonite] Church, 1971), 19.
41. Elsie Bender to HSB, Apr. 15, 1920, f. 4, b. 2, G&EKB papers; Florence Bender, interviewed by John Bender at Elkhart, Ind., Dec. 22, 1977, p. 14, transcript of tape in BOHC.
42. George Bender to J. E. Hartzler, Aug. 29, 1916, f. G. L. Bender, b. 6, Goshen College presidential papers, AMC.
43. Elsie Bender to HSB, Apr. 15, 1920, f. 4, b. 2, G&EKB papers; Florence Bender, interviewed by John Bender at Elkhart, Ind., Dec. 22, 1977, p. 14, transcript of tape in BOHC.
44. Schlabach, *Gospel Versus Gospel* (see n. 3), 87.
45. Umble, *Mennonite Pioneers* (see n. 8), 114.
46. J. C. Meyer, "In College, June 1914-1916" (n.d.), f. 1, b. 6, J. C. Meyer papers, AMC.
47. Turner, "My Family" (see n. 13), 11.
48. George Bender to HSB, Apr. 24, 1919, f. 5, b. 1, G&EKB papers.

49. George Bender to HSB, Apr. 15, 1920, f. 4, b. 1, f. 4, G&EKB papers.
50. Dr. Larue Carter to HSB, Apr. 29, 1920, f. 16, b. 1, G&EKB papers.
51. Letters of Elsie Bender to HSB and George Bender to Elsie Bender, passim, 1920, f. 4, b. 2, G&EKB papers.
52. Elsie Bender to HSB, Apr. 15, 1920, f. 4, b. 2, G&EKB papers.

**Chapter 2**
1. Dora Gehman, interviewed by John Bender at Goshen, Ind., May 26, 1989, tape in BOHC.
2. Orie B. Gerig to HSB, Oct. 1, 1920, f. 1, b. 2, Bender papers.
3. Aunt Cinda to HSB, July 17, 1900, f. 6, b. 2, Bender papers.
4. Aunt Cinda to Elsie Bender, May 2, 1907, f. 2, b. 14, G&EKB papers.
5. Violet B. Turner, "My Family: An Informal Narrative Written for My Children" (n.d.), 20, b. 11, G&EKB papers.
6. HSB to Lloyd Blauch, Jan. 16, 1919, f. 2, b. 1, Bender papers.
7. Florence Bender to HSB, Oct. 11, 1916, f. 1, b. 2, Bender papers.
8. John C. Wenger, interviewed by John Bender, May 26, 1989, tape in BOHC; see also Paul Erb, *Orie O. Miller: The Story of a Man and an Era* (Herald Press, 1969), 34-35.
9. Guy F. Hershberger, "Harold S. Bender and His Time," in *Harold S. Bender: Educator, Historian, Churchman*, ed. John C. Wenger et al. (Herald Press, 1964), 11-12.
10. HSB, letter in *Words of Cheer* 34 (Apr. 25, 1909): 4.
11. Dora Gehman, interviewed by John Bender at Goshen, Ind., May 26, 1989, tape in BOHC.
12. HSB's Elkhart High School transcript, 1914, f. 1, b. 108, Bender papers; also John C. Wenger, interviewed by John Bender at Goshen, Ind., May 26, 1989, tape in BOHC.
13. HSB to Dear Papa, June 3, 1914, f. 7, b. 2, Bender papers.
14. Ibid.
15. HSB letters to Family, passim, f. 7, b. 2, Bender papers.
16. *Maple Leaf*, 1918, 113.
17. Susan Fisher Miller, *Culture for Service: A History of Goshen College, 1894-1994* (Goshen, Ind.: Goshen College, 1994), 53-54.
18. *Maple Leaf*, 1915, 50.
19. Ibid. (1918), 108.
20. Ibid. (1915), 80.
21. Ibid. (1915), 17.
22. HSB's academic record, 1914-1915, f. 30, b. 2, J. C. Wenger papers, AMC.
23. Ibid.
24. *Goshen: Sesquicentennial Edition, 1831-1981* (Goshen, Ind.: 1981), 58.
25. George Bender to HSB, Sept. 10, 1916, f. 5, b. 1, Bender papers.
26. HSB to Dear Folks, Sept. 11, 1916, f. 7, b. 2, G&EKB papers. See also George Bender to J. E. Hartzler, Aug. 29, 1916, f. G. L. Bender, b. 6, Goshen College presidential papers, AMC.
27. HSB to Lloyd Blaugh, Jan. 16, 1916, f. 2, b. 1, G&EKB papers.
28. HSB to Raymond Hartzler, Mar. 2, 1919, f. 19, b. 19, Raymond Hartzler papers, AMC.
29. Quoted in John Sylvanus Umble, *Goshen College, 1894-1954* (Goshen, Ind.: Goshen College, 1955), 60.
30. *The Goshen College Record*, Sept. 1913, 2; for a quick survey of connections between the national Christian rural life movement and Mennonite manifestations of a similar sort, see Theron F. Schlabach, *Gospel Versus Gospel: Mission and the Mennonite Church, 1863-1944* (Herald Press, 1980), 263ff.
31. *Maple Leaf*, 1916, passim.
32. Ibid., 1916, 92.

33. Ibid., 1916, 43.
34. *The Goshen College Record*, Feb. 1916, 10.
35. HSB to Dear Folks, Sept. 11, 1916, f. 7, b. 1, Bender papers.
36. HSB to Dear Folks, Feb. 18, 1916, f. 7, b. 1, Bender papers.
37. Jesse Smucker to HSB, Feb. 7, 1917, f. 3, b. 4; Aug. 8, 1917, f. 7, b. 4; Bender papers.
38. HSB to Dear Folks, Sept. 3, 1916, f. 7, b. 2, Bender papers.
39. HSB to Dear Folks, Feb. 18, 1917, f. 7, b. 2, Bender papers.
40. HSB to Dear Folks, Sept. 11, 1916, f. 7. b. 2; Elsie Bender to HSB, Sept. 14, 1916 f. 1, b. 2; Bender papers.
41. George Bender to Ernest Miller, Sept. 6, 1918, f. 1, b. 7, Mennonite Board of Missions papers, AMC.
42. For a good survey of the college and history surrounding it in this period, see Miller, *Culture for Service* (see n. 17), chap. 3.
43. Umble, *Goshen College* (see n. 29), 73.
44. *Maple Leaf*, 1918, 128.
45. HSB's Goshen College transcript, f. 1, b. 108, Bender papers.
46. *Maple Leaf*, 1918, 114-115, 130.
47. *Maple Leaf*, 1918, 130.
48. Elizabeth Horsch, "The Quest of an Ideal," *CM*, Sept. 1913, 271-272.
49. Mary Eleanor Bender, interviewed by Albert Keim at Goshen, Ind., July 1991, notes in BOHC.
50. *Goshen College Record*, June-July, 1918, 7.
51. *Maple Leaf*, 1918, 42
52. Ibid., 1918, 35.
53. Elizabeth Horsch, "Ignorance vs. Error," *Goshen College Record*, Jan. 1918, 9-10.
54. J. B. Smith to Mennonite Board of Education, Feb. 18, 1918, J. B. Smith papers, MSHLA.
55. Ibid.; see also John Horsch to Dear Brother Smith, Feb. 11, 1918, b. 5, E. G. Gehman papers, MSHLA.
56. Payson Miller to HSB, Sept. 17, 1918, f. 9, b. 3, Bender papers.
57. Minutes, Conference of Historic Peace Churches (Chicago, Sept. 18-19, 1936), f. 41, E. L. Harshbarger papers, MLA; Noah A. Keim, interviewed by Albert Keim in Charlottesville, Va., Apr. 2, 1994, notes in BOHC. A young Old Order Amish minister at the time, Noah Keim attended a meeting at the Beech Mennonite congregation near Louisville, Ohio, where Bender met with a group of young Mennonite men employed at a Youngstown steel plant. The date was spring 1943, and Bender was at Beech church to try to persuade the young men to give up such employment. Bender told the story of his work for Goodyear during the summer of 1918 as an example of a mistake of his own which he regretted.
58. George Bender to HSB, June 20, 1918, f. 1, b. 5, G&EKB papers.
59. See n. 57.
60. Elsie Bender to HSB, Aug. 2, 1918, f. 2, b. 2, Bender papers.
61. Ernest Miller to George Bender, Sept. 20, 1918, f. 1, b. 7, Mennonite Board of Missions papers, AMC.
62. George Bender to Ernest Miller, Sept. 6, 1918, f. 1, b. 7, Mennonite Board of Missions papers, AMC.

**Chapter 3**
1. John Sylvanus Umble, *Goshen College, 1894-1954* (Goshen, Ind.: Goshen College, 1955), 92.
2. Elsie Bender to HSB, Aug. 2, 1918, f. 2, b. 2, G&EKB papers.
3. Jesse Smucker to HSB, June 26, 1919, f. 3, b. 4, Bender papers.
4. HSB to Uncle Dan, Mar. 25, 1918, f. 3, b. 1, G&EKB papers.

5. Daniel Bender to George Bender, Feb. 2, 1920, f. 15, b. 1, G&EKB papers.
6. HSB, "Answer to Questionnaire," f. 4, b. 1, Bender papers.
7. HSB to George Bender: Apr. 19, 1919; Mar. 22, 1920; f. 7, b. 2, G&EKB papers.
8. George Bender to Henry Symsma, Feb. 1920, f. 8, b. 2, G&EKB papers.
9. *Bulletin* of Goshen College (July 1922): 6.
10. Mary Miller, *A Pillar of Cloud: The Story of Hesston College* (North Newton, Kan.: Mennonite Press, 1959), 24-25.
11. Based on observations of photographs of all the college classes in those years.
12. HSB to George Bender, Dec. 2, 1918, f. 7, b. 2, G&EKB papers.
13. George Bender to HSB, Dec. 20, 1918, f. 5, b. 1, G&EKB papers.
14. HSB to Raymond Hartzler, Sept. 17, 1918, f. 19, b. 19, Raymond Hartzler papers, AMC.
15. HSB to George Bender, Sept. 28, 1919; George Bender to HSB, Sept. 25, 1919; f. 5, b. 1, G&EKB papers.
16. HSB to George Bender, Dec. 2, 1918, f. 7, b. 2, G&EKB papers.
17. HSB to Raymond Hartzler, Sept. 17, 1918, f. 2, b. 1, Raymond Hartzler papers, AMC.
18. O. B. Gerig to HSB, Oct. 13, 1920, f. 1, b. 2, Bender papers.
19. Daniel Bender to HSB, Apr. 16, 1918, f. 4, b. 1, G&EKB papers; HSB to Raymond Hartzler, Sept. 17, 1918, f. 19, b. 19, G&EKB papers.
20. Various letters of Harold to his family, b. 2, G&EKB papers.
21. *Hesston Academy Journal* (Nov. 1918): 6.
22. Ibid. (Dec. 1918): 7.
23. Ibid. (Feb. 1919): 7.
24. Daniel Kauffman to HSB: Feb. 13, 1919; Mar. 14, 1919; f. 1, b. 3, Bender papers.
25. *Hesston Academy Journal* (Apr. 1919): 5.
26. HSB to Raymond Hartzler, May 14, 1919, f. 19, b. 19, G&EKB papers.
27. George Bender to HSB, Dec. 20, 1918, f. 5, b. 1, G&EKB papers.
28. HSB to George Bender, Apr. 19, 1919, f. 7, b. 2, G&EKB papers.
29. George Bender to HSB, Apr. 24, 1919, f. 5, b. 1, G&EKB papers.
30. Daniel Bender to George Bender, Jan. 26, 1929, f. 15, b. 1, G&EKB papers.
31. T. K. Hershey to HSB, Mar. 11, 1919, f. 15, b. 3, Bender papers.
32. Joseph S. Shoemaker to HSB, July 1, 1919, f. 15, b. 3, Bender papers; HSB to George Bender, May 27, 1919, f. 12, b. 1, G&EKB papers.
33. HSB to George Bender, Sept. 15, 1919, f. 7, b. 2, G&EKB papers.
34. Abram Metzler, interviewed by Albert Keim at Goshen, Ind., July 26, 1991, tape in BOHC.
35. HSB to Raymond Hartzler, Mar. 2, 1919, f. 2, b. 1, Raymond Hartzler papers, AMC.
36. HSB to Raymond Hartzler, May 12, 1919, f. 2. b. 1, Raymond Hartzler papers, AMC.
37. George Bender to HSB, Jan. 17, 1920, f. 5, b. 1, Bender papers.
38. On the formation and history of MCC, see the following: John D. Unruh, *In the Name of Christ: A History of the Mennonite Central Committee and Its Services, 1920-1951* (Herald Press, 1952); Wesley J. Prieb, *Peter C. Hiebert* (Hillsboro, Kan.: Center for Mennonite Brethren Studies, 1990); a special issue entitled "Mennonite Central Committee, 1920-1970," *MQR* 44 (July 1970): esp. 213-244, Guy F. Hershberger, "Historical Background to the Formation of the Mennonite Central Committee."
39. Paul Erb, *Orie O. Miller: The Story of a Man and an Era* (Herald Press, 1969), 143.
40. Raymond Hartzler to HSB, Mar. 20, 1919, f. 3, b. 2, Bender papers.
41. HSB to Raymond Hartzler, May 19, 1919, f. 2, b. 1, Raymond Hartzler papers, AMC.

42. HSB to Raymond Hartzler, May 12, 1919, f. 2, b. 1, Raymond Hartzler papers, AMC.
43. Ibid.
44. *CM*, Apr. 12, 1919, 114.
45. J. C. Meyer to HSB, Aug. 5, 1919, Meyer Corres., b. 3, Bender papers.
46. Ibid.
47. Ibid.
48. HSB to Raymond Hartzler, May 17, 1919, f. 2, b. 1, Raymond Hartzler papers, AMC.
49. Ibid.
50. *Hesston Academy Journal* (Aug.-Sept. 1919): 4.
51. HSB to George Bender, Sept. 28, 1919, f. 7, b. 2, G&EKB papers.
52. *Hesston Academy Journal* (Dec. 1919): 14.
53. *Hesston College Journal* (Feb. 1920): 7.
54. HSB to George Bender, Sept. 28, 1919, f. 7, b. 2, G&EKB papers.
55. Ibid.
56. *Hesston College Journal* (June 1920): 23.
57. Bender family album possessed by Mary Eleanor Bender, Goshen, Ind.
58. *Hesston College Journal* (1919-1920): passim.
59. *Hesston College Journal* (Mar. 1920): 16.
60. HSB to Dear Mother, Dec. 28, 1919, f. 7, b. 2, G&EKB papers.
61. HSB to Dear Father, Dec. 21, 1919, f. 7, b. 2, G&EKB papers.
62. HSB to Dear Mother, Dec. 23, 1919, f. 7, b. 2, G&EKB papers.
63. HSB to Dear Father, Dec. 21, 1919, f. 7, b. 2, G&EKB papers.
64. Harold to Dear Mother, Dec. 28, 1919, f. 7, b. 2; Elsie Bender to HSB, Mar. 11, 1920, f. 4, b. 2; G&EKB papers.
65. HSB to Dear Father, Mar. 22, 1920, f. 7, b. 2, G&EKB papers.
66. George Bender to HSB, Sept. 25, 1919, f. 5, b. 1, G&EKB papers.

**Chapter 4**
1. J. C. Meyer to Samuel Musselman, June 8, 1920, f. 10, b. 2, J. C. Meyer papers, AMC.
2. John Sylvanus Umble, *Goshen College, 1894-1954* (Goshen, Ind.: Goshen College, 1955), 96.
3. Vernon Reiff to Dr. Larue Carter, June 2, 1920, f. 16, b. 1, G&EKB papers. Fortunately C. H. Musselman, one of George Bender's good friends, had given the mission board a $15,000 gift, part of which was for George Bender's care. After an appeal for help in *GH* 13 (June 24, 1920): 250, there was also an inpouring of gifts from many other people,
4. Elsie Bender to HSB, June 24, 1920, f. 4, b. 2, G&EKB papers.
5. Ibid.
6. C. F. Yake to HSB, Sept. 23, 1930, f. 11, b. 4, Bender papers.
7. J. B. Smith to HSB, Oct. 12, 1920, f. 16, b. 3, Bender papers.
8. Ernst Correll to Elizabeth Bender, Sept. 30, 1935, f. 4, b. 6, Bender papers.
9. Paul Horsch, interviewed by Albert Keim at Pittsboro, N.C., Oct., 1991, tape in BOHC.
10. Harold S. Bender, "John Horsch, 1867-1941: A Biography," *MQR* 21 (July 1947): 132.
11. Paul Horsch, interviewed by Albert Keim, at Pittsboro, N.C., Oct. 1991, tape in BOHC.
12. Ibid.
13. Ibid.; see also Menno Horsch, interviewed by Albert Keim at Frankenmuth, Mich., July 25, 1992, notes in BOHC.
14. Bender, "John Horsch, 1867-1941," *MQR* 21 (July 1947): 134.
15. Paul Horsch, interviewed by Albert Keim at Pittsboro, N.C., in Oct. 1991, tape

in the BOHC.

16. Ibid.

17. Mary Ellen Meyer, "Elizabeth Horsch Bender," *MQR* 60 (July 1986): 238ff.

18. John A. Hostetler, *God Uses Ink: The Heritage and Mission of the Mennonite Publishing House After Fifty Years* (Herald Press, 1958), 72.

19. Levi Miller, "The Growth and Decline of Mennonites near Scottdale, Pennsylvania, 1790-1890," *Pennsylvania Mennonite Heritage* (Oct. 1990): 12.

20. For a survey, see Hostetler, *God Uses Ink*, 79ff.

21. Edward Yoder, "A Bibliography of the Writings of John Horsch," *MQR* 21 (July 1947): 205-228.

22. The numbers are cited in Bender, "John Horsch, 1867-1941," *MQR* 21 (July 1947): 143.

23. John Horsch, "The Danger of Liberalism," *GH* 1 (June 20, 1908): 178-179.

24. James C. Juhnke, *Vision, Doctrine, War: Mennonite Identity and Organization in America, 1890-1930*, The Mennonite Experience in America, vol. 3 (Herald Press, 1989), 263.

25. HSB to John C. Wenger, Jan. 7, 1937, f. 27, b. 2, Bender papers.

26. John Horsch to HSB, May 11, 1921, f. 7, b. 2, Bender papers. The letter from Bender to Horsch has been lost, but the evidence is clear in Horsch's letter to Bender.

27. Elizabeth Horsch Bender, "My Seasons of Life," *MQR* 60 (July 1986): 234.

28. Menno Horsch, interviewed by Albert Keim at Frankenmuth, Mich., July 25, 1992, notes in BOHC.

29. Paul Horsch, interviewed by Albert Keim at Pittsboro, N.C., Oct. 1991, tape in BOHC.

30. Menno Horsch, interviewed by Albert Keim at Frankenmuth, Mich., July 25, 1992, notes in BOHC.

31. Ibid. In the interviews with both sons, the pressure to conform to the prevailing standards of nonconformity imposed by bishops Daniel Kauffman and Aaron Loucks was a salient part of their memories.

32. "Report of the Young People's Conference," *CM*, Nov. 1920, 724-726.

33. Guy F. Hershberger, "Historical Background to the Formation of the Mennonite Central Committee," *MQR* 44 (July 1970): 223.

34. Ibid.

35. "Open Letter to the Mennonite Brotherhood from the Mennonite Brethren in Relief Work in France," *GH* 12 (May 8, 1919): 109.

36. Ibid.

37. "Report of the General Conference of Mennonites in France in Reconstruction Work: Held at Clermont-en-Argonne, Meuse, France, June 20-22, 1919," MHL and elsewhere.

38. Ibid.; see also J. C. Meyer, "The Young People's Conference Held in Clermont, France, June 20-22, 1919," f. 1, b. 1, Orie O. Miller papers, AMC.

39. O. B. Gerig, "Mennonite Young People's Conference," *GH* 13 (Apr. 15, 1920): 61.

40. J. L. Stauffer, "Meditations on the Report of the General Conference of Mennonites in France in Reconstruction Work," *GH* 12 (Feb. 19, 1920): 891.

41. O. B. Gerig to J. C. Meyer, Mar. 5, 1920, f. 10, b. 2; see also Vernon Smucker to J. C. Meyer, Mar. 5, 1920, f. 20, b. 4; Orie O. Miller papers, AMC.

42. Letters, 1920, passim, f. 6, b. 4, Bender papers.

43. J. L. Stauffer to HSB, May 31, 1920, f. 6, b. 4, Bender papers.

44. Ibid.

45. HSB to J. L. Stauffer, May 18, 1920, f. 6, b. 4, Bender papers.

46. George R. Brunk to HSB, June 16, 1920, f. 6, b. 1, Bender papers.

47. Ibid.; orig. copy is in H. S. Bender file, b. 2, George R. Brunk I papers, MSHLA.

48. O. B. Gerig to HSB, Mar. 2, 1920, f. 1, b. 2, Bender papers.

49. Ibid.
50. Ibid.
51. Ibid.
52. Ibid.
53. O. B. Gerig, "Mennonite Young People's Conference," *GH* 13 (Apr. 15, 1920): 61.
54. Daniel Kauffman, "Editorial," *GH* 13 (Apr. 15, 1920): 49.
55. HSB to J. L. Stauffer, May 18, 1920, f. 6, b. 4, Bender papers.
56. Ibid.

Chapter 5
1. Jesse Smucker to HSB, Nov. 22, 1920, f. 3, b. 4, Bender papers.
2. *Maple Leaf*, 1921, 140.
3. Ibid., 14.
4. Ibid., 16.
5. Ibid.
6. Paul Erb to HSB, Aug. 11, 1920, f. 14, b. 1, Bender papers.
7. Ernest E. Miller to YPC exec. comm., Sept. 2, 1920, f. 1, b. 92, Bender papers. See also "Echoes from the Young Peoples Conference, 1920," f. 6, b. 92, Bender papers.
8. Jesse Smucker to HSB, Oct. 25, 1920, f. 3, b. 4, Bender papers.
9. HSB to Oscar Burkholder, Oct. 7, 1920, f. 9, b. 1, Bender papers.
10. Ibid.
11. *GH* 12 (Sept. 4, 1919): 418.
12. Ibid.
13. HSB to Daniel Bender, Dec. 15, 1920, f. 5, b. 1, Bender papers.
14. *Goshen College Record*, Jan. 1921, 18.
15. Violet B. Turner, "My Family: An Informal Narrative Written for My Children" (n.d.), 11, box 11, G&EKB papers.
16. J. C. Meyer to C. H. Musselman, Jan. 26, 1921, f. 17, b. 8, Orie O. Miller papers, AMC.
17. Jesse Smucker to HSB, Jan. 19, 1921, f. 3, b. 4, Bender papers.
18. Aaron Loucks to HSB, Jan. 16, 1921, f. 5, b. 3, Bender papers.
19. HSB to YPC exec. comm., Feb. 1, 1921, f. 7, b. 92, Bender papers.
20. Turner, "My Family," 11.
21. Notes, passim, f. 5, b. 18, G&EKB papers.
22. Florence Bender, interviewed by John Bender at Goshen, Ind., Dec. 22, 1977, transcript of a tape, BOHC; see also various items in f. 5, b. 18, G&EKB papers.
23. John Ellsworth Bender, interviewed by Albert Keim in Philadelphia, Pa., Oct. 11, 1991, notes in BOHC.
24. Ibid.
25. Frederick A. Norwood, *From Dawn to Midday at Garrett* (Evanston, Ill.: Garrett Evangelical Theological Seminary, 1978), 91, 104.
26. Ibid.
27. Daniel Kauffman to HSB, Apr. 4, 1921, f. 1, b. 4, Bender papers.
28. HSB to Daniel Kauffman, May 5, 1921, f. 1, b. 3, Bender papers.
29. HSB to Orie O. Miller, July 29, 1921, f. 1, b. 34, Orie O. Miller papers, AMC.
30. Ibid.
31. See Bender's notes in f. 2, b. 100, Bender papers.
32. John Horsch to HSB, May 11, 1921, f. 7, b. 2, Bender papers.
33. C. Henry Smith to HSB, May 9, 1921, f. 2, b. 4, Bender papers. See books by C. Henry Smith: *The Mennonites of America* (Goshen, Ind.: C. Henry Smith, 1909); and *The Mennonites: A Brief History* (Berne, Ind.: Mennonite Book Concern, 1920).
34. Jesse Smucker to HSB, Apr. 13, 1821, f. 3, b. 4, Bender papers.
35. Ibid.
36. Art Slagel to HSB, Oct. 1, 1922, f. 6, b. 4, Bender papers.

37. HSB to Dear Brethren: Aug. 15, 1921; Sept. 15, 1921; f. 7, b. 21, Bender papers.

38. HSB to S. C. Yoder, Aug. 20, 1921, f. 7, b. 92, Bender papers.

39. S. C. Yoder to HSB, Aug. 22, 1921, f. 7, b. 92, Bender papers.

40. HSB to Dear Brethren, Sept. 18, 1921, f. 7, b. 92, Bender papers.

41. Menno Horsch, interviewed by Albert Keim at Frankenmuth, Mich., July 25, 1992, notes in BOHC.

42. Noah Oyer to HSB, Sept. 15, 1921, f. 4, b. 3, Bender papers.

43. Hubert Pellman, *Eastern Mennonite College, 1917-1967* (Harrisonburg, Va.: Eastern Mennonite College, 1967), 266.

44. *Princeton Seminary Catalog*, 1922-23, 64.

45. HSB to Noah Oyer, Nov. 22, 1922, f. 4, b. 3, Bender papers.

46. Noah Oyer to HSB, Apr. 10, 1921, f. 11, b. 3, Bender papers.

47. HSB to Noah Oyer, Nov. 22, 1922, f. 11, b. 3, Bender papers.

48. Machen's most accessible work is J. Gresham Machen, *Christianity and Liberalism* (New York: Macmillan, 1923); a good biography, helpful for delineating Machen's theology, is Ned B. Stonehouse, *J. Gresham Machen: A Biographical Memoir* (Grand Rapids: Eerdmans, 1954).

49. Quoted in George Marsden, *Understanding Fundamentalism and Evangelicalism* (Grand Rapids: W. B. Eerdmans, 1991), 191.

50. Ibid.

51. Notes passim, f. 15, b. 100, Bender papers.

52. HSB to John Horsch, Apr. 29, 1924, b. 2, Horsch papers.

53. HSB to John C. Wenger, Jan. 7, 1937, f. 27, b. 2, Bender papers.

54. This view of Vos's work is found in Mark A. Noll, *Between Faith and Criticism: Evangelicals, Scholarship, and the Bible in America* (San Francisco: Harper & Row, 1986).

55. For an overview of Presbyterian history in the 1920s and Erdman's role, see Lefferts A. Loetscher, *The Broadening Church: A Study of Theological Issues in the Presbyterian Church Since 1869* (Philadelphia: Fortress, 1954).

56. HSB to Elsie Bender, Feb. 25, 1923, f. 8, b. 2, Bender papers.

57. HSB to Orie O. Miller, Dec. 13, 1921, f. 1, b. 34, Orie O. Miller papers, AMC.

58. Ibid.

59. Ibid.; see also Paul Erb to HSB, Aug. 16, 1921, f. 6, b. 32, Bender papers.

60. HSB to Orie O. Miller, Dec. 13, 1921, f. 1, b. 34, Orie O. Miller papers, AMC.

61. HSB to S. C. Yoder, Feb. 4, 1922, f. 13, b. 4, Bender papers.

62. Daniel Bender to HSB, May 11, 1922, f. 5, b. 1, Bender papers.

63. Notes, passim, f. 10, b. 99, Bender papers.

64. Ibid.

65. Ibid.

66. "Report," *CM*, Sept. 1922, 658ff.; see also materials in folders. 8 and 10, b. 92, Bender papers.

67. Editorial, *GH* 15 (May 25, 1922): 145-146.

68. "The Young People's Conference," *CM*, July 1922, 551; "Report of the Young People's Conference," *CM*, Sept. 1922, 658-661.

## Chapter 6

1. HSB to John Horsch, July 22, 1922, b. 2, Horsch papers.

2. Ibid.

3. Art Slagel to HSB, Oct. 1, 1922, f. 1, b. 4, Bender papers.

4. *Princeton Seminary Catalog*, 1922-23, 64.

5. *Princeton Seminary Bulletin*, Nov. 1922, 5, 13.

6. Ibid.

7. For notes and exhibits, see f. 10, b. 100, Bender papers.

8. HSB to Noah Oyer, Nov. 22, 1922, f. 11, b. 3, Bender papers.

9. Ibid.

10. HSB to Elsie Bender, Feb. 18, 1923, f. 8, b. 2, G&EKB papers.

11. HSB to Elsie Bender, Dec. 13, 1922, f. 8, b. 2, G&EKB papers.

12. Ibid.

13. HSB to Elsie Bender, Jan. 7, 1923, f. 8, b. 2, G&EKB papers.

14. HSB to Noah Oyer, Apr. 12, 1923, f. 11, b. 3, Bender papers.

15. *Princeton Seminary Bulletin*, July-Aug. 1923, 6.

16. HSB to Noah Oyer, Apr. 12, 1923, f. 11, b. 3, Bender papers.

17. HSB to Noah Oyer, May 4, 1923, f. 11, b. 3, Bender papers.

18. HSB to Noah Oyer, Nov. 22, 1922, f. 11, b. 3, Bender papers.

19. Ibid.

20. Ibid.

21. *Princeton Seminary Bulletin*, May 1923, 1.

22. The wedding was later reported in *GH* 16 (June 17, 1923): 192, and in *Goshen Daily News*, June 14, 1923, in the "Society and Personals" section; see notes in f. 3, b. 121, Bender papers.

23. HSB to Elsie Bender, Feb. 25, 1923, f. 8, b. 2, G&EKB papers.

24. HSB to Elsie Bender, Apr. 22, 1923, f. 8, b. 2, G&EKB papers.

25. Paul Horsch, interviewed by Albert Keim at Pittsboro, N.C., in Oct. 1991, tape in BOHC.

26. HSB to Elsie Bender, May 1, 1923, f. 8, b. 2, G&EKB papers.

27. "Notice," *GH* 16 (June 14, 1923): 216.

28. HSB to Elsie Bender, Mar. 8, 1923, f. 8, b. 2, G&EKB papers; *GH* 16 (July 12, 1923): 312.

29. HSB to Noah Oyer, June 2, 1923, f. 11, b. 3, Bender papers.

30. Ibid.

31. Ibid.

32. John Sylvanus Umble, *Goshen College, 1894-1954* (Goshen, Ind.: Goshen College, 1955), 103.

33. Editorial, *GH* 16 (Apr. 26, 1923): 65.

34. His attitude seems obvious, although I have no succinct statement of it.

35. John C. Wenger, *The Mennonites in Indiana and Michigan* (Herald Press, 1961), 42ff.

36. "Program of the Young People's Conference" (June 15-17, 1923), f. 9, b. 92, Bender papers.

37. "Call for a Young People's Conference," *GH* 16 (June 14, 1923): 219.

38. Editorial, *GH* 16 (June 28, 1923): 257.

39. Bender family album, in the possession of Mary Eleanor Bender, Goshen, Ind.

40. HSB to Noah Oyer, Nov. 13, 1923, f. 11, b. 3, Bender papers.

41. Ibid.

42. Ibid.

43. Ibid.

44. Ibid.

45. Paul Horsch, interviewed by Albert Keim at Pittsboro, N.C., Oct. 1992, tape in BOHC.

46. HSB to Noah Oyer, Nov. 13, 1923, f. 11, b. 3, Bender papers.

47. HSB, "Report on the Work of the Christenpflicht," *GH* 16 (Oct. 4, 1923): 561-562. John Horsch also wrote articles in the *CM* on the same subject.

48. HSB to John Horsch, July 22, 1922, b. 2, Horsch papers. Actually, the *Goshen Daily News* (June 14, 1923) announcement of the marriage indicated that Bender planned to attend Leipzig University; what may have changed his plan is unclear.

49. HSB to Noah Oyer, Nov. 13, 1923, f. 11, b. 3, Bender papers.

50. Ibid. See also "Notes," *Christian Exponent* 1 (Mar. 14, 1924): 96; 1 (June 6, 1924): 192.

51. HSB to Noah Oyer, Nov. 13, 1923, f. 11, b. 3, Bender papers.
52. Ibid.

**Chapter 7**
1. Maynard L. Cassady to J. Harvey Brumbaugh, Nov. 19, 1923, Admin. Corres., J. Harvey Brumbaugh papers, Juniata College Archives, Huntingdon, Pa.
2. *Der Grosse Brokhaus* (Tübingen, 1934), 163-164.
3. HSB to John Horsch, Jan. 23, 1924, b. 1, Horsch papers. Stauffer's essay was published in *Zeitschrift für Kirchengeschichte* 51 (1933): 545-598; in 1945 Robert Friedmann translated it and Bender published it with the English title "The Anabaptist Theology of Martyrdom," *MQR* 19 (July 1945): 180-214.
4. HSB to John Horsch, Jan. 23, 1924, b. 1, Horsch papers.
5. Ibid. Wellhausen summarized his ideas in his book *Prolegomena zur Geschichte Israels* (Berlin: G. Reimer, 1899).
6. Ingemar Holmstrand, *Karl Heim on Philosophy, Science and the Transcendence of God* (Uppsala: Uppsala Univ., 1980), 5. Homstrand offers a good introduction to the thought of Karl Heim.
7. Ibid., 7.
8. Ibid., 16.
9. HSB to John Horsch, Feb. 11, 1924, b. 7, Horsch papers.
10. HSB to John Horsch, Jan. 23, 1924, b. 2, Horsch papers.
11. Ibid. J. Gresham Machen, *Christianity and Liberalism* (New York: Macmillan, 1923).
12. HSB to John Horsch, Jan. 23, 1924, b. 2, Horsch papers.
13. HSB to John Horsch, Jan. 21, 1924, b. 2, Horsch papers.
14. HSB to John Horsch, Feb. 11, 1924, b. 7, Horsch papers.
15. John Horsch to HSB, Feb. 21, 1923, f. 7, b. 2, Horsch papers.
16. Ibid.
17. *CM*, Jan.-Feb. 1924, passim.
18. For biographical information on Christian Hege, see *ME*, 2:689.
19. For biographical information on Christian Neff, see *ME*, 3:820.
20. HSB to John Horsch, Feb. 11, 1924, b. 7; HSB to Horsch, June 20, 1924, b. 2; Horsch papers.
21. HSB to John Horsch, Feb. 11, 1924, b. 7, Horsch papers.
22. HSB to John Horsch, Jan. 23, 1824, b. 2, Horsch papers.
23. Sanford Yoder to HSB, Oct. 2, 1923, f. 13, b. 4, Bender papers.
24. HSB to Sanford C. Yoder, undated [from internal evidence, about Oct. 15 or 16, 1923], f. 13, b. 4, Bender papers.
25. Ibid.
26. Sanford C. Yoder to HSB, Dec. 1, 1923, f. 13, b. 4, Bender papers.
27. Ibid.
28. Ibid.
29. John Horsch to HSB, Jan. 13, 1924, f. 7, b. 2, Bender papers.
30. Vinora Weaver Salzman, *Day by Day—Year by Year* (n.p.: the author, 1982), 26, 17-18.
31. Vernon Smucker to HSB, July 30, 1924, f. 4, b. 4, Bender papers.
32. See James C. Juhnke, *Vision, Doctrine, War: Mennonite Identity and Organization in America, 1890-1930*, The Mennonite Experience in America, vol. 3 (Herald Press, 1989), 267-269.
33. Sanford Yoder to HSB, Mar. 12, 1924, f. 13, b. 4, Bender papers.
34. Sanford Yoder to John Horsch, Mar. 12, 1924, f. 1, b. 4, Sanford C. Yoder papers, AMC.
35. Vernon Smucker to HSB, July 30, 1924, f. 4, b. 4, Bender papers.
36. HSB to John Horsch, May 13, 1924, b. 2, Horsch papers.
37. Daniel Kauffman to HSB, Mar. 10, 1924, f. 1, b. 3, Bender papers.

38. HSB to John Horsch, Apr. 29, 1924, b. 2, Horsch papers.
39. Sanford C. Yoder to HSB, June 7, 1924, f. 13, b. 4, Bender papers. (Bender's letter of protest apparently is lost, but Yoder referred explicitly to Bender's protest.)
40. Ibid.
41. HSB to Sanford Yoder, July 5, 1924, f. 1, b. 4, Bender papers.
42. HSB to Noah Oyer, Nov. 13, 1923, f. 11, b. 3, Bender papers.
43. Note in *Christian Exponent*, Mar. 14, 1924, 19.
44. John Horsch to HSB, Mar. 27, 1924, f. 7, b. 2, Bender papers.
45. HSB to John Horsch, May 13, June 6, 1924, b. 2, Horsch papers.
46. HSB to John Horsch, June 6, 1924, b. 2, Horsch papers.
47. Donald Durnbaugh, "Ernst H. Correll and Juniata College," *MQR* 67 (Oct. 1993): 481ff.
48. HSB to John Horsch, June 29, 1924, b. 2, Horsch papers.
49. HSB to John Horsch, Oct. 1, 1924, b. 2, Horsch papers.
50. HSB to John Horsch, Oct. 1, 1924, b. 2, Horsch papers.
51. Two letters, HSB to Orie O. Miller, Jan. 20, 1925, Orie O. Miller papers: f. 4, b. 42; f. 10, b. 1.
52. Paul Horsch, interviewed by Albert Keim at Pittsboro, N.C., Oct. 1991, tape in BOHC.
53. Ibid.
54. "Bender Family Obligations, 1931," f. 6, b. 121, Bender papers.
55. John Ellsworth Bender, interviewed by Albert Keim in Philadelphia, Pa., Oct. 11, 1991, tape in BOHC.
56. *Goshen: The First 150 Years* (Goshen, Ind., 1981), 130 and passim.
57. Ibid.
58. Ibid.
59. Ibid.
60. *Maple Leaf*, 1925, 92.

Chapter 8
1. *Christian Exponent*, Oct. 10, 1924, 336.
2. *Maple Leaf*, 1926, 84.
3. HSB to John Horsch, Sept. 28, 1925, b. 3, Horsch papers.
4. *Maple Leaf*, 1931, 82-83.
5. HSB to Violet Bender, Oct. 17, 1928, f. 7, b. 4, Bender papers.
6. See Paul Erb, *Orie O. Miller: The Story of a Man and an Era* (Herald Press, 1969).
7. HSB to Orie O. Miller, Oct. 19, 1925, f. 4, b. 42, Orie O. Miller papers, AMC.
8. HSB to Orie O. Miller, Nov. 26, 1925, f. 4, b. 42, Orie O. Miller papers, AMC.
9. Ibid.
10. HSB to Orie O. Miller, Oct. 11, 1928, f. 1, b. 49, Orie O. Miller papers, AMC.
11. Orie O. Miller to HSB, Oct. 16, 1928, f. 8, b. 3, Bender papers.
12. HSB to Orie O. Miller, Feb. 1, 1926, f. 3, b. 44, Orie O. Miller papers, AMC.
13. HSB to John Horsch, Jan. 8, 1926, b. 4, Horsch papers.
14. HSB to Orie O. Miller, Dec. 12, 1926, f. 3, b. 44, Orie O. Miller papers, AMC; see also HSB to John Horsch, Dec. 12, 1926, b. 3, Horsch papers.
15. Harold S. Bender, "The Need for the Support of the Study of Mennonite History," *GH* 18 (Mar. 18, 1926): 1050-1051.
16. Ibid.
17. Harold S. Bender, "What Can the Church Do for Her Historical Work?" *GH* 20 (various issues, Apr.-May 1927): 58, 90-92, 107, 138, 154, 170, 202.
18. Ibid.
19. HSB to Daniel Kauffman, Mar. 9, 1927, f. 1, b. 3, Bender papers.
20. See "Constitution of the Mennonite Historical Society of Goshen College," f. 9, b. 82, Bender papers.

21. Silas Hertzler diary, Nov. 3, 1924, b. 2, Silas Hertzler papers, AMC.

22. Harold S. Bender, "Mennonite Historical Society," *Goshen College Record*, Oct. 1924, 5-6; every subsequent issue for the next year carried accounts of historical activity, by students or staff.

23. See also Susan Fisher Miller, *Culture for Service: A History of Goshen College, 1894-1994* (Goshen, Ind.: Goshen College, 1995), 147-150.

24. See Ernst Correll, H. S. Bender, and Edward Yoder, "A Letter from Conrad Grebel to Andreas Castelberger," *MQR* 1 (July 1927): 41-53.

25. John Horsch to HSB, Mar. 15, 1925, f. 7, b. 2, Bender papers.

26. HSB to John Horsch, Mar. 17, 1925, b. 7, Horsch papers.

27. HSB to John Horsch, Mar. 2, 23, 1925, b. 7, Horsch papers.

28. HSB to John Horsch, Feb. 11, 1924, b. 2; Horsch to HSB, Feb. 4, 1925, b. 3; Horsch papers.

29. Quoted by Daniel Kauffman in a letter to Dear Brethren, May 12, 1924, f. 1, b. 3, Bender papers.

30. Ibid.

31. HSB to John Horsch, July 18, 1924, b. 2, Horsch papers.

32. Harold S. Bender, "Editorial," *Goshen College Review Supplement*, May-June 1926.

33. Ibid.

34. Harold S. Bender, review of John Ellsworth Hartzler, *Education Among the Mennonites of America* (Danvers, Ill.: Central Mennonite Publishing Co., 1925), in *Goshen College Review Supplement* 8 (May-June 1926): 35-44.

35. HSB to John Horsch, Feb. 1, 1926, b. 3, Horsch papers.

36. "To the Administration of Goshen College" (Nov. 10, 1926), f. 13, b. 4, Bender papers.

37. F. W. Loetscher to HSB, Mar. 2, 1927, f. 11, b. 3, Bender papers. See also "Recommendations for the Complimentary List, 1927," f. 7, b. 83, Bender papers.

38. "To the Youth of the Mennonite Church," *MQR* 1 (Jan. 1927).

39. "Editorial," *MQR* 1 (Jan. 1927): 1-8.

40. HSB to John Horsch, Oct. 4, 1926, b. 3, Horsch papers.

41. HSB to John Horsch, July 14, 1926, b. 3, Horsch papers.

42. HSB to John Horsch, Dec. 12, 1926, b. 3, Horsch papers.

43. HSB to John Horsch, Nov. 9, 1925, b. 3, Horsch papers.

44. HSB, "Editorial," *MQR* 1 (Jan. 1927): 5-6.

45. Harold S. Bender, *Two Centuries of American Mennonite Literature* (Mennonite Publishing House, 1929), vii.

46. Ibid.

47. HSB to Orie O. Miller, Sept. 10, 1927, f. 5, b. 46, Orie O. Miller papers, AMC.

48. Ibid.

49. Harold S. Bender, "Experiences and Plans in Gathering Materials for a Mennonite History," *GH* 21 (May 31, 1928): 186-187.

50. HSB to John Horsch, Feb. 28, 1928, b. 4, Horsch papers.

51. HSB, "Report to the Historical Committee," f. 2, b. 81, Bender papers.

52. HSB to John Horsch, Nov. 9, 1925, b. 3, Horsch papers.

53. HSB to John Horsch, Dec. 28, 1926, b. 3, Horsch papers.

54. Letters, passim, 1926, f. 16, b. 3, Horsch papers.

55. HSB to John Horsch, Apr. 10, 1928, b. 4, Horsch papers.

56. HSB to John Horsch, May 14, 1927, b. 4, Horsch papers.

57. Ibid.

58. HSB to John Horsch, Oct. 2, 1928, b. 4, Horsch papers.

59. Ibid.

60. HSB to Noah Oyer, July 9, 1929, f. 1, b. 4, Bender papers.

61. "Heart of Europe Tour" brochure, f. 27, b. 2, J. C. Wenger papers, AMC; HSB to John Horsch, July 18, 1929, b. 4, Horsch papers.

62. HSB to John Horsch, July 18, 1929, b. 4, Horsch papers.
63. HSB to Ernst Correll, June 1, 1929, f. 11, b. 1, Bender papers.
64. HSB to S. C. Yoder, July 9, 1929, f. 1, b. 4, Bender papers.
65. HSB to Noah Oyer, July 19, 1929, Noah Oyer papers, AMC; HSB to Sanford Yoder, Aug. 2, 1929, S. C. Yoder papers, AMC.
66. Harold S. Bender, "A Flying Trip Through Russia," *Goshen College Record*, Dec. 1929, 26.
67. "Russian Trip, 1929" (HSB diary), f. 1, b. 120, Bender papers.
68. Ibid.
69. Postcards to Noah Oyer, Aug. 20, Aug. 27, 1929, f. 13, b. 3, Noah Oyer papers, AMC.
70. Harold S. Bender, "What of the Morrow?" (Sept. 1929), f. 37, b. 101, Bender papers.
71. Ibid.
72. Ibid.
73. HSB to Members, "Heart of Europe Tour" (Nov. 7, 1929), f. 3, b. 1, Bender papers.

**Chapter 9**
1. HSB to Ernst Correll, July 31, 1930, f. 1, b. 81, Bender papers.
2. HSB to Lester Hostetler, July 21, 1926, f. 9, b. 2, Bender papers.
3. HSB to John Horsch, Aug. 27, 1926, b. 3, Horsch papers.
4. John Horsch to HSB, May 11, 1921, and also Jan. 16, 1924, f. 7, b. 2, Bender papers.
5. John Horsch to HSB, Jan. 16, 1924, f. 7, b. 2, Bender papers.
6. HSB to Irvin E. Burkhart, Dec. 7, 1929, f. 7, b. 1, Bender papers.
7. HSB to Irvin E. Burkhart, May 15, 1931, f. 14, b. 5, Bender papers.
8. John Horsch to HSB, Jan. 13, 1924, b. 7, Horsch papers.
9. HSB to John Horsch, Feb. 11, 1924, b. 7, Horsch papers.
10. John Horsch, *The Mennonite Church and Modernism* (Mennonite Publishing House, 1924).
11. HSB to John Horsch, Jan. 6, 1924, b. 7, Horsch papers.
12. Ibid.
13. HSB to John Horsch, Jan. 16, 1926, b. 3, Horsch papers.
14. HSB to Orie O. Miller, Aug. 23, 1928, f. 1, b. 49, Orie O. Miller papers. During this visit bishop Brunk informed Bender that he was beginning a new paper to be called *The Sword and Trumpet*. Reporting the events to Orie O. Miller, Bender kidded Miller: "Better subscribe on the ground floor. It is only $.50 a year."
15. HSB to N. E. Byers, May 24, 1926; N. E. Byers to HSB, June 3, 1926; f. 2, b. 1, Bender papers.
16. Harold S. Bender, "Fundamentals Should Be Taught These Days," *GH* 18 (Jan. 21, 1926): 887.
17. Harold S. Bender, "The Christian Life and Faith," *GH* 19 (Oct. 28, 1926): 660.
18. Harold S. Bender, "Detecting Modernism, *CM*, June 1928, 161; see also his "Biblical Test of Orthodoxy," *GH* 21 (Apr. 19, 1928): 69-71.
19. Harold S. Bender, "Criticism, Desired and Undesired," *Goshen College Record*, July-Aug. 1925, 30.
20. John H. Mosemann to Sanford Yoder, Sept. 12, 1925, f. 2, b. 2, S. C. Yoder papers, AMC.
21. Sanford Yoder to John H. Mosemann, Jan. 4, 1926, f. 2, b. 2, S. C. Yoder papers, AMC.
22. HSB to Elizabeth Bender, Feb. 22, 1930, f. 2, b. 1, Bender papers.
23. See Frank H. Epp, *Mennonites in Canada, 1920-1940: A People's Struggle for Survival*, Mennonites in Canada, vol. 2 (Toronto: Macmillan of Canada, 1982), chap. 7; see also Epp's *Mennonite Exodus: The Rescue and Resettlement of the Russian Men-*

*nonites Since the Communist Revolution* (Altona, Man.: D. W. Friesen and Sons for the Canadian Mennonite Relief and Immigration Council, 1962).

24. Epp, *Mennonites in Canada, 1920-1940*, 322.

25. Orie O. Miller to HSB, July 12, 1930, f. 38, b. 50, Bender papers; in this letter Miller gives Bender full credit for getting the refugee movement directed to Paraguay.

26. A brief account may be found in *ME*, 4:117; Epp, *Mennonite Exodus*, 257-258.

27. Telegrams, Apr. 17, 1930, f. 1, b. 53, Orie O. Miller papers.

28. HSB to Noah Oyer, Apr. 29, 1930, f. 2, b. 1, Bender papers.

29. Ibid.

30. Ibid.

31. HSB to John Horsch, July 20, 1930, b. 5, Horsch papers.

32. HSB to John Horsch, July 19, 1930, b. 5, Horsch papers.

33. HSB to Ernst Correll, July 31, 1930, f. 1, b. 83, Bender papers.

34. HSB to John Horsch, July 19, 1930, b. 5, Horsch papers.

35. HSB to Ernst Correll, July 31, 1930, f. 1, b. 83; HSB to Elsie Bender, Mar. 3, 1930, f. 8, b. 2; Bender papers.

36. HSB to Sanford Yoder, undated letter, f. 1, b. 4, S. C. Yoder papers, AMC.

37. HSB to Elsie Bender, Mar. 3, 1930, f. 8, b. 2, Bender papers.

38. HSB to Noah Oyer, July 14, 1930, f. 1, b. 2, Bender papers.

39. Ibid.

40. Ibid.

41. Sanford Yoder to HSB, July 25, 1930, f. 13, b. 4, Bender papers.

42. HSB to Christian Neff, July 11, 1930, f. 12, b. 3, Bender papers; HSB to John Horsch, July 20, 1930, b. 5, Horsch papers.

43. HSB to John Horsch, July 20, 1930, b. 5, Horsch papers.

44. HSB to Levi Mumaw, May 28, 1930, f. 1, b. 53, Orie O. Miller papers, AMC.

45. HSB to Ernst Correll, July 31, 1930, f. 1, b. 83, Bender papers.

46. David Toews memo, 1930, f. 5, b. 60, Bender papers.

47. Regarding Klassen, see Herbert and Maureen Klassen, *Ambassador to His People: C. F. Klassen and the Russian Mennonite Refugees* (Hillsboro, Kan.: Kindred Press, 1990).

48. MCC exec. comm. minutes, Jan. 3, 1931, f. 4, b. 50, Bender papers.

49. HSB to Walter Landes, Nov. 15, 1930, f. 27, b. 51, Bender papers.

50. John Sylvanus Umble, *Goshen College, 1894-1954* (Goshen, Ind.: Goshen College, 1955), 136.

51. Ibid.

52. A. D. Wenger and C. K. Lehman to Dear Brethren, Feb. 5, 1927, C. K. Lehman papers, MSHLA.

53. Ibid.

54. S. C. Yoder and Noah Oyer to Dear Brethren, undated, f. EMS, b. 4, Noah Oyer papers, AMC.

55. HSB to Violet Bender, Oct. 17, 1928, f. 7, b. 4, Bender papers.

56. Paul Horsch, interviewed by Albert Keim at Pittsboro, N.C., in Oct. 1991, tape in the BOHC.

57. HSB to Violet Bender, Oct. 17, 1928, f. 7, b. 4, Bender papers.

58. HSB to Father Horsch, Nov. 22, 1928, b. 4, Horsch papers.

59. "Suggestions for John Horsch—Guggenheim Application," f. 8, b. 2, Bender papers.

60. Harold S. Bender, "The Founding of the Mennonite Church in America at Germantown," *MQR* 7 (Oct. 1933): 227-250.

## Chapter 10

1. Faculty minutes, Feb. 26, 1931, b. 5, Dean's Files, Goshen College papers, AMC.

2. Harold S. Bender, "Noah Oyer, 1891-1931," *CM*, May 19, 1931, 142-144.

3. HSB to John Horsch, Mar. 3, 1931, b. 5, Horsch papers.

4. HSB to Orie O. Miller, Jan. 12, 1931, f. 3, b. 55, Orie O. Miller papers, AMC.
5. HSB to Orie O. Miller, Jan. 29, 1931, f. 3, b. 55, Orie O. Miller papers, AMC.
6. For the campus context around the events of 1930-31, see Susan Fisher Miller, *Culture for Service: A History of Goshen College, 1894-1994* (Goshen, Ind.: Goshen College, 1994), 140ff.
7. John Horsch to HSB, Mar. 14, 1931, f. 1, b. 8, Bender papers.
8. HSB to John Horsch, Mar. 26, 1931, b. 5, Horsch papers.
9. HSB to John Horsch, Apr. 18, 1931, b. 5, Bender papers.
10. Orie O. Miller to C. L. Graber, Mar. 24, 1931, f. 4, b. 55, Orie O. Miller papers, AMC.
11. Silas Hertzler diary, Mar. 13, 1931, Silas Hertzler papers, AMC.
12. Ibid., Mar. 14, 1931.
13. Sanford Yoder to Orie O. Miller, Apr. 14, 1931, f. 4, b. 5, Orie O. Miller papers, AMC.
14. C. L. Graber to Orie O. Miller, Mar. 19, 1931, f. 4, b. 55, Orie O. Miller papers, AMC.
15. Sanford Yoder to Orie O. Miller, June 25, 1931, f. 4, b. 56, Orie O. Miller papers, AMC.
16. HSB to John Horsch, Mar. 3, 1931, b. 5, Horsch papers.
17. Orie O. Miller to HSB, Mar. 31, 1931, f. 8, b. 10; also, see other letters passim, f. 4, b. 10; Bender papers. President Yoder used better judgment: he returned one letter with the comment that probably Mosemann would not want the Oyer family to see the letter.
18. Silas Hertzler diary, May 4, 1931; Aug. 1, 1931; Silas Hertzler papers, AMC.
19. Administrative Committee minutes, May 27, 1931, f. 16, b. 62, Bender papers.
20. Faculty meeting minutes, June 1, 1931, f. 16, b. 62, Bender papers.
21. Silas Hertzler diary, 1931, passim, Silas Hertzler papers, AMC.
22. Orie O. Miller to HSB, Apr. 26, 1932, f. 8, b. 10, Bender papers.
23. Sanford Yoder to Orie O. Miller, July 28, 1932, f. 1, b. 58, Bender papers.
24. HSB to Orie O. Miller, May 25, 1933, f. 1, b. 58, Bender papers.
25. Orie O. Miller to HSB, Mar. 2, 1933, f. 8, b. 10, Bender papers.
26. HSB to Orie O. Miller, Apr. 12, 1933, f. 2, b. 58, Bender papers.
27. C. L. Graber to Orie O. Miller, Apr. 4, 1934, f. 3, b. 59, Orie O. Miller papers, AMC.
28. C. L. Graber to Orie O. Miller, Dec. 29, 1931, f. 4, b. 55, Orie O. Miller papers, AMC.
29. Orie O. Miller to HSB, Apr. 23, 1932, f. 8, b. 10, Bender papers.
30. HSB to Orie O. Miller, Mar. 8, 1932, f. 1, b. 57, Bender papers.
31. Miller, *Culture for Service* (see n. 6), 140ff.
32. C. L. Graber to Orie O. Miller, Apr. 4, 1934, f. 1, b. 51, Orie O. Miller papers, AMC.
33. Silas Hertzler, "Attendance at Mennonite Schools and Colleges" (two articles), *MQR* 6 (Oct. 1932): 268; 18 (Jan. 1945): 62.
34. Daniel Kauffman to HSB, Apr. 26, 1933, Dean's Files, Goshen College papers, AMC.
35. Harold S. Bender, "A Program for Goshen College, 1933," Dean's Files, Goshen College papers, AMC.
36. *GH* 26 (Aug. 10, 1933): 410-411.
37. Bender, "A Program for Goshen College, 1933."
38. Faculty meeting minutes, 1931 and 1932, f. 1, b. 64, Bender papers.
39. *Goshen College Bulletin*, May 1934, 36.
40. *Goshen College Catalog*, Apr. 1936, 38-42.
41. John Sylvanus Umble, *Goshen College, 1894-1954* (Goshen, Ind.: Goshen College, 1955), 145.

42. Faculty meeting minutes, Feb. 14, 1939, Dean's Files, Goshen College papers, AMC.

43. See relevant issues of *Goshen College Bulletin*.

44. Sanford Yoder to HSB, Oct. 31, 1938, Dean's Files, Goshen College papers, AMC.

45. HSB to Samuel Yoder, Dec. 16, 1937, f. 12, b. 13, Bender papers.

46. Ibid.

47. Letters, 1934, passim, f. 1, b. 8, Bender papers.

48. HSB to John Horsch, May 10, 1934, f. 1, b. 8, Bender papers.

49. C. L. Graber to Orie O. Miller, Feb. 17, 1934, f. 3, b. 59, Orie O. Miller papers, AMC.

50. HSB to Daniel Kauffman, Jan. 1, 1933, f. 4, b. 6, Bender papers.

51. HSB to J. C. Wenger, Dec. 31, 1936, f. 27, b. 2, J. C. Wenger papers, AMC.

52. HSB to J. C. Wenger, Oct. 4, 1936, f. 6, b. 13, Bender papers.

53. J. C. Wenger to HSB, Oct. 14, 1939, f. 6, b. 13, Bender papers.

54. HSB to J. C. Wenger, Oct. 27, 1936, f. 27, b. 2, J. C. Wenger papers, AMC.

55. HSB to J. C. Wenger, Nov. 11, 1936, f. 27, b. 2, J. C. Wenger papers, AMC.

56. John C. Wenger, interviewed by John Bender, May 26, 1989, at Goshen, Ind., tape in BOHC.

57. HSB to Fritz Blanke, Mar. 26, 1937, f. 7, b. 13, Bender papers.

58. Fritz Blanke to HSB, July 7, 1938, f. 12, b. 5, Bender papers.

59. Carl Kreider, interviewed by Albert Keim at Goshen, Ind., Nov. 1991, tape in BOHC.

60. HSB to Carl Kreider, Sept. 13, 1936, f. 5, b. 9, Bender papers.

61. HSB to Clarence Pickett, Jan. 21, 1937, f. 5, b. 9, Bender papers.

62. Carl Kreider to HSB, Feb. 3, 1939, f. 5, b. 9, Bender papers.

63. See, e.g., Bender's directive assistance to Lois Gunden (Clemens) in 1938 and 1939. He not only explored admissions questions on her behalf at several universities but finally decided she should go to Peabody University because Peabody promised she could finish her M.A. work in three semesters. With that schedule, she could return to teach language at Goshen sooner than if she atended the University of Chicago or Ohio State University—materials in f. 12, b. 7, Bender papers.

64. Quoted in HSB to Carl Kreider, Mar. 30, 1938, f. 5, b. 9, Bender papers.

65. Ibid.

66. Quoted by Carl Kreider, interviewed by Albert Keim at Goshen, Ind., in Nov. 1991, tape in the BOHC.

67. Bible School faculty minutes, Nov. 19, 1939, Dean's Files, Goshen College papers, AMC.

68. Library brochure, f. 34, b. 101, Bender papers.

69. Daniel Kauffman to HSB, Dec. 20, 1938, f. 7, b. 8, Bender papers.

70. Edward Yoder, *Edward: Pilgrimage of a Mind*, ed. Ida Yoder (Wadsworth, Ohio: Ida Yoder, 1985), 217.

71. *Maple Leaf*, 1941, 92.

72. HSB to Orie O. Miller, Feb. 8, 1941, f. 22, b. 52, Bender papers.

73. See Miller, *Culture for Service* (see n. 6), 164ff.

Chapter 11

1. HSB to Walther Köhler, Jan. 29, 1935, f. 1, b. 86, Bender papers.

2. HSB to John Horsch, Feb. 17, 1935, f. 2, b. 8, Bender papers.

3. HSB to John Horsch, Feb. 27, 1935, f. 2, b. 8, Bender papers.

4. HSB to James Twaddell, Oct. 28, 1938, f. 13, b. 2, Bender papers.

5. Notes from courses Bender took—in fs. 2, 3, 4; b. 111, Bender papers.

6. HSB to Orie O. Miller, May 6, 1935, f. 8, b. 10, Orie O. Miller papers, AMC.

7. HSB to John Horsch, Aug. 5, 1935, f. 2, b. 8, Bender papers.

8. "Beitrag: Zulassung zur mündlichen Prüfung für die Promotion," Aug. 1, 1935, f. 1, b. 86, Bender papers.

9. HSB to John Horsch, Sept. 4, 1935, b. 6, Horsch papers.

10. HSB to John Horsch, Aug. 5, 1935, f. 2, b. 8, Bender papers.

11. "Für Geburtstag und Hochzeit am 20 Juli 1935," f. 9, b. 17, Bender papers.

12. HSB to John Horsch, Aug. 5, 1935, f. 2, b. 8, Bender papers.

13. Ibid.

14. HSB to John Horsch, Sept. 4, 1935, b. 6, Horsch papers.

15. HSB to Wilbur Bender, Nov. 4, 1935, f. 10, b. 5, Bender papers.

16. Walther Köhler to HSB, Mar. 20, 1935, f. 5, b. 8, Bender papers.

17. HSB to John Horsch, Aug. 5, 1935, f. 2, b. 8, Bender papers.

18. John Horsch to HSB, Oct. 7, 1935, f. 2, b. 8, Bender papers.

19. Cornelius Krahn, "The Conversion of Menno Simons: A Quadricentennial Tribute," MQR 10 (Jan. 1936): 46-54.

20. John Horsch to HSB, Oct. 7, 1935, f. 2, b. 8, Bender papers.

21. Harold S. Bender, "Conrad Grebel, der erste Führer der Schweizer Täufer" (Th.D. dissertation, theological faculty, Univ. of Heidelberg, 1936).

22. See Annemarie Lohmann, Zur geistigen Entwicklung Thomas Müntzers (Leipzig and Berlin: B. G. Teubner, 1931).

23. HSB to John Horsch and Ernst Correll, May 26, 1935, b. 6, Horsch papers.

24. Ibid.

25. Ibid.

26. Ibid.

27. See Harold S. Bender, Conrad Grebel (Mennonite Publishing House, 1950), 273, n. 30a.

28. Ernst Correll to HSB, Aug. 17, 1935, f. 4, b. 6, Bender papers.

29. Ernst Correll to Elizabeth Bender, Sept. 30, 1935, f. 4, b. 6, Bender papers; Correll reported the content of the cable.

30. John Horsch to HSB, Oct. 7, 1935, f. 2, b. 8, Bender papers.

31. Christian Neff to HSB, Oct. 17, 1935, f. 12, b. 11, Bender papers.

32. HSB to Christian Neff, Sept. 15, 1935, f. 12, b. 11, Bender papers; see also HSB to John Horsch, Sept. 4, 1935, b. 6, Horsch papers.

33. HSB to John Horsch, Sept. 4, 1935, b. 6, Horsch papers.

34. Ibid.

35. Ibid.

36. HSB to Orie O. Miller, Mar. 6, 1936, f. 9, b. 10, Bender papers.

37. Harold S. Bender, "Report of the Third Mennonite World Conference, June 29-July 3, 1936," f. 12, b. 90, Bender papers.

38. Ibid.

39. Daniel Kauffman, "Editorial," GH 29 (Sept. 24, 1936): 556-558; John H. Mosemann, "The Proposed Fourth Mennonite World Conference," GH 29 (Oct. 15, 1936): 637.

40. HSB to John Horsch, Mar. 25, 1937, b. 6, Horsch papers.

41. HSB's Paraguay trip diary, June 14, 1938, f. 3, b. 120, Bender papers.

42. Harold S. Bender, "Report on Trip to Brazil and Paraguay" (MCC, 1938), b. 50, Orie O. Miller papers, AMC.

43. Orie O. Miller to HSB, July 12, 1930, f. 38, b. 50, Bender papers; Miller gives Bender full credit for getting the refugee movement directed to Paraguay.

44. Frank H. Epp, Mennonite Exodus: The Rescue and Resettlement of the Russian Mennonites Since the Communist Revolution (Altona, Man.: D. W. Friesen and Sons for the Canadian Mennonite Relief and Immigration Council, 1962), 257-259.

45. Harold S. Bender, "With the Mennonite Refugee Colonies in Brazil and Paraguay—A Personal Narrative," MQR 15 (Jan. 1939): 59-70; Bender, "Report on Trip to Brazil and Paraguay."

46. Ibid.
47. Ibid.
48. HSB, Paraguay trip diary, July 2, 1938, f. 3, b. 120, Bender papers.
49. John D. Unruh, *In the Name of Christ: A History of the Mennonite Central Committee and Its Services, 1920-1951* (Herald Press, 1951), 35-36.
50. HSB, Paraguay trip diary, Aug. 10, 1938, f. 3, b. 120, Bender papers.
51. C. L. Graber to Orie O. Miller, Sept. 28, 1938, f. 2, b. 2, Orie O. Miller papers, AMC.
52. Ibid.
53. HSB to Orie O. Miller, Oct. 4, 1938, f. 2, b. 2, Orie O. Miller papers, AMC.
54. C. L. Graber to Orie O. Miller, Oct. 25, 1934, f. 3, b. 59, Orie O. Miller papers, AMC.
55. Robert Friedmann to HSB, Mar. 24, 1943, f. 5, b. 4, Bender papers.
56. Robert Friedmann to HSB, Apr. 24, 1943, f. 5, b. 4, Bender papers.
57. Irvin E. Burkhart, "Menno Simons on the Incarnation," *MQR* 4 (Apr.-July 1930): 113-139, 178-207; for Horsch's attitude, see HSB to Irvin E. Burkhart, Dec. 7, 1929, f. 7, b. 1, Bender papers.
58. Gustav Heinrich Enss, "Christianity and Religion," *MQR* 6 (July 1932): 133-143.
59. HSB to John Horsch, Jan. 12, 1933, b. 5, Horsch papers.
60. Gustav Enss, "Notes," *MQR* 7 (Jan. 1933): 61-63. Professor James C. Juhnke has pointed out that Enss was probably the first American Mennonite to express a Barthian position: "Gustav A. Enss, Mennonite Alien (1885-1965)," *Mennonite Life* 36 (Dec. 1981): 9-15.
61. Quoted in John Horsch to HSB, Aug. 7, 1933, f. 1, b. 8, Bender papers.
62. HSB to Orie O. Miller, Oct. 18, 1945, f. 4, b. 21, Bender papers.
63. HSB to A. J. Metzler, Nov. 13, 1941, f. 9, b. 20, Bender papers.
64. Ibid.

Chapter 12
1. HSB to Wilbur Bender, Aug. 28, 1937, f. 10, b. 5, Bender papers.
2. HSB letters to R. H. Kolb, July 1939, passim, f. 13, b. 18, Bender papers.
3. HSB to John Horsch, Feb. 7, 1934, f. 1, b. 8, Bender papers.
4. Paul Horsch, interviewed by Albert Keim at Pittsboro, N.C., in Oct. 1991, tapes in BOHC.
5. HSB to Lieber Onkel Michael, Nov. 15, 1939, f. 42, b. 53, Bender papers.
6. HSB to John Horsch, Apr. 29, 1938, b. 6, Horsch papers; Millie Graber Stoltz-fus, interviewed by Albert Keim at Harrisonburg, Va., Dec. 28, 1993, notes in BOHC.
7. HSB to John Horsch, Dec. 2, 1936, b. 6, Horsch papers.
8. Letters, passim, f. 3, b. 5, Bender papers.
9. S. C. Yoder to Orie O. Miller, July 25, 1934, f. 3, b. 60, Orie O. Miller papers, AMC.
10. Local board minutes, Jan. 6, 1936, f. 1, b. 14, Orie O. Miller papers, AMC.
11. Notes in f. 6, b. 62, Bender papers.
12. HSB to Ernst Correll, letters, f. 4, b. 6, Bender papers.
13. HSB to Florence Bender, Oct. 15, 1936, f. 3, b. 5, Bender papers.
14. HSB to John Horsch, Dec. 25, 1933, f. 1, b. 8, Bender papers.
15. Salary accounts, f. 5, b. 121, Bender papers.
16. HSB to Florence Bender, Oct. 25, 1936, f. 3, b. 5, Bender papers.
17. HSB to John Horsch, Aug. 6, 1937, f. 2, b. 8, Bender papers.
18. HSB to president of Montgomery Ward, Feb. 18, 1937, f. 2, b. 10, Bender papers.
19. HSB to Florence Bender, May 26, 1937, f. 3, b. 5, Bender papers.
20. HSB to Paul Horsch, Oct. 12, 1938, f. 13, b. 7, Bender papers.
21. HSB to John Horsch, Nov. 25, 1936, f. 2, b. 8, Bender papers.

22. HSB to Goshen city council, Sept. 6, 1941, f. 1, b. 7; Edwin Yoder to HSB, Apr. 5, 1945, f. 4, b. 24; Bender papers.

23. Harold S. Bender, Goshen, Ind., as quoted from Oct. 1935, in *Goshen: Sesquicentennial Edition, 1831-1981* (Goshen, Ind., 1981), 70.

24. John Horsch to Peace Problems Committee, Feb. 27, 1935, b. 6, Horsch papers.

25. HSB to John Horsch, Mar. 9, 1935, b. 6, Horsch papers.

26. HSB to Sanford Yoder, May 16, 1935, f. 13, b. 13, Bender papers.

27. HSB to John Horsch, Mar. 9, 1935, b. 6, Horsch papers.

28. *Goshen College Record*, Aug. 1937, 15.

29. Edward Yoder, *Edward: Pilgrimage of a Mind*, ed. Ida Yoder (Wadsworth, Ohio, Ida Yoder, 1985), 274.

30. *Maple Leaf*, 1936, 22; 1937, 62.

31. *Goshen College Record*, Nov. 1936, 19.

32. HSB to Alfred Kinsey, Apr. 11, 1938, f. 4, b. 8, Bender papers.

33. *Maple Leaf*, 1940, 98.

34. Daniel Kauffman to HSB, Dec. 26, 1932, f. 7, b. 8, Bender papers.

35. Ibid.

36. HSB to John Horsch, Aug. 6, 1937, f. 2, b. 8, Bender papers.

37. *Report of the Twentieth Mennonite General Conference Held at Turner Oregon, August 25-27, 1937*, 15, 123-128.

38. Ibid.

39. Ibid.; see also a discussion in Guy F. Hershberger, *The Mennonite Church in the Second World War* (Scottdale, Pa.: Herald Press, 1952), 251.

40. Harold S. Bender, "In Time of Peace, Prepare for War," *GH* 25 (Apr. 21, 1932): 70-71.

41. Ibid.: 70.

42. Ibid.: 71.

43. HSB comments in Conference of Historic Peace Churches minutes, Sept. 18-19, 1936, f. 34, E. L. Harshbarger papers, MLA.

44. "Mennonite Conference on War and Peace" (Goshen College, Feb. 15-17, 1935), Peace Problems Committee papers, AMC.

45. "Tentative Program for the Conference of Historic Peace Churches, Nov. 2, 1935," MLA.

46. "Report of a Conference of Mennonite Peace Groups" (Mar. 10, 1939), f. 143, Hiebert papers, MLA.

47. Peace Problems Committee minutes, Sept. 30, 1939, f. 6, b. 15, Bender papers. For more on the "Plan of Action," see chap. 13. It has been printed in various places, most conveniently in Melvin Gingerich, *Service for Peace: A History of Mennonite Civilian Public Service* (Akron, Pa.: MCC, 1949), 431-433.

48. "Minutes of the Meeting of Church Representatives" (Oct. 21, 1939), b. 39, Guy F. Hershberger papers, AMC.

49. HSB to John Horsch, May 23, 1939, b. 6, Horsch papers.

50. Guy F. Hershberger, *War, Peace, and Nonresistance* (Herald Press, 1944).

51. David Yoder to Orie O. Miller, May 30, 1938, f. 1, b. 2, Orie O. Miller papers, AMC.

52. Ibid.

53. Ibid.

54. Sanford Yoder to Orie O. Miller, Jan. 12, 1939, f. 3, b. 2, Orie O. Miller papers, AMC.

55. C. L. Graber to David Yoder, Jan. 12, 1939, f. 3, b. 2, Orie O. Miller papers, AMC.

56. Sanford Yoder to Orie O. Miller, Jan. 12, 1939, f. 3, b. 2, Orie O. Miller papers, AMC.

57. Letters, passim, fs. 2 and 3, b. 2, Orie O. Miller papers, AMC.

58. Ernest Miller to Faculty, Feb. 22, 1944, f. 21, b. 2, Bender papers.
59. Ibid.
60. For an evaluation of Ernest Miller's presidency, see Susan Fisher Miller, *Culture for Service: A History of Goshen College, 1894-1994* (Goshen, Ind.: Goshen College, 1994), 164-170 and passim.

**Chapter 13**
1. Gladys Graber Beyler and Millie Graber Stoltzfus, interviewed by Albert Keim at Harrisonburg, Va., on Jan. 3, 1944, transcript in BOHC.
2. HSB to M. R. Zigler, Sept. 14, 1939, f. 13, b. 24, Bender papers.
3. Albert N. Keim and Grant M. Stoltzfus, *The Politics of Conscription: The Historic Peace Churches and America at War, 1917-1955* (Herald Press, 1988), 73.
4. Melvin Gingerich, *Service for Peace: A History of Mennonite Civilian Public Service* (Herald Press, 1949), 35, 43.
5. HSB to E. L. Harshbarger, Oct. 26, 1939, f. 15, E. L. Harshbarger papers, MLA.
6. HSB to Robert Balderston and Paul Bowman, Dec. 18, 1939, f. 16, E. L. Harshbarger papers, MLA.
7. E. Raymond Wilson to Robert Balderston, Dec. 26, 1939, f. 16, E. L. Harshbarger papers, MLA.
8. Ibid.
9. P. C. Hiebert to E. L. Harshbarger, Jan. 13, 1949, f. 16, E. L. Harshbarger papers, MLA.
10. Orie O. Miller to HSB, Sept. 26, 1939, f. 19, b. 52, Bender papers.
11. Notes in f. 6, b. 62, Bender papers.
12. HSB to Orie O. Miller, Mar. 9, 1940, f. 20, b. 52, Bender papers.
13. HSB to P. C. Hiebert, May 11, 1940, f. 9, b. 32, Bender papers.
14. Paul Horsch, interviewed by Albert N. Keim at Pittsboro, N.C., in Oct. 1991, tape in BOHC; see also HSB to Michael Waldner, Nov. 11, 1941, f. 18, b. 23, Bender papers.
15. HSB to Orie O. Miller, June 19, 1940, f. 21, b. 52, Bender papers.
16. HSB to C. L. Graber, July 24, 1940, f. 7, b. 17, Bender papers.
17. Ernest Bennett, interviewed by Albert N. Keim at Akron, Pa., Apr. 22, 1992, notes in Keim's possession.
18. Harold S. Bender, "Report of a Visit to Mennonite Relief Work in Europe" (Newton, Kan., Sept. 14, 1940), f. 17, b. 52, Bender papers.
19. Ibid.
20. Ibid.
21. Ibid.
22. Ibid.
23. HSB to Herbert Hoover, Mar. 20, 1941, f. 10, b. 17, Bender papers.
24. *Maple Leaf*, 1941, 85.
25. Trip information in f. 4, b. 120, Bender papers.
26. Harold S. Bender, "Report of a Visit to Mennonite Relief Work in Europe" (Newton, Kan., Sept. 14, 1940), f. 17, b. 52, Bender papers.
27. See pamphlet by Lois Gunden Clemens, *At Brenner Park Hotel* (Akron, Pa.: MCC, 1945).
28. See Albert N. Keim and Grant M. Stoltzfus, *The Politics of Conscience: The Historic Peace Churches and America at War, 1917-1955* (Herald Press, 1988), chap. 4.
29. Ibid., 107.
30. HSB to Orie O. Miller, Sept. 26, 1940, f. 21, b. 52, Bender papers.
31. HSB to Orie O. Miller, June 19, 1940, f. 21, b. 52, Bender papers.
32. HSB to Orie O. Miller, Sept. 21, 26, 1940, f. 21, b. 52, Bender papers.
33. Keim and Stoltzfus, *The Politics of Conscience*, 108-109.
34. Clarence Pickett, *For More Than Bread: An Autobiographical Account of Twen-*

ty-two Years' Work with the American Friends Service Committee (Boston, Mass.: Little, Brown and Co., 1953), 324.
35. HSB to Paul Comly French, Mar. 18, 1941, f. 63, b. 56, Bender papers.
36. Paul Comly French to HSB, Mar. 21, 1941, f. 63, b. 56, Bender papers.
37. HSB to Paul Comly French, Mar. 24, 1941, f. 63, b. 56, Bender papers.
38. Henry Fast to HSB, Dec. 2, 1940, f. 1, b. 52, Bender papers.
39. John D. Unruh, In the Name of Christ: A History of the Mennonite Central Committee and Its Services, 1920-1951 (Herald Press, 1952), chap. 11.
40. "Minutes of the Meeting of the Peace Section of the MCC" (Washington, D.C., Jan. 13, 1942), f. 55, b. 56, Bender papers.
41. Ernest Miller to Orie O. Miller, Sept. 24, 1940, f. 6, b. 21, Bender papers.
42. Ibid.
43. HSB to Orie O. Miller, Aug. 14, 1943, f. 26, b. 52, Bender papers.
44. Sanford Shetler to Orie O. Miller, Jan. 20, 1943, f. 26, b. 52, Bender papers.
45. HSB to Orie O. Miller, Aug. 27, 1943, f. 4, b. 21, Bender papers.
46. HSB to Milo Kauffman, June 30, 1943, f. 6, b. 181, Bender papers.
47. HSB to G. Thomas Robbins, Jan. 27, 1943, f. 73, b. 55, Bender papers.
48. HSB to Ralph Hernley, Nov. 4, 1943, f. 67, b. 55, Bender papers.
49. HSB to Orie O. Miller, Nov. 11, 1943, f. 26, b. 52, Bender papers.
50. HSB to J. C. Hiebert, Jan. 5, 1944, f. 9, b. 52, Bender papers.
51. For details on the Malcolm story, see Guy F. Hershberger, The Mennonite Church in the Second World War (Herald Press, 1950), 246-264.
52. Harold S. Bender, ed., Mennonites and Their Heritage: A Series of Six Studies Designed for Use in Civilian Public Service Camps (Akron, Pa.: MCC, 1942)—six pamphlets. Vol. 1 is by Bender, Mennonite Origins in Europe, 72 pages.
53. HSB to Roland Bainton, May 11, 1940, f. 5, b. 14, Bender papers.
54. Leonard Gross, ed., "Conversations with Robert Friedmann," MQR 48 (Apr. 1974): 152.
55. HSB to Father Horsch: July 20, 1930, b. 5, Horsch papers; Dec. 24, 1930, f. 8, b. 2, Bender papers. See also Gross, "Conversations with Robert Friedmann," 146-150.
56. Gross, "Conversations with Robert Friedmann," 151.
57. Gross, "Conversations with Robert Friedmann," 151-153.
58. HSB to Roland Bainton, Mar. 13, 1940, f. 5, b. 14, Bender papers.
59. Roland Bainton to HSB, Mar. 11, 1940, f. 5, b. 14, Bender papers.
60. HSB to Roland Bainton, May 18, 1940, f. 5, b. 14, Bender papers.
61. HSB to Roland Bainton, June 20, 1940, f. 5, b. 14, Bender papers.
62. Gross, "Conversations with Robert Friedmann," 155.
63. Ibid.
64. Ibid.
65. Ibid., 157-158.
66. Letters to Robert Friedmann, Ernest E. Miller, Orie O. Miller, the Carl Schurz Fund, et al., f. 12, b. 16, Bender papers.
67. HSB to Melvin Gingerich, Nov. 11, 1944, f. 2, b. 8, Bender papers.

Chapter 14
1. Robert Friedmann, "Anabaptism and Pietism," MQR 14 (Apr.-July, 1940): 90-128, 149-169; Harold S. Bender, "Editorial," MQR 14 (Apr. 1940): 66. For an understanding of Pietism different from that of Friedmann, see Dale W. Brown, Understanding Pietism (2d ed., Nappanee, Ind.: Evangel Publishing House, 1996).
2. For a more systematic discussion of this matter, see Theron Schlabach, Gospel Versus Gospel: Mission and the Mennonite Church, 1863-1944 (Herald Press, 1980), esp. the last part of chap. 1; also J. Denny Weaver, "The Quickening of Soteriology: Atonement from Christian Burkholder to Daniel Kauffman," MQR 61 (Jan. 1987): 5-45; and Weaver, Keeping Salvation Ethical: Mennonite and Amish Atonement Theology in the Late Nineteenth Century (Herald Press, 1997).

3. John Sylvanus Umble, *Goshen College 1894-1954* (Goshen, Ind.: Goshen College, 1955), 153.

4. See Earl McGrath to HSB, Sept. 18, 1941, f. 1, b. 20, Bender papers.

5. Susi Friedmann to Elizabeth Bender, July 7, 1941, f. 12, b. 16; HSB to Mrs. Primrose, Sept. 13, 1941, f. 1, b. 27; Bender papers.

6. HSB to Robert Freidmann, June 23, 1942; see also Robert Freidmann to HSB, June 25, 1942; f. 12, b. 16, Bender papers.

7. HSB to Robert Freidmann, July 2, 1942, f. 12, b. 16, Bender papers.

8. HSB to Edward Yoder, May 13, 1941, f. 8, b. 24, Bender papers.

9. J. C. Wenger to HSB, Sept. 15, 1942, f. 2, b. 24, Bender papers.

10. Harold S. Bender, *Conrad Grebel, 1498-1526: Founder of the Swiss Brethren* (Goshen, Ind.: Mennonite Historical Society, 1950).

11. Robert Friedmann, *Mennonite Piety Through the Centuries: Its Genius and Its Literature* (Goshen, Ind.: Mennonite Historical Society, 1949).

12. John C. Wenger, *Glimpses of Mennonite History* (Mennonite Publishing House, 1940).

13. Guy F. Hershberger, *War, Peace, and Nonresistance* (Herald Press, 1944).

14. Edward Yoder, *Edward: Pilgrimage of a Mind*, ed. Ida Yoder (Wadsworth, Ohio: Ida Yoder, 1985), 488.

15. HSB to A. J. Metzler, Nov. 27, 1943, f. 4, b. 20, Bender papers.

16. Edward Yoder, with Jesse W. Hoover and Harold S. Bender, *Must Christians Fight? A Scriptural Inquiry* (Akron, Pa.: MCC, 1943).

17. HSB articles in the *GH* 35-36 (Jan.-Apr. 1943), passim.

18. Harold S. Bender, "The Content of the Bible School Curriculum," *GH* 35 (Feb. 18, 1943): 1015-1016.

19. Matthew Spinka to HSB, Jan. 11, 1932, f. 1, b. 5, Bender papers.

20. Harold S. Bender, "Conrad Grebel, the Founder of Swiss Anabaptism," *Church History* 5 (June 1938): 157-179.

21. See program of the American Society of Church History, 1940, in *Church History* 10 (Mar. 1941): 60-72.

22. HSB to Thomas C. Pears Jr., Feb. 24, 1943, f. 1, b. 11, Bender papers.

23. Thomas C. Pears Jr. to HSB, Mar. 25, 1943, f. 1, b. 11, Bender papers.

24. E. R. Hardy Jr. to HSB, June 4, 1943, f. 1, b. 11, Bender papers.

25. HSB to E. R. Hardy Jr., Oct. 9, 1943, f. 9, b. 17, Bender papers.

26. HSB to E. R. Hardy Jr., Dec. 16, 1943, f. 9, b. 17, Bender papers.

27. Ibid.

28. HSB to Orie O. Miller, Dec. 24, 1943, f. 26, b. 52, Bender papers.

29. Minutes, *Church History* 11 (Mar. 1944): 57.

30. See correspondence, passim: f. 9, b. 17; f. 1, b. 5; and f. 1, b. 11; Bender papers.

31. Leonard Gross, "Conversations with Elizabeth Bender," *Mennonite Historical Bulletin* 47 (July 1986): 6.

32. HSB to Roland Bainton, Jan. 31, 1939, f. 5, b. 14, Bender papers.

33. HSB and Ernst Correll, "C. Henry Smith's *The Story of the Mennonites*," *MQR* 16 (Oct. 1942): 273; see also Keith Sprunger, "C. Henry Smith's Vision of Mennonite History," *Mennonite Life* 50 (Mar. 1995): 4-11.

34. C. Henry Smith, "A Communication from C. Henry Smith Concerning the Review of His Book *The Story of the Mennonites*," *MQR* 17 (Oct. 1943): 249.

35. Roland Bainton, "The Left Wing of the Reformation," *Journal of Religion* (Apr. 1941): 124-134.

36. Ibid.

37. Harold S. Bender, "The Anabaptist Vision," *Church History* 13 (Mar. 1944): 4.

38. Ibid., 8.

39. Ibid.

40. Ibid., 13.

41. Ibid., 13-14.

42. Ibid., 18.
43. Ibid., 20.
44. Harold S. Bender, "The Literature and Hymnology of the Mennonites of Lancaster County, Pennsylvania," *MQR* 6 (July 1932): 156-168; Bender, "The Founding of the Mennonite Church in America at Germantown, 1683-1708," *MQR* 7 (Oct. 1933): 227-250.
45. HSB letter, *Christian Exponent*, Apr. 11, 1924, 127. The J. E. Hartzler article was part of a series entitled "The Faith of Our Fathers," and published in the Feb. 1, 1924, issue of *Christian Exponent*. See also C. Henry Smith, *The Mennonites: A Brief History* (Berne, Ind.: Mennonite Book Concern, 1920).
46. Ernst Correll's doctoral dissertation as published was entitled *Das Schweizerische Täufer-Mennonitentum* (printed in Tübingen, 1925); in 1942 his essay "The Sociological and Economic Significance of the Mennonites as a Culture Group in History," *MQR* (July 1942): 161-166, emphasized the main point of his 1924 dissertation.
47. HSB to John Horsch, July 19, 1930, b. 5, Horsch papers. Bender's considerable regard for Köhler was transformed into reverence when he learned after the war that when Köhler died in 1943, his deathbed utterance was that "he would have preferred to die a Mennonite." See note in *MQR* 24 (Jan. 1950): 91.
48. See note in Harold S. Bender, *Conrad Grebel, Founder of the Swiss Brethren, Sometimes Called Anabaptists* (Herald Press, 1950), 280. The books by Dietrich Bonhoeffer are *Nachfolge* (Munich: C. Kaiser, 1937); and its English translation, *The Cost of Discipleship*, trans. R. H. Fuller (London: SCM Press, 1948).
49. Harold S. Bender, "Recent Progress in Research in Anabaptist History," *MQR* 8 (Jan. 1934): 3-17.
50. Ibid.
51. Ethelbert Stauffer, "Märtyrer-theologie und Täuferbewegung," *Zeitschrift für Kirchengeschichte* 52 (1933): 545-598.
52. Robert Friedmann, "Conception of the Anabaptists," *Church History* 8 (Dec. 1940): 341-365.
53. Ibid., 357.
54. John Horsch, "The Faith of the Swiss Brethren," *MQR* 4 (Oct. 1930): 251, n. 30.
55. Harold S. Bender, "Editorial," *MQR* 14 (Apr. 1940): 66.
56. Robert Friedmann, "Anabaptism and Pietism," *MQR* 14 (July 1940): 156.
57. Ibid., 156-157.
58. Harold S. Bender, *Mennonite Origins in Europe* (Akron, Pa.: MCC, 1945), 35.
59. Robert Friedmann, "The Anabaptist Genius and Its Influence on Mennonites Today" (unpublished paper, 1942), 21, b. 24, Robert Friedmann papers, AMC.
60. Robert Friedmann to HSB, Oct. 2, 1943, f. 12, b. 16, Bender papers.
61. J. C. Wenger to HSB, Dec. 23, 1943, f. 2, b. 24, Bender papers.
62. Ibid.
63. Robert Friedmann, "Anabaptism and Pietism" (see n. 56), 157-158. Daniel Kauffman's *Manual of Bible Doctrines* (Elkhart, Ind.: Mennonite Publishing Co., 1989) appeared in expanded versions as *Bible Doctrine* (MPH, 1914) and *Doctrines of the Bible* (MPH, 1928).
64. Stanley Shenk, "Journal" (entry for Dec. 30, 1991), box 9, Stanley Shenk papers, AMC.
65. HSB to Ernst Correll, Jan. 22, 1944, f. 13, b. 15; HSB to Matthew Spinka, May 11, 1944, f. 10, b. 22; Bender papers.
66. Hans-Jürgen Goertz, "The Confessional Heritage in Its New Mold: What Is Mennonite Self-Understanding Today?" in Calvin Redekop and Samuel Steiner, eds., *Mennonite Identity: Historical and Contemporary Perspectives* (Lanham, Md.: Univ. Press of America, 1988), 7.
67. Donovan Smucker, "The Theological Triumph of the Early Anabaptist Mennonites: The Re-Discovery of Biblical Theology in Paradox" *MQR* 19 (Jan. 1945): 5-26; Harold S. Bender, "Editorial," ibid., 176.

68. Ibid., 6, n. 4.
69. Ibid., 19.
70. Ibid., 7.
71. Ibid., 7, n. 6.
72. Harold S. Bender, "Editorial," *MQR* 19 (July 1945): 178.
73. Stauffer, "Märtyrer-theologie und Täuferbewegung" (see n. 51); now republished as Ethelbert Stauffer, "The Anabaptist Theology of Martyrdom," *MQR* 19 (July 1945): 179-214.
74. Harold S. Bender, "Editorial," *MQR* 19 (July 1945): 178.
75. Ibid.
76. Ibid.

**Chapter 15**
1. *Goshen College Record*, Dec. 1944, 6-8; see also *GH* 37 (Oct. 20, 1944): 576.
2. See Gerald W. Schlabach, "A New Wineskin for the Old Wines: A Changing Ministry, Harold S. Bender and a New Mennonite Seminary" (unpublished History Seminar paper at Goshen College, 1978), MHL.
3. HSB to Ernest Miller, Dec. 1, 1943, f. 2, b. 21, Bender papers.
4. Ibid.
5. Ibid.
6. HSB to Olive Wyse, Mar. 28, 1944, f. 3, b. 24, Bender papers.
7. HSB to C. F. Yake, Oct. 28, 1944, f. 5, b. 24, Bender papers.
8. HSB to John C. Wenger, Dec. 20, 1937, f. 2, b. 27, J. C. Wenger papers, AMC.
9. HSB to John Leatherman, July 14, 1943, f. 5, b. 19, Bender papers.
10. Bible School faculty minutes, Oct. 19, 1940, Dean's Files, Goshen College papers, AMC.
11. See Mennonite Board of Education (MBE) minutes (Oct. 7-9, 1942), Minutes and Reports, MBE papers, AMC; C. F. Yake to Board of Education members, Dec. 14, 1942, f. 5, b. 24, Bender papers; "New Draft Regulations Concerning Students Preparing for Church Work," *GH* 37 (July 14, 1944): 292.
12. Bender quoting Lehman in HSB to J. Irvin Lehman, July 25, 1944, f. 5, b. 19, Bender papers.
13. HSB to J. Irvin Lehman, July 25, 1944, f. 5, b. 19, Bender papers.
14. *Goshen College Bulletin*, Dec. 1944, 6-8.
15. J. L. Stauffer to HSB, July 1, 1944, f. 5, b. 23, Bender papers.
16. Harold S. Bender, "Our Bible Schools: What They Are and What They Are Not," *GH* 37 (Aug. 11, 1944): 373.
17. HSB to Eastern Baptist Seminary registrar, Mar. 27, 1943, f. 4, b. 16, Bender papers.
18. David Yoder to Goshen College Congregation, June 10, 1944, f. 1, b. 4, David Yoder papers, AMC.
19. J. C. Wenger to D. A. Yoder, May 29, 1943, b. 4, J. C. Wenger papers, AMC.
20. Ibid.
21. J. C. Wenger, interviewed by John Bender at Goshen, Ind., in 1989, tapes in BOHC.
22. HSB to Ezra Yordy, Feb. 1, 1945, f. 4, b. 24, Bender papers.
23. HSB to J. D. Hartzler, Feb. 9, 1945, f. 9, b. 17, Bender papers.
24. "Annual Report of the Dean of the Seminary," Dec. 5, 1947, f. 2, b. 21, Bender papers; see also *Fellowship*, July 1946, 2 (newsletter published by the seminary, perhaps only with this issue), MHL.
25. Bible School faculty minutes, Mar. 16, 1944, Dean's Files, Goshen College, AMC.
26. Ibid., Nov. 7, 1944.
27. Ibid., Nov. 28, 1945.
28. Ibid., Aug. 12, 1942.

29. Ibid., Sept. 18, 1945; see also Lois Johns Yoder, interviewed by Albert Keim at Waverly, Ohio, June 10, 1993, notes in BOHC.

30. Bible School faculty minutes, Sept. 18, 1945, Dean's Files, Goshen College papers, AMC.

31. "Memorandum Concerning the Granting of the B.D. Degree by Goshen College" (Feb. 1946), f. 3, b. 7, Bender papers; Steve Nolt, "An Evangelical Encounter: Mennonites and the Biblical Seminary in New York," *MQR* 70 (July 1996): 389-417.

32. *Fellowship* (see n. 24), July 1946, 1. See n. 31, Nolt.

33. "Memorandum Concerning. . . ."

34. Ibid.

35. Ibid.

36. Harold S. Bender, "The Content of the Bible School Curriculum," *GH* 35 (Feb. 18, 1943): 1015-1016.

37. Ibid.

38. "Bible School Teachers' Loads Survey," Dean's Files, Goshen College papers, AMC.

39. This observation was made by a number of Bender's colleagues who had been his students; material in BOHC, passim. E.g., Roy Umble, who had been a student in the late 1930s and then a longtime Goshen faculty member, commented that Bender "often seemed preoccupied with concerns other than his teaching, giving the impression to his students that he wasn't giving [them] his best." Umble, interviewed by Albert Keim at Goshen, Ind., Sept. 20, 1991, tapes in BOHC.

40. Criticism of Bender's teaching was nearly universal among some forty of his former students who were interviewed for the Bender Oral History Project. E.g., Karl Massanari remembered that he had found Bender to be an interesting teacher, but that "he seemed to never give us all that he had to offer, possibly because he did didn't take time to prepare." Massanari, interviewed by Albert Keim in Goshen, Ind., Sept. 25, 1991, tapes in BOHC.

41. Olive Wyse to HSB, Mar. 17, 1944, f. 3, b. 24, Bender papers.

42. The author's conclusions are based on some forty interviews with former colleagues and students of Bender who almost universally agreed that the prevailing intent at the seminary was to be theologically safe and conservative. E.g., Millard Lind (later a professor at Associated Mennonite Biblical Seminaries), who studied to earn a Th.B. at the Bible school in the early 1940s, has reminisced: the school was "fundamentally conservative.' One had to have a literal understanding of Scriptures to be acceptable." One reason for that conservatism, Lind thought, was "Bender's considerable concern about church relationships." Lind, interviewed by Albert Keim, Goshen, Ind., Nov. 14, 1991, tape in BOHC.

43. HSB to P. H. Richert, Nov. 15, 1944, f. 4, b. 22, Bender papers.

44. Daniel Kauffman, "Editorial," *GH* 36 (Sept. 30, Oct. 7, 1943): 545-546, 562.

45. Harold S. Bender, "The Responsibility of the Mennonite Church High School and College for the Preservation and Extension of Mennonitism" (program for "Week-End Institute," Apr. 5-7, 1946), f. 41, b. 55, Bender papers.

46. Ibid.

47. Ibid.

48. Paul Erb, "Editorial," *GH* 37 (Aug. 11, 1944): 371; see also Sanford Shetler, "The Mennonite Church Today," *GH* 37 (Aug. 11, 1944): 369-370.

49. *Proceedings of the* [MC] *Mennonite General Conference*, Aug. 18-24, 1943 (Herald Press, 1943), 51-52.

50. Ibid.

51. Harold S. Bender, "The Function and Authority of General Conference," *GH* 37 (July 14, 21, 1944): 289-290, 306, 316.

52. Ibid.: 306.

53. Ibid.: 316.

54. For an interesting exchange about the articles, see Sanford Shetler to HSB, July

24, 1944; HSB to Sanford Shetler, July 31, 1944; f. 9, b. 22, Bender papers.
55. Guy F. Hershberger, "Introduction," in Edward Yoder, *Edward: Pilgrimage of a Mind*, ed. Ida Yoder (Wadsworth, Ohio: Ida Yoder, 1985), ix.
56. Ibid.
57. Ibid., xx.
58. Ibid.
59. "The Meetings in Indiana," *GH* 37 (Aug. 25, 1944): 412-413.

Chapter 16
1. HSB to A. J. Metzler, Apr. 13, 1944, f. 4, b. 20, Bender papers.
2. Ibid.
3. J. Winfield Fretz, "Mutual Aid Among Mennontes," *MQR* 13 (Jan., July, 1939): 28-58, 187-209.
4. HSB to Orie O. Miller, Apr. 13, 1939, f. 4, b. 21, Bender papers.
5. Guy F. Hershberger, "Nonresistance and Industrial Conflict," *MQR* 13 (Apr. 1939): 135-154.
6. *Mennonite Weekly Review*, Sept. 17, 1942.
7. Melvin Gingerich, "Is There a Need for a Mennonite Rural Life Publication?" *Proceedings of the First Conference on Mennonite Cultural Problems* (Mennonite Colleges and Schools, 1942), 60-66.
8. O. E. Baker, "The Effects of Urbanization on American Life and the Church," *MQR* 19 (Apr. 1945): 117.
9. Harold S. Bender, "The Mennonite Conception of the Church and Its Relation to Community Building," *MQR* 19 (Apr. 1945): 90.
10. Ibid.: 100.
11. "Minutes of the Organization Meeting of the Mennonite Community Association" (at Smithville, Ohio, June 3, 1946), f. 1, b. 79, Bender papers.
12. See Theron Schlabach, "To Focus a Mennonite Vision," in J. R. Burkholder and Calvin Redekop, eds., *Kingdom, Cross and Community* (Herald Press, 1976), 32-40.
13. "Minutes of the Organizational Meeting of the Mennonite Research Fellowship" (at Bluffton, Ohio, Aug. 23, 1945), f. 2, b. 90, Bender papers.
14. Ibid.
15. Ibid.
16. Ibid.
17. "Report of the Committee on the *Mennonite Lexikon* to the Mennonite Research Fellowship" (unpublished, 1946), f. 2, b. 90, Bender papers.
18. HSB to Dear Brethren, Mar. 11, 1946, f. 29, b. 2, Bender papers.
19. "Report of the Committee on the *Mennonite Lexikon*."
20. Ibid.
21. Ibid.
22. See James Harder, "Driven by Economic Forces or by Member Commitment?" *MQR* 71 (July 1997): 377-394.
23. See *ME*, 2:635.
24. HSB to Orie O. Miller, Dec. 10, 1936; Feb. 6, 1937; f. 4, b. 21, Bender papers.
25. Guy F. Hershberger, *The Mennonite Church in the Second World War* (Herald Press, 1951), 195ff.
26. Ibid.
27. Ibid.
28. John Horst to HSB, Dec. 18, 1943, f. 8, b. 18, Bender papers.
29. John Mumaw to John Horst, Apr. 25, 1944, f. 8, b. 18, Bender papers.
30. Ibid.
31. John Horst to HSB, Apr. 22, 1944, f. 8, b. 18, Bender papers.
32. HSB to John Horst, Dec. 7, 1944, f. 8, b. 18, Bender papers.
33. HSB to John Horst and Orie O. Miller, Feb. 15, 1945, f. 8, b. 18, Bender papers.
34. HSB to John Horst, Jan. 23, 1945, f. 8, b. 18, Bender papers.

35. HSB to John Mumaw, June 27, 1945, f. 1, b. 55, Bender papers.
36. HSB to John Horst, July 13, 1945, f. 8, b. 18, Bender papers.
37. Harold S. Bender, "Report," *GH* 37 (July 24, 1944): 277.
38. HSB to Orie O. Miller and John Horst, Apr. 21, 1945, f. 4, b. 21, Bender papers.
39. HSB to John Horst, May 8, 1945, f. 8, b. 18, Bender papers.
40. Ibid.
41. Hershberger, *Mennonite Church in the Second World War* (see n. 25), 206.
42. HSB to John Horst, Aug. 30, 1945, f. 8, b. 18, Bender papers.
43. Orie O. Miller to C. F. Klassen, Nov. 5, 1945, f. 41, b. 51, Bender papers.
44. "Mission Board Report," *GH* 38 (June 15, 1945): 194.
45. HSB to C. F. Klassen, Jan. 25, 1945, f. 15, b. 52, Bender papers.
46. P. C. Hiebert to HSB, Oct. 12, 1945, f. 9, b. 52, Bender papers.
47. HSB to P. C. Hiebert, Oct. 22, 1945, f. 9, b. 52, Bender papers.
48. HSB to P. C. Hiebert, July 24, 1945, f. 9, b. 52, Bender papers.
49. William Snyder, interviewed by Robert Kreider at Akron Pa, Mar. 1, 1982, MCC Oral History Project, transcript text, p. 143, at MCC offices, Akron, Pa.
50. Ibid.
51. HSB to John Horst, Apr. 22, 1944, f. 8, b. 18, Bender papers; see also *ME*, 5:917.
52. HSB to John Horst, Apr. 22, 1944, f. 8, b. 18, Bender papers.
53. "Report of the Standing Committees," *GH* 39 (July 14, 1946): 131-132; see also Laurence Horst to HSB, Mar. 19, 1947, f. 45, b. 55, Bender papers.
54. *Goshen College Bulletin*, June 1945, 3.
55. HSB to Orie O. Miller, July 6, 1946, f. 29, b. 52, Bender papers.
56. Ibid.
57. HSB to the alumni of the class of 1933, *Alumni Newsletter*, Sept. 1, 1945, Dean's Files, Goshen College papers, AMC.

Chapter 17
1. John D. Unruh, *In the Name of Christ: A History of the Mennonite Central Committee and Its Services, 1920-1951* (Herald Press, 1952), 81, 84.
2. Minutes of the Conjoint Executive and Relief Committees, MBMC (Goshen, Ind., Apr. 25, 1946), f. 1, b. 78, Bender papers.
3. Robert Kreider, interviewed by Albert Keim at North Newton, Kan., July 14, 1994, tapes in the BOHC.
4. Ibid.
5. Ibid.
6. Ibid.
7. Ibid.
8. A. J. Metzler to Christian Neff, Sept. 23, 1946, f. 5, b. 20, Bender papers.
9. "Vereinbarung zwischen Prof. Harold S. Bender von Goshen (USA) und Prediger D. Chr. Neff, Weierhof," f. 5, b. 91, Bender papers.
10. HSB to Paul Erb, Oct. 5, 1946, f. 74, b. 53, Bender papers.
11. Cornelius Krahn to HSB, Nov. 2, 1946, f. 4, b. 19, Bender papers.
12. Robert Kreider, interviewed by Albert Keim at North Newton, Kan., July 14, 1994, tapes in the BOHC.
13. HSB to Walter Landes, June 7, 1946, f. 27, b. 55, Bender papers.
14. HSB to Walter, Menno, and Paul Horsch, Sept. 10, 1946, f. 27, b. 55, Bender papers.
15. Robert Kreider, interviewed by Albert Keim at North Newton, Kan., July 14, 1994, tapes in the BOHC.
16. HSB to Ernst Correll, May 10, 1947, f. 13, b. 15, Bender papers.
17. HSB to Ernst Crous, Dec. 26, 1946, f. 16, b. 15, Bender papers.
18. Robert Kreider to HSB, Aug. 12, 1946, f. 27, b. 55, Bender papers.
19. Unruh, *In the Name of Christ* (see n. 1), 146.
20. Harold S. Bender, "Biographical and Research Notes," *MQR* 24 (Jan. 1950): 91.

21. Robert Kreider to Dear Loved Ones, Nov. 3, 1946, Kreider files, MCC papers, AMC.
22. Ibid.
23. Robert Kreider, interviewed by Albert Keim at North Newton, Kan., July 14, 1994, tapes in the BOHC.
24. HSB to Orie O. Miller, Oct. 4, 1946, f. 29, b. 52, Bender papers.
25. Ibid.
26. Robert Kreider to MCC exec. comm., Aug. 27, 1945, Kreider files, MCC papers, AMC.
27. Ibid.
28. HSB to Henry Fast, Dec. 5, 1946, f. 1, b. 52, Bender papers.
29. "Report of H. S. Bender on His Work as Special Commissioner to Belgium, Oct. 1946," f. 27, b. 55, Bender papers.
30. J. L. Stauffer to HSB, Dec. 13, 1946, f. 5, b. 13, Bender papers.
31. Orie O. Miller to J. L. Stauffer, Dec. 17, 1946, f. 29, b. 52, Bender papers.
32. HSB to Jacob Ter Meulen, Aug. 15, 1946, f. 71, b. 56, Bender papers.
33. Emma Loewen to HSB, Oct. 7, 1946, f. 71, b. 56, Bender papers.
34. Orie O. Miller to S. J. Goering, May 1, 1946, f. 53, b. 53, Bender papers.
35. HSB to J. C. Wenger, May 21, 1947, f. 2, b. 24, Bender papers.
36. See overall story in Frank Epp, *Mennonite Exodus: The Rescue and Resettlement of the Russian Mennonites Since the Communist Revolution* (Altona, Man.: D. W. Friesen and Sons for the Canadian Mennonite Relief and Immigration Council, 1962), 371-376.
37. Ibid., 374-375.
38. HSB to Ernst Correll, Feb. 6, 1947, f. 13, book 15, Bender papers.
39. Ibid.
40. HSB to Atlee Beechy, Jan. 4, 1947, f. 34, b. 51, Bender papers.
41. "Suggestions on Plan of Work for H. S. Bender, June 1947-Aug. 1948" (MCC Peace Section), f. 68, b. 56, Bender papers.
42. Ibid.
43. HSB to Orie O. Miller, Feb. 27, 1947, f. 30, b. 52, Bender papers.
44. Ibid.
45. HSB to C. L. Graber, June 12, 1947, f. 8, b. 57, Bender papers.
46. Lois Yake Kenagy, interviewed by Albert Keim at Harrisonburg, Va., in Feb., 1994, notes in BOHC.
47. Ibid.
48. Harold S. Bender, "Report #1 and #2" (MCC), f. 70, b. 56, Bender papers.
49. Ibid.
50. HSB to Domine Golterman, June 23, 1947, f. 53, b. 53, Bender papers.
51. Bender, "Report #1 and #2."
52. Ibid.
53. Ibid.
54. Ibid.
55. Ibid.
56. HSB to Ruth Hilty, Oct. 31, 1947, f. 22, b. 52, Bender papers.
57. Ruth Hilty to HSB, Oct. 5, 1947, f. 22, b. 55, Bender papers.
58. Ibid.
59. HSB to Ruth Hilty, Oct. 21, 1947, f. 22, b. 55, Bender papers.
60. Ibid.
61. HSB to Orie O. Miller, Sept. 15, 1947, f. 9, b. 52, Bender papers.
62. HSB to J. C. Wenger, Aug. 30, 1947, f. 10, b. 57, Bender papers.
63. Ibid.
64. HSB to Orie O. Miller, Sept. 15, 1947, f. 10, b. 52, Bender papers.
65. HSB to Orie O. Miller and Edna Ramseyer, Sept. 27, 1947, f. 31, b. 52, Bender papers.

Chapter 18

1. Lois Yake Kenagy, interviewed by Albert Keim at Harrisonburg, Va., Mar. 12, 1992, notes in BOHC.
2. Ibid.
3. Ibid.
4. HSB to Elsie Bender, Sept. 27, 1947, f. 2, b. 24, Bender papers.
5. HSB to J. C. Wenger, Sept. 27, 1947, f. 2, b. 24, Bender papers.
6. HSB to Robert Kreider, Oct. 11, 1947, f. 17, b. 52, Bender papers.
7. Atlee Beechy to Cornelius Dyck, Oct. 18, 1947, f. 17, b. 52, Bender papers.
8. HSB to Orie O. Miller, Oct. 11, 1947, f. 31, b. 52, Bender papers.
9. Ibid.
10. Irvin Horst to HSB, Jan. 13, 1947, f. 14, b. 31, Bender papers.
11. Ibid.
12. Robert Kreider, interviewed by Albert Keim at North Newton, Kan., July 14, 1994, tapes in the BOHC; confirmed by Keim's conversations with Irvin B. Horst.
13. HSB to Irvin Horst, Mar. 17, 1847, f. 14, b. 31, Bender papers.
14. HSB to Irvin Horst, Apr. 20, 1947, f. 14, b. 31, Bender papers.
15. HSB to Irvin Horst, May 10, 1947, f. 14, b. 31, Bender papers.
16. HSB to Irvin Horst, July 21, 1948, f. 14, b. 31, Bender papers.
17. H. S. Bender, Director, "Review of Activities—MCC Peace Section in Europe, June 13-Oct. 31, 1947," f. 31, b. 52, Bender papers.
18. HSB to Christian Landes, Oct. 29, 1947, f. 51, b. 53, Bender papers.
19. "Niederschrift" (minutes of the meeting at the Thomashof, Nov. 28, 1947, compiled by the secretary, H. Braun), f. 3, b. 55, Bender papers.
20. John D. Unruh, *In the Name of Christ: A History of the Mennonite Central Committee and Its Services, 1920-1951* (Herald Press, 1952), 341.
21. Ibid.
22. HSB to Orie O. Miller, Dec. 12, 1947, f. 31, b. 52, Bender papers.
23. Ibid.
24. Peter Dyck, interviewed by Albert Keim at Akron, Pa., in Mar. 1993, notes in the BOHC.
25. HSB to Robert Kreider, Dec. 23, 1947, f. 17, b. 52, Bender papers.
26. Cable, HSB to Cecil Bender, Dec. 24, 1947, Bender papers.
27. HSB to Melvin Gingerich, Dec. 30, 1947, f. 2, b. 17, Bender papers.
28. HSB to Orie O. Miller, Jan. 20, 1948, f. 6, b. 36, Bender papers.
29. Robert Kreider to HSB, Apr. 26, 1947, f. 44, b. 53, Bender papers.
30. HSB to P. C. Hiebert, June 1, 1948, f. 28, b. 57, Bender papers.
31. Ibid.
32. Ibid.
33. Complete series of *Der Mennonit* may be seen in most of the academic Mennonite historical libraries.
34. *Der Mennonit*, Mar. 1948.
35. HSB to Jacob ter Meulen, Apr. 27, 1939, f. 1, b. 20, Bender papers.
36. HSB to W. F. Golterman, Oct. 28, 1947, f. 1, b. 17, Bender papers.
37. J. L. Stauffer to Orie O. Miller, Nov. 15, 1947, f. 31, b. 53, Bender papers.
38. Orie O. Miller to HSB, Nov. 15, 1947, f. 31, b. 53, Bender papers.
39. "Committee on Counsel and Guidance—All Mennonite World Conference" (Jan. 7, 1948), f. 9, b. 52, Bender papers.
40. P. C. Hiebert to My Dear Harold, Feb. 10, 1948, f. 9, b. 52, Bender papers.
41. Mennonite World Congress, *News Bulletin*, nos. 1-2 (Jan. 20, June 30, 1948), f. 43, b. 57, Bender papers.
42. Orie O. Miller to HSB, Feb. 23, 1948, f. 34, b. 57, Bender papers.
43. T. O. Hylkema to HSB, Jan. 23, 1948, f. 9, b. 32, Bender papers.
44. HSB to Orie O. Miller, Feb. 16, 1948, f. 34, b. 57, Bender papers.
45. Orie O. Miller to HSB, Feb. 23, 1948, f. 34, b. 57, Bender papers.

46. HSB to Ernest Miller, June 26, 1948, f. 3, b. 36, Bender papers.
47. HSB to Fritz Gerber, Jan. 27, 1948, f. 1, b. 30, Bender papers.
48. HSB to Ross Martin, Mar. 28, 1948, f. 21, b. 57, Bender papers.
49. HSB to John Horst, Apr. 14, 1948, f. 1, b. 32, Bender papers.
50. Atlee Beechy to Others, June 8, 1948, f. 17, b. 57, Bender papers.
51. HSB to Fritz Blanke, June 30, 1948, f. 10, b. 26, Bender papers.
52. Paul Peachey, interviewed by Albert Keim at Harrisonburg, Va., June 30, 1995, notes in BOHC.
53. HSB to Adolf Enns, July 19, 1948, f. 3, b. 28, Bender papers.
54. Delbert Gratz to HSB, Aug. 31, 1948, f. 13, b. 30, Bender papers.
55. HSB to Andre Pasteur, July 21, 1948, f. 1, b. 29, Bender papers.
56. HSB to D. Krzeszewski, Dec. 24, 1948, f. 1, b. 31, Bender papers.
57. HSB to Atlee Beechy, Aug. 17, 1948, f. 17, b. 57, Bender papers.
58. P. C. Hiebert, ed., *Fourth Mennonite World Conference Proceedings* (Akron, Pa.: MCC, 1950), 313-316.
59. HSB to Orie O. Miller, et al., Aug. 18, 1948, f. 28, b. 57, Bender papers.
60. Hiebert, ed., *Fourth Mennonite World Conf.*, 313-316.
61. Ibid.

**Chapter 19**
1. HSB to Orie O. Miller, Jan. 6, 1949, f. 6, b. 36, Bender papers.
2. Ibid.
3. Handwritten letter, marked confidential, Paul Mininger to HSB, Jan. 6, 1948, f. 9, b. 36, Bender papers; Mininger reported that he had heard of Orie O. Miller's discussion with Bender about giving up the seminary deanship to devote more time to writing and to MCC work.
4. HSB to Orie O. Miller, June 17, 1948, f. 3, b. 57, Bender papers.
5. Paul Mininger to HSB, Apr. 30, 1949, f. 9, b. 36, Bender papers.
6. A. J. Metzler to HSB, Oct. 26, 1948, f. 10, b. 35, Bender papers.
7. HSB to A. J. Metzler, Nov. 29, 1948, f. 10, b. 35, Bender papers.
8. A. J. Metzler to HSB, Dec. 23, 1948, f. 10, b. 35, Bender papers.
9. HSB to Paul Mininger, Nov. 12, 1948, f. 9, b. 36, Bender papers.
10. HSB to A. J. Metzler, Nov. 29, 1948, f. 10, b. 35, Bender papers.
11. A. J. Metzler to HSB, Dec. 23, 1948, f. 10, b. 35, Bender papers.
12. HSB to Orie O. Miller, Nov. 16, 1948, f. 34, b. 57, Bender papers.
13. Ibid.
14. Ibid.
15. Ibid.
16. HSB to A. J. Metzler, Nov. 29, 1948, f. 10, b. 35, Bender papers.
17. Paul Mininger to HSB, Dec. 30, 1948, f. 9, b. 36, Bender papers.
18. HSB to Orie O. Miller, Jan. 6, 1949, f. 6, b. 36, Bender papers.
19. HSB to Orie O. Miller, Nov. 16, 1948, f. 34, b. 57, Bender papers.
20. See *Discipleship*, Winter 1950-51, 3-4; *Discipleship* was the bulletin of Goshen College Biblical Seminary, begun in the winter of 1950-51, published three times a year but not 1953-55.
21. HSB to Dean Edward H. Roberts, Dec. 10, 1952, f. 1, b. 34, Bender papers.
22. HSB to John W. Miller, Oct. 18, 1948; John W. Miller to HSB, Dec. 22, 1948; HSB to Dean Edward H. Roberts, Dec. 27, 1952; Dean Edward Roberts to HSB, Jan. 26, 1949; f. 5, b. 36, Bender papers.
23. John W. Miller to HSB, Oct. 14, 1948; HSB to John W. Miller, Dec. 15, 1950; f. 5, b. 36, Bender papers.
24. HSB to John W. Miller, Oct. 15, 1948, f. 5, b. 36, Bender papers. For fuller reference, see: B. B. Warfield, *Revelation and Inspiration* (New York: Oxford Univ. Press, 1927); J. Gresham Machen, *The Origins of Paul's Religion* (New York: The Macmillan Co., 1921); Cornelius Van Til, *The New Modernism* (Philadelphia: The Presbyte-

rian and Reformed Publishing Co., 1946); Carl F. H. Henry, *Fifty Years of Protestant Theology* (Boston: Wilde Publishing Co., 1950).

25. HSB to John W. Miller, Oct. 15, 1948, f. 5, b. 36, Bender papers.
26. John W. Miller to HSB, Apr. 13, 1950, f. 5, b. 36, Bender papers.
27. HSB to John W. Miller, Mar. 10, 1951, f. 5; Ernest Miller to HSB, July 25, 1952, f. 4; b. 36, Bender papers.
28. HSB to Carl Kreider, Oct. 10, 1950, f. 4, b. 34, Bender papers.
29. Ibid.
30. HSB to Ernest Miller, Dec. 15, 1950, f. 3, b. 36, Bender papers.
31. Donovan Smucker to HSB, Nov. 22, 1950, f. 4, b. 40, Bender papers.
32. HSB to Paul Mininger, May 4, 1953, f. 9, b. 36; HSB to Hugh R. Peterson, May 30, 1953, f. 3, b. 39; Bender papers.
33. J. Lawrence Burkholder to HSB, Nov. 14, 1953, f. 17, b. 26, Bender papers.
34. J. Lawrence Burkholder to HSB, Nov. 19, 1953, f. 17, b. 26, Bender papers. Actually, as early as September 1950, Bender had submitted a plan to reduce faculty loads, but president Miller had ignored the proposal; see HSB to Nelson Kauffman, Sept. 13, 1950, f. 3, b. 33, Bender papers.
35. J. Lawrence Burkholder to HSB, Nov. 14, 1953, f. 17, b. 26, Bender papers.
36. HSB to J. Lawrence Burkholder and Norman Kraus, Nov. 19, 1953, f. 17, b. 26, Bender papers.
37. Ibid.
38. HSB to John Mumaw, Sept. 23, 1954, f. 17, b. 26, Bender papers.
39. HSB to Julia Van Delden, Apr. 23, 1951, f. 1, b. 28, Bender papers.
40. "The Evangelism Policy of the Goshen College Biblical Seminary" (mimeographed Mar. 17, 1952), 3, f. 8, b. 12, Orie O. Miller papers, AMC.
41. Orie O. Miller to HSB, Mar. 26, 1952, f. 8, b. 12, Orie O. Miller papers, AMC; see also HSB to Ernest Miller, May 18, 1950, f. 3, b. 36, Bender papers.
42. "The Evangelism Policy of the Goshen College Biblical Seminary," 3.
43. HSB to J. H. Enns, Apr. 26, 1956, f. 7, b. 26, Bender papers.
44. George Brunk to HSB, June 12, 1953, f. 7, b. 27; HSB to George Brunk, May 2, 1953, f. 7, b. 26; Bender papers.
45. HSB to H. H. Janzen, Oct. 2, 1951, f. 11, b. 32, Bender papers.
46. Milo Kauffman to HSB, Mar. 15, 1951, f. 2, b. 33, Bender papers.
47. HSB to J. Lawrence Burkholder and Norman Kraus, Nov. 4, 1953, f. 1, b. 34, Bender papers.
48. HSB to Simon Gingerich, Nov. 6, 1950, f. 1, b. 30, Bender papers.
49. HSB to Paul Mininger, July 12, 1954, f. 9, b. 36, Bender papers.
50. Seminary faculty minutes, May 29, 1947, Seminary Dean's files, Goshen College Biblical Seminary papers, AMC.
51. Letters, passim, fall 1950, f. 10, b. 32, Bender papers.
52. Orie O. Miller to HSB, Nov. 20, 1951, f. 30, b. 57, Bender papers.
53. HSB to A. K. Mann, Sept. 24, 1954, f. 1, b. 35, Bender papers.
54. HSB to Paul Mininger, July 26, 1956, f. 9, b. 36, Bender papers.
55. HSB to Orie O. Miller, Feb. 16, 1952, f. 6, b. 35; Donovan Smucker to HSB, Jan. 10, 1952, f. 4, b. 40; Bender papers.
56. For a more detailed discussion of the merger process which led, after nearly two decades, to the creation of the Associated Mennonite Biblical Seminaries, see Samuel F. Pannabecker, *Venture of Faith: The Story of the Mennonite Biblical Seminary* (Elkhart, Ind.: Mennonite Biblical Seminary, 1975).
57. Erland Waltner, interviewed by Albert Keim at Elkhart, Ind., June 2, 1995, notes in BOHC.
58. HSB to Erland Waltner, Apr. 27, 1954, f. 6, b. 41, Bender papers.
59. Erland Waltner to HSB, Aug. 7, 1954, f. 6, b. 41, Bender papers.
60. HSB to Erland Waltner, Oct. 14, 1954, f. 6, b. 41, Bender papers.
61. HSB to J. Winfield Fretz, Oct. 21, 1954, f. 7, b. 29, Bender papers.

62. HSB to Erland Waltner, Nov. 3, 1954, f. 6, b. 41, Bender papers.
63. HSB to Edmund Kaufman, Oct. 17, 1955, f. 4, b. 33, Bender papers.
64. "MBS Board of Directors' Resolution" (Oct. 26, 1955), f. 6, b. 41, Bender papers.
65. HSB to C. N. Hostetter, Oct. 29, 1955, f. 6, b. 37, Bender papers.
66. HSB to Donovan Smucker, Oct. 31, 1955, f. 4, b. 40, Bender papers.
67. HSB to Calvin Redekop, Dec. 1, 1955, f. 3, b. 38, Bender papers.
68. Paul Miller to HSB, Apr. 6, 1956, f. 7, b. 36, Bender papers.
69. HSB to Calvin Redekop, June 2, 1955, f. 3, b. 39, Bender papers.
70. Ibid.
71. "Minutes of the Meeting for Consultation Regarding the Proposed Plan of Association of Mennonite Biblical Seminaries" (Atlantic Hotel, Chicago, Ill., Dec. 21, 22, 1955), f. 7, b. 37, Bender papers.
72. HSB to Paul Miller, Feb. 10, 1956, f. 7, b. 36, Bender papers.
73. Memorandum, HSB to Paul Mininger, Feb. 14, 1956, f. 9, b. 36, Bender papers.
74. I. E. Burkhart to Paul Mininger, Mar. 23, 1956, f. 4, b. 25, Bender papers.
75. Erland Waltner to HSB, Apr. 24, 1956, f. 6, b. 41, Bender papers.
76. Ibid.
77. HSB to Erland Waltner, Apr. 26, 1956, f. 6, b. 41, Bender papers.
78. Paul Mininger to HSB, May 11, 1956, f. 9, b. 35, Bender papers.
79. Nelson Kauffman to Arthur Rosenberger, Aug. 8, 1956, f. 3, b. 33, Bender papers.
80. HSB to Donovan Smucker, May 22, 1956, f. 4, b. 40, Bender papers.
81. HSB to Orie O. Miller, June 26, 1956, f. 50, b. 61, Bender papers.
82. *Goshen College Bulletin*, Oct. 1959.
83. HSB to John E. Hartzler, Nov. 7, 1955, f. 1, b. 31, Bender papers.

**Chapter 20**
1. The handwritten text, trans. into German by Elizabeth Horsch Bender, f. 10, b. 26, Bender papers.
2. "Gedenkfeier abgehalten in Zurich, am 15. Aug. 1952," f. 10, b. 26, Bender papers; also, report in Zurich newspaper *Zeichen der Zeit*, Aug. 17, 1952, 10-11.
3. The same as n. 2.
4. *Fünfte Mennonitische Weltkonferenz, 10. bis 15. Aug. 1952 auf St. Chrischona bei Basel, Schweiz* (published program booklet of the conference), f. 10, b. 26, Bender papers.
5. See HSB to Henry Fast, Dec. 21, 1951, f. 27, b. 57, Bender papers.
6. Preparatory Commission minutes, June 19-20, 1951, f. 3, b. 5, Bender papers.
7. HSB to H. A. Fast, Dec. 31, 1951, f. 27, b. 57, Bender papers.
8. Paul Peachey to HSB, Apr. 26, 1952, f. 9, b. 37, Bender papers.
9. HSB to Paul Peachey, May 5, 1952, f. 9, b. 37, Bender papers.
10. HSB to B. B. Janz, Apr. 29, 1952, f. 11, b. 32, Bender papers.
11. The young men were Irvin Horst, John W. Miller, Paul Peachey, Calvin W. Redekop, David A. Shank, Orley Swartzentruber, and John Howard Yoder; the meeting which generated the communion idea was the first Concern meeting, held in mid-April 1952 in Amsterdam.
12. HSB to Henry Fast, Mar. 13, 1952, f. 27, b. 57, Bender papers.
13. Irvin Horst to HSB, July 21, 1952, MWC papers, AMC.
14. HSB to Carl MacIntire, Mar. 9, 1951; Arthur Holt to HSB, Apr. 21, 1952; MWC papers, AMC.
15. HSB to Orie O. Miller, Feb. 25, 1952, f. 36, b. 57, Bender papers.
16. Ibid.
17. See various letters of HSB, to Paul Erb, Orie O. Miller, Henry Fast, Cornelius Krahn, and others, in f. 10, b. 57, Bender papers.

18. Bender papers, passim: e.g., Rose Crous to Dear Friends, July 8, 1952, f. 10, b. 27.

19. Fritz Blanke to HSB, July 7, 1952, f. 10, b. 26, Bender papers.

20. Fritz Blanke to HSB, May 5, 1952, f. 10, b. 26, Bender papers.

21. HSB to Fritz Blanke, July 7, 1952; also see another letter, Der Stadtrat von Zürich an Herrn [the mayor of Zurich to the honorable] Professor H. S. Bender, July 25, 1952); f. 10, b. 26, Bender papers.

22. HSB to Walter Landes, July 7, 1952, f. 6, b. 39, Bender papers.

23. Harold S. Bender, news release (Apr. 1952), f. 6, b. 5, Bender papers.

24. See *Die Gemeinde Christi und Ihr Auftrag: Vorträge und Verhandlungen der fünften Mennonitischen Weltkonferenz* (Karlsruhe, Germany: printed by H. Schneider, 1953), 369-370.

25. A. J. Metzler to Ellrose Zook, Aug. 15, 1952, MWC papers, AMC.

26. Joan Strauss to Gladys Stoltzfus, Sept. 9, 1952, f. 9a, b. 40, Bender papers.

27. Ibid.

28. HSB to Margarethe (Grete) Mecenseffy, Dec. 15, 1952, f. 7, b. 35, Bender papers.

29. Rachel Waltner, "From Anabaptism to Mennonitism: *The Mennonite Encyclopedia* as a Historical Document" (Bethel College Social Science Seminar paper, Apr. 15, 1982), 12, MLA; a version of Waltner's paper appeared in *Mennonite Life* 37 (Dec. 1982): 13-19.

30. "Publication and Research Projects in Anabaptist-Mennonite History," *MQR* 23 (Jan. 1949): 57; Harold S. Bender, "Preface," *ME*, 1:vii.

31. Waltner, "From Anabaptism to Mennonitism," 12-15.

32. HSB to Paul Erb, Nov. 15, 1948, Erb file, drawer 5, *ME* papers, AMC.

33. Paul Erb to HSB, July 20, 1949, Erb file, drawer 5, *ME* papers, AMC.

34. Cornelius Krahn to HSB, Feb. 19, 1951, Krahn file, drawer 7, *ME* papers, AMC.

35. Melvin Gingerich to Cornelius Krahn, Oct. 10, 1950, Krahn file, drawer 5, *ME* papers, AMC.

36. Cornelius Krahn to HSB, Aug. 6, 1951, Krahn file, drawer 7, *ME* papers, AMC.

37. HSB to Cornelius Krahn, July 3, 1959, Krahn file, drawer 8, *ME* papers, AMC.

38. The *ME* correspondence between Bender and Friedmann, Friedmann file, drawer 6, *ME* papers, AMC.

39. Robert Friedmann to HSB, Feb. 3, 1957, Friedmann file, drawer 6, *ME* papers, AMC.

40. Robert Friedmann to HSB, Oct. 5, 1958, Friedmann file, drawer 6, *ME* papers, AMC.

41. Cornelius Krahn to HSB and Melvin Gingerich, Mar. 28, 1951, Krahn file, drawer 5, *ME* papers, AMC.

42. HSB to Robert Friedmann, Nov. 28, 1958, Friedmann file, drawer 6, *ME* papers, AMC.

43. Robert Friedmann to HSB, Dec. 7, 1958, Friedmann file, drawer 6, *ME* papers, AMC.

44. Robert Friedmann to HSB, July 8, 1959, Friedmann file, drawer 7, *ME* papers, AMC.

45. Specific documentation is elusive, but Elizabeth Horsch Bender's prodigious effort is abundantly shown through the *ME* papers, and the author has often discussed these matters with Liesel Widmer throughout a forty-year acquaintance. Bender and Krahn acknowledged the two women's work in "Preface," *ME*, 4:4-5.

46. A. J. Metzler to HSB, Feb. 2, 1950, Bender file, drawer 5, *ME* papers, AMC.

47. A. J. Metzler to HSB, Feb. 2, 1950, Bender file, drawer 5, *ME* papers, AMC; also, [MC] *Mennonite General Conference Proceedings*, Aug. 25-27, 1959, 15.

48. George Williams to HSB, Nov. 10, 1959, f. 19, b. 49, Bender papers.

49. "Report of the Editor," Aug. 11, 1959, Bender file, drawer 5, *ME* papers, AMC.

50. HSB to Robert Friedmann, July 12, 1958, f. 8, b. 44, Bender papers.

51. A. J. Metzler to HSB, Aug. 13, 1959, Bender file, drawer 5, *ME* papers, AMC.
52. Nelson Kauffman to Ernest Miller, Jan. 30, 1952; see also Ernest Miller to Dear Brethren, Mar. 27, 1952; both in f. 2, b. 17, Orie O. Miller papers, AMC.
53. Ernest Miller to Dear Brethren, Mar. 27, 1952, f. 2, b. 17, Orie O. Miller papers, AMC.
54. Handwritten note, undated, f. 2, b. 17, Orie O. Miller papers, AMC.
55. Nelson Kauffman to HSB and I. E. Burkhart, Dec. 3, 1952, f. 3, b. 33, Bender papers.
56. Orie O. Miller, "thots," May 3, 1953, f. 1, b. 17, Bender papers.
57. HSB to Orie O. Miller, Jan. 14, 1952, f. 2, b. 17, Orie O. Miller papers, AMC.
58. Ibid.
59. Orie O. Miller to Dear Brethren, Aug. 18, 1952, f. 8, b. 12, Orie O. Miller papers, AMC.
60. HSB to Dear Brethren, Oct. 24, 1952, f. 3, b. 17, Orie O. Miller papers, AMC.
61. HSB to Dear Brethren, Mar. 23, 1953, f. 1, b. 17, Orie O. Miller papers, AMC.
62. Carl Kreider to Paul Mininger, July 29, 1953, f. 1, b. 17, Orie O. Miller papers, AMC.
63. Ibid.
64. Menn. Bd. of Educ. exec. comm. minutes, Apr. 29-30, 1953, f. 1, b. 17, Bender papers.
65. J. C. Wenger, "Memorandum Submitted to the Mennonite Board of Education Executive Committee" (Sept. 9, 1953), f. 1, b. 17, Orie O. Miller papers, AMC.
66. HSB to Dear Brethren, Mar. 23, 1953, f. 1, b. 17, Orie O. Miller papers, AMC.
67. HSB to Nelson and Orie, Sept. 5, 1953, f. 2, b. 17, Orie O. Miller papers, AMC.

Chapter 21
1. "Bender Receives Anniversary Volume," *Goshen College Alumni Newsletter*, Sept. 1957, 2; Guy F. Hershberger, ed., *The Recovery of the Anabaptist Vision: A Sixtieth Anniversary Tribute to Harold S. Bender* (Herald Press, 1957).
2. "European Study Conference of American Mennonite Students in Europe" (Apr. 14-25, 1952), f. 3, b. 1, Orie O. Miller papers, AMC. The major primary source for the Concern movement's ideas is a series of pamphlets under the title *Concern*, published annually 1954-1971. *The Conrad Grebel Review* 8 (Spring 1990) is entirely on the movement and includes retrospectives by Concern participants as well as comments by others; in that issue, an introductory essay by Paul Toews, "The Concern Movement: Its Origins and Early History," 109-126, offers a helpful overview. Also see Steven M. Nolt, "Anabaptist Visions of Church and Society," *MQR* 69 (July 1995): 283-294; J. Lawrence Burkholder, "Concern Pamphlets Movement," *ME*, 5:177-180.
3. "European Study Conference. . . ."
4. Paul Peachey, "Summary of the Conference: 'The Decline of the West' " (Amsterdam, The Netherlands, Apr. 1952), f. 9, b. 37, Bender papers.
5. "Reflections on the Irrelevance of certain Slogans to the historical Movements they represent. Or, the Cooking of the Anabaptist Goose, Or, Ye garnish the sepulchres of the righteous" (sic, Yoder's capitalization; Apr. 25, 1952), f. 6, b. 47, Bender papers.
6. John H. Yoder to HSB, July 31, 1952, f. 6, b. 42, Bender papers.
7. Yoder, "Reflections, . . . Cooking of the Anabaptist Goose."
8. Irvin Horst to Dear Comrades, June 17, 1952, f. 3, b. 1, Bender papers.
9. Irvin Horst to Dear Comrades, July 17, 1952, f. 3, b. 1, Bender papers.
10. John H. Yoder to HSB, July 5, 1956, f. 6, b. 47, Bender papers.
11. John H. Yoder to HSB, May 5, 1954, f. 6, b. 42, Bender papers.
12. Ibid.
13. Ibid.
14. HSB to John H. Yoder, July 2, 1954, f. 6, b. 42, Bender papers.
15. John H. Yoder to HSB, July 2, 1954, b. 11, John H. Yoder papers, AMC.
16. HSB to John H. Yoder, Aug. 10, 1948, f. 6, b. 42, Bender papers.

17. John H. Yoder to HSB, Aug. 17, 1948, f. 6, b. 42, Bender papers.
18. Ibid.
19. HSB to John H. Yoder, Aug. 10, 1948, f. 6, b. 42, Bender papers.
20. John H. Yoder to HSB, Dec. 13, 1949, f. 6, b. 42, Bender papers.
21. Ibid.
22. John H. Yoder to HSB, Mar. 1, 1950, f. 6, b. 42, Bender papers.
23. HSB to John H. Yoder, May 29, 1950, f. 6, b. 42, Bender papers.
24. HSB to John H. Yoder, June 24, 1950, f. 6, b. 42, Bender papers.
25. HSB to John H. Yoder, Jan. 17, 1950, f. 6, b. 42, Bender papers. During 1950 the "Anabaptist Vision" essay was translated into French and German.
26. John H. Yoder to HSB, Jan. 12, 1951, f. 6, b. 42, Bender papers.
27. HSB to John H. Yoder, Jan. 19, 1951, f. 6, b. 42, Bender papers.
28. Ibid.
29. HSB to John H. Yoder, Mar. 21, 1951, f. 6, b. 42, Bender papers.
30. John Yoder to David Shank, Nov. 10, 1952, f. 6, b. 42, Bender papers.
31. Ibid.
32. Ibid.
33. John Yoder to David Shank, Mar. 6, 1952, f. 6, b. 42, Bender papers.
34. Ibid.
35. John Yoder to David Shank, July 6, 1954, f. 6, b. 42, Bender papers.
36. John Yoder to Dear Brethren, Aug. 6, 1954, f. 6, b. 42, Bender papers.
37. For a more extended description of the lines of such discussions, see Nolt, "Anabaptist Visions of Church and Society" (see n. 2), 283-294.
38. "Program of the Church Organization and Administration Conference," Chicago, Ill., Mar. 28-29, 1955, vertical files, MSHLA.
39. HSB to John Yoder, July 2, 1954, f. 6, b. 42, Bender papers; see also Paul Peachey, "Anabaptism and Church Organization," MQR 30 (July 1956): 213-228. Bender's editorial introduction of Peachey's article was less than enthusiastic and expressed reservations with Peachey's argument that congregationalism was the basic form of the New Testament church and of the Anabaptists.
40. See brief report of the conference, in "Freedom . . . to Obey" (n.d.), f. 6, b. 42, Bender papers.
41. John H. Yoder, "A Study in the Doctrine of the Work of Christ" (unpub. paper from seminar at Domburg, The Netherlands, Apr. 27, 1954), f. 6, b. 42, Bender papers.
42. Ibid.
43. Ibid.
44. Ibid.
45. John Yoder to Dear Brethren in Concern, Aug. 6, 1954, f. 6, b. 42, Bender papers.
46. John C. Wenger, Introduction to Theology: An Interpretation of the Doctrinal Content of Scripture, Written to Strengthen a Childlike Faith in Christ (Herald Press, 1954).
47. Ibid.
48. John H. Yoder, "The New Testament Conception of the Ministry," GH 48 (Feb. 8, 1955): 121-122.
49. HSB to John Yoder, Feb. 18, 1955, f. 6, b. 42, Bender papers.
50. John H. Yoder and David Shank, "Biblicism and the Church," Concern 2 (1955), 26-69.
51. Reference by Yoder in John Yoder to HSB, June 16, 1955, f. 6, b. 42, Bender papers.
52. John Yoder to HSB, June 10, 1955, f. 6, b. 42, Bender papers.
53. HSB to John Yoder, June 27, 1955, f. 6, b. 42, Bender papers.
54. Ibid.
55. Author conversation with C. Norman Kraus in Harrisonburg, Va., in 1995.
56. Paul M. Miller to HSB, Dec. 31, 1956, f. 7, b. 36, Bender papers.

57. Paul Peachey to HSB, Aug. 26, 1957, f. 9, b. 37, Bender papers.
58. Heinz Kloppenburg to HSB, July 23, 1962, f. 7, b. 46, Bender papers.

### Chapter 22
1. For Klassen's biography, see Herbert and Maureen Klassen, *Ambassador to His People: C. F. Klassen and the Russian Mennonite Refugees* (Hillsboro, Kan.: Kindred Press, 1990).
2. C. F. Klassen to Orie O. Miller, Sept. 22, 1951, f. 66, b. 58, Bender papers.
3. For a good analysis of C. N. Hostetter Jr. and MCC's situation in the early 1950s, see E. Morris Sider, *Messenger of Grace: A Biography of C. N. Hostetter, Jr.* (Nappanee, Ind.: Evangel Press, 1982).
4. Paul Miller to HSB, Apr. 6, 1956, f. 7, b. 36, Bender papers.
5. Sider, *Messenger of Grace*, 171-172.
6. HSB to Orie O. Miller, July 8, 1954, f. 36, b. 60, Bender papers.
7. C. F. Klassen to Orie O. Miller, Sept. 22, 1951, f. 66, b. 58, Bender papers.
8. John D. Unruh, *In The Name of Christ: A History of the Mennonite Central Committee and Its Services, 1920-1951* (Herald Press, 1952), Appendix IV.
9. HSB to Orie O. Miller, Jan. 9, 1951, f. 36, b. 57, Bender papers.
10. C. F. Klassen to Orie O. Miller, f. 66, b. 58, Bender papers.
11. C. F. Klassen to Orie O. Miller, Sept. 22, 1951, f. 66, b. 58, Bender papers.
12. C. F. Klassen to HSB, Feb. 19, 1951, f. 66, b. 58, Bender papers.
13. HSB to Orie O. Miller, Jan. 9, 1951, f. 36, b. 57, Bender papers.
14. Ibid.
15. Harold S. Bender, "Our Relief Program in Danger," *GH* 44 (Feb. 27, 1951): 196.
16. Harold S. Bender, "Shall We Continue Our Relief Work, Voluntary Service, and I-W Service?" *GH* 48 (Aug. 17, Nov. 8, 1955): 1057-1058.
17. Ibid.
18. HSB to C. F. Klassen, Feb. 23, 1952, f. 66, b. 58, Bender papers.
19. Ibid.
20. Paul Peachey to HSB, Jan. 10, 1951, f. 75, b. 58, Bender papers.
21. HSB to C. F. Klassen, Feb. 23, 1952, f. 66, b. 58, Bender papers.
22. HSB to William T. Snyder, Oct. 17, 1958, f. 41, b. 60, Bender papers.
23. Atlee Beechy to Orie O. Miller, Jan. 5, 1949, f. 31 b. 57, Bender papers.
24. Paul Peachey to HSB, Feb. 1, 1950, f. 75, b. 58, Bender papers.
25. Orie O. Miller to Guy F. Hershberger, Feb. 24, 1950, f. 27, b. 58, Bender papers.
26. HSB to Cornelius Wall, Aug. 6, 1951, f. 3, b. 59, Bender papers.
27. See MCC exec. comm. minutes, May 15, 1954, b. 3, MCC papers, AMC.
28. Ibid., Aug. 29, 1956.
29. See "Journal" of Bender's 1956 Soviet trip, f. 7, b. 120, Bender papers.
30. Orie O. Miller to Ambassador Dmitri S. Shuvahin, Apr. 4, 1956, f. 50, b. 61, Bender papers; see also Harold S. Bender, "Mennonites in the Soviet Union Today," *GH* 48 (Aug. 16, 1955): 775.
31. Bender, "Mennonites in the Soviet Union Today," 775.
32. See "Journal" of Bender's 1956 Soviet trip.
33. Comments made to me in 1996 by Walter Sawatsky of Associated Mennonite Biblical Seminary, author of *Soviet Evangelicals Since World War II* (Herald Press, 1981).
34. HSB to Mr. T. Gostjev (U.S.S.R. Minister of Cults), Nov. 15, 1956, f. 48, b. 61, Bender papers.
35. HSB to Cornelius Krahn, July 3, 1950, Drawer 7, *ME* papers, AMC.
36. HSB to Members of MCC Peace Section, July 10, 1950, f. 5, b. 58, Bender papers.
37. Lewis B. Hershey, *Outline of Historical Background of Selective Service and Chronology* (Washington, D.C.: Government Printing Office, 1952), Table 3, 38-40.

38. *News Notes* (monthly newsletter from the National Council of Churches, Jan. 1951), 4.

39. A. Stauffer Curry to Board of Directors, National Service Board for Religious Objectors, May 22, 1951, American Friends Service Committee, f. 5, SCPC (Swarthmore College Peace Collection, Swarthmore, Pa.).

40. *Religious News Service*, Jan. 2, 1951, 6, National Service Board for Religious Objectors (NSBRO) files, SCPC.

41. HSB to Albert Gaeddert, Jan. 30, 1951, f. 1, b. 30, Bender papers.

42. Consultative Council Minutes, Jan. 1951, NSBRO files, SCPC.

43. Conference Report (House N a535), June 7, 1951, *Congressional Record*, Eighty-Second Congress, First Session, 6247.

44. Ibid.

45. HSB to All Bishops and Ministers in the Mennonite Church in the United States, Jan. 9, 1952, f. 29, b. 2, J. C. Wenger papers, AMC.

46. Albert N. Keim and Grant M. Stoltzfus, *The Politics of Conscience: The Historic Peace Churches and America at War, 1917-1955* (Herald Press, 1988), 141-146.

47. American Friends Service Committee Board Meeting Minutes, Sept. 17, 1952, 1-2, American Friends Service Committee files, SCPC.

48. Edgar Metzler, "Another Alternative for Draft-Age Youth," *GH* 52 (Nov. 17, 1959): 977-978.

49. Harold S. Bender, "When May Christians Disobey Government?" *GH* 53 (Jan. 12, 1960): 25.

50. Edgar Metzler to HSB, Dec. 31, 1951, f. 10, b. 47, Bender papers.

51. To find ample materials on the I-W program, see Willard Swartley and Cornelius Dyck, eds., *Annotated Bibliography of Mennonite Writings on War and Peace, 1930-1980* (Herald Press, 1987), section I.

52. See Donald F. Durnbaugh, ed., *On Earth Peace: Discussions on War/Peace Issues Between Friends, Mennonites, Brethren, and European Churches, 1935-1975* (Elgin, Ill.: Brethren Press, 1978), esp. chaps. 3-6.

53. See Nicholas W. Dick, "The Church Peace Mission" (paper presented to a class at Associated Mennonite Biblical Seminaries, Elkhart, Ind., Apr. 29, 1959), copy at AMBS. For HSB's understanding of the CPM program, see HSB to Dear Brethren, May 14, 1962; copy of his speech, "One Program of Christian Pacifism"; both, f. 5, b. 52, Bender papers.

54. Durnbaugh, *On Earth Peace*, chap. 5.

55. See items in f. 10, b. 61, Bender papers; for overview, see Durnbaugh, *On Earth Peace*, chaps. 9-21.

56. See report by Heinz Kloppenburg, f. 6, b. 43, Bender papers.

57. "Guiding Principles on Participation in East-West Peace Conferences" (MCC Peace Section exec. comm. minutes, May 27, 1960), Peace Problems Committee folder, b. 61, Guy F. Hershberger papers, AMC.

58. HSB to Harold E. Fey, Sept. 7, 1961, f. 43, b. 12, Bender papers; see also Bender's report in the *GH* 54 (Sept. 19, 1961): 825, and his "Report of the Peace Section Observer Delegation to the First All-Christian Peace Assembly at Prague, Czechoslovakia, June, 1961," f. 9, b. 61, Bender papers.

59. Douglas Steere to Dear Friends, Jan. 9, 1962, f. 6, b. 49, Bender papers.

60. Douglas Steere to Friends, Feb. 2, 1962, f. 6, b. 49, Bender papers.

61. HSB to Douglas Steere, Feb. 7, 1962, f. 6, b. 49, Bender papers.

Chapter 23

1. The "Kunstbuch" actually exists in manuscript form, with the original at the Bürgerbibliothek, a division of the Stadt- und Universität Bibliothek, Bern, Switzerland; mircroform copies are at the historical library of Bluffton College and in the MHL; no doubt it will eventually be published in the series so-called Täuferakten (Quellen zur Geschichte der Wiedertäufer [from 1940, Täufer]). For further details, see: *ME*, 3:259;

notes in *MQR* 30 (Jan. 1956): 75-77; 31 (Oct. 1957): 294-295; Heinold Fast, "Pilgram Marbeck und das oberdeutsche Täufertum: Ein neuer Handscrhriftenfund," *Archiv für Reformationsgeschichte* 47/2 (1956): 212-242; and William Klassen, "Pilgram Marpeck in Recent Research," *MQR* 32 (July 1958): 211-229.

2. Robert Friedmann to HSB, Sept. 23, 1955, f. 8, b. 29, Bender papers.

3. HSB to Heinold Fast, Sept. 24, 1955, f. 2, b. 29, Bender papers.

4. HSB to Delbert Gratz, Mar. 30, 1956, f. 13, b. 30, Bender papers.

5. HSB to Jan Kiwiet, June 29, 1956, f. 14, b. 32, Bender papers; see also Kiwiet's doctoral dissertation, "Pilgram Marbeck: sein Kreis und seine Theologie (ca. 1495-1556)" (Univ. of Zurich, 1955), typescript copy in MSHLA.

6. Ibid.

7. Ibid.

8. HSB to Dear Friends and Brethren, undated, f. 6, b. 4, Robert Friedmann papers, AMC.

9. Ibid.

10. HSB editorial comments, *MQR* 31 (Oct. 1957): 226.

11. HSB to Robert Friedmann, June 27, 1957, f. 6, b. 4, Robert Friedmann papers, AMC.

12. Cornelius Krahn, "Anabaptist-Mennonitism in Doctoral Dissertations," *Mennonite Life* 36 (Apr. 1958): 83-86.

13. HSB to Fritz Blanke, Sept. 24, 1955, f. 10, b. 26, Bender papers.

14. HSB editorial, *MQR* 32 (July 1958): 179; HSB to George Williams, Dec. 15, 1961, f. 19, b. 49, Bender papers.

15. Fritz Blanke, *Brüder in Christo: Die Geschichte der ältesten Täufergemeinde, Zollikon, 1525* (Zurich: Zwingli-Verlag, 1955); Blanke, *Brothers in Christ: The History of the Oldest Anabaptist Congregation, Zollikon, near Zurich, Switzerland*, trans. Joseph Nordenhaug (Herald Press, 1961).

16. HSB to Friedmann, Aug. 15, 1956, f. 13, b. 41, Bender papers.

17. George Williams to Elizabeth Horsch Bender, July 5, 1956, f. 13, b. 41, Bender papers.

18. HSB to George Williams, June 4, 1955, f. 13, b. 41, Bender papers.

19. Robert Friedmann to HSB, July 12, 1953, f. 6, b. 29, Bender papers.

20. HSB to George Williams, Feb. 18, 1957, f. 13, b. 41, Bender papers.

21. HSB to George Williams, July 14, 1958, f. 19, b. 49, Bender papers.

22. Cornelius J. Dyck to Carl S. Meyer, Aug. 7, 1958; Cornelius J. Dyck to Hans Hillerbrand, Jan., 28, 1959; f. 2, b. 44, Bender papers.

23. Guy F. Hershberger, ed., *The Recovery of the Anabaptist Vision: A Sixtieth Anniversary Tribute to Harold S. Bender* (Herald Press, 1957).

24. The essay was also published in the *MQR* 29 (Jan. 1953): 3-16.

25. Harold S. Bender, *These Are My People: The Nature of the Church and Its Discipleship* (Herald Press, 1962), viii.

26. Personal observations of the author, a college student at EMC at the time.

27. See John Bright, *The Kingdom of God: The Biblical Concept and Its Meaning for the Church* (New York,: Abingdon, 1953), esp. chaps. 7-8.

28. For the New Testament, see Paul Minear, *Images of the Church in the New Testament* (Philadelphia: Westminster, 1960); cf. John Driver, *Images of the Church in Mission* (Herald Press, 1997), chaps. 10-11.

29. Bender, *These Are My People*, 68.

30. Ibid., 75.

31. Ibid., 81.

32. Harold S. Bender, "Our Witness for Nonconformity in Dress in the Future" (n.d.), f. 10, b. 100, Bender papers.

33. John C. Wenger, *Introduction to Theology: An Interpretation of the Doctrinal Content of Scripture, Written to Strengthen a Childlike Faith in Christ* (Herald Press, 1954).

34. Donovan E. Smucker, review of J. C. Wenger, *Introduction to Theology*. . . , in *MQR* 28 (Oct. 1954): 310-313.
35. [MC] *Mennonite General Conference Proceedings* . . . (Aug. 25-27, 1957), 51.
36. Ibid., 40-44.
37. HSB to J. C. Wenger, July 10, 1960, f. 29, b. 2, J. C. Wenger papers.
38. Harold S. Bender, "Outside Influences on Mennonite Thought," *Proceedings of the Ninth Conference on Mennonite Educational and Cultural Problems* (Hesston, Kan., June 18-19, 1953), 37-41.
39. Ibid., 37.
40. Ibid., 38.
41. Ibid., 39.
42. Ibid., 41.
43. See Harley J. Stucky, "The Agricultural Revolution of Our Day," *Mennonite Life* 39 (July 1959): 117-118.
44. Quotations from Perry Bush, *Two Kingdoms, Two Loyalties: Mennonite Pacifism in the Twentieth Century* (Baltimore: Johns Hopkins, 1997), 380-381.
45. Bender, "Outside Influences . . . " (see n. 38), 40.
46. [MC] *Mennonite General Conference Proceedings* . . . (Aug. 23-26, 1955), 86-89.
47. High School Study Committee minutes, 1952, f. 12, b. 72, Bender papers.
48. [MC] *Mennonite General Conference Proceedings* . . . (Aug. 12-18, 1955).
49. Ibid., 16-17.
50. HSB to John Mosemann and Paul Mininger, May 28, 1956, f. 9, b. 36, Bender papers.
51. HSB to Roy Roth, Feb. 10, 1955, f. 10, b. 38, Bender papers.
52. HSB to C. L. Garber, Sept. 10, 1955, f. 1, b. 30, Bender papers.
53. HSB to Gentlemen, Mar. 20, 1952, f. 9, b. 32, Bender papers.
54. HSB to Orie O. Miller, Mar. 30, 1956, f. 3, b. 39, Bender papers.
55. Mary Eleanor Bender, interviewed by Eileen K. Saner at Goshen, Ind., Mar. 4, 1989, tapes in BOHC.
56. Paul Mininger to HSB, Nov. 15, 1957, f. 9, b. 36, Bender papers.
57. HSB to Paul Mininger, Nov. 28, 1957, f. 9, b. 36, Bender papers.
58. Ada Schrock to Irene Hershberger, July 8, 1961, f. 3, b. 49, Bender papers.
59. HSB to J. L. Stauffer, Jan. 18, 1954, f. 7, b. 40, Bender papers.
60. William H. Day to HSB, Feb. 19, 1962, f. 16, b. 43, Bender papers.
61. Atlee Beechy to HSB, Sept. 26, 1958, f. 8, b. 43, Bender papers. Also see HSB to Nelson Kauffman, Oct. 24, 1952, f. 3, b. 33, Bender papers.
62. Paul Erb to HSB, July 28, 1958, f. 4, b. 44, Bender papers.
63. HSB to Paul Peachey, Oct. 23, 1953, f. 7, b. 45, Bender papers.
64. HSB to John C. Wenger, July 19, 1957, f. 29, b. 2, Wenger papers.
65. HSB to Paul Mininger, July 19, 1961, f. 13, b. 47, Bender papers.
66. Ibid.
67. Ada Schrock to Irene Hershberger, Nov. 10, 1961, f. 3, b. 49, Bender papers.
68. Ada Schrock to Irene Hershberger, Mar. 14, 1962, f. 3, b. 49, Bender papers.
69. Ada Schrock to Irene Hershberger, Sept. 9, 1961, f. 3, b. 49, Bender papers.
70. Bender to Paul Mininger, June 22, 1962, f. 13, b. 47, Bender papers.
71. Guy F. Hershberger to Franklin Littell, Sept. 16, 1962, f. 12, b. 12, Guy F. Hershberger papers, AMC.
72. John Drescher, "Mennonite World Conference—1962," *GH* 55 (Aug. 21, 1962): 729.
73. "The Proceedings of the Seventh Mennonite World Conference" (Kitchener, Ont., Aug. 1-7, 1962), 5-6, MWC papers, AMC.
74. Ibid.
75. Minutes of the meeting of the presidium of the seventh MWC (Kitchener, Ont., Aug. 1-7, 1962), MWC papers, AMC.

76. "The Proceedings of the Seventh Mennonite World Conference," 264, MWC papers, AMC.

77. John C. Wenger, interviewed by John Bender at Goshen, Ind., in 1989, tapes in the BOHC.

78. HSB to Paul Burkholder, Aug. 29, 1962, f. 4, b. 43, Bender papers.

79. MCC exec. comm. minutes, Sept. 7-8, 1962, b. 4, Orie O. Miller papers, AMC.

80. Robert Kreider, interviewed by Albert Keim at North Newton, Kan., Oct. 22, 1995, notes in the BOHC.

81. "World Conference President and Seminary Dean Dies in Chicago," *Mennonite Weekly Review*, Sept. 27, 1962, 1.

82. Franklin H. Littell to Friends of Harold S. Bender, Jan. 1, 1963, f. 29, b. 2, Wenger papers.

# Sources and Bibliography

## Archives

The Archives of the Mennonite Church (AMC) at 1700 South Main St., Goshen, Indiana, house rich source materials. The huge Harold S. Bender collection there, comprising more than 100 boxes of material, was the key resource for this book. Also consulted at the AMC were the papers of Guy F. Hershberger, Sanford Calvin Yoder, Orie O. Miller, John C. Wenger, George and Elsie Kolb Bender, John F. Funk, Robert Friedmann, and others.

Sources used continually were the minutes and documents of such organizations as Mennonite Central Committee, the Mennonite World Conference, the Mennonite Board of Missions and Charities (later, Mennonite Board of Missions), the Mennonite Church (MC) Peace Problems Committee, and the Mennonite Relief Committee, plus various papers of Goshen College, Goshen, Indiana, and its Biblical Seminary, and the materials supporting *The Mennonite Encyclopedia*. Also quite valuable were tapes, transcripts, and notes of oral interviews with colleagues, friends, and family of Harold S. Bender in the Bender Oral History Collection (BOHC). All of these sources are in the AMC.

Other key sources were the papers of Chester K. Lehman, Amos D. Wenger, John L. Stauffer, and George R. Brunk, plus published materials, located in the Menno Simons Historical Library and Archives (MSHLA) at Eastern Mennonite University, Harrisonburg, Virginia. Published and unpublished materials in the Mennonite Historical Library (MHL), located at Goshen College, and others in the Mennonite Library and Archives (MLA) at Bethel College, North Newton, Kansas, also deserve special mention.

Abbreviations are listed on pages 429-430. Books by Herald Press or Mennonite Publishing House are published at Scottdale, Pennsylvania, and at Kitchener or (from 1990) Waterloo, Ontario.

## Selected General Bibliography

Bainton, Roland. "The Left Wing of the Reformation." *Journal of Religion* 20 (Apr. 1941).

Baker, O. E. "The Effects of Urbanization on American Life and the Church." *MQR* 19 (Apr. 1945).

Bender, Elizabeth Horsch. "My Seasons of Life." *MQR* 60 (July 1986).

Bender, Harold S., and Ernst Correll. "C. Henry Smith's *The Story of the Mennonites.*" *MQR* 16 (Oct. 1942).

Blanke, Fritz. *Brothers in Christ: The History of the Oldest Anabaptist Congregation.* Herald Press, 1961.

Bright, John. *The Kingdom of God: The Biblical Concept and Its Meaning for the Church.* New York: Abingdon Press, 1953.

Burkholder, J. Lawrence. "The Limits of Perfection: Autobiographical Reflections." In Rodney Sawatsky and Scott Holland, eds., *The Limits of Perfection: Conversations with J. Lawrence Burkholder.* Waterloo, Ont.: Institute of Anabaptist-Mennonite Studies, Conrad Grebel College, 1993.

Bush, Perry. *Two Kingdoms, Two Loyalties: Mennonite Pacifism in the Twentieth Century.* Baltimore: Johns Hopkins Univ. Press, 1997.

Clemens, Lois Gunden. *At Brenner Park Hotel.* Akron, Pa.: Mennonite Central Committee, 1945.

Correll, Ernst. *Das schweizerische Täufermennonitentum: ein soziologischer Bericht.* Tübingen: J. C. B. Mohr (P. Siebeck), 1925.

_____. "The Sociological and Economic Significance of the Mennonites as a Culture Group in History." *MQR* 16 (July 1942).

Driedger, Leo. "Mennonite Community Change: From Ethnic Enclaves to Social Networks." *MQR* 60 (July 1986).

Eitzen, Dirk W., and Timothy R. Falb. "An Overview of the Mennonite I-W Program." *MQR* 56 (Oct. 1982).

Epp, Frank H. *Mennonite Exodus: The Rescue and Resettlement of the Russian Mennonites Since the Communist Revolution.* Altona, Man.: Canadian Mennonite Relief and Immigration Council, 1962.

_____. *Mennonites in Canada, 1920-1940: A People's Struggle for Survival.* Toronto: Macmillan of Canada, 1982.

Erb, Paul. *Orie O. Miller: The Story of a Man and an Era.* Herald Press, 1969.

Fretz, J. Winfield. "Mutual Aid Among Mennonites." *MQR* 13 (Jan., July, 1939).

Friedmann, Robert. "Conception of the Anabaptists." *Church History* 8 (Dec. 1940).

_____. "Anabaptism and Pietism." *MQR* 14 (Apr., July, 1940).

_____. *Mennonite Piety Through the Centuries: Its Genius and Its Literature.* Goshen, Ind.: Mennonite Historical Society, 1949.

Gates, Helen Kolb. *Bless the Lord, Oh My Soul: A Biography of Bishop John Fretz Funk, 1835-1930.* Herald Press, 1964.

Gingerich, Melvin. "Is There a Need for a Mennonite Rural Life Publication?" *Proceedings of the First Conference on Mennonite Cultural Problems.* Mennonite Colleges and Schools, 1942.

_____. *Service for Peace: A History of Mennonite Civilian Public Service.* Herald Press, 1949.

Goertz, Hans-Jürgen. "The Confessional Heritage in Its New Mold: What Is Mennonite Self-Understanding Today?" In Calvin W. Redekop and Samuel J. Steiner, eds., *Mennonite Identity: Historical and Contemporary Perspectives.* Lanham, Md.: Univ. Press of America, 1988.

Graber, J. D. *100 Years: Prairie Street Mennonite Church.* Elkhart, Ind.: The [Prairie Street Mennonite] Church, 1971.

Gross, Leonard. "Mennonite Leadership: Holding the Church Together." *Mennonite Historical Bulletin* 47 (Apr. 1986).

Hart, Darryl G. *Defending the Faith: J. Gresham Machen and the Crisis of Conservative Protestantism in Modern America.* Baltimore: Johns Hopkins Univ. Press, 1994.

Hartzler, John Ellsworth. *Education Among the Mennonites of America.* Danvers, Ill.: Central Mennonite Publishing Co., 1925.

Henry, Carl F. H. *Fifty Years of Protestant Theology.* Boston: Witte Publishing Co., 1950.

Hershberger, Guy F. "Nonresistance and Industrial Conflict." *MQR* 13 (Apr. 1939).

_____. *War, Peace, and Nonresistance.* Herald Press, 1944.

_____. *The Mennonite Church in the Second World War.* Herald Press, 1952.

_____. "Harold S. Bender and His Time." In John C. Wenger et al., eds., *Harold S. Bender: Educator, Historian, Churchman.*

Herald Press, 1964.

_____. "Historical Background to the Formation of the Mennonite Central Committee." *MQR* 44 (July 1970).

_____, ed. *The Recovery of the Anabaptist Vision: A Sixtieth Anniversary Tribute to Harold S. Bender.* Herald Press, 1957.

Hershey, Lewis B. *Outline of Historical Background of Selective Service and Chronology.* Washington, D.C.: Government Printing Office, 1952.

Holmstrand, Ingemar. *Karl Heim on Philosophy, Science, and the Transcendence of God.* Uppsala: Uppsala Univ., 1980.

Horsch, John. *The Mennonite Church and Modernism.* Mennonite Publishing House, 1924.

_____. "The Faith of the Swiss Brethren." *MQR* 4 (Oct. 1930).

_____. "The Danger of Liberalism." *GH* 1 (June 20, 1908).

Hostetler, Beulah Stauffer. *American Mennonites and Protestant Movements: A Community Paradigm.* Herald Press, 1987.

Hostetler, John A. *God Uses Ink: The Heritage and Mission of the Mennonite Publishing House After Fifty Years.* Herald Press, 1958.

Juhnke, James C. "Mennonite Church Theological and Social Boundaries, 1920-1930—Loyalists, Liberals, and Laxitarians." *ML* 38 (June 1983).

_____. "Mennonite History and Self-Understanding: North American Mennonitism as a Bi-Polar Mosaic." In Calvin W. Redekop, ed., *Mennonite Identity: Historical and Contemporary Perspectives.* Lanham, Md.: Univ. Press of America, 1988.

_____. *Vision, Doctrine, War: Mennonite Identity and Organization in America, 1890-1930.* The Mennonite Experience in America, 3. Herald Press, 1989.

Keim, Albert N., and Grant M. Stoltzfus. *The Politics of Conscription: The Historic Peace Churches and America at War, 1917-1955.* Herald Press, 1988.

Keim, Albert N. "The Anabaptist Vision: The History of a New Paradigm." *The Conrad Grebel Review* 12 (Fall 1994).

Klassen, Herbert and Maureen. *Ambassador to His People: C. F. Klassen and the Russian Mennonite Refugees.* Hillsboro, Kan.: Kindred Press, 1990.

Kraus, C. Norman. "American Mennonites and the Bible." *MQR* 41 (Oct. 1967).

Loetscher, Lefferts A. *The Broadening Church: A Study of Theological Issues in the Presbyterian Church Since 1869.* Philadelphia: Westminster Press, 1954.

Machen, J. Gresham. *The Origins of Paul's Religion.* New York: Macmillan, 1921.

Machen, J. Gresham. *Christianity and Liberalism.* New York: Macmillan, 1924.

Marsden, George R. *Fundamentalism and American Culture: The Shaping of Twentieth-Century Evangelicalism, 1870-1925.* New York: Oxford Univ. Press, 1980.

MCC [Fiftieth] *Anniversary Issue,* i.e., *MQR* 44 (July 1970).

Miller, Levi. "The Growth and Decline of Mennonites near Scottdale, Pennsylvania, 1790-1890." *The Pennsylvania Mennonite Heritage* (Oct. 1990).

Miller, Mary A. *A Pillar of Cloud: The Story of Hesston College, 1909-1959.* North Newton, Kan.: Mennonite Press, 1959.

Miller, Susan Fisher. *Culture for Service: A History of Goshen College, 1894-1994.* Goshen, Ind.: Goshen College, 1994.

Minear, Paul. *Images of the Church in the New Testament.* Philadelphia: Westminster Press, 1960.

"Minutes of the Fifty-Fifth Consecutive Meeting of the American Society of Church History, December 28 and 29, 1943." *Church History* 11 (Mar. 1944).

Noll, Mark A. *Between Faith and Criticism: Evangelicals, Scholarship, and the Bible in America.* San Francisco: Harper & Row, 1986.

Durnbaugh, Donald F., ed. *On Earth Peace: Discussions on War/Peace Issues Between Friends, Mennonites, Brethren, and European Churches, 1935-1975.* Elgin, Ill.: The Brethren Press, 1978.

Pannabecker, Samuel F. *Ventures of Faith: The Story of the Mennonite Biblical Seminary.* Elkhart, Ind.: Mennonite Biblical Seminary, 1975.

Peachey, Paul. "Toward an Understanding of the Decline of the West." *Concern* 1 (June 1954).

Pellman, Hubert. *Eastern Mennonite College, 1917-1967.* Harrisonburg, Va.: Eastern Mennonite College, 1967.

Pickett, Clarence. *For More Than Bread: An Autobiographical Account of Twenty-Two Years' Work with the American Friends Service Committee.* Boston, Mass.: Little, Brown and Co., 1953.

Redekop, Calvin W. *Mennonite Society.* Baltimore: Johns Hopkins Univ. Press, 1989.

Redekop, Calvin W., ed. *Mennonite Identity: Historical and Con-*

*temporary Perspectives*. Lanham, Md.: Univ. Press of America, 1988.

Sawatsky, Rodney. "The Influence of Fundamentalism on Mennonite Nonresistance 1908-1944." M.A. thesis, Univ. of Minnesota, 1973.

Schlabach, Gerald W. "A New Wineskin for the Old Wines: A Changing Ministry, Harold S. Bender, and a New Mennonite Seminary." History seminar paper at Goshen College, 1978, copy in MHL.

Schlabach, Theron F. "To Focus a Mennonite Vision." In J. R. Burkholder and Calvin W. Redekop, eds., *Kingdom, Cross and Community: Essays on Mennonite Themes in Honor of Guy F. Hershberger*. Herald Press, 1976.

_____. *Gospel Versus Gospel: Mission and the Mennonite Church, 1863-1944*. Herald Press, 1980.

Sider, E. Morris. *Messenger of Grace: A Biography of C. N. Hostetter Jr.* Nappanee, Ind.: Evangel Press, 1982.

Smith, C. Henry. "A Communication from C. Henry Smith Concerning the Review of His Book *The Story of the Mennonites*." *MQR* 17 (Oct. 1943).

_____. *The Mennonites of America*. Goshen, Ind.: The Author, 1909.

_____. *The Mennonites: A Brief History*. Berne, Ind.: Mennonite Book Concern, 1920.

Smucker, Donovan. "The Theological Triumph of the Early Anabaptist Mennonites: The Re-Discovery of Biblical Theology in Paradox." *MQR* 19 (Jan. 1945).

Sprunger, Keith. "C. Henry Smith's Vision of Mennonite History." *Mennonite Life* 50 (Mar. 1995).

Stauffer, Ethelbert. "Märtyrer-Theologie und Täuferbewegung." *Zeitschrift für Kirchengeschichte* 52 (1933).

Stayer, James, Werner Packull, and Klaus Depperman. "From Monogenesis to Polygenesis: The Historical Discussion of Anabaptist Origins." *MQR* 49 (Apr. 1975).

Swartley, Willard M., and Cornelius J. Dyck, eds. *Annotated Bibliography of Mennonite Writings on War and Peace, 1930-1980*. Herald Press, 1987.

Toews, John B. *With Courage to Spare: The Life of B. B. Janz (1877-1964)*. Winnipeg: Board of Christian Literature, General Conference of the Mennonite Brethren Churches, 1978.

Toews, Paul. "The Long Weekend or the Short Week: Mennonite

Peace Theology, 1925-1944." *MQR* 60 (Jan. 1986).

_____. "The Concern Movement: Its Origins and Early History." *The Conrad Grebel Review* 8 (Spring 1990).

_____. *Mennonites and American Society, 1930-1970: Modernity and the Persistence of Religious Community*. The Mennonite Experience in America, 4. Herald Press, 1996.

Turner, Violet B. "My Family: An Informal Narrative Written for My Children." Undated. Copy in AMC.

Umble, John Sylvanus. *Mennonite Pioneers*. Mennonite Publishing House, 1940.

_____. *Goshen College, 1894-1954: A Mennonite Venture in Christian Higher Education*. Goshen, Ind.: Goshen College, 1954.

Unruh, John D. *In The Name of Christ: A History of the Mennonite Central Committee and Its Services, 1920-1951*. Herald Press, 1952.

Van Til, Cornelius. *The New Modernism*. Philadelphia: The Presbyterian and Reformed Publishing Co., 1946.

Waltner, Rachel. "From Anabaptism to Mennonitism: *The Mennonite Encyclopedia* as a Historical Document." *Mennonite Life* 37 (Dec. 1982).

Warfield, B. B. *Revelation and Inspiration*. Grand Rapids: Baker Book House, 1981 (reprint).

Weaver, Abraham A. *A Standard History of Elkhart County, Indiana*. Chicago: American Historical Society, 1916.

Weaver, J. Denny. *Keeping Salvation Ethical: Mennonite and Amish Atonement Theology in the Late Nineteenth Century*. Herald Press, 1997.

_____. "The Quickening of Soteriology: Atonement from Christian Burkholder to Daniel Kauffman." *MQR* 61 (Jan. 1987).

Wellhausen, Julius. *Prolegomena zur Geschichte Israels*. Berlin: G. Reimer, 1899.

Wenger, John C. *Glimpses of Mennonite History*. Mennonite Publishing House, 1940.

_____. *Introduction to Theology: An Interpretation of the Doctrinal Content of Scripture, Written to Strengthen a Childlike Faith in Christ*. Herald Press, 1954.

_____. *The Mennonites in Michigan and Indiana*. Herald Press, 1961.

_____ et al., eds. *Harold S. Bender: Educator, Historian, Churchman*. Herald Press, 1964.

Yoder, Edward. "A Bibliography of the Writings of John Horsch."
    *MQR* 21 (July 1947).
_____. *Edward, Pilgrimage of a Mind: The Journal of Edward
    Yoder, 1931-1945.* Ed. Ida Yoder. Wadsworth, Ohio: Ida Yoder,
    1985.
Yoder, John Howard. "The Anabaptist Dissent: The Logic of the
    Place of the Disciple in Society." *Concern* 1 (June 1954).
_____. "Anabaptist Vision and Mennonite Reality." In A. J.
    Klassen, ed., *Consultation on Anabaptist-Mennonite Theology.*
    Fresno, Calif.: Council of Mennonite Seminaries, 1970.
Yoder, Sanford Calvin. *The Days of My Years.* Herald Press, 1959.

## Selected Publications by Harold S. Bender
(in chronological order within each category)

### Books and Pamphlets Published

*Two Centuries of American Mennonite Literature: A Bibliography
    of Mennonitica Americana, 1727-1928.* Goshen, Ind.: Menno-
    nite Historical Society, 1929.
With John Horsch. *Menno Simons' Life and Writings: A Quadri-
    centennial Tribute, 1536-1936.* Mennonite Publishing House,
    1936.
*Mennonite Origins in Europe.* Akron, Pa.: Mennonite Central Com-
    mittee, 1942.
*Conrad Grebel, c. 1498-1526: The Founder of the Swiss Brethren,
    Sometimes Called Anabaptists.* Studies in Anabaptist and Men-
    nonite History, 6. Goshen, Ind.: The Mennonite Historical
    Society, 1950.
*Biblical Revelation and Inspiration.* Mennonite Publishing House,
    1959.
*These Are My People: The Nature of the Church and Its Disciple-
    ship According to the New Testament.* Herald Press, 1962.

### Major Works Edited

*The Mennonite Quarterly Review.* Vols. 1-36. Goshen, Ind.: Menno-
    nite Historical Society, 1927-1962.
*Der Mennonit.* Basel: Mennonite Central Committee, 1948-1951.
With Ernst Crous and Gerhard Hein. *Mennonitisches Lexikon.* Vol.
    3, no. 37, through vol. 4, no. 48. Karlsruhe: Druck and Verlag
    Heinrich Schneider, 1951-1962.

580 *Harold S. Bender*

With C. Henry Smith. *The Mennonite Encyclopedia.* Vols. 1-4. Mennonite Publishing House; Newton, Kan.: Mennonite Publications Office; Hillsboro, Kan.: Mennonite Brethren Publishing House; 1955-1959. Cornelius Krahn served as Associate Editor, Melvin Gingerich as Managing Editor, and Elizabeth Horsch Bender as Assistant Editor. (A fifth, auxiliary volume was published in 1990, ed. Cornelius J. Dyck and Dennis Martin.)

**Articles in *The Mennonite Quarterly Review* (or Its Predecessor)**
With Ernst H. Correll. "Conrad Grebel's Petition of Protest and Defense to the Zurich Council in 1523." *Goshen College Record Review Supplement* 27 (Jan. 1926): 23-32.

"Important New Acquisitions by the Mennonite Historical Library at Goshen College." *Goshen College Record Review Supplement* 28 (Sept. 1926): 44-47.

"The Discipline Adopted by the Strasbourg Conference of 1568." Trans. and ed. H. S. Bender. *MQR* 1 (Jan. 1927): 57-66.

"New Source Material for the History of the Mennonites in Ontario." *MQR* 3 (Jan. 1929): 42-53.

"A Letter from Pennsylvania Mennonites to Holland in 1773." *MQR* 3 (Oct. 1929): 225-234.

"An Amish Church Discipline of 1781." *MQR* 4 (Apr. 1930): 140-148.

"The Correspondence of Martin Mellinger: Translations of the Correspondence of Martin Mellinger with Relatives in the Rhenish Palatinate, 1807-1839." Trans. and ed. H. S. Bender. *MQR* 5 (Oct. 1931): 231-244.

"The Literature and Hymnology of the Mennonites of Lancaster County, Pennsylvania." *MQR* 6 (July 1932): 156-168.

"The Founding of the Mennonite Church in America at Germantown, 1683-1708." *MQR* 7 (Oct. 1933): 227-250.

"Recent Progress in Research in Anabaptist History." *MQR* 8 (Jan. 1934): 3-17.

"Conrad Grebel, the First Leader of the Swiss Brethren (Anabaptists)." *MQR* 10 (Jan. 1936): 5-45; 10 (Apr. 1936): 91-137; 10 (July 1936): 151-160.

With Orie O. Miller. "A Brief Account of the Third Mennonite World Conference Held at Amsterdam, Elspeet, and Witmarsum, Netherlands, June 29 to July 3, 1936." *MQR* 11 (Jan. 1937): 68-82.

"The Mennonites of the United States." *MQR* 11 (Jan. 1937): 68-82.
"The Theology of Conrad Grebel." *MQR* 12 (Jan. 1938): 27-54;
12 (Apr. 1938): 114-134.
"With the Mennonite Refugee Colonies in Brazil and Paraguay: A
Personal Narrative." *MQR* 1 (Jan. 1939): 59-70.
"Conrad Grebel as a Zwinglian, 1522-1523." *MQR* 15 (Apr. 1941):
67-82.
"The Anabaptist Vision." *MQR* 18 (Apr. 1944): 67-88.
"The Mennonite Conception of the Church and Its Relation to
Community Building." *MQR* 19 (Apr. 1945): 90-100.
"John Horsch, 1867-1941: A Bibliography." *MQR* 21 (July 1947):
131-144.
"C. Henry Smith: A Tribute." *MQR* 23 (Jan. 1949): 5-21.
"The Anabaptist Theology of Discipleship." *MQR* 24 (Jan. 1950):
25-32.
"Mennonite Peace Action Throughout the World." *MQR* (Apr.
1950): 149-155.
"The Zwickau Prophets, Thomas Münzter, and the Anabaptists."
*MQR* 26 (Jan. 1953): 3-16.
"Mennonites in Art." *MQR* 27 (July 1953): 187-203.
"The Anabaptists and Religious Liberty in the Sixteenth Century."
*MQR* 29 (Apr. 1955): 83-100.
"The Pacifism of the Sixteeth-Century Anabaptists." *MQR* 30 (Jan.
1956): 5-18.
"The Hymnology of the Anabaptists." *MQR* 31 (Jan. 1957): 5-10.
"The Historiography of the Anabaptists." *MQR* 31 (Apr. 1957): 88-
104.
"Mennonite Inter-Group Relations." *MQR* 32 (Jan. 1958): 48-58.
"Walking in the Resurrection: The Anabaptist Doctrine of Regenera-
tion and Discipleship." *MQR* 35 (Apr. 1961): 96-110.
"A Tribute to Robert Friedmann." *MQR* 35 (July 1961): 242.
"The Response of Our Anabaptist Fathers to the World's Challenge."
*MQR* 36 (July 1962): 196-207.
"Pilgram Marpeck, Anabaptist Theologian and Civil Engineer."
*MQR* 38 (July 1964): 231-265.

**Articles in Other Periodicals**
"Dear Readers." *Words of Cheer* 34, Apr. 25, 1909, 4.
"The Life and Work of Adam Smith." GCR 20, Oct. 1918, 1; 20,
Nov. 1918, 2.
"Principles of Good Manners." *Hesston College Journal* 6, Feb.

1920, 10.

"University Life in Germany," *CM* 16 (May 1924): 532-535.

"Currents of Religious Life in Germany Today." *Christian Exponent* 1 (May 9, 1924): 150; 1 (May 23, 1924): 168-169.

"Journey in the Land of the Mennonite Fathers." *CM* 17 (series, Jan. to July, 1925).

"One Central Standard College for the Mennonite Church." *GCR* 27, July-Aug. 1925, 10.

"Fundamentals Should Be Taught These Days." *GH* 18 (Jan. 21, 1926): 885-887.

"The Need for the Support of Study in Mennonite History." *GH* 18 (Mar. 18, 1926): 1050.

"What Can the Church Do for Her Historical Work?" A series in *GH* 20: (Apr. 21, 1927): 58; (Apr. 28, 1927): 90-92; (May 2, 1927): 107; (May 12, 1927): 138; (May 19, 1927): 154; (May 26, 1927): 170; (June 2, 1927): 202.

"Biblical Test of Orthodoxy." *GH* 21 (Apr. 19, 1928): 69-71.

"Experiences and Plans in Gathering Material for a New Mennonite History." *GH* 21 (May 31, 1928): 171; (June 7, 1928): 203; (June 14, 1927): 235; (June 21, 1928): 251.

"Detecting Modernism." *CM* 20 (June 1928): 161.

"A Flying Trip Through Russia." *GCR* 31 (Dec. 1929): 3.

"From Siberia to Paraguay with Russian Mennonite Refugees." *GCR* 32 (Oct. 1930): 1.

"In Time of Peace, Prepare for War." *GH* 25 (Apr. 21, 1932): 70-71.

"Has Mennonitism a Contribution for Our Day?" *GCR* 35 (Mar. 1934): 6.

"The Bible Department in Goshen College." *GCR* 37 (Feb. 1936): 5.

"What the Sunday School Did for the Mennonite Church." *CM* 32 (Oct. 1940): 312-314.

"In the Midst of War: Thoughts for Nonresistants." A series in *GH* 35:

"I. Farming and Fighting." (Jan. 29, 1943): 938.

"II. The High School Victory Corps." (Feb. 4, 1943): 954.

"III. Mennonite Men in the Army." (Feb. 11, 1943): 986.

"IV. Money and War." (Feb. 18, 1943): 1002.

"V. War Hysteria." (Mar. 4, 1943): 1050.

"VI. Rationing." (Mar. 11, 1943): 1074.

"VII. Marriage in the Midst of War." (Mar. 18, 1943): 1090.

"VIII. Civilian Defense." (Mar. 25, 1943): 1105.

"IX. Support of Dependents of Drafted Men." (May 1, 1943):

1117.
"The Content of the Bible School Curriculum." *GH* 35 (Feb. 18, 1943): 1015.
"Daniel Kauffman and His Times." *GH* 36 (Feb. 10, 1944): 962.
"The Anabaptist Vision." *Church History* 13 (Mar. 1944): 3-24.
"The Function and Authority of General Conference." *GH* 37 (July 14, 1944): 289-290; 37 (July 21, 1944): 306.
"Inaugural Address" (as dean of the Bible School). *GCR* 45 (Dec. 1944): 6-8. Also in *GH* 36 (Oct. 20, 1944): 576.
"Nonresistant Nurses and the Draft." *GH* 37 (Feb. 8, 1945): 901.
"Mennonite Service Units for the Summer of 1946." *GH* 38 (Mar. 22, 1946): 994.
"The Work of the Mennonite Research Foundation." *GH* 39 (May 20, 1947): 172.
"The Historical Background of Our Present Ministerial Offices." *Christian Ministry* 4 (July 19, 1949): 134-137.
"Miracles, Signs, and Wonders: An Attestation of the Gospel." *Christian Ministry* 3 (Apr. 1950): 1-4.
"Our Relief and Refugee Program in Danger." *GH* 44 (Jan. 2, 1951): 2.
"Die Gemeinde Jesu Christi in der Urtäuferischen Schau." *Gemeindeblatt der Mennoniten* 82 (Oct. 1, 1951): 97.
"The Anabaptists and Religious Liberty in the Sixteenth Century." *Archiv für Reformationsgeschichte* 44 (1953): 32-51.
With Millard C. Lind and Chester K. Lehman. "The Revised Standard Version: An Examination and Evaluation." *GH* 46 (May 12, 1953): 433; 46 (May 19, 1953): 460; 46 (May 26, 1953): 484.
"World Conference Committee at Work." *GH* 47 (Mar. 16, 1954): 244.
"Bethany Christian High School." *Christian Living* 1 (Sep. 1954): 5.
"The New Testament Doctrine of the Church." *Christian Ministry* 8 (Jan. 1955): 9-16.
"Communion—Close or Open?" *GH* 48 (Jan. 11, 1955): 25.
"The Pacifism of the Sixteenth-Century Anabaptists." *Church History* 2 (June 1955): 119-131.
"Report from Russia." *GH* 49 (Dec. 11, 1956): 1147.
"Explanatory Statement on the Proposed Modification of the Plan of Cooperation for the Associated Mennonite Biblical Seminaries." *Discipleship* 3 (Winter 1956/1957).
"The Usage of the Term "Church" in the New Testament." *GH* 51

(Jan. 7, 1958): 21.

"The Jerusalem Conference—and Our Conference." *GH* 51 (Feb. 18, 1958): 150.

"A Serious Hour in World Affairs." *GH* 52 (June 23, 1959): 579.

"The Mennonite World Conference, 1962." *GH* 52 (Oct. 20, 1959): 885.

"When May Christians Disobey the Government?" *GH* 53 (Jan. 12, 1960): 25.

"In the Name of Christ." *GH* 54 (Apr. 26, 1960): 361.

"Lessons to Be Learned from Past Divisions." *GH* 53 (May 17, 1960): 441.

"The Prague Peace Conference." *The Mennonite* 66 (Sep. 19, 1961): 597.

"What Is the Mennonite World Conference?" *GH* 54 (Nov. 14, 1961): 997.

"I Robbed Churches—Paul." *GH* 55 (Sep. 4, 1962): 773.

"Follow Thou Me." *GH* 56 (July 30, 1963): 649, 652, 667.

# Index

# The Author

ALBERT N. KEIM has taught history at Eastern Mennonite University for more than thirty years.
His specialty is recent American
history, with a focus on issues of
religion and the state. His Ph.D.
dissertation at Ohio State University was a biographical study of
John Foster Dulles as a churchman engaged in statecraft.

Keim, born into an Old
Order Amish family near Union-
town, Ohio, has published books
on the Amish and public education. He has also written on
public policy issues surrounding
the refusal of the Historic Peace Churches to participate in World
War II and in the Korean War.

Albert Keim's spouse, Leanna Yoder Keim, is a former teacher
and currently a self-employed potter. They have a daughter, a son-
in-law, and two grandsons. The Keims are members of Park View
Mennonite Church, Harrisonburg, Virginia.

# The Editor

FOR THE PAST two decades, Theron F. Schlabach has been a leading, well-recognized historian of Mennonites in America. During a career as a teacher of American history at Goshen College in Indiana, he has written articles and two major books in American Mennonite history, served for nearly twenty years as a chief editor of the Studies in Anabaptist and Mennonite History book series, and as editor of the four-volume Mennonite Experience in America series.

Schlabach has also served as a consulting editor and as interim editor of *The Mennonite Quarterly Review*. From that broad background, the Mennonite Historical Society appointed him to serve as chairperson and main editor in the Bender biography project.